Twentieth Century Writing

A Reader's Guide to Contemporary Literature

Twentieth Century Writing

A Reader's Guide to Contemporary Literature

Edited by Kenneth Richardson
Associate Editor R. Clive Willis

NEWNES BOOKS
LONDON · NEW YORK · SYDNEY · TORONTO

Published for Newnes Books by The Hamlyn Publishing Group Limited,
London, New York, Sydney, Toronto,
Hamlyn House, 42 The Centre, Feltham, Middlesex

SBN 600 40292 4

Printed in Great Britain by Morrison & Gibb Limited,
London and Edinburgh

Introduction

Twentieth Century Writing is first and foremost a reader's guide. It is designed to answer questions like 'what sort of novels does Lawrence Durrell write?'; 'What are Ionesco's plays all about?'; 'How should I approach T. S. Eliot?'; 'Would I enjoy D. H. Lawrence?'; 'Why is Sartre thought so important?'—as well as the simpler factual queries such as 'Who is Cavafy?'; 'What are Peter Cheyney's best-known titles?'; 'Who are the leading Spanish and Portuguese writers of today?' and 'Who wrote *An American Tragedy* and when?'. Some 1200 individual authors are dealt with; and since the primary aim is to provide guidance to their principal writings, the biography and bibliography has been limited to what is considered necessary for this purpose.

While the articles on the most celebrated contemporary figures will provide a sound introduction for the student of literature, there is a breadth of scope that will enable the general reader to see in perspective the various kinds of writer at work today: the *avant-garde* poet, novelist and playwright, the conventional 'middle-brow', and writers in particular genres such as the crime thriller and science fiction. The degree of catholicity aimed at in this work, inevitably limited by considerations of size, reflects the editors' belief that it is a mistake to attempt a clear-cut distinction between 'serious' and 'popular' writers.

The reader coming for the first time to the works of a particular author will not be best served by esoteric or eccentric value judgments. Generally, therefore, contributors have indicated the contemporary standing of a given work rather than express an individual evaluation; and the editors have made their inclusions, exclusions and space-allocations in the light of the consensus of critical opinion wherever such a consensus exists. In many instances, however, opinion is divided; and here the editors have endorsed those trends which have seemed to be gathering rather than losing momentum. Thus the increasing importance attached by some critics to the literatures of Africa, of Latin America and of the English-speaking Commonwealth countries is reflected in the number and length of the entries on authors from these areas.

The principle of letting the length of entry reflect an author's importance is subject to some important qualifications. These are as follows:

Two-thirds of the space is given to English-language writers. This does not imply any pre-eminence for English literature, but simply caters for the average reader's predominant interest in reading books originally written in his own language.

The quantity of a writer's output, and the space needed for an adequate exposition, vary enormously, and are important factors determining the length of an article.

In the articles on writers whose original language is a foreign one, the availability of a writer's works in English has generally been made an important criterion.

In view of the relative inaccessibility, in every sense, of literature written in the oriental and African languages, the foreign-language authors are limited to those writing in a European language (Turkish and Hebrew being treated as European for this purpose). Latin American writers are thus included, as are English-language writers from the African and Asian parts of the Commonwealth, and French-language African and West Indian writers.

For the purpose of this work, an author is generally considered to be a twentieth-century figure if he lived and wrote for one decade into the century and had a substantial amount of his major work published after 1 January 1900.

Finally, a word should be said about the methods of guidance adopted by the editors and contributors. The contributors' approaches to different entries vary considerably. In the case of the longest articles it has generally been possible to provide a comprehensive and chronological survey of the writer's publications in book form (novels, plays, collections of poems or short stories), with any omissions made good in a short concluding paragraph rather than in a repetition of the complete list as a formal bibliography. In the shorter ones the aim has been either to devote the bulk of the space to an examination of the writer's best-known work or works or to give an account of the general character of his writings—depending on whether or not he is known chiefly by one or two outstanding books, and also on which approach is thought likely to be most helpful.

The English translation given in square brackets following a foreign title is in italics when it is the title of a published English version—as with Barbusse's *L'Enfer* [*Hell*]; it is in roman and enclosed by single quotation marks when it is the literal English rendering of a title which has not been published in English—as with the same author's *Les Pleureuses* ['Weeping women'].

The editors regret that it has not always been possible to obtain the birth dates of living authors.

The arrangement of the entries in alphabetical order recognises that the reader's chief method of use will be to look up the name of an author in order to obtain information and guidance about his writings. There is also a comprehensive index of authors, book titles, and countries.

Acknowledgments

The editors and publishers are grateful to the following for permission to quote copyright passages from the works named:

William Empson and Chatto & Windus Ltd., for *Seven Types of Ambiguity*
Roy Fuller, Andre Deutsch Ltd., and Curtis Brown Ltd., for *Brutus's Orchard*
The Trustees of the Hardy Estate and Macmillan & Co. Ltd., for *The Collected Poems of Thomas Hardy*
The Society of Authors as the literary representative of the Estate of the late A. E. Housman, and Messrs Jonathan Cape Ltd., publishers of A. E. Housman's *Collected Poems*
Alun Lewis and George Allen & Unwin Ltd., for *The Raider's Dawn* and *Ha Ha Among the Trumpets*
Mr Harold Owen and Chatto & Windus Ltd., for *Poems* by Wilfred Owen
The Literary Estate of Isaac Rosenberg, Chatto & Windus Ltd., and Schocken Books Inc., for Rosenberg's *Collected Poems*
The Trustees for the Copyrights of the late Dylan Thomas and J. M. Dent & Sons Ltd., for Thomas's *Collected Poems*
Philip Larkin and Marvell Press Ltd., for *Wants*
Laurie Lee and Laurence Pollinger Ltd., for *Collected Poems*
A. P. Watt & Son, for Yeats's *Collected Poems*
A. P. Watt & Son, and Doubleday & Co. Inc., for Kipling's *Rewards and Fairies*
Angus & Robertson (U.K.) for *Woman to Man* and *The Gateway* by Judith Wright, and 'Australia' by A. D. Hope in *Australian Poetry*
Jonathan Cape Ltd., and A. D. Peters & Co., for *Collected Poems* by C. Day-Lewis
Jonathan Cape Ltd., and Holt, Rinehart & Winston Inc., for *The Complete Poems of Robert Frost*, and *Chicago Poems* by Carl Sandburg
Constable & Co. Ltd., for *Turns and Movies* by Conrad Aiken
Curtis Brown Ltd., for *Adamastor* by Roy Campbell
J. M. Dent & Sons Ltd., for *Verses from 1929* by Ogden Nash
Edwards & Shaw, of Sydney N.S.W., for *The Wandering Islands* by A. D. Hope
Eyre & Spottiswoode (Publishers) Ltd., for *Poems* by Dom Moraes
Faber & Faber Ltd., for *Selected Poems 1923–1958* by e. e. cummings; *Collected Poems 1909–1962* by T. S. Eliot; *The Hawk in the Rain* by Ted Hughes; *Collected Poems* by Marianne Moore; and *Hugh Selwyn Mauberley* by Ezra Pound.

Faber & Faber Ltd. and Random House Inc., for *For the Time Being* and *The Shield of Achilles* by W. H. Auden, and *Collected Poems* by Stephen Spender
Faber & Faber Ltd., and Harcourt, Brace & World Inc., for *Lord Weary's Castle* by Robert Lowell, and *Ceremony and Other Poems* by Richard Wilbur
Faber & Faber Ltd., and Oxford University Press (New York), for *The Collected Poems of Louis MacNeice*
Faber & Faber Ltd., and Mr George Sassoon, for *Collected Poems* by Siegfried Sassoon
Faber & Faber Ltd., and Alfred A. Knopf Inc., for *Harmonium* by Wallace Stevens
Faber & Faber Ltd., and Mrs Mary Jarrell, for *Little Friend, Little Friend* by Randall Jarrell
Victor Gollancz Ltd., for *Son of Man* by Augusto Roa Bastos
Macmillan & Co. Ltd., for *Poems* by Robert Conquest
Macmillan & Co. (New York), for *The Man against the Sky* by Edwin Arlington Robinson
Methuen & Co. Ltd., for *One Way Song* by Wyndham Lewis
John Murray (Publishers) Ltd., for *Collected Poems* by John Betjeman
Oxford University Press, for *Insurrection* by David Gascoigne
Secker & Warburg Ltd., for *Trial of a Poet* by Karl Shapiro
The Society of Authors as the literary representative of the Estate of the late John Masefield, for *Dauber*
Thames & Hudson International Ltd., for *Six Poets of Modern Greece*

Abercrombie, Lascelles (1881–1938), English poet, dramatist and critic, was primarily a metaphysical and philosophical poet. *Interludes and Poems* (1908), his first volume of verse, began a period lasting until 1914, during which he wrote much of his best poetry including the much praised 'Ryton Firs' (in *Twelve Idylls*, 1928), a poem that combines a wry humour with a near-parody of Wordsworth, and in which the fallen fir trees stand as a symbol for a Europe felled by war. His other works include *Emblems of Love* (1912), *Thomas Hardy, a Critical Study* (1912) and *Four Short Plays* (1922). A notable edition of his poetry is *Poems of L. Abercrombie* (Oxford Poets series, 1930).

Abercrombie's work is interesting because it demonstrates all the influences that lead English poetry to and away from the crossroads of the first world war. He remains a minor poet because at the crossroads he takes no positive route but remains dancing beneath the signposts.

G. S.; D. L. P.

Abrahams, Peter (1919–   ), productive South African writer. A Negro from Johannesburg, he is best known for his autobiography *Tell Freedom* (1954). Most of his work was written while in England, but he subsequently moved to Jamaica. His other publications include *The Path of Thunder* (1948), *Wild Conquest* (1951), a historical novel; and his most praised work, the novel *A Wreath for Udomo* (1956). *Dark Testament* (1942), his first publication, contains the sensitive impressions of his youth.

C. P.

Abramov, Fyodor (1920–   ), Soviet writer, is not well known outside the Soviet Union, but he did strike the literary headlines in 1963 with his short novel *Vokrug da okolo* [*The New Life: a Day on a Collective Farm*], which observes through the eyes of the 'New Life' kolkhoz manager the countless problems arising during the course of a day. With quiet humour and sympathy, and forgoing the limiting demands of 'socialist realism' in the interests of genuine description, Abramov shows how the manager and his workers react to these problems, portraying the general frustration still to be found on the kolkhozes and something of the apathy and discontent of some of the workers. The result is an unexpectedly sensational account of rural Russia and the Soviet collective system.

B. W.

Achebe, Chinua (1930–), Nigeria's most impressive novelist. His widely acclaimed first novel *Things Fall Apart* (1958) contrasts the externally imposed moral codes of African tribal custom and those of Christian ethics and Roman law brought by the Europeans. Both falling short, Achebe postulates man's need to develop an inner standard to determine his social behaviour. *No Longer at Ease* (1960) follows, saga-like, the destiny of the same clan, bringing the conflict more up to date. *The Sacrificial Egg* (1962) is a collection of short stories which more simply reveal Achebe's didactic strength, while *Arrow of God* (1964) is the assured, complex and dramatic evocation of ancestral village life. *A Man of the People* (1966) is his first—and very telling—direct political satire. C. P.

Adams, Arthur H. (1872–1936), Australian poet, novelist and playwright, was born and educated in New Zealand, then spent three years in London, after which he returned to make his home in Australia. His poems are still encountered in anthologies and are characterised by their deliberately detached and almost cynical observation of the Australian countryside and its people. His astringent comments are given further bite by a technical competence which marks him out from his Australian contemporaries. S. R.

Adams, Henry Brooks (1838–1918), American historian and man of letters. Adams is primarily a historian whose philosophy centres on the fragmentation of human society by the ideas of science. His nine-volume history of the U.S.A. during the administrations of Jefferson and Madison (published 1889–91) bridges the period of the reorientation of his country from European to native American influence. Adams's philosophy is primarily determinist; he does not see man as capable of deciding the course of the world. His best-known works, *Mont Saint-Michel and Chartres* (1913) and *The Education of Henry Adams* (1918), illustrate the dichotomy he finds between the unity of spiritual force and the chaos which science formulates of man and nature. The contrasting symbols of the Virgin and the Dynamo are intended to illustrate the disintegration of man from the thirteenth century, as epitomised by the aesthetic and spiritual beauty of Chartres cathedral, to the nineteenth and twentieth centuries, where the dynamo symbolises the pressure of the outer forces of nature and science destroying the inner unity of faith.

Adams's pessimistic, deterministic philosophy expresses a need for religious faith but discovers only an intellectual chaos. His view that art, too, must be chaotic to express real chaos underpins many of the problems of American literature in the early twentieth century. D. L. P.

Adams, Léonie (1899–), American poet whose early girlish ecstasy has been modified into the restrained emotions and controlled but vivid imagery of maturity. She is a writer capable of expressing, in imaginative and almost metaphysical form, her mystical sense of wonder in Nature. She is by no means a major poet but one or two of her poems are to be found in most anthologies of American verse. Her published volumes include *Those Not Elect* (1925), *High Falcon* (1925), *This Measure* (1937) and *Poems: A Selection* (1954). D. L. P.

Ade, George (1866–1944), American humorist and playwright. He worked as a journalist and produced for the *Chicago Record* a series of fictional, likeable rogues who became immediate favourites with the reading public. Ade wrote in an urban slang that caught at the essence of the genteel liars, the bootblacks and the warm-hearted blusterers he depicted. The characters were popular enough for their creator to translate his journalistic techniques into book form in *Artie* (1896), *Pink Marsh* (1897) and *Doc' Horne* (1899). Further stories in journalese style were collected in *Fables in Slang* (1898). Ade worked also on musical comedies and films and produced a number of successful plays including *The County Chairman* (1903) which propaganded against political corruption.

D. L. P.

Ady, Endre (1877–1919), Hungarian poet, was the most controversial literary figure in Hungary during the early part of the century. His Calvinist education was followed by a formative period of journalism in Nagyvárad (now Oradea, Rumania), where he met the lady whom he later calls 'Léda' in his verses, and followed her to Paris. His *Új versek* ['New poems'] (1906), though not his first volume, began a new era in Hungarian verse. They were lyric poems, extremely subjective and couched in symbolist language of passionate intensity. Ady's subjects ranged from erotic love to religious and patriotic themes, all considered in a highly personal form; his world is entirely his own, pierced through by savage visions and prophecies which have been seized upon by almost every radical cause. He has a startling feeling for colour and the music of poetry. Completely self-centred, he broke off relations with Léda only to marry later a young wife, 'Csinszka', who nursed him through his last years of sickness.

Ady also wrote many articles and short stories, but in these he rarely found the release that is the mark of his verse. English versions of the latter include *Poems* (trans. René Bonnerjea; Budapest, 1941) and selections in W. Kirkconnell, *The Magyar Muse* (1933); but the English language is a poor vehicle for his muse. The most complete edition of his poems is *Összes versek* (ed. Földessy; 1961). G. F. C.

Æ was the pen-name of George William Russell (1867–1935), Irish writer and painter. 'Æ' combined a mystical imagination with involvement in the Irish national movement. He was, like Yeats, interested in Buddhism and theosophy, which interests he combined with practical involvement in co-operative ideals. In 1899 he published, together with Yeats, a book of critical essays. In 1904 he issued a volume of imaginative stories entitled *The Mask of Apollo*. In 1916 there appeared *The National Being, Thoughts on an Irish Policy*. His semi-mystical concept of Ireland and his lyrical gifts are seen at their best in his first three volumes of verse: *Homeward: Songs by the Way* (1894), *The Earth Breath* (1897) and *Divine Vision* (1903), all put out in collected form in 1913. D. L. P.

Afinogenov, Alexandr Nikolayevich (1904–41), Soviet playwright who specialised in melodramas which portray Soviet and foreign life filled with labour struggles, spies and sabotage. At first a favourite with officialdom, he was later to be arrested for his views.

Despite its obvious flaws and conventional ending, his play *Strakh* [*Fear*] (1930) caused a tremendous sensation when produced in Moscow. The hero, a relic of the pre-revolutionary intelligentsia, is a professor who finds personal freedom is too restricted under the Soviet régime. As a result of his research into the stimuli which activate the behaviour of the Soviet people he has discovered that the most potent force is fear. Eventually the old scientist's opposition to the Soviet system is overcome and he repents of his errors. His observations, however, were very real to the audiences of the time and the play and its author were only saved by the latter's wise introduction of an old Bolshevik whose job was to show that the fear which gripped people in Czarist times had been overcome by the working classes. Afinogenov's other work is not of the same high standard. It consists of *Dalyokoye* [*Distant Point*] (1936), *Vtoriye puti* [*The Secret Track*] (1939), and *Nakanunye* [*On the Eve*] (1941) which deals with the German attack on the Soviet Union. One month after its completion Afinogenov was killed in a German air-raid on Moscow. B. W.

Agate, James (1877–1947), English theatre critic, essayist and diarist. Much of his most durable writing on the drama—both on the classics and on the works of his own time—first appeared in the *Manchester Guardian* from 1906 onwards. His essays and diaries take their colour from the expression of his own vigorous and subtle personality: the latter being published under the title *Ego* (9 vols. 1935–48). K. R. R.

Agee, James (1909–55), American novelist, film writer and poet, achieved posthumous fame with the second of his two novels *A Death in the Family* (1957); both the novel itself, and its subsequent adaptation for the stage, winning Pulitzer prizes. The novel portrays an ordinary family in a small town in Tennessee experiencing the sudden and premature death of the husband and father. As in his earlier novel, *The Morning Watch* (1954), recording a day in the life of a twelve-year-old boy, Agee has been primarily concerned to convey the quality of human experience; but *A Death in the Family* is also an effective piece of story-telling.

To many addicts of the cinema, Agee's name will be best known for his screen plays and film criticism, which have been collected in two volumes entitled *Agee on Film* (1958 and 1960). K. R. R.

Agnon, Samuel Joseph (formerly Czaczkes; 1888–), Israeli writer and joint winner of the 1966 Nobel prize, was born in (then Austrian) Galicia, a province of Polish-Ukrainean-German-Jewish ethnic and cultural condominium now incorporated in the U.S.S.R. He had a traditional Jewish education in Bible and Talmud, taught in Yiddish, his mother tongue. Hebrew was the (not spoken) language of his Jewish studies, German the channel of Europe's literary and cultural influences. Poland, Germany and Israel are the main scenes of his narrative dramas. Jewish tradition, human existence and modern Europe form the themes and essence of his writings.

As early as 1903 he began publishing book reviews and Yiddish poems. In 1904 his first Hebrew poem was published in Cracow. He soon joined the Zionist movement and, in 1907, emigrated to Palestine. There he published his first story *Agunot* ['Forbidden to marry'] (1908), with a Freudian plot in a Jewish-traditional framework, and written in a mediaeval Hebrew idiom in contradistinction to the then familiar modern Hebrew style. In assonance to 'Agunot' he signed himself as 'Agnon', which name he later adopted.

With *Agunot* Agnon started the process of a revival of the talmudic-rabbinic manner of speech and thought as an idiomatic and dialectical instrument of modern Hebrew narrative creation. In that idiom his first book, *Wehayah He-Akov Le-Mishor* [*And the Crooked Shall Be Made Straight*], was published in Jaffa in 1916.

To widen his European cultural horizon, he went in 1913 to Germany where he stayed, caught up by the first world war, until 1924, when he returned to Palestine. In the same year, while still in Germany, Agnon, a book lover and expert collector, lost his invaluable library of rare books and manuscripts, including that of his (never restored) autobiographical novel *Bitzror Ha-Chayyim* ['In the bundle of life']. This time it was fire. When the disaster occurred a second time in Jerusalem in 1929, rioters did the destruction. In Agnon's own work the themes of books, writers and writings loom prominently.

In 1930 Agnon revisited Germany and his native town Buczacz. In that year appeared *Hakhnasat* [*The Bridal Canopy*], a novel with a Don Quixote pattern set against an early nineteenth-century chassidic background. The result of his visit to Galicia was *Oreach Natah Lalun* ['A guest for the night'] (1939), a superb epical jeremiad on the decline and destruction of Jewish life in the diaspora. Another product of this period was *Bilvav Yamim* [*In the Heart of the Seas*] (1935). In 1949 the Palestine novel *Temol Shilshom* ['Only yesterday'] appeared, a tragedy in narrative form (with a Kafka-like dog-allegory) dealing with the conflict between the old and the new as reflected in the cultural and social set-up in the rebuilt land of Israel. Earlier, in 1935, *Sippur Pashut* ['A simple story'] had forecast Agnon's later preoccupations with the Jewish spiritual crisis; while from 1932 Kafkaesque stories of *Sepher Ha-Maasim* ['The Book of Acts'] had been appearing as well as further Freudian stories including *Panim Acherot* ['Other faces'], *Shevuat Emunim* ['Betrothed'; in *Two Tales*, London 1966] and many others.

A major element in Agnon's work is Jewish myth, legend and tradition. Themes like love, land-of-Israel, language, literature, Jews and Gentiles are dealt with in the framework of tradition. Irony, satire and humour permeate his whole writing—irony as a counter-point to myth, satire as a weapon against the travesty of tradition and its true values; humour as an attitude to man and his behaviour. In his Kafkaesque stories, for example, *Pat Sheleymah* ['A whole loaf'] and *Ha-Avtobus Ha-Acharon* ['The last bus'] he shows man's alienation from God and his fellow-man, his frustrations and impotence, his schizophrenic state of mind when actions and reactions are needed. In later allegorical tales, like *Ido w' Eynam* ['Ido and Eynam'; in *Two Tales*, London 1966], we are witnessing the fatal split in the mind of the modern Jew in his approach towards the fount of his spiritual existence.

English translations of Agnon's writings have been published in New York, Jerusalem and London. His stories have also been translated into Yiddish, German, French, Italian and Swedish. His two important anthologies *Yamim Noraim* [*The Days of Awe*] and *Attem Reitem* ['You have seen'], containing literary material stretching over three thousand years, about the New Year and the Day of Atonement, and Pentecost, are also widely translated. M. G.

Albee, Edward (1928–), American writer, has achieved a minor reputation as an *avant-garde* playwright. His first four plays were performed off Broadway and his first full-length play became a critical and popular success. He is generally admired as an 'anti-formalist' though his plays are always carefully structured, sometimes, as in the case of *Who's Afraid of Virginia Woolf* (1961–62), being elaborate allegories of the sickness of contemporary American society. The same theme occurs in *The American Dream* (1959–60) which like its later elaboration concerns itself with the creation of ideals that bear no relation to reality. In both cases this is represented by a mother searching for a son. His other plays like *The Sand Box* (1961) and *The Death of Bessie Smith* (1959) have similar pre-occupations and concern themselves with death. In the former, he shows its inevitable victory, contrasted to a denial by the father of its existence
s a fact of life, and in the latter he portrays the death of the great Negro
lues singer who was refused entrance into white hospitals.

K. G.-Y.

erti, Rafael (1902–), Spanish poet. Of those who emerged in the
0s Alberti is the poet whose style has most mirrored the changing
ry forms of an age of crisis. Both his poetry and his own life have
characterised by a series of reactions to inhibiting situations. Born
n impoverished branch of a respectable Catholic family of wine
ers in Puerto de Santa María (Cádiz), he has become a communist
rried a divorced woman. As a child he rebelled against his Jesuit
asters and against the family's move to Madrid in 1917—he saw
s a *Marinero en tierra* ['Sailor on land'], the title of his first
of traditional poems published in 1925.
lready achieved fame as a painter, he was only widely accepted
hen *Marinero en tierra* was awarded the National Prize for
924–25. His next two works *La amante* ['The lover'] (1926)
del alhelí ['Wallflower dawn'] (1927) were also written in
rms but *Cal y canto* [*Quicklime and Song*] (1929) is a
e Góngora tercentenary celebrations of 1927. Alongside
ex exercises in neo-baroque technique we find ironic and
contemporary life. Beneath the gay, elegant surface of
wever, there is a sense of dissatisfaction, and in 1927 this
The poet suffered a breakdown. He lost his religious
confidence and experienced strange dreams in which he
il angels. These creatures, evidently symbols of the
him in his personal crisis, form the subject matter of
Concerning Angels] (1929), Alberti's masterpiece. It
tion of a world of order—religious and temporal—

Aidoo, Christina Ama Ata (1940–), Ghanaian playwright. *The Dilemma of a Ghost* (1965) dramatises cultural conflict especially in terms of a young American-educated Ghanaian's mental turmoil regarding the family (having children, women drinking, etc.). She has also published short stories and poems.

C. P.

Aiken, Conrad (1899–), American poet, novelist, short-story writer and critic, is singularly representative of the influences felt by the American writer of the early twentieth century. He attended Harvard with T. S. Eliot and Walter Lippman. His work is affected by Freud, Havelock Ellis, William James and Henri Bergson; it is influenced both by a self-conscious intellectuality and by a consciousness of sex, and it retains a morbidity that probably reflects back to childhood and the violent deaths of his parents.

Aiken, a precocious child, wrote his first poem at the age of nine and subsequently published a volume of verse when he was fifteen. However, it is with *The Charnel Rose* and *Senkin and Other Poems* (both 1918) that he began to attract critical recognition. The latter volumes contain echoes of Eliot's 'Prufrock' but the force of imagination tends to destroy itself in a quality of fantasy bordering on obscurity. *Preludes for Memnon* (1931) is a rather more disciplined book, but here too the combination of Freudian imagery and seductive musical form risk a blurring of impact on the reader both in terms of intellectual force and of emotional energy. And these are the very grounds on which Aiken attacked Amy Lowell and the early imagists. *Brownstone Eclogues* (1942) is more definitely disciplined, and at the same time shows a return to the tender lyricism of 'Music I heard with You' (*Turns and Movies*, 1916):

> Music I heard with you was more than music,
> And bread I broke with you was more than bread;
> Now that I am without you all is desolate;
> All that was once so beautiful is dead.

Aiken's novels demonstrate his involvement in psychology and fantasy, *Ushant* (1952) being the most outstanding. His short stories involve a similar probing into the psyche, but here the sureness of touch comes near the quality of terror to be found in Poe. A prolific critic, Aiken was largely responsible for the revival of interest in Emily Dickinson, with the introduction to the English reader in 1924 of her *Selected Poems*. However, the award of a Pulitzer prize in 1930, for Aiken's own *Selected Poems* (1929), indicates that his principal claim to recognition is as a poet.

His other novels include *Blue Voyage* (1927), *Great Circle* (1933), *King Coffin* (1935) and *Conversation* (1940). His verse, stories and essays are collected in *Collected Poems* (1953); *Collected Short Stories* (1960); and *Reviewer's ABC: collected criticism of Conrad Aiken from 1916 to the present* (1958). D. L. P.

Akhmatova, Anna (Anna Andreyevna Gorenko; 1888–1966), Soviet poetess who despite frequent official disapproval of her work has always been popular among the young intellectuals. Her first published work appeared in 1912, two years after her marriage to the acmeist poet Nikolay Gumilyov. Her early work followed the pattern of the acmeist movement with its clear description and firm manner, although basically her preoccupation with religion and the sadness and disillusionment occasioned by love is so very personal that it is hard to fit her into one category; what can be said is that it belongs to that range of Soviet literature which lays itself wide open to criticism from communist literary officials.

In 1912 she published *Vecher* [*Evening Collections*]; this was followed by *Chotki* [*The Rosary*] (1914) and *Byelaya staya* [*The White Flock*] (1917). She divorced her husband in the year after the revolution and married Vladimir Shileyko, a minor poet. Some of her best mature poetry appeared in 1921 in *Anno Domini MCMXXI* [*Anno Domini MCMXXI*]. After 1923 she refused to prostitute her poetic soul for the new government's literary demands and except for a few useful studies of Pushkin published little until in the 1940s she was able to take advantage of the growing literary freedom and publish again her reflective lyric poetry. She produced a remarkable war poem called 'Muzhestvo' ['Courage'], but in 1946 the thaw ended and she was expelled from the Union of Soviet Writers. She was called, because of her preoccupation with religion and love, 'half-nun, half-prostitute, or rather both since her prostitution is mingled with prayer'.

For the greater part of two decades Akhmatova's voice was virtually silenced, though she did make an unheralded reappearance at the second Congress of Soviet Writers in 1954. (Four years earlier, to save the life of her son, she had published some indifferent verses praising Stalin which she subsequently deleted from anthologies of her works.) Yet she demonstrated that she had not entirely abandoned her independence when she refused to condemn the young radical writers in 1963, an independence which had already won her the admiration of the poet Alexey Surkov when he wrote in 1961 that her position in contemporary poetry had not been acquired by any moral or creative compromise. The year before she died she travelled to Britain to receive an honorary doctorate from Oxford University. B. W.

Aksionov, Vasily Parlovich (1932–), Soviet writer of 'little' novels about young people and their problems. He has acquired a good reputa-

tion among the reading public and is a prominent member of the liberal group of Russian writers. He began writing while working as a doctor and he published his first short story in 1959. Next year his novel *Kollyegi* [*Colleagues*] was published. Drawing on his own experiences as a doctor he described with obvious sincerity how three newly graduated doctors faced the world and how all the main characters found a positive role t
play in their chosen profession.

Zvezdniy bilyet [*A Starry Ticket*] (1961) tells the story of two brot
one who conforms and one who dares to rebel. Despite its enthu
reception it did not win official approval as *Colleagues* had done
theless, Aksionov continued to publish his tales, written in the
language typical of modern Russian youth. *Na polputi k lun*
to the Moon] (1962) and *Papa, chto eto znachit?* [*Daddy, Wh*
Spell?] (1962) are two very perceptive short stories, whil
Morokko [*Oranges from Morocco*] (1963) is a review of
conditions found at the 'Wasted Labour' co-ope
Criticised for writing nothing new and showing none
of life, Aksionov wrote an official apology and then
on some new themes.

Alain-Fournier (Henri Alban Fournier; 1886–19
in La Chapelle d'Angillon (Cher) the son of a s
an unsuccessful scholastic career at the Ly
military service he worked as a private s
published a novel *Le Grand Meaulnes* [T
September 1914 was reported missing du
His literary reputation rests on *Le Gran*
posthumous collection of poems, sto
ance (1905–14) with Jacques Rivière
which had left a deep imprint up
allegory of the gulf between
Augustin Meaulnes returns to
days, during which he has w
de Galais lives with his sis
in love. The adventure be
idyllic existence. Yet wh
element—Meaulnes's p
Valentine Blondeaux
finds Valentine, reun
has died in childbi
of an adolescen
romanticism.

and the poet's struggle to erect a new cosmos, founded on man's awareness that he is alone.

In the thirties Alberti emerged from his crisis to become a Marxist 'poet in the streets'. Identifying with the workers in their class struggle, his concern was now political where formerly it had been spiritual liberty. After the civil war, in which he played an active role, he carved out a new life in Argentina editing texts, painting once more and writing poetry. But his later work seldom approaches the intensity of *Sobre los ángeles. A la pintura* [*Homage to Painting*] (1948) is a virtuoso performance in the manner of *Cal y canto*, while *Retornos de lo vivo lejano* [*Returns of the Far and the Living*] (1952) is a magnificent evocation of the exile's yearning for Spain—Alberti is always at his best when sighing for the unattainable.

His production now numbers twenty-five books of poetry, eleven plays and an autobiography; his most recent poetry *Abierto a todas horas* ['Open at all hours'] (1965) showing a return to the traditional forms and technical exercises of the twenties. There is an anthology of English versions by Ben Belitt (University of California Press, 1966).

D. H. G.

Aldanov, Mark (Mark Alexandrovich Landau; 1886–), is an emigré Russian writer who has been a most successful historical novelist. He analyses the fundamental part played by chance in history. His best-known work deals with the French revolution, in a cycle of novels called *The Thinker*. This includes *Devyatoye termidora* [*The 9th Thermidor*] (1923), *Chortov most* [*The Devil's Bridge*] and *Zagovor* [*The Conspiracy*] (1927). His finest novel, however, is probably *Desyataya simfoniya* ['The 10th symphony'] (1931) which delves into the unhappiness and frustration in the life of Beethoven.

B. W.

Aldington, Richard (1892–1962), English poet, novelist and biographer. He married the American poet Hilda Doolittle (H.D.) in 1913. His early poetry appeared with that of Pound, Eliot and H.D. herself in the imagist anthologies of the first world war, poetry designed simply to catch at the clearly seen and felt momentary impression. While Aldington is not derivative he echoes the techniques of Eliot in using direct quotation and indirect reference.

Both his poetry and prose find substance in strong anti-war sentiments as with *Images of War* (1919) and his novel *Death of a Hero* (1929). The latter is concerned ostensibly with the effect of George Winterbourne's death in action in 1918 on his father, mother, wife, mistress and friend. The fact that there is very little effect starts the author on a series of violent blows against the shallow attitudes of the English middle class, working class, upper class and intellectual groupings before, during and after the first world war. George stands up in the heat of battle and allows his chest to be riddled with the bullets from a German machine-gun not only because a stupid war run by stupid people has left him shell-shocked and indifferent but because he has reached the culminating point in the destruction of his spirit—destruction set in train by weak, ignorant and selfish parents, by oppressive schooling, by the educated but superficial women with whom he has become involved and above all by the hypocrisy and superficiality of English life. Aldington's style is a mixture of aggressive resentment, deeply felt irony, wit that sears and a sexual maturity unusual for novels of the period.

Aldington is also well known as a controversial (at times almost malicious) biographer, writing the lives of Wellington (1946), of D. H. Lawrence (1950) and of Lawrence of Arabia (1955). He published his autobiography in 1941.

D. L. P.

Aldiss, Brian W. (1925–), English science-fiction novelist. He has perhaps been most influential as an anthologist and philosophical critic of SF (he edited all the first three volumes of *Penguin Science Fiction*), but is also a prolific author of novels and short stories. The volume *The Airs of Earth* (1963) gives a good illustration of his versatility, ranging from earthbound political stories to poetic fantasies like the brilliant 'O Moon of my Delight'. A collection of *Best Science Fiction Stories of Brian W. Aldiss* was published in 1965; and *The Saliva Tree and Other Strange Growths* (1966) is another notable volume.

C. B.

Alegría, Ciro (1909–), Peruvian novelist. A member of the political movement known as APRA (American Popular Revolutionary Alliance), he was imprisoned in 1931 and voluntarily went into exile in 1934. His novels realistically reflect his social and political preoccupations with the situation of the oppressed Indians in Peru. He has produced three prize-winning books. *La serpiente de oro* [*The Golden Serpent*] (1935) lacking a definite argument or plot, consists of a number of legends and pictures of the local way of life in the area of the river Marañón. *Los perros hambrientos* ['The hungry dogs'] (1939) is similar, but *El mundo es ancho y ajeno* [*Broad and Alien is the World*] (1941) centres on a story—a long narrative concerning the conflict between whites and Indians, with frequent digressions into ideas and customs, and with descriptions of the geography of Peru.

P. R. B.

Aleixandre, Vicente (1900–), Spanish poet, a leading member of the so-called '1927 Generation' which emerged in Spain during the 1920s and which found a focus for its activities in the Góngora tercentenary celebrations of 1927. An intermittent invalid whose verse has largely been written in the restored vitality of convalescence, Aleixandre has produced poetry that is characterised by an illogical, sensual imagery reminiscent of surrealism, deployed in complex baroque structures. In *La destrucción o el amor* ['Destruction or love'] (1935) he evokes the cosmos as bound in erotic union, nature being uncontaminated by man and his civilisation. Disillusion with present reality is still more marked in *Sombra del paraíso* ['Shadow of paradise'] (1944). For Aleixandre paradise is in the past, and specifically in Málaga, his childhood home. The world is corrupt for man has rejected his destiny. Only certain higher mortals—his father, children, peasants, lovers—are not separated nature. Aleixandre's vision changes fundamentally, however, in *Historia de un corazón* ['A heart's story'] (1954) and *En un vasto dominio* ['In a vast domain'] (1962). He now writes a poetry of engagement—with man depicted as a social, not a fallen, being.

D. H. G.

Algren, Nelson (1909–), American novelist and short-story writer, specialises in chronicling the hopeless lives of the flotsam and jetsam of American society. In his early writings—e.g. the strongly Marxist *Somebody in Boots* (1935)—their wretched lot is related to economic and social conditions: but in the more sensational, non-dogmatic later works by which he is best known it is more often assumed that there always will be down-and-outs, prostitutes, drug addicts and compulsive gamblers. These are, simply, the people to whom Algren is drawn, and in his adoption of their language—not only in reported conversation but also in his own narration—he identifies himself with them.

His best-known works are the novels *A Walk on the Wild Side* (1956) and *The Man with the Golden Arm* (1949), set in New Orleans and Chicago respectively. The former traces the erratic progress of the gentle simpleton Dove Linkhorn to the great Southern city, and his educative though ultimately destructive experiences there. The early part is uneven in quality, but there is a vividness and warmth in Algren's descriptions of the city's bars and brothels, and in particular of the girls whom varying circumstances have brought there from all over the country and from every walk of life. *The Man with the Golden Arm*, the story of a heroin-addicted gambler with a 'golden arm' for dice and cues, whose attempts to escape from his environment are doomed to failure, has a stronger narrative; but it is in descriptive power and in the narration of individual episodes that Algren excels and it is arguable that his best work is contained in his less well-known volume of short stories, *The Neon Wilderness* (1947).

K. R. R.

Aliger, Margarita Iosifovna (1915–), Soviet poetess whose early work shows the influence of Anna Akhmatova. She achieved popularity with her sensitive war poems. Her best-known work is an emotional narrative poem *Zoya* [*Zoya*] (1942) which relates how a Komsomol girl, Zoya Kosmodemyanskaya, fights with the Russian underground against the German invaders and is caught, tortured and killed by them in a vain effort to extract information. Aliger's post-war writing displays an interest in the theme of reconstruction. After the 'thaw' in 1956 she wrote *Spravedlivost'* [*Rightness*] vividly describing an encounter with an old friend who has just spent seventeen years in a concentration camp on a false charge. In later years she encountered disapproval for her failure to respond to official criticism, but her poetry continued to be published after an appropriate expression of loyalty. B. W.

Allen, Hervey (1889–1949), American poet, biographer and historical novelist. Allen was born in Pittsburgh, Pennsylvania. He produced a number of volumes of verse, of which *New Legend* (1929) is a representative sample, and an authoritative biography of Poe entitled *Israfel, Life and Times of Edgar Allan Poe* (1926). As a novelist he wrote a series between 1943 and 1948 under the general heading of *The Disinherited.* He is chiefly remembered, however, for the massive historical novel *Antony Adverse* (1933) which was one of the first American best-sellers, going to well over a million copies. D. L. P.

Allen, Walter (1911–), English novelist and critic, author of *The English Novel* (1954) and of a notable sequel on the contemporary novel entitled *Tradition and Dream* (1963). In his own fiction he has recreated with sympathy and imagination the social and political scene of working-class England from the turn of the century, most effectively in *All in a Lifetime* (1959), where an old man recalls his childhood in a large family characterised by its poverty and its high principles. In the most important people in his life—his sternly non-conformist elder brother, and his greatest friend, originally a fellow-student at the evening institute and later a Labour M.P.—we see a personification of important strands in England's history; these being followed through into more recent times in the lives of his four sons. S. R.

Allingham, Marjorie (Mrs Philip Youngman Carter; 1904–66), English novelist, had her first success with *Crime at Black Dudley* (1929). Her earlier novels were simply light and entertaining, but the characterisation, depth and style of her later ones have placed her in the front rank of English detective-story writers. Among her many memorable characters are the mild bespectacled detective Albert Campion and his ex-criminal manservant Mr Lugg.

Apart from a brief excursion into the realm of social history, she has remained loyal to the detective story and reached her peak with *Tiger in the Smoke* (1952). Her plots are always unusual and complex, but in her later books she has shown a tendency towards overcomplexity and tortuousness. Other titles include *Fashion in Shrouds* (1938), *More Work for the Undertaker* (1949) and *The Mind Readers* (1965). K. M. H.

Aluko, Timothy Mofolorunsho (1918–), Nigerian prose satirist. *One Man—One Wife* (1959) and *One Man—One Matchet* (1962) contain rich and sharp observations of the social and political perils that may attend the wholesale and ill-considered transplanting of 'exotic' mores. C. P.

Álvarez Quintero, Serafín (1871–1938) and Joaquín (1873–1944), Spanish playwrights. Their copious production largely consists of gentle comedies of manners set in their native Andalusia, written in a witty, brilliant Spanish that at its best represents perfectly the speech of that region. Much of their work now seems trivial and ephemeral, but *El amor que pasa* [*Love Passes By*] (1906), *Doña Clarines* [*Doña Clarines*] (1909), *Puebla de las mujeres* [*A Woman's Town*] (1912) and the more pretentious *Malvaloca* [*Malvaloca*] (1912) possess more lasting merit. D. H. G.

Amado, Jorge (1912–), Brazilian novelist, and best-known writer among the authors of the Brazilian 'novel of the northeast'. He was born and brought up on his father's cacao plantation in the district of Ferradas (Itabuna) in southern Bahia. He began his studies in the Colégio Antônio Vieira run by the Jesuits in Bahia, but after a dramatic escape he transferred to the Ginásio Ipiranga. Amado was a negligent student, but an avid reader of European and contemporary Brazilian literature. At the age of sixteen he began to contribute articles and reviews to *Diário da Bahia* and he became an active member of the 'academy of rebels' founded by young enthusiasts of the *modernista* movement in Brazil. The group launched two short-lived publications *A Semana* and *Meridiana* and Amado contributed regularly until the group disbanded in 1930. That same year he left for Rio de Janeiro to finish his studies and in 1931 he enrolled as a law student.

His first novel, *O País do Carnaval* ['Carnival land'], appeared in 1932 and, despite its technical immaturity, its concern with political and social issues set a pattern for his later works. In his second novel literary form is once again sacrificed to thesis. With crude realism *Cacáu* ['Cacao'] (1933) depicts the shameless exploitation of Negro and mulatto workers on the plantations. The work attracted immediate attention and Amado was arrested for twenty-four hours on charges of subversive propaganda. *Suor* [*Slums*] (1934) offers the same depressing picture of poverty and vice now set in the festering slums of Bahia.

The same setting appears in his fourth novel *Jubiabá* (1935), but while *Suor* is little more than a series of sketches drawn from life, *Jubiabá* reveals considerable development in matters of structure and technique. The adventures of the protagonist Antônio Balduíno represent the Negro's uphill struggle against social oppression. Balduíno belongs to the new age of social progress and enlightenment while Jubiabá the venerable *pai de santo* (high priest) of the *candomblé* and *macumba* rituals becomes the symbol of the African past which is gradually disappearing. In 1936 Amado published *Mar morto* ['The dead sea'], the first of his novels which describes at length the maritime life of the city. Combining elements of adventure and local superstition the work is an eloquent example of his lyrical vein. The following year he undertook an extensive tour of North and South America. Under the Vargas régime writers suffered persecution and Amado's outspoken disapproval and radical left-wing views made him an obvious target for censure and further arrests. *Capitães da Areia* ['The beach waifs'] (1937) makes a compassionate study of city urchins and social outcasts and the novel reaffirms Amado's fundamental belief in the primitive purity of the lower classes.

Amado's next novel did not appear until 1942. With *Terras do Sem Fim* [*The Violent Land*] he achieved a novel of epic grandeur and this tale of conflict between rival planters for possession of the cacao groves is unanimously considered his masterpiece. *São Jorge dos Ilhéus* ['St George of Ilhéus'] (1944) belongs to the same cycle and like *Terras do Sem Fim* integrates much biographical material. The scene changes to the Brazilian interior in *Seara Vermelha* ['Red harvest'] (1946) which owes something to *Os Sertões* by Euclydes da Cunha with its scenes of violence and fanaticism among the hungry masses impoverished by the crippling *latifundia* system. Here, too, Amado derives his interpretation of social disorders from Marxist doctrine and both plot and characters are designed to support Marx's theory that the masses must unite against their oppressors.

From 1948 to 1952 Amado went into exile with his family, and his travels took him to Europe, the Soviet Union, China and Mongolia. He published a vivid account of these travels in *O Mundo da Paz* ['The world of peace'] (1950). In 1953 he made a second trip to Europe and in the following year wrote *Os Subterrâneos da Liberdade* ['The subterraneans of freedom']. In 1957 he visited the Far East and returned to achieve unanimous acclaim with the publication of *Gabriela Cravo e Canela*

[*Gabriela, Clove and Cinnamon*] (1958), *Os Velhos Marinheiros* [*Home is the Sailor*] (1961) and *Os Pastores da Noite* [*Shepherds of the Night*] (1964).

Much criticised for his political bias, his stereotyped characters and his morbid obsession with sexual disorders and perversions, Amado must be recognised nevertheless as a compelling narrator whose vivid descriptions of Bahia are without parallel. His novels have been translated into thirty languages and works like *Terras do Sem Fim* and *Jubiabá* have been adapted with success for stage, radio and cinema. G. P.

Ambler, Eric (1909–), English novelist, began writing spy stories about 1936, and some of his most successful books were written in the period 1936–40, including *Dark Frontier* (1936), *Uncommon Danger* (1937), *Epitaph for a Spy* (1938), *Cause for Alarm* (1938), *The Mask of Dimitrios* (1939) and *Journey into Fear* (1940). These last two were reissued in the volume *Intrigue* (1965). He is an accomplished craftsman and his novels are well constructed and full of tension without the gratuitous violence which is present in so many modern thrillers. His heroes are not supermen of the James Bond type.

Ambler has also written many very successful film scenarios, including *The Way Ahead*, *The Card*, *The Cruel Sea* and *The Yangtse Incident*. His later novels include *The Light of Day* (1962), *To Catch a Spy* (1964) and *Dirty Story* (1967). K. M. H.

Amis, Kingsley (1922–), English novelist and poet, became well known with his first comic novel *Lucky Jim* (1954), a satire on life in an English provincial university. Dullness, pomposity and a variety of half-baked attitudes (to scholarship, culture, sex) combine to provoke Jim Dixon, an already irreverent young lecturer failing to adapt to the social stratum into which his education has borne him, into increasingly outrageous behaviour, culminating in a drunken display of academic debunking in a special history lecture. The story ends with Dixon's escape to the metropolis with a strong uncomplicated girl and the opportunity to chart his own values.

His next novel, *That Uncertain Feeling* (1955), creates another background of provincial dowdiness and parochialism, the 'hero' here being a librarian in a small Welsh town who escapes temporarily from his nappy-bound home life by having an affair with the nymphomaniac wife of one of the town's leading citizens. Their class difference gives the story another dimension, and links it with other examples of the literature of protest of the 1950s—e.g. Osborne's plays and Braine's novels. *I Like It*

Here (1958) was followed by *Take a Girl Like You* (1960), which describes a long and often unscrupulous campaign conducted by a young grammar school master Patrick Standish, to relieve the modest but unfairly luscious Jenny Bunn of the burden of her virginity. The book explores almost all the variants of sexual persuasion and pursuit and is a most accurate and devastating comedy of contemporary sexual mores and manners. The ending, it may be objected, is unpleasant, with Patrick successfully seducing Jenny while she is drunk; but there is sufficient compassion throughout in the description of their moral indecision—Patrick feeling forced to conform to the expectations of lechery while experiencing the desire to be good and noble, Jenny feeling a dissatisfaction with the narrow and unhelpful morality inculcated in her and longing to be bad—to make the book a very satisfying experience.

The succeeding years saw Amis's involvement with science fiction, in which he combines a serious regard for the genre with a certain 'cocking the snook' at the literary establishment. As well as editing the *Spectrum* science-fiction anthologies with Robert Conquest he became the first English author to write a full-length critical survey of the genre in *New Maps of Hell* (1961). He also published further novels, including *One Fat Englishman* (1963), *The Egyptologists* (with Conquest; 1965) and *The Anti-Death League* (1966). This last proved to be Amis's weightiest work to date: complex, full of ambivalences, and embodying positive values beyond anything previously found in his writings. It is about attitudes to death; it is also about the technologies of administering it, of preventing others from administering it, and of healing the human mind that has been sickened by it. The book has two unmistakable heroes (who between them have several of the characteristics of the traditional Amis anti-hero), in the young and generally inexperienced army officer James Churchill who is outraged by the incidence of arbitrary death and suffering, and his alcoholic-homosexual fellow-officer Max Hunter who vents his feelings through a series of sick practical jokes, including the anonymous founding of an 'anti-death league'. Ironically, it is neither of these, but, rather, those who have been willing to go through with a preventive war of a peculiarly horrific nature, who by their elaborate skill and cunning have effectively combated avoidable death. That they have done so enables Churchill's girl-friend Catharine to reclaim her lover from the state of paralysis and withdrawal into which he has retreated. Yet we are repelled by their technology: and even more by that of the detestable psychiatrist Dr Best who has treated both Hunter and Catharine and who numbers among his patients a man with Churchill's symptoms of withdrawal. Hunter, partly at least as the final practical joke which he perpetrates out of his loathing for the man, frames Best as a spy and precipitates the latter's own retreat into madness: such incidents serving to cast Best as the book's scapegoat.

Amis's poetry reveals similar qualities to those found in his novels: dislike of romanticism, hostility to snobbery and pretentiousness and the taking on of the persona of the average man. Despite the cool irony and sharp intelligence of his work one can sympathise with those critics who find it unsatisfactory because the poet plays the role of the cynical and satirical realist without offering any positive values to salvage the civilisation which he simply mocks. But Amis does offer verse which has strong, positive and feeling content besides technical skill and mocking cynicism, though perhaps less often than one could wish. Poetry published includes *Bright November* (1947), *A Frame of Mind* (1953) and *A Case of Samples* (1956). K. R. R.; D. L. P.

Anderson, Maxwell (1888–1959), American playwright, wrote prolifically on topical and historical subjects. He is probably best known for the verse-tragedy *Winterset* (1935), his second play about the Sacco-Vanzetti case. The story is of a son's attempt to clear the name of his father, an executed Italian radical who had been framed on a murder charge. Mio's faith in his father's innocence wavers when he meets a reformed member of the murderer's gang, and he falls in love with his sister: with the result that when the murderer appears in person and is shocked by an unexpected confrontation into an admission of guilt, the boy hesitates to denounce him to the police. With such knowledge he cannot be allowed to survive, and the two lovers are soon added to the toll of death. The power of love to modify a steadfast and high-minded seriousness of purpose links this play with Anderson's other major success, *High Tor* (1936), where the hero has initially dissociated himself from the cynical materialism of twentieth-century America and renounced all that it can offer him.

K. R. R.

Anderson, Sherwood (1876–1941), American short-story writer and novelist, drew much of his material from his early life in Ohio. His first novel was *Windy MacPherson's Son* (1916); but the work which first showed the full extent of his talents was *Winesburg, Ohio* (1919), a collection of related stories portraying characters in varying states of psychological conflict, generally sexual in origin, against a sombre background of life in a small town. Grotesque in their internal derangement, or alienated from society by their maladjustment to it, they nonetheless are sympathetically, almost lovingly, portrayed: as if, in the repressed society in which they live, to be alienated or grotesque is better than to be successfully adjusted and 'normal'. The stories are integrated through the ubiquitous, almost priest-like figure of George Willard, a newspaperman like Anderson himself.

As in the emphasis on sexuality in *Winesburg, Ohio*, so also in his ambivalent chronicling of the process of industrialisation in his impressive novel *Poor White* (1920), there is to be found Anderson's much remarked affinity with D. H. Lawrence. In his succeeding works, such as *Many Marriages* (1923) and *Dark Laughter* (1925), Lawrence's influence is consciously invoked; but the unsuited role of the prophet, together with the new self-conscious artistic seriousness of a man who had now given up his other work to be a full-time writer, overload and distort the talent of the reporter, and they are generally agreed to be much inferior. Of his other works of this period, among the most readable are his autobiographical studies *Tar—a Mid-West Childhood* (1926), *A Story-Teller's Story* (1924) and *Sherwood Anderson's Notebook* (1926), though deliberately romanticised and inaccurate; and the collection of short stories *Horses and Men* (1923).

In 1926 he settled in Virginia where he bought and edited several local papers. He was married four times. G. S.; K. R. R.

Andres, Stefan (1906–), German novelist, is one of the many German writers whose work has been influenced by the political and moral conditions of the society in which they found themselves. A Rhinelander and a Catholic, Andres originally intended to become a priest; but he turned aside from this vocation and after university studies turned to the vocation of letters. His first novel, *Bruder Luzifer* ['Brother Lucifer'] (1932), is clearly autobiographical, dealing with the steps by which a young monk is drawn away from the monastic life by the blandishments of the world. Travelling widely, he yet produced two novels in 1934, *Eberhard in Kontrapunkt* ['Contrapuntal Eberhard'] and *Die unsichtbare Mauer* ['The Invisible Wall'], stories of young provincials who make their way in the world by hard work and study. But with *El Greco malt den Grossinquistor* ['El Greco paints the Great Inquisitor'] (1936) Andres approached the theme which was increasingly to preoccupy him: the conflict between the Christian view of life and the values of the world, and the conflict between those Christians who see God as a God of Love and those who see him as a stern and exacting Judge. By 1937 Andres had settled in Italy, a self-imposed exile which reflected both his love for the South and his distaste for the Nazi régime in his own country; and just as the English Catholic novelist Graham Greene was to find in the Mexican revolution the background to one of his best novels *The Power and The Glory* so Andres found in the Spanish civil war the background for his great work *Wir sind Utopia* [*We are Utopia*] (1942). This novel deals with a runaway monk turned soldier who finds himself captured and imprisoned in the very monastery he had voluntarily entered years previously. He recalls the facts which led him to leave the cloister, his attempts to justify the pagans who could worship their gods in nature itself and who thus did not sin ever in their most sensual pleasures. His thoughts are interrupted by the villainous commander of the prison who asks him to hear his confession: the gaoler has become the prisoner for a brief moment, and the ex-monk has it in his power to kill his captor and escape. But rather than refuse absolution he forces himself to confess the wretch before him and chooses death with his fellow prisoners rather than escape. It is a novel of brilliant antithesis, a study of man's eternal problems in a particular historical context.

This preoccupation with man's spiritual predicament reached its climax in the trilogy *Die Sintflut* ['The Flood'], the first book of which, *Das Tier aus der Tiefe* ['The Animal from the Depth'], was published in 1949 after Andres' return to Germany. The trilogy symbolises the rise and fall of Nazi Germany: in the first volume a renegade priest enters politics and becomes a dictator, in *Die Arche* ['The Ark'] (1951) the modern totalitarian state is ruthlessly exposed, and the final volume *Der Regenbogen* ['The Rainbow'] (1959) completes the account with the aftermath of a crushing war. During his years in Italy, Andres had published several novels reflecting his delight in the Mediterranean countries, such as *Der Mann von Asteri* ['The Man from Asteri'] (1939) and *Der gefrorene Dionysos* ['The frozen Dionysus'] (1941) later retitled *Die Liebesschaukel* ['Love's swing'] (1951) when published in Germany. Even after his return *Ritter der Gerechtigkeit* ['Knight of Justice'] (1948) and *Das goldene Gitter* ['The Golden Gate'] (1948) showed his love for the South; but *Die Sintflut* remains as his finest work, a work evoked by the history of his own country. G. W.

Andreyev, Leonid Nikolayevich (1871–1919), Russian short-story writer and dramatist. He had tried to support himself at his legal studies by painting portraits. On several occasions he tried to commit suicide. He was unsuccessful as a lawyer, turning to journalism in order to earn his living. Gorky encouraged him and introduced him to a gathering of young writers. Andreyev impressed his audience with his story *Molchaniye* ['Silence'] (1900). Within the year his collection of short stories had sold out and his reputation was made.

In his realistic short stories Andreyev expressed his disgust with life under the czar and his scorn for middle-class smugness. He possessed a fertile imagination and soon added the more lucrative subjects of sex and horror to his wide repertoire. The early Tolstoyan realism in his work was eventually replaced by a modernistic symbolism, yet he still leaned heavily on other writers, especially in his horror stories.

His early realistic writing consisted of *Mysl'* [*Thought*] (1902), *T'ma* [*In the Fog*] (1902), *Gubernator* [*The Governor*] (1906), *Yeleazar* [*Lazarus*] (1906), *Iuda Iskariot* [*Judas Iscariot*] (1907) and *Rasskaz o syemi povyeshennikh* [*Seven who were Hanged*] (1908). These stories are written with a great deal of sympathy but Andreyev's preoccupation with the ubiquity of sex and death tends to make everything else in life seem a vague illusion. *Krasniy smyekh* [*The Red Laugh*] (1904) is an important, stylised work which shows how a soldier can go mad after experiencing the horrors of war. An early example of his later, symbolic work is *Zhizn' chelovyeka* [*The Life of Man*] (1906), a morality play where all the characters are abstractions.

After 1910 Andreyev's popularity waned until he produced his remarkable poetic fantasy, the play *Tot kto poluchayet poshschechiny* [*He Who Gets Slapped*] (1914). This is set in a circus where 'He' arrives to offer his services. He might be described as a refugee intellectual messiah, seeking ways of communicating his lofty ideals to other people. The circus people are able to communicate directly with their audience because of their simplicity; whereas He's intellect is a barrier, not allowing him to communicate simply. By acting the great man who smiles while being slapped he thus directly conveys the intellectual's ridiculous and lonely predicament. The struggle between Lust and Love is also enacted, and because He interferes he is killed.

Andreyev's influence on Soviet literature is slight, though traces of it can be found in Pilnyak's and Gladkov's work. His importance is mainly historical: few other writers of his day being so much in tune with the disillusionment of the Russian intelligentsia, especially after the failure of the 1905 revolution. B. W.

Andrić, Ivo (1892–), Yugoslav novelist and short-story writer, and 1961 Nobel prize winner, notable also as a poet. He was born in the small Bosnian town of Travnik, and his writings are firmly rooted in the customs, language and history of his native land, which formed part of the Ottoman empire until 1878 and of Austro-Hungary until the first world war. As a diplomat between the two wars, Andrić published two volumes of prose poems *Ex Ponto* and *Nemiri* ['Restlessness'], both of which appeared in 1918, and three volumes of short stories. The basic experience of the tragic condition of man contained in the prose poems forms the foundation of Andrić's future work. He spent the war years writing his three novels, all published in 1945: *Travnička Hronika* [*Bosnian Story*], *Na Drini Ćuprija* [*The Bridge on the Drina*] and *Gospodjica* [*The Woman from*

bâtis plus beau' (Down with the world, I shall build it more beautiful). These and subsequent volumes of verse showed Aragon to be a lyric poet of considerable stature, with a gift for word-play amounting almost to preciosity.

He was, however, also a man of action. A life-long communist, he rose to be a member of the French Communist Party's central committee and its leading spokesman on cultural matters. He was influenced in his youth by J.-J. Rousseau and Maxim Gorky, and his poetry can be traced back to Victor Hugo, in its powerful rhetoric, as much as to Rimbaud and the surrealists. This is particularly apparent in the enormously successful *Crève-coeur* ['Heart-break'] (1941), a volume of poetry inspired by the war, the exodus from Paris and the 1940 armistice. In this Aragon really spoke for the people of France and he subsequently became one of the intellectual leaders of the French resistance.

His themes change. Humanity, courage, patriotism, love are the main subjects of the series of volumes that now followed: *Cantique à Elsa* ['Song for Elsa'], *Les Yeux d'Elsa* ['Elsa's Eyes'] (1942), *Brocéliande* ['Brocéliande'], *Le Musée Grévin* ['The Grévin Museum'] (1943), *Je te salue, ma France* ['France, I salute thee'] (1944), *La Diane Française* ['The French Diana'] (1944), etc.

Aragon has also had a distinguished career as a novelist. His first novel *Le Paysan de Paris* ['The Peasant of Paris'] (1926) was surrealist, but with *Les Cloches de Bâle* [*The Bells of Basel*] (1934) and *Les Beaux Quartiers* ['The Fasionable Districts'] (1936) he undertakes the description of the 'real world' while dreaming of a future in which 'books will be written for men who are peaceful and masters of their own destiny'. His early years in the French Communist Party, founded in 1920, provide material for *Aurélien* ['Aurélien'] (1944). This was followed by the vast five-volume fresco *Les Communistes* ['The Communists'] (1949). In 1958 appeared *La Semaine sainte* [*Holy Week*], written in an entirely different, 'Stendhalian', style. Aragon also wrote an immense number of political articles and a history of the U.S.S.R. from Lenin to Krushchev (1964), which has been published in both the U.S.A. and the U.K. A. L. W.

Arden, John (1930–), English playwright, born in Yorkshire, began writing plays while studying architecture, and became known when they were successfully produced at the Royal Court Theatre in the late 1950s. Arden is essentially a poetic dramatist who finds his material in the everyday life of England past and present—on a housing estate (*Live Like Pigs*, 1958), the army at the time of the Crimean war (*Sergeant Musgrave's Dance*, 1959), in municipal politics (*The Workhouse Donkey*, 1963) or amongst the turbulent Borderers of the sixteenth century (*Armstrong's*

Last Goodnight, 1964). Despite the catastrophic endings of several of his plays, his is essentially a comic theatre, celebrating 'the old essential attributes of Dionysus', the Greek wine-god who personified the irrational and the uncontrolled in human behaviour.

Civilisation exists to impose reason and order on these forces: in so doing, Arden's plays suggest, it may kill that which is most vital and truly human, and victimise those who have remained immune from it. The disorderly vitality of the gypsies who 'live like pigs' next door to a respectable middle-class family constitutes a threat to civilised standards, as a result of which their own way of life is put in jeopardy. Alderman Butterthwaite, 'the workhouse donkey' alias 'the Napoleon of the north', is a law unto himself, and must eventually so offend against all the rules of public life as to precipitate the downfall of his own full-blooded and generous personality. The 'mad' Sergeant Musgrave whose recruiting speech becomes a tirade against war clearly cannot be left at large; and the troublesome borderer Armstrong of Gilnockie, whose irresponsible and egotistical marauding is an embarrassment to the peacemakers of England and Scotland, must somehow be disposed of, however treacherous the means. That the one is protesting against war and the other is a threat to peace is not the main point: it is, rather, civilisation's treatment of the anarchic individual—a deed, in Gilnockie's case, whose baseness will long outlast the peace it secures and which gains extra horror from its having been engineered by a man who, though he represents the Scottish king's authority, is in his own nature most like Gilnockie in his humanity and independence. K. R. R.

Arlen, Michael (born Dikrān Kouyoumdjian; 1895–1956), English novelist of Armenian origin, became celebrated for his best-selling book *The Green Hat* (1924). His books are comic-romantic and sometimes melodramatic, and his favourite topics are the love lives of the Mayfair set of the 1920s. Other titles include *These Charming People* (1920) and *Hell! Said the Duchess* (1934). K. R. R.

Arrabal (Fernando Arrabal Téran; 1932–), Spanish dramatist. Arrabal was born in Melilla, but spent his youth in Iberian Spain, studying law at Madrid. In 1954, disillusioned by family and artistic difficulties, he moved to Paris and now writes in French. Arrabal's vision is the product of a civil-war society: in his work—which is deeply Spanish—we find a dislocation of values, a curiously amoral search for good, an awareness of death, and of man's hypocrisy, all of which stem from that background. Thus in his earliest plays—written in 1952 when Arrabal had heard of neither Beckett nor Jarry, nor of any of the other writers who have allegedly influenced him—there occur typical situations. *Oraison* [*Orison*] shows us Fidio and Lilbe, seated on the coffin of the child they have killed, with a Louis Armstrong 'blues' playing in the background, discussing how they can be 'good', live according to the tenets of Christianity; while in *Pique-nique en campagne* ['Picnic in the field'] the parents of a soldier have a day's outing, visiting their son at the front. Arrabal's main device is the use of such devastating contrasts: the reading of the Gospels over the coffin of the murdered child, the middle-class outing to the battlefield. In *Les Deux Bourreaux* [*The Two Executioners*] (1956) Arrabal probes the motives, the hypocrisy, of bourgeois society, while in *Guernica* ['Guernica'] (1959) he presents the archetypal man and woman, Fanchu and Lira, trapped in a ruined house during the bombing of the Basque capital by the Germans. Fanchu's mixture of tenderness and sadism towards Lira mirrors that of Fando towards the paralysed Lis in *Fando et Lis* [*Fando and Lis*] (1956): Fanchu has an amoral innocence that strikes a deep chord in the contemporary audience. Recently Arrabal has evolved the concept of 'Panic' theatre, based on the view that 'Life is memory and man is chance'. But his work need not rest on so tenuous a basis: Arrabal is a highly relevant dramatist, already translated into twenty languages. He has also published three novels. D. H. G.

Artaud, Antonin (1896–1948), French poet and critic. At once a twentieth-century caricature of the late Romantic *poète maudit* and a forerunner of contemporary apostles of social disaffection, his belated posthumous recognition contrasts all the more savagely with the obscure tragedy of his wretched life. He is now considered essential reading for anyone interested in the wider implications of surrealism; of the literature of alienation—confined to mental hospitals for some nine years in later life, he is today studied and respected by several existential psychiatrists; of drug addiction—he sampled peyotl in Mexico; and of the theatre of cruelty, which is not only deeply indebted to his theories but, so it is claimed, was actually founded by his 1935 production of Shelley's *The Cenci*. *N.R.F.* began publishing the *Oeuvres complètes* ['Complete works'] in 1956; as yet only his collected dramatic criticism, *Le Théâtre et son double* [*The Theatre and its Double*] (1938), and the excellent introductory *Artaud Anthology* edited by Jack Hirschman are available in English translation. M. D. E.

Arzak, Nikolay. See **Daniel,** Yuri.

Asch, Sholem (1880–1957), Polish-born American Jewish novelist, dramatist and poet, began to write about Jewish life when nineteen, his first success being *Dos Shtelt* [*The Town*] (1904). His play *God of Vengeance* was produced in Berlin in 1910 by Max Reinhardt. He settled in America in 1914 and was naturalised in 1920 (though he later lived in England and Israel), becoming one of the most popular of Yiddish authors. His later works, sometimes characterised by a disregard for historical religious differences and an attempt to bring Christian and Jewish viewpoints closer, include *Salvation* (1934); a trilogy on the life of Christ—*The Nazarene* (1939), *The Apostle* (1940) and *Mary* (1945); and also the popular *East River* (1946) and *Tales of My People* (1948). G. S.

Aseyev, Nikolay Nikolayevich (1889–), Russian poet, was a friend and disciple of Vladimir Mayakovsky. In 1923 he helped to organise the 'Left Front of Art' and the magazine *Lef*. He entered the realm of literature in 1914, and shocked his readers with the vulgar images he deliberately used. He made famous the phrase 'The world is an ugly mug'. The restraining effect of the Soviet régime saw this futurist poet begin to follow a more conventional line. *Semyon Proskakov* [*Semyon Proskakov*] (1926), a romantic poem about the civil war, is notable but he is best known for his long socialist 'elegy' *Mayakovsky nachinayetsya* [*Mayakovsky Emerges*] (1940), which was actually written in an attempt to produce a work conforming to the demands of socialist realism. This long description of the poet's life is a vigorous poem written in traditional forms, though it lacks the strength of Mayakovsky's own work. B. W.

Ashton-Warner, Sylvia (–), New Zealand novelist, achieved success with her first novel *Spinster* (1958), interesting for its remarkable portrait of Anna Vorontsov, the schoolmistress spinster of the title, a most striking and unusual creation. *Incense to Idols* (1960) is an ambitious attempt to enter the mind of another extraordinary woman, the *femme fatale* Germaine de Beauvais, for whose beauty four men ruin their lives and who in turn destroys herself for love of an indomitable priest. Though the style—seeking to capture the sophisticated thought patterns of a Frenchwoman—at times seems lamely provincial, the central theme of the conflict in a human soul between the calls of God and mammon is most convincingly portrayed. S. R.

Asimov, Isaac (1920–), American writer of science fiction (and of scientific books for children), is by profession a biochemist teaching at Boston University School of Medicine. His novels nearly all deal with the remote future, but a strong belief in the continuity of human experience gives his characters an immediacy and reality not too common in this genre—even when they inhabit the galaxy of a million years into the future. Robotics and psychology play prominent parts in his stories: the former provides the basis of *The Caves of Steel* (1958), but is perhaps best developed in a series of fine short stories published under one cover, *I Robot* (1950). Psychology underpins the whole structure of Asimov's most ambitious work: the *Foundation* trilogy (1951–53), one of the most imaginative and wide-ranging science fiction sagas written. In these books he postulates a whole new science, psychohistory—'that branch of mathematics which deals with the reactions of human conglomerates to fixed social and economic stimuli'. The trilogy covers a period of galactic history lasting some four hundred years: a period during which the first great galactic empire decays, anarchy arises and eventually the hope of a new empire appears. Other titles include *Fantastic Voyage* (1966). G. D. G.

Asturias, Miguel Ángel (1899–), Guatemalan novelist, poet, playwright and 1967 Nobel prize winner. The doyen of Central American writers, he has spent much of his life abroad in study, the diplomatic service and political exile; he is now Guatemalan ambassador in Paris. As a young man he earned academic recognition with *Religiones y mitos de la América indígena* ['Religions and myths of the indigenous Americans'] (1923–6), *Leyendas de Guatemala* ['Legends of Guatemala'] (1930), a work highly praised by Valéry, and a version of the sacred writings of the Guatemalan Quichés, the cosmogonical *Popol Vuh.* This longstanding devotion to the myths, traditions and folklore of the oppressed and impoverished descendants of the Maya Indians, who today form the majority of his fellow-countrymen, nourishes and conditions a disturbingly potent, quasi-surrealist imagination; and yet it rarely involves a circumscribed exoticism, neither in the chromatic poems and plays nor in the vivid parochialism of such novels as *Hombres de maiz* ['Men of maize'] (1949), *Mulata de tal* [*The Mulatta and Mr Fly*] (1963), and the anti-imperialist trilogy *Viento fuerte* [*Cyclone*] (1950), *Papá verde* ['Green daddy'] (1954), *Los ojos de los enterrados* ['The eyes of the buried'] (1960). The book on which his international fame rests, *El Señor Presidente* [*The President*] (1946), demonstrates perfectly his ability to represent the ocean in a rock-pool; an essentially poetic re-creation of a particular political nightmare—the 1898–1922 Estrada Cabrera régime—its graphic denunciatory passion assaults all tyranny, whatever its cause, wherever its provenance. According to legend, 'The weight of the dead makes the earth turn by night, and by day it is the weight of the living . . . When there are more dead than living there will be eternal night, night without end, for the living will not be heavy enough to bring the dawn . . .' In such predicaments we have need of revolutionaries. M. D. E.

Atherton, Gertrude (1857–1948), prolific American novelist, biographer and historian, is best remembered for *The Conqueror* (1902), a fictional biography of the early American statesman Alexander Hamilton. Her novels sometimes exhibit a sensationalist streak—e.g. the glandular rejuvenation of the heroine in *Black Oxen* (1923)—and in the early stages of her writing career she was branded as a member of 'the erotic school'. Her last work, published in her ninetieth year, was a book about her native city, *My San Francisco* (1947). K. R. R.

Aub, Max (1903–   ), Spanish novelist and playwright. Although born in France, Aub is a naturalised Spaniard and writes in Spanish. Having emerged in the twenties as an *avant-garde* dramatist, during the thirties and above all after the civil war Aub revealed himself as primarily a novelist. His outstanding work is *El laberinto mágico* ['The magic labyrinth'] (1943–   ), a diffuse collection of twenty-seven novels and sketches portraying the torn Spain of the civil war. As a virtuoso performance it is almost matched by *Jusep Torres Campalans* [*Jusep Torres Campalans*] (1958), which purports to recount the life of an 'unknown' Catalan post-impressionist painter. The reader is provided with a catalogue of his work, technical notes and some reproductions.

D. H. G.

Auchincloss, Louis (1917–   ), American novelist. Auchincloss's career as a successful lawyer complements his skill as a writer. Superficially his stories and novels might be described as case histories. He does not produce the panoramic epic novels of some of his contemporaries, but careful, incisive studies of individuals within closed communities.

His first book *The Indifferent Children* (1947) was published under the pen-name of Andrew Lee. In 1950 he brought out a volume of stories under the title of *The Injustice Collectors* with the common theme of characters unconsciously and masochistically pursuing punishment. In 'The Fall of the Sparrow', for example, Auchincloss condenses the whole theatre of the Pacific war to create a situation which objectively is insignificant but in which the hero, Victor, is minutely delineated in his mishandling of the simple task of bringing one boat alongside another. In *Portrait in Brownstone* (1962) he exposes the tensions between the characters in the novel over a period of fifty years but restricts his intensive examination to the relations between a few people in a tight family group.

In *The Rector of Justin* (1965) a young teacher at a New England boarding school comes to terms spiritually both with himself and his environment, the latter symbolised by the towering eighty-year-old rector. Auchincloss's genius for precise analysis of individuals in close relationships, which become the boundaries of their world, is here seen at its best.

D. L. P.

Auden, W. H. (Wystan Hugh Auden; 1907–   ), English-born poet, dramatist, editor and critic, has been one of the leading writers of English verse since the 1930s. Some critics feel that Auden can be assimilated into the great moral and philosophical school of poets containing such figures as Milton. He is a moralist attempting to reform not by the technique of the preacher but by creating self-awareness in the reader and focusing this awareness on the leading intellectual questions of the age against the background of the universal problems of man. In this sense he is a didactic poet.

Auden was born in York, educated at Gresham's School, Holt and Christ Church, Oxford. His early career did not suffer from lack of variety. In 1929 he visited Berlin where he met the American psychologist Homer Lane, whose ideas influenced his later writing. In the early 1930s he was a school teacher in England and Scotland while publishing *Poems* (1930) and *The Orators* (1932). In 1935 he went to Iceland with Louis MacNeice, subsequently publishing *Letters from Iceland* (1937); in 1937 he was a stretcher bearer for the Republicans in the Spanish civil war. In 1938 he went to China with Christopher Isherwood, and in 1939 went to live permanently in America. During this whole period he edited numerous books of verse and even wrote scripts for films, including the verse commentary on the G.P.O. film *Night Mail*, on which he worked with Benjamin Britten.

He also collaborated in writing a number of plays with Isherwood.

These plays, *The Dog Beneath the Skin* (1935), *The Ascent of F 6* (1936) and *On the Frontier* (1938), are morality plays tuned not to the emotions but to the intellect of the audience. Essentially they are anti-romantic. Even the leading characters represent attitudes of mind rather than complete human beings. There is little development of character through dramatic conflict, only static contrast. The plays work out Auden's own concept that drama deals with the general and universal, not with the particular and local.

In *The Ascent of F 6* the hero, Michael Ransom, comes closest to real individuality. His strength of character and purpose is contrasted with the average man represented by Mr and Mrs A and with his brother James whom he dislikes and distrusts, a politician whose own strength is sustained by popular acclaim. Michael agrees to lead the climb on the mountain F 6 but is financed under political circumstances that threaten his integrity. His fierce idealism slowly disintegrates on the mountain under the pressure of holding together the disparate members of his party. The narrative form of the play breaks up when Michael, near death at the summit of the mountain, has a series of dreams or hallucinations including a symbolic chess game with his brother and an image of lying in the lap of his mother; the mother who had denied him love as a child in order to make him strong. Michael's apparent strength and subsequent collapse due to the heavy working out of an Oedipus complex derives from Auden's preoccupation with academic psychology, especially that of Homer Lane.

In the years during and after the second world war Auden continued to publish quantities of varied material, including (in verse) *For the Time Being* (1944), *The Sea and the Mirror* (1944), *Collected Poetry* (1945), *The Age of Anxiety* (1947), *The Shield of Achilles* (1955) and *About the House* (1966). Aside from teaching in American universities and editing, Auden worked on the libretti of a number of operas, usually collaborating with Chester Kellman. In 1942 he worked with Benjamin Britten on an operetta, in 1951 on Stravinsky's *The Rake's Progress*, in 1956 on Mozart's *The Magic Flute*, in 1961 on the latter's *Don Giovanni*. In the mid-1960s he was living and writing in Austria.

Given the details of his career it becomes immediately clear that Auden is a writer of enormous breadth and complex involvements. Despite general recognition of his stature he has, however, been received dubiously by his critics. Leavis and the major English literary magazine of the 1930s, *Scrutiny*, saw him as glib and superficial. Post-war American critics tended to regard him as a builder of sleek generalisations over fundamental uncertainties. Reasons for this treatment are not hard to find. With Auden's range of interests there is a continual tension between the broad perspective, the general truth, and the intimacy and compassion of immediate insight. The delicate detail of one man's mind and emotions tends to be blurred by the over-riding patterns of politics or religion or history or sex. There is often an intellectual cross-referencing that is difficult to follow. Auden is interested, for example, both in politics—the study of people in society—and in psychology—the study of individual behaviour. In *The Orators* these two elements combine, the poet being concerned with social decay and the degeneration of the young and the talented. Politically apparently Marxist, he looks towards the idealism of Russia but merges the general enemy represented by social decay with a particular projection of individual inner tension and aggressiveness.

Auden's scientific knowledge, and his preoccupation not only with psychology but with sociology and biology, leads to categorisation and generalisation. He has been accused of taking central ideas from, say, Marx or Adler and kicking them into poetry, a technique liable to lead into the dangerously facile. The lack of the intimate, the desire to see man in perspective, promotes a tendency for Auden to speak like a Greek chorus, for all men rather than for just one man here and now. In 'Solo and Chorus' from *For the Time Being* he writes:

> Let number and weight rejoice
> In this hour of their translation
> Into conscious happiness:
> For the whole in every part,
> The truth at the proper centre . . .

The same reflective intelligence seems at work in *The Shield of Achilles*:

> The mass and majesty of this world, all
> That carries weight and always weighs the same
> Lay in the hands of others; they were small
> And could not hope for help and no help came . . .

The process of intellectualisation seems to accelerate after 1940, coincident with Auden's reconversion to Christianity. Philip Larkin has described the poetry written before the war as exciting, that which came after as verbose and over-intellectual. Certainly the early lyric poetry written by Auden attains an effectiveness and quality which become diffused over the longer, more formally structured pieces.

It is evident, however, that technically Auden is brilliantly versatile, turning his hand from drama to lyric, from traditional sonnet form to a modification of the syllabic mobiles of Marianne Moore—as in his verse drama *The Sea and the Mirror*, a delicately constructed and intellectually agile version of Shakespeare's *The Tempest* in which art and order are unified. Given the poet's technical mastery and conceptual capacity the question remains as to whether he actually has anything to say. His retention of objectivity, his consciously avoiding imposing his own person on the reader, might be justified if his real function as a writer is seen to be the ability to make clear the broad implications of man's position in western culture, leaving the reader free to make his own individual moral decisions in areas which have been elucidated for him.

Auden's quality as a poet is substantially opposed to that of Eliot. He has not the focused depth or spiritual intensity to be found in *Four Quartets* or *The Waste Land*. It is his totality that gives him grandeur, a unity of expression and feeling that like that of Wallace Stevens goes beyond not particularly original ideas into another sphere of understanding. Honours he has received include the King's Medal for Poetry, a Pulitzer prize, a Bollingden prize and election to the American Academy of Arts and Letters. He was Professor of Poetry at Oxford between 1956 and 1961.

D. L. P.

Austin, Alfred (1835–1913), English poet, appointed Poet Laureate in 1896. Austin wrote conventional lyric poetry, inspired usually by nature. It is little read today. In 1894 his prose work *The Garden that I Love* gave him some popularity but his public verse—after his appointment as Poet Laureate—was heavily criticised, especially his hasty praise of the Jameson Raid. His autobiography was published in 1911. D. L. P.

Awoonor-Williams, George (1935–), Ghanaian poet whose restrained yet powerful epic style informs and distinguishes *Rediscovery* (1964), a volume that gives impressive evidence of the effect of his interest in vernacular poetry. C. P.

Ayala, Francisco (1906–), Spanish novelist, essayist and sociologist, whose real merit lies in the novel and *conte*. Born in Granada, Ayala moved to Madrid in 1923 to study law, at the same time producing his early novels. By 1929 his collection *El boxeador y el ángel* ['The boxer and the angel'] shows the influence of the dehumanised experimentalism of the twenties. From 1930 there is a gap in his imaginative output until *El hechizado* [*The Bewitched*] (1944). Subsequently Ayala, exiled from Spain, has been highly productive: no longer is the experimentalism—flashbacks, interior monologue, the use of 'documents' to give an apparent objectivity—mere gratuitous trickery, but the necessary expression of a coherent world-view. In *Historia de macacos* ['A tale of apes'] (1955) we find a writer at the summit of his powers; and the portraits of a sinning world in *Muertes de perro* [*Death as a Way of Life*] (1958) and *El fondo del vaso* ['The bottom of the class'] (1962) are masterly accounts of life in a tropical dictatorship. Ayala's method is, by a sober yet bitter linguistic montage, to satirise humankind and its pretensions. He is a novelist of the highest quality. D. H. G.

Aymé, Marcel (1902–1967), French writer. Born in the Jura, he had several jobs before becoming known as a writer. His main early works are novels: *Brûlebois* ['Burnwood'] (1926), *La Table aux crevés* [*Poor Man's Table*] (1929), *La Jument verte* [*The Green Mare*] (1933), the last of which is generally regarded as his masterpiece and has made a very successful film. His early novels reflect his knowledge of peasant life and often present a depressing picture of its savagery. In addition to the novels, among which one must also mention *Travelingue* [*The Miraculous Barber*] (1941), *Uranus* [*Fanfare in Blémont*] (1948) and *Les Tiroirs de l'inconnu* [*Conscience of Love*] (1960), he has written short stories—*Les Contes du chat perché* [*Wonderful Farm*] (1939), *Le Passe-muraille* [*Walker through Walls*] (1943)—which use the miraculous to satirise contemporary attitudes;

and also numerous plays—notably *Lucienne et le boucher* [*Lucienne and the Butcher*] (1948), *Clérambard* [*Clerambard*] (1950), *La Tête des autres* [*The Heads of Others*] (1952). He is known today as a witty satirist, whose works, of keen observation and cutting style, are essentially non-committed entertainment, often very funny, always viewing the world from an unusual angle. D. E. A.

Ayres, Ruby Mildred (Mrs Reginald William Pocock; 1883–1955), English novelist, doyen of the genre of light romantic fiction, began writing fairy tales as a child and later turned to writing romantic serials for magazines and newspapers. It might be argued that she never stopped writing fairy stories as all her love stories are variations of the Cinderella theme with 'love conquering all' and a 'happy-ever-after' ending. It is difficult to pick out any outstanding examples from her phenomenal output of novels, but some representative titles which speak for themselves are *Long Lane to Happiness* (1915), *Girl Next Door* (1919), *Much Loved* (1934) and *Man in Her Life* (1935). K. M. H.

Azorín (José Martínez Ruiz; 1873–   ), Spanish essayist. A close friend of Baroja, Azorín invented the term '98 Generation' to describe the group of disillusioned writers who, emerging around the crisis year of 1898, sought to understand themselves and their country. In his essays and novels Azorín has evolved a minor art form peculiar to himself: his descriptions of a countryside, or a literary or historical figure, always serving to reveal the author's central preoccupation, the passage of time in his own and Spain's life. His detailed yet lyrical art is best seen in the essays *Los pueblos* ['The country towns'] (1905), *La ruta de Don Quijote* ['Don Quixote's route'] (1905) and *Una hora de España* [*An Hour of Spain*] (1924). D. H. G.

Azuela, Mariano (1873–1952), Mexican novelist, who studied and practised medicine. Violently opposed to the dictatorship of Porfirio Díaz, he supported Madera's rebel movement and later joined the revolutionary forces in action against Huerta. Azuela's novels illustrate, with evidence of personal involvement and first-hand experience, the various phases of the Mexican revolution from its period of violent rebellion to the system that emerged afterwards. His point of view is that of the lower classes, but he captures—possibly with excessive pessimism—not only the political corruption of the ruling body but the defects inherent in all human nature. *Mala yerba* [*Marcela*] (1909) is a notable early work denouncing the despotism of local bosses before the revolution. In 1916 appeared *Los de abajo* [*The Underdogs*], Azuela's major work and the first novel of the

Mexican revolution. It traces the military events from 1913 to 1915, focusing on a band of rebels led by the likeable Demetrio Macías. These peasant farmers have taken up arms in reaction against personal affronts and oppression; they have no conception of an ideal, nor of the broad sweep of the revolution. After a brief period of victory they lapse into aimless and wanton plunder and brutality, to be carried ultimately to destruction by their own impetus. In contrast, *La malhora* ['That woman Malhora'] (1923) narrates—often in an *avant-garde* manner—the misfortunes of a village girl, and describes Mexico's proletariat life. *La luciernaga* ['The firefly'] (1932), a social and psychological analysis, is the most important of the remaining novels, although English translations have been made of *Los caciques* [*The Bosses*] (1917), *Las moscas* [*The Flies*] (1918) and *Las tribulaciones de una familia decente* [*The Trials of a Respectable Family*] (1938). P. R. B.

B

Babel, Isaak Emanuilovich (1894–1941), Russian short-story writer, was born in Odessa of Jewish parentage. His father was a merchant and he educated his son in Hebrew. Until he was sixteen Isaak had to study the Bible and the Talmud, and his only relaxation came from attending the commercial high school. These early impressions play a large part in his later stories. When he was twenty-one he travelled to Petersburg where he endured great hardships. He met Gorky when he tried to sell his stories to various magazines and Gorky helped him a great deal. However, Babel's stories at this time were highly erotic and legal proceedings were only stopped by the outbreak of the 1917 revolution. Babel spent the next seven years wandering about, working, fighting, gaining experience.

It was the recounting of the remarkable experiences he obtained while serving with General Budionni's cavalry regiment on the Polish front that led to the compilation of his major work *Konarmia* [*Red Cavalry*] (1926). He had begun these sketches in 1920, their popularity leading to their publication in one volume. The sketches do not give a balanced picture of the cavalry nor of the Polish campaign; rather do they portray the author's experiences of the absurd violence of men who kill without reason and often without malice. They also include a large number of non-war stories. Babel saw the violence and brutality through the bespectacled eyes of an intellectual and was struck by the malevolent ironies of life. At first his work was well received by the Soviet critics but later they began to suspect that Babel's stories reflected a lack of enthusiasm for the Red cause, occasioned no doubt by the absence of any political shading which was a feature of his work. Many people wrongly regarded these tales as realistic portrayals instead of impressionistic sketches.

With the appearance of *Konarmia* Babel also began to publish his *Odesskiye rasskazy* [*Odessa Tales*] (1927). For these he drew heavily on his experiences in the Moldavanka quarter of Odessa, although not all the stories take place there. Mostly they revolve around the exploits of the legendary Jewish gangster, Benya Krik, who terrorised the Odessa police, but other stories deal with episodes of life in Paris and Petersburg.

In the following years Babel was seen less frequently, and although he made an appearance at the Writers' Conference in 1934, he apologised for his lack of productivity saying that he was working in the new genre of 'silence'. He did produce other work at this time, however, including a play *Maria* [*Maria*] (1934) which was to be his last completed work. The plot is based on life in Petersburg during the early revolutionary years when corruption was rife and Bolshevism the ideal, and it admirably portrays the atmosphere of that time.

Gorky had told the young Babel at the beginning of his career that the way would be strewn with nails. In 1939 Babel disappeared; it appeared later that he had been arrested on trumped-up charges, and had died in 1941 still in gaol. He was rehabilitated in 1954. Much of his previously unpublished work appeared in English translation, compiled by his daughter, in *The Lonely Years*—1925–39 (1964). B. W.

Bacchelli, Riccardo (1891–), Italian poet, novelist and journalist. Among his early successful works is *Il diavolo al Pontelungo* [*The Devil at the Long Bridge*] (1927), an attempt to re-create the background to Bakunin's bid to organise a revolutionary movement in Emilia in the 1870s. He experimented in an entirely different genre with *La città degli amanti* [*Love Town*] (1929). Enrico De Nada, a married man serving as a lieutenant in the Italian army, falls in love with Cecchina Gritti and goes with her to Mexico where an American businessman has founded a community of eroticists run on scientific lines. When the couple become dissatisfied with the hygienic impersonality of Love Town they decide to resume their place in society in spite of the obstacles presented by the conventional moral code. Bacchelli's reputation as a writer rests, however, on *Il mulino del Po*, a powerful epic in prose in three volumes of which the first two, *Dio ti salvi* [*God Save You*] (1938) and *La Miseria viene in barca* [*Trouble Travels by Water*] (1939), were published together in English under the title *The Mill on the Po* in 1952 while the third, *Mondo vecchio sempre nuovo* [*Nothing New under the Sun*] (1940), was not published in English until 1955. This trilogy embraces a century in the history of a family of millers, the Scacernis, against the background of Italy's struggle for its independence and unification. Bacchelli's post-war production includes *L'incendio di Milano* [*The Fire of Milan*] (1951), an account of the tragic adventures of a group of people during the momentous events of 1943, and *Il figlio di Stalin* [*Son of Stalin*] (1955), the romantic story of the last days of Stalin's son Jacob until his untimely death as a prisoner of war in Germany. Bacchelli's style is original and rich with descriptions, and presents a characteristic mixture of romantic themes combined with sensual undertones and a taste for the baroque element in literature. D. B.

Bachmann, Ingeborg (1926–), Austrian poetess who first achieved prominence in the 1950s. Her two collections of poems *Die gestundete Zeit* ['Borrowed time'] (1953) and *Anrufung des Grossen Bären* ['Invocation of the great bear'] (1956) established her as one of the most sensitive of the post-war poets. Her work also includes stories, radio plays and libretti for Hans Werner Henze. A collection of her translated stories appeared under the title *The Thirtieth Year* (1964). The BBC has broadcast translations of some of her radio plays, and translations of individual poems are to be found in *Modern German Poetry* (ed. Michael Hamburger and Christopher Middleton; 1962) and *German Writing Today* (Penguin Books, 1967). R. C. W.

Bagnold, Enid (Lady Roderick Jones; 1889–), English novelist and playwright, wrote the once popular novel *National Velvet* (1935) about a girl jockey who wins the Grand National steeplechase. She is best known today as the author of successful plays such as *The Chalk Garden* (1956) and *The Chinese Prime Minister* (1961). K. R. R.

Baker, Ray Stannard (1870–1946), American essayist and biographer, won a Pulitzer prize for his eight-volume biography *Woodrow Wilson—Life and Letters* (1927–39). He published several volumes of essays including *Adventures in Contentment* (1907), written under the pseudonym David Grayson; and was author of the 'muck-raking' publication *The Railroads on Trial* (1906). K. R. R.

Balchin, Nigel (1908–), English novelist, worked as scientific adviser to the army during the 1939–45 war. This is the background to one of his best-known novels, *The Small Back Room* (1943), which describes the inventor on a shoe-string budget resisting an inflexible and insular Civil Service that attempts to shape his activities in terms of its own organisation. The hero endures also the solitary fear of dealing with anti-personnel bombs and his conquest of this fear enables him to survive his personal weaknesses. The novel thus brilliantly depicts the hero doing battle both with the outside world and with his inward self.

Balchin had previously followed a business career, and under the pseudonym of Mark Spade had written two humorous satires on the business world, *How to Run a Bassoon Factory* (1934) and *Business for Pleasure* (1935). Many of his post-war novels are psychological studies, notably *Mine Own Executioner* (1945) and *A Sort of Traitors* (1949), but they lack the compelling power of *The Small Back Room*. Other titles include *Lord I was Afraid* (1947), *Anatomy of Villainy* (1950), *Sundry Creditors* (1953), *Seen Dimly before Dawn* (1962) and *In the Absence of Mrs Petersen* (1966). K. M. H.; D. L. P.

Baldwin, James (1924–), American writer, is probably the most widely known Negro writer and is potentially one of the most important novelists now writing in English. At his best, he achieves what Conrad defined as the novelist's task, to make the reader hear, feel, see. The opening section of *Another Country* (1963)—the story of Rufus, a young Negro jazz musician, a tragedy of beauty and life going to waste and being destroyed—is the work of a great novelist, a masterpiece of observation and creation; the artist making articulate the despair of those who are less articulate. Sadly, Baldwin senses he has a prophetic mission: prophecy (the advocacy of one particular solution to the problems of life) involving a denial of diversity, a narrowing down and simplifying of the complexity of human experience, the individuality of individual existence. Eric, the central figure of the latter part of the novel, stands as an ideal embodiment of certain virtues of love and sympathy which Baldwin seems to offer elsewhere (in, for example, many of his essays, the prose of which at times becomes rhetorically over-insistent) as a panacea to the problems arising from the spiritual captivity of modern man: the war between the sexes, the war between the races, the war between man and himself (which are all really the same war). Thus, when he makes love to the young writer Vivaldo, he is presented as helping Vivaldo to surrender that pride of self-consciousness that is the greatest barrier to genuine human communication, and thus to find himself, and learn compassion and forgiveness. Yet the reader remains unconvinced: unconvinced that Vivaldo would so surrender, and unconvinced that the experience could be transcendental in this way. One feels that Vivaldo has, in fact, been forced to surrender his individuality, to betray the guts and integrity he has displayed in his lonely quest for love and artistic truth. The prophet has betrayed the artist, twice over.

If Baldwin's great novels were yet to come, his earlier achievements had certainly also been substantial. His previous novel, *Giovanni's Room* (1957), deserves to be singled out as one of the most striking evocations of a homosexual love affair, unmarred by the false notes struck in its more ambitious successor. No other writer has so captured the terrors that beset such a relationship even in a society that does not make it a criminal offence: the panic of the normally heterosexual who finds himself propelled by rival tendencies into an area of experience felt to be beyond the pale of acceptability, and the confirmed homosexual's even greater dread of losing the precious rarity of a true love and being condemned by instinctual necessity to surrender to a lifetime of sordid physical relationships. There is an awe-inspiring purity to the vengeance enacted by the tormented Giovanni on the jealous, aging Guillaume when the latter, having spitefully deprived him of his job at discovering his precarious happiness with the sexually ambivalent American student David, has been the exultant instrument of his degradation after David's desertion to rejoin his fiancée.

Other titles include *Go Tell it on the Mountain* (1954), and various powerful non-fiction pieces on the situation of the Negro in America including *The Fire Next Time* (1963). J. L.; K. R. R.

Ballantyne, David (1924–), New Zealand novelist, is concerned with social documentation of working-class urban life. The best example of his work is the long novel *The Cunninghams* (1948), a study of a family dominated by the mother, who dwarfs both husband and son. He has also written a volume of short stories *The Last Pioneer* (1963); and plays for television, *And the Glory* (1963) and *Passing Throng* (1961). S. R.

Ballard, James Graham (1930–), English science-fiction writer noted for his particularly credible physical and geographical catastrophes as in *The Drowned Planet* (1963) and *The Crystal World* (1966), the latter describing the gradual petrification of matter in an African forest and the deadly attraction of its gem-like static beauty. S. R.

Bandeira, Manuel (1886–), Brazilian poet and critic, born in Recife (Pernambuco), was educated in Rio de Janeiro at the Colégio Pedro II, and subsequently in São Paulo where his study of architecture was cut short by tuberculosis. During a lengthy convalescence he experimented with *vers libre* under the influence of Apollinaire; in 1913 he left for Europe and entered a sanatorium near Davos-Platz where he met Paul Eluard. When the first world war broke out Bandeira returned home intent upon a literary career and his first book of verse *A Cinza das Horas* ['The dust of the hours'] appeared in 1917. This was well received, and although it was influenced by Parnassian and symbolist models, there are echoes of the traditional Portuguese lyrics. Meanwhile, Bandeira also contributed poems to a number of *avant-garde* periodicals which were helping to launch *modernismo*, like *Klaxon*, *Terra Roxa* and *Revista de Antropofagia*. Bandeira's metrical innovations develop further in *Carnaval* ['Carnival'] (1919) and the poems of this collection together with those of *O Ritmo Dissoluto* ['Dissolved rhythm'] (1924) fully express the spirit of the 1922 generation of poets. He was hailed as the 'São João Batista da Nova Poesia' (St John the Baptist of the new poetry') and his correspondence and mutual collaboration with Mário de Andrade during the twenties assured the movement's success.

Libertinagem ['Libertinism'] (1930) is not only the poet's most representative contribution to *modernismo* but it also includes the most characteristic examples of Bandeira's lyricism—colloquial, ironic, and often infused with a tragic humour. His clear conception of the aesthetic principles and aims which inspired the Semana de Arte Moderna ('Week of Modern Art') is evident in the numerous articles he wrote for *Mês*

Modernista, Ariel and *Diário da Noite* among other periodicals and newspapers. With *Estrêla da Manhã* ['The morning star'] (1936) he further refined his experiments in free verse and metrical innovations and began to explore the Negro folklore of Brazil, sometimes with a social intention.

In 1938 Bandeira returned to the Colégio Pedro II to teach literature, and in 1943 became Professor of Spanish-American Literature at the Federal University in Rio de Janeiro. These were also years of varied literary activity. In 1937 he edited an *Antologia dos Poetas Brasileiros da Fase Romântica* ['Anthology of Brazilian Poets of the Romantic Phase'] and a companion anthology on the Parnassian poets of Brazil followed in 1938. Other editions include the poetry of Alphonsus de Guimaraens, Antero de Quental and Gonçalves Dias. The first edition of his own *Poesias completas* ['Complete poems'] appeared in 1940, the year that he was elected to the Brazilian Academy of Letters. Subsequent editions were augmented to include *Belo Belo* (1948); *Mafuá do Malungo* (1948) and *Opus 10* (1952). The evolution and range of his poetry clearly emerges from his self-effacing autobiographical essay *Itinerário de Pasárgada* ['The Itinerary of Pasargada'] (1954) and from the numerous prose writings published in 1958.

Important translations represent another facet of Bandeira's work. His *Poemas Traduzidos* ['Translated poems'] were first published in 1945. His remarkable versions of *Macbeth* and Schiller's *Maria Stuart* have been successfully performed in Brazil and translations of Cocteau, Sean O'Casey and Richard Nash followed. Recent publications include an important comprehensive anthology of Brazilian poetry *A Poesia do Brasil* (1961). Translations of his poetry are available in the Dudley Fitts *Anthology of Contemporary Latin-American Poetry* (1942), in selections of *Modern Brazilian Poetry* edited by Leonard S. Dounes (1954) and John Nist (1962) and in *The Poem Itself* edited by Stanley Burnshaw (Pelican, 1964). The poet's eightieth birthday in 1966 was marked by tributes in Brazil and Portugal and Bandeira became the first Brazilian poet to receive a national decoration.

G. P.

Banks, Lynne Reid (–), English novelist, wrote *The L-Shaped Room* (1960), the classic tale of bedsitter life in a decaying part of London. The heroine is a single girl who has become pregnant, and eventually decides to have the child. The changing reactions of the other inhabitants of the house—a characteristic assortment of the flotsam and jetsam of bedsitterland—form one of the most appealing aspects of her book, and the arrival of the baby provides a focus for their otherwise near-purposeless existence. Her second novel, *End to Running*, was published in 1962.

K. R. R.

Barbusse, Henri (1873–1935), French novelist. Born at Asnières Barbusse entered journalism at the age of sixteen. He made his literary debut in 1896 with a volume of poems entitled *Les Pleureuses* ['Weeping Women'], indicative of a very sensitive nature that reacted to every fleeting impression of the reality of modern life. This was followed by the novel *L'Enfer* [*Hell*] (1908) in which Barbusse was very obviously following in Zola's footsteps. It contains some powerful descriptions but suffers from Barbusse's inability to resist turning it into a philosophical analysis of his time—the handling of abstract ideas not being the area where his talent lay. It lay rather at the opposite extreme of powerful and limpid emotion, compounded of great sincerity and fervour. No doubt it was these qualities, applied to the tragedy of the first world war, that made his book *Le Feu* [*Fire*] (1916) France's biggest best seller. Subtitled 'Diary of a Company', it presents, as no other book has ever done, an exact description of life in the trenches as seen through the eyes of the *poilu*, the French 'tommy'. Thus there is no artifice whatever in the moving intensity and virile humour with which are depicted attacks, 'spud bashing' and the behaviour of his fellow soldiers. The book also contains bitter satire on the division of France into 'two foreign countries, the front and the rear'. The tragic sobriety and simplicity of *Fire* makes it the most powerful picture of the horror and hatefulness of war that has ever been penned. Henri Barbusse devoted the rest of his life to progressive causes.

A. L. W.

Barclay, Florence (1862–1921), English popular novelist, wrote the best-selling romance *The Rosary* (1909) about a plain girl who will not marry the artist who has fallen in love with her for fear that he will lose interest in her afterwards.

K. R. R.

Barea, Arturo (1897–1957), Spanish writer. After an unsettled youth, and a harrowing spell as a conscript in Spanish Morocco in the twenties, Barea worked for the Republicans during the civil war, censoring the dispatches of foreign correspondents and directing broadcasts to the rest of Europe. In 1938 he moved to England where he remarried, took British citizenship and lived by his pen. Barea is best known for his autobiographical trilogy *La forja de un rebelde* [*The Forging of a Rebel*] (1941–44), wherein the uprooted exile seeks and discovers a sense to the frustrations and tensions he finds in himself and in Spain. Barea's only true novel *La raiz rota* [*Broken Root*] (1951), written in his characteristically anglicised Spanish, is the uneven and tendentious account of an exiled Republican's return to post-war Spain. Barea does not enjoy the same reputation in Spain as elsewhere. He wrote well, if ungrammatically, but he lacked a sense of construction and his attitudes seem dated and foreign. He also published critical essays on García Lorca and Unamuno.

D. H. G.

Baring, Maurice (1874–1945), English writer. A gift for languages led him into the diplomatic corps (1898–1904) before he became a correspondent for the *Morning Post* in Manchuria and Russia. He learnt Russian and developed an abiding sympathy for the Russian people. Besides various volumes of poems, parodies and critical essays he wrote several novels, the first titles being *Passing By* (1921), *Cat's Cradle* (1925) and *Daphne Adeane* (1926), which were set in the social circles in which he had moved. Other works include *The Russian People* (1911), *Gaston de Foix* (a play, 1903) and *Puppet Show of Memory* (1922).

G. S.

Barker, George (1913–), English poet. Barker's poetry is violently romantic, mystical, visionary, declamatory, extravagant and belongs with the work of Robinson Jeffers in America and Blackburn and Clemo in England. Barker was born in Essex, educated at an L.C.C. school and then at Regent Street Polytechnic. He has lectured in English literature in Japan and lived for a time in America.

Barker hovers between religious ecstasy and vision on the one hand and violence, horror and terror on the other; his is poetry of extremes of mood. The brilliance and vividness of his imagery, matched by technical skill, loses its force in a lack of overall coherence in the poetry as a whole. *The True Confession of George Barker* (1950) omitted from *Collected Poems* (1957) is an account of the poet's sexual development which is as lewd and scatological as it is honest and powerful. It demonstrates the tensions between mysticism and sexual experience which seem to preoccupy a number of English poets of Barker's era. The problem is not one of close human relationships but of the dichotomy between animal sex and spiritual intensity. He has Swift's horror of the body and of reproduction, as when in *The True Confession* he describes:

> The act of human procreation
> —The rutting tongue, the grunt and shudder . . .

Barker is involved with political and social questions but he is seldom free from a profusion of images and a nihilistic philosophy that together blur the intellectual content of his verse. Like Jeffers he is a compelling and a striking poet rather than an integrated artist. Other volumes include *The View from a Blind I* (1962) and *Dreams of a Summer Night* (1966).

D. L. P.

Barnes, Djuna (1892–   ), American dramatist, novelist and short-story writer. Djuna Barnes had a series of three plays produced during 1919 and 1920 but has since concentrated more on the short story and novel forms. She published in 1923, and revised in 1929, a mixed bag of prose and poetry called simply *A Book* which dealt in depth with characters whose non-intellectual empathy lay in the direction of the simplicity of animals. *Rhyder* (1928) is a satirical novel in the prose style of the later James Joyce dealing with the relations between a man and the various women in his life. *Nightwood* (1936) bears an introduction by T. S. Eliot comparing its starkness and sense of impending tragedy with the gloomiest aspects of the seventeenth-century revenge tragedies of Tourneur and Webster. The book deals with the problems of a psychopathic group and highlights the author's intense involvement with the psychology of the abnormal. Djuna Barnes's other work includes *Antiphen*, a surrealistic play published in 1958. D. L. P.

Baroja, Pío (1872–1956), Spanish novelist. Baroja is a unique figure, individualistic and disillusioned, a Basque compound of 'spleen' and sincerity. His friend Azorín (q.v.) characteristically assigned him to the '98 Generation' of writers preoccupied with the problem of Spain: Baroja equally characteristically refused to acknowledge the existence of such a generation, feeling himself distinct from Unamuno, Azorín and his other contemporaries. Baroja is important as the writer who demolished the stereotyped form of the nineteenth-century novel—he typically depicts a semi-autobiographical anti-hero in a plot-less structure—and both technically and stylistically he remains a dominant influence on Spanish novelists. His major production covers the years 1900–12: the later novels re-elaborate the basic themes emerging in these initial works, which form the foundation of Baroja's reputation.

In the Basque novels *El mayorazgo de Labraz* [*The Lord of Labraz*] (1903) and *Zalacaín el aventurero* ['Zalacaín the adventurer'] (1909) we find Baroja's characteristically tragic *dénouement* and the archetypal heroes—Don Juan de Labraz, weak and irresolute; Martín Zalacaín, the man of action. In 1904–05 he wrote the novels *La busca* [*The Quest*], *Mala hierba* [*Weeds*] and *Aurora roja* [*Red Dawn*] which form the sombre trilogy *La lucha por la vida* ['The struggle for life']. Set in the slums of Madrid, they show how the wretched milieu determines and corrupts the life of Manuel Alcázar. The atmosphere of these early works is sullen and pessimistic and their protagonists are failures—as, for example, Andrés Hurtado, in *El árbol de la ciencia* ['The tree of knowledge'] (1911); César Moncada, whose political ambitions founder in married stagnation in *César o nada* [*Caesar or Nothing*] (1910); Silvestre Paradox, the collapse of whose utopian republic is witheringly described in *Paradox, rey* [*Paradox, King*] (1906); and Quintín García Roelas, the unscrupulous protagonist of *La feria de los discretos* [*The City of the Discreet*] (1905). Only the 'men of action' achieve worthwhile self-affirmation, as in the balanced figure of the Basque seaman in *Las inquietudes de Shanti Andía* [*The Restlessness of Shanti Andía*] (1911). Baroja's idealisation of such characters and his peculiarly formless novels earned him the admiration of Hemingway. He died in Madrid in 1956. D. H. G.

Barrie, J. M. (Sir James Matthew Barrie; 1860–1937), Scottish novelist and playwright. Working as a journalist in Nottingham, and from 1885 in London, his first book *Better Dead* appeared in 1887. In 1888 *Auld Licht Idylls,* sketches of life in Kirriemuir, revealed his mastery of humour and pathos. *A Window in Thrums* (1889), in similar sentimental vein, led to his being described as a master of the Kailyard school, a group of Scottish novelists who exploited their background and excluded the harsher side of Scottish life. By 1900 he was well known as a novelist; but by 1925 he had become probably the most popular living dramatist with the success of such plays as *Quality Street* (1901), *The Admirable Crichton* (1903) and *Peter Pan* (1904). *Peter Pan,* the story of the little boy who does not want to grow up, and his friends who fly with him to Never-Never Land, continues to delight thousands of children every Christmas, and has been adapted as a Disney film.

Barrie became skilful at balancing comedy and pathos, and in most of his later work there is an appeal to become as simple as little children and to discard too-worldly success. *The Twelve-pound Look* (1910), on this theme, was his best one-act comedy. The whimsicality and sweetness in much of his work have proved less palatable to later generations, though *Quality Street* and *What Every Woman Knows* (1908) have been turned into musicals. Other plays include *The Little Minister* (1897); *Dear Brutus* (1917); and *Mary Rose* (1920). G. S.

Barrios, Eduardo (1884–1963), Chilean novelist, who has followed various occupations including circus acrobat, director of public libraries, and minister of education. His novels reveal a fundamentally romantic sensibility and are of either psychological or regional themes. *El niño que enloqueció de amor* ['The boy who went mad with love'] (1915), claimed to be the first psychological novel of South America, is the diary of a hypersensitive ten-year-old who falls in love with a woman, losing his reason through her betrothal to another. Barrios' most important work *El hermano asno* ['Brother ass'] (1922) is the intimate self-analysis of a Franciscan monk, Brother Lázaro, who records in brief passages of lucid, sensitive, often poetic prose the mental and spiritual crisis incurred when his feelings for a woman, María, stir old memories and conflict with his vocation. Meanwhile he also gives an impressionistic account of the increasing saintliness of Brother Rufino, a mentally unbalanced fighter. Ultimately Rufino assaults María (for self-abasement? through lust? to save Lazaro?) and dies. Lázaro resolves his own conflict through self-sacrifice, assuming responsibility for the act. Of later novels, *Gran señor y rajadiablos* ['Feudal lord and proud oppressor'] (1948) is the most significant, describing the life of a wealthy Chilean landowner, against a vivid social and historical background. P. R. B.

Barry, Philip (1896–1949), American playwright, wrote a series of sophisticated social comedies including *Hotel Universe* (1930) and *Philadelphia Story* (1939). The film version of the latter has become a classic of the cinema. K. R. R.

Barstow, Stan (1928–), English novelist who achieved success with his book *A Kind of Loving* (1960), an accurate and moving account of the contemporary pressures on love and marriage: on Vic the boy, of the sexual bragging of his companions and of titillating magazines, and on Ingrid the girl, of her dread of losing him. The resolution—after a hasty marriage precipitated by Ingrid's pregnancy, incompatibility exacerbated by their living in the same house as her mother, quarrels and separation—is a qualified one as Vic comes to recognise that the best he can hope for is 'a kind of loving'. The sequel, *The Watchers on the Shore* (1965), is rather more melodramatic in its incidents and its characterisation, and suggests that the frail optimism that was the best feature of the first novel was unjustified. Barstow's other publications include *The Desperadoes and Other Stories* (1961), *Ask Me Tomorrow* (1962) and *Joby* (1964), which describes adolescence as it happens to, and the adult world as it is seen by, an eleven-year-old boy. S. R.

Barth, John (1930–), American novelist, whose titles include *The Floating Opera* (1956), *The End of the Road* (1960), *The Sot-Weed Factor* (1962) and *Giles Goat Boy* (1967). These display an interesting combination of serious analysis of human predicaments with an academic detachment which make his subjects comic, and vehicles for the portrayal of pessimistic humour.

A professor of English, Barth clearly achieves a scholarly enjoyment from experimenting with style, and using his initial plot as a hub of philosophical and psychological discussion. Always, however, this is done coherently and hardly ever to the detriment of the structure of the novel. *The Sot-Weed Factor*—a historical piece of story-telling about the adventurous and bawdy transplantation of parts of seventeenth-century English society to the American colonies—is possibly the most fragmented of his works and apparently the least concerned with analysing ordinary and foreseeable situations. The latter are made painfully clear in *The End of the Road*, which (despite its being written in the first person) is a detached narration of the cataclysmic effects of Jake, the narrator, upon the marriage of a colleague and friend. Superficially, the novel is a *tour de force* of comic disaster; but it also conveys penetrating and disturbing insights into American college life, and into the nature of a not untypical academic marriage.

If, because of this, Barth can be compared to Edward Albee, in his subsequent and longest work *Giles Goat Boy* he can be compared to Jonathan Swift or Wyndham Lewis. For this work is a long and inventive allegory in which the ethical and political life of modern man in a nuclear age are presented against a panoramic and mythical background. All human society is contained within a university campus, the conflicting sections of which are controlled by WESCAC and EASCAC—the giant computers and the students of which live in a permanent state of 'cool riot'. This is the situation in which George, or Giles, a boy from the outer world who has been reared among goats by an aging don, is inspired to prove himself the Messiah and become the Grand Tutor. The book is consistently inventive with Barth borrowing academic language for the coining of words to convey the moral and cultural codes of the society. This novel is an important, if pessimistic, work. Even if it does not present an answer to the problem of need for meaning in a technological, secularised society, it is powerfully and ironically amusing in the way it poses the question. S. M.

Bass, Eduard (1888–1946), Czech writer. As a journalist he acquired prodigious knowledge of various fields which he exploited in his unpretentious novels. His *Klapzubova jedenáctka* [*The Chattertooth Eleven*] (1922) parodies the world of international soccer and *Cirkus Humberto* [*Umberto's Circus*] (1941) is a chronicle of a Czech circus family. K. B.

Bassani, Giorgio (1916–), Italian novelist and short-story writer, born in Ferrara of Jewish origin. Formerly better known as the editor of *Botteghe Oscure* and the proponent of Lampedusa's *The Leopard*, he has won both the Strega and Viareggio prizes as well as a Charles Veillon award. In *Cinque Storie Ferraresi* [*A Prospect of Ferrara*] (1956), provincial compromise with, domination by and opportune rejection of, fascism is minutely dissected with fastidious aplomb. *Gli Occhiali d'oro* [*The Gold-rimmed Spectacles*] (1958) introduces Dr Fadigati who comes to Ferrara in the restless years of emergent fascism. He gains provisional acceptance as a cultured gentleman and capable physician but is eventually rejected and driven to suicide after a humiliating, homosexual alliance with a particularly nasty student. *Il Giardino dei Finzi-Contini* [*The Garden of the Finzi-Continis*] (1962) recalls Ferrara's richest Jewish family, obsessively fascinating like Proust's Guermantes, effortlessly remote like Pasinetti's Partibons, yet vulnerable and, ultimately, exterminated. Ferrara comes vividly, illuminatingly alive in Bassani's reticent, ironical evocations, impinging on the narrator's wealthy Jewish consciousness of racial antagonism and political affiliation as a microcosm of the banality behind the despicably decent ostracism of the outsider, the minority, the unconventional. Complaisant respectability and spineless probity, not prejudice, are the real cancer. M. D. E.

Bastos, Augusto Roa (1917–), Paraguayan novelist. On the one hand an historically improbable Arcadia visited by Candide, on the other, a rumoured refuge for unsavoury political delinquents, Paraguay has long been a country of the mind. Two excellent travel journals, Gerald Durrell's *The Drunken Forest* (1956) and Gordon Meyer's *The River and The People* (1965), together with an admirable brief history, George Pendle's *Paraguay* (1954), supplied valuable ballast for our imagination but, if the national physiognomy had recently become more familiar, until the advent of Señor Bastos there had been no Paraguayan characterisation of the national reality. Born in Asunción, the capital, variously journalist, broadcaster, lecturer, diplomat and political exile, Bastos demanded and obtained international attention with an engrossing parable of his country's contemporary situation, *Hijo de hombre* [*Son of Man*] (1961), a virtuoso exercise in psychological excoriation which exposes the nerve ends of history, a history made by the Europeans and endured by the Indians. In this novel modern Paraguay reflects on its past—the Chaco War of 1932–5 in which Bastos fought, the traumatic years of the War of the Triple Alliance, 1865–70, which decimated the male population, the arrival of the Jesuits, the Spanish Conquest—and in reflecting invents its future, a future when, in the words of the Guarani Indian Hymn of the Dead which the author cites as an epigraph:

> . . . My voice shall be heard again among the dead . . .
> And my word shall once more be made flesh . . .
> When this age is over and a new age begins . . .

Two further works are as yet untranslated, a novel, *El trueno entre las hojas* ['The Thunder among the Leaves'] (1961), and a collection of short stories, *El Baldío* ['Derelict'] (1966). M. D. E.

Bates, H. E. (Herbert Ernest Bates; 1905–), English novelist. His early short stories showed the clarity of style, sympathetic evocation of the countryside, and portrayals of the concerns and emotions of country people which are to be found in much of his work. A different inspiration was provided during the war when the government commissioned him to write about the R.A.F., and about the war in Burma. As well as the novels published under the name of Flying Officer X, his war stories *Fair Stood the Wind for France* (1944) and *The Cruise of the Breadwinner* (1947) were widely read for their feeling for the time and characters involved, allied with factual accuracy. The novels in which he draws on his knowledge of Burma and Kashmir, *The Purple Plain* (1947), *The Jacaranda Tree* (1949) and *The Scarlet Sword* (1951), have a particular colour and intensity in atmosphere, scenes and relationships. For his later novels *The Darling Buds of May* (1958) and *Oh! To Be in England* (1963) he has returned to the rural and domestic. His mastery of the short story can be seen in any of the various collections, *My Uncle Silas* (1939), *The Wedding Party* (1965) and others. J. W.

Bates, Katherine Lee (1859–1929), American poetess, whose *Selected Poems* was published posthumously in 1930. Her best-known poem 'American the Beautiful' was purportedly inspired by the view from the top of Pike's Peak in Colorado. D. L. P.

Bates, Ralph (1899–), English novelist, best known for his writings about Spain and Spanish political life in the years preceding the civil war, in which he himself fought. These include *Sierra* (1933), *The Lean Men* (1934) and *The Olive Field* (1936). K. R. R.

Baum, Vicki (1888–1960), Viennese-born novelist who settled in Germany, wrote in English after one of her earlier novels *Grand Hotel* (1930) was dramatised (and later filmed) in America. In this, one of her most successful books, she used the technique of the 'group novel' to bring together a number of varied personalities in one setting. Many of her earliest written works appeared quite late in her life; among her numerous titles in English are *Falling Star* (1934), *Weeping Wood* (1943), *Danger from Deer* (1951) and *Ballerina* (1958). K. M. H.

Baxter, James K. (1926–), New Zealand poet and critic, was acclaimed upon the appearance of the youthful *Beyond the Palisade* (1944). *Blow,*

Wind of Fruitfulness (1948) revealed a development towards more serious content and a note of sober wintry pessimism. His first volume of criticism *Recent Trends in New Zealand Poetry* (1951) showed authority and discernment and provided evidence of his belief that poetry should affirm a moral truth. He attempted to demonstrate this in his next collection *The Fallen House* (1953). His more recent poetry, particularly some poems written for inclusion in the *New Zealand Poetry Yearbook* for 1964, is characterised by a harsh satire of modern life and sexuality and led to the issue's losing its government grant. Other publications include *The Fire and the Anvil* (1955) and a series of parodies *The Iron Breadboard* (1957) and *Howrah Bridge* (1962). S. R.

Bazin, Hervé (Jean Hervé-Bazin; 1911–), is the great-nephew of René Bazin, member of the Académie Française. He has published some poetry, but his first novel *Vipère au poing* [*Viper in the Fist*] obtained a *succès de scandale* on its publication in 1948. It is the story of an aristocratic family, the Rezeau, and of the mutual hatred felt by the narrator and his mother. The vivacity and savagery of the descriptions of the development of this feeling are remarkable, and it is not surprising that the story should be continued in later works by Bazin. He went on to write *La Tête contre les murs* [*Head against the Wall*] (1949), *La Mort du petit cheval* [*Death of the Little Horse*] (1950), *Lève-toi et marche* [*Take up thy Bed and Walk*] (1952), *L'Huile sur le feu* [*Oil on the Fire*] (1954), the last of these being the story of a fire-raiser, whose exploits and their results are seen through the eyes of a child. Subsequent titles included *Qui j'ose aimer* [*Tribe of Women*] (1955) and *Au nom du fils* [*In the Name of the Son*] (1961). All his works, whether they be continuations of the Rezeau story or not, are inspired by the same intensity of feeling and rapidity and quality of intelligence which were noticeable in his first work. D. E. A.

Beach, Rex (1877–1949), American novelist, wrote tales of the Alaska outback. His first four novels were collected in *Alaskan Adventures* (1935); his last was *The World in His Arms* (1945). K. R. R.

Beauvoir, Simone de (1908–), French writer. Born in Paris, she specialised in philosophy, teaching in Marseilles, Rouen and Paris. As a philosopher, her attitude is similar to that of Jean-Paul Sartre, whose close friend she is; and her work is in particular a plea for personal and social liberty, based on the existentialist premise of personal responsibility and involvement. Thus for her the problem of good and evil has to be redefined as the problem of the personal creation of a scheme of values.

Her novels are means for her to illustrate and exemplify her philosophy, and, as such, pose the particular problems and dilemmas appropriate to her thought. *L'Invitée* [*She Came to Stay*] (1943), still regarded as probably her best work, poses that of the existence of others and of the dilemma of choice when the other is inimical to one's own consciousness. Among her other novels are *Le Sang des autres* [*The Blood of Others*] (1944), *Tous les hommes sont mortels* [*All Men are Mortal*] (1947) and *Les Mandarins* [*The Mandarins*] (1954). This novel, the Goncourt prize-winner for 1954, illustrates the problems of commitment which so preoccupied the French intelligentsia after the last war; the 'mandarins' are those whose commitment fails and who can thus merely write, not act.

Her essays and philosophical and political works include *Pyrrhus et Cinéas* ['Pyrrhus and Cineas'] (1941), *Pour une morale de l'ambiguité* [*The Ethics of Ambiguity*] (1947) and *Le Deuxième Sexe* [*The Second Sex*] (1949), an uncompromisingly feminist study of the position of woman in society, which is 'existentialist' in the sense that it shows how the history of attitudes towards woman has determined her own views of her role. *La Longue Marche* [*The Long March*] (1957), a report on China, other pieces on America, on the Algerian war and on features of modern society (for example a lecture on 'Brigitte Bardot and the Lolita syndrome') show that she sees her role as that of the committed intellectual. Nonetheless, she has won popularity with subsequent autobiographical and semi-autobiographical works such as *Mémoires d'une jeune fille rangée*[*Memoirs of a Dutiful Daughter*] (1958) and *La Force de l'âge* [*The Prime of Life*] (1960); and with a further novel *Les Belles Images* ['The beautiful images'] (1966). D. E. A.

Beckett, Samuel (1906–), Irish-born novelist and playwright writing both in French and English, only became widely known in the English-speaking world with the theatrical success in the mid-1950s of *Waiting for Godot* (*En attendant Godot*, 1953). The comic and pathetic poetry of this enigmatic work gave it an appeal far beyond the expectations of its promoters, but there was no agreement as to what it was all about. Prior to this success, however, Beckett had written five largely unread novels —*Murphy* (1938) and *Watt* (written 1942–44; published 1953) in English, and a trilogy in French (written 1947–49) consisting of *Molloy* (1951), *Malone meurt* [*Malone Dies*] (1951) and *L'Innommable* [*The Unnamable*] (1953); and the reader who wishes to arrive at a clearer understanding of his plays must be prepared to make an intellectual pilgrimage through their challenging territory.

Most of the literary techniques that Beckett employs need not trouble anyone who is familiar with Joyce (whose companion Beckett was in

Paris during the years 1928–31): but to those who are unlearned in the philosophical ideas of Descartes, of Wittgenstein, and of the existentialists, and who have never been seriously troubled by (for instance) the idea that their own existence might be an illusion, the despairing nihilism of Beckett's world, for all its humour and pathos, may not seem very meaningful. Some of his characters (e.g. Murphy) are chiefly obsessed with the need to unite their own personal nonentity with the cosmic nothingness, in an almost Buddhist quest for nirvana: others (e.g. Watt) are tormented by this universal nothingness and meaninglessness to the extent that they seek refuge in words and numbers which at least have a meaningful existence in relation to each other. The predominant philosophy of these two first novels is summed up in the names of the two chief characters of *Watt*, signifying respectively the eternal universal question and the inevitable negative answer: Watt himself ('What?'), and his elusive, arbitrary employer, the householder Mr Knott ('Not').

A more compellingly tragic quality is present in the trilogy, whose protagonists are symbolically either maimed, paralysed or in a state of disintegration: the crippled, decaying Molloy crawls to a standstill; the already immobile Malone's existence takes place between 'dish' and 'pot', feeding and excreting; while the grotesque figure of 'the Unnamable' lives legless and armless in a jar. All three are engaged in a hopeless quest for meaningful identity; in Molloy, this takes the form of a search for an 'other' person (his mother) in whose mind he can exist, while Malone and the Unnamable increasingly derive their identity from the creations of their own minds.

Even in an age when man's physical insignificance in relation to the infinities of time and space has reached correspondingly infinitesimal proportions, there will be many readers who find themselves out of sympathy with the philosophical content of these novels (or simply unable to understand it): but few will deny the validity of these images of decomposition, increasing impotence and depersonalisation, and their capacity to speak for something in the state of man. And both in the progressive detachment of the mind from the body that can be traced in the trilogy (Malone's approaching death, for instance, being accompanied by an increasing objectivisation of his body's extremities), and in the recurring idea that no one is ever identical with the person that existed or will exist a short distance away in time (embodied in Beckett's sequence of protagonists, all of whom may be seen as manifestations of the same 'person'), there is a lucid statement of the problem expressed in the question 'Who am I?'—or, what exactly, in this psychophysical unity that bears my name, is really designated by that name or by the pronoun 'I'?

Although it is often said that there is little in Beckett's plays that is not to be found in his novels, it is difficult to imagine his rapid ascent to the status of a major literary figure had he not decided to re-interpret his ideas in dramatic form. Whether the pairs of 'characters' to be found in *En attendant Godot* [*Waiting for Godot*] (1953) and *Fin de partie* [*Endgame*] (1957) express different components of the same personality, or are the embodiments of opposing attitudes, or even represent in simplified form the polarisation of any relationship into opposite roles (e.g. master-servant)—and it seems likely that all these interpretations, and many more, are equally and co-existently valid—they make much greater impact on a stage than in the pages of a novel. The cross-fire of dialogue, punctuated by a certain amount of significant action and only the occasional burst of philosophical monologue, expresses the essential sadness and humour, horror and farce, of Beckett's philosophy in a form to which theatre audiences have responded the world over.

Endless discussions have centred on the identity of Godot, but it seems fairly certain that the apparently central allusion—to God—is intentional; though it should be remembered that this would not be immediately clear to the play's original French audience, and that any attempt to give a precise meaning would amount, in Beckett's philosophy, to naming the unnamable and defining the indefinable. The play is largely a static portrayal of a human situation, and the fact that the two tramps Vladimir and Estragon are still waiting at the end should occasion no sense of anti-climax. But against the cyclic pattern in the dialogue of this mutually complementary pair (dialogue which at times takes on overtones of a music-hall act) must be set the distinct degeneration of the other pair, the worldly Pozzo and his idealistic slave Lucky, between their two appearances, when they have become blind and dumb respectively in the course of Pozzo's unsuccessful attempts to sell Lucky at a fair.

The Pozzo-Lucky relationship, with its hint of the domination of the body over the mind or the soul, and leading in this case to the body's desire to prostitute the mind/soul and the ensuing blindness of the body and dumbness of the mind/soul (a level of meaning which, it must be repeated, is only one of many), is repeated, with variations, in the Hamm-Clov relationship in *Endgame*: and the degeneration of these two becomes the central metaphor for the whole of the latter play, with its sense of the clock of time gradually running down. Here the cast is completed by Hamm's legless parents, Nagg and Nell, who inhabit a pair of dustbins, thus vividly embodying the past in a play that is chiefly concerned with escape from the tyranny of time. Outside, in the 'real' world, death and destruction already prevail: in the inner, subjective world we are witnessing the final stages in a game of chess which can never end in the desired checkmate. At the beginning, for the blind Hamm it is already 'nearly finished': but at the end, with the clock ticking ever more slowly, there is still an infinite distance to go.

If the picture of Hamm and Clov waiting for the end represents Beckett's return to less universally meaningful subject matter (as might be suggested by the play's much diminished popularity), his next play *Happy Days* (1961), with Winnie, its one major character, already half-buried, carries the process a stage further. It has been argued that Winnie's 'happiness', which results from her indifference to her fate and which is preserved by her ability to misuse language so as to erect a smoke-screen between her and reality, makes the play a more despairing play than *Endgame*. What is undeniable is that her partial disappearance into the ground makes a powerful image for the loss of identity—whether or not that is considered desirable.

Winnie's relationship with her husband Willie forms a continuous thread through her long monologues and occasional dialogue: and there is a suggestion also in Beckett's sixth novel *Comment c'est* [*How it is*] (1961) that a human relationship, however rudimentary, constitutes something positive and real amidst the universal void. Such a view is lent further force by the positively idyllic references to the relationship between the young Krapp and his girl in the one-act play *Krapp's Last Tape* (1958), a dialogue between the now ageing Krapp and his previous selves in the form of a series of tape-recordings of his own voice. As an alternative to this somewhat conventional lifebelt, some critics have pointed to the religious elements in *Waiting for Godot* and *Endgame* (in the last scene of which Clov sights through the window a small boy—a possible Christ-figure—resurrected from the ruins of the world outside). The Christian allusions—though ambivalent—are even stronger in the radio play *All That Fall* (1957).

Other later titles include *Imagination Dead Imagine* (1965), the shortest novel ever published, which was also included in the collection of shorter prose works *No's Knife* (1967), one of several volumes published in honour of Beckett's sixtieth birthday. K. R. R.

Beeding, Francis (H. St G. Saunders, 1898–1951; J. L. Palmer, 1885–1944), name used by an English thriller-writing partnership whose products included *The Seven Sleepers* (1927) and *The Six Proud Walkers* (1928).

K. R. R.

Beerbohm, Max (1872–1956), English novelist, essayist and caricaturist. Beerbohm made his name as a wit and satirical essayist in the 1890s, contributing his first caricatures 'Club Types' to the *Strand* magazine in 1892, writing for the *Yellow Book*, and in 1898 succeeding George

Bernard Shaw as dramatic critic of the *Saturday Review*. Beerbohm's satire was aimed at social and literary hypocrisy. *A Christmas Garland* (1912) parodied Bennett, Conrad, Chesterton and Wells. *The Works of Max Beerbohm* were published as early as 1896 and a whole series followed, including *More* (1899), *Yet Again* (1909) and *And Even Now* (1920). *Zuleika Dobson* (1911) is the best-known novel, a fantasy of a young and phenomenally beautiful girl turning the world of Oxford upside down. Beerbohm's caricatures were always signed 'Max'; *A Book of Caricatures* was published in 1907.

Essentially Beerbohm's wit and his sensitive adjustment of style were used to expose the eccentricities of men in society rather than the tragedies of man in the universe. He retired in 1910 to live with his wife on the Italian riviera. He was knighted in 1939. D. L. P.

Behan, Brendan (1923–64), Irish writer. He drew on his experiences in the Irish Republican Army and prison for most of his work. His most important play is *The Quare Fellow* (1956) which is an impressionistic description of the twenty-four hours prior to an execution seen through the responses of other prisoners and the warders of the prison. Here he creates the tragedy behind the macabre comedy which culminates in everyone playing roles forced on them by their situation or occupation. The only other play *The Hostage* (1958) also ends with the death of a prisoner. An English soldier is held hostage by the I.R.A. in the hope that this will force the British to reprieve one of its own men. Its strength lies in the way it describes Behan's disillusion with the movement which is chaotically organised and lacking in informed members. The shooting is an accident and terrifies them all. Its weakness lies in his noticeably over-relaxed style which is, at times, puerile in its determination to obtain an easy laugh. In this he resembles the late Dylan Thomas.

His other works are either anecdotal or autobiographical. The most important of these is *Borstal Boy* (1958) which is a romanticised account of what appears to have been his period of formal education. Its style is rambling and repetitive, but conveys his broad eclectic humour better than his later works of this kind. *The Scarperer* (1966) is his only novel. K. G. Y.

Beier, Ulli (1922–), German-born editor and translator who lived in Nigeria, editing *Black Orpheus*, a leading African literary magazine, and has compiled and edited *Yoruba Poetry* (with B. Gbadamosi; 1959) and *African Poetry* (1966). C. P.

Belasco, David (1859–1931), American dramatist, is best known as the author and part-author of plays on which two of Puccini's operas are based—*The Girl of the Golden West* (1905) and *Madame Butterfly* (1900). K. R. R.

Belloc [Joseph] Hilaire (1870–1953), English poet, historian and essayist. Belloc was born near Paris into a family whose paternal ancestors had a military history going back to the campaigns of Napoleon. Apart, however, from a brief period of national service in the French artillery Belloc was educated in England, at Birmingham and at Oxford where he became president of the Union. He is best known for light satirical verse written with more technical skill than is evident from its surface simplicity. *Verses and Sonnets* was published in 1895, *The Bad Child's Book of Beasts* in 1896 and *Cautionary Tales* in 1907. His witty and elegant essays are collected in volumes which include *On Nothing* (1908), *On Everything* (1909) and *On Anything* (1910). Like his friend Chesterton, Belloc was a Catholic polemicist and joined in the latter's attacks on writers like Shaw and Wells. Belloc's travel books include *The Path to Rome* (1902) which combines humour and information with his Catholic viewpoint. Novels, often illustrated by Chesterton, include *Pongo and the Bull* (1910). *A History of England* was published between 1925 and 1927. D. L. P.

Bellow, Saul (1915–), American novelist. Born in Canada of Jewish parentage, he has taught at various universities. Bellow is an introspective writer who is consciously in sharp contrast with the 'hard-boiled' school and the later imitators of Hemingway. His first novel *Dangling Man* (1944) is in the form of a journal, of a man called Joseph who has given up his job in anticipation of his call-up for military service. He fills the vacuum thus created in his life by scrutinising his environment; and with the picture of the state of man that he finds himself inducing from it he is soon in a condition of acute self-torment, and increasing paralysis of the will to do anything constructive with his freedom. The book ends with him taking steps to hasten his drafting into the army—to fight in a war which has previously been one of the things preying on his mind; and he embraces the regimentation of army life as a blessed release.

Joseph becomes alienated from the world he lives in precisely because he finds himself with the time to stand and stare. Leventhal in *Victim* (1947) is also alienated, though in his case this is largely the result of his Jewishness, a characteristic which he shares with several other Bellow characters. His alienation becomes crystallised, during his wife's temporary absence, in a bizarre relationship with a drunken anti-Semitic bum called Allbee who moves into his flat to torment him on the dubious grounds that

Leventhal was once indirectly responsible for his losing his job. Eventually they work their way to a degree of mutual acceptance, leaving Leventhal in a happier state when his wife returns. If (as has been suggested by some critics) Allbee is seen as his victim's *alter ego*, or Jungian shadow, the story acquires an extra and enriching dimension.

Augie and his elder brother Simon in *The Adventures of Augie March* (1953) are also complementary. They are effectively brought up by an adopted Grandma—a tough old Russian Jewess whose axioms for survival in the world, and in Chicago in particular, are to 'trust nobody', and to be always tough, realistic and unsentimental. (If the boys' mother had been like this, she argues, she would never have got herself landed with three children, and no father to support them.) Simon follows her teaching and effectively hardens himself: he does not flinch from putting their idiot brother in an institution, and their weak-minded near-blind mother in a home—in both cases the 'practical' solutions. Nor is he slow to grasp that he can only turn in the right money for the newspapers he sells in his spare time and win a profit for himself, if he gives short change to the gullible customers to cover his losses from being swindled by others. He clearly has the key to worldly success; and when he eventually underwrites his business career by marrying for money, he has carried Grandma's teaching to its logical conclusion. We are left in no doubt, however, that something in him has been violated in the process: in between his outbursts against Augie for failing to emulate him, he lavishes genuine affection on him, as if he is his own 'better self'. He also finds it necessary to seek affection outside his marriage; and at times the strain is so great that he hints at suicide.

Augie is very much influenced by him—as he is by everyone else who tries to build him into their plans. In addition to Simon, there is the boyhood friend who has become a successful crook and wants him as an accomplice; the childless society couple who have taken him into their fashionable clothing concern and want to adopt him; and the beautiful heiress who takes him to Mexico to train an eagle to hunt iguanas. Always he ends up disengaging himself: he cannot commit himself to any situation where he is not being true to himself—and in particular to that 'something' in himself (call it integrity: or, in his words, 'axial lines') that Simon has violated. The difficulty is that he is constantly in doubt about himself, the world, and his role in it: as with Joseph in *Dangling Man*, involvement does at least keep one occupied, and (on the surface at least) sane.

Augie is the first of a succession of larger-than-life questing heroes, and the book has an extrovert exuberance that contrasts strongly with its predecessors. The second of these heroic figures occurs in *Henderson*,

The Rain King (1959): a book whose mythical proportions are far more striking than those of *The Adventures of Augie March* (despite the latter's constant emphasis on historical analogues), and whose symbolism of rebirth and renewed fertility in primitive Africa enriches it with the dimension of psychological significance to be found in *Victim*. The third figure in this sequence is the title-character of *Herzog*, perhaps the most interesting of Bellow's heroes in that though fundamentally extrovert he is in the grips of neuroticism. Herzog is an aging but still virile academic with a moderately successful career. However, as Bellow strides into an exploration of his psychological upheaval he emerges for the reader as a huge and viable personality. Following the desertion by Madeleine, his maddeningly attractive and destructive second wife, he gropes about for answers to his problem of why he seems an unsuitable candidate for happiness. His relationships with others, especially women, and his incessant letter-writing to, among others, Napoleon, the American president and Spinoza (with whom he closely identifies), contain testaments to the active concern of a man sufficiently gentle to accept anything and sufficiently strong to want to understand why it happens to him. K. R. R.; S. M.

Bemelmans, Ludwig (1898–1962), American humorist, whose most durable published volumes include *My War with the United States* (1937), based on his army experiences, and *Dirty Eddie* (1947), inspired by his experience of Hollywood. *The World of Bemelmans* (1955) is an omnibus edition. He also published *Are You Hungry, Are You Cold* (1960), and a successful play entitled *Now I Lay Me Down to Sleep* (1944). K. R. R.

Benavente, Jacinto (1866–1954), Spanish playwright, winner of the 1922 Nobel Prize for Literature. Son of a well-known children's doctor, Benavente was able from his youth to indulge his passion for the theatre. His early plays—together with those of the novelist Pérez Galdós—revolutionised the Spanish stage during the 1890s, replacing the gratuitous outbursts of Echegaray by the analysis and revelation of character through plot. In *La gobernadora* [*The Governor's Wife*] (1901) and *Los malhechores del bien* [*The Evil Doers of Good*] (1905) the naturalistic style is a perfect vehicle for middle-class satire, but Benavente's disillusioned outlook achieves its best expression in the *commedia dell' arte* types of *Los intereses creados* [*The Bonds of Interest*] (1907), in which the cynical and worldly Crispín uses others' self-interest to achieve the prosperity of his idealistic master Leandro. The influence of D'Annunzio in *La noche del sábado* [*Saturday Night*] (1903), and the sentimentality of *Rosas de otoño* [*Autumnal Roses*] (1905), hardly prepare us for the treatment of the theme of incest in the rural drama *La malquerida* [*The Passion Flower*] (1913), Benavente's most solid achievement. Though popular in its day, Benavente's later output, often doctrinal in tone, now seems excessively facile. D. H. G.

Benchley, Robert (1889–1945), American humorist, is best remembered for his self-satirising *My Ten Years in a Quandary* (1936). He also wrote *20,000 Leagues Under the Sea, or, David Copperfield* (1928) and *Chips Off the Old Benchley* (1949). K. R. R.

Benét, Stephen Vincent (1898–1943), American writer, was a prolific poet, novelist, dramatist and short-story writer. Among his work are included two major pieces of writing: the epic poem *John Brown's Body* which won a Pulitzer Prize in 1929, and the short story, 'The Devil and Daniel Webster' (from *Thirteen O'Clock*, 1937).

Benét was born in Pennsylvania, brought up in California and Georgia and educated at Yale. Between 1915 and his death he published a great deal. Several collections of poetry included verse in ballad form, notably *Ballads and Poems 1915–1930* (1931), possessing a high level of technical dexterity. *John Brown's Body*, almost a novel in verse form, describes the civil war with realism and sympathy and in considerable breadth. It had a widespread popular success but differing critical receptions varying from acceptance as 'the American epic' to Harriet Monroe's pejorative 'cinema epic'. In perspective it is none the less significant for being a popular work and not attempting to be great literature in an altogether different category. Benét's novels include *John Huguenot* (1923) and *James Shore's Daughters* (1934). His collections of short stories also include *Tales Before Midnight* (1939) and *The Last Circle* (1946).

D. L. P.

Bennett, [Enoch] Arnold (1867–1927), English novelist. Bennett was born at Hanley, Staffordshire, the son of a solicitor. He was educated at Burslem and Middle School, Newcastle; he subsequently gave up a training in law and turned to journalism, becoming editor of the magazine *Woman*. This gave him useful experience for a sympathetic understanding of female characteristics—experience which was to be translated into his novels. Bennett is primarily known as a novelist of the pottery towns: Burslem, Tunstall, Hanley, Stoke-on-Trent and Longton. Although his private life became sophisticated with success—he married a French wife, lived at Fontainebleau and bought a yacht—the subject matter of his books is essentially the provincial world of 'the five towns'.

Bennett's first book, *A Man From the North* (1898), describes his early experiences in London where he came as a reviewer. The first major novel, *Anna of the Five Towns* (1902), is written in what is generally described as a naturalistic style after the manner of the French novelist Zola. It certainly deals realistically and unromantically with middle and lower-middle class values and life. Anna, the wealthy but repressed daughter of a narrow Wesleyan father, is forced by the habit of obedience to reject her lover and ruin his father financially, only to marry the respectable, dull, self-interested suitor of her father's choice. The novel ends with the dramatic suicides of both her lover and his father. Its portrayal of the sordid industrial background of the Potteries does bear resemblance to Zola's realism; but the book lacks the latter's intensity and ferocity. The French writer's *Germinal*, for example, has a similar realism coupled to melodrama, but a more profound level of involvement in fundamental human problems.

The Old Wives' Tale (1908) grafts on to the provincial atmosphere of the industrial north the European cultural influences that Bennett felt keenly. Two sisters, Sophia and Constance Barnes, live contrasting lives. One is deserted by her lover in Paris and makes her way amidst the upheavals of that European capital, which include the 1870 siege; the other marries at home and inherits the respectability of her father's business.

Clayhanger (1910) describes the conflict between an insular and puritan father and the aspirations of his sensitive son, Edwin Clayhanger, who wishes to work and marry outside his father's control. The plot is complicated by the discovered bigamy of the husband of Edwin's lover, and eventually resolved by the death of the elder Clayhanger. A subsequent novel, *Hilda Lessways* (1911), relates the same story from the point of view of Edwin's future wife—a technique which pre-empts Laurence Durrell's idea of the relativity of judgment in time. *These Twain* (1916) and *The Roll Call* (1918) continue the family story of the Clayhangers. All of these novels are remarkable for their detailed and realistic accounts of the lives of apparently ordinary people.

The Card (1911) has the realism of the others but is a richly comic novel concerned with the opportunism and rise to fortune of Denry, a cheeky, brash, intelligent materialist and the son of a washerwoman. He begins his adult career by forging an invitation to a ball, gaining an evening suit by forging a second invitation for the tailor, and taking society by storm when he dances with a duchess. He goes from opportunist strength to opportunist strength, building a business and becoming the youngest mayor of his home town by employing the neat political and popular device of buying a star player for the declining local football team. There is only a hint of Bennett's European experiences, when Denry and his bride honeymoon in Switzerland.

Bennett possesses in his novels a strong sense of the passage of time and its effect upon developing personality. He gets to grips with north-country character, its resignation to sordidness, its strong individuality, its stoicism and grim humour. He makes the ordinary fascinating, not in a style that is at all derivative of Zola or Flaubert—however much these influenced his original attitudes—but in a manner that is distinctively his own. D. L. P.

Benson, E. F. (Edward Frederic Benson; 1867–1940), prolific English novelist, popular for his novels portraying from the inside the exclusive world of upper-class society (*Dodo*, 1893), or of a public school and a Cambridge college (*David Blaize*, 1916; *David of Kings*, 1924). He also wrote several volumes of reminiscences including *As We Were* (1930). S. R.

Benson, Stella (1892–1933), English novelist, short-story writer and travel writer. She loved adventure and worked in many different occupations, travelling widely, before marrying in China and settling there. She vividly described the strange characters and places she knew from her travels. Her novel *Tobit Transplanted* (1931) won the Femina Vie Heureuse prize. G. S.

Bentley, Edmund Clerihew (1875–1956), English detective novelist and nonsense writer, first won literary fame with *Biography for Beginners* (1905), a collection of nonsense rhymes in a verse form made up of four lines of varying length, which became known as clerihews. Then came *Trent's Last Case* (1913) which has been described by critics as one of the great masterpieces of detective fiction. It marked the end of the dominance of Sherlock Holmes in this field and heralded a new type of naturalistic detective story. Bentley was greatly influenced in his writing by his school-friend G. K. Chesterton; but despite his great success with *Trent's Last Case* his literary output was not high. Though he published further volumes of nonsense verse (*More Biography*, 1929, and *Baseless Biography*, 1939), he only wrote two other detective stories, *Trent's Own Case* (1936) written in collaboration with Warner Allen, and *Trent Intervenes* (1938). *Those Days* (1940) is an autobiography. K. M. H.

Bentley, Phyllis (1894–   ), English novelist, whose works are chiefly characterised by their regional (Yorkshire) background. Her first book

Environment (1922) was followed by a succession of titles including *The Inheritance* (1932) and *A Modern Tragedy* (1934), the latter dealing with the effects of the depression. Among her later ones are *The House of Moreys* (1953), *A Man of His Time* (1966) and the autobiographical *O Dreams, O Destination* (1962). K. R. R.

Beresford, John D. (1873–1947), English novelist, is best remembered for his painstaking portrayal of adolescence in his first novel *Jacob Stahl* (1911), the opening part of a trilogy which was completed by *A Candidate for Truth* (1912) and *The Invisible Event* (1915). Other titles include *The Old People* (1931), the first part of another trilogy; and the posthumous *Hampdenshire Wonder* (1948). K. R. R.

Bergengruen, Werner (1892–), prolific German novelist. A Catholic convert and critic of the Nazis he has devoted himself mainly to historical novels in the manner of the Swiss C. F. Meyer. Presenting parallels with the present, his positive criticism of the past has a remarkable immediacy. His best-known works are *Der Grosstyrann und das Gericht* [*A Matter of Conscience*] (1935) and *Am Himmel wie auf Erden* [*In Heaven as on Earth*] (1940). R. C. W.

Berger, Yves (1933–), French novelist, born at Avignon. Berger's first novel, *Le Sud* [*The South*], was published in 1962 and won the Prix Fémina. The novel is the story of a man who brings up his daughter and his son in the beliefs of pre-white civilisation Red Indians. After his death, his daughter Virginia initiates her brother into the delights of love and becomes his mistress. Despite this amorality, and the difficult style of a novel whose author is consciously trying to create 'literature', the virtues of the writer are great—his poetical view of Provence, his narrative powers, his rich imagination. He has also written a biography of Boris Pasternak. D. E. A.

Bergson, Henri (1859–1941), French philosopher and winner of the Nobel Prize for Literature, 1927. He achieved prominence with *L'Evolution créatrice* [*Creative Evolution*] (1907). He championed the powers of human intuition and indicated that the principles of duration and flux are of extreme importance in analysing patterns of human behaviour and consciousness. He exercised profound influence on many novelists, most notably Proust. Bergson was also the philosophical spokesman for the French symbolist poets. He believed that the intellect performs a simplifying process which distorts the real world, the latter being apprehended by a totality of the senses, the intellect and the emotions. The symbolist poets attempted to evoke in the reader a sensation or apprehension of the outside world involving total being rather than a clear but very over-simplified projection of the mind. R. C. W.; D. L. P.

Bernanos, Georges (1888–1948), French novelist. Born in Paris, Bernanos was educated by the Jesuits. A journalist on *Action Française*, a Catholic nationalist newspaper, he spent the first world war in the trenches and became an insurance agent afterwards. In 1926 he published *Sous le soleil de Satan* [*The Star of Satan*], two intermingled stories, of Mouchette, a rejected girl who is finally possessed by Satan, and the priest Donissan, whose trials and temptations before he finally conquers Satan echo those of Mouchette. Bernanos' world is one of torment and temptation, and in *L'Imposture* [The Imposture'] (1927) and *La Joie* [*Joy*] (1929) the themes of damnation and redemption, of evil and saintliness, are met again. Bernanos sees the world as a place in which the priest, God's representative, fights, often physically, against Satan, in the form of monstrous beings and situations conjured from an involved imagination. Childhood is the time of innocence; sin is the sin against childhood or against the innocence of childhood. *Le Journal d'un curé de campagne* [*The Diary of a Country Priest*] (1936) is the story of a sick, gauche and inexperienced young priest's contacts with the indifference of his parish, his gradual assumption of its evil, his success by his sacrifice of himself. In *Nouvelle Histoire de Mouchette* [*Mouchette*] (1937) Bernanos re-echoes his concern with the innocence of childhood; and *Monsieur Ouine* [*Monsieur Ouine*] (1946) sees the disintegration of a parish from the point of view of an adolescent.

Bernanos has a very personal style; his novels are often chaotic, tormented, over-imaginative, but the intensity of this personal vision, of his personal distress and emotion, the horror he feels at evil, have created works which are immensely powerful, which reflect his own violent and neurotic personality, his own faith. A militant Catholic, he was prepared to condemn Franco in *Les Grands Cimetières sous la lune* [*Great Cemeteries beneath the Moon*] (1938), Munich in *Scandale de la vérité* ['The scandal of truth'] (1939) and Pétain in *Lettres aux anglais* ['Letters to the English'] (1942); and his polemical and propagandist essays are as violent as his novels. He has also written a play, *Dialogues des Carmélites* [*The Restless Heart*] (1949). D. E. A.

Bethell, Mary Ursula (1874–1945), New Zealand poet, published *From a Garden in the Antipodes* (1929), a collection of verses sent in correspondence to England, dealing with simple and familiar subjects but written with great technical felicity in that she varies her style to suit, or to make ironic contrast with, her topic. Her poetry became a medium for meditative and philosophical speculations on the fundamentals underlying the landscape and incidents she describes. This can be seen in later collections—*Day and Night, Poems, 1924–34* (1939) and the posthumous anthology *Collected Poems* (1950). S. R.

Beti, Mongo (Alexandre Biyidi; 1932–), Cameroonian novelist writing in French. His *Mission terminée* [*Mission to Kala*] (1957) is the swift, delightfully Rabelaisian story of a young *lycée* student's mission to retrieve the runaway life of a cousin. *Le Roi miraculé* [*King Lazarus*] (1958) has thematically much in common with Laye's *The Radiance of the King*. C. P.

Betjeman, John (1906–), English poet. Betjeman has probably the largest reading audience of the practising English poets. Ostensibly his work is light, nostalgic, sentimental and guaranteed to appeal to the middle-aged middle classes. On closer examination his poetry can be seen to have more to offer than the merely comprehensible.

Betjeman was educated at Marlborough and Magdalen College, Oxford. He was a contemporary of Auden. Besides writing verse he has been a book reviewer, an author of Shell Guides, a broadcaster, a church warden and an authority on architecture and churches, editing and contributing a masterly introduction to *Collins's Guide to English Parish Churches* (1958). His public image is of a nostalgic sentimentalist looking back to the security of middle-class life in the Victorian and Edwardian eras and casting a moist eye on the pseudo-Gothic of St Pancras Station or Temple Meads, Bristol. *Summoned by Bells* (1960) reflects this image, revealing a sheltered life of privilege in a verse autobiography. It was, however, acclaimed by at least one eminent critic and poet, Philip Larkin, and also received the popular accolade of serialisation in the Sunday press.

Betjeman's serious claims to recognition lie in three areas: he is a mature descriptive poet of nature, he is preoccupied by the universal problems of humanity, and he is a reflective poet dealing compassionately with death. His style is not contemporary in structure, deriving rather from the nineteenth- and early twentieth-century work of Tennyson and Hardy; but he carves out an individual manner which achieves depth in his awareness of the fragility of man:

> With the tap upon polished parquet
> of inflexible nurses' feet . . .

And say shall I groan in dying,
as I twist the sweaty sheet
Or gasp for breath uncrying,
as I feel my senses drown'd
While the air is swimming with insects
and children play in the street?

Editions of his poems include *Selected Poems* (1948) and *Collected Poems* (1958). D. L. P.

Betti, Ugo (1892–1953), Italian poet, short-story writer and dramatist, was born at Camerino (Macerata) and educated in Parma, becoming a student of law at Parma University. He soon developed his interest in politics, and in his doctoral thesis he interpreted the history of European civilisation in terms of man's innate egotism—a view of human nature which is consistently reflected in his plays.

Betti's career was rudely interrupted by the outbreak of war. He was commissioned in the artillery and was awarded a military decoration; then in 1917 he was taken prisoner by the Germans during the Caporetto campaign. These wartime experiences radically altered his political outlook. Betti soon recognised the futility of war and the urgent need to reconcile ideological differences—convictions which he was to develop much later as secondary themes in two plays with political overtones, *La regina e gli insorti* [*The Queen and the Rebels*] (1949) and *L'aiuola bruciata* [*The Burnt Flower-bed*] (1951–52).

After the first world war Betti resumed his legal studies and his literary activities, and in the years that followed his loyalties continued to be divided between his professional duties and his interest in creative writing. He began work on a lengthy dissertation on certain aspects of railway law which incorporated some interesting views on the central question of individual responsibility. His earliest book of verse *Il re pensieroso* ['The pensive king'] appeared in 1922. This collection included poems that he had composed in a German prison camp. They are lyrics of imagination and fantasy predominantly elegiac in tone. But in time his poetic world deepened and his best lyrics are those of a later period which portray the tragic solitude of modern man.

In 1928 Betti published his first collection of short stories, *Caino* ['Cain']. His first play *La padrona* ['The landlady'] (1929) gained first prize in a competition organised by a Roman periodical. *La casa sull'acqua* ['The house on the water'] followed in 1928 and *L'isola meravigliosa* ['The wonderful island'] in 1929. He married in 1930 and settled in Rome where he held office as magistrate in the High Court throughout the period of fascist dictatorship. After the purge of 1943 he withdrew from the judiciary and became archivist in the Rome Palace of Justice. Biographical details and allusions to legal archives appear in plays like *Corruzione al palazzo di giustizia* [*Corruption in the Law Courts*] (1944–45) and in *Acque turbate* [Turbulent waters] (1948–49).

Between 1941 and 1953 his literary output accelerated with some thirteen plays and numerous contributions to newspapers and periodicals. At his death his writings included three volumes of original verse, three collections of short stories, a novel, essays, articles and twenty-five dramatic works. Much of this, including *Ultime liriche, 1937–53* ['Last lyrics'], was published posthumously. Today Betti is best remembered for his important contribution to contemporary Italian drama. His plays give eloquent expression to the spiritual crisis of modern man torn between human egotism and his innate desire for harmony and justice. Apart from a handful of comedies, among which *Il paese delle vacanze* [*Summertime*] (1937) is an outstanding success, Betti concentrated on tragedies which are often violent and bizarre. His relentless pursuit of human justice, sanity and tolerance in a world of evil where men are condemned to exile in their obstinate and fatal disregard of God emerges most strongly in *Frana allo Scalo Nord* [*Landslide at the North Station*] (1932) and *La fuggitiva* [*The Fugitive*] (1952–53). Betti himself has left behind a critical essay of some importance in *Religione e teatro* ['Religion and theatre'] which throws considerable light on the symbolism and significance of his drama. G. P.

Biely, Andrei (Boris Nikolayevich Bugayev; 1880–1934), Russian symbolist poet and novelist who was more popular with writers than with the reading public because of his ornamental and highly mannered style. He belonged to that group of artists who sought ultimate truth in image, metaphor and suggestion, rather than in reason. Many subsequent authors were influenced by Biely's original use of language and symbolism, which is best represented by his autobiographical work *Kotik Letayev* [*Kotik Letayev*] (1918), reconstructing a child's awaking conception of the world around him. In his memoirs (4 vols., 1922–33) Biely hailed the revolution as the catharsis of Russia, but he felt let down by the Soviet régime and thereafter sought a mystical regeneration of Russian spiritual culture. B. W.

Biggers, Earl Derr (1884–1933), American novelist, is chiefly read today for his stories of the Chinese detective Charlie Chan, the first of which was *The House Without a Key* (1925). K. R. R.

Binyon, Laurence (1869–1943), English poet, dramatist and art historian. Binyon taught poetry at Harvard in the 1930s; his own *Collected Poems* were published in 1931 and a posthumous volume, *The Burning of the Leaves*, in 1944. The famous memorial poem 'For the Fallen' was published in *The Four Years* (1918). As a dramatist he was principally concerned with the revival of blank-verse drama in England; representative of his poetic drama are *Paris and Oenone* (1906), *Attila* (1907) and *Boadicea* (1925). Binyon was made a Companion of Honour in 1932. D. L. P.

Birmingham, George A. (Canon James Owen Hannay; 1865–1950), Irish novelist. An Irish Protestant clergyman, he wrote travel and religious books under his own name but is chiefly known for his prolific output of humorous novels of Irish life. His works include *The Major's Niece* (1911), *Spanish Gold* (1908), *Good Conduct* (1920) and *General John Regan* (a play, 1913). G. S.

Birney, Earle (1904–), Canadian poet and writer who has travelled widely in Europe, Mexico and Spain, yet whose central concern remains the nature of the Canadian creative contribution. This has led him to take a vigorous part in the literary activity of his country as editor, supervisor of broadcasts, and university lecturer. His works include *David and Other Poems* (1942), the title piece of which is a long and moving narrative poem of a fatal mountain climb; *Now is Time* (1945), containing descriptive and philosophical poems on war; and *The Strait of Anian* (1948), a perceptive and lyrical tour of the variety and vastness displayed by the regions of Canada. He extended his scope still further in subsequent years—publishing a verse radio-play in his volume *Trial of a City and Other Verse* (1952); exploring the wider world and international problems for his inspiration in *Ice Cod Bell or Stone* (1962); and turning to prose for his widely known comic novel *Turvey* (1949), concerning a soldier in Canada's wartime, and the political *Down the Long Table* (1955). S. R.

Birrell, Augustine (1850–1933), English essayist and biographer. His publications include two collections of *Obiter Dicta* (1884 and 1887), followed by *More Obiter Dicta* (1924); and biographies of Charlotte Brontë (1885), Hazlitt (1902) and Marvell (1905). K. R. R.

Bishop, Elizabeth (1911–), American poet, belongs to the period of consolidation after the great surge forward in the American literature of the 1920s and 1930s. All of her poetry has been published since the second world war, beginning with *North and South* (1946). She was born in New England, educated at Vassar and subsequently made her home in Brazil.

Elizabeth Bishop possesses a range of moods from perceptive wittiness to disciplined fantasy. The easy conversational tone of the poetry is deceptive since the images and attitudes she presents are very delicately blended and tightly controlled. Superficially she gives an impression of being an academic poet, an impression reinforced by her appointment as a consultant in poetry to the Library of Congress. But the formal discipline of the verse (it has been described as 'quartzlike') does not detract from the depth and breadth of her involvements, as, for example, in 'The Fish' or 'A Cold Spring' in *North and South—A Cold Spring* (1955).

Elizabeth Bishop's published volumes are relatively few but she is represented in numerous anthologies, especially since her *Poems* (1956) won a Pulitzer prize. D. L. P.

Blackburn, Thomas (1916–), English poet. Blackburn is a religious, almost mystical poet, distrustful of the world of reason. His avowed poetic aim is to make the world of complex human individuals understandable to themselves. The poet's fascination with myth and legend parallels that of Yeats and the luxuriance of his imagery is partly influenced by Dylan Thomas. The resonance of his metre and his forceful images are less rigorously controlled than those of Yeats but the looseness is countered by the energy of the rhythm.

Blackburn is concerned to record the movement of the human spirit in terms of the fight against inward darkness. *The Next Word* (1958), for example, joins the theme of speculation on the nature of identity with the idea of the fusion of suffering and imaginative creativity. We see the poet involved in the struggle through evil and suffering to grace.

Other volumes include *The Outer Darkness* (1951); *The Holy Stone* (1954); *In the Fire* (1956); and *A Smell of Burning* (1961). D. L. P.

Blackmur, R. P. (Richard Palmer Blackmur; 1904–65), American critic and poet. Blackmur's poetry—*Jordan's Delight* (1937), *The Second World* (1942) and *The Good European* (1947)—is both intellectual and spiky with earthy common sense. It is as a critic, however, that he is better known. *The Double Agent* (1935) examines the relations in verse between form and content. *Language as Gesture* (1952) takes this theme further in probing the relationships between linguistic expression and the shades of underlying meaning it carries. Blackmur was also one of the first American critics to introduce, in America, the close analytical and critical methods of F. R. Leavis and the *Scrutiny* school of literary critics. D. L. P.

Blackstock, Charity, is the pseudonym of Ursula Torday (1888–), English novelist of mixed Hungarian and Scots parents. In one of her first novels *Dewey Death* (1956) she drew on her experiences as a typist at the National Central Library for the background to a psychological thriller set in an imaginary centre for the interloan of books; but it was with the later *Briar Patch* (1960) that she first attracted the attention of the critics. Her novels are generally a mixture of psychological study and thriller, but in *Exorcism* (1961) she makes an attempt at a supernatural study which does not quite come off. Other titles include *Foggy Foggy Dew* (1958), and *When the Sun Goes Down* (1965); and a number of rather stereotyped historical romances written under the name of Paula Allardyce.

K. M. H.

Blackwood, Algernon (1869–1951), English novelist, whose books are characterised by their preoccupation with the occult. *John Silence* (1908) was the first of a series of novels featuring a detective endowed with remarkable psychic powers. The craftsmanship of his short stories is illustrated by the ease with which they were translated into effective television playlets in the 1960s. K. R. R.

Blake, George (1893–1961), Scottish novelist born in Greenock. A critic of the Kailyard School, Blake believed in presenting a complete picture of Scottish life including its harsher sides. He excelled at describing the Scottish landscape, particularly the area around the Clyde, and his novel *The Shipbuilders* (1935) is a sympathetic and informed picture of Glasgow and Clydeside during the depression. Other works include *Late Harvest* (1938), *The Valiant Heart* (1940), *The Constant Star* (1945), *The Voyage Home* (1952) and *The Innocence Within* (1955). He was also author of *Barrie and the Kailyard School* (1951) and *The Firth of Clyde* (1951). G. S.

Blake, Nicholas. See **Day Lewis,** Cecil.

Blasco Ibáñez, Vicente (1867–1928), much-translated Spanish novelist, last of the great nineteenth-century Realists. A lifelong anti-clerical, Blasco worked for radical causes both in jail and parliament, while as a novelist he developed a sort of bastard naturalism in the early regional novels (1894–1902) which form his enduring contribution. These provide a complete portrait of Valencia: its fishermen in *Flor de Mayo* [*Mayflower*]; the degrading living conditions of its agricultural hinterland in *La barraca* [*The Cabin*]—more lyrically presented in *Entre naranjos* [*The Torrent*]; its rice-growers in *Cañas y barro* [*Reeds and Mud*]. The later output never again achieves such intensity. In the so-called 'novels of rebellion' Blasco presents the diverse ills of Spain in non-Valencian contexts: clericalism in

La Catedral [*The Shadow of the Cathedral*] (1903); the Jesuits in *El intruso* [*The Intruder*] (1907); the intolerance of the landlord and drunkenness among the working classes in *La bodega* [*The Fruit of the Vine*] (1905). Much better known, however, are *Sangre y arena* [*Blood and Sand*] (1908), and *Los cuatro jinetes del Apocalipsis* [*The Four Horsemen of the Apocalypse*] (1916), a war novel wherein violence is not gratuitous but inspires disgust with war and hope for the future. In following Julio Desnoyers from his Argentinian home to a soldier's death in France, Blasco successfully combines reportage with a legitimate novelistic intention. D. H. G.

Blixen-Finecke, Karen. See **Dinesen,** Isak.

Blok, Alexandr Alexandrovich (1880–1921), was the outstanding Russian symbolist poet of the early twentieth century. He was born in St Petersburg into a cultured intellectual family, and began writing at an early age. When his parents obtained a divorce Blok stayed with his mother, who encouraged his literary tastes and remained close to him all his life. Blok was early influenced by the mystical philosophy of Solovyov and from about 1898 had devoted his energies to exalting the female personification of Divine Wisdom. In 1904 he published a book of *Stikhi o prekrasnoi damye* [*Verses about the Beautiful Lady*], a work whose significance was not immediately understood although its author's talent was recognised by the leading poets of the time. Blok's marriage in 1903 was at first a very happy affair, and his wife received the adulation of his friends as the Beautiful Lady. However, the forces of his mysticism began to dwindle after 1903 and Blok's disillusion is illustrated by his replacing his beautiful lady with an unidentifiable prostitute. Blok's poetry is very personal, sonic and melodious, and full of symbols.

After the failure of the 1905 revolution Blok's disillusion deepened into despair; yet he still retained his faith in his beloved Russia, despite its contradictions and backwardness. His faith crystallises in his masterpiece written in 1918 *Dvenadtsat'* [*The Twelve*]. The poem opens with a series of pictures of the old Russia which has been overthrown. The heroes are twelve rough and ready Soviet soldiers representing the revolution. As they march through the symbolic frost and blinding snow, the figure of Christ appears at their head. This serves to symbolise the spiritual nature of the victory of the revolution, and put Blok's seal of approval on it.

The enthusiasm with which he greeted the 1917 revolution was not maintained, partly because of his endless search for something he could not find in the new utopia. He died a revered but melancholy poet just three months after he had been enthusiastically received at a 'personal' evening in the Petersburg Theatre of Drama. B. W.

Bloom, Harry (1913–), South African novelist and librettist. *Episode* (1956), a brilliant reportage novel, briskly and graphically portrays the life of an African 'location' (ghetto) and the rhythm of a political 'emergency' such as was later to be occasioned by the Sharpeville-Langa shootings in 1960. *King Kong* (1961), an 'African jazz opera', also has African location life as its centre, and features the career of the boxer Ezekiel Dhlamini. C. P.

Bloom, Ursula (–), English romantic novelist. Her first book *Tiger* was published privately when she was seven years old and with this early start to her career she went on to become one of the most widely read of the romantic novelists. Her novels are usually love stories with moral undertones, but she has also written a number of light historical romances under her own name and under the pseudonym of Lozania Prole. Her writing is at its best in her family reminiscences and studies of Edwardian life, as in *Elegant Edwardian* (1957). Her later works include *Quiet Village* (1965) and *Rosemary for Stratford on Avon* (1966).

K. M. H.

Blunden, Edmund Charles (1896–), English poet and critic. Educated at Christ's Hospital and Queen's College, Oxford, he served in the first world war and subsequently held university posts in English at Tokyo, Oxford and Hong Kong. In 1966 he became Oxford's Professor of Poetry in succession to Robert Graves.

Blunden's poetry is often characterised by the critics as Georgian, which term indicates a feeling for pastoral poetry of a generally Wordsworthian character. Terms like 'delicacy', 'formality', 'Augustan' are applied to his work. However, it is given weight by a tendency to reflection and meditation of a genuinely Wordsworthian stamp, combined with a strain of intellectual discipline from his academic background and a haunted quality derived from memories of trench warfare. The poem 'Old Homes' characteristically evokes nostalgia of youth, tending to the pastoral life of the enclosed village and to the imagined delights of life in the country as opposed to the gloom of philosophy and age. The poetry is marked not so much by its philosophical strength as by its ascetic fineness; the pastoral qualities of an environment are neither merely described nor philosophised upon but are finely transmuted through an artist's eye. And Blunden departs in other ways from conventional Georgian verse. There is an interesting sense of Browning's indifferent Nature—violence and death are never far below the surface of tranquility.

Volumes of his verse include *Poems 1914–1930* (1930), *Poems 1930–1940* (1940) and *Poems of Many Years* (1957). Apart from his poetry Blunden has published biographies of Leigh Hunt, Charles Lamb, John Taylor and Shelley and also discovered new poems by John Clare. His reflections on the first world war, *Undertones of War* (1928), he himself rates as highly as any of his poetry and it is certainly comparable with the similar autobiographies of Graves and Sassoon—two writers whose poetry has followed markedly different directions from that of Blunden's. D. L. P.

Bobrowski, Johannes (1917–1965), East German poet and novelist. Born at Tilsit on the old East Prussian-Lithuanian frontier, he began writing in the early 1940s but, apart from the still neglected *Hans Clauert, der märkische Eulenspiegel* ['Hans Clauert, the Poor Man's Eulenspiegel'] (1956), little of his work appeared in print before his inclusion in the anthology *Deutsche Lyrik auf der anderen Seite* ['German Lyric Poetry from the Other Side'] (1960) brought him to the attention of West European and American critics. Two volumes of poetry, *Sarmatische Zeit* ['Sarmatian Days'] (1961) and *Schattenland Ströme* ['Shadowland Streams'] (1962)—also available under one title in paperback, *Das Land Sarmatien* ['Sarmatia'] (1967)—earned him the 1962 Preis der Gruppe 47. A third volume, *Wetterzeichen* ['Storm-signal'] (1967), was published posthumously and too late, unfortunately, for any of the poems in it to be translated by Ruth and Matthew Mead in their excellent English language selection, *Shadow Land* (1966). Two prose works, *Boehlendorff und andere* ['Boehlendorff Etcetera'] (1965) and *Mäusefest* ['Mouse Fair'] (1965), and two novels, *Levins Mühle: 34 Sätze über meinen Grossvater* ['Levin's Mill: 34 Essays about my Grandfather'] (1964) and *Litauische Claviere* ['Lithuanian Pianos'] (1966), displayed a late, accomplished and perhaps largely unexpected extension of his talents without departing in any way from the fundamental themes and sensibilities of his poems; and it remained for the publication of his collected occasional criticism, especially the formal exposition of his unorthodox Christian Socialism, *Fortgeführte Überlegungen* ['Further Reflections']—hitherto somewhat adrift in Union Verlag's *Antikommunismus und Proexistenz* ['Anti-communism and Pro-existence'] (1965)—plus a few remaining short stories, to enable one to assess his complete works. Some of the excitement aroused by Bobrowski's sudden eminence was due, inevitably, to political considerations; he was, as it were, a German Pasternak. However, such qualifications should not, nor indeed can obscure his undeniable excellence. A uniquely individual voice, immediately recognisable above the contemporary cacophony, as isolated and lonely as was Hölderlin, his titles alone are a sufficient indication of his nostalgic evocation of the ancient telluric deities, his Chagall-like awareness of the unconscious persistence of a half-forgotten and not necessarily inferior cosmology. The past continues to inform the present and Bobrowski, totally absorbed by the social, cultural and psychological legacies of the old Balto-Slavic mythology, in exploring their interaction glimpsed the future far behind him. M. D. E.

Bogan, Louise (1897–), American poet. Louise Bogan was born in Maine and educated at Boston University. She was poetry critic of the *New Yorker*, has held the Chair of Poetry at the Library of Congress and lectured at a number of American universities.

Her poetry is objective in tone, spare in form, subtle and sensitive in expression. She writes the polished minor poetry one might expect from a critical and intellectual mind in the twentieth century. It is dependent on a literary environment but not obviously derived from any particular author or movement. *Collected Poems* was published in 1956.

D. L. P.

Böll, Heinrich (1917–), German novelist, born in Cologne, spent his infancy in an area occupied by Allied troops, his adolescence in a country staggering under the effects of economic repression and the rise of National Socialism, and his early manhood in an infantry battalion fighting a bitter war. Wounded four times, he knew the life of the common soldier from personal experience; he shared his hopes and fears, his preoccupation with food, sleep and love. It was natural that this should form the basis of his first literary exercise, the short story *Der Zug war pünktlich* [*The Train Was On Time*] (1949) which described three days and nights spent on leave by battle-weary soldiers. This was an immediate success, as was the collection of twenty-five *Novellen* published under the title of *Wanderer, kommst du nach Spa* [*Traveller, If You Come to Spa*] (1950) which treated of the soldier's life at the front and on leave, and his return to a defeated country.

War and its aftermath became the major theme of Böll's writing. Novels have appeared almost at annual intervals since the publication of *Wo warst du Adam* [*Adam Where Art Thou*] (1951) which describes the chaos of the retreat from Rumania and the final capitulation of Germany in 1945. *Und sagte kein einziges Wort* [*Acquainted with the Night*] (1953) examined the conditions of life in a bomb-shattered town, and the effect of these conditions on the people. In particular, it stressed the role of the wife in creating a stable society. The novel centres on a demobilised soldier with shattered nerves who turns to drink and the pin-table saloon to escape from the realities of life in one room. His wife, secure in her religious faith, finds the strength necessary to overcome her material poverty and eventually draws back her husband to herself.

It would have been easy for Böll, given the hardship of his own military career, to devote himself to the violence of war; but as the years progressed, he began to produce novels with a closer analysis of the long-term effects of war on society. *Haus ohne Hüter* [*The Unguarded House*] (1954) once again dealt with family life under stress, this time as seen by two schoolboys whose fathers were both killed in the war. The mother of one of them finds refuge from the harsh realities of her life in the cinema, which becomes more real than the world in which she lives; the mother of the second boy tries desperately to find some stability in men, but fails to attain it because of the frenzy of her search. The two central characters of the story are therefore failures, 'anti-heroes'.

By 1959 Böll had developed into a craftsman of letters, regarded by many as the most hopeful writer in post-war Germany. *Billard um halbzehn* [*Billiards at Half-past Nine*] (1959), which was in some ways a deliberate attempt to discover the past in a less directly personal manner, marked a reinvigoration of the old German prose form. It was hailed as an extraordinarily powerful work by critics in both England and America, and was at once translated in both countries. Less successful was his first play *Ein Schluck Erde* ['A mouthful of earth'] which met with a barrage of hostile criticism on its first performance in 1962. Subsequent fiction has included *Ansichten eines Clowns* [*The Clown*] (1963), *Entfernung von der Truppe* [*Absent without Leave*] (1964) and *Ende einer Dienstfahrt* ['End of a mission'] (1966).

There has been some criticism of Böll in recent years which maintains that his success and his fluency have been too easy and that he has been weakened as an artist in consequence; but the continued irony of his style has more admirers than detractors and he remains within the select handful of first-class post-war German writers. G. W.

Bolt, Robert (1924–), English playwright. In the 'new drama' Robert Bolt occupies a middle position, and it is probably because of this that even his earlier plays were produced by a wholly commercial company. This has perhaps induced some critics to brand his work as commercial theatre. Undoubtedly in such works as *Flowering Cherry* (1958) and *The Tiger and the Horse* (1960) he is writing solidly professional works in the tradition of family analysis, even though he may go beyond mere realism when he enters the uncharted realms of the mind with Jim Cherry's vision of escape into the country or Gwendoline Dean's scene of insanity. His *A Man for All Seasons* (1960), however, on the life and death of Sir

Thomas More, has more of interest in it, whether it be in the staging—for example in the device of the common-man narrator who is at the same time a participant in the action; or in the study of the characters of those concerned and what made them act in the way they did; or in its general theme—that there is a point beyond which even an ordinary man will not go because to do so would be to betray the little that is really him.

J. B. M.

Borges, Jorge Luis (1899–   ), Argentinian critic, poet, essayist and short-story writer, born in Buenos Aires. He was educated in Switzerland and studied English at the University of Cambridge. In 1921 he returned to Argentina and began to contribute to *avant-garde* periodicals like *Prisma*, *Proa* and *Martín Fierro* which were influenced by German expressionism, ultraism and other literary trends recently imported from Europe. His first book of verse *Fervor de Buenos Aires* ['Fervour of Buenos Aires'] (1923) was well received. *Luna de enfrente* ['The moon across the street'] followed in 1925, *Cuaderno San Martín* ['St Martin notebook'] in 1929 and his collected *Poemas* in 1943.

In his poetry, Borges soon departed from the traditional themes of lyric verse in favour of metaphysical fantasies—the myths of time, the universe and human personality. Meantime he prepared numerous translations and editions of national and European works, and began to write his remarkable series of essays, entitled *Inquisiciones* ['Inquiries'] (1925); *El tamaño de mi esperanza* ['The size of my hope'] (1926); *Historia de la eternidad* ['History of eternity'] (1926); *El idioma de los argentinos* ['The language of the Argentinians'] (1928); *Evaristo Carriego* (1930); *Discusión* ['Discussion'] (1932); and *Otras inquisiciones* ['Other inquiries'] (1952). These reveal a writer of unique talent who uses innumerable themes and sources and combines the technical virtuosities of Poe, Hoffman and Kafka only to surpass them.

From his essays Borges derives the style and themes of the short stories in which he has come to excel. His first collection *Historia universal de la infamia* ['Universal history of infamy'] (1935) consists of narrative sketches borrowed or sometimes translated from other authors. But his individual talent emerges in *El jardín de los senderos que se bifurcan* ['The garden of bifurcated paths'] (1941) and *La muerte y la brújula* ['Death and the compass'] (1951), jointly published in English translation under the title of *Ficciones* (1962), where Borges has been able fully to exercise his extraordinary powers of invention and imagination. These stories also mark his progression from experimentation to reflection, from an exaggerated cult of metaphor to a prose style of greater simplicity and firmer control of logical structure. Themes are conditioned by his basic scepticism which rejects theological doctrine, historical facts and philosophical maxims. The accepted reality of man's existence is dissolved, and in its place Borges constructs a cosmos of myths and hypotheses which engenders aesthetic pleasure with its interplay of metaphysics and lyricism, erudition and fantasy. Many of the stories are connected and complementary in this intellectual game with its carefully organised structure of idea, situation, dénouement, phrase and word.

His *Obras completas* ['Complete Works'] began to appear in 1954, and Borges in 1961 published his *Antología personal* [*A Personal Anthology*] which includes selections of prose and verse. Translations of his poetry are available in the Dudley Fitts *Anthology of Contemporary Latin-American Poetry* (1942). Extracts from his collections of prose and poetry have appeared in translation in several issues of *Encounter*. Recent anthologies of translated extracts have appeared under the titles *Labyrinths* (1962; augmented 1964) and *Dreamtigers* (1964). G. P.

Bosman, Herman Charles (1905–51), South African short-story writer, poet, novelist and essayist. His astringent humour reminds one of Saki, while his sharp characterisation recalls Maupassant; structurally his work has affinities with that of O. Henry and his shifts of mood might be called Runyonesque. *Mafeking Road* (1947) and *Unto Dust* (1963) convey the flavours of the northern Transvaal, fully savoured by a loving satirist; *Jacaranda in the Night* (1946) is the first of his two complex and visionary novels which nonetheless emerge as distinctive. C. P.

Bottome, Phyllis (Mrs Ernan Forbes-Dennis; 1884–1963), English novelist and short-story writer. She was influenced by Adler, the psychoanalyst, and this is reflected in *Private World* (1934). *The Mortal Storm* (1937) warned readers against fascism. Her autobiographical works *Search for a Soul* (1947), *The Challenge* (1953) and *The Goal* (1961) contain some of her most sensitive and brilliant writing. The short story was a form in which her clarity and directness were particularly successful and several collections were published, including *Fortune's Finger* (1950), *Man and Beast* (1954) and *Walls of Glass* (1958). J. W.

Bottomley, Gordon (1874–1948), English poet and dramatist. Bottomley's verse form tends towards technical freedom; and the descriptive detail of his poetry can be seen as a rather crude forerunner to the imagist school of writing. *Poems of 30 Years* was published in 1925. As a dramatist Bottomley was concerned, like Binyon, to revive English verse drama. His plays include *The Crier by Night* (1902), *King Lear's Wife* (1915) and *Gruach and Britain's Daughter* (1921). D. L. P.

Boulle, Pierre (1912–), French novelist, born in Avignon. He is known particularly for *Le Pont de la Rivière Kwai* [*The Bridge on the River Kwai*] (1952), a story which recalls Somerset Maugham and Kipling and which was made into a very successful film. The background to this story, the far east, became known to Boulle through his stay there from 1936 to 1944. Boulle has published a number of other novels and stories with and without this background—*William Conrad* (1952), *Le Sacrilège malais* [*Sacrilege in Malaya*] (1951), *Contes de l'absurde* [*Stories of the Absurd*] (1953), *La Face* [*Saving Face*] (1953), *Le Bourreau* [*The Chinese Executioner*] (1954), *L'Epreuve des hommes blancs* [*White Man's Test*] (1955), $E=mc^2$ (1957), *La Planète des Singes* [*Monkey Planet*] (1963), *Un métier de seigneur* [*For a Noble Cause*] (1960).

D. E. A.

Bowen, Elizabeth (1899–), English novelist, is the author of some eight novels, short stories collected in six volumes, and several autobiographical and historical works. The influence of Henry James and Virginia Woolf, on both her style and her themes, has been frequently remarked. Her subject is most often innocence confronted by experience—usually with tragic results because experience is sheltering behind a façade and has nothing but compromise and disillusionment to offer. Although she has an acute ear for social nuance (reserving her sharpest satire for a merciless rendering of the middle class at home), her novels do not provide an obvious social commentary: the settings—hotels, the occupation of Ireland before the 1922 Treaty, London in wartime—serving to supply a physical counterpart to her characters' feelings of rootlessness. However, she has a painter's eye for visual effects, and it is often her descriptions of seasons and of landscapes that linger most vividly in the mind.

Her first novel was *The Hotel* (1927), a story of English people wintering on the Italian Riviera, many of the characters betraying the restlessness of the post-war years. Its heroine, Sydney Warren, is of a type to be repeated in other novels: intelligent and sensitive but unable to cope with real life, and destined to make an unsatisfactory compromise in the choice of a husband. This was followed by *The Last September* (1929), still considered by many to be her best novel, a lyrical evocation of a period—the troubles in Ireland. The young girl of the 'Great House' (probably Elizabeth Bowen's own ancestral home, Bowen Court) falls in love with a young British officer, but he is too poor and socially unacceptable for the match to be approved. Physical violence, rare in the novels, resolves the situation, as first her lover is killed and then the Great House is burnt down.

Next came two fairly straightforward novels: *Friends and Relations* (1931) and *To the North* (1932). The first concerns a father's attempt to protect his children from the influence of their grandmother, a divorcee with a lover. The second is interesting for its containing the first portrait of a male character central to the story: the previous works, and to a large extent the later ones, revolving chiefly around women. *The House in Paris* (1935) marks an extension of the scope of her work, both in subject matter and technique. Leopold, a young boy, spends a few hours in passing at the house in Paris: and a long flashback takes us into the life of his mother. But throughout it is of the dark brooding house as a linking force that we are chiefly conscious.

However, it is *The Death of the Heart* (1938) that is considered by many to be the most complete statement of a theme common to many of the books. The heroine, Portia, an awkward adolescent, is unexpectedly inherited by Anna and Thomas Quayne, whose marriage is cool and detached and who find her claims on them embarrassing. The young girl, intensely lonely and rejecting the arid life they lead in their large immaculate Regents Park house, records her observations in great detail in her diary. This Anna discovers and reads—and to Portia such an act is complete betrayal. The girl is betrayed on two more occasions. First she is let down by Eddie, one of Anna's lovers, a gay witty childish philanderer, when he becomes frightened by the strength and straightforwardness of her attachment, which he incorrectly assumes to be physical. In the end it is to Major Brutt, the pitiful unemployed remnant of the Indian army who has been kind to her, that she turns: only to be deserted by him when his sense of social inadequacy makes him feel that he cannot be her source of strength. As he hands her back to the Quaynes, we are left wondering how many such betrayals Portia can survive before her heart is as dead as theirs and their friends'.

In *The Heat of the Day* (1949), Stella Rodney, a woman long since divorced with a grown-up son, finds love in wartime with Robert Kelway. She is informed by Harrison, who is in love with her, that Robert is a spy, but that he is safe if she will become Harrison's lover. This rather melodramatic story is actually unfolded very quietly as Stella's love falls prey successively to incredulity, suspicion and hopelessness. In contrast to this main plot are two very interesting minor ones: one involves her son and his discovery that his mother was in fact the innocent party in her divorce; and the second introduces a simple factory girl who, though connected to Stella and Harrison by the slenderest threads of coincidence, allows them both to assume tremendous personal significance for her, completely misinterpreting their real relationship. This theme of deception and wrong interpretation of human actions is brilliantly echoed in the long passage in which newspaper reportage, with its emotional patriotic fervour and its over-simplification of facts, is revealed as comic, tragic, and yet absolutely necessary.

In contrast to this wartime realism, we next meet the insubstantial dream-like fabric of *A World of Love* (1955). In this book the heroine falls in love with a man already dead—through reading a cache of his letters which she has discovered. Such is the fanciful charm and delicacy of this book that the reader's disbelief may well be suspended: but it does not compare in stature with its two predecessors. A more solid achievement was *The Little Girls* (1964), the much praised story of a reunion of three school friends after nearly fifty years and the recall of the fierce emotions of childhood—in their case crystallised around the existence of a mysterious buried box. It is written with her usual distinctive and unsentimental evocation of women. *A Day in the Dark* (1965) is a volume of short stories. S. R.

Bowen, John (1924–), English novelist, is a satirical writer who employs fable and allegory to criticise the habit of generalisation which labels a group, and which in so doing submerges the individuals thus irrelevantly described and demands that they live by standards unrelated to their real situation. The conjunction of the elaborately worked-out structure, the tendency to symbolism and the sharply observed factual reporting of events emphasises the absurdities he sees, and achieves a comic as well as satiric effect. His novels include *The Truth Will Not Help Us* (1956), *After the Rain* (1958), and *A World Elsewhere* (1965). He has also written critical essays and children's books. J. W.

Bowen, Marjorie. See **Long,** [Gabrielle] Margaret.

Bowles, Paul (1910–), American novelist whose books have recalled the horror stories of Poe and the philosophical ideas of the French existentialists. As a setting for his horrific parables of meaninglessness Bowles has chosen the rotting squalor of North Africa, as in *The Sheltering Sky* (1949), or the nightmarish jungle of Central America, as in *Up Above the World* (1967). K. R. R.

Boyd, Martin (1893–), Australian writer, himself a member of the upper-middle class society which he describes in all his novels. His characters are the snobbish descendants of the early settlers in Victoria who still feel close ties with England and who never fully identify themselves with Australia. So much is Martin Boyd writing about people and attitudes that he knows well, that if one reads his autobiography *A Single Flame*

(1939) many of the characters and incidents in his novels can be traced to his own experience. His most well-known works are *The Montforts* (1928), a family saga in three parts; *Lucinda Brayford* (1946), a long novel tracing the life of Lucinda and her son Stephen; *The Cardboard Crown* (1952); and *A Difficult Young Man* (1955). The sophistication, wit and sensitivity of his style is as unusual to find in Australian writing as is his choice of milieu, and it is for his documentation of little-charted territory that he is most significant. Later titles are *Outbreak of Love* (1957) and *When Blackbirds Sing* (1962). S. R.

Bradbury, Malcolm (1932–), English novelist and academic. Bradbury has much in common with Kingsley Amis: he, too, is an academic knocking at the pomposity of university life. Educated at London, Indiana and Manchester universities, with a spell at Yale in 1958, Bradbury was appointed to the department of English Literature at Hull in 1959. He has written for *Punch*, the *Spectator*, *Atlantic Monthly* and *Saturday Review*. His novel *Eating People is Wrong* (1959) is more broadly comic and less sharply satirical than Amis's *Lucky Jim*. Professor Treece is a kind of successful Jim Dixon: the head of an English department in a provincial university, he allows himself to drift into an unsatisfactory sexual relationship with Dr Viola Masefield, one of his senior staff. He eventually achieves a short-lived fulfilment with one of his postgraduate students, Emma Fielding, who is healthily normal. The plot is complicated by a brilliant but unstable undergraduate, Louis Bates, who attempts suicide when rejected by Emma: Bates being a classic example of the intellectual whose I.Q. has outstripped his emotional maturity, leaving him prone to sudden, disjointed and unpredictable actions. The general tone of the novel is set by an incident at a college dance when Treece is asked whether he can supply a student with a contraceptive for immediate use; he is prepared to go through the motions of searching his wallet, knowing full well he has not got one; whereupon the student disappears to 'risk it'. Later titles include *Stepping Westwards* (1965). D. L. P.

Bradbury, Ray (1920–), prolific, popular and highly praised American writer in various genres. His short stories appeared in a multitude of American magazines specialising in science fiction before 1945, but it is the publication of his collections and full-length novels since then that has established his reputation. One of the features of his science fiction is the strong accent of probability that underlies his creations: the reader feels that the world of the future he describes is all too recognisably present in embryo in this one.

The stories in *The Illustrated Man* (1952), linked together by the fact that they appear as short moving films on the skin of a tattooed man, provide a series of horrifying and macabre little object lessons. Both the warmth and sympathy with which characters of the stories are drawn, and the effective and subtle symbolic device through which their total significance is expressed, are typical of Bradbury's work. For example, in *Fahrenheit 451* (1953), books (particularly the classics) are regarded as so inflammatory and destructive of the *status quo* that the task of firemen is to burn them—and history has even been rewritten to the effect that this has always been their duty. Bradbury's explanation of how this happened pictures an apathetic civilisation valuing above all things conformity, protection, and not happiness but rather absence of unhappiness.

However, the most remarkable quality to be found in his work and one uncommon in science fiction, which is more often given to pointing dreadful warnings, is his positive and unashamed belief in human values—witness the close of *Fahrenheit 451* with its band of wanderers carrying the works of great writers in their heads; the title story of *The Day it Rained Forever* (1959) in which harp music simulates the patter of the longed-for rain and brings peace to the listeners; or 'Dark They Were and Golden-Eyed' from the same collection, a lyrically beautiful story about a family humble enough to learn from a new environment rather than determined to dominate and destroy it. His work as a whole is characterised by detailed rendering of settings as diverse as Mexico, Ireland and the mid-west of the U.S.A. (*The Machineries of Joy*, 1964). His main characters often represent the grotesque and bizarre extremes of the human condition—desperately poor, enormously fat, very small or malformed—who in their plight have carved out a precarious reason for existence. His subject is the remarkable variety of ways in which man embraces love and death; his mood is one of romantic optimism; his style pure poetry freshly minted for each new story. Other titles include *Dark Carnival* (1947), *The Martian Chronicle* (1950; English title *The Silver Locusts*), *The October Country* (1956), and *The Golden Apples of the Sun* (1953), which is now a secondary-school text in England.

S. R.

Brahms, Caryl (Doris Caroline Abrahams; 1901–), English novelist and theatre critic (especially on ballet). As a novelist she has written a dozen books in collaboration with 'S. J. Simon' (Simon J. Skidelsky). The most popular, *Don't Mr Disraeli* (1940) and *No Bed for Bacon* (1941), may best be described as historical romps. As Miss Brahms herself has said, 'if history has looked in now and then it is only to raise an eyebrow'. She also collaborated with Ned Sherrin in writing the novel *Cindy-Ella* (1962).

K. M. H.

Braine, John (1922–), won immediate fame with his best-selling novel *Room at the Top* (1957), about a young man determined to get to the top at any price. He gets there finally by marrying the daughter of the wealthiest man in town, a girl he does not love; the price is the sacrifice of his true love-relationship with an older woman and her subsequent suicide, a catastrophe for which his arrival at the top proves no compensation. Appearing the year after Osborne's *Look Back in Anger*, Braine's novel, with its vivid class-consciousness and its realistic portrayal of lower-middle-class life in a drab provincial town, led to his being associated with the so-called 'kitchen-sink' school of literature and with the 'angry young men' who produced much of it. However, the passionate and joyous intensity of Joe Lampton's relationship with Alice, and his double agony first at losing her and subsequently at feeling that he has virtually murdered her, lift it clear of any such categorisation.

Before *Room at the Top*, Braine had worked principally as a librarian in his native Yorkshire; afterwards he was for a time a journalist, still living in the north. Neither his sequel *Life at the Top* (1962), nor the intervening novel *The Vodi* (1959), achieved anything like the same success, but with *The Jealous God* (1964) he re-established himself as an important writer, drawing his inspiration again from the West Riding. The book opens with as bleak a landscape—physical and human—as the unfamiliar reader could imagine, with the thirty-year-old Catholic bachelor schoolmaster Vincent Dungarvan the odd man out in a community that admits of only two vocations: marriage or the priesthood. He is unenthusiastic about the latter; but the marriages of his two brothers, and of almost all the people he knows, characterised by the twin interests of children and material goods and by an acceptance that physical love is a thing of short duration, do not appeal to him either. Under pressure from his mother to become a priest, tormented by unquenched sexual desire, he wanders around the dreary town that his crude Irish forebears settled in, joylessly drinking its beer in dismal bars or playing records to himself at home. Then he meets Laura, a Protestant girl of his own intelligence and sensitivity, with the characteristic Yorkshire virtues of honesty, courage and toughness but also with the capacity for joy that is rarely to be found in Vincent's world. For the first time, he falls in love: only to be brought up with a jolt by the news, obtained by his now watchful family (who embody the proprietary jealousy of the God they serve), that she is divorced.

So strong is the influence of his religion that he finds himself unable to consummate their love: but so acute are his sexual needs that shortly afterwards he commits adultery with his sister-in-law, who has long suppressed a passion for him. When, eventually, he and Laura fulfil their love, their brief ecstasy begins to founder again, this time on Vincent's realisation that he cannot marry a woman who, in his church's eyes, still has a husband; and the rupture comes when Laura's ex-husband, summoned by an unsigned note, reappears on the scene. From now on we see Laura, increasingly conscious of a spiritual vacuum in her own outlook, grow into an awareness of the indissolubility of her marriage and a determination to try again. The attempt ends disastrously, with her ex-husband's suicide; but the way is now open for Vincent and Laura, who both share a measure of guilt, to start a life together in another part of the country. K. R. R.

Braithwaite, E. R. (Eustace Edward Ricardo Braithwaite; 1920–), West Indian novelist, worked as a teacher in London. His first book, *To Sir With Love* (1959), attracted considerable interest as a record of courage and humour in overcoming the difficulties presented by a tough class in an East End school. In *Paid Servant* (1962), drawing on the experiences he gained for the L.C.C. Department of Child Welfare, Braithwaite describes some of the individual problems which arise in trying to find homes with foster or adoptive parents for non-white children. *A Kind of Homecoming* (1963), as the title suggests, gives an account of his reaction to several African countries which he visited; *Choice of Straws* (1965) deals with racialism in London. J. W.

Bramah, Ernest (Ernest Bramah Smith; 1868–1942), English writer of the delightful 'Kai Lung' stories *Kai Lung Unfolds His Mat* (1928); *The Wallet of Kai Lung* (1900) in which he uses the literary idiom, social system and mythology of ancient China, often in order to satirise modern Western society. Every word and phrase is chosen with fastidious care, so that the result is as ingenious and fascinating as an intricate Chinese carpet.
J. T. M.

Brandes, Georg (1842–1927), former influential Danish literary critic, whose impact was felt particularly in Scandinavia towards the end of the nineteenth century and in the early years of the twentieth. Radical in outlook, he demanded the rejection of abstract idealism and that literature should concern itself with reality and progress. Many of his numerous critical works are available in English. R. C. W.

Branner, Hans Christian (1903–), prominent Danish novelist and playwright. After a relatively unsuccessful early career on the stage he turned to literature in the late 'thirties, his principal achievements lying in the field of the novel. Noteworthy is his acute psychological analysis of the human condition, its fears and loneliness, its greed for power and the resultant dangers. His chief novels are *Legetøj* ['Toys'] (1936), *Barnet leger ved Stranden* ['The child lies on the beach'] (1937), *Drømmen om en Kvinde* ['Dream about a woman'] (1941), the radio-novel *Historien om Børge* ['The story of Børge'] (1942), *Rytteren* [*The Riding Master*] (1949) and *Ingen kender Natten* ['Nobody knows the night'] (1956). Other works include the *novella* entitled *Angst* ['Fear'] (1947); two collections of *novelle* and stories, *Om lidt er vi borte* [*In a Little While We Shall Be Gone*] (1939) and *To Minutters Stilhed* [*Two Minutes of Silence*] (1944); an antecedent dramatisation of *Rytteren* (produced only in 1950); and the play *Søskende* [*The Judge*; in *Contemporary Danish Plays*, ed. Elias Bredsdorff, 1955] which had a long and successful run in 1952. Branner's keen comprehension of the psychology of children is often apparent in his work and nowhere more than in *Historien om Børge*. His most effective novel is undoubtedly *Ingen kender Natten*, set in Copenhagen during the German occupation, which probes the intellectual's struggle to work free from the spiritual and moral lethargy and inertia of the period. R. C. W.

Brasch, Charles (1909–), New Zealand poet and founder in 1947 of the literary periodical *Landfall*, a publication which has had considerable influence on New Zealand letters. He has lived abroad for several periods and displays an ambivalent attitude towards his country in the poems published in *The Land and its People* (1939) and *Disputed Ground* (1948). Only with *The Estate* (1957) do Brasch's contradictions appear to be resolved, and corresponding poetic maturity attained. Recent titles include *Ambulando* (1964). S. R.

Brecht, Bertolt (1896–1956), German writer for the theatre born in Bavaria, was a dramatist of the world scene whose work became internationally renowned in his own lifetime. His initial university studies were in science and philosophy, but he abandoned these after the first world war to devote himself to writing. His first plays, *Baal* [*Baal*] (1922) and *Trommeln in der Nacht* ['Drums in the Night'] (1922), were immediately successful, especially the latter, dealing as it did with a soldier who returns from the war to find his wife living with another man. His collection of ballads under the satiric title *Die Hauspostille* [*Book of Family Devotions*] (1927) were stark and realistic, as were his plays of this period. It was the success of *Die Dreigroschenoper* [*The Threepenny Opera*] (1928), however, that established Brecht as a major figure, and indicated his full acceptance of Marxism as a social philosophy. A bitingly witty adaptation of the eighteenth-century *The Beggar's Opera*, it was set to music by Kurt Weill and rapidly translated for foreign consumption. It also indicated Brecht's abandonment of expressionism and his wholehearted conversion to the 'epic theatre' or the 'epic opera'. For him, the audience were not to be persuaded that the people and the events on the stage were real; they were to be constantly reminded that the stage was a stage and the actors really actors. As means to this end, Brecht allows his characters occasionally to explain to the audience directly who they are and what they are doing; to prevent the audience from becoming too involved in the people or stage, they deliberately 'blow up' in their lines, or as in *Herr Puntila und sein Knecht Matti* [*Puntila*] (1948) adopt increasingly ugly make-up. This was not done just for the sake of novelty; Brecht believed that the theatre was a place where 'social experiments' could be carried out, where audiences could be subjected directly to a Marxist message by means of actions which were accompanied by their interpretation. Music, loudspeakers, cycloramas, film excerpts, all were incorporated into the epic treatment. It follows that to be a spectator of one of his plays was both an exciting and disturbing experience, and to be one of his actors demanded a rejection of accepted practice.

Having found his genre, Brecht began his fantastically prolific output of 'epics'; many of these have become part of world literature. *Aufstieg und Fall der Stadt Mahagonny* [*The Rise and Fall of the Town of Mahagonny*] (1929) was a thoroughly Marxist attack on the cultural barbarism of the modern city; *Die heilige Johanna der Schlachthöfe* [*St Joan of the Stockyards*] (1932) turned the spotlight on capitalism and its exploitation of the working class and even of religion. Joan Dark, a Salvation Army type of girl, organises a strike in the Chicago stockyards; her main opponent is Pierpoint Manler who controls the markets. Admiring Joan's courage he is yet unmoved by her arguments; her death produces tributes from him and his confrères, but the system still survives.

With the advent of Hitler in 1933, Brecht went into self-imposed exile, first in Denmark, then Finland, and finally in the United States which he reached in 1941. At first, despite a steady output, his work might appear to have declined a little in quality, but this would be to misunderstand the circumstances in which plays written in the 'thirties came to be produced only in the late 'forties and early 'fifties. Shortly before the war, however, *Galileo Galilei* [*The Life of Galileo*] (1942), *Die Geschäfte des Herrn Julius Caesar* ['The business of Julius Caesar'] (1949), *Der gute Mensch von Sezuan* [*The Good Person of Sezuan*] (1942) and the outstanding *Mutter Courage und Ihre Kinder* [*Mother Courage and Her Children*] (1941) were written. The latter, dealing with a vulgar woman owner of a travelling canteen who follows the troops and lives indirectly off their trade, has become a world classic; losing her sons in the fighting and her dumb daughter Katrin who, unable to shout, is shot as she beats a drum to warn of an attack, Mother Courage learns nothing and follows the troops. The theme, in lesser hands, might well have led to an idealisation of the poor and the ignorant. Brecht made no concessions, showing Mother Courage for nothing better than she is, cunning, stubborn, bawdy. The play also includes examples of Brecht's concept of alienation. A young girl tries on a prostitute's hat while a Lutheran hymn is being sung; thus religion and its expression are 'alienated' by the sort of thing which actually happens in real life.

During his exile in the United States, Brecht openly attacked Nazi Germany in short plays, published in 1941 as *Furcht und Elend des dritten Reiches* [*Anxiety and Misery of the Third Reich*]. His Marxism caused him to be called before a senate committee in 1946, where he denied membership of the Communist Party. Despite his return to East Berlin the following year events seem to indicate that this was the truth. Invited by the East German authorities, provided with a theatre and a first-class company in the Berliner Ensemble, having a first-class actress Helene Weigel to interpret his leading roles, he had plays which had been written years before produced with the full support of a government not unaware of the value of their championship of the dramatic arts. Thus it was that Galileo, Mother Courage, the poor Chinese prostitute heroine of *The Good Person of Sezuan*, and the servant girl who adopts an unwanted baby in *Der Kaukasiche Kreidekreis* [*The Caucasian Chalk Circle*] (1947) passed into the repertory of the world's theatre. It is possible that some of his earlier plays written in exile might have secured as much success had they been as brilliantly produced, but Brecht had only a few years left to produce his works. He revealed himself as a dedicated artist; despite the committed nature of much of his writing, he showed himself strangely ambivalent to the events of the Berlin rising in 1953, and the same aloofness caused him to produce his opera *Lucullus* ['Lucullus'] in a political environment not likely to secure its acceptance. In the opera, the Roman general renders an account for his actions before a tribunal of the shadows; it was withdrawn after the first night by government decree. Brecht may have consciously scored his revenge when he produced *The Life of Galileo* which shows that despite the apparent victory of the forces of the Church, the old astronomer still won and knew himself to have won: truth will last —'*eppur si muove*' ('and yet it does move'). Consciously critical or not, Brecht's death in 1956 was a tragedy for the theatre of the world and for the theatre of ideas. His wife and company maintain his work, and reveal his extraordinary powers, both as a dramatist and as a lyric poet. G. W.

Brennan, Christopher J. (1870–1932), Australian poet, has long been regarded by critics as a major figure but has only recently received appreciation on any scale from the public. Of the collections published while he was alive, only *Chant of Doom* (1918), expressing his anger and indignation with Germany, found a wide market and then mainly because of the topical nature of his subject. *Poems: 1913* is a volume more representative of the philosophical basis underlying his poetry—that man is a wanderer and that his ultimate goal is consciousness of self. This theme is developed in language of great beauty appealing to the senses with its imagery and music, and to the intellect with the profundity of its subject. His work is now collected in *The Verse of C. J. Brennan* (1961) and *The Prose of C. J. Brennan* (1962). S. R.

Brent of Bin Bin, pseudonym used by the Australian author (probably Miles Franklin, q.v.) responsible for a number of novels dealing with the isolated lives of the squatters of New South Wales: such as *Up the Country* (1928) and *Ten Creeks Run* (1930). In *Back to Bool Bool* (1931) we see the second generation leave Australia for Europe—some returning to their childhood surroundings, but viewing them with new eyes. Since 1950 three further volumes, previously held back by their mysterious author, have been published. S. R.

Breton, André (1896–1966), French poet. Breton, at first a student of medicine, soon took to writing poetry and founded a review *Littérature* in 1919. Friendly with Aragon, Soupault and Apollinaire, Breton used his review to support dadaïsm but in 1922, having broken with this movement, took the leadership of the surrealists. Accepted as the theoretician of the group, he published three *Manifestes* ['Manifestos'] in 1924, 1930 and 1942 to explain and codify the beliefs of the group. During this period he also published collections of his poems: *Les Champs magnétiques* ['Magnetic fields'] (1919; with Soupault); *Les Pas perdus* ['Time to waste'] (1924). *Légitime défense* ['Legitimate defence'] (1926) opposes any external control of the artist, whether by reason or political ideology. More collections followed, *Le Revolver à cheveux blancs* ['The revolver with white hair'], *Les Vases communicants* ['Communicating vessels'] (1932), and the prose-poems *Nadja* (1928) and *Arcane 17* (1945).

In 1941 Breton went to America, returning after the war. As the leader of surrealism he formulated the doctrine that the subconscious should be allowed to enter the world of literature, but the political connections of the movement had now led to its eventual disappearance. Breton also published *Jeunes cerisiers garantis contre les lièvres* [*Young Cherry-trees Protected from Hares*] (1946) and *Yves Tanguy* (1946), as well as many articles, interviews and reviews. A. L. W.

Brett Young, Francis (1884–1954), English novelist and poet. Although the distinguished *Portrait of a Village* was published in 1951 and his patriotic long poem, *The Island*, in 1944, he was still most admired for his earlier works, *Deep Sea* (1914), *Portrait of Clare* (1927), *My Brother Jonathan* (1928), and *The House under the Water* (1932). He was a doctor and drew on his medical experience as well as on his knowledge of the sea for his subjects. He wrote with delicate perception and charm, and occasionally, sentimentality. In his accounts of pre-war South Africa, *They Seek a Country* (1937) and *The City of Gold* (1939), history and imagination effectively merge. J. W.

Brickhill, Paul (1916–), Australian writer who recreated vividly events and personalities of the second world war. A member of the R.A.A.F. he became a prisoner of war in Stalag Luft III, from where the ill-fated escape, described in *The Great Escape* (1951), was made. The dramatic bombing of the Mohne dam was the subject of *The Dam Busters* (1951). These two books and *Reach for the Sky* (1954), the life of Douglas Bader the crippled air hero, have been filmed. J. W.

Bridie, James (Dr O. H. Mavor; 1888–1951), Scottish dramatist who began writing plays at the age of forty and quickly became known by, among others, *The Anatomist* (1931) and *Tobias and the Angel* (1932); the latter, based on a story from the Apocrypha, being perhaps one of his most successful achievements. He continued his career as a physician and surgeon in Glasgow until 1938. His writing has the vigour, argument and incident associated with Scottish literature, although his hopes of reviving Scottish theatre were hardly realised. He again took Biblical subjects for *Jonah and the Whale* (1932), and *Susannah and the Elders* (1938), and was fond of debating Scottish problems, as in *Mr Bolfry* (1943), a religious play with a strong element of the supernatural. Observation of character and a gift for forthright, witty dialogue give his plays a lively astringency that is not without sympathy, and they are only marred by weaknesses of co-ordination and structure. These have perhaps been most successfully overcome in *Mr Bolfry*, which also revealed a depth of seriousness new to Bridie. The last play by which he is remembered, *Daphne Laureola* (1948), is a comedy. J. W.

Bridges, Robert (1844–1930), English poet. Bridges was educated at Eton and Oxford. He qualified in medicine at St Bartholomew's Hospital but retired from practice in 1882 to devote his time to literature. He was made Poet Laureate in 1913. One major contribution to English literature was his publication of the works of Gerald Manley Hopkins in 1918.

Bridges's own style was based on a veneration for the classical form of the eighteenth century but like his friend Hopkins he was involved in experimentation. The immensely successful long poem *The Testament of Beauty* (1929) is founded on a loose Alexandrine line. Its fusion of poetry with Platonic philosophy tends however to suspend the reader's involvement and lose him in remote speculation. Bridges's best poetry is in the shorter lyrics which combine deep personal feeling with the firm technical skill that is characteristic of the poet. *The Poetical Works of Robert Bridges* was published in 1936. D. L. P.

Brighouse, Harold (1882–1958), English playwright, was one of a group of writers who helped to introduce working-class themes into the English theatre in the first decades of the century. His best-known play *Hobson's Choice* (1916) was revived by the National Theatre in the 1960s.

K. R. R.

Brittain, Vera (1896?–   ), English novelist. Born in Newcastle, she went to Oxford in 1914. The first world war which interrupted her studies there influenced her very profoundly. She describes her early life very movingly in *Testament of Youth,* which was published in 1933. Apart from *Verses of a V.A.D.* (1918), her first published work was a novel *Dark Tide* (1923). Her most outstanding work apart from *Testament of Youth* is *Testament of Friendship* (1940) in which she tells the story of her great friend Winifred Holtby. A passionate feminist, her subsequent works include *Lady into Woman* (1953), a history of women from Victoria to Elizabeth II; *Testament of Experience* (1957); and *Envoy Extraordinary* (1965), a study of Vijaya Lakshmi Pandit. K. M. H.

Broch, Herman (1886–1951), Austrian-born novelist, experienced the disintegration of the Hapsburg empire and saw the collapse of the Third Reich from the security of the United States. Strongly affected by these experiences, he nevertheless treated them in an extremely personal way. He was influenced by James Joyce and by Hofmannstal whose works he translated into English; it was while he was Professor of German at Yale that he began to be recognised as one of the leaders in the new literary school of metaphysical or magic realism. He turned from literary criticism to literature itself only in his late forties; and his first novel *Die unbekannte Grösse* ['The unknown factor'] (1933) did not indicate clearly the direction he was taking. This was revealed in his trilogy *Die Schlafwandler* [*The Sleepwalkers*] (begun 1931), a brilliant chronicle of middle-class life in imperial Germany, dominated by the military and losing its faith in its own social and religious values. He reached his peak with *Der Tod des Vergil* [*The Death of Virgil*] (1945). Past, present and future are skilfully blended together in this account of the poet's sadness at his own inadequacies as he looks back over his life. Broch was to use this technique again in *Die Schuldlosen* ['The guiltless'] (1950), when he continued *Die Schlafwandler* to portray the advent of the totalitarian state in Germany. His posthumous work *Die Versucher* ['The tempters'] (1954) moved from the grand canvas to the small cameo; here he symbolises Hitler as Marius who wrecks the old social cohesion of a hitherto contented mountain village. His translated *Short Stories* appeared in 1966. G. W.

Bromfield, Louis (1896–1956), American novelist. His first book *The Green Bay Tree* was published in 1924 and was followed by *Possession* (1925) and *Early Autumn* (1926) which won a Pulitzer prize. Many of his best-known novels, notably *The Rains Came* (1937), set in India, and *Mrs Parkington* (1943), won him added popularity because they were filmed, but they lacked the quality of his earlier writing and seemed to have been written with one eye on Hollywood. During the last period of his life his autobiographical reminiscences about Malabar, the farm he bought in 1933—*Pleasant Valley* (1945) and *Malabar Farm* (1948)—have more literary value than any of his other writings, possibly excepting *Wild Country* (1948), the story of a young boy in Missouri. K. M. H.

Brooke, Rupert (1887–1915), English poet. Brooke's early poetry comes into the general pastoral category known as Georgian. The best-known poem is the often quoted 'The Old Vicarage at Grantchester' (1912) which finishes:

Ah God! to see the branches stir
Across the moon at Grantchester!

oh! yet
Stands the Church clock at ten to three?
And is there honey still for tea?

Some of the later poetry, however, derives wit and depth from the influence of the seventeenth-century metaphysicals.

As a war poet Brooke is limited by the fact that he died in 1915 and did not succeed to the disillusioned realism of Owen or Rosenberg. He left behind a group of sonnets titled *1914* which upon his death gained immense popularity from a combination of almost jingoistic patriotism and a sense of the sentimental in the eclipse of youth. These sonnets included 'The Soldier' with the famous opening:

If I should die, think only this of me:
That there's some corner of a foreign field
That is for ever England.

Brooke's *Letters from America* with an introduction by Henry James was published in 1916. *The Complete Poems* was issued in 1932. D. L. P.

Brooke-Rose, Christine (1926–), English novelist, characterised by an analytic wit and unusual perception. Her best-known books include *The Middle Men* (1961), a satirical novel of the world of public relations; and *Out* (1964), a novel set in 'Afro-Eurasia' after a major world disaster the nature of which is never revealed. The latter is the story of a sick white man of lost identity and his struggle to adjust himself to life in a world rendered totally unfamiliar through catastrophe. Later titles include *Such* (1966), a volume of short stories. P. E.

Brooks, Van Wyck (1886–1963), American critic. His Pulitzer prize-winning book *The Flowering of New England, 1815–65* (1936) is one of five semi-sociological volumes dealing with American cultural evolution. He had earlier written *The Wine of the Puritans* (1908), a critical account of the repressive puritan heritage. K. R. R.

Brophy, Brigid (1929–), Irish-born novelist. In her first, much admired novel, *Hackenfeller's Ape* (1953), Miss Brophy protests, with wit, against a world which will struggle to preserve an animal in captivity and yet will send it into the incomprehensible suffering of a space flight. She brings her ironic humour and sympathy to her later novels, *Flesh* (1962) and *The Snow Ball* (1964), in which the relationships between her characters are anatomised in acutely observed settings which enhance the whole satiric picture. Apart from novels Miss Brophy has written *Black Ship to Hell* (1962), a psychoanalytical discussion of the causes of war, and *Mozart the Dramatist* (1964). Her essays have been frequently published in the *New Statesman* and the *London Magazine.* J. W.

Brophy, John (1899–), English novelist, father of Brigid Brophy. Prolific and wide-ranging in his subject matter, he embraces religious and political as well as military and romantic themes. His titles include *The Bitter End* (1928), *Waterfront* (1934), *Immortal Sergeant* (1942), *Julian's Way* (1949) and *The Day they Robbed the Bank of England* (1959). More recently he has written *The Meaning of Murder* (1963), *A New Look at Murder* (1966) and *The Left in Western Europe since 1789* (1966).

K. R. R.

Broster, D. K. (Dorothy Kathleen Broster; 1878–1950), English historical novelist. Her first novel *Chantermerle*, a romance of the Vendéan war in

1792, appeared in 1911 and was followed in 1913 by *Vision Splendid*, both being written in collaboration with G. W. Taylor; but she won her real reputation with a trilogy based on the adventures of Prince Charles the Young Pretender, beginning with the Jacobite rebellion of 1745: *The Flight of the Heron* (1925), *The Gleam in the North* (1927) and *The Dark Mile* (1929). Her other popular works include *Almond, Wild Almond* (1933), *Child Royal* (1937), and her last novel *The Captain's Lady* which was published in 1947. K. M. H.

Brutus, Dennis (1924–), South African poet now exiled in London. His political experiences form the bedrock of some intensely felt and sensuously expressed personal and protest poems in *Sirens, Knuckles and Boots* (1963). While in gaol on Robben island—where as a political prisoner (and subsequently as a 'banned' man) he could not write for publication—Brutus wrote a further series of poems in the form of letters; these *Letters to Martha* (London, 1966, in a volume also including earlier and other unpublished poems) are quietly controlled, taut and deeply contemplative distillations of his experiences during the eighteen months of his imprisonment. The tone and style—simple, lucid and expressive, at once movingly personal and strongly public—are in marked contrast to *Sirens*, and the range of feeling and subject are wider and more profound. C. P.

Bryant, Sir Arthur (1899–), English writer on historical subjects, who has made events in British history enthralling to a wide public. His popular success began with his book on *King Charles II* (1931), and great interest was aroused by his three-volume life of Pepys: *Samuel Pepys: the Man in the Making* (1933), *Samuel Pepys: the Years of Peril* (1935), and *Samuel Pepys: the Saviour of the Navy* (1938). These are based on Pepys's diaries and convey the immediacy of the events observed by the diarist. In *English Saga* (1940) he charted the history of the United Kingdom over the last hundred years, up to Dunkirk. The problems facing the country during the French revolution and the Napoleonic wars are described in *The Years of Endurance* (1942), *The Years of Victory* (1944) and *The Age of Elegance* (1950). Among his many other works are *Stanley Baldwin* (1937) and *The Age of Chivalry* (1963). J. W.

Bryusov, Valeri Yakovlevich (1873–1924), Russian symbolist poet and prose-writer, whose hatred of the czarist régime led him together with Blok into supporting the Bolsheviks. His 'decadent' poetry was officially frowned upon for its erotic opulence and imagery. He drew inspiration both from antiquity and from the civilisation of the modern city, which he treats symbolically in his poem *Kon' bled* [*Pale Horse*] (1904). His prose style was influenced by the fantasy of Poe and his best work, about magic in Germany, is *Ognenniy angel* [*Fire Angel*] (1907); however, perhaps his best-known work, which seemed to contradict his admitted Bolshevik sympathies, is *Respublica yuzhnovo kryesta* [*Republic of the Southern Cross*] (1907). His survey of five years of Russian poetry up to 1922 seems today a surprisingly unreliable and misguided appreciation of contemporary acmeist, futurist and symbolist poets. B. W.

Buchan, John, Baron Tweedsmuir (1875–1940), Scottish novelist and statesman. Buchan's career combines success as a public figure with a vast volume of writing. He was born in Perth and educated at Glasgow university and Oxford where he became president of the Union. He was called to the bar and then accompanied Lord Milner to South Africa. His first mature novel *Prester John* (1910) is a romance of South Africa. During the first part of the first world war Buchan served in France. He became Director of Information in 1917, subsequently writing a twenty-four-volume history of the war. He later represented the Scottish universities in parliament and was appointed Governor-General of Canada in 1935.

Buchan's writings include *Poems, Scots and English* (1917) and biographies which include those of *Montrose* (1913), *Scott* (1932), *Julius Caesar* (1932), *Oliver Cromwell* (1934) and *Augustus* (1937). He is best known, however, for his adventure novels which are in the romantic tradition of Robert Louis Stevenson. *The Thirty-Nine Steps* (1915), *Greenmantle* (1916) and *The Three Hostages* (1924) feature Richard Hannay as the hero. The first of these uses the technique of the hero accidently fallen among villains, who in this case gradually unravels and exposes a plot to reveal the naval plans of his country in time of war. The device of the central character pursued both by police and spies sets a pattern for many spy and detective novels of the twentieth century. The climax of the book is Hannay's desperate bid to cross the rough Scottish countryside pursued by an unrelenting enemy. The later novels *The Path of the King* (1921) and *A Prince of Captivity* (1933) reveal a compelling interest in the supernatural. D. L. P.

Buck, Pearl (1892–), American author of numerous best-selling novels. The sensitivity and craftsmanship of her books about China, where her parents were missionaries, earned her considerable respect, culminating in the award of the Nobel prize in 1938.

Her most famous book is *The Good Earth* (1931), the story of a simple Chinese peasant Wang-Lung who becomes a rich land-owner and head of an important family. Wang is distinguished by his practical intelligence and strength of character, which equip him to survive many vicissitudes; but most of all by his love of 'the good earth'—this, rather than any capitalistic greed, driving him to invest his savings in more and yet more land, rather than in the pleasures of the moment. Early on, he timidly visits the great house of Hwang in the nearby city to acquire the slave O-lan to be his wife; and eventually he himself ends up living there—partly through his diligence and enterprise in using his own acres, partly through the decline of a family whose extravagant life has lost all relation to the capacity of its land to produce wealth. Ironically, his success has enabled his own sons to lead lives divorced from the land that has nourished them, and when he dies they are planning to sell it. Even Wang and O-lan are not unaffected: the second wife that Wang purchases, when the luxuries of the town's tea-house have awakened in him a desire of feminine beauty, proving a cruel thorn in the faithful O-lan's flesh.

The Good Earth was followed by two sequels, forming a trilogy entitled *The House of Earth*. Other well-known titles include *Pavilion of Women* (1946) and *Death in the Castle* (1966). K. R. R.

Buckler, Ernest (1908–), Canadian novelist, is the author of *The Mountain and the Valley* (1952), a depressing allegory of the Canadian creative predicament. Significantly, it has as its hero a mute artist who escapes from an unsatisfactory reality into a private world of his own. The book ends with his ascent of a mountain which overwhelms him with the vastness and colourlessness of its expanse of snow. S. R.

Buechner, Frederick (1926–), American novelist who established his reputation with *A Long Day's Dying* (1949), a somewhat free interpretation of the Philomela myth in the context of an American widow's sexual escapade on the campus of the university where her son is a student. The book's symbolism is often far from clear, and the style tends to the artificial, but its fantastic, sometimes gruesome, qualities make it compelling reading. Other titles include *The Return of Ansel Gibbs* (1958).

K. R. R.

Buero Vallejo, Antonio (1916–), Spanish dramatist. Buero is a tragic writer, examining 'the conflict between necessity and liberty'. In *Historia de una escalera* ['The story of a staircase'] (1949) that conflict is between the inhibiting environment of a Madrid tenement and the aspirations of its inhabitants; while *En la ardiente oscuridad* ['In burning darkness'] (1950), set in a school for the blind, contrasts Carlos's unquestioning acceptance of his infirmity with the dissatisfied longings of Ignacio. Buero has recently probed socio-political problems in three historical tragedies. The finest is *El concierto de San Ovidio* ['The concert of Saint Ovide'] (1962), another play about the blind, set in pre-revolutionary Paris: with David, a blind musician forced to play in a burlesque orchestra, murdering Valindín the impresario. In *En la ardiente oscuridad* blindness had symbolised man's tragic unfulfilment; here it represents his degradation and exploitation by capitalist society. Buero's courageous treatment of such themes confirms him as the major figure to have emerged in the Spanish theatre since the civil war. D. H. G.

Bulatović, Miodrag (1930–), Yugoslav novelist and short-story writer. He is a controversial figure and his novel *Hero on a Donkey* (London 1966) has been banned in Yugoslavia. Bulatović aroused public attention with his first volume of stories *Djavoli Dolaze* ['The devils are coming'] (1955), written in a highly individual style: symbolic and disjointed, with the outside world being presented through the eyes and emotions of a number of characters, generally poor and often outside social conventions. One of the stories in this volume, *Ljubavnici* ['The lovers'], was included in *New Fiction* in 1962. Starting from sympathy for the outcast and the mass of ordinary people, Bulatović enters into characters and situations and illuminates them in their essential stark and fantastic colours. His second volume of stories *Vuk i Zvono* ['The wolf and the bell'] (1958), where the symbol of fire is used as a leitmotif in the treatment of contemporary situations, established his reputation within Yugoslavia, and his novel *Crveni Petao leti prema Nebu* [*The Red Cockerel*] (1959) made him known abroad. This work centres on the symbol of the cockerel which alone is free to rise above the filth, sin and pettiness of human life. Bulatović's first play *Godot has Arrived* has been produced in Düsseldorf (June 1966) and described as 'one of the most heartening dramas to come out of eastern Europe in recent times'. C. W.

Bulgakov, Mikhail Afanasievich (1891–1940), Soviet novelist, dramatist and satirist, born and educated in Kiev. He preferred a literary profession to one in medicine and acquired great success with his autobiographical first novel *Byelaya gvardiya* [*White Guard*] (1924). It is outstanding in Soviet literature because its heroes are White officers. The dramatised version *Dni turbinykh* [*The Days of the Turbins*] (1925) subsequently attracted the close attentions of the censorship; after a series of mordant short stories or dramatic satires culminating in *Krasnaya ostrova* [*The Crimson Island*] (1928), which is a sharp attack on the censorship, he was obliged to restrict his literary genius to dramatising biographies or the novels of other writers. In 1938 he wrote his strange masterpiece *Magister i Margarita* [*The Master and Marguerita*] (published 1967). Immensely varied in its themes and moods, it conveys memorably the Devil's visit to Moscow. In 1939 Bulgakov went blind and in great pain dictated to his wife his delightfully and originally humorous semi-autobiographical story *Chorniy syneg* [*Black Snow*] (1965). B. W.

Bullett, Gerald (1893–), English poet and novelist. Bullett's poetry includes *Dreams O' Mine* (1915) and *The Bubble* (1934). His novels include *The History of Egg Pandervil* (1928), *The Jury* (1935) and *The Trouble at Number Seven* (1952). He edited an admirable anthology of *Silver Poets of the 16th Century* (1947). D. L. P.

Bunin, Ivan Alexeyevich (1870–1953), Russian poet and novelist who, despite much official hostility after his emigration to France in 1919, continued to have a large number of admirers in the Soviet Union. He was born at Voronezh, of noble stock. Near his family estate were places frequented by well-known literary figures, and so a feeling for literature was absorbed by the young Bunin. His first work was of a poetic nature. He was one of the finest pre-symbolist poets, a Parnassian, whose lyrics consisted mainly of his impressions of nature. However, he is best known for his prose works, which fall into two main categories: the stark and terse, and the exotic. The first is usually retained for Russian topics, while the second is for stories from abroad. This system is ignored, however, in his best-known work, *Gospodin iz San Francisco* [*Gentleman from San Francisco*] (1915), where the very terse language, reminiscent of Tolstoy's, heightens the horror and irony of death in the story of an American millionaire who, having spent a lifetime acquiring his wealth, rather belatedly takes a world cruise in order to enjoy spending it, only to die as he reaches the isle of Capri.

His other works of note are *Derevnya* [*The Village*] (1910), *Sny Changa* [*Dreams of Chang*] (1916), the semi-autobiographical *Zhizn' Arsenyeva* (*Yunost'*) [*Well of Days*] (1927) and *Dyelo korneta Yelagina* [*The Elaghin Affair*] (1927). He received the Nobel literature prize in 1933, went on to write *Tyomniye alleyi* [*Dark Alleys*] (1943), and published his *Vospominaniya* [*Memoirs and Portraits*] in 1953. Bunin tended to be a rather sad writer, and preoccupied with love and death. He expressed his dislike of the Soviet régime right up to his own death, but his qualities as a writer of outstanding style allowed him to retain a place of importance in Russian literature. B. W.

Burdick, Eugene (1918–), American author or co-author of books featuring controversial aspects of the American way of life: such as *The Ugly American* (1958), which deals with U.S. foreign policy in south-east Asia; *Fail Safe* (1962), with nuclear-weapons escalation; *The 480* (1964), with the manipulation of public opinion by admass methods during a campaign for the presidency; and *Sarkhan* (1966), with Washington politics and the threat of communism. *Nina's Book* (1965) is partly set in a concentration camp. S. R.

Burgess, Anthony (1917–), English novelist whose work is characterised by an unusual, almost fiendish wit and a remarkable power of imagination, often of a near-Rabelaisian kind. His titles include *A Clockwork Orange* (1962), a picaresque novel in the form of an alarming confession from a juvenile delinquent written in his own distinctive slang; *The Wanting Seed* (1962), a wickedly and grotesquely funny study of overpopulation, with cannibalism proposed as a solution; *The Eve of St Venus* (1964) in which Venus interrupts the arrangements for a wedding and claims the groom for herself; *A Vision of Battlements* (reissued 1965), a highly comic novel set in Gibraltar where a garrison looks forward with apprehension to the readjustment which the end of the war will entail; and the ribald thriller *Tremor of Intent* (1966).

He has also written *Here Comes Everybody* (1965), an introduction for the cautious reader to the works of James Joyce, which he followed up in 1966 with an edited, shortened version of Joyce's *Finnegan's Wake*; a story of Shakespeare's love life entitled *Nothing Like the Sun* (1964); and a group of novels originally published under the pseudonym Joseph Kell, notably *Inside Mr Enderby* (1962) in which the hero finds asylum and literary inspiration in a lavatory. P. E.

Burgess, [Frank] Gelett (1866–1951), American humorist, wrote *Goops and How to be Them* (1900), followed by several other books about 'goops' (his own invention). He also coined other now-familiar words, including 'blurb'; and his name is preserved in anthologies of comic verse by the poem beginning 'I've never seen a purple cow'. K. R. R.

Burnett, W. R. (William Rodgers Burnett; 1899–), American novelist, a leading exponent of the 'hard-boiled' school of writing with its terse, near-casual treatment of the violent and the sordid and its naturalistic low-life dialogue. His first book *Little Caesar* (1929) was a big commercial success, and was made into a notable film; like several others, it dealt with prohibition-era gangsterism. Of his later works, *The Asphalt Jungle* (1949), also filmed, must be reckoned one of the most powerful evocations of the criminal life of a big city. K. R. R.

Burns, John Horne (1916–53), American novelist, made his name with *The Gallery* (1947), a loosely connected series of episodes set in Naples at the time of the American occupation, vividly portraying a variety of soldiers and civilians. His subsequent books, *Lucifer with a Bible* (1949) and *A Cry of Children* (1952), were less successful. K. R. R.

Burroughs, Edgar Rice (1875–1950), American writer of adventure stories, was the creator of the jungle-hero Tarzan. *Tarzan of the Apes* (1914) was the first of over thirty titles, some of which have been translated into over fifty languages. He has also written crude science fiction. K. R. R.

Burroughs, William (1914–), American writer, sometimes loosely identified with the beat movement, whose books have aroused either a sense of outrage for their detailed and often nauseating description of sexual and more often homosexual activity and of drug addiction, or unstinted praise for creating a new and radically different form of expression and so indicating where to go next after the Joycean 'stream of consciousness'.

Much has been made of Burroughs's increasingly arbitrary 'construction' of his books. Sometimes it is his own writing that he reorganises, slicing pages and shuffling them so that events appear in random order; sometimes it is the work of other writers, or headlines, captions, paragraphs from newspapers and magazines, that he 'cuts' or 'folds' in. It has been suggested that this serves two purposes—to detach the reader from a steady forward plot of narrative, and to surround him instead with words, detached and floating, and with fragments of incidents that blur the boundaries of past and present, memory and actuality, fact and dream. This could be said to be both a poetic aim and a poetic form—but it is the subject matter itself that brings the reader up short. This is indeed designed to shock him out of his supposed familiar trance of a private masturbatory reaction to the printed innuendo that has been the stock-in-trade of romantic and pornographic writer alike, by actually spreading on the printed page his inner fantasy.

Burroughs's books *The Naked Lunch* (1959) and *Nova Express* (1966) concern travellers—through cities, countries, space—who report on the life they find in a combination of factual description, supported by occasional scholarly footnotes, and wildly exotic, forbidden and perverted day-dreams. All is escape: characters frequently float, thus defying the restraints of gravity; experience unflagging sexual desire, achieve countless orgasms, thus triumphing over the usual effects of satiety and fatigue; take drugs and find release from the sober bounds of the imagination; hang themselves and revive, and so cheat death.

It could be that in thus turning the tables on our concept of literature, Burroughs is saying that his is the more honest and accurate version of what the writer and reader want with each other. It could also be taken as it is presented—as the singularly unvarnished record of a man's hallucinations under drugs. For it is most interesting to read Burroughs's non-fiction pronouncements—articles in magazines where he writes with great lucidity and insight about drugs, their effects and cures (*Evergreen*, no. 34; 1964) and about his theories of writing (seen put into practice in *The Yage Letters*; 1963, written 1953), or in which he talks about his work (*Paris Review*, no. 35).

Other titles include his early and comparatively straightforward *Junkie* (1953, published under the pen-name of 'William Lee'); *Dead Fingers Talk* (1963); and *The Soft Machine* (1964). S. R.

Butler, Guy (1918–), South African playwright, poet, anthologist and critic. His plays *The Dam* (1953) and *The Dove Returns* (1956) chiefly explore the relationships between the English- and Afrikaans-speaking communities in South Africa. *Stranger to Europe* (1960) contains strong, controlled, thematically rich and varied poetry. C. P.

Butor, Michel (1926–), French novelist. Michel Butor took a degree in philosophy and taught widely in France and abroad (U.S.A., Greece, Egypt, England) from 1950 to 1957. He published his first novel, *Le Passage de Milan* [*Journey from Milan*], in 1954, and has since published both novels and critical and theoretical works. He has said that the novel, being a 'story' whose truth cannot be checked against outside facts, is therefore a literary form in which outside reality can be studied most closely. So the form of the novel is of prime importance, and should allow the reader to free himself of his own reality in order to attain that of the story. It is the task of the novelist to provoke his readers to this new assessment of reality; otherwise he will merely contribute to the malaise of the reader of today who cannot integrate or assimilate the world around him. Furthermore, the creation of new forms for the novel at all levels, in language, style, technique, composition, structure, leads to a new view of the novel and its social function.

Although Butor is generally considered to form part of the '*nouveau roman*' group, and although he shares with them both a distrust of psychological novels of analysis, and that awareness of the world of objects which has led to the labelling of the group as 'the school of description', he is nonetheless much less ready to dismiss (as does Robbe-Grillet in *La Jalousie* for example) the category of time. In *L'Emploi du temps* [*Passing Time*] (1956) the hero tries to recall, seven months after they occurred, events during his stay in a small Welsh mining town. *La Modification* [*Second Thoughts*] (1957) stresses again the time element: a man boards a train for Rome, determined to return to Paris with his mistress and to break with his wife; during the journey his thoughts (he speaks to himself as '*vous*' throughout) show a gradual transformation in a mixture of description, reminiscence and reflexion until he arrives in Rome, having taken the decision to allow things to continue as before. *Degrés* ['Degrees'] (1960) is the story, by a teacher of history and geography, of a session with a class, including the relation of the lesson, the life of the teacher, of his nephew, of some of his colleagues, of some of his pupils. The attempt at total description of this reality in terms of a time framework is found again in *Mobile* (1962), 'a study for a representation of the United States'; and *Réseau aérien* ['Air network'] (1962) examines the effect of air travel on our awareness of time and space. *6,810,000 litres d'eau par seconde* ['6,810,000 litres of water per second'] (1965) describes Niagara. D. E. A.

Buzzati, Dino (Dino Buzzati Traverso; 1906–), Italian novelist and short-story writer. He stands out in the Italian literary world for the frequent use of a type of surrealism often compared with that of Kafka. His best-known novel is *Il deserto dei Tartari* [*The Tartar Steppe*] (1940), fraught with obvious symbolism: Giovanni Drogo, a young officer, is seconded to a fortress standing on the border of a vast desert land. The fortress garrison live in the constant expectation of an enemy attack, but only when Drogo reaches old age and the end of his career do the first signs of an impending onslaught by enemy troops emerge. Buzzati, whose writing is politically uncommitted, relies on the ability to represent the irrational and often contradictory elements in human existence by evoking an uncanny, sometimes hallucinatory atmosphere, coupled with frequent symbolism and yet the use of plain everyday language. On the other hand *Un amore* [*A Love Affair*] (1963) combines a more realistic background with inroads into the world of psychology in depicting the moral decline of a middle-aged man through his liaison with a prostitute.

Buzzati is also the author of several collections of surrealistic short stories of which there are selections in English under the headings *The Scala Scare* (1961) and *Catastrophe* (1966). There are also English translations of his novel *Il grande ritratto* [*Larger than Life*] (1960), on the 'rebellion' of an electronic brain equipped with human intelligence and feelings, and of his book for children *La famosa invasione degli orsi in Sicilia* [*The Bears' Famous Invasion of Sicily*] (1946). D. B.

Byrne, Donn (Brian Oswald Donn-Byrne; 1889–1928), Irish-American novelist and short-story writer, wrote the best-selling romantic novel *Messer Marco Polo* (1921). His other books include *Blind Raftery* (1924), the story of a nineteenth-century Gaelic poet. K. R. R.

C

Cabell, James Branch (1879–1958), American novelist, best remembered as the author of the once notorious *Jurgen* (1921). Cabell stands apart from the mainstream of contemporary American fiction, preferring to express his perception of the human predicament in pure fantasy rather than in anything which could be construed as realistic on any plane whatsoever. Yet it would be a mistake to dismiss his writing as being of little or no significance; for even at the times when he does appear to be indulging in fantasy for fantasy's sake, he is often attacking the philistinism and prudery of his own society.

Jurgen is in many ways typical of his writings, celebrating as it does the richness of the human imagination, and asserting the significance of man's fantasies. Jurgen the middle-aged hen-pecked pawnbroker—in whom there still lives something of Jurgen the young poet, and lover of the beautiful Dorothy—journeys through the land of man's imagination and of his own desires: he meets the young Dorothy again and sees history repeat itself; he becomes the consort of a fertility goddess, is sated and eventually bored; he also encounters Queen Guinevere and Helen of Troy, becomes the lover of a hamadryad and a vampire, and visits both Hell and Heaven. When he returns from his journey it is to become once more, by choice, a middle-aged hen-pecked pawnbroker. K. R. R.

Cain, James (1892–), American novelist, scored a success with his first novel, the violent and fast-moving crime-melodrama *The Postman Always Rings Twice* (1934), which established him as a member of the 'hard-boiled' school of fiction. Later titles include *This Man and This Woman* (1951) and *Mignon* (1955). K. R. R.

Caine, [Thomas Henry] Hall (1853–1931), English writer. The author of immensely popular, romantic and picturesque novels, mostly set in the Isle of Man, his success began with *The Deemster* (1887) and continued with *The Bondman* (1890) and *The Scapegoat* (1891). *The Eternal City* (1901) sold over a million copies and *The Christian* (1897) almost as many. *The Manxman* (1894) showed his real knowledge of the Manx people. Many of his stories were dramatised and filmed. Other titles include *The Prodigal Son* (1904). G. S.

Caldwell, Erskine (1903–), American novelist of the Deep South, is the outstanding chronicler of its 'poor white' community, whom he portrays in a near-animal state of ignorance and degradation, with sex as one of the few recreations open to them. *Tobacco Road* (1932) and *God's Little Acre* (1933), his best-known works, contain much that from an ordinary human viewpoint would be tragic, but so sub-human are most of his characters that they remain essentially comic. They are not truly outcasts in the sense that Nelson Algren's characters are, but they are generally equally lacking in the hope for anything better.

Caldwell's later works, generally less successful, include *Claudelle Inglish* (1959), and several volumes of short stories. K. R. R.

Calisher, Hortense (1911–), American novelist and short-story writer of great sophistication and occasional obscurity. Among her most interesting works is the long short-story 'The Scream' first published in the *New Yorker* in which a lonely and neurotic woman hears a scream in the anonymity of her apartment. *Journal from Ellipsia* (1966), an excursion into a type of science fiction, introduces a visitor from another planet on which exists the order and perfection that we strive for, who arrives on earth to marvel at our complex, painful and individual world. S. R.

Callaghan, Morley (1903–), Canadian novelist and short-story writer who was born and has lived in Toronto except for a brief period during the 1920s spent in Paris, where he associated with Hemingway and Fitzgerald. This experience is movingly described in his book *That Summer in Paris* (1963). Callaghan first met Hemingway when both were young newspapermen in Toronto and some similarities in the milieu described in his early work to that of Hemingway's led critics to look on Callaghan as a follower of the American author's; but he has always had an intensely personal style and a deep commitment to moral questions which is entirely his own. Callaghan's first fame came from his short stories, more than 100 of which were published, many in the *New Yorker*, in the 1920s and 1930s. They have been collected in *A Native Argosy* (1929), *Now That April's Here* (1936), and *Morley Callaghan's Stories* (1959). Some critics argue that these stories, in which deep revelations of character turn on seemingly unimportant incidents, are his finest work, but Callaghan virtually ceased writing short fiction in the 1940s as he became increasingly involved with complex themes which demanded longer treatment.

His first novel, *Strange Fugitive* (1928), was followed by *It's Never Over* (1930) and *A Broken Journey* (1932), but it was with the appearance of *Such Is My Beloved* (1934) that he became a novelist of major importance. This tale of a Roman Catholic priest's attempt to redeem two prostitutes, which ends in failure and his disgrace, revolves around Callaghan's two central concerns: the ambiguity of human motives and the nature of love. Callaghan leaves it to the reader to decide whether the priest's interest in the prostitutes is prompted by Christian love or carnal lust. The same ambiguity surrounds the heroine's love for the Negroes of Montreal in *The Loved and the Lost* (1951), and becomes a question of selflessness or selfishness in the public relations man who is the hero of *The Many Coloured Coat* (1960). In *A Passion in Rome* (1961) the story is a simpler one of a love affair between two expatriates in Rome, but it also raises the wider and deeper philosophical and moral questions which permeate all his work.

The complexity with which Callaghan invests outwardly simple relationships, his deliberately understated, sometimes flat style and his use of unromantic Canadian cities as the background for personal crises of almost unbearable intensity have alienated many critics. Others, like the American critic Edmund Wilson who compared him to Dostoevsky, see him as a writer of the first rank dealing in his unique way with problems which may be unfashionable in the middle of the twentieth century but which are central to the human condition. K. W.

Calvino, Italo (1923–), Italian novelist and short-story writer. An arts graduate of Turin University, he took part in the resistance movement and now belongs to the Italian left-wing intelligentsia. He has published several collections of stories, in which the themes of the Italian resistance movement, realistically treated, alternate with a typically Calvino-esque tendency to surrealism. Calvino's happy qualities as a blender of reality and fantasy have found their most successful outlet in the 'fairy-tale' trilogy of novels *I nostri antenati* ['Our forefathers'] comprising *Il visconte dimezzato* [*The Cloven Viscount*] (1952), *Il barone rampante* [*Baron in the Trees*] (1957) and *Il cavaliere inesistente* [*The Non-existent Knight*] (1959). *Il visconte dimezzato*, fundamentally a protest against the rigidity of social conventions, relates the adventures of a viscount, Medardo, who is dissected by a cannon ball into two halves, one good and the other bad, which become re-united in the end: an obvious symbol of the dichotomy of modern man. In *Il barone rampante* Baron Cosimo as a boy climbs a tree in a fit of rage against his parents, gradually decides not to come down again and eventually settles down to his new existence which includes a good deal of travelling on tree tops. The last novel of the trilogy is about Charlemagne's paladin Agilulfo, who does not in fact exist but is simply a voice and a strong-willed mind within a suit of armour. His adventures and battles are the background for an attempt to recapture the nobility of the past ages.

Calvino's stories have been collected in English translation with the titles of *The Path to the Nest of Spiders* and *Adam, One Afternoon and Other Stories*. Although Calvino is an advocate of social reforms, his works do not indulge in analyses of environment or social conditions but reflect a genuine interest in nature and the fundamentals of humanity.

D. B.

Cameron, Norman (1905–53), English poet, is known as a distinguished translator for his *A Season in Hell* (1949) from Rimbaud, his *Villon: Poems translated in the original forms* (1952) and his *Candide* (1947), although he is also remembered for his own *Collected Poems* (1957). A natural linguist, possessed of great verbal skill, his work is distinguished by its simplicity, wit, precise language and sure rhythm. P. E.

Campbell, Roy (Ignatius Roy Dunnachie Campbell; 1901–57), South African poet. Campbell's poetry retains the colour and aggression of his own life. In his teens he fought in World War I. He was a bronco-buster and a professional bullfighter in the twenties and thirties and fought for Franco in the Spanish civil war. He was permanently incapacitated while fighting as a volunteer in the British army in the second world war and retired to live in Portugal where he was killed in a car crash in 1957.

Campbell's political fascism and his rough upbringing in South Africa are present in his poetry, barely subdued by technical virtuosity:

True sons of Africa are we,
Though bastardized with culture;
Indigenous, and wild, and free
As wolf, as pioneer and vulture . . .

A large number of books of verse were issued during Campbell's lifetime: his *Collected Poems* were published in 1949 and 1957. *Light on a Dark Horse* (1952) is an autobiography. D. L. P.

Camus, Albert (1913–60), French novelist, dramatist and philosophical essayist. Born in Algeria, Camus took a degree in philosophy before becoming a journalist in Algiers and Paris. During the war in Paris he was editor of *Combat*, a resistance newspaper; after the war his political activity remained strong. A number of articles and statements surrounded his break with Sartre in 1953. In 1957 he gained the Nobel prize, but died in 1960 after a car accident.

His early works *L'Envers et l'endroit* [*The Right Side and the Wrong Side*] (1937) and *Noces* [*The Wedding*] (1938), poetical essays, were followed in 1942 by *L'Etranger* [*The Outsider*] in which Meursault, the 'outsider' hero, conscious of the absurdity of our daily life and the meaninglessness of existence, lives a life of indifference in which all events, even the death of his mother or his own act in murdering an Arab, leave him unmoved. The scene of his trial for this murder allows Camus to show to what extent society (bourgeois society) reflects in its attitudes the basic absurdity of life; Meursault is condemned not so much because he has killed, as because he has been honest enough to show that the events of everyday life are meaningless, that a show of emotion is pointless. The basic honesty of Meursault, allied to the philosophy of the absurd as expressed in *L'Etranger* and in *Le Mythe de Sisyphe* [*The Myth of Sisyphus*] (1943), was to provide the ideal of post-war Paris and of the existentialist generation of the forties and fifties. In the latter, a collection of essays, Camus attempts to define his answer to the problem of the absurdity of life, to the feeling caused by the confrontation of the disorganised chaos of existence and man's need for order and comprehension. It is an answer which denies the possibility of a 'leap' towards God or towards hope; an answer which offers the possibility only of a life of 'experience', a life whose ideal is a succession of moments before an always conscious mind.

Camus had also been interested at Algiers in drama and his plays include *Le Malentendu* [*Cross Purpose*] (1944), *Caligula* [*Caligula*] (1944), *L'Etat de siège* [*Siege*] (1948), and *Les Justes* [*The Just*] (1950); he also produced a stage adaptation of Dostoevsky's *The Possessed.* While reflecting his view of the horror of our human fate, these present a dramatic version of Camus's answer. This answer, the revolt of the intellectual against the constraint of circumstances, is again put forward in *L'Homme révolté* [*The Rebel*] (1951) and in novel form in *La Peste* [*The Plague*] (1947). This latter novel is the story of an outbreak of plague at Oran, in Algeria. The narrator, the doctor Rieux, relates the stages of the epidemic, the attitudes of the town's inhabitants, the effects on them of their isolation when the town is closed, and their different answers to the problem of living side-by-side with violent death. Father Paneloux, for example, preaches two sermons, the first 'explaining' the plague as God's answer to man's evil, and thus the occasion for submission and acceptance; the second, after a harrowing experience at the bedside of a dying child, presenting faith as necessarily blind, as a belief which must accept without exception. The journalist Rambert, who is caught by the closure of the town, tries all possible methods to escape to rejoin his love, but decides finally to remain to help. The fundamental problem posed by *La Peste* is to know how to reply to evil, both external and internal; how to be a saint without God. The novel can be read on several levels as a story, as a picture of the effect of Nazi occupation on France or as an allegory of human fate; the answer proposed is perhaps that man must fight, must never accept. *La Chute* [*The Fall*] (1956), a monologue of seeming defeat, is a complete contrast to the tenseness of *La Peste*.

Camus also published a series of short stories *L'Exil et le royaume* [*The Exile and the Kingdom*] (1957) and many of his articles for *Combat* were assembled in several volumes called *Actuelles* (1950–58). D. E. A.

Canetti, Elias (1905–), German-language writer. Born in Bulgaria of Ladino-speaking, Spanish-Jewish parents and educated in England, Switzerland, Austria and Germany, Canetti came to England in 1938. His works include plays, a study in crowd psychology *Masse und Macht* [*Crowds and Power*] (1960), and one novel *Die Blendung* [*Auto-da-fé*] (1935). Kien, an eminent sinologist, lives only for his work and his library. His obsessive world is shattered when his housekeeper tricks him into marriage, then, abetted by the concierge, drives him out of the house into the nightmare underworld of the sinister expressionist city, where he is exploited by a hunchbacked chess-playing criminal dwarf. Apparently mad, and not responding to the attempts of his psychiatrist brother, another eccentric, to cure him, Kien regains the flat, sets fire to his books and dies in the blaze, laughing 'louder than he had ever laughed in all his life'. Opinion of this novel in Britain has been very divided, despite the book's continental fame, both on its first appearance in English in 1946 and on its reissue in 1962. Some critics see it as gratuitously unpleasant, a gothic horror tale with metaphysical embellishment; others as a profound, misanthropic exploration of the human condition in the central European tradition of Broch, Kafka, Hašek or Musil.

M. D. E.

Cantwell, Robert Emmett (1908–), American proletarian novelist. *Laugh and Lie Down* (1931) and *The Land of The Plenty* (1934) are concerned with the rough life and the industrial strife in a timber mill town; the latter's second part, entitled 'The Educating of a Worker', being a memorable account of a sensitive young man's initiation into the grim experiences of a strike. Cantwell has also been involved as editor for a number of magazines including the *New Republic*. D. L. P.

Čapek, Karel (1890–1938), Czech novelist, dramatist and essayist, was the son of a country doctor, studied philosophy in Prague, Berlin and Paris and later worked as a journalist. A liberal and humanist, he was the defender of the natural order of things and of the middle-class society of the common man which he depicted with love and gentle humour. Most of his plays and novels are mild protests against both technology and the spiritual concepts menacing his ideal humanity; in his trilogy—*Hordubal* (1933), *Meteor* (1934), *An Ordinary Life* (1934)—he is occupied with the problems of the plurality of man's personality. His witty essays are reminiscent of a world which has since disappeared.

His other novels include *The Absolute at Large* (1922), *Krakatit—An Atomic Phantasy* (1924), *War with the Newts* (1936), *The First Rescue Party* (1937) and *The Cheat* (1939); he has also published several volumes of short stories, including such titles as *Tales from Two Pockets* (1929) and *Apocryphal Stories* (1932). His plays include the robot-play *RUR* (1920), *The Life of the Insects* (with his brother Josef Čapek; 1921) otherwise known as *The Insect Play*, and *The Macropoulos Secret* (1922). Among his most popular volumes of essays are his *Letters from England* (1924) and similar volumes from Spain, Italy and Holland. K. B.

Capote, Truman (1925–), American novelist and short-story writer, became widely known abroad only when his long short-story *Breakfast at Tiffany's* was filmed. However, he had earlier acquired an enthusiastic following in New York and Paris with his first novel *Other Voices, Other Rooms* (1948), written while 'retired' on a farm in his native Louisiana. *Other Voices, Other Rooms* is set in one of the weirder backwaters of the Deep South with a population of exotic individuals: the centenarian Negro Jesus Fever and his granddaughter Missouri ('Zoo'), who has survived having her throat cut by her husband Keg and lives in fear of his return; the adolescent hellcat Idabel and her twin Florabel; the aged hermit Little Sunshine who concocts charms in the derelict Cloud Hotel in the heart of the forest, amidst the ghosts of the fashionable guests who peopled it in his boyhood; and the bizarre household at Skully's Landing—Amy, her charming and sexually ambivalent cousin Randolph, and her husband Ed, who has been paralysed and practically speechless since being accidentally shot by Randolph. It is in this dream-like world that Ed's thirteen-year-old son Joel (by his first marriage), who has been decoyed there by Randolph, experiences his adolescence. It proves every bit as fantastic as those 'other rooms' of Joel's imagination, in which he has previously taken refuge from the drabness of his aunt's home in New Orleans: but having spent his boyhood escaping into fantasy, he now finds himself a prisoner of it, unable to return to normality. For much of the book, a mystery hangs over the person of Joel's father whom he is not allowed to meet: when he knows the truth and is anxious to escape, he is prevented by the wily Randolph, into whose corrupting power he finally falls.

Breakfast at Tiffany's (1958) is set in New York. Holly Golightly, its heroine, has all the superficial characteristics of the itinerant playgirl of the gossip columns, and she is escorted by middle-aged men who give her 'fifty dollars for the powder room'. But beneath the veneer of blasé sophistication, there is an innocent, naive and frightened child, who is taken for a ride by a wealthy South American while insisting that he is intending to marry her; who goes berserk at the death of a brother; and who becomes unwittingly involved in a narcotics racket. It transpires that she is in flight from the experience of being an orphan and child-wife; as her card says, she is constantly 'travelling', never alone but always lonely.

Other writings by Truman Capote include the controversial 'non-fiction' novel *In Cold Blood* (1966), an account of the quadruple murder of an innocent Kansas farming family by two escaped convicts and of their subsequent conviction and execution; and a number of short stories.

K. R. R.

Carossa, Hans (1878–1956), Bavarian writer and physician. His works include verse, short stories and autobiography. Best known are *Eine Kindheit* [*A Childhood*] (1922), *Rumänisches Tagebuch* [*Rumanian Diary*] (1924) and *Der Arzt Gion* [*Doctor Gion*] (1933). R. C. W.

Carpentier, Alejo (1904–), Cuban novelist, poet and short-story writer. A cosmopolitan polymath of Russian-French descent, sometime musicologist, literary theorist and social historian of repute, variously active in films, advertising, theatre and politics, his novels have won him international acclaim. An early familiarity with and respect for Afro-Cuban and Amerindian music, myth, rite and custom soon suggested a broader theme, the cultural potential of Latin America in the problematical future of Western civilisation; only hinted at in an elegant re-creation of the Haitian past, *El reino de este mundo* [*The Kingdom of this World*] (1949), its most successful elaboration is *Los pasos perdidos* [*The Lost Steps*] (1953). The narrator, during a highly symbolical journey up the Orinoco, an allegorical return to the parting of the waters, 'uncovers his face and talks and vomits what he has swallowed and lays down his load', namely, the sterile nonsense of a modish, commercial aesthetic, and abandons his sophisticated mistress in favour of Rosario, in whom 'had fused . . . the great races of the world, the most widely separated, the most divergent, those which for centuries had ignored the fact that they inhabited the same planet'. Thus the lost steps are retraced and a fresh start made. Carpentier continued his 'Adam's task of naming things' in *El siglo de las luces* [*Explosion in a Cathedral*] (1962). Ostensibly an episode in the career of Victor Hugues, who conquered Guadeloupe for the French Revolutionaries and participated in the 'Brigands' War', it is actually an exhaustive, chromatic, Caribbean encyclopaedia, an intrepid, superbly executed exercise in tropical baroque, a vision of a new civilisation in a new context. M. D. E.

Carr, John Dickson (1906–), American writer of thrillers, son of a lawyer, after a brief spell studying in Paris embarked on a life of wandering and writing. He has written about fifty novels, most of them stories of mystery and suspense. Many of them feature his well-known detective Dr Fell, but some of his most successful thrillers are historical period pieces with macabre and supernatural settings, for example *Devil in Velvet* (1951). His other titles include *Most Secret* (1964), *The House at Satan's Elbow* (1965) and thrillers under the pseudonym Carter Dickson.
K. M. H.

Carson, Rachael (1907–64), American writer on scientific topics, worked for the U.S. Bureau of Fisheries as a marine biologist. Her first book *Under the Sea Wind* appeared in 1941, but it was *The Sea Around Us* (1951) which brought her real fame. She is that rare phenomenon, a writer who combines scientific ability and observation with a command of the English language, and it is probably her hauntingly beautiful style rather than the unlikely appeal of a biological study of the ocean that made *The Sea Around Us* into a best-seller.

She followed up her success with another scientific work *The Silent Spring* (1963), a book with powerful emotional appeal, being an angry tract against the use of chemicals in the soil and the consequent indiscriminate destruction of wild life. K. M. H.

Cartland, Barbara (1904–), English romantic novelist. Her books include conventional love stories, for example *Armour Against Love* (1945) and *Desire of the Heart* (1954); historical romances such as *Outrageous Queen* (1956), the story of Christina of Sweden; and two volumes of autobiography *Isthmus Years, 1919–1939* (1943) and *Years of Opportunity, 1939–1945* (1948). Amongst the hundred or more books she has written are a number of swashbuckling romances under her married name Barbara McCorquodale, and a volume recounting the history of woman's struggle for equality, entitled *Woman the Enigma* (1965). K. M. H.

Cary, [Arthur] Joyce (1888–1957), English novelist. Though he has never quite reached the ranks of the great English authors of this century, his books display a gift for story-telling and an ability to create a great diversity of characters; and he writes with a combination of dedicated craftsmanship, imaginative invention and seriousness of intent.

Joyce Cary was raised and educated in England, though he spent a considerable part of his childhood with relations in Ireland (in the semi-autobiographical *A House of Children*, 1941, he is both Evelyn Corner and the elder brother Harry). He studied art in Edinburgh and Paris, read law at Oxford and, in search of action, fought in the Balkan war of 1912–13 (recorded in *Memoirs of the Bobotes*; published posthumously, 1964). Finally he went to Africa, where he remained for six years, for part of the time a member of the colonial administration in Nigeria, part of the time as a soldier. He left the political service in 1920 owing to ill health, settled in Oxford and set himself to serve an apprenticeship to the craft of writing. After careers as varied, as active and as formative as those he had followed, he felt that a period of study, reading and reflection, and above all reassessment of values, was vital. For twelve years he published nothing but the occasional short story, though he was in fact writing a great deal and developing the method of composition that he was to use for the rest of his life. He would fill notebooks with observations, snatches of dialogue, whole chapters, beginnings and ends of books from which he would later select and combine until the material was shaped into a novel. This method, whatever its virtues, does result in occasional inconsistencies and slightly jerky progress of plot, and, more serious than these minor flaws, a predetermination of the outcome of the story that can rob his characters of spontaneous and unpredictable growth.

The first series of novels published, set in the Africa that had concerned him for a significant section of his life, reveals both his versatility and his liberalism. In characterisation, he shows himself equally able to enter the mind of native subject and of white administrator. *Aissa Saved* (1932) depicts the confusion caused by the grafting of Christianity on to the primitive tribal beliefs already held by the native girl Aissa—though stressing man's deep-seated need for a faith of some kind. In *An American Visitor* (1933) he attempts to disentangle the motives underlying the liberalism of the visitor Marie Hasluck and of the whites with whom she comes in contact. The next theme he approaches, in *The African Witch* (1936), is the fascination of the power exerted by rhetoric (later to be explored further in the political career of Chester Nimmo in his second trilogy), embodying it here in one of his most vivid characters, Elizabeth Aladai, the witch of the title.

Best of all these African novels is the last, *Mister Johnson* (1939), which centres on a naïve, boundlessly enthusiastic and open-hearted young native clerk, who feels nothing but admiration for all things British. This book, which deals with the double-edged benefits of progress, contains a tragic picture of an impossible friendship between Johnson and the magistrate roadbuilder, Rudbeck, that is as moving as anything else Cary wrote. By a bitter irony Johnson's vitality and child-like optimism are silenced by the letter of British justice, a death Johnson finds tolerable only when he persuades the man he most admires, Rudbeck, to administer it.

Charley is My Darling (1940), dealing with the war-time evacuation of London children to the country, is closely akin in mood to *Mister Johnson*, despite the different settings. The young city boy's energy, his half-understood sexual desires, his craving for recognition and need to make his mark in the world, lead him inexorably into conflict with authority and end in his being labelled with the adult term for the individual and rebellious child—juvenile delinquent.

However, Cary's major achievements are in the genre of his own ambitious form of trilogy, a triptych of widely differing characters whose lives overlap, and through whose vivid and distinctive speech a tri-personal picture is evoked not only of the common events and relationships in which they have themselves been involved but of a whole period of social history. The first novel of the first trilogy, *Herself Surprised* (1941), concerns Sara Munday, formerly cook-housekeeper-mistress and almost wife to Thomas Wilcher, the old, pursed-up lawyer of *To Be a Pilgrim* (1942), and also one-time mistress and model to the voluble eccentric artist Gulley Jimson of *The Horse's Mouth* (1944). Sara is writing her memoirs for the Sunday papers while in prison for robbing her former employer, Wilcher, so that her book has the quality of an apologia; Wilcher is writing his journal and at seventy-one is trying to make sense of his life; while Jimson is dictating his rambling and explosive thoughts on his deathbed, using words because for the first time in his life he is unable to communicate through paint. Sara is the eternal woman, the life force in its physical, domesticating manifestation; she acts impulsively on a combination of maternal and sexual instincts, ever generous and loving towards her men, but afterwards is perplexed by her remembrance of less flexible moral codes. Wilcher is conservative, slow to change but endowed with a sense of the past, of history and of religious faith that enables him to see life as a pilgrimage. Gulley Jimson is the personification of the life force in its creative, untamable guise; he operates on exuberance and visionary insight and a personal philosophy which he finds elsewhere only in the work of Blake. It is a measure of Cary's skill that he has presented us with characters the world would rate of no account, a lax and thieving housekeeper, an old crabby man given to indecent exposure, and an impossibly anti-social and eccentric artist—and thus illumined them from within.

The social history that emerges from such a chronicle as this first trilogy is described even more vividly in *A Fearful Joy* (1949), another excursion into the relationship of fundamental woman and vital bounder, a relationship which is again a source of life and of the joy of the title. But more remarkable still is the second trilogy, for its insight into the fascination political power can exert and for its description of a whole stratum and era of English non-conformity and radical politics. In *A Prisoner of Grace* (1952) the career of Chester Nimmo, his initial idealism, growing ruthlessness and what seems more and more to be his expediency is described in the first person by his ex-wife Nina who allowed him to marry her only when she was threatened by the scandal of an illegitimate pregnancy (by her cousin Jim Latter), and who has thereafter felt 'a prisoner of grace'. *Except the Lord* (1953) goes back not forward in time and has Chester himself speaking, describing his evangelical non-conformist childhood and his involvement in politics as part of this faith. However, the book ends before he meets Nina and it is for the reader to reconcile the two rather puzzlingly inconsistent portraits of the great man. The third volume *Not Honour More* (1955) is the soldier Jim Latter's story, written in prison while awaiting trial for the murder of his wife Nina. The third section of the lives of the three is now revealed, Nina's marriage to Jim and the continual intrusions upon it by Chester. In this furious indictment of Chester, his politics, his morals, his equivocation, Jim reveals his own intransigence and his inability to understand Nina. The impossibility of reaching a political decision based on the alternatives offered by Jim and Chester is symbolised by Nina's failure ever to choose one of them exclusively as a man: thus indicating what to Cary is the essential dilemma of the nature of freedom—conflict and compromise.

Cary's last novel, not quite finished but published posthumously, was *The Captive and the Free* (1959), which takes religion rather than politics as a symbol of man's creativity and tells of the conflict between a faith-healer and an Anglican curate and of the manipulation of the battle by a journalist of the popular press. All three men are mouthpieces for 'the truth', and yet the differences between the versions lead to violence, libel actions, and imprisonment for the Anglican.

Cary's seriousness and dedication to writing has resulted in a body of fiction that is always interesting and often profound. In its warm sympathy for the ugly and unfortunate, it transcends the occasional lapse of the dialogue into monotony and woodenness. Each book is a *tour-de-force* of impersonation or identification, and in the two trilogies he has suppressed his own authority as the author to the extent that when one puts down the last book there is no real sense of resolution, of ends neatly tied, of a verdict given. The multi-faceted vision remains as kaleidoscopic as it is in real life. That Cary himself realised and even intended this is clear from his statement in a letter: 'My work does not reveal any subjective centre. It deals as far as I can manage it with the whole landscape of existence; and though that landscape is seen from one point of view, the especial nature of the point of view does not appear in the books.' S. R.

Casey, Gavin S. (1907–   ), Australian short-story writer and novelist, chooses most often to depict the rather seamy side of Australian life, sometimes on the goldfields, sometimes in the suburbs, which he does with considerable humour and sympathy. His works include *Downhill is Easier* (1945), about a man's gradual descent into criminal life; followed by *The Wits are Out* (1947), *City of Men* (1950) and *Amid the Plenty* (1962).

S. R.

Casona, Alejandro (Alejandro Rodríguez Álvarez; 1903–65), Spanish playwright. An Asturian, the son of school teachers and himself an inspector of schools until the civil war, Casona left Spain in 1937 for Latin America where he wrote nearly all his best-known plays. Returning to Spain in 1962 he achieved considerable theatrical success, often with works first produced twenty years previously. Casona's theatre is characterised by two features: first, the *dénouement* gives rise to ethical conclusions (the pedagogue being inseparable from the playwright); secondly, the plot-structure consistently employs a blend of illusion and reality. Thus in *La sirena varada* ['The stranded mermaid'] (1934) Ricardo, who hates all that is rational and prosaic, Daniel the blindfolded painter and María the deranged 'mermaid' are all forced to abandon their fantasies and face up to reality. Illusion is only legitimate if based upon life-enhancing love, as in Dr Ariel's sanatorium in *Prohibido suicidarse en primavera* ['No suicides in spring'] (1937). In *Los árboles mueren de pie* ['Trees die upright'] (1949), Mauricio's fantasies are condemned since his intentions are suspect. The Devil effects the illusion in *La barca sin pescador* ['The boat with no fisherman'] (1945); while in *La dama del alba* [*The Lady of the Dawn*] (1944) Death, personified in the Pilgrim, persuades Angélica, presumed dead by the Mother, to commit suicide and thus redeem her wretched existence. Such a suicide is beautiful and 'beauty is the other form of truth'. Not surprisingly, such views have not gone unchallenged in Spain, and recently Casona's theatre has been the object of sharp attacks by the younger critics. D. H. G.

Cassola, Carlo (1917–   ), Italian novelist and short-story writer. Born in Rome, he took an arts degree, fought in the resistance movement in Tuscany and subsequently devoted himself to school teaching. His experiences in Tuscany, notably as a resistance fighter, have prompted the setting of almost all of his stories and novels. In *Fausto e Anna* [*Fausto and Anna*] (1952) Fausto, who comes from a middle-class background, and has become increasingly disaffected from his parents' world, causes Anna to break off their relationship through ideological incompatibility, then joins the communist resistance fighters, but is soon disillusioned by their ruthless methods. When he meets Anna again, he finds her married and has to give her up although his feelings for her are unchanged. *La ragazza di Bube* [*Bebo's Girl*] (1960), which won Cassola the Strega literary prize in the same year, is the dramatic account of the sacrifice of a young girl, Mara, who becomes involved with a former resistance hero, Bube. When Bube is sentenced to a long term of imprisonment, Mara's love is challenged and enhanced by this supreme test and she decides to wait for him. A different facet of Cassola's literary activity is to be found in *Un cuore arido* [*An Arid Heart*] (1961), which depicts with stark realism the tragedy of an unsophisticated young girl Anna, who, after two unfortunate love affairs, withdraws into the estrangement of a spiritually empty world.

The most outstanding features of Cassola's art are his fundamentally pessimistic attitude to the problems of human communication, combined however with faith in the worthiness of the devotion to a cause and, in particular, in the values of the resistance movement; and on a stylistic plane, a colourless yet effective prose re-echoing the Tuscan tradition of literary realism. Among his other works are several collections of short stories often reprinted under different titles. D. B.

Castillo, Michel del (1934–　　), French novelist of Spanish extraction who has very frequently used Spain as a backcloth to his novels. To date his works are *Tanguy* [*Tanguy*] (1956), *La Guitare* [*The Guitar*] (1957), *L'Afficheur* [*The Billsticker*] (1958), *La Mort de Tristan* [*The Death of Tristan*] (1959), *Le Manège espagnol* [*Through the Hoop*] (1960) and *Tara* ['Tara'] (1963). Of all these the most artistically successful is the exquisite and deeply moving *La Guitare*. Replete with the sombre and superstitious atmosphere of Spanish Galicia, it relates the tragic destiny of a hideous, hunchbacked dwarf. Shunned and stoned by the peasants, he learns to play the guitar expertly, hoping to achieve communication through the magic of its voice, but to the peasants this is no less than sorcery. *L'Afficheur* portrays the prelude to the Spanish civil war and the early fighting in the Madrid area; its bitter yet curiously detached narrative is notable for some compelling character studies. In *La Mort de Tristan* Castillo abandoned his customary milieu, choosing the setting of a Parisian Christmas to illustrate in lighter vein the birth and death of a man's self-indulgent romantic passion and its replacement by mature love. A somewhat tedious yet humorous analysis of the kaleidoscope of contemporary Spain is the essence of *Le Manège espagnol*; using the basic theme of a young student who claims to have had an extraordinary visitation from Christ, Castillo establishes a remarkable background of corruption, hypocrisy and moral indifference. R. C. W.

Cather, Willa (1876–1947), American novelist and short-story writer. She was brought up amongst immigrant farmers on the Nebraska prairies. In 1895 she graduated and entered journalism, travelling in Europe and studying writing. In 1903 she published a volume of poetry, followed by *Troll Garden*, short stories, in 1905 and a novel *Alexander's Bridge* in 1912. However, it was with *O Pioneers* in 1913 that she achieved recognition; this being followed by *The Song of the Lark* (1915) and *My Antonia* (1918). In much of these early writings her subjects were the lives of immigrant farmers set in the scenes of her childhood. A contemplative and symbolic writer, she rejected the disorder and feverishness of contemporary life and sought perfection of mind and spirit. The deserts of the American south-west, which she described in some unrivalled passages in *The Professor's House* (1925), were the setting for one of her most important novels *Death Comes for the Archbishop* (1927), a composite study of differing characters and backgrounds illumined by the faith and intelligence of the bishop and his soulmate Father Vaillant. Other works include *One of Ours* (1922), *Shadows on the Rock* (1931) and *The Old Beauty* (1948). G. S.

Cato, Nancy (1917–), Australian poet who in choosing the simplest subjects and using a variety of verse forms achieves a truth and clarity often missed by more ambitious and experimental poets. Her work is published in *The Darkened Window* (1950) and *The Dancing Bough* (1957). S. R.

Cau, Jean (1925–), French novelist and playwright. A journalist and former secretary of Sartre, he won the Prix Goncourt for 1961 with his sixth and first truly successful novel *La Pitié de Dieu* [*The Mercy of God*], which portrays four cell-mates all serving life sentences for the murder of women. A penetrating examination of the nature of objective truth, this novel presents the creeping insanity due to confinement which besets the four prisoners. Truth and fantasy merge; their accounts of their crimes differ vastly after constant retelling. One suffers from epilepsy, another imagines he is training for a boxing bout, another for a cycling championship. Eventually their identities become confused. A new inmate is totally ignored and commits suicide. Ultimately their individuality is lost in a collective consciousness which comes to recognise the epileptic as God. Cau's treatment of the problems of objectivity and truth was strikingly similar to that of his German contemporary Uwe Johnson. R. C. W.

Cavafy, Constantine (Konstantinos P. Kabaphes; 1863–1933), Greek poet. Born in Alexandria, the youngest son of a Greek merchant,

E. M. Forster's 'gentleman in a straw hat, standing absolutely motionless at a slight angle to the universe' spent seven childhood years in England. Three more in Istanbul, with his mother's Phanariot relatives, stimulated his idiosyncratic Byzantine and Hellenistic preoccupations, but for thirty years the most important figure in modern Greek literature worked obscurely in his native city, a clerk in the Ministry of Irrigation. Even today he is, perhaps, best known as the legendary 'poet of the city' in Lawrence Durrell's *Alexandria Quartet*. Cavafy's technical and linguistic virtuosity elude the English reader, yet the characteristic stance persists and of all great poets he probably loses least in translation. Professor Mavrogordato's *The Poems of C. P. Cavafy* (1951), the best English collection, is out of print. Rae Dalven's version, *Complete Poems* (1961), is the easiest to find. The standard text is *Poiemata* ['Poems'] (Athens, 1963).

Typically modern in his search for a viable poetic myth, Cavafy was particularly fortunate in his birthplace. Cut off from the Greek tradition, he found his roots in the racial heterogeneity of the Alexandrian past, the impotent splendour of a declining Panhellenism:

> We: the Alexandrians, the Antiochians,
> the Seleukeians, and the countless
> other Greeks of Egypt and of Syria,
> and those of Media, and of Persia, and all the rest.

His unromantic patriotism is pride in language,

> the Common Greek Tongue
> which we carried into Bactria, to the Indians,

and culture—

> a Hellene: mankind has no quality more precious

rather than country. Puritanical myopia has censured Cavafy as a derivative Levantine decadent. Certainly a pagan aesthete and homosexual erotic, he was also a scholar, a poet-historian whose ironical despair, wry observation and delicate sincerity, expressed in simple direct statements stripped of metaphor and simile, evolved analogues of universal application and enduring validity, appropriate to a cyclic interpretation of historical vicissitude. Cavafy was rigorously critical of his own work. That which survives is correspondingly slight, the greater part written after he turned forty; but it is this sense of balance, reticence and discipline that with rare exceptions preserves it from sentimental indulgence or superficial brilliance, without inhibiting its individuality. A tolerant humanity redeems the cynical appraisal of political ephemera, transient passion and opportunist morality. Courage, humour and resignation inform the urbanity, not least in the pervasive nostalgia, the laconic irreverence, the sense of exile, no less acute because temporal rather than spatial. M. D. E.

Cecil, Lord [Edward Christian] David (1902–), English biographer and critic. A literary scholar, he became Goldsmith's Professor of English Literature at Oxford in 1948. His first biography, a life of William Cowper entitled *The Stricken Deer* (1929), is probably his most penetrating study as he felt himself to have certain affinities with the poet. He has also written a political biography of Lord Melbourne (two vols, 1939 and 1954). His work is characterised by a delicate understanding, clear appraisal and a polished and elegant style. Other titles include *Sir Walter Scott* (1933); *Early Victorian Novelists* (1934); *Poets and Storytellers* (1949); *Walter Pater* (1956); *Max* (Beerbohm)*; a Biography* (1964). G. S.

Cecil, Henry (Henry Cecil Leon; 1902–), English judge and novelist, whose light-hearted stories revolve round the application of English law, making full use of its comic potential. Titles include *Brothers in Law* (1944), which has been filmed. H. C.

Cela, Camilo José (1916–), Spanish novelist—in his own view, the most important since the Masters of the '98 generation, Azorín, Baroja, Valle-Inclán and Unamuno. A Galician with Italian and English ancestors, Cela's early life—as student, soldier, clerk—shows the restlessness of the outsider. His first published work, *La familia de Pascual Duarte* [*The Family of Pascual Duarte*] (1942), an overnight success, brought new preoccupations and language to the Spanish novel. Duarte, a peasant awaiting execution for a series of murders, recounts his life: a portrait emerges of a simple man whose violence is a necessary reaction to the inhibitions of an unjust society. *Pabellón de reposo* [*Rest Home*] (1944) is a more delicate work, the letters and diaries of patients in a sanatorium. The harsher side to Cela's art triumphed, however, in *La colmena* [*The Hive*] (1951), his undoubted masterpiece: it describes three days in the life of working-class Madrid, with poverty and economic injustice engendering not violence but sexual licence. *La colmena* typifies Cela's distinctive style which, owing much to Baroja and Valle-Inclán, involves highly convoluted patterns of repetition and expressions of extreme crudity.

Of his subsequent novels only *La catira* ['The blond'] (1955) merits comparison with *La colmena*. Indeed since 1947 Cela's production has consisted largely of short stories, and travel books dealing with Spain. Of the latter the best is *Viaje a la Alcarria* [*Journey to the Alcarria*]

(1947), a vivid account abounding in rich characters and conveying a typically disabused vision. D. H. G.

Celan, Paul (1920–), Austrian poet born and reared in Czernowitz, Rumania, who was interned by the Nazis in a forced labour camp, 1942–43, and is now a French subject living in Paris. Much of his work has been concerned with translations from Rimbaud, Valéry, Blok, Yesenin and Mandelstam. His main reputation rests, however, on five verse-collections: *Sand aus den Urnen* ['Sand from the urns'] (1949), *Mohn und Gedächtnis* ['Poppy and memory'] (1952), *Von Schwelle zu Schwelle* ['From doorstep to doorstep'] (1955), *Sprachgitter* ['Speech-grill'] (1959) and *Die Niemandsrose* ['Rose without an owner'] (1963). Characterised by strains of symbolism and surrealism, his highly hermetic verse and the calm, formal purity of his diction have stamped him as a leading figure among the post-1945 generation of poets. English translations of individual poems have appeared in the *New Statesman*, in *Modern German Poetry 1910–60* (ed. M. Hamburger and C. Middleton, 1962) and in *German Writing Today* (Penguin, 1967). R. C. W.

Céline, Louis-Ferdinand (Louis-Ferdinand Destouches; 1894–1961), French novelist and physician. Childhood privations and factory work in his early teens helped formulate a misanthropic nihilism. His personal history was reflected in his novel *Voyage au bout de la nuit* [*Journey to the End of the Night*] (1932). A *succès de scandale*, it related the driftings of the cynical Ferdinand Bardamu, a deserter in World War I and later a physician in the U.S.A. and Africa, and his successive reactions to military, industrial and tropical hell. The physician's view of moral and physical squalor was reiterated in *Mort à crédit* [*Death on the Instalment Plan*] (1936) in which all existence was rejected as evil or insane. Many found repellent the desperate philosophy and coarse slang of Céline's various works. *Mea Culpa* [*Mea Culpa*] (1937) recorded his disillusionment with communism after a visit to Russia. Finding new scapegoats in the Jews and the 'degenerate' Third Republic he became a fascist collaborator and pamphleteer. Fleeing to Denmark after the fall of Vichy France, he returned only after his sentence was suspended. Continuing to publish tracts and minor novels until the end, this talented yet perverse novelist died a destitute outcast. R. C. W.

Cendrars, Blaise (1887–1961), French writer. A colourful novelist and poet, he published, after wide travels and varied experiences in the world, long poems and novels based on them. *Le Panama ou les aventures de mes sept oncles* [*Panama or the Adventures of my Seven Uncles*] (1918) is a notation of feelings in poem form, borrowing its material from very varied sources. *Du Monde entier* [*From the Entire World*] (1919), in the same vein, was followed by novels—*L'Or* [*Sutter's Gold*] (1924), *Moravagine* [*Moravagine*] (1926), *Rhum* [*Rum*] (1930), *La Vie dangereuse* [*Dangerous Life*] (1938). After the war he also published more autobiographical works—*La Main coupée* [*The Cut-off Hand*] (1946), *L'Homme foudroyé* [*Thunderstruck Man*] (1945), *Le Lotissement du ciel* [*Heaven in Lots*] (1949). His complete poetry was published in 1954, and in 1957, *Trop, c'est trop* ['Too much']. D. E. A.

Cernuda, Luis (1904–63), Spanish poet. Born in Seville, where he took a degree in law and studied literature under Salinas, Cernuda's excessive timidity prevented him from publishing until *Perfil del aire* ['Profile of the air'] (1927). He taught in France for two years, returning to Spain in 1930. The mood of his poetry now evolved rapidly from passionate elegance to the disabused and choleric tone apparent in most of *La realidad y el deseo* ['Reality and desire'], the collected edition of his verse published in 1936. Influenced by surrealism, the poet's solidarity with communism and his equivocal relationships, this work is deeply imbued with the tragic sense of man's solitude. Cernuda never knew real happiness. After the civil war, in Britain, the United States and finally Mexico, he added new sections to *La realidad y el deseo*: the themes of loss and loneliness are only rarely attenuated by a sense of affirmation and fulfilment. Cernuda was also an incisive literary critic. D. H. G.

Césaire, Aimé (1913–), West Indian poet writing in French. Born in Martinique, prominent in Antillean local government, metropolitan politics and international polemics, he, like St John Perse, is one of the great exotic masters of the French language and no comprehensive evaluation of surrealist, existentialist or Marxist literature—nor, indeed, any serious discussion of the contemporary irruption, efflorescence and reassessment of mythological thought—can afford to ignore him. Ironically however, this seeming paragon of assimilation is esteemed not for his espousal of European intellectual or anti-intellectual values but for that careful scrutiny and qualified rejection of Western tradition, implicit in the concept of true racial and cultural parity, which he and Senghor made the basis of the *négritude* movement.

Césaire was the first to give vivid, poetic expression to the emotions, insights and ideas discovered by a subsequent generation in the uncompromising prose of his fellow countryman Frantz Fanon's *Les Damnés de la terre* [*The Wretched of the Earth*] (1961); yet despite this, or perhaps, because of it, and the praise of Sartre and Breton notwithstanding, his literary reputation has been eclipsed by that of the apparently more palatable Senghor. Regrettably, he remains virtually untranslated apart from various articles in the bi-lingual quarterly *Présence Africaine*; even his masterpiece, one of the finest long lyrical poems in French literature, *Cahier d'un retour au pays natal* [*Memorandum of My Martinique*] (1939), has been out of print for many years in its American-English version. Among his more important works are the collections of poetry, *Les Armes miraculeuses* ['The miraculous weapons'] (1946), *Ferrements* ['Clapped in irons'] (1960), *Cadastre* ['Cadastral survey'] (1961); the plays *Et les chiens se taisaient* ['And the dogs were silent'] (1956), *La Tragédie du Roi Christophe* ['The Tragedy of King Christophe'] (1963); the brilliant pamphlets *Discours sur le colonialisme* ['Discourse on colonialism'] (1950), *Lettre à Maurice Thorez* [*Letter to Maurice Thorez*] (1956); and a provocative study of the eighteenth-century Haitian revolutionary leader *Toussaint Louverture* [*Toussaint Louverture*] (1961). M. D. E.

Chandler, Raymond (1888–1959), American novelist. Chandler established detective-story writing as a respectable and respected art. The hero of his novels, Philip Marlowe, is hard, tough, honourable; an average sensual man except in terms of an almost brutal integrity that does not wilt in face of beatings-up and police corruption but faces up with stoicism and melancholy to a largely hostile world. In one sense Marlowe is the romantic hero, isolated in the jungle of big city life, having to forge his own moral and metaphysical values from the meaninglessness of his environment. Inevitably his security takes the form of a sexual relationship; not the coupling of satyr to nymphomaniac as with Fleming's James Bond but the resignation of a rich girl in love to the hard values and low income of a private detective. Chandler's novels are well worth reading: they include *The Big Sleep* (1939), *Farewell My Lovely* (1940) and *The Long Goodbye* (1954). *The Simple Art of Murder* (1950) is a collection of short novels, short stories and an essay on the art of writing crime fiction.

D. L. P.

Char, René (1907–), French poet, born in Provence, whose first works—*Arsenal* ['Arsenal'] (1929), *Arline* ('Arline'] (1930), *Le Marteau sans maître* ['The hammer without a master'] (1934)—were influenced by surrealism. He broke with the movement in 1937 however, and published after the war poems and prose poems in *Seuls demeurent* ['Only they remain'] (1945) and *Feuillets d'Hypnos* [*Hypnos Waking*] (1946). In *Les Matinaux* [*The Early Risers*] (1950), Char gives the clearest expression of his '*art bref*', poetry made of aphorisms and enigmas in as brief and concise a form as possible. He has also published *À une sérénité crispée*

['To an anxious calm'] (1951), *Recherche de la base et du sommet* ['Search for the base and the summit'] (1955), *Fureur et mystère* ['Fury and mystery'] (1948), and *La Parole en archipel* ['The word in archipelago'] (1961).

D. E. A.

Charteris, Leslie (Leslie Charles Bowyer Lin; 1907–), American novelist, the son of a Chinese surgeon and an Englishwoman. He published his first story at the age of seventeen and before he took up fiction writing seriously had worked as a planter, a pearl fisher, a showman, a barman, a gold prospector and a seaman. The Saint, the fictional character at the centre of his books, is that fairly well-established literary and historical figure, the well-intentioned, highly moral, in a fundamental kind of way, never caught gentleman criminal. The Saint is a boy's adventure-book hero, quite pleasant, quite ubiquitous but without the lechery of Fleming's James Bond or the romanticism of Chandler's Philip Marlowe. Saint books include *Enter the Saint* (1930), *Alias the Saint* (1931), *The Saint in Miami* (1940), *The Saint Goes West* (1942), and many, many more.

D. L. P.

Chase, James Hadley (1906–), English crime and adventure novelist, is best known for his sensational and trend-setting *No Orchids for Miss Blandish* (1939). The generally amoral quality of Chase's early fiction makes him a forerunner of the kind of adventure stories popular in the 1950s and 1960s. His later titles include *The Way the Cookie Crumbles* (1965) and *You Have Yourself a Deal* (1966). K. R. R.

Cheever, John (1912–), American novelist and short-story writer who made his name through his contributions to the *New Yorker*, is now widely known for his best-selling humorous novel *The Wapshot Chronicle* (1957) satirising the doings of government departments, and its sequel *The Wapshot Scandal* (1964). K. R. R.

Chesterton, Gilbert Keith (1874–1936), English novelist, poet, essayist, journalist, biographer and historian. Like Hilaire Belloc, Chesterton tends to Catholic values in his writing but combining with his polemicism a refreshing wit and humour. He was born at Campden Hill, London, and educated at St Paul's School and the Slade School of Art. As a journalist, he became well known for a series of light and humorous weekly articles and essays. One of the many collected volumes of essays is *On Running After One's Hat* (1908). Chesterton's novels include a number which are imaginatively futuristic in the sense of placing man in unusual contexts. *The Napoleon of Notting Hill* (1904) predicts an uninspiring London where the people elect a king who restores the excitement of mediaeval pageantry and creates autonomous areas within the city. The Provost of the Notting Hill area objects to a road-making scheme and his resistance takes the form of subtly organised battles based on mediaeval concepts of war. *The Man Who Was Thursday* (1908) takes a Catholic theme of the sanctity of order and applies it to a fantasy plot of spies and detectives.

Chesterton's popular reputation rests with the 'Father Brown' stories. These are based on a lovable, eccentric, apparently absent-minded Catholic priest who in reality possesses an analytical brain comparable with that of Sherlock Holmes. The individual flavour of the stories lies in the incredible situations which arise from a priest, with the combination of qualities described, pursuing criminals whom he happens upon by accident and catches by applying a blend of sympathetic understanding and logic. Five volumes of these stories were issued between 1911 and 1935. The collected edition, *The Father Brown Stories*, was first published in 1929 and has been reissued a number of times since. Chesterton's social criticism is contained in volumes like *Heretics* (1905), *Orthodoxy* (1908) and *What's Wrong with the World* (1910). His dislike of capitalism and socialism alike led to his theory of Distribution, concerned with the individual possession of land. The writer's conversion to Catholicism in 1922 seems in retrospect an inevitable consequence of both his controversial social writing and his fictional work. His subsequent theological writing combines wit, ingenuity and high seriousness, the best-known books being *St Francis of Assisi* (1923) and *St Thomas Aquinas* (1933). *The Everlasting Man* (1925) is an outline of history from a religious point of view.

Chesterton's reputation as a literary critic and biographer is based on a serious scholarship shaped by a zestful style. *Robert Browning* was published in 1903, *Charles Dickens* in 1906, *George Bernard Shaw* in 1909, *William Blake* in 1910 and *The Victorian Age in Literature* in 1913. His own verse is a mixture of propaganda, polemic and the hilariously funny, his best results being achieved in ballad form. *Lepanto* (1911) is written in a sober style; *Ballad of the White Horse* (1913) is intensely patriotic; *The Flying Inn* (1914) presents a set of drinking songs. *Collected Poems* was published in 1927.

Despite his exuberance, his wit and his subtlety, the overall feeling and philosophy of Chesterton's work expresses gratitude and humility before the wonder of life. His *Autobiography* was published in 1936. D. L. P.

Chevallier, Gabriel (1895–), French novelist, who at first devoted himself to the psychological novel as in *La Peur* ['Fear'] (1930), *Clarisse Vernon* ['Clarisse Vernon'] (1933) and *Durand* ['Durand'] (1934). Turning to humorous fiction, he was highly successful with *Clochemerle* [*Clochemerle*] (1934) and pursued this course, though never again with quite the same impact, in *Propre à rien* [*Good-for-nothing*] (1938), *Les Héritiers Euffe* [*The Euffe Inheritance*] (1945), *Sainte-Colline* [*Sainte-Colline*] (1946), *Ma petite amie Pomme* [*Cherry*] (1950) and *Clochemerle-Babylone* [*Clochemerle Babylone*] (1954). The narrative of *Clochemerle*, later the subject of a hilarious film, centres on the construction of a public urinal in a Beaujolais village. Rich in characters and episodes, this satirical almost Rabelaisian novel remains his masterpiece. R. C. W.

Cheyney, Peter (Reginald Evelyn Peter Southouse-Cheyney; 1896–1951), English poet and novelist. Cheyney published two volumes of verse before becoming established as a detective-story writer: *Poems of Love and War* (1916) and *To Corana* (1917). The style of his novels is tough and thrilling. The heroes are hard-bitten adventurers or private detectives who like blondes and enjoy shooting villains but they do not have quite the sadistic overtones of Spillane's heroes, nor quite the sexual sophistication of Fleming's James Bond. The novels include *This Man is Dangerous* (1936), *Don't Get Me Wrong* (1938), *It Couldn't Matter Less* (1941) and *Dance Without Music* (1947). D. L. P.

Childers, Erskine (1870–1922), Anglo-Irish writer on history and politics, is best known for his only novel *The Riddle of the Sands* (1903), a spy story dealing with the possibility of an invasion of England by Germany from the North Sea coast, which remained credible forty years later. The book influenced British naval policy, and has provoked thought as well as pleasure ever since, being both authoritative and undated in style: its account of the adventures of two diverse, likeable young men in a small yacht among the tides and sands of the Frisian islands being based on the author's own experiences. Decorated for his part in World War I, Childers returned to Ireland to work for her independence, joined the Republican army, was arrested and shot. H. C.

Choromański, Michał (1904–), Polish novelist and playwright now living in Montreal. He started his literary career by writing in Russian and translating Polish authors into Russian. One of his earliest works was a short novel *Biali bracia* ['The white brothers'] (1931). Choromański is best known for his novel *Zazdrość i medycyna* [*Jealousy and Medicine*] (1932). A collection of short stories *Opowiadania dwuznaczne* ['Man of action'] (1934), where the imaginary elements are deliberately commonplace, the events around which the stories are woven trivial and the stories themselves consciously blown up and extended, was followed by his play *Człowiek czynu* ['Ambiguous tales'] (1935). However, the enormous success in Europe of the strikingly original novel that preceded them has tended as a result to eclipse Choromański's interesting tales and his other work even among Polish readers. An original writer who probes deep into human psychology, he employs symbols profusely. B. M.

Christie, Agatha (1891–), English crime novelist and dramatist. Her first novel, *The Mysterious Affair at Styles* (1920), introduced that incomparable Belgian detective Hercule Poirot, and with her great gift for story-telling Miss Christie has now been acknowledged, more than fifty novels later, as one of the widest-read crime novelists in the English language. Her plots have endings which are almost inevitable in their unexpectedness, and one of her best novels *The Murder of Roger Ackroyd* (1926) has the ultimate in trick endings with the narrator unmasked as the criminal.

In 1930, having divorced her first husband Archibald Christie, she married Max Mallowan, an archaeologist, whom she accompanied on many expeditions; and these expeditions inspired many of her later novels, notably *Murder in Mesopotamia* (1936). Her more recent novels, such as *At Bertram's Hotel* (1965), have featured another detective Jane Marple, elderly, genteel and very astute.

In her later years Miss Christie has also won a considerable reputation as a dramatist and among her plays which have been produced with outstanding success are *The Mouse Trap* (1952) and *Witness for the Prosecution* (1953). K. M. H.

Church, Richard (1893–), English poet, novelist and critic. His verse includes *Collected Poems* (1948) and *North of Rome* (1960); among his best-known novels are *Over the Bridge* (1955) and *Calm October* (1961). Church also wrote *The Growth of the English Novel* (1951), a small volume rather infelicitously comparing the novel in England with the developing undergrowth, foliage and trees of a great forest. But perhaps his most interesting work is *Prince Albert* (1965), a novel concerned with close domestic relations on a farm owned by one Matthew Burbage who with his wife Anna attempts to make life meaningful within the regular pattern and rhythm of the countryside. The book is also involved with the close relationship between Burbage's small daughter Madelaine and his farm-hand Tom, a slow enigmatic man, close to the soil. Prince Albert, needless to say, is a horse. D. L. P.

Churchill, Winston (1871–1947), American novelist, wrote a number of best-selling historical novels, including *Richard Carvel* (1899), a tale of the American revolution, and *The Crisis* (1901), a civil war novel. The historical romanticism of much of his early writing was followed by an interest in contemporary politics, as in *Coniston* (1906); and he himself ran for the governorship of New Hampshire in 1913. Finally, he became preoccupied with religion; though the novels of this period—*A Far Country* (1915) and *The Dwelling Place of Light* (1917)—were much less popular than their predecessors. A quarter-century later he was still writing about religion—as in *The Uncharted Way: The Psychology of the Gospel Doctrine* (1940). K. R. R.

Churchill, Winston Leonard Spencer (1874–1965), English statesman, historian and biographer. He entered the army in 1895 and his service in the campaigns of 1897 and 1898 provided him with material for two brilliant books *The Story of the Malakand Field Force* (1898) and *The River War* (1899). During the Boer War, 1899–1902, he was correspondent for the *Morning Post* and wrote *London to Ladysmith via Pretoria* (1900) and in the same year a novel *Savrola* and *Ian Hamilton's March.* In 1906 he published an authoritative and outstanding biography of his father *The Life of Lord Randolph Churchill.* Between *My African Journey* (1908) and *The World Crisis* (four volumes, 1923–29), his account of World War I, he was vigorously pursuing his political career, having been first elected an M.P. in 1900. His subsequent spell in the political wilderness was a period of vigorous literary activity, producing *My Early Life* (1930), *The Eastern Front* (1931), *Great Contemporaries* (1937), and his major work *Marlborough* (1933–38), a four-volume biography of his ancestor, the first duke. After his second tenure of the centre of the political arena came his greatest literary achievement, for which he was awarded the Nobel Prize for Literature in 1953. This was his six-volume history *The Second World War* (1948–54). His personal involvement in the story, his unique opportunity to acquire material, his strong patriotism, his force and wit and his dramatic style, combined to create a masterly chronicle. Other works include his *History of the English-Speaking Peoples* (four volumes, 1956–58), and many volumes of speeches. G. S.

Cialente, Fausta (1900–), Italian writer. She has spent several years in Egypt where she took part in anti-fascist propaganda activities during the second world war. She has written a number of novels of which the most successful one, *Ballata levantina* [*The Levantines*] (1961), re-creates the stages of a changing era in the cosmopolitan atmosphere of pre-war and wartime Egypt through the eyes of an Italian girl, Daniela, who graduates from an opulent childhood on the fringe of respectable society to her involvement with the intellectual exile sets, before her mysterious and untimely disappearance. D. B.

Clark, John Pepper (1935–), Nigerian poet and author of *Three Plays* (1964), a volume which contained *The Masquerade*, *The Raft* and *Song of a Goat*. Typical of his themes is the need for man to feel assured of his potency—and critics have claimed that his work has something of the stark simplicity, tragedy and universality found in Greek drama. He has also published an attack on the American way of life drawn from his experiences while studying there, *America, their America* (1964). S. R.

Clarke, Arthur C. (1917–), English novelist, mainly in the genre of science fiction. Himself an astronomer, he combines poetic imagination with scientific expertise: many of his ideas have been realised in practice and he anticipated Telstar, for instance, by twenty years. His fiction covers the full range from the near future and the solar system—*The Sands of Mars* (1951), *Earthlight* (1955)—to remote future and distant galaxies as in *The City and the Stars* (1956). His masterpiece *Childhood's End* (1954) is a transitional book, about the first impact on Earth of extra-terrestrial intelligence. His short stories have a similar range and excellence. Among his other work is *Profiles of the Future* (1962; non-fiction prophecy) and the screenplay for Stanley Kubrick's film *Space Odyssey 2001 A.D.*

C. B.

Clarke, Austin (1896–), Irish poet, novelist and verse dramatist whose work is inspired by the legends and history of Ireland. His many published works include *Collected Poems* (1936) and *Collected Later Poems* (1961); the novels *The Singing Men at Cashel* (1936) and *The Sun Danced at Easter* (1952); *Collected Plays* (1963); and a volume of memoirs, *Beyond the Pale* (1966). P. E.

Claudel, Paul (1868–1955), French poet, dramatist and prose writer. Born in the village of Villeneuve-sur-Fère-en-Tardenois in the Aisne department, Paul Claudel spent his childhood at Bar-le-Duc, Rambouillet and Compiègne until his family went to Paris in 1882. Already he had begun to write. As he tells us in the autobiographical volume *Contacts et Circonstances* ['Contacts and circumstances'] (1940), he felt a great spiritual hunger during his adolescence. His salvation—a central theme of all his work—he owed to two things: the work of the poet Arthur Rimbaud, who showed him a way out of his 'materialist prison' by giving him a 'living and almost physical impression of the supernatural'; and his conversion to Catholicism on Christmas day 1886 in Notre Dame de Paris, 'near the second pillar at the entrance to the choir, on the right, the sacristy side'. Claudel's varied literary work, in poetry, prose and the drama, flowed from these two fundamental experiences.

Claudel was a career diplomat and his whole life was spent abroad, first in the U.S.A., then the far east (China and Japan) from 1895 to 1909, then Europe (Germany and Czechoslovakia) until 1914, then Latin America, Asia and the U.S.A. (1928–33), and Europe once again till his retirement in 1936. It was during his first long stay in the far east that his first major works were published: *Connaissance de l'est* [*The East I Know*] (1895–1905), *Connaissance du temps* ['Knowledge of time'] (1903) and *Traité de la connaissance du monde et de soi-même* ['Knowledge of the world and of oneself'] (1904), these last two being the theoretical basis for his very unique style; and *Partage de midi* [*Break of Noon*] (1906).

His *Grandes Odes* ['Great Odes'], Claudel's major poetic works, were published between 1904 and 1908. In them he finally fixed his verse style, which is reminiscent of the Bible, and of the ancient Greek dramatist Aeschylus or the poet Pindar. In them the poet undertakes to name the world, as Adam was invited in Genesis to continue the creation by naming the animals. Thus the poet continues the creation, he is a 'maker'. This Claudelian rhetoric, based on the verset, is used even in his dramas and prose works.

His great dramas were written after his return from the far east: *L'Otage* ['Hostage'] (1909), *L'Annonce faite à Marie* [*Tidings Brought to Mary*] (1910), *Le Pain dur* [*Crusts*] (1914), *Le Père humilié* [*The Humiliated Father*'] (1916), and finally *Le Soulier de satin* ['*The Satin Slipper*'] (1924). It is on these that Claudel's reputation mainly stands. His early plays *Tête d'or* [*Golden Head*] (1889) and *La Ville* [*The City*] (1890) had dealt with the conflict between temporal order or revolt and man's quest for the eternal, for God. The great plays all deal, in a variety of situations, contemporary, historical or imaginary, with the central Christian themes of purity, pride, charity, sin and redemption. A. L. W.

Clemo, Jack (1916–), English poet. Clemo, the son of a Cornish clay worker, finished his formal education at the age of thirteen. Most of his life has been lived in Cornwall, together with his mother, in a granite cottage. His poetry is based on deeply held Calvinist beliefs struggling with an erotic mysticism. Other influences include Nietzsche, Kierkegaard, Hardy and Lawrence. The spiritual energy in his work complements a style which is perhaps too heavily based on nineteenth-century declamatory romanticism.

Clemo's bodily suffering, including bad sight and hearing, he has felt to be trials sent by God and his best verse stems from his struggle through pain to the redeeming faith in Christ. However, much of his poetry is concerned with the tensions between the dogma of religion and sexual eroticism, the latter providing a remarkably vivid feature of his work as in the poem 'The Excavator':

> I fondle and understand
> In lonely worship this malicious tool.

Published volumes include *The Clay Verge* (1951) and *The Map of Clay* (1961). D. L. P.

Cloete, Stuart (1897–), Paris-born English writer of numerous novels and short stories principally set in Africa. For a long time he farmed cattle in the Transvaal, and many of his books have the high veld and the bush veld as their setting (*The Soldier's Peach*, 1959; *The Looking Glass*, 1963); but other parts of Africa such as the Congo and Mozambique also feature as backgrounds (*Mamba*, 1955; *Gazella*, 1958). The time range of his work is equally wide, spanning the Great Trek of the 1830s, (*Turning Wheels*, 1939; *Watch for the Dawn*, 1939), the Boer war period *Rags of Glory* (1963), and a present-day Paris in which an old man nostalgically relives his libidinous youth at the turn of the century (*The Thousand and One Nights of Jean Macaque*, 1965). In general his evocation of Africa is in the epic mode—steeped in mystery, lusty adventure, and vastness of emotional appetite: it is in the style of Haggard brought up to date with sensation, sensuality and realism. C. P.

Clostermann, Pierre (1921–), French author and aviator. His reputation rests entirely on one work *Le Grand Cirque* [*Flames in the Sky*] (1948) which has been widely translated. In a manner which bears comparison with that of Antoine de Saint-Exupéry, he relates in this work the adventures and trials of a French fighter-pilot in the second world war. R. C. W.

Cobb, Irwin (1876–1944), American humorist, was the author of the popular *Old Judge Priest* (1915), a collection of stories about a kindly if unorthodox Kentucky judge. In addition to several sequels, Cobb wrote scripts for Hollywood and himself acted with Will Rogers. *Exit Laughing* (1941) is his autobiography. K. R. R.

Coccioli, Carlo (1920–), Italian-born novelist writing in both the Italian and French languages. Born in Leghorn, he has travelled extensively and has been an officer and resistance fighter during the second world war. He is the author of a number of novels, better known abroad than in Italy itself, in most of which emotional and religious problems are interwoven with a pessimistic appraisal of modern society. *La piccola valle di Dio* [*The Little Valley of God*] (1948) relates the difficulties besetting a Tuscan parish priest through a succession of unusual events in an out-of-the-way valley during a hot summer. On the other hand Coccioli breaks away from his more usual pattern and points to a possible redemption of human nature with *Il cielo e la terra* [*Heaven and Earth*] (1950), the story of the conscientious dilemmas of a priest and his difficult progress to the supreme test of personal sacrifice.

An unconventional theme is treated in *Fabrizio Lupo* [*The Eye and the Heart*] (1952), the chronicle of an *outré* relationship between two young artists. With *La Ville et le sang* [*Daughter of the Town*] (1955) Coccioli reverts to the posing of emotional-religious problems against a background of pessimism: the young Luciano is haunted by a passion for the seventeen-year-old Giuditta, who eventually yields to his advances but takes revenge by publicly stabbing him during a religious ceremony interpreted as an act of purification. *Manuel le Mexicain* [*Manuel the Mexican*] (1956) is an attempt to penetrate the complex spiritual structure of Mexico viewed as a combination of traditional myths and Christian faith. In *Le Caillou blanc* [*The White Stone*] (1958) the Italian priest Ardito Piccardi recovers his lost faith after numerous vicissitudes which include several encounters with the power of evil in disguise. D. B.

Cocteau, Jean (1889–1963), French poet, playwright, novelist, film-maker, had one of the most extraordinary literary careers of the entire twentieth century. 'Jean, astonish me!' said Diaghilev to him in 1913: and from then until the end of his life he did so assiduously, whether in the *Boeuf sur le Toit* cabaret or in the French Academy. By 1913 he had already written a few light-weight works. But his meeting with Diaghilev and the influence of Stravinsky's *Rite of Spring* caused him to reconsider his whole position. The crisis he went through is recounted in *Le Potomak* (1919), a sort of allegorical confession. Cocteau had some extraordinary adventures during the first world war. In particular, he became a close friend of the great flying ace Roland Garros, doing aerobatics with him; and his volume of poetry *Cap de Bonne-Espérance* ['Cape of Good Hope'] (1919), cubist in inspiration, was dedicated to Garros. His *Poésies* ['Poems'] (1920), which were inclined to be Dadaist (Cocteau was nothing if not fashionable), were published about the same time, as well as an ode to Picasso. It was also during this period that Cocteau conceived his theory of 'celestial calculations', it being the poet's job to 'make a transfer of the invisible'.

But he also rediscovered Greece with its myths and tragedy. Above all he discovered Orpheus, who became the central theme of Cocteau's infinitely varied work. He made a play on *Orpheus* (1927) and two films (1951 and 1959). Just as Orpheus sought to defeat death with the music of his lyre, so for Cocteau poetry became the exercise of the magic power of words and the experience of the consequences thereof. All magic is astonishing, and all astonishment is magic. Poetry is the electric current that passes between these two poles. Magic mixes up appearance and reality, the object and its reflection in a mirror, truth and illusion. 'I am', says the poet, 'a lie which always tells the truth.' Jean Cocteau devoted his life and his work to the attempt to embody in language these necessary exchanges between incompatible terms.

Cocteau was a real jack-of-all-trades. (History will judge whether he was also a master of none.) He tried all registers of the real and surreal, every refinement of sensation and spiritual exaltation. He even had mystical tendencies, as witness his relations with Claudel, Maritain and Mauriac. But it was magic above all which held him. He introduced it into tragedy: *Oedipe-Roi* [*Oedipus Rex*], published in 1928, *La Machine Infernale* [*The Infernal Machine*] (1934) and *Renaud et Armide* ['Renaud and Armide'] (1948); into the ballet: *Phèdre* ['Phaedra'] (1950) and *La Dame à la Licorne* ['The lady on the unicorn'] (1953); into films: *La Belle et la Bête* ['Beauty and the beast'] (1954), *Orphée* [*Orpheus*] (1951) and Le *Testament d'Orphée* ['The testament of Orpheus'] (1959); and the novel: *Thomas l'Imposteur* [*The Imposter*] (1923) and *Les Enfants Terribles* [*Holy Terrors*] (1929). But his favourite medium was poetry. After his first volumes of poetry in 1919–20 came *Vocabulaire* ['Vocabulary'] in 1922, *Plain-Chant* ['Plainsong'] in 1923, *L'Ange Heurtebise* ['The angel Heurtebise] in 1925, and *Opéra* ['Opera'] in 1927. This ended his first period during which he evolved his poetic style and language. Following a long *entr'acte* devoted to the theatre, novel, cinema, ballet and graphic art, he returned to poetry with *Allégorie* ['Allegory'] in 1941, followed by *Le Chiffre Sept* ['The figure seven'] in 1952, *Appoggiatures* ['Appoggiatura'] in 1953 and *Clair-Obscur* ['Chiaroscuro'] in 1954.

Cocteau's entire life was surrounded by an aura of legend and ambiguity which the poet did nothing to demolish. In the years following his death it seemed it would take a number of years to winnow out what would last of his work from what was merely modish and superficial. A. L. W.

Colette, Sidonie-Gabrielle (1873–1954), French novelist. Her euphoric Burgundian childhood and remarkable mother are lyrically evoked in *La Maison de Claudine* [*My Mother's House*] (1922) and *Sido* [*Sido*] (1929). Far superior to the titillatory *Claudine* quartet (1900–03; instigated by their putative author, her first husband 'Willy', sometime pornographer, critic and libertine), these together with *L'Etoile Vesper* ['Evening star'] (1946), *Le Fanal bleu* [*The Blue Lantern*] (1949) and the unjustly neglected *La Naissance du jour* [*Break of Day*] (1928) constitute her credo —insofar as a credo can be abstracted from her corpus of novels, essays, dramatic criticism, journalism, plays and a libretto (*Ballet for my Daughter*, 1916; for Ravel's *L'Enfant et les sortilèges*).

An early work of note, set against the seedy glamour of the music halls in which she mimed and danced following her divorce, is *La Vagabonde* [*The Vagabond*] (1910), which with its characteristically slight plot sustains the perennial feminine conflict of intellect and sexuality. Renée, the emergent new woman, weighs career and emancipated loneliness against marriage and dependence on her rich suitor Max. Colette's resolution of the problem, a 'denial of happiness through love of liberty', is surprisingly existential, while its exposition anticipates the mature ability, to endow universal figures with individual attitudes, of her masterpiece *Chéri* [*Chéri*] (1920). Born in the enervating world of fashionable venality to which Colette returned in *Gigi* [*Gigi*] (1944), Chéri's initiation into the rites of civilised debauchery is entrusted to Léa, a courtesan. Wholly sympathetic, the latter is realised with a subtle eroticism which pervades her clothes, her flat, even her food and reveals Colette's outstanding stylistic quality, the imaginative persuasion of eye, ear, nose and touch. Ironically, Léa, who lives by and for sexual pleasure, falls genuinely in love with Chéri before the disparity in their ages brings Colette's perceptive, classically spare analysis to a celebrated tragic climax. In *La Fin de Chéri* [*The Last of Chéri*] (1926), published after a sensitive portrait of precarious adolescence, *Le Blé en herbe* [*Ripening Seed*] (1923), the spoilt, handsome Narcissus has returned from the war to a marriage and society which his emotionally debilitating association with Léa and the disillusionment fostered by military experience have rendered increasingly distasteful. We sense a precocious alienation, a foretaste of nausea, but Chéri, immured like Bassington in the elegant promise of his golden youth, drifts into decline and suicide.

Content in a third marriage and honoured by the Académie Goncourt, Colette wrote *Chambre d'hôtel* [*Chance Acquaintances*] (1940), *Julie de Carneilhan* [*Julie de Carneilhan*] (1941) and Gigi which testify to the resilience of her omnivorously impressionistic talent, her huge vocabulary and her superb style, admired by Proust. Her characters, often epicene, frequently amoral, derive from the paradoxically masculine conventionality of a small, circumscribed, yet varied world whose expensive tarts, music hall artists and wealthy bourgeois Bohemians avoid intellectual discussion, social, political or religious involvement. Desire, jealousy, animals, children, food and drink, flowers, a pagan veneration of the young and beautiful, an aesthetic hedonism reminiscent of Gide, a new poetic sensibility compounded of sensuality, feline grace, anarchic independence, and a compassionate humanity leavened by robust humour, these are the constants in her life and work.

M. D. E.

Colum, Padraic (1881–   ), Irish poet and dramatist, who settled in America in 1914. He helped found the *Irish Review* and with Yeats, Lady Gregory, Synge and Æ was involved in the creation of the Irish National Theatre. Colum's plays, for example *The Fiddler's House* (1907), are reminiscent of the early Ibsen. His poetry, of which *Wild Life* (1907) is a representative sample, is centrally based on country lore. A number of the poet's lyrics have been transformed into folk music, and a volume on travel and folklore called *The Poet's Circuits* was issued in 1960.

D. L. P.

Compton-Burnett, Ivy (1892–   ), distinguished English author of some seventeen novels. *Dolores* (1911) is interesting to read because the theme is quite the reverse of that developed in all her later novels, in that it explores a life of sacrifice and concludes that such selflessness can be uplifting and rewarding. However, *Pastors and Masters* (1925) is the first novel to exhibit her distinctive style, bare of description and composed almost entirely of a number of dialogue scenes, consisting of conversations of great length and verbal fluency occasionally barbed with an acid or outrageous observation. In *Brothers and Sisters* (1929) the theme of incest, the epitome of the inbred relationship, first appears—the man and wife discovering that they are half-brother and sister, and striving (unsuccessfully) to keep this revelation a secret. The novel is thronged with other pairs of brothers and sisters in various stages of dependence and involvement.

These and subsequent titles indicate the main preoccupations of her novels—the ingrown extended family and its servants and tutors in an Edwardian England; the complex balance of power within it; and the resultant cruelty that members employ towards one another. Thus one recurring feature is the tyrant: in *A House and its Head* (1935) it is Duncan Edgeworth, a weak man who, when a son not his own is born to his beautiful second wife, gasses the child; in *Daughters and Sons* (1937) there are two tyrants, a grandmother and her daughter; while in *Men and Wives* (1931) the mother, Lady Haslam, so dominates her family that when she feigns suicide (more from malice than anguish) and is moved to a mental home, they discover delightful freedom without her, and on her return her son murders her.

These murders are paralleled in a great many of her novels. For example, in *More Women than Men* (1931) the headmistress of a girls' school is so consumed with possessive passion for her nephew that she brings about the death of his young wife during an attack of pneumonia. Many critics were alert to, some perplexed by, this disconcerting combination of a late-Victorian-Edwardian setting and Greek or even barbaric acts of murder, incest and forgery. It was becoming clear that these events had a poetic reality of their own; that here were the suppressed desires and forces common to any relationships as unsought and confined as those within a family being actually voiced or acted out. Once viewed in this light, the cool detached prose and the surprising deeds of wickedness present a world the reverse of the one which we inhabit: character as we know it is turned inside out—thoughts becoming words, and desires, actions. So used are we to interpreting the secrets of the heart by a thousand surface signs, that when the heart itself is laid bare the territory revealed is almost unrecognisable.

Such an approach makes sense, for example, of the otherwise preposterous *Elders and Betters* (1944) in which some extraordinary acts are performed and the most startling accusations made and answered. The newly arrived cousin Anna so ingratiates herself with the aging great-aunt Sukey that the latter in one of her tantrums names her the beneficiary in her will, excluding her own family who have borne with her for so long. The old woman relents, but dies in the act of asking Anna to destroy the petulant new will; Anna instead destroys the old one and proceeds to use the money to 'buy' her cousin Terence, a sensitive young man, for her husband by offering to support him and thus relieve him of the dreaded necessity of earning a living. No less bizarre, but, equally, no less intelligible are the many sub-plots—such as the near-incestuous love of a father for his daughter, and she for him; or the antics of a pair of children who serve as a sounding board for the events described through their blunt, even rude responses when expected to conform to hypocritical adult protestations of grief or joy.

The preoccupation with inheritance has previously featured in *A Family and a Fortune* (1939); while these remarkable children are echoed by the two sons in *Manservant and Maidservant* (1947) who, having suffered at the hands of their domineering father for years, even after he reforms, hesitate to warn him that the bridge he intends to cross is rotten. Children also feature in *Parents and Children* (1941) and in *Two Worlds and Their Ways* (1949), where two young children at school struggle to reconcile the absurd expectations their parents hold for them with the impossibility of achieving them except by immoral means—in their case, cheating.

Later novels do show evidence that Miss Compton-Burnett was attempting to modify her writing in the direction suggested by some critics—there were more descriptions of characters' physical appearance, of their actions during the long conversations, and perhaps a greater element of compassion. However, the effect of any such conscious changes remained defiantly her own. *Mother and Son* (1955) makes reference to the pouring of tea for the son Rosebery. This innocent act, repeated throughout the first chapters (his mother insists that he likes sugar, has always liked sugar—the companion knows that he doesn't), assumes the proportions of a battleground. But this novel still observes the all-important convention established in the earlier books, whereby actions represent the expressions of desires: a convention which explains the absence of retribution even for the most violent of behaviour. Proposals and engagements take place here, as in many of the books, without any overtures or preliminaries. They are settled in a few exchanges of dialogue often shortly after the two characters have been introduced, and are often broken off soon afterwards when others concerned have protested—or the offer of marriage may be simply withdrawn at the end of the conversation in which it was introduced. Thus Miss Compton-Burnett is portraying in bold strokes the primitive mating impulse that underlies the whole social situation. There is also the same remorseless exposure of the truth. When Rosebery's mother is on her death-bed, her husband confesses that his 'nephew' and 'niece' are his natural children by his late mistress; that same evening papers are found which prove that she too has been similarly guilty. This novel is a particularly good example of the 'onion-skin' progress of the author's plots: layer after layer of truth being exposed until there is no one left to point a moral finger.

Here lies the greatest strength of her writing. The novels have an absolutely consistent and unsentimental vein of honesty and it is this that provides the strong basis of morality. Such plain-speaking cannot but make the reader feel humble. That she was abundantly clear about her intentions is shown by her statement in a broadcast: 'I think there are signs that strange things happen, though they do not emerge. I believe it would go ill with many of us if we were faced with temptation, and I suspect that with some of us it does go ill.'

Other later titles include *Darkness and Day* (1951), *The Present and the Past* (1953), *A Father and His Fate* (1957), *A Heritage and its History* (1959), *The Mighty and Their Fall* (1961) and *A God and His Gifts* (1963).

S. R.

Connolly, Cyril (1903–   ), English essayist and critic, wielded great influence through the literary journal *Horizon* which he founded in 1939 and which he edited until it closed in 1949. The journal was of great help to young writers, reflecting a variety of revolutionary attitudes which developed into an aggressive optimism during the early war years; and in his work as a critic he was acknowledged leader of the intellectual *avant-garde*. Selections of Connolly's editorial writing are included in *Ideas and Places* (1953). In 1944, under the pseudonym of Palinurus, Connolly produced *The Unquiet Grave*, a slim collection of literary reflections and commentaries—*pensées littéraires*—which, despite detraction from the critics, became a best-seller. His other notable works include a novel *The Rock Pool* (1936) and essays collected in *Enemies of Promise* (1938) and *The Condemned Playground* (1945); amongst his later titles is *The Modern Movement* (1965), a volume of literary criticism. R. A. K.

Connor, Ralph (Rev. Charles William Gordon; 1860–1937), Canadian novelist who achieved sudden success with a series of books combining a religious theme with a vigorous and stirring story—*Black Rock* (1898), *The Sky Pilot* (1899) and *The Man from Glengarry* (1901). He drew on his boyhood experiences to present, against a background of the Canadian frontier, the conflict between two standards and the confrontation of the cynics and the believers. It could be said that the popularity of these and of his many later works was due to the simple and often violent working-out of the story and to the romantic settings. S. R.

Conquest, Robert (1917–), English poet and editor. Conquest was educated at Winchester and Magdalen College, Oxford. He served in the infantry between 1939 and 1945. Subsequently he became a diplomat, a research fellow at the London School of Economics and a lecturer in American universities. Apart from his own poetry he is well known for his interest in science fiction, editing the *Spectrum* series of science-fiction short stories with Kingsley Amis. Equally important was his editorship of *New Lines* (1956) which introduced a fresh series of English poets—Larkin, Enright, Davie, Gunn, Amis, Wain, Jennings—all apparently with common themes. These poets, whose attitudes have since diverged, became at that time the nucleus of what was known as 'The Movement', being held together by certain predominating involvements. These were a reaction against 'pop' public relations, devotion to literature as a serious moral force, a sense of the necessity to infuse poetry with some intellectual criteria (scepticism, empiricism, coolness, irony), and a need for precise, analytical but elegant statements of truth. This empiricism in poetry was hard with intellectual integrity.

These general statements may serve as a guide to Conquest's own work, as exemplified in the following extract:

> Till then, or till forever, those who've sought
> Philosophies like verse, evoking verse,
> Must take, as I beneath these junipers,
> Empiric rules of joy and thought,
> And be content to break the idiot calm . . .

His *Poems* was published in 1955. D. L. P.

Conrad, Joseph (Teodor Josef Korzeniowski; 1857–1924), English novelist of Polish origin. Son of a poet and revolutionary he was a sailor for over twenty years before becoming a writer. That a sailor should have become a writer of his calibre is not so remarkable as that he should have become a sailor at all, except that every voyage, as later every novel, was more than a physical outgoing; it was an extroversion of vitality and perception. His early reading had included translations of the adventure stories of Fenimore Cooper and Marryat, and it is likely that they appealed so much to the romantic in him that he decided to go to sea, at the age of fifteen, though he had not by then even seen the sea. His romantic ideas were shortly disillusioned but his career at sea was successful and adventurous, including gun-running for the Carlists in Spain, and his own command at the age of thirty-one. He joined an English ship in 1878, thus becoming an English sailor, and it was from his fellows, as well as from reading, that he learnt the language he was later to adorn. His first novel, *Almayer's Folly*, which was started as 'impressions' for a Polish newspaper, and continued to fill in time, was published by Fisher Unwin in 1895, when Joseph Conrad—the book appeared under that name—was thirty-seven. For some time past he had been dissatisfied with his life at sea and had considered other employment: until now it had not occurred to him to be a professional writer. At the suggestion of Edward Garnett, Conrad began another book (*An Outcast of the Islands*, 1896), and found himself, willy-nilly, an author. He married in 1896 and did not go to sea again.

The sea naturally provided the subject-matter for much of his work. Some of the novels and stories are autobiographical insofar as their motif is taken from an actual incident or sequence of incidents in his life, and many of his characters are portraits of real people. He had been in a typhoon in the Pacific which provided the subject for *Typhoon* (1901); and most of the crew in *The Nigger of the Narcissus* (1898), perhaps the most powerful of his early writings, were drawn from the actual crew of the *Narcissus* in which Conrad had sailed. Most of these early works (and even the masterpieces that followed) can be read, and indeed often are, as straightforward and realistic adventure stories. What distinguishes them as literature is perhaps best conveyed in Einstein's observation, 'The most beautiful thing we can experience is the mysterious. It is the source of all true art and science.' A typhoon in Conrad is more than a meteorological phenomenon; and the power that the dying Negro exerts over the crew of the *Narcissus* has a supra-human dimension.

Conrad took no interest in social relationship; rather he sought for the scene, the atmosphere of situations as the context wherein an individual reveals himself. In the situations he presents, an individual is often tested in his capacity for fidelity (to those for whom he carries responsibility, to the ideals he has set up for himself, or simply to the code of his profession). The title figure of *Lord Jim* (1900) is a young man who on one occasion—when mate of a dangerously overloaded pilgrim ship—has failed on all counts by taking to the sea in a moment of panic, and the novel is concerned with his attempt to redeem himself. That in the second crucial test of his life, Tuan ('Lord') Jim—as he is called by the Malayan natives whom he has befriended—should again fail those who have put their trust in him, is a cruel irony: in that this time it is not his physical courage that requires to be exercised. With Jim's second and mortal failure we are forced to look for the agency of a malignant power—embodied in this case in the unscrupulous exploiter Brown whose threat to the lives of Jim's new dependants has created the situation that precipitates the latter's downfall.

One of Conrad's methods of creating atmospheric effect—now commonplace, but remarkable in 1900 when *Lord Jim* was published—was his use of retroaction in the plot, whereby the reader is moved alternately between past (in which the events occurred) and present (in which they are narrated): the effect being to achieve a double perspective on the events narrated. Conrad's technique for doing this in *Lord Jim*, and in several other works (for example, *Heart of Darkness*, 1902; *Chance*, 1913), was to introduce the person of a narrator, the ex-seaman Marlowe: thus enabling him at the same time to be 'detached but not remote'—aloof as well as sympathetic towards his subject. The interpolation of personal comment in an impersonal narrative had been his previous way of bridging the gap, but it was crude, and Conrad had now solved this problem by the simple device of allowing a narrator to make his comments for him. Jukes's letter at the end of *Typhoon* had had a similar effect of personal comment. Neither Marlowe nor Jukes speaks Conrad's thoughts directly, but each opens a wider, or a different view from that which the chronicle alone affords. They do not, any more than Conrad himself, give a facile solution to the problem of factual objectivity and the artist's (and hence the reader's) subjective participation in it.

In the short novel (or long short-story) that followed, *Heart of Darkness* (1902)—based on his own miserable experiences as a riverbound seaman on the Congo, which gave him poor health for the rest of his life—Conrad used the same technique to convey, this time with overpowering effect, the sense of that ubiquitous supra-natural malignancy already hinted at in the downfall of Lord Jim. Thames and Congo merge, in the fusion of present and past, and the 'heart of darkness' encountered in the upper Congo is felt to be beating out through the whole of human civilisation. In *Nostromo* (1904), however, the technique differs, though the malignancy is still present, embodied in the silver that is being mined in an imaginary

Latin American republic—a lodestone for the conduct of the various characters whose lives become involved with it. It is the only major novel that does not focus on one central character. From the points of view of most of the characters, the conclusion does not represent any logical synthesis, wherein either good or evil is defeated and an indication given of a more or less happy future. This, for Conrad, would have been an intolerable contrivance: the end that he achieves being contained in the greatness of his characters and the feeling in the reader that the journey has been worth the making. The future is obscure: but the journey has contained tragedy, in which one is personally involved, and comedy, which one observes uncommitted. Both may be expressed within an ironical humour—the kind that impels laughter as an emotional release.

The Secret Agent (1907) represents a return to a familiar pattern, of a simple character involved in an unfamiliar situation. For the first two-thirds of its progress, *The Secret Agent* reads like a straightforward—though supremely authentic—spy story. Just as Conrad's sea stories have that elusive quality that we call 'larger than life'—a quality of being at once both ordinary and *extra*ordinary—so too does this tale of the seedy Mr Verloch, boosting the earnings from his seamy business by carrying out various shady diversionary assignments for a foreign embassy, and the assortment of neurotics and misfits whose anarchistic and revolutionary politics his activities are designed to discredit. But only when the climax has been reached, in the bomb outrage at Greenwich observatory, do we realise that the character on whom the tale pivots is Winnie, the woman who has married Verloch in order to provide a home for her backward young brother Stevie. Her maternal protectiveness is a straightforward characteristic of an essentially uncomplicated person: but when the awful truth dawns on her that Stevie has been blown up by the bomb destined for the observatory, we see this attachment to be the centrepiece of her life, its violation engendering the need to execute a terrible vengeance, the murder of her husband.

With the minor role of the Assistant Commissioner Conrad found himself, almost unexpectedly, with a man who had all the qualities of one of his favourite heroes: detached but not remote, with a past in the Foreign Office and slightly at odds with his new profession, sensitive, cautious even, but prepared for any risk on the strength of deep-felt though scarcely formulated principles. This man's ratiocinations may retard the narrative, but they project the primitive irrationality of the conspirators, while his excursions into the drawing-rooms of politics and society indicate more clearly, and make more real, the background of pathos and squalor.

Even in his later works—*Under Western Eyes* (1911), *The Secret Sharer*

(1912), *Chance* (1913), *Victory* (1915) and *The Shadow-Line* (1917), books in which a partial disappearance of the sense of mystery, and a partial abandonment of the technique of multiple vision, are accompanied by an increasing conventionality of moral judgment and a tendency to rhetoric —Conrad displays the discernment of the true artist: in the wealth of detail, in the longest periods and, indeed, among the many, varied characters that throng them (and the women are as accurately and profoundly observed as the men) there is seldom an irrelevancy, and never a caricature or unnecessary role. Nonetheless, Conrad once said, 'I am writing towards some fixed event or scene I can see, but I do not know how I shall ever get there'.

Conrad had the passion of the Pole and the loves of the English: his bequest is international, for he dealt with life itself which is contradictory and universal, and he has the contradictory qualifications of a creator, being both inexorable and kind. Conrad said, 'A work that aspires, however humbly, to the condition of art, should carry its justification in every line. And art itself may be defined as a single-minded attempt to render the highest kind of justice to the visible universe, by bringing to light the truth, manifold and one, underlying its every aspect.' The effect of any of Conrad's works is to make the reader feel exalted, as well as humble.

H. C.; K. R. R.

Cooper, William (Harry S. Hoff; 1910–), English novelist in whose early work *Scenes from Provincial Life* (1950) critics later thought they could detect the first signs of the kind of comedy characterised by the self-deprecating anti-hero, the revived male preoccupation with breasts and sex, the stifling provincial background, the escapist fantasy—crystallised four years later in Kingsley Amis's *Lucky Jim*. *The Ever-Interesting Topic* (1953) is a slightly less funny account of the problem of sex for the boys and masters of a small public school. This was followed by *Young People* (1958) in which an attempt is made to portray the contemporary scene as it is, and clear it of cant by abstaining from moral judgments. Next came a sequel to the earlier novel, *Scenes from Married Life* (1961)—said to portray Cooper's close friend and one-time colleague C. P. Snow. Cooper's interest in the world that Snow himself portrays is very marked in the choice of character and setting (and even in the title) of *Memoirs of a New Man* (1966); but here the restriction of the form of the novel to a journal allows him to withdraw completely from commenting on his character's ethics. S. R.

Cope, Jack (1913–), versatile and widely sympathetic South African writer of verse, drama, short stories, translations and novels. *The Fair*

House (1955), his first novel, deals with the end of the last Zulu rebellion, led by Bambatta. However, the main theme of this and the other works of this committed writer, including his stories in *The Tame Ox* (1960), is the distance between, and the hope of the reconciliation and co-operation of, the various groups, black and white, in South Africa. C. P.

Coppard, A. E. (Alfred Edgar Coppard; 1878–1957), English short-story writer and poet. Self-educated and at one time a professional sprinter, he started full-time writing in 1919. Collections of his stories, written in a style that gives the impression of his speaking aloud, include *Adam and Eve and Pinch Me* (1921), *The Black Dog* (1923), *Ninepenny Flute* (1937), *Fearful Pleasures* (1946) and *The Dark Eyed Lady* (1947). *Collected Poems* was published in 1928. D. L. P.

Corelli, Marie (Mary Mackay; 1855–1924), English novelist. She was a writer of popular fiction, mainly of a lofty and sentimental nature, and had an enormous following at the turn of the century. Her second book *Barabbas* (1893) was a quick success, and of the many others she wrote the most popular was *The Sorrows of Satan* (1895). Later titles include *The Love of Long Ago* (1920). R. A. K.

Cornford, Frances Crofts (1886–1960), English poet. A grand-daughter of Charles Darwin, she wrote pleasant, delicate pastoral poetry. *Collected Poems* was published in 1954. D. L. P.

Corso, Gregory (1930–), American beat poet. Corso has the same refreshing and irreverent wit as Ferlinghetti (q.v.). His poetry builds upon images, constructing, with apparent lack of logic, one sequence upon another. It often plays around themes made up of words grouped together by sound or meaning, sometimes to the point of frivolity. Corso's work shows the usual beat rejection of conventional social values, and when he is fully in control of his material a surge of almost romantic melancholy underpins an impressive technique. Published work includes *The Vestal Lady of Brattle* (1953), *Gasoline* (1958) and *The Happy Birthday of Death* (1960). D. L. P.

Cortázar, Julio (1914–), Argentinian novelist. Formerly Professor of Literature in the University of Buenos Aires, he moved to Paris in 1951, where he worked thereafter as a part-time UNESCO translator. Between 1949 and 1962 he published five collections of short stories and *novelle* and a translation of the prose works of Edgar Allan Poe. His most successful stories were republished in *Cuentos* ['Stories'] (1964). Bearing technical affinities with the work of Kafka, Joyce and Borges, these stories were mainly dream-fantasias in which ordinary events and situations assumed a gradual, almost imperceptible distortion. His reputation was vastly enhanced by his two novels, *Los premios* [*The Winners*] (1960) and *Rayuela* (*Hopscotch*] (1963). The former continued the basic mood of the short stories, while the latter contrived elaborate experiments with time sequence, typography and language as well as posing searching questions about the identity of people and places. Its malcontent anti-hero, Oliveira, is essentially an ordinary person deliberately setting himself against convention. His quest for a metaphysic through human relations leads him to suicidal bewilderment. Cortázar's later titles include the collections *Todos los fuegos el fuego* [*The End of the Game*] (1966) and *La vuelta al día en ochenta mundos* ['Round the day in eighty worlds'] (1966). R. C. W.

Corvo, Baron. See **Rolfe,** Frederick.

Costain, Thomas Bertram (1885–1965), Canadian novelist whose lurid historical romances, written after he retired from a successful career as a magazine editor in Canada and the United States, achieved wide popularity in both countries. He also published several popular works of non-fiction on Canadian history. Costain's titles, several of which were made into Hollywood movies, include *For My Great Folly* (1942), *Ride With Me* (1944), *The Black Rose* (1945), *The Moneyman* (1947), *High Towers* (1949), *The Conquerors* (1949), *Son of a Hundred Kings* (1950), *Magnificent Century* (1951), *The Tontine* (1955), *The Darkness and the Dawn* (1959), *The Chord of Steel* (1960) and *The Last Love* (1963). K. W.

Cottrell, Leonard (1913–   ), English author who is best known for his archaeological writings among which are *The Lost Pharaohs* (1950), *The Bull of Mines* (1953), *The Lion Gate* (1963) and *The Land of Shinar* (1965). He has also edited the *Concise Encyclopaedia of Archaeology* (1960). P. E.

Couperus, Louis (1863–1923), Dutch novelist. A wide traveller and dedicated cosmopolite, he wrote more than thirty novels and numerous minor works. He began his literary career by writing verse in the manner of Hérédia, but after the success of his first novel, *Eline Vere* [*Eline Vere*] (1889), he found his true métier, dedicating himself to writing both realist and historical novels. At the time of his death he was a leading contender for the Nobel prize. His work is characterised by his remarkable powers of observation, particularly of The Hague society of his contemporaries, and by a deep sense of fatalism, a sense that destiny outweighed moral choice; a considerable stylist, he also evinced a keen and accurate comprehension of psychological motivation. Many of his works and most of his novels are available in English. His most successful novels were his realist studies of life in The Hague, of contemporary society and of the problems of old age; most noteworthy in this context are *Eline Vere*, *Noodlot* [*The Law Inevitable*] (1891), *De stille kracht* [*The Hidden Force*] (1900), The four-volume *De boeken der kleine zielen* [*Small Souls*] (1901–1904) and *Van oude menschen* [*Old People*] (1906).

A gradually developing interest in the historical and the exotic, fomented by his travels in warmer climes, led in 1907 to his complete abandonment of his former themes. Turning in particular to the exploration of the romantic past, he composed a series of novels which drew their material from the tropical and Graeco-Roman worlds. In the main these works were somewhat superficial and pedestrian, although *De komedianten* [*The Comedians*] (1917), *Xerxes* [*Arrogance*] (1919), and *Iskander* ['Alexander'] (1920) were of a quality to maintain his earlier reputation.

R. C. W.

Courage, James (1905–63), New Zealand-born novelist, resident in England, most of whose novels take as their subject memories of his New Zealand childhood. This gives detachment though some distortion to his picture of the squatters (i.e. prosperous landowners) who formed the upper classes of the province of Canterbury. He shows them living as nearly English a life as they can manage, which leads to their decay and degeneracy. His most successful works are *Desire Without Content* (1956) and *The Young Have Secrets* (1954). S. R.

Coward, Noël (1899–), English playwright and composer. His most significant work was produced between the wars, and he showed early brilliance in his comedy *The Young Idea* (1923) and in a naturalistic play *The Rat Trap* (1924). He has always had a strong sense of the theatre and of the art of creating dramatic surprise, combined at his best with a brittle wit; the latter being particularly effective in the plays that mirrored the smart life of the twenties with its new and often tedious bohemianism. *The Vortex* (1924), *Hay Fever* (1925) and *Private Lives* (1930) are comedies of manners redolent of the atmosphere of this period with dialogue that is crisp, irreverent and often with intent to shock and surprise.

In the more ambitious dramatic work *Cavalcade* (1931) he shows a grasp of the spectacular and a skill in tapping veins of sentimentality often of a jingoistic nature. The latter is often evident, too, in his sketches and lyric pieces, in such songs as 'Mad Dogs and Englishmen' or 'The Stately

Homes of England', where he pokes fun at this sentimentality from the inside.

The wartime *Blithe Spirit* (1941) was a gracefully conceived little comedy without the brittle quality of earlier work, and memorable for the characterisation of the eccentric medium Madame Acarti; it was followed by *This Happy Breed* (1943) and other pieces for stage and screen (notably *Brief Encounter*, 1945) that are outstanding in their evocation of the period. In the post-war years, when he has largely lived abroad, he has continued to score successes on both the London and New York stage, for example with *Nude with Violin* (1959). R. A. K.

Cozzens, James Gould (1903–), American novelist, became widely known outside his own country with the appearance in 1957 of *By Love Possessed*, the work by which he is best known today. However, before this Cozzens had been writing novels of a high quality for nearly thirty years.

Among his early works the most readable is probably the sea story *S.S. San Pedro* (1931) which has been favourably compared with Wouk's better-known *The Caine Mutiny*. But Cozzens's most characteristic works are the series of novels dealing with man in society, *Men and Brethren* (1933), *The Just and the Unjust* (1943), *Guard of Honour* (1948) and *By Love Possessed* (1957). In these books Cozzens explores the inner conflicts and tensions that arise through a man's involvement in the social fabric, especially in his professional capacity. In the first three the men concerned are chiefly clergymen, lawyers and servicemen; in each case, situations arise where professional ethics, responsibilities and commitments clash with individual conscience. By virtue of having accepted a public appointment in, say, the church, the army or the judiciary, one is pledged to obey certain rules and to act in the interests of the community one serves: how far, Cozzens asks, is a man entitled to break those rules and damage those interests in order, say, to succour an individual in distress?

In *By Love Possessed* the emphasis has shifted. The professional ethics of the late Arthur Winner, sen., were inseparable from a faith in Reason. Its antithesis—an indulgence in the dictates of one's own personal feelings—is the 'love' by which in some form or other, all the relations, friends and colleagues of his son Arthur Winner, jun., appear one by one to be possessed. And, to quote the words inscribed on the antique clock that the son has inherited from the father, *amor vincit omnia*. There is the blind maternal love of the orphaned Helen Detweiler for her younger brother Ralph: a love which, having bred him to be irresponsible and inconsiderate, is prepared to subvert the law to protect him. There is the sexual passion of Marjorie Penrose, semi-widowed by the paralysis of her husband (who is Winner's partner), for Arthur Winner himself: and the subsequent religious ecstasy that drives her to confess the adulteries that had stemmed from her unavoidable frustration and his loneliness following the death of his first wife (a lapse that Reason would have discreetly covered rather than wound the third party). Different again is the deep sense of personal loyalty that has made Noah Tuttle, the senior partner, feel himself responsible for the financial losses of a client who had acted on his advice: an emotional fidelity that has led him to make vast borrowings from money entrusted to him by others in order to salvage something from the wreckage of his client's business.

For the greater part of the book Arthur Winner's behaviour is, even by his own standards, unimpeachable; and his reputation is untarnished. One by one he sees those around him yield to a love which is stronger than public morality or the dictates of Reason. The climax comes when he becomes involuntarily an accessory after the fact in respect of Noah's conversions. His professional standards—everything he has ever stood for—demand a public admission of the facts: but his love for all the people who stand to lose by such an action is great enough to prevent it. *Amor vincit omnia.* K. R. R.

Crane, Hart (1899–1932), American poet. The tragedy of Hart Crane was the combination of outstanding brilliance with a severe lack of personal, and sometimes, poetic discipline. His life was a parody of the popular conception of the Greenwich Village artist. With a highly strung nervous system, made more unstable by the incompatibility of his parents, Crane went to New York in 1916 where he ignored formal education and immersed himself in the new literary movement. Disowned by his father, dissipated, homosexual, in poverty and supported only by patronage, Crane worked in fits and starts. Finally, returning by boat from a wasted fellowship in New Mexico, he threw himself overboard.

Crane's early poetry, contained in *White Buildings* (1926), comes under the fashionable influences of the period: Eliot, Pound, Rimbaud, Laforgue and the resurrected English metaphysical poets. His work is heavy with symbolism and preoccupied with the sensation rather than the meaning of words. Influenced by Eliot, he is, however, in reaction against him and against what he regards as the negative, academic attitudes of 'The Waste Land'. He is concerned with the fusion of past and present but in terms of passionate perception, not intellectual and cultural pessimism.

Crane's poetry, then, is dependent on the experimental methods of the period and on the influence of Eliot, but his main involvement goes back to Whitman and the desire to create an American myth. This is the function of *The Bridge* (1930), which is an attempt to fuse poetic ecstasy with a creative vision. The symbol of the bridge is the link interconnecting the past, the present and the future of America. Dependent on an uneven level of inspiration the epic is necessarily a formal failure, especially in view of Crane's limited acquaintance with American history and his lack of intellectual consistency. But whatever its structural failure it is a major achievement of American literature, containing individual passages which can certainly be described under the heading of ecstatic vision. 'The Tunnel', for example, based on the underground railway between Manhattan and East River, is an incredibly persuasive picture of an earthly hell. *The Bridge* must rate as the most brilliant formal failure of American poetry in the twentieth century.

A posthumous publication of Crane's verse is *Collected Verse* (1933). Also of interest are his *Letters* (1952). D. L. P.

Creasey, John (1908–), prolific English writer of crime stories. His works feature a number of specific characters in series—there are, for instance, the Inspector West, Gideon and Toff series. His novels appear also under a number of pseudonyms including J. J. Marric, Gordon Ashe, Michael Halliday, Anthony Morton and Jeremy York. R. A. K.

Croce, Benedetto (1866–1952), Italian historian, philosopher and critic, born at Pescaseroli (Aquila). As a young child he was taken to Naples where he was to live most of his life, apart from odd intervals mostly spent in Rome. After the loss of his parents in the Casamicciola earthquake and a short period spent studying law in Rome, Croce settled in Naples with his books and private research. A natural scholar, he began to write erudite essays on various aspects of Neapolitan history. *I teatri di Napoli XV–XVII* ['The theatres of Naples during the sixteenth, seventeenth and eighteenth centuries'] (1889–91), *Studî storici sulla rivoluzione napoletana del 1799* ['Historical studies on the Neapolitan revolution of 1799'] (1897) and *Storie e leggende napoletane* ['Histories and legends of Naples'] (1905) prepared the way for his more ambitious *Storia d'Italia 1871–1915* ['A history of Italy 1871–1915'] (1928). In numerous essays and articles Croce investigated at length the nature and function of history. He discussed the concept of history as an art form in *La storia è una scienza o un'arte?* ['Is history a science or an art?'] (1893) and developed this theme in other writings prior to his *Teoria e storia della storiografia* [*Theory and History of Historiography*] which appeared in 1917. His controversial study on *La critica letteraria* ['Literary criticism'] (1894) questioned the status of literary criticism in Italy.

Alongside these studies on history and literature Croce began to develop his interest in the field of philosophy. An important essay on

Marxist doctrine, *Materialismo storico ed economia marxistica* ['The history of materialism and Marxist economy'] (1900), analysed the Marxist theory of social regeneration through labour and Croce himself remained convinced of the importance of the economic factor in human affairs. Other philosophical writings betray his debt to Vico's *Scienza nuova* [*New Science*] and to the critical studies of De Sanctis. In 1902 he published the first of his major philosophical works, *Estetica come scienza dell'espressione e linguistica generale* [*Aesthetic as Science of Expression and General Linguistic*], and a succession of companion works covered other branches of philosophy. In collaboration with Giovanni Gentile he founded *La Critica* ['Criticism'] in 1903, his own contributions on a wide variety of literary and philosophical topics amounting to more than a hundred essays, which were subsequently collected into a series entitled *La letterature della nuova Italia* ['The literature of the new Italy'] (1940). The collection includes remarkable studies on Carducci, De Sanctis, Verga, D'Annunzio and Fogazzaro. In 1906 he published a study of Hegelian doctrine *Ciò che è vivo e ciò che è morto della filosofia di Hegel* [*What is living and what is dead of the Philosophy of Hegel*]. Other works covered aesthetics, logic, economics and ethics, and his philosophical programme is clearly stated in *Logica come scienza del concetto puro* [*Logic as the Science of the Pure Concept*] (1905) and *Filosofia della pratica. Economia ed etica* [*Philosophy of the Practical. Economics and Ethics*] (1909). Croce referred to his philosophy as *filosofia dello spirito* ['philosophy of the spirit'] and based his doctrine on the central conviction that the world is solely a manifestation of the spirit. Later he re-studied and modified his theories in new or revised editions of his works. In 1910 he published *Problemi di estetica e contributi alla storia dell'estetica italiana* ['Aesthetic problems and contributions to the history of aesthetics in Italy'] and in 1913 his much-quoted *Breviario di estetica* ['Breviary of Aesthetics']. His *Nuovi saggi di estetica* ['New essays in aesthetics'] appeared in 1920 and a few years later he contributed a lengthy article on aesthetics for the 1929 issue of the *Encyclopaedia Britannica.*

Croce's contribution to the study of poetics dates from an early essay on *Poesia e non poesia* ['Poetry and non-poetry'] (1923). A number of studies followed on this subject. *Poesia popolare e poesia d'arte* ['Popular poetry and art poetry'] appeared in 1933 and *La Poesia* ['Poetry'] in 1936—an important analysis of poetic creation and the critic's interpretation of poetry. In addition to the essays which appeared in *La Critica*, Croce wrote innumerable studies on individual authors. Of particular note are his essays on Goethe, Dante and Carducci and a single volume on Ariosto, Shakespeare and Corneille. G. P.

Crofts, Freeman Wills (1879–1957), Irish-born detective novelist, began writing in 1919 to pass the time during an illness. His first story *The Cask* (1920) became one of the classics of detective fiction, and in 1929 he gave up his work as an engineer in order to devote his full time to writing. His detective stories are all in the classic vein with closely written intricate plots, and his chief character Inspector French has a reputation for the painstaking unravelling of clues and close attention to police routine. His other works include *Inspector French's Greatest Case* (1925), *12.30 from Croydon* (1934), *Death of a Train* (1946) and *French Strikes Oil* (1951). K. M. H.

Cronin, A. J. (Archibald Joseph Cronin; 1896–   ), Scottish-born novelist who practised medicine until ill-health turned him to writing. His first novel, *Hatter's Castle* (1930), was a tremendous success. Setting a tale of innocent, doomed love against the background of a tyrannical father's equally doomed pursuit of worldly success, it had a mordant impact and showed a sensitivity of feeling that he never quite attained in his later novels. The world of medicine provided the subject-matter of *The Citadel* (1937), which opens in the Black Country and traces a young doctor's progress to affluence, taking a long hard look at the darker side of Harley Street. His other notable works include *The Stars Look Down* (1935); the deeply religious *The Keys of the Kingdom* (1941) set in China; *The Spanish Gardener* (1950); and *The Life of Riley* (1964), the narrative of a professional beggar. His portrayal of the Scottish G.P.s in some early stories has given rise to one of the most successful of television series, *Dr Finlay's Casebook.* R. A. K.

Cross, Ian (1925–   ), New Zealand novelist, whose best-known work *The Backward Sex* (1960) is a fresh and funny account of the adolescent stirrings of sexual desire in a young small-town New Zealand boy and the intolerable temptations set in his path by a somewhat ravaged but still voluptuous divorcee. The book strikes an unusual note with the thread of steely desperation that develops in the boy in reaction to the dizzying mixture of rebuffs, enticements and humiliations he receives. Cross's first book, *The God Boy* (1958), first published in the U.S.A. and received with great acclaim, deals with a young boy trying to come to terms with an only partly comprehended tragedy and blaming God angrily for his failure to intervene. Ian Cross has also written *After Anzac Day* (1961). S. R.

Cummings, E. E. (1894–1962), is the gadfly of the American literary renaissance that followed the first world war. One gains the impression of critic after critic throwing up his hands in horror at the poet's typographical eccentricities, at his anarchism, both literary and social. If adjectives employed at one time or another were strung together, Cummings could be described as a nihilistic, eccentric, shocking, obscene, superficial, satirical, adolescent dadaist. In fact, he is a fairly orthodox and lyrical romantic with a flair for unusual typography. Despite the latter his strong command of verse form is easy on the ear and nowhere as difficult to the eye as many would like to believe:

> - - - - - - my
> self etcetera lay quietly
> in the deep mud et
>
> cetera
> (dreaming
> et
> cetera of
> your smile
> eyes knees and of your etcetera)

from 'my sweet old etcetera' (*Is 5*, 1926)

Cummings's first major published work was a novel, *The Enormous Room* (1922), based on his experiences in a French jail during the first world war. In it he manifests the horror of the organised and official and the love for the individual and eccentric which are predominant themes of his poetry. *Tulips and Chimneys* (1923) develops in verse this theme of the worth of the individual as opposed to the mass, organised by the politicians and the advertisers. As a romantic he is accused of lack of development, of retaining his boyish affectations, of never stepping out of the mould created in his early work. Perhaps this is true but equally, by doing so, Cummings has retained a convincing feeling for the saving graces of love, whether erotic or obscene, which does not degenerate through irony to despair and bitterness in the manner of many of his contemporaries. He does not, for example, resort to the cult of the hero which is the refuge of Wallace Stevens.

Cummings can be obscenely abusive, he can be delicately satirical as in 'the Cambridge ladies' (*Tulips and Chimneys*), but essentially he is an unspoiled romantic concerned with human love. He is not a great poet but, despite the fact that his typography employs a small 'i' and large gaps in the middle of words, he is a delightful one.

Editions of his poems include *Collected Poems* (1938), *Poems 1923–1954* (1954) and *95 Poems* (1958). Also of interest is *I, Six Non-lectures* (1953).

D. L. P.

Curnow, Allen (1911–), New Zealand writer, is known chiefly for his poetry, though he has written one play, *The Axe* (1949). In his subject-matter he fuses New Zealand's present with her historic past, as in the volume *Not in Narrow Seas* (1939). His early style was often satirical, notably in *Enemies* (1937), but in later works such as *Island and Time* (1941) and *At Dead Low Water* (1949) critics have noted a meditative detachment that suggests greater maturity and depth. S. R.

Cusack, Dymphna (–), Australian writer, best known as part-author of the sensational novel *Come in Spinner* (1951) which describes wartime Sydney and the influx of American servicemen through the eyes of six women working in the beauty parlour of a large hotel. Despite the notoriety it attracted for its description of sexual encounters, the book is worthy of attention for the excellent portrayals of urban working-class Australian society, which in later novels she portrays from an increasingly committed left-wing viewpoint, *Say No to Death* (1951) is a tender story of a casual affair that suddenly, to the surprise of the lovers, becomes serious when it is discovered that the girl has tuberculosis. She has also published *Southern Steel* (1953); *Sun in Exile* (1955), set in England; and *Picnic Races* (1962). S. R.

D

Dahlberg, Edward (1900–), American novelist, whose *Bottom Dogs* (1930) belongs in the same category as Farrell's Studs Lonigan trilogy and the early novels of Nelson Algren. Less well endowed by nature even than Lonigan, Dahlberg's bottom dog Lorry Lewis never has a chance: his succession of hopeless and de-humanising environments blocking any possibility of human development and reducing him swiftly to a state of pessimistic apathy. Dahlberg's subsequent writings did not fulfil the promise of this early work. K. R. R.

Dane, Clemence (Winifred Ashton; 1888–1965), English novelist and playwright, who also won success as a painter and as an actress. Her first book, which drew on her experience as a teacher, and which was written while she was recuperating from an illness, was the novel *Regiment of Women* (1917), the story of the teachers in a girls' school. It was an immediate success, and she continued to write. She was persuaded to dramatise her third novel *Legend* (1919), and the resulting *Bill of Divorcement* (1921) has remained one of her most powerful plays. One of her best-known novels is *Broome Stages* (1931), the story of a theatrical family. Her others include *He Brings Great News* (1944), a story of the Napoleonic era, and *Flower Girls* (1954).

Clemence Dane with her experience of the stage was naturally attracted to playwriting and among her many successes were *Will Shakespeare* (1921), *Wild Decembers* (1932) and *Cousin Muriel* (1943). If in her plays as in her novels she falls short of greatness in her writing, it is probably because of the diversity of her interests which lessens her power in any one field. K. M. H.

Daniel, Glyn (1914–), English academic, writer on archaeology and author of sophisticated crime fiction. Titles in the former category, which are scholarly but not lacking in popular appeal, include *The Three Ages* (1942), *A Hundred Years of Archaeology* (1950) and *The Megalith Builders of Western Europe* (1958). His detective thrillers are entitled *The Cambridge Murders* (1945) and *Welcome Death* (1954). K. M. H.

Daniel, Yuri (1926–), Soviet writer who was arrested with Sinyavsky ('Abram Tertz') for publishing allegedly anti-Soviet works in the West under the name of Nikolay Arzak. His writing displays a masterly style in his work *Ruki* ['Hands'] (1963) which tells how a member of the Cheka loses his nerve when he sees his bullets (unknown to him exchanged for blanks) have no effect during the execution of a priest. The equally impressive *Govorit Moskva* [*This is Moscow Speaking*] (1961) is a short story describing the reaction of people conditioned by terror to the state's cynical announcement of a Public Murder Day.

B. W.

Daninos, Pierre (1913–), French writer. Born in Paris, Pierre Daninos went to the U.S.A. in 1934 as a reporter; he was mobilised in 1939 and came to England as liaison officer with a British unit. His first novel, *Le Sang des hommes* ['The blood of men'], was published in 1940. On his return from a period in South America he published *Méridiens* ['Meridians'] (1945), and in 1946 *Eurique et Amérope* ['Eurica and Amerope'] and *Le Roi sommeil* ['The sleep king']. In 1947 he received the Prix Interallié for *Les Carnets du Bon Dieu* ['God's notebooks']. In 1949 he published *L'Eternel Second* ['The eternal second'], and in 1952 *Sonia, les autres et moi* ['Sonia, the others and me']. However, his best-known character is Major Thompson, the mythical Englishman who married a Frenchwoman as his second wife and whose notebooks and journal describing the differences between the French and the English attitudes to love, sex, marriage, food, life and other people have made both French and English laugh. He appears in *Les Carnets du Major Thompson* [*Major Thompson lives in France*] (1954), and *Le Secret du Major Thompson* [*The Secret of Major Thompson*] (1956). These were followed in 1958 by *Vacances à tout prix* ['Holidays at any price'], and in 1960 by an analysis of French national characteristics in *Un Certain M. Blot.* [*A Certain Monsieur Blot*].

This perceptive humorist, who has also been described as an eminent sociologist, has assembled, in *Le Jacassin* ['The chatterbox'] (1962)—a dictionary of clichés, in words and attitudes—in *Snobissimo* (1964) and in *Daninoscope* (1963), a selection of quotations and reflections derived from his books, a selection which together makes up a variety of observations, half-humorous and half-serious, half-psychological and half-sociological, that go far to explain the mental make-up of the French of today.

D. E. A.

D'Annunzio, Gabriele (1863–1938), Italian patriot, poet, novelist and playwright, born at Pescara (Abruzzi) on the Adriatic coast. He achieved early prominence in Roman literary circles (1881–91), followed by periods in Naples, the Abruzzi, Florence, and Moulleau near Arcachon (France) where he spent five years before returning to Italy to play a prominent part in political events.

He started to compose verse at the age of ten and his first collection of poems *Primo vere* ['In early spring'] (1879) appeared when he was still at school. Although immature and largely imitative, these poems offer an early example of D'Annunzio's remarkable facility with language and metre and the poet's natural feeling for descriptive verse. His next two volumes *Canto novo* ['New canto'] (1882) and *Intermezzo di rime* ['Intermezzo of rhymes'] (1883) develop these powers into an opulent virtuosity. Here the poetry is rich in that decadent extravagance and ultrasophisticated aestheticism which became synonymous with D'Annunzio's name. His prose style became equally characteristic and the same sensual descriptions and brilliance of vocabulary abound in *Terra vergine* ['Virgin land'] (1882) and in *Il libro delle vergini* ['The book of virgins'] (1884). In 1886 he published *Isaotta Guttadauro ed altre poesie* ['Isaotta Guttadauro and other poems'] and six years later *Elegie Romane* ['Roman elegies'] (1892). That same year *Odi navali* ['Naval odes'] appeared, which expressed the poet's love of the sea and ships while extolling the importance of the sea in warfare between nations.

Apart from the *Poema paradisiaco* ['A poem of gardens'] (1893) with its evocations of childhood, little verse of importance appeared until 1899 when he published *Laudi del cielo, del mare, della terra e degli eroi* ['Praises of the sky, of the sea, of the earth and of heroes']. Only four of the subsequent volumes here projected were completed, each bearing the title of one of the Pleiades: *Maia* (1903), *Elettra* ['Electra'] (1904), *Alcione* ['Alcyone'] (1904) and *Merope* (1912). The *Laudi* celebrate life's pleasures, the overwhelming beauty of nature, the joys of sensuous experience, art, poetry and legend, described in great detail within an elaborate framework of allegory. *Alcione* is outstanding with nature poems of great beauty. These describe the sensuous pleasures of a Tuscan summer—its colours, melodies, silences and perfumes, the voices of the sea, the winds, the rivers and the air.

Among D'Annunzio's numerous prose writings *Le novelle della Pescara* [*Tales of my Native Town*] (1902) still offer an interesting picture of provincial life in a regional setting. His first novel *Il piacere* [*The Child of Pleasure*] appeared in 1889, and five years later *Trionfo della Morte* ['The triumph of death'] which is probably his most substantial prose work. His novels, however, are generally weak in characterisation and consistently pessimistic in tone despite their unique quality of description and verbal harmony. In 1898 D'Annunzio began to write plays in both Italian and French. *La Ville morte* [*The Dead City*] was the first of a succession of dramas which he continued to write until 1914. Notable successes include *La Gioconda* [*La Gioconda*] (1899); *Francesca da Rimini* [*Francesca da Rimini*] (1901), in which Eleonora Duse triumphed;

and *La Figlia de Iorio* [*The Daughter of Jorio*] (1904), his most significant contribution to Italian drama with its skilful dramatisation of regional life in the Abruzzi.

During the first world war D'Annunzio played a prominent role in operations on the Adriatic. He occupied Fiume in 1919 where he published orations, messages and pamphlets on political and military topics. After the war he withdrew to 'Il Vittoriale', a luxurious villa on the shore of Lake Garda. There after his retirement he prepared his memoirs.

G. P.

Darío, Rubén (1867–1916), Nicaraguan poet. The leading exponent of 'modernism', it was he who carried the movement to Europe, playing an essential part in the revitalisation of Spanish and Spanish American poetry. Reporter and customs officer in Chile, correspondent of *La Nación* of Buenos Aires, and representative abroad of the Nicaraguan government, he travelled widely throughout the Americas and Europe until his bohemian existence destroyed his health. Owing a good deal to French Parnassian, 'decadent' and symbolist poets, he adhered to the theory of art for art's sake, considered the poet as a man set apart (a 'tower of God'), and wrote from his ivory tower with his eyes turned away from immediate reality in search of beauty. 'You will see in my verse', he wrote, 'princesses, kings, imperial things, visions of distant or impossible lands.' This is the content of *Azul* ['Blue'] (1888), a book mainly of short stories and descriptions in poetic prose. *Prosas profanas* ['Profane prose'] (1896) is a book of poetry, the zenith of 'modernism'. These poems, in which content seems almost a by-product to form, sing of beauty, riches, mythology and the immediate pleasures of life. But Darío reveals a more profound preoccupation with reality and death in *Cantos de vida y esperanza* ['Songs of life and hope'] (1905), where some of the colour and ornateness have yielded to a deeper melancholy and a more personal, heart-felt expression. English versions of his poetry are included in various anthologies, but he is best represented in *An Anthology of Spanish Poetry* (ed. Flores; 1961). P. R. B.

Dark, Eleanor (1901–), Australian novelist, is distinguished by the polish and ease of her style. Her early novels are characterised by introspective and penetrating psychological studies and at the same time by their containment of an impressive range of character development within strict devices of form (e.g. an adherence to the unities of time, place and action to be found in Greek tragedy). In *Prelude to Christopher* (1933) a series of flashbacks over the space of four days sketch the background to Christopher, a child not yet conceived, and by a couple not yet united.

We see the tragic history of a case of insanity, callously predicted, perhaps manifesting itself precisely because of its prediction. In *Return to Coolami* (1936), four characters are confined in a car for a two-day journey and during this period remarkable changes take place in the personal development of each one. In *Sun Across the Sky* (1937) the action is restricted to a single day and yet the unfolding of the story is so skilled that not until the end does one become aware of the significance of the title. Her later and more voluminous novels are in the main historical: *The Timeless Land* (1940) deals with Governor Phillip's years as the first governor of New South Wales, and contrasts the reactions of both newcomers and aborigines to this strange land; *The Storm of Time* (1948) covers a later period, of Governors Hunter, King and Bligh, and the clash of public with private interests; *No Barrier* (1953) concentrates on the relationship of man to his natural surroundings, attempting to show how the conflicting influences at work in a new land may be resolved in the face of common problems. S. R.

Davie, Donald (1922–), English poet and critic. Davie was educated at Barnsley Grammar School and St Catherine's College, Cambridge. He served in the navy during the war and subsequently was a university lecturer in Britain and America. Davie, as a poet and as a critic, is concerned to resist the movement to provincialism of writers like Larkin and Amis. Like Charles Tomlinson he feels that English poetry should take full advantage from the roads opened up by Pound and Eliot. However, he is not as directly influenced by the French symbolists as the latter, relying on an intelligence and lucidity that is more Augustan in form. He admires Johnson and Pope and his poetry reflects a concern with the technique of verse structure; imagination and severe discipline combining for him in a sensibility that is largely anti-romantic. Davie is constantly concerned to enlarge the boundaries of his art but not at the expense of technical excellence. *A Sequence for Francis Parkman* (1961), for example, extends his intellectual involvement beyond European into American spheres of influence but retains a form that is as much a vehicle for an eighteenth-century concept of reasonableness as for the universal values with which he is concerned. Other volumes include *Brides of Reason* (1955), *A Winter Talent* (1957) and *The Forest of Lithuania* (1959).

D. L. P.

Davies, Robertson (1913–), Canadian novelist, playwright and essayist chiefly known for his affectionate satirical portraits of life in a small Canadian university town. *Tempest Tost* (1951) and *Leaven of Malice* (1954) both deal in comic fashion with the feuds and jealousies of the would-be intellectuals of this inbred community. *A Mixture of Frailties* (1958) tells with more tenderness but equal humour the story of a young girl from the same town of Salterton who goes to England to train as a singer and falls in love with a famous, and much older, conductor. Davies has also written many one-act and full-length plays, and collections of his humorous, satirical and critical occasional writings have been published in *The Diary of Samuel Marchbanks* (1947), *The Table Talk of Samuel Marchbanks* (1949) and *A Voice from the Attic* (1960). K. W.

Davies, W. H. (William Henry Davies; 1871–1940), Welsh-born English poet and autobiographer. Davies was born in Newport, Monmouthshire, and became a tramp in England, travelling to America when he was twenty-two where he picked fruit and punched cattle; he injured his leg permanently when jumping trains in the best hobo style. He returned to England and published a book of verse *The Soul's Destroyer* in 1907. He was befriended by Edward Thomas and George Bernard Shaw, and patronised by the former he wrote his *Autobiography of a Super Tramp* (1908) which was instantly successful. A second autobiography *Later Days* was published in 1925.

Davies's verse is associated with the Georgian school of nature poets, but despite apparent Wordsworthian influence it combines a distinctive freshness with earthy realism in an individual style which seems quite spontaneous. *Collected Poems* were published in 1928 and 1943.

D. L. P.

Davin, Dan (1913–), New Zealand novelist who settled in England, explores the problems of the young and culturally ambitious in the colonies. Occasionally his work is set abroad—in Cairo or London, for example—but even at this distance his central preoccupation is a small area back in New Zealand that he knows well, settled by Irish Catholics. His publications include *Cliffs of Fall* (1945), *Roads from Home* (1949), *For the Rest of our Lives* (1947), *The Sullen Bell* (1956) and *No Remittance* (1959). He has also produced a highly praised book of short stories *The Gorse Blooms Pale* (1947). S. R.

Daviot, Gordon. See **Tey,** Josephine.

Davison, Frank Dalby (1893–), Australian short-story writer and novelist, is the author of the prize-winning *Manshy* (1931), a story of cattle on a station in Queensland, now regarded as a classic of its kind. He has produced several other works including *Children of the Dark People* (1936), but the one which approaches most closely the quality of

Manshy is *Dusty* (1950), the story of a killer dingo and the attempts of the local farmers to destroy him. He has since published *The Road to Yesterday* (1964). S. R.

Day, Clarence (1874–1935), American writer whose frank and tender family studies made his parents household words. *God and My Father* appeared in 1932 and was followed by *Life With Father* (1935), *Life With Mother* (1936) and *Father and I* (1940); *Life With Father* was dramatised in 1939. One of Day's lesser-known works is *This Simian World* (1920), a brilliant work illustrated with his own sketches describing what would have happened if man had descended from an animal other than the ape. K. M. H.

Day Lewis, Cecil (1904–   ), Irish-born English poet, critic and novelist. Day Lewis, related distantly to Oliver Goldsmith, was educated at Sherborne School and Wadham College, Oxford. He was a schoolmaster until 1935 and has written a number of children's books including *Poetry for You* (1945). As a detective novelist under the pen-name of Nicholas Blake he has written in the intellectual 'problem-solving' style, with such titles as *The Case of the Abominable Snowman* (1941) and *The Worm of Death* (1961). In 1968 he became Poet Laureate.

Day Lewis's poetry was associated in the pre-World War II period with the socialist, Marxist aspirations of Auden and Spender. His work of those years is steeped in images of industry and society and tends to a polemic line. A number of Marxist literary essays which he wrote included *Revolution in Writing* (1935). His later poetic style is more flexible than during this earlier didactic period. *An Italian Visit* (1953) contains interesting parodies of poets ranging from Hardy to Dylan Thomas. Like Auden's, Day Lewis's tone is seldom personal or intimate; his poetry is at its best when he is reflecting on general and universal themes, with the controlling effect of a powerful rhythmic technique, as in the following passage from 'The Chrysanthemum Show', in *Collected Poems* (1954):

> And today when I see chrysanthemums,
> I half envy that boy
> For whom they spoke as muffled drums
> Darkly messaging, 'All decays
> But youth's brief agony can blaze
> Into a posthumous joy'.

Other volumes include *The Room and Other Poems* (1965). D. L. P.

Deeping, Warwick (1877–1950), English novelist. After qualifying as a doctor, and working as a general practitioner in the country for a year, he began his literary career with the publication of the historical novel

Uther and Igraine (1903), which was followed by *The Red Saint* (1909); but he won his first big success with *Sorrell and Son* (1925), the product of his own experiences during and after the first world war, and dealing with the plight of an ex-officer reduced in peacetime to working as a hotel 'boots' to support his son and himself. Tracing his rise to the post of hotel manager, this novel was frankly sentimental especially in its treatment of the father-son relationship, and it set the pattern for all his future writing including *Old Pybus* (1928) and *Kitty* (1928). The *New York Times* rather scornfully wrote of his 'well woven plots, full of British solidity and gentlemanly goodness', but although his novels were sentimental with inevitable happy endings, they were about real people and appealed to a wide reading public. K. M. H.

Deighton, Len (1929–), English novelist and gastronome. Deighton, the son of a governor of the Windward Islands, was educated at Eton and Worcester College, Oxford, where he became president of the Union. Subsequent jobs included being a deckhand on a Japanese whaler. His most celebrated novel *The Ipcress File* (1962) is an offbeat, slightly fragmented, spy thriller. The hero, transferred from the regular army to a spy unit under the brilliant Dalby, is arrested for supposed treason while visiting an American space base. He is then supposedly captured by the Russians and whisked off to the Soviet Union. However, on escaping from his prison he discovers himself in the heart of London, the victim of an elaborate plot to break him down. Eventually he discovers Dalby to be the real traitor and that he himself has been used as bait to catch the fish which the authorities have been all along trying to land. The novel is sophisticated but superficial. The hero's main personality trait is his disposition to be a gourmet, an interest presumably inherited from Deighton's earlier cookery books. Other thrillers include *Horse Under Water* (1963), *Funeral in Berlin* (1964), and the far-fetched *Billion Dollar Brain* (1966). D. L. P.

Delafield, E. M. (Edmée Elizabeth Monica de la Pasture; 1890–1943), English novelist, daughter of a French nobleman who settled in England. Her mother Mrs Henry de la Pasture was also a novelist of some note. Her upbringing in a typical Edwardian family provided the background for many of her books, but it was during the first world war that her first novel *Zella Sees Herself* (1917) appeared. She married in 1919 and from the early twenties, through the thirties, hardly a year passed without the publication of one of her books. Amongst her better-known works are *Thank Heaven Fasting* (1932); *Nothing is Safe* (1937), an indictment of the harm caused to children by easy divorce; and *Messalina of the*

Suburbs (1923), the reconstruction of a notorious crime. But she is best remembered for the *Diary of a Provincial Lady* (1930) and its sequels. 'The Provincial Lady' first appeared in *Time and Tide* of which E. M. Delafield was a director, and the gentle humour of this revealing picture of life in an upper-middle-class family has won it a lasting place in the literature of the period. K. M. H.

De la Mare, Walter (1873–1956), English poet, whose poetry is a good antidote to the griefs of our civilisation. He sought not a means of escape but a means of expression, and found it through a child-like simplicity of vision. He himself was beloved by children, but his work is not primarily for them; a measure of its success is that, enjoyed by the averagely intelligent child, it is appreciated more as the child grows older, and is discovered with equal satisfaction by the adult.

His genius springs from those seconds between sleeping and waking when not only the good but the perfect are within one's ambit; similarly his poems are short and incandescent, with a clarity and joy that could not survive in a longer work without becoming obscured and sentimentalised. *Songs of Childhood* (1902) made clear what was to become characteristic, a lyrical and subtle use of varied metres which never become artificial, and a dream quality which includes the dingy and the fearful together with innocence and 'the smooth-plumed bird'. Subsequent editions included *Peacock Pie* (1913), *Poems 1901–1918* (1920) and *Poems 1919–1934* (1935).

De la Mare's poetry dazzles his achievement as a story-teller, in such volumes as *The Three Mulla-Mulgars* (1910), *Memoirs of a Midget* (1921) and several collections of short stories; but all of these have the same uncloying grace as his poems in verse-form. H. C.

Delaney, Shelagh (1939–), English dramatist, achieved fame and several awards with Joan Littlewood's Theatre Workshop production of her *A Taste of Honey* in 1958. Written when she was eighteen, the play is both funny and sad, set in and capturing the flavour of the author's own town of Salford. It tells a simple story of an illegitimate pregnancy; its originality lies in the fact that the characters involved are the flotsam and jetsam of society, parodies of the roles they fill, yet absolutely believable and not demanding pity. Josephine (Jo) is a wary but resilient schoolgirl in a constantly warring, curiously adult relationship with her improvident promiscuous mother, who deserts her daughter to marry her latest lover. Jo is befriended briefly by a Negro sailor and becomes pregnant. Geof, a young homosexual art student, prim, neat and affectionate, comes to share Jo's ramshackle attic and takes over preparations for the baby. Part of the play's impact derives from the way in which the daughter's life repeats the pattern of the mother's; and for all the squalor of the events and environment, there is 'a taste of honey' in the bizarre relationships between mother and daughter and between the unmarried-teenage-mother and her effeminate companion. Shelagh Delaney has since had performed a more ambitious but much less successful work, *The Lion in Love* (1960), interesting for portraying a similar mother-daughter relationship and for its development of a note of myth; and *Sweetly Sings the Donkey* (1964). S. R.

De la Roche, Mazo (1885–1961), Canadian novelist. Her first novel *Explorers of the Dawn* did not appear until 1922, and was not very successful; but she won the *Atlantic Monthly* 10,000-dollar prize with her next book *Jalna* (1927). This was the first of the famous Whiteoaks series, chronicling the life of a Canadian family from early pioneering days up to the present time. Mazo de la Roche created several generations of memorable characters, the most colourful being the indomitable Adeline Whiteoak who in a life spanning over a hundred years is a central figure in many of the Whiteoaks novels. The narrative moves backwards and forwards in the stories; *The Building of Jalna* is the first in history but did not appear until 1944. Other titles in the series include *Finch's Fortune* (1931), *Master of Jalna* (1933), *Young Renny* (1935), *Renny's Daughter* (1951), and *Whiteoak Brothers* (1953). K. M. H.

Deledda, Grazia (1871–1936), Italian novelist born at Nuoro (Sardinia). Although largely self-educated and isolated in a remote and primitive island, Deledda began to write in her teens and her collections of *novelle* and early novels brought her native Sardinia into literary prominence. In 1900 she married and moved with her husband to Rome where she established a reputation as the leading exponent of the regionalist novel in Italy. Her publications during the next thirty years amounted to some twelve collections of *novelle* and some twenty-five additional novels.

The most successful and greater part of her novels are set in the mountainous central area of Sardinia and filled with reminiscences of the island's primitive occupations, its poverty, customs, superstitions and acts of violence. Her early work is darkly pessimistic. Two novels of this period are available in translation: *Dopo il divorzio* [*After the Divorce*] (1902) and *Cenere* [*Ashes*] (1904). Later a note of resignation and final acceptance of the harsh conditions of life in this abandoned region gradually creeps into her work. Her most important novels adhere to the classical definition of tragedy. *Elias Portolu* (1903) is a tragic novel based on the theme of temptation and offers a notable example of the conflict between violent instinctive passion and the ensuing sense of guilt, which characterises also the tensions of *L'Edera* ['The Ivy'] (1906), *Canne al vento* ['Reeds in the wind'] (1913), *Marianna Sirca* (1915), *Le colpe altrui* ['The faults of others'] (1914) and *La madre* [*The Mother*] (1919). A novelist of reality rather than realism, Deledda writes with biblical simplicity and clear individual characterisation. In 1927 she received the Nobel prize for literature. G. P.

Delibes, Miguel (1920–), Spanish novelist, born in Valladolid where he lectures in the College of Commerce and edits a daily newspaper. Away from Madrid, Delibes has quietly achieved a solid reputation—despite his somewhat archaic technique, constructing his novels around a thesis, and often conveying the sense by a specific symbol. Thus in *La sombra del ciprés es alargada* ['The shadow of the cypress is lengthy'] (1948) the gloom of the tree—found in every Spanish cemetery—reflects the pessimistic philosophy of Pedro, the narrator. The thesis obtrudes less in *El camino* [*The Path*] (1950), a beautifully structured novel and his most successful work to date. Daniel, aged eleven, spends the night reliving his childhood in the village which he is reluctantly to leave the next day for boarding school. *Las ratas* ['The water-rats'] (1962) is a bitter study of Castilian villagers struggling against the harshness of their environment and of society. D. H. G.

Delius, Anthony (1916–), South African poet, playwright and journalist. *An Unknown Border* (1954) and *A Corner of the World* (1962) pursue poetic paths which are, in subject-matter, not unlike those of Guy Butler; while the rumbustious satirical vein of *The Last Division* (1959) marks Delius as the heir to Roy Campbell's genius. Another, slighter, political satire—but in prose—is *The Day Natal Took Off* (1963); while *The Fall* (1960) seeks to delineate Rhodes, the man rather than the empire-builder. C. P.

Dell, Ethel Mary (1881–1939), English novelist, began writing as a child, but she first achieved popularity with *The Way of An Eagle* (1912) and repeated her success with *Rocks of Valpré* (1914). Almost all her thirty-four novels feature the same type of hero: strong and silent with a titillating strain of sadism, albeit very genteel. They could best be described as a series of cardboard representations of Jane Eyre's Mr Rochester.

Her other novels include *The Knave of Diamonds* (1913), *The Hundredth Chance* (1917) and *Serpent in the Garden* (1938). K. M. H.

De Morgan, William Frend (1839–1917), English novelist. De Morgan, the son of a mathematician, eventually became a manufacturer of artistically acclaimed but only mildly commercially successful pottery. In his early sixties he turned to writing and produced eight novels before his death. The first, *Joseph Vance* (1906), was very successful and evinced comparisons with Dickens; it was followed by *Alice-for-Short* in 1907. *The Old Man's Youth* (1921) was published posthumously. De Morgan's style was moral, sentimental and socially aware. Not unnaturally his books were popular. They are not widely read today. D. L. P.

Dennis, C. J. (Clarence Michael James Dennis; 1876–1938), Australian author of the enormously popular *Songs of a Sentimental Bloke* (1915), a series of comic poems in ripe dialect chronicling the courtship and final domestication of a belligerent but soft-hearted larrikin by his girl Doreen. The phenomenal success of Dennis's verse can be attributed to the reassuring ordinariness of the events described, the outrageous spelling and slang, his swinging rhythms and the strong chords of sentimentality. Further volumes dealt with the exploits of other characters sketched in the early volume. *The Moods of Ginger Mick* (1916), *Digger Smith* (1918) and *Doreen* (1917). S. R.

Dennis, Nigel (1912–), English critic, playwright and novelist. His critical works include *Dramatic Essays* (1962) and *Jonathan Swift, a Short Character* (1964). His interest in Swift indicates the nature of his plays which are satirical though they tend to be cerebrally constructed. His most considered play is *Cards of Identity* (1958) written in the same year as *The Making of Moo*. The former was later produced as a novel, where he shows a number of characters being broken down and reshaped in forms they cannot constitutionally support. It reflects his attitude to post-war Britain in a less direct way than the play *August for the People* (1962) which concerns itself with a diplomat's approach to his work. The latter culminates in a drunken speech describing the failure of democracy, containing a plea for an attempt to find another path out of the present spiritual wilderness. For all the brilliance of his initial ideas Dennis fails to resolve the problems he poses within his works. This is, perhaps, not the task he has set himself and his disillusion with contemporary society may reflect a romantic approach to the past. 'What slowly dies', he says in his work on Swift, 'is the old gaiety, strangled to death by circumstances, wilfulness, chagrin and illness.' This is an indication of the themes of his work. Other titles include *A House in Order* (1966), a novel. K. G.-Y.

Déry, Tibor (1894–), Hungarian novelist and short-story writer, came of a wealthy family and was sent to learn the timber trade which supported it. Here he came into contact with radical ideas and soon joined the communists. Much of his life between the two world wars was spent in exile, where he began to write his lengthy novel *A befejezetlen mondat* ['The unfinished sentence'] (1947), describing the activities of the illegal communist party. *Felelet* ['Response'] (1952) describes Hungarian society before the second world war, but questions the application of ready-made solutions to its problems; it thus started a fierce controversy in the country. Déry's critical mind put him among the leaders of the 1956 uprising, when his *Niki* [*Niki*] (1958) unveiled some of the barbarous inhumanity of the previous years. After spending some four years in prison, he began to publish again. A volume of short stories both early and new appeared in 1963, entitled *Szerelem* ['Love'], and his satirical Utopian novel *G. A. ur X-ben* ['Mr G. A. in X'] in 1964. Parts of the latter are translated in *New Hungarian Quarterly*, Budapest, Vol. IV, no. 10. His long novels tend to be turgid in style and slow-moving, but his short stories are models of the genre, clear and concise. Good examples of the latter are to be found in *The Giant* (1964) and *The Portuguese Princess and other Stories* (1967). G. F. C.

Descalzo, Martín. See **Martín Descalzo,** Ignacio.

Deutsch, Babette (1895–), American poet and critic. Her poetry combines quality of intellect with emotional involvement in the social problems of her day. *Banners* (1919), *Honey Out of the Rock* (1925) and *Animal, Vegetable and Mineral* (1954) are representative of her work. *One Part Love* (1939) is a passionate denunciation of society's lack of spiritual involvement. In addition to three novels, Babette Deutsch has produced a number of critical books: *Potable Gold* (1929) and *This Modern Poetry* (1935) were combined as *Poetry in Our Time* (1952). The author's *Coming of Age: New and Selected Poems* was published in 1959. D. L. P.

Dhlomo, Herbert E. (1905–57), South African poet and playwright. *Valley of a Thousand Hills* (1941) contains sonorous, romantically evocative descriptions of landscape in a style derived from Tennyson and Wordsworth. *The Girl Who Killed to Save* (1935) is a historical play centred on the role played by Nong-quase in the 'national suicide' of the Ama-Xhosa during the governorship of Sir George Grey in the Cape Colony. C. P.

Dickens, Monica (1915–), English writer. A great-granddaughter of Charles Dickens, she worked first as a domestic help and later as a nurse. Her humorous accounts of these two experiences were published as *One Pair of Hands* (1939) and *One Pair of Feet* (1942), both books being much sought after as light relief from the grimness of war. She continued her chapters of autobiography with *My Turn to Make the Tea* (1951) describing her experiences on the staff of a small provincial newspaper. She has written several novels including *The Happy Prisoner* (1946), *Flowers on the Grass* (1949) and *The Room Upstairs* (1966). G. S.

Dinesen, Isak (Baroness Karen Christence Blixen-Finecke; 1885–1961), Danish short-story writer and novelist who sometimes wrote under her own name and also used the pseudonym Pierre Andrézel. The daughter of a prominent author and explorer, she inherited her father's wanderlust; after study at an art academy she married into the Danish nobility and settled with her husband in Kenya where they farmed from 1914 to 1931. While in Kenya she found herself doctor, teacher and judge to the native farmhands working on the Blixen estate and frequently regaled them and their families in the evenings with her highly imaginative and often fantastic stories. Her first collection was issued in English in 1934 entitled *Seven Gothic Tales*, only appearing in Danish the following year. Thereafter were published virtually simultaneously in English and Danish five further collections: *Out of Africa* (1937), *Winter's Tales* (1942), *Last Tales* (1957), *Anecdotes of Destiny* (1958) and *Shadows on the Grass* (1962, Danish ed. 1961). Late in life she wrote two novels, the thriller *Gengaeldelsens Veje* [*The Angelic Avengers*] (1944) and the comic pastoral novel *Ehrengard* [*Ehrengard*] (1963). Her literary attitude to life frequently bore the clear imprint of the teaching of her compatriot Kierkegaard.
R. C. W.

Diver, Maud (*c.* 1867–1945), English novelist born in India, a country which she loved and was to portray in her novels of British India. These began with the immensely successful *Captain Desmond, V.C.* (1906); later titles included *Ships of Youth* (1931) and *Kabul to Kandahar* (1935). K. R. R.

Doderer, Heimito von (1896–), Austrian novelist, passed his early youth in Vienna before serving in the army. Captured on the eastern front, he was a prisoner of war in Siberia, not returning home until 1920. His first publication *Gassen und Landschaft* ['Lanes and countryside'] (1923) was lyric poetry, but he became famous as a novelist of contemporary society, especially of Viennese society. *Das Geheimnis des Reichs* ['The secret of the empire'] (1930) treated with the collapse of imperial Russia. *Ein Mord, den jeder begeht* ['A murder that everyone commits'] (1938) deals with a man searching for the murderer of his sister-in-law. During the second world war Doderer served in the air force; on his return to Vienna he resumed work on his monumental *Die Dämonen*

[*The Demons*], finally published in 1956. This treats of the intermingling of the lives of the highest members of inter-war society in Vienna with the lowest strata of society; the lives of prostitutes are ruthlessly exposed. Earlier he had published *Die Strudelhofstiege* ['Strudelhof stairs'] (1951), in which the hero is introduced as a lieutenant in the army; at the end he is a retired civil servant, the sort of man who always makes clumsy mistakes in his life. There is a tremendously Dickensian quality about Doderer's work which has established his reputation and caused him to be compared also to the English novelist Laurence Sterne. Later novels include *Die Merowinger* ['The Merovingians'] (1962), *Die Wasserfälle von Slunj* ['The waterfalls of Slunj'] (1963) and *Unter schwarzen Steinen* ['Under black stones'] (1966). G. W.

Dolci, Danilo (1924–), Italian social reformer and essayist, winner of the Lenin Peace Prize in 1959. Born near Trieste, he joined Father Zeno Saltini at the boys' town of Nomadelfia, and in 1952 moved to western Sicily where he has since lived and worked for the social rehabilitation of the destitute peasants and fishermen of this area, alternating his work with books and visits abroad aimed at giving publicity to his reformist views and action. His foremost works directly concerned with the social issues of western Sicily are *Banditi a Partinico* [*The Outlaws of Partinico*, also containing essays and reports published earlier] (1955), *Inchiesta a Palermo* [*To Feed the Hungry*] (1956) and *Spreco* [*Waste*] (1960). In his collection of essays *Verso un mondo nuovo* [*A New World in the Making*] (1964), Dolci airs his views on the methodics of social and economic planning and reviews what has been achieved in this field in emergent countries. Dolci's writings are composed in the flat style of a chronicle and are often interspersed with statistical data, quotations from eye-witnesses' reports and opinions of local inhabitants, yet they exude a magnetic force which makes them compulsory reading, and are suffused with a sympathetic and compassionate outlook on the plight of the needy. D. B.

Donleavy, James Patrick (1926–), American writer of Irish extraction, acquired fame with a novel set in Dublin, where he had himself been a student at Trinity College. Sebastian Dangerfield in *The Ginger Man* (1956)—a book that is farcical, bawdy, often genial, at times almost elegiac, but consistently less pretentious than some critical adulation would suggest—is at first sight an amiable feckless parasite, becoming a rather less attractive figure in his treatment of his unfortunate wife Marion: who is certainly not wanting in the all-important characteristic of desiring to go to bed with Sebastian, and whose only fault is to be distressed at such happenings as the failure of the plumbing and subsequent cascading of excrement through the ceiling on to her herself and her unfortunate baby. However, with Marion finally departed, Sebastian comes more clearly into focus as a would-be child of nature, only wanting to live off his environment without toiling or spinning: and he is certainly as good (in his own particular way) to the frustrated virgins and spinsters of Catholic Ireland, as he expects the world to be to him in providing him with a living. The course of his life in Dublin, and the inevitable failure (despite hopes of a legacy) of his illusion, is counterpointed by the career of his fellow student Kenneth O'Keefe, whose laborious attempts to achieve both sustenance and sexual satisfaction by the opposite method of unremitting effort do not even bring him the measure of peace and contentment that does from time to time illuminate Sebastian's life.

Donleavy's subsequent publications include *Fairy Tales of New York* (1960), *A Singular Man* (1964), and *The Saddest Summer of Samuel S.* (1967). K. R. R.

Doolittle, Hilda. See **H. D.**

Dos Passos, John Roderigo (1896–), American novelist, is today a writer more talked about than read. For the greater part of the two decades following the second world war, little of his major work of the twenties and thirties was in print outside America, and in each succeeding generation it is read by progressively fewer people. Yet his reputation as one of the leading figures in American literature between the wars still remains, thus providing a measure of the impact he made on his contemporaries. One possible reason for the apparently ephemeral quality of his work is the disappearance into history of the economic and social conditions that were the breeding ground for his best work; while a second factor could be the unsatisfactory nature of his technical experiments, which when taken in conjunction with the revolutionary nature of his subject matter appeared at the time to mark him out as a literary prophet but which today seem of dubious value.

His work is characterised by a tortuous emotional involvement with America as a collective human phenomenon, heavily coloured by his commitment to the cause of the proletariat in an era of gross injustice. Too close a personal identification with the struggle of the unions, and with the activities of revolutionary political organisations (he himself was an active member of the I.W.W.), may have prevented him from producing a novel as durable as Steinbeck's *The Grapes of Wrath*, where the indignation of the writer has not dissolved his necessary artistic detachment and made him unable to see the universal in the particular. At the same time his attempts to convey the totality of human America (in the *U.S.A.* trilogy), or of the city of New York (in *Manhattan Transfer*), in techniques often reminiscent of Joyce, are never as successful as Joyce's evocation of Ireland and Dublin for the simple reason that his human dramas merely contribute to the cumulative picture, without imposing any unifying pattern on it.

Dos Passos's first work of any importance was *Three Soldiers* (1921), one of the best of the crop of anti-militaristic novels produced in the aftermath of the first world war. In the next four years he was to publish a volume of poetry, a play and another novel *Streets of Night* (1923) before producing the key work *Manhattan Transfer* (1925). As with the main figures of the two previous novels, we get a full portrait of the background, parentage and childhood of the two principal characters, Jimmy Herf and Ellen Thatcher: and like the three soldiers', their reactions to the conditions surrounding their young adult lives are governed by the experiences of their childhood. Here, however, the city of New York, in its diversity of physical and human manifestations, counts for much more than the conditions of warfare, and exerts a dominating personality of its own. In it, a man can get lost: and the birth of Ellen in the book's first paragraph is immediately followed by the arrival on the Manhattan ferry of Bud Korpenning who has committed a crime of violence and is seeking refuge in anonymity. But it can also wreak havoc with a man's life, and in the closing pages Jimmy takes the ferry in the opposite direction, knowing only that he must go 'pretty far'.

Such movement—not only in and out, but up and down, converging and diverging, waxing and waning—is of the very essence of a city whose physical landscape is itself in a state of flux; and it is displayed kaleidoscopically in the personal relationships, economic fortunes and social status of a multiplicity of vividly portrayed characters. People come and go, sometimes staying only long enough for a brief glimpse before they disappear again in the crowd. To the very end, new characters are constantly introduced; and if it is not grasped that their existence is subordinate to the life of the city, the reader may be baffled and irritated. As for the physical framework for all this flesh and blood, it is constantly in evidence, and its various elements (focused in chapter headings such as 'Tracks', 'Rollercoaster', 'Skyscraper') provide a pattern for the narrative.

Manhattan Transfer was in many senses a curtain-raiser for the gigantic *U.S.A.* trilogy, which attempts to do for America as a whole what its predecessor had done for New York. There are twelve principal characters, representing the spheres of business, labour, the armed services and the arts, as well as a variety of social and regional backgrounds.

There is also an apparently inexhaustible fund of minor characters many of whom exist for their public or personal relationships with one of the twelve. But there are also three new technical devices, designed to fill out the canvas. A total of 68 'Newsreels' locate the fictional narrative in actual history, their highly selective content serving to reinforce the political slant of the novels. Secondly, to remedy the necessary limitations in creating a representative list of characters, there are a series of biographies of notable Americans of the period, including Presidents Theodore Roosevelt and Woodrow Wilson, the banking family of John Pierpont Morgan, the inventor Thomas Edison, the writer Thorstein Veblen, and the newspaper magnate William Randolph Hearst. The third device is a series of stream-of-consciousness passages entitled 'The Camera Eye', expressing cinematically the free associations of a roving focus of consciousness from different points in the fabric of American life.

The 42nd Parallel (1930), the first part, introduces us to Fainy McCreary, a labour leader who becomes compromised by marriage, and J. Ward Moorhouse, a successful public relations consultant whose chief mission is to heal the breach between capital and labour. Mac represents, as do the numerous other union organisers, the agitating and therefore divisive forces in injustice-ridden pre-war America, and much of this first book is taken up with attempts to precipitate revolution by the I.W.W. In this context, J. Ward Moorhouse represents the cohesive, and therefore reactionary, forces. The social origins of the two are not dissimilar, but their destinies have been shaped by different social conditions. We also meet two of the women in Moorhouse's life: the designer Eleanor Stoddard who becomes his friend, and Janey Williams his secretary. The fifth of the twelve, Charley Anderson, who as an aviation mechanic is later to represent the knowledge, skill and inventiveness on which industry is based, is introduced at the end.

Nineteen Nineteen (1932), the second part, takes us into the war years, with America coming in 'to save the Morgan loans'. Much of the story centres on the anti-war movement—the cynicism and depravity of the liberal intellectuals who are serving with the American Red Cross (as exemplified by the Harvard-educated Richard Ellsworth Savage), and the victimisation of the left-wing agitators at home (represented by the Jewish boy Ben Compton, previously glimpsed in the first part). Savage irresponsibly takes his own toll of human life, seducing and then deserting the young Texan relief-worker Anne Elizabeth French ('Daughter') who fatally persuades a drunken French pilot to take her flying in a suspect craft. A large section of the narrative is assigned to Janey Williams's brother Joe, whose wearisome struggle to better himself in the merchant navy never gets off the ground, with the social gulf between brother and sister constantly widening; and whose ignominious death in a drunken brawl counterpoints, as does Anne Elizabeth's, the tragic futility of the deaths at the front. At the peace treaty Moorhouse and his entourage—now extended to include Eveline Hutchins, previously introduced as Eleanor Stoddard's partner and friend—are much in evidence. We see Eveline undone by Moorhouse's boyish charm, but she eventually stakes her near-desperate hopes of happiness on a marriage to an inexperienced and idealistic boy. The second part ends with a bitter 'biography' of an unknown soldier, 'The Body of an American'.

The Big Money (1936) takes us into the post-war era, with fortunes made and lost on the stock exchange and the stark contradictions of unbridled capitalism. The chief character throughout the greater part of the novel is Charley Anderson whose wartime experiences as an aviator have made him potentially a valuable asset to the new industry. But first we see him as a member of the great army of unemployed ex-war heroes, socially celebrated but economically redundant. Eventually the extrepreneurs exploit his productive capacity, and he finds a reasonably comfortable niche. However, he acquires their habit of pursuing wealth on the stock market, and the spectacular rise in his fortunes is followed by an equally dramatic collapse. Meanwhile, he has a series of unsatisfactory relationships with the women of the economic class into which his success has brought him, and the combination of personal unhappiness and financial misfortune drive him to more and more heavy drinking and reckless driving, which culminate in his fatal collision with a train on a level crossing.

This final part of the trilogy has also introduced us to the last two of its twelve main characters, the future film star Margo Dowling and the social worker and future union organiser Mary French. The fortuitous rise of the orphaned Margo from obscurity to Hollywood stardom counterpoints Anderson's career; while Mary French serves as a focus for the agony of the underprivileged, in their struggles for a better deal, and of the fragmenting but always heroic left-wing groups. Towards the end we meet again the Red Cross set from *1919*, the total waste of their lives contrasting with the well-nigh hopeless work of the indomitable Mary.

By 1936 Dos Passos's disenchantment with the revolutionaries was such as to make him vote for Roosevelt and the New Deal. He went to Spain but left when he found that the communists had taken control of the Republican side. His next three novels—subsequently loosely grouped as a Roosevelt-era trilogy entitled *District of Columbia*—are broadly concerned with communist perfidy in the labour movement (*Adventures of a Young Man*, 1937), corruption in American politics (*Number One*,

1943; based on the Louisiana dictator Huey Long), and the sell-out to international communism in the treaties that ended the second world war (*The Grand Design*, 1947). But neither in these nor in the subsequent group—of which the most ambitious is *Midcentury* (1961)—is there the same singleness of vision that makes the earlier novels memorable.

K. R. R.

Douglas, Lloyd C. (1877–1951), American clergyman who became a popular novelist when over fifty, is best known for *The Robe* (1942), a dramatic story about the robe of Jesus, for which the Roman soldiers cast lots. Its successor, *The Big Fisherman* (1948), about St Peter, was also widely read.

K. R. R.

Douglas, [George] Norman (1868–1952), English author of travel books, essays, novels—works difficult to classify yet so distinctive and outrageous in their implications that he has always aroused strong reactions in his readers and critics. He is erudite yet wears his learning effortlessly; his books on Mediterranean countries, *Siren Land* (1911) and *Old Calabria* (1915), contain such a wealth of information on the language, idioms, customs, history and the personality of the people that they make some other descriptions of the same areas seem the thin and undigested observations of amateurs. The best known of his three novels *South Wind* (1917) puts an Anglican bishop returning from a dispiriting diocese in Africa on the balmy Mediterranean island of Nepenthe, inhabited by exiles, eccentrics and exotics. He finds there every kind of amorality and immorality, all of which are described with the tongue-in-cheek style of a fable. Douglas shocks more with his asides, and with his and his bishop's acceptance of such goings-on, than with any controversial avowals. Douglas stands for, as far as one can make out, an aristocratic tradition of excellence, reticence, beauty, privilege and individuality; he is against Christianity, puritanism, morality, social levelling (he felt it would always be downward), caution and moderation.

His other titles include *Fountains in the Sand* (1912), *Alone* (1921), *Together* (1923), which are travel books; *They Went* (1921) and *In the Beginning* (1927), novels; and the autobiographical essays *Paneros* (1931) and *Looking Back* (1933).

S. R.

Doyle, Sir Arthur Conan (1859–1930), English novelist and short-story writer. Doyle's best-known creation is essentially a nineteenth-century figure although a large number of Sherlock Holmes adventures were published in the early twentieth century. The analytical intelligence which the famous detective employs in his deductive methods was based on the personality of Dr Joseph Bell under whom Doyle had worked as a surgeon. Holmes was introduced to the public in *A Study in Scarlet* (1882) and a number of subsequent stories appeared in the *Strand Magazine*. The author tried to kill off the detective in *The Memoirs of Sherlock Holmes* (1894), but his popularity with the reading public led to his resurrection. Further Holmes stories include *The Return of Sherlock Holmes* (1905), *The Hound of the Baskervilles* (1902), *His Last Bow* (1917) and *The Casebook of Sherlock Holmes* (1927). The attraction of Doyle's hero is essentially contained in the simple logic he applies with clarity to seemingly bizarre and unconnected aspects of human behaviour to produce in the end a credible pattern of events. Holmes believed that if one eliminated the absolutely impossible one was necessarily left with the incredible but true.

Science fiction owes a great deal to the adventures of Professor Challenger who combines a logic similar to Holmes with animal energy and personal dogmatism. *The Lost World* (1912) takes Challenger and a small party of explorers into the jungle to find a plateau containing the last survivors of the prehistoric period, both animal and near-human. *The Poison Belt* (1913) is one of the first science-fiction novels to plunge the earth into apparent disaster as it passes through a cloud of poison gas in space. The world survives—with the aid of Challenger's logical mind. D. L. P.

Drabble, Margaret (1939–), English novelist who explores with astringent wit and great insight the reactions of the intelligent young woman to love, marriage and child-bearing—familiar enough territory but appearing fresh and new in her hands. In *The Garrick Year* (1964) she describes the growth to a certain peace and maturity of an actor's wife, mother of two small children, forced to spend a season in a provincial town, and similarly in *The Millstone* (1965) that of a girl Rosamund, pregnant and unmarried, who goes through with having her child. Later titles include *Jerusalem the Golden* (1967). S. R.

Dreiser, Theodore (1871–1945), American novelist, was one of the first American writers to depart from the genteel proprieties of nineteenth-century fiction, and he saw his first book *Sister Carrie* (1900) virtually withdrawn through the moral objections of the publisher's wife to a plot which allowed a 'fallen' woman to end up happy and unpunished. Like his first heroine, Dreiser came to Chicago from a small middle-western town: like her, he experienced both the reality of poverty and the appeal of wealth, and in his subsequent novels the contrast between penury and affluence is frequently in evidence. Some readers are irritated by the unevenness of his style and the occasional inconsistencies in his plots; but the imperfections of his literary craftsmanship are compensated by the power of his narratives.

The grinding poverty of the Hansons, with whom their sister Carrie lodges when she comes to Chicago, and the arduous and dispiriting manual labour with which Carrie earns herself a pittance, constitute a situation from which her liberation by the amiable salesman Drouet is seen more as a rescue than a seduction. She has not been living long with him when she begins to be courted, with mounting passion, by Drouet's friend, the prosperous club-manager Hurstwood, a man who in material terms has everything he could wish but whose relationship with his wife and children is totally devoid of any deep feeling. Aware of this emotional vacuum he lets himself be carried away by his infatuation with Carrie; and when, having discovered that her wooer has a wife and has deceived her, she refuses to see him again, he forcibly abducts her, at the same time embezzling money so that he can start a new life with her somewhere else. They end up in New York, under a new name; but disillusion is not long in setting in, and when in a new environment Hurstwood finds he lacks the capital to repeat his business success, he sinks into a decline. Meanwhile Carrie launches out on a career on the stage, and the book ends with her looking beyond her new-found affluence to the possibility of a higher set of values—values, it is implied, that become feasible once material welfare is secured. For Hurstwood, however, the ending is an ignominious suicide after a period of abject poverty in which he has degenerated into a bum.

The disaster that overtook the first edition of *Sister Carrie* was the beginning of a decade during which Dreiser wrote very little indeed, and which saw him sink into almost Hurstwood-like poverty and despair. The partial recognition which followed its republication by another publisher in 1907 spurred him to new efforts, the chief result of which was his successful second novel *Jennie Gerhardt* (1911): a story with a similar pattern to its predecessor, with Jennie, a personality of rather greater depth than Carrie, being made pregnant by a senator who subsequently dies.

There followed a period of great activity, during which Dreiser developed the fictional genre of the 'business novel' by which he is most generally known. His years in the economic wilderness had, if anything, increased his fascination for the world of business and finance, and he was now to endow a series of business heroes with the proportions of the popes and potentates of the renaissance—or, in *The 'Genius'* (1915), with the calibre of an artist. His most important creation of the period is the character of Cowperwood, first encountered in *The Financier* (1912), and again in

The Titan (1914). Dreiser was subsequently to build these two novels into a trilogy, but the third part was unfinished when he died.

However, perhaps Dreiser's most enduring work is *An American Tragedy* (1925) which appeared after a spate of comparatively less important works and was the first to raise a question mark over the idea of the business hero. If the successful careerist is the hero, what of the careerist who fails? And as for that saving lack of superfine moral scruples, that necessary degree of amorality which is a prerequisite for the emergence of the post-Jamesian type of business hero: where does one draw the line between what is permissible and what is not? And, finally, what kind of judgment must one pass on a society in which the perfectly natural and laudable urge to escape from poverty can be so inflamed by that society's inequalities, and so perverted by its materialism, that a young person will stop at nothing—literally nothing—to achieve worldly success? The penniless Clyde Griffiths, in the raw material of his own nature, is no better and no worse than Carrie Meeber: that he will murder the pregnant girl he once loved, rather than see his carefully built-up but still precarious social position (with his virtual engagement to a beautiful heiress as its lynch-pin) collapse overnight, is a condemnation of the society that makes such things as social and economic status a matter of life and death. With ironical appropriateness, that society duly condemns him: to the electric chair. That, given a little luck, Clyde might never have been found out—in which case, his worldly success would have been assured—gives this already compelling and almost unendurably painful book a richness of implication that transcends the occasional clumsiness of its narrative and the gaucheness of its dialogue.

Dreiser's later titles included the posthumously published *The Bulwark* (1946) and *The Stoic* (1947), the unfinished third part of the Cowperwood trilogy.

K. R. R.

Drummond de Andrade, Carlos (1902–), Brazilian poet, born in Itabira (Minas Gerais). He was educated at Belo Horizonte and Friburgo and graduated in pharmacy. His chequered career included teaching and journalism and after he moved to Rio de Janeiro in 1933 he joined the staff of the Patrimônio Histórico e Artístico Nacional ('National Trust of History and Art'). He began to write poetry as a member of the *modernista* group which sprang up in Minas Gerais around 1925.

His first book of poems, *Alguma poesia* ['Some poetry'], appeared in 1930. His technique aims at simplicity of statement, objective descriptions without commentary and detached observation of the world around him. But his verse also carries a note of indecision, sometimes vaguely humorous, cautious or even gauche. In *Brejo das almas* ['Swamp of souls'] (1943) his mood is generally pessimistic. Life is something dark and anguished and humanity shares this fate. The poet searches for a path of escape; he is filled with sudden impulse and the determination to break the bonds of his misery—or perish.

The climate changes in *Sentimento do mundo* ['Feeling for the world'] (1940) where the poet, faced by deaths, war and collective destruction, is filled with remorse. He must consolidate his efforts with those of his fellow-creatures and share their sufferings in their fight with injustice and cruelty. Only then can men hope for a better world. Drummond de Andrade develops this theme of human solidarity further in his *Poesias* ['Poems'] (1942) alongside reminiscences of his childhood, his family and his native city.

Political and social preoccupations are frequently voiced in the poems of *A rosa do povo* ['The rose of the people'] (1945) and *Poesia até agora* ['Poetry until now'] (1947) but the poet is careful not to sacrifice artistic expression to versified propaganda. This sense of mission persists in *Claro enigma* ['Bright enigma'] (1951) and *Fazendeiro do ar* ['Planter of the air'] (1954) but the mood is generally more tranquil. Odd moments of irritation, despair, and guilt reappear, but the spectacle of the world now '*pede ser visto e amado*' ('asks to be seen and loved') and the poet reaches a new understanding of the world and himself.

Translations of his poetry are available in the Dudley Fitts *Anthology of Contemporary Latin-American Poetry* (1942) and in selections of *Modern Brazilian Poetry* edited by Leonard S. Dounes (1954) and John Nist (1962). Drummond de Andrade is also the author of numerous chronicles, essays and short stories. G. P.

Drury, Allen (1918–), American novelist, for many years a Washington correspondent, is best known for his evocation of the personal and public drama of American political life in his Pulitzer prizewinner *Advise and Consent* (1959). Later titles include *That Summer* (1965) and *Capable of Honour* (1967). K. R. R.

Dudintsev, Vladimir (1918–), Soviet writer, was born into an intellectual and musical household and at an early age demonstrated his literary talent. He resisted being absorbed into the approved literary circles, but nevertheless was not antagonistic to the Soviet system. After the war he wrote for *Komsomolskaya Pravda* and in 1955 he began writing his most famous novel *Ne khlebom yedinim* [*Not by Bread Alone*] (1956). It described the struggle of individualism against oppressive and stultifying officialdom. The characters of the book are not particularly well drawn; and the problem is not really resolved at the end, for although the individual inventor Lopatkin triumphs, the bureaucratic Drozdov and his kind are still left holding the managerial reins of power. The theme is repeated in his short fantasy *Novogodnaya skazka* [*A New Year's Tale*] (1960), which is filled with political significance. Dudintsev's early ideals of selfless devotion to the good are illustrated, but he was sharply criticised in official circles even though Khrushchev himself overtly supported him. His works represent a landmark in the development of the Soviet novel and a continuation of the traditions of pre-revolutionary literature.

B. W.

Duffy, Maureen (1933–), English novelist whose treatment of human relationships embraces a celebrative earthiness, a reverence for the emotionally intimate, and a sharp eye (though less reliable ear) for the often-sordid social setting. The much acclaimed *That's How it Was* (1962) was followed by *The Single Eye* (1964), in which the life-history of a young photographer's artistically paralysing love for a destructive neurotic, and his eventual escape into a creative relationship with his brother's wife, is underpinned by a religio-biological philosophy derived from Teilhard de Chardin. A third novel, *The Paradox Players*, was published in 1967.

K. R. R.

Duggan, Alfred (1903–64), English historical novelist, the son of a rich Irish-Argentinian, and stepson of Lord Curzon. Duggan was brought up in a patrician atmosphere and dissipated a large fortune. In 1924 he sailed to the South Seas on a natural history expedition and later travelled extensively in Greece and Turkey where he took part in excavations at Constantine's palace in Istanbul. Having fought as a private soldier in World War II he published his first book *Knight with Armour* (1950) at the age of forty-seven. This described the First Crusade through the eyes of a young pilgrim. He returned to this period of history many times in his later novels, and his last book *Count Bohemond* (1964) continues the story of Bohemond I, Prince of Antioch whose story began in *Knight with Armour*. While his writings are basically serious, they contain a rich humour and are sometimes very funny, notably *Family Favourites* (1960). His characters behave recognisably, and romance and accuracy are enhanced, never obscured, by his religious conviction, ironic wit and impersonal style. His other titles include *Conscience of the King* (1951),

Devil's Brood (1957), *God and My Right* (1955) and *Leopards and Lilies* (1960). He also wrote several historical stories for children including *Growing Up in the Thirteenth Century* (1962). H. C.; K. M. H.

Duhamel, Georges (1884–), French novelist. Georges Duhamel belongs to the generation which made of the years 1920–40 'a golden age of the novel'. Duhamel was not, however, to start with a literary profession. He was a military surgeon during the first world war. This inculcated in him a profound compassion for man and hatred for all that disfigured him. He was also a lover of poetry, the theatre and music. So in Duhamel's work we find a continual attempt to reconcile realism and idealism, the struggle between man's desire for correct action and mental and moral equilibrium and the powerful material forces that oppose this. His early works *Vie des martyrs* [*New Book of Martyrs*] (1917) and *Civilisation* [*Civilization*] (1918) denounce the murderous violence of the 1914–18 war; while *Scènes de la vie future* [*America: the Menace*] (1930) condemns the slaughterhouses of Chicago. Together with *La Possession du monde* [*Possession of the World*] (1919) these works constitute a literature of action, humanism, vigilant pacifism, command over machine civilisation, the defence of culture—the whole expressed with powerful conviction. These were an excellent preparation for Duhamel's life work which is contained in two novel cycles: *Salavin* [*Salavin*] (1920–32) and *La Chronique des Pasquier* [*The Pasquier Chronicles*] (1933–41).

The Salavin series is composed of the following novels: *La Confession de minuit* [*Confession at Midnight*] (1920), *Deux Hommes* [*Two Men*] (1924), *Journal de Salavin* [*Salavin's Journal*] (1927), *Le Club de Lyonnais* [*The Lyonnais Club*] (1929), and *Tel qu'en lui-même* [*End of Illusion*] (1932). Salavin is employed by a pasteurised milk firm. His job is therefore utterly commonplace and he would like to pull himself out of it, out of his background and out of himself. But he is constantly, grievously and ironically aware of a sense of failure. Whatever he does, he will never be able to change. Whatever his illusions and vain calls for help, he will always remain the same, likeable in his congenital weakness. 'The fault, dear Brutus, lies not in our stars, but in ourselves, that we are underlings.'

The Pasquier Chronicles is made up of ten volumes: *Le Notaire du Havre* [*News from Havre*] (1933), *Le Jardin des bêtes sauvages* [*Caged Beasts*] (1934), *Vue de la terre promise* [*The Sight of the Promised Land*] (1934), *La Nuit de la Saint-Jean* [*St John's Eve*] (1935), *Le Désert de Bièvres* [*The House in the Desert*] (1936), *Les Maîtres* [*Pastors and Masters*]

(1937), *Cecile parmi nous* [*Cecile*] (1938), *Le Combat contre les ombres* [*The Fight against the Shadows*] (1939), *Suzanne et les jeunes hommes* [*Suzanne and the Young Men*] (1941) and *La Passion de Joseph Pasquier* [*The Passion of Joseph Pasquier*] (1941). The form of this immense novel is the journal of the doctor and biologist Laurent Pasquier. It is basically autobiographical, but around this central character it builds up a broad picture of a society in crisis. The social and psychological envelope to this personal tale is very rich. The great problem of the relations between science and humanism is perhaps the central theme of the whole.

A. L. W.

Du Maurier, Daphne (1907–   ), English novelist, daughter of the actor Gerald Du Maurier. Her first novel *The Loving Spirit* appeared in 1931, but it was with *Jamaica Inn* (1936), a colourful story about smuggling, that she achieved popular success. Then in 1938 came what is probably her most famous novel, *Rebecca.* This romantic novel, set like so many of her novels in Cornwall, has all the ingredients of a best seller, with its brooding Gothic atmosphere, rich and moody hero and shy penniless heroine.

Her later novels *Hungry Hill* (1943) and *The King's General* (1946) were less well received but she returned to the successful formula of *Rebecca* for *My Cousin Rachel* (1951). Subsequent titles include *The Flight of the Falcon* (1965). She has also written two interesting family studies, *Gerald* (1934) and *The Du Mauriers* (1937), and two of her plays *The Years Between* (1945) and *September Tide* (1948) have been produced with great success.

K. M. H.

Dumitriu, Petru (1924–   ), Rumanian novelist. His father was a Rumanian army officer, his mother a member of the Hungarian provincial nobility; he published his first book in 1945 after studying philosophy at Munich, won the State Prize for Literature in 1949, 1952 and 1954, on the third occasion with *Pasărea furtunii* [*Stormy Petrel*] (1954), became the director of the State Publishing House, Bucharest, and then in 1960 while on a cultural mission defected to the west. He now lives in Germany.

Family Jewels and *The Prodigals* are the abridged translations of the first two books of *Cronică de familie* (1956–57), not technically a trilogy but a long novel in three volumes, none of which bears an individual title in the original. The first deals with the period 1862–1907. The Coziano family, wealthy boyars enviably well endowed with vices and the means of their gratification, typify the amoral ruling class of that epoch; unscrupulous hedonists, implacable in their reactionary politics, insatiable in their self-indulgence, inexorable in their demands on a desperate peasantry. Readers of Rebreanu's *The Uprising* will appreciate their mentality, shared by Nadina, and the insurrection of 1907 which temporarily restrained them. Similarly, enthusiasts of Olivia Manning's Balkan novels should read the *The Prodigals*, a narrative covering the events of 1914–44, the years of Madame Lupescu and her king, the Iron Guard and fascism, the German occupation and, finally, the arrival of the Russians, when 'all that mattered was to be on the winning side, even if it meant starting again at the beginning'. Some ideological gymnasts succeeded, many lacked the necessary agility, a few were sufficiently limber but declined to perform the more humiliating feats deemed obligatory by the new dispensation. Two works comparable in their verve and ambition to the most celebrated examinations of the modern political conscience, *Rendez-vous au jugement dernier* [*Meeting at the Last Judgement*] (1961) and *Incognito* [*Incognito*] (1962), which is not the third part of *Cronică de familie* as is generally believed, study the genesis of their refusal and its retribution. Entitled in the original Rumanian, respectively, *Întâlnire la judecata din urmă* and *Incognito*, both remain unpublished in that language. Sebastian, the hero of the latter, is told by his time-serving brother, 'The West doesn't exist any more! They're spiritually devastated, impoverished and dehumanised. There's nothing left but a technological, economic and biological superstructure. . . . They're an empty shell. . . .' *L'Extrême Occident* [*Westward Lies Heaven*] (1964), another extraordinarily dextrous assessment of contemporary mythology, written in French not Rumanian, is Dumitriu's initial appraisal of the carapace. A further novel, *Le Sourire sarde* ['The Sardinian smile'], appeared in 1967. M. D. E.

Duncan, Ronald (1914–   ), English poet, dramatist, essayist and journalist, with an experience of farming, has been described as a combination of poet and peasant largely because his work draws strength from a close connection with the earthy world of nature and from an apparent sympathy with ordinary, fallible and simple people—qualities to be found for instance in his essays for the *Evening Standard*, published in *The Blue Fox* (1951).

Other examples of his work more notable for their artistic sophistication include *The Eagle has Two Heads* (1946), a play adapted from the French of Jean Cocteau, and *The Rape of Lucretia* (1946), a libretto for the opera by Benjamin Britten. The play *Stratton* (1948), again with music by Britten, is fatalistic and almost mystical in its approach to human destiny. Stratton, killing those whom he has loved, and himself tortured by his own personality, closes the play with a vision of man as 'both crucified and crucifier', and as a desert on which he calls down the rain of Christ's compassion.

Volumes of Duncan's poems include *The Solitude and Other Poems* (1960). An autobiography *All Men are Islands* was published in 1964.

D. L. P.

Dundy, Elaine (1927–), American novelist whose first novel *The Dud Avocado* (1958), the high-spirited story of a young girl in Paris, was extremely successful. Her second, *The Old Man and Me* (1964), is a wise-cracking account of a gold-digging American girl's pursuit of a wealthy, elderly Englishman. P. E.

Dunne, Peter Finlay (1867–1936), American humorist, was the creator of 'Mr Dooley', a Chicago-Irish saloon-keeper who comments and philosophises on day-to-day affairs. *Mr Dooley in Peace and War* (1898) and succeeding volumes were originally written as journalistic pieces. Dunne's 'informal memoirs' *Mr Dooley Remembers* (1963) were edited by his son Philip. K. R. R.

Dunsany, Lord (Edward John Plunkett; 1878–1957), Irish dramatist, helped to found the Abbey Theatre, where his play *The Glittering Gates* (1909) was produced by Yeats. He wrote a number of successful one-act plays in the years that followed. K. R. R.

Duras, Marguerite (1914–), French writer. She studied law before establishing herself as a novelist in the early 1940s. The difficulty of reconciling her popularity to the limited appeal of the 'new novel' has encouraged allegations of opportunism and stylistic insincerity, but a comparison of her later, better-known work with even the relatively untypical *Un Barrage contre le Pacifique* [*A Sea of Troubles* or *The Sea Wall*] (1950), a sombre story of frustrated colonial endeavour in French Indo-China where she was born, is sufficient to vindicate her consistency and integrity. She is a cartographer of those accidental meetings, usually on hot boring Mediterranean holidays with wives, husbands, children or the past in obtrusive attendance, which provoke the banal germination and maturation of passion. Certain traits, the skilful evocation of place and atmosphere, the deft substitution of external violence, a murder or fatal accident, for psychological motivation, syncopated dialogue for explicatory narrative, recur in the principal plays, novels and scenarios: *Le Marin de Gibraltar* [*The Sailor from Gibraltar*] (1952), *Les Petits Chevaux de Tarquinia* [*The Little Horses of Tarquinia*] (1953), *Le Square* [*The Square*] (1955), *Moderato* *cantabile* [*Moderato Cantabile*] (1958), *Dix heures et demie du soir en été* [*10.30 on a Summer Night*] (1960), *Une aussi Longue Absence* [*Une Aussi Longue Absence*] (1961), *L'Après-midi de Monsieur Andesmas* [*The Afternoon of Monsieur Andesmas*] (1962) and her finest achievement, the magnificent film script *Hiroshima mon amour* [*Hiroshima, Mon Amour*] (1961); but the singularity and distinction of Mme Duras' approach consists in her attitude to time, which she regards as the vital protagonist, the dramatic catalyst and crucible, not as an inert problem of technique.

Later titles include *Le Ravissement de Lol V. Stein* [*The Rapture of Lol V. Stein*] (1964), *Le Vice-consul* ['The vice-consul'] (1966) and *L'Amante anglaise* ['The English girl-friend'] (1967). M. D. E.

Durrell, Gerald (1925–), English writer about animals, the brother of Lawrence Durrell, is an animal-collector and zoologist. Born in India, he lived between the ages of ten and fifteen on the island of Corfu where he kept many local animals as pets. This experience is recounted with great perception and charm in *My Family and Other Animals* (1956). Other titles include *The Overloaded Ark* (1952) and *Menagerie Manor* (1964). G. C.

Durrell, Lawrence (1912–), English poet, novelist and 'travel writer', is most celebrated today for the four novels that comprise his *Alexandria Quartet* (1957–60). The fame of this monumental work rapidly dwarfed his previous modest reputation as the author of the banned Milleresque *Black Book* (Paris, 1938), the highly praised poetry volume *Cities, Plains and People* (1946) and the three very readable if lightweight Mediterranean island portraits—*Prospero's Cell* (1945), *Portrait of a Marine Venus* (1953) and *Bitter Lemons* (1957) portraying respectively Corfu, Rhodes and Cyprus.

His newly acquired status as a major writer led to the first publication in the English-speaking world (New York, 1960) of *The Black Book*, a highly personal and often well-nigh unintelligible work which is important both as an account of a spiritual journey, and as a technical precursor of his later *magnum opus*. Durrell had come to England at the age of eleven after a childhood spent in view of the Himalayan peaks; he abandoned it in his mid-twenties to settle in the Mediterranean world that was to inspire the bulk of his mature work. Working through the metaphor of continuous physical journeying, *The Black Book* records the psychological odyssey that had ended with his resurrection from 'the English death', from the hypocrisy and prudery, the cold, the dark and the damp, of 'that mean, shabby little island'. The reader is constantly reminded of Henry

Miller, with whom Durrell had struck up a warm personal friendship; but there is also much—even in the bizarre accounts of the variegated eroticism to be found blooming in the dismal wilderness of south London—that marks out the originality of the author's mind.

The period of the war years and the decade that followed saw Durrell first as a teacher of English in Greece, and then as a member of the diplomatic corps, a rôle which he continued to fill (and which allowed him limited time for writing) for most of the next decade, providing him with the material for his spy thriller *White Eagles over Serbia* and the humorous *Esprit de Corps* (both 1957, the same year in which he published both his first Alexandrian novel and his third island-portrait). It was also a period packed with important personal events and relationships: divorce from his first wife (Nancy), his second and third marriages (Eve and Claude), and the birth of two children. Both his public and private life, as well as the environment in which they were set, were preparing him for the vast literary complex he was to create in the years that followed.

Much has been said, both by Durrell himself and by his critics, about the structure of the quartet—*Justine* (1957), *Balthazar* (1958), *Mountolive* (1958) and *Clea* (1960)—and about the philosophical basis of its technique. It has been said by some that his application to fiction of the Einsteinian ideas of relativity and the space-time continuum amounts to little more than the presentation of the same nexus of events and flux of relationships from four different standpoints: but it is undoubtedly Durrell's contention that there cannot even be any absolute truth—any more than one's position in the physical universe, or any physical motion within it, can be given an absolute definition. It can be argued that the physical death of the necromancer Capodistria (reported in *Justine*, disproved in *Clea*) either did or did not take place: but a man's purely physical death is as much a partial truth as any of the 'selected fictions' by which all the characters live. *Mountolive* does in fact give an 'objective', historian's account of the events, creating a truth which is just as relative as those of the other three. It must be added that no observer can obtain a detached picture, since he himself is part of that picture, exerting his own influence on it and being at the same time influenced by it: this being equally true in Einsteinian physics and Durrell's fiction. Any observer distorts the fields of influence that radiate from and between the phenomena he is observing, like a man trying to read a compass with a magnet in his pocket. The Einsteinian concept of the space-time continuum—with its three dimensions of space and one of time—led Durrell to deploy his material both spatially (in the first three books) and temporally (in *Clea*). Each novel contains different configurations of the matter that is common to all of them: and it is suggested at the end that any number of additional volumes could be written, starting from different 'workpoints'—the focal points potentially infinite in number in his four-dimensional continuum of human life.

It will be clear from the foregoing structural analysis that any attempt to give an outline of the quartet in linear fashion is impossible. If, however, one looks at the development in the character of the narrator—the writer Darley, whose initials are significantly L. D.—it is possible to say that the quartet traces his emotional education and its preparation of him for the rôle of the artist. In the first book all his experiences and observations are related to his love affair with Justine, the enigmatic Jewish wife of the Coptic aristocrat Nessim: anything mysterious in the latter's behaviour, for instance, being attributed to his membership of the religio-philosophical Cabal or to his suspicions of his wife's infidelity. In the second book, we see Darley's version of the events corrected by an interlinear written by Balthazar, a doctor, also a member of the Cabal: Justine it seems was merely using Darley as a decoy while she was the infatuated mistress of the writer Pursewarden, now dead. In the third, 'historical' book, dominated by the personality of Mountolive, the English ambassador, we see Nessim and Justine hand-in-glove in a political intrigue, their marital relationship fired by their shared adventure, with Justine cold-bloodedly exploiting her English contacts. Finally, we see Darley's return visit to Alexandria, its centre of gravity now provided by his relationship with the artist Clea, in which he tries to find the truth about Justine, about his relationship with her, hers with Pursewarden and her marriage with Nessim, and learns instead—through the writings of the dead Pursewarden—the nature of truth. His experiences, and his progressive understanding of them, have made it possible for him to have a more satisfactory relationship with Clea, the other character whose emotional education can be traced: and the latter's new-found maturity as a painter matches Darley's coming-of-age as a writer.

Darley's and Clea's preparation has consisted in erotic experiences, and the quartet can be viewed as a panorama of sexual experience. To the many gradations of heterosexual eroticism—from the romantic-idealistic to the purely physical—are added rape, incest, male homosexuality, lesbianism, child-prostitution and transvestism. Durrell's Alexandrians, a people of mixed Mediterranean (predominantly Levantine) stock, are driven to lurid, soul-tormenting extremes of sexuality by the extremities that are of the very nature of the city itself and of its climate. True, sex is for Durrell (as for Miller) the most important of all human activities: but the key point here is that it is through the extremes (sometimes ecstatic, more often agonising) of sexual experience that true understanding is born—of oneself, of others, and of life in general. For Durrell, there is no category of sexual behaviour that is intrinsically good or bad: the quartet's chief positive values emerging as the brave honesty and the equally brave tenderness which make possible the warm vital human relationships that alone can resurrect a man from the deadly solipsism of *The Black Book.*

The reader who is not put off the quartet by the seaminess of the early part of Justine (perhaps half-intended to shock the more squeamish Anglo-Saxon reader) will be rewarded by a feast of exotic poetry, human drama and intellectual pyrotechnics. Whether all this adds up to the timeless masterpiece that the Durrell addicts claim it to be—or whether, like his next work *Tunc* (1968), it comes to be praised chiefly for its technical virtuosity—time alone will tell. K. R. R.

Dürrenmatt, Friedrich (1921–), Swiss-German dramatist, born into a religious family. His early studies were in art and architecture, but he never completed his university career and from the age of twenty-four turned to writing for a living. As a Swiss-German he had avoided close personal contact with the war and could look with some detachment on the post-war scene; writing in German he found his public obviously outside Switzerland, and he began his literary career at a time when very few creative writers were being produced by Germany itself. In 1947 he married an actress, Lotti Giessler, and that same year produced his first play *Es steht geschrieben* [*It is Written*]. Since then he has concentrated on the drama, both for the theatre and the radio. His international reputation was established with the production of *Die Ehe des Herrn Mississippi* [*The Marriage of Mr Mississippi*] (1952), but he is probably most famous in England as the author of *Die Physiker* [*The Physicists*] (1962) and *Der Besuch der alten Dame* [*The Visit*] (1956). In the latter play, a rich elderly woman returns to the town from which she had been hounded as a girl because of an affair with a man who still lives there. Gradually, by playing on the cupidity of the townsfolk, she wins them over to her side in a monstrous plot to avenge herself on her seducer. *The Physicists* is set in the closed atmosphere of a lunatic asylum where three physicists stay voluntarily, feigning madness, each from different motives. Mobius, for example, who pretends to receive revelation from King Solomon, prefers the asylum because only there can he pursue research in freedom. His research is crowned by complete success, but his findings are absolutely dangerous for mankind.

Son of a pastor as he is, there is little Christian optimism present in Dürrenmatt's work. He concentrates on the extreme situation and persuades us that life is impersonal and cruel; and indeed supernatural beings can do nothing to alleviate the human condition. *Ein Engel kommt nach Babylon* [*An Angel comes to Babylon*] (1953) is an ironic parable, because the Angel brings not peace, but a sword, creating chaos wherever he passes. But his work is not defeatist; however stark the message may be, Dürrenmatt implies constantly that faced with such a life, man must continue to assert himself against the cruel pressures of life itself.

Amongst his prose-fiction is to be found one noteworthy novel, *Das Versprechen* [*The Pledge*] (1958). G. W.

Durych, Jaroslav (1886–1962), Czech writer. An army surgeon by profession, Durych combined naturalism with mysticism in his historical novels which are often situated in the baroque period. His monumental novel on Wallenstein (*Bloudění*, 1929) was published in an abridged English version under the title *The Descent of the Idol* (1935). K. B.

Dyson, Edward (1865–1931), Australian balladist and short-story writer, dealt mainly with life in the Ballarat goldfields, and later in urban factory settings. Representative of his work are the collections *Below and On Top* (1898), later reissued as *The Golden Shanty* (1929); and *Fact'ry 'Ands* (1906). S. R.

E

Eberhart, Richard (1904–   ), American poet. Like Wallace Stevens, Eberhart has had a successful career in business as well as in teaching and writing. This duality is instanced by his becoming vice-president of a wax and polish company in 1946 and a consultant in poetry to the Library of Congress between 1956 and 1961.

Eberhart's poetry, contained in most anthologies of American literature, while academic and intellectual is also imaginative, and sometimes macabre. He is fond of extending from the object of perception and description to universal statements about the nature of man. His philosophy is saved from an over-intellectual dryness by a delicate sense of rhythm and an imaginative command of metaphor. Much of his work is contained in *Collected Poems 1930–1960* (1960). D. L. P.

Echegaray, José (1832–1916), Spanish nineteenth-century dramatist deservedly forgotten by posterity, was joint winner of the 1904 Nobel Prize for Literature. A leading engineer and politician, Echegaray wrote of death, dishonour and tragic madness. The tragedies *O locura o santidad* [*Madman or Saint*] (1877) and *El gran galeoto* [*The World and His Wife*] (1881) exemplify his high-pitched melodramatic romanticism. D. H. G.

Edelman, Maurice (1911–   ), English writer, and a Labour M.P. since 1945. His first book *Birth of the 4th Republic* appeared in 1945 but it is for his novels that he is best known. In *Who Goes Home* (1953) he drew on his knowledge as an M.P. to recreate the atmosphere of the House of Commons. Most of his novels have a political background and in *Fratricides* (1963) he wove his story around the troubled times in Algeria. His other works include *The Minister* (1961), *Shark Island* (1967) and a biography *Ben Gurion* (1965). K. M. H.

Egbuna, Obi B. (1938–   ), Nigerian novelist, essayist and playwright of great potential. His novel *Wind Versus Polygamy* (1964) achieved success in its dramatised form, and his published play *The Anthill* (1965) is a compelling (though wordy), almost surrealistic play about the relationship between an African student and an English ex-soldier. C. P.

Ehrenburg, Ilya Grigorievich (1891–1967), prominent Soviet poet and novelist, was born into a middle-class Jewish family in Kiev. He was educated in Moscow, then lived many years abroad especially in France, and was one of the few Soviet writers to possess a good inside knowledge of the western way of life.

Ehrenburg began his literary career with verse that was frankly imitative of French models. He had a very devious political career, but usually managed to be on the right side. During the Spanish civil war he was a Russian newspaper correspondent, and in 1945 he went to the United States; he was actually in Paris when the Germans began their advance during World War II and his book *Padeniye Parizha* [*The Fall of Paris*] (1941), his most ambitious work, displays despite its overt political message a deep sympathy for the French. As he grew older, Ehrenburg realised that an artist had to be true to his conscience and so began to advocate very firmly more creative freedom. His novels *Ottepel* [*Thaw*] (1954) and *Vyesna* [*Spring*] (1956) with their symbolic titles are manifestations of his firm stand as well as indications of the greater literary freedom that obtained after the death of Stalin. It was with his full-blooded satirical novel *Neobyknovennoye priklyucheniya Julio Jurenito* [*The Extraordinary Adventures of Julio Jurenito*] (1959) that he became world-famous.

But perhaps his most important work is his memoirs published in 1960, in which he tried to rehabilitate officially ignored writers and artists as well as presenting accepted figures in a new and truer light. Ehrenburg wrote in an unpolished journalistic style and his works have been tremendously popular; but since he was primarily a chronicler of contemporary events, much of his earlier work is already forgotten, and his future position as an original writer is uncertain. B. W.

Eich, Günter (1907–), German poet, was born in Lebus in what is now Polish territory. He pursued both legal and oriental studies, but he very early turned to poetry and earned a considerable reputation for his *Hörspiele*, lyrical radio plays, of which the collected edition appeared in 1966. By 1932 he had become a freelance writer, and in the succeeding years continued to extend the range and depth of his work. During the war he served in the army and was captured by the Americans. His post-war work, by which he has become well known, reflects the disillusionment of his generation; he has written not only about the problems of youth and the post-war world, but also turned to mysticism and theology. Noteworthy is *Der Tiger Jussuff* [*Tiger Jussuff*] (1952), a study of the savage beast in man, and *Träume* [*Dreams*] (1950), a fantastic collection of five poems which first appeared in 1953.

Several of Eich's radio plays have been broadcast in translation by the B.B.C. Selections of his more recent poetry are to be found in translation in *German Writing Today* (Penguin, 1967). G. W.

Ekwensi, Cyprian (1921–), productive Nigerian novelist, is interesting for his concentration on western, urban themes rather than on tribal or historical subjects. *Jagua Nana* (1961), his best-known novel, is a study of jealousy between an older woman and a young girl over a young man who is in the process of educating himself. C. P.

Eldershaw, Barnard M. (Flora Eldershaw, 1897–1956; Marjorie Barnard, 1897–), Australian literary partnership, probably best known for their first book *A House is Built* (1929), a saga tracing personal fortunes and the growth of a family business against a background of early Sydney and New South Wales. The theme of the elusive nature of love and of happiness is underlined by the use of chance and accident to develop the plot. A similar vein of ironic fatalism can be detected in their later works *The Glasshouse* (1936), *Plague with Laurel* (1937) and *Tomorrow and Tomorrow* (1947). S. R.

Eliot, T. S. (Thomas Stearns Eliot; 1888–1965), Anglo-American poet, dramatist, critic and publisher, was born in St Louis, Missouri. He was educated at Harvard, Oxford and the University of Paris, settled in England in 1915, and became a British subject in 1927. He became a director of the publishing firm of Faber and Faber. His enormous influence on English and European literature was recognised by the award in 1948 of the Order of Merit and the Nobel Prize for Literature.

Eliot is commonly regarded as a 'difficult' poet. He assumes in his readers a familiarity with European and Classical literature and mythology which very few can hope to possess; and he writes in a poetic idiom which many people brought up on Keats, Wordsworth and Tennyson may find daunting—just as those familiar with the music of Bach, Mozart and Beethoven may find that of Schönberg and Webern baffling and impenetrable. Indeed, Eliot, and his early master Ezra Pound, represent in poetry a break with the past as radical as that achieved by the latter composers. It is safe to say that without Eliot—who has been described as the 'greatest poet and critic of our time'—modern English poetry would be unrecognisable.

It is therefore almost inevitable that the newcomer to Eliot, while he will certainly find much that is immediately beautiful and intriguing, will also find much that at a first, and even at a fifth reading, he may feel to be exasperatingly obscure. It would therefore be wise for him to start with those passages which have an immediate appeal, whether by reason of their irony, their humour or their beauty; and none of these is hard to find. Such passages appear, for instance, in the Sweeney poems; in the verse-drama *The Rock* (1934); in the choruses from *Murder in the*

Cathedral (1935); and in some parts of the *Four Quartets* (1944). Much of Eliot's power lies in his skilful juxtaposition of the sublime and the deliberately profane:

Gloomy Orion and the Dog
Are veiled: and hushed the shrunken seas;
The person in the Spanish cape
Tries to sit on Sweeney's knees.

The astringent and cultivated irony of these lines informs all his work, and goes to produce those passages of savage and outrageous humour to be found in *The Waste Land* (1922), such as the conversation in the pub., and in *Sweeney Agonistes* (1924):

Any man might do a girl in
Any man has to, needs to, wants to
Once in a lifetime, do a girl in.

In reading such passages one becomes insensibly more familiar with Eliot's idiom, and gradually more of his verse becomes accessible. However, the reader will miss a great deal of Eliot's significance unless he is prepared to undertake a fairly strenuous intellectual and spiritual pilgrimage. And this he can hardly do without the aid of some of the excellent and readable guides to Eliot's work. The poet's own critical and sociological writings—his prose is much less 'difficult' than his verse—will also prove helpful: as, for instance, those to be found in *The Use of Poetry and the Use of Criticism* (1933), *The Idea of a Christian Society* (1939), *Notes Towards the Definition of Culture* (1948) and elsewhere (a useful anthology being the *Selected Prose*, ed. John Hayward). These all help to elucidate the nature and growth of Eliot's views and the significance of his verse, from the early *Prufrock* (1917) and *Poems* (1919), through the long poetic works of the twenties and the verse dramas of the thirties, to the Quartets and the post-war plays.

The Waste Land is often regarded as the most difficult, as it is certainly the most seminal, of Eliot's works. Using the symbolism of the Fisher King legend, the poem describes the spiritual 'waste land' of the commercial and cosmopolitan world of the 1920s: barren, unwatered, fragmented, decadent; a stricken country in which all one can know is

A heap of broken images, where the sun beats
And the dead tree gives no shelter, the cricket no relief,
And the dry stone no sound of water. . . .

In the final section, the poem evokes the hope that the rain and thunder of renewal may fall. The theme of death and rebirth is implicit throughout, as it is in so much of Eliot's work, for example in 'The Journey of the Magi'. Evident also is his preoccupation with time. It is significant that Eliot's immediate predecessors, the Georgian poets, had averted their eyes from the modern commercial world which was his concern, and had instead clung nostalgically to the peace and beauty of a rural England that was already passing away. Thus they had in effect tried to bring time to a halt:

> . . . oh! yet
> Stands the church clock at ten to three?

asked Rupert Brooke in 'Grantchester'. In *The Waste Land* we find by contrast an intense and sometimes desperate awareness of the passage of time; the conversation in the pub. is repeatedly interrupted by the yell of the barman:

HURRY UP PLEASE ITS TIME

And the subjection of man to 'time past' and 'time future' is to form the central theme of the Quartets.

The Rock, the first of the verse dramas, was written specifically for a popular audience and makes an immediate appeal to the general reader—or listener. In it, Eliot's religious faith is explicit, and biblical imagery is used with great effect to comment, in the accents of the prophet, on the economic and spiritual malaise of the 1930s and on the miseries of chronic unemployment:

> No man has hired us
> With pocketed hands
> And lowered faces
> We stand about in open places.

The message of *The Waste Land* is made more explicit:

> There shall be left the broken chimney
> The peeled hull, a pile of rusty iron
> In a street of scattered brick where the goat climbs
> Where My Word is unspoken.

Nor do the suburbs escape—'the land of lobelias and tennis flannels'—where

> . . . the wind shall say: 'Here were decent godless people:
> Their only monument the asphalt road
> And a thousand lost golf balls.'

Murder in the Cathedral portrays the events leading up to and culminating in the martyrdom in 1170 of Archbishop Thomas Becket at the hands of the knights of King Henry II; it contains some of Eliot's finest choral verse. It is characteristic that the title of the play might be that of an Agatha Christie novel, and that embedded in the dialogue between Thomas and one of the Tempters are several lines lifted almost word for word from a Sherlock Holmes story. After the murder, the four knights, in a superbly ironical anti-climax, address the audience directly, attempt to win their sympathy, and in so doing lay bare the extent to which the issues and values of twelfth-century England are also those of today.

Of the remaining verse dramas, the most important are *The Family Reunion* (1939) and *The Cocktail Party* (1950). They are both in a sense extensions of *The Waste Land* and *The Rock*; but whereas the earlier works give us sweeping panoramas of a landscape, we are here presented with a microcosm, a waste land within the relationships between the members of a family, or between the guests at a cocktail party. Also, while redemption and renewal have previously been no more than hoped-for possibilities, we are now able to witness the process of their realisation. In both plays one is tempted to suspect the influence on Eliot of modern dynamic psychology, and indeed *The Family Reunion* anticipates in a quite remarkable way the thesis that underlies what is today known as 'family psychiatry'—the belief that one member of a family may find himself unwittingly carrying the problems of all the others. In *The Cocktail Party* the relationship of redemption and reconciliation to neurosis is made quite explicit—though in terms that many psychotherapists would indignantly, and perhaps rightly, repudiate.

The *Four Quartets* are considered by many to be the summit of Eliot's poetic achievement, and they may be expected to endure not only for their poetry but also as examples of supreme verbal craftsmanship. Their grave, austere, delicate harmonies may not be heard immediately, and they are often thought obscure. However, the quality of their 'obscurity' is less tangible than that of *The Waste Land*: they do not assume in the reader a familiarity with esoteric literature, but rather the capacity to listen with more than usual receptivity. They need to be read—and read aloud—as one listens to unfamiliar music: without asking continually 'what does it mean?' (Eliot's own recorded readings should be heard if possible.) The 'meaning' of them has of course been well elucidated by critical writers; but when one speaks of their obscurity and need for explanation one should perhaps recall the poet's own dictum, that 'the ordinary reader, when warned against the obscurity of a poem, is apt to be thrown into a state of consternation very unfavourable to poetic receptivity. . . . The more seasoned reader does not bother about understanding; not, at least, at first.' No better guidance could be given to the newcomer to Eliot's poetry. J. T. M.

Ellison, Ralph (1914–), American novelist, established his reputation with his powerful first novel *Invisible Man* (1952). The Negro hero (significantly unnamed), in the course of a life of protest and struggle for Negro rights, progressively loses his identity: becoming, to both sides, simply a Negro, totally invisible as an individual human being. K. R. R.

Elsner, Gisela (1937–), German novelist. Born in Bavaria, she won the 1965 Prix Formentor with *Die Riesenzwerge* [*The Giant Dwarfs*] (1964), which she describes as *ein Beitrag*, a contribution, rather than a novel, to indicate the intentional lack of development or progression. There would appear to be no limit, save fatigue, to the possible extension of her process since each chapter is self-contained in a startling catalogue of human stupidity, brutality, lust, greed and regimentation, tenuously linked by the presence of Lothar, the five-year-old narrator. This technique fortifies her satirical, nightmare world as the grossness is presented through the innocent eyes of the child in a deadpan, uncommitted, factual manner which obviates overt moral judgment. Unrelieved by the pathos of its silent stupid suffering or by the extraordinary comic richness of the more successful pieces, it inevitably recalls the visual horrors of Bosch and Grosz. Yet we are disturbingly well able to recognise ourselves in the absurd exaggeration and violent caricature of the surrealistic bestiary.

M. D. E.

Eluard, Paul (1895–1952), one of the greatest French lyric poets of the twentieth century. His first volume of importance, *Capitale de la douleur* ['Capital of grief'], appeared in 1926, to be followed by *L'Amour de la poésie* ['Love of poetry']. This was his surrealist period, which ended in 1934 with *La Rose publique* ['The public rose']. A new period opened with *Les Yeux fertiles* ['Fertile eyes'] in 1936, marked by simplicity of language allied with dreamlike imagination. Eluard sought thus through poetry to make contact with common humanity. The Spanish civil war caused him to commit himself definitely to the left. This is illustrated by *Cours naturel* ['Natural course'] (1938), *Le Livre ouvert* ['Open book'] (1942), *Poésie et vérité* ['Poetry and truth'] (1942–43), *Au Rendez-vous allemand* ['German rendezvous'] (1944) and *Poèmes politiques* ['Political poems'] (1948). His continuing and parallel search for linguistic perfection is exemplified in *Poésie ininterrompue* ['Uninterrupted poetry'] (1946). English translations of his verse are contained in *Thorns of Thunder* (Europa Press, 1936), *Le Dur Désir de durer* (ed. Stephen Spender and Frances Cornford; Trianon Press, 1950) and *Selected Writings* (Routledge, 1952).

A. L. W.

Empson, William (1906–), English poet and critic, and a major literary figure of our time, was an original exponent of the 'practical' method of criticism as the author of *Seven Types of Ambiguity* (1930), and subsequently the writer of a body of passionately concentrated, allusive poetry (*Collected Poems, 1955*).

Empson wrote *Seven Types* while still at Cambridge, with enthusiastic encouragement from Professor I. A. Richards. The attitude he adopts to poetry is essentially and primarily personal; his personal reaction is then taken apart and analysed to see in what way the poet has achieved his effect. A final judgment is consistently refused, on the ground that no objective criteria are available. The term 'ambiguity' is used to denote any word or phrase in which more than one meaning or shade of meaning can be glimpsed. Empson distinguishes two kinds of critic: the appreciative and the analytical. To quote:

> An appreciator produces literary effects similar to the one he is appreciating, and sees to it, perhaps by using longer and plainer language, or by concentrating on one element of a combination, that his version is more intelligible than the original to the readers he has in mind. . . . The analyst is not a teacher in this way; he assumes that something has been conveyed to the reader by the work under consideration, and sets out to explain, in terms of the rest of the reader's experience, why the work has had the effect on him that is assumed.

Empson's own poems have the reputation of being difficult. True, many of them are so tight-packed with images that the full intended poetic impact may only come with reading the poet's own extensive and helpful notes. (Though a reader familiar with the metaphysical poets of the seventeenth century, Donne and Herbert in particular, will find Empson's style of expression very similar.) Gone is the soft romantic language of the nineteenth century, the narrative or purely sensory poem; instead there is imagery, and indeed (as in the poems 'To an Old Lady' and 'Arachne') complete poetic structures, derived from the physical world of science. In each of these the image runs through the poem almost as powerful in its self-contained meaning as the actual theme. In 'Doctrinal Point' the real theme, the justification of Christianity, is never precisely stated but is slid into the reader's awareness by the use of certain words and phrases bearing religious associations: for instance 'Free by predestination in the blood, Saved by their own sap, shed for themselves', 'Whether they burgeon, massed wax flames, or flare, Plump spaced-out saints, in their gross prime, at prayer' and 'This is the Assumption of the description'.

Complications of language may overlie the passionate feeling and conviction of Empson's original concept, especially under the discipline of a very regular poetic form, but this is not always the case. 'Courage means Running' and 'Missing Dates' are extremely passionate in effect, even on first reading, yet thick with verbal image. The short poem 'Let it go' shows his style at its plainest and the impact is devastating. 'Ignorance of Death' mixes image and direct comment with perhaps even greater effect: 'Liberal hopefulness regards death as a mere border to an improving picture' or 'It is the trigger of the literary man's biggest gun'.

Empson's other published works include: *Some Versions of Pastoral* (1935), *The Structure of Complex Words* (1951) and *Milton's God* (1961).

G. C.

Enright, Dennis Joseph (1920–), English poet and novelist, has taught in universities in Alexandria, Japan and England, and his work reflects his different milieux. His learning is evident but never obtrudes, and his joy in words is always controlled to make his short, sophisticated poems models of clarity and relevance. Perhaps the most successful are those where he treats of suffering (especially loneliness) and pity. In all of them, including the comic, his feelings are of regret rather than rage, but they are vitalised by their author's compassion for humanity and by its astringent expression. Published titles include *The Laughing Hyena* (1953), *Bread Rather than Blossoms* (1956) and *The Old Adam* (1965).

His novels (*Academic Year*, 1955; *Heaven Knows Where*, 1957; and others) express the same attitude and his characters are keenly and charitably observed. They all deal with rootless, essentially benevolent people seeking, occasionally in Utopia, security for themselves and an outlet for their generosity. H. C.

Enzensberger, Hans Magnus (1929–), German poet, was born in Bavaria and as a youth fought in the *Volksturm* at the end of the second world war. After graduation he worked for the South German radio, travelled widely, and acquired a growing reputation as a distinctive lyric poet. It was not so much the quality of his verse as the nature of his subjects which attracted attention. Modern industry, the tourist trade, the film and newspaper world were all attacked in poems later published as *Sammlung theoretischer Arbeiten* ['Collected theoretical works'] (1962). For Enzensberger poems are scalpels with which to expose the corruption of modern society; and he has kept true to this concept since as a young man he wrote an item entitled 'Verteidigung der Wölfe Gegen die Lämmer' ('The Defence of the Wolves against the Lambs'). His subsequent work includes a 'museum of modern poetry' in sixteen languages and an elaborate collection of nursery rhymes. Selected poems in translation have appeared in *German Writing Today* (Penguin, 1967). G. W.

Erskine Lindop, Audrey (–), English novelist and playwright whose best-known play *Beware of Angels* (1959) was written in collaboration with her husband Dudley Leslie. The most widely known of her novels is probably *The Singer Not the Song* (1953), which is set in Mexico and presents a conflict between good and evil in the persons of a priest and a bandit. Others include *I Thank a Fool* (1958), the central figure of which is a girl of exquisite beauty who appears simple-minded but is in reality gifted with rare insight; *The Way to the Lantern* (1961), dealing with the French revolution and the subsequent reign of terror; *Nicola* (1964); and *I Start Counting* (1966). P. E.

Ervine, St John (1883–), Irish playwright and novelist. His earlier plays were tragedies within the tradition of the Irish National Theatre, and included *John Ferguson* (1915), a tragedy of conflict between a farmer and a brutal moneylender. Later Ervine moved to England and wrote for the commercial theatre a number of successes in different theatrical styles, including *The Lady of Belmont* (1925), a costume drama, and *The First Mrs Fraser* (1928), a comedy of manners. His novels include *Mrs Martin's Man* (1917) and *The Wayward Man* (1927). R. A. K.

Evans, Caradoc (1883–1945), Welsh journalist and novelist, wrote the bitingly satirical *My People* (1915), followed by a series of portrayals in similar vein of various aspects of Welsh life. K. R. R.

F

Fadeyev, Alexandr Alexandrovich (A. A. Bulyga; 1901–56), Soviet novelist, was born in Siberia. He joined the Communist Party in 1915 and began writing soon after. He wrote political speeches and essays on proletarian literary theory and eventually produced his civil war novel *Razgrom* [*The Rout*] (1927), which tells of the débâcle of a Red cavalry unit. Some of the characters are well drawn but the new Soviet hero—Levinson—does not come to life. In 1928 Fadeyev began an unfinished epic inspired by the *The Last of the Mohicans* by Fenimore Cooper: *Poslednyi iz Udege* [*The Last of the Udegs*] being the story of a remote Russian tribe coming into contact with the paraphernalia of Soviet communism. *Molodaya gvardiya* [*The Young Guard*] (1946) tells of guerrilla resistance to the German invasion, but because of adverse criticism Fadeyev rewrote some of it to show the Communist Party in a more active rôle.

As a Soviet writer Fadeyev firmly believed in socialist realism, but his artist's conscience sought inspiration from Tolstoy to help him achieve a better technique. He gradually withdrew from literature after becoming secretary to the Writers' Union and was its official spokesman during the Stalinist period. He shot himself in 1956 just after the 'thaw' and his failure to be re-elected to his secretarial post. B. W.

Fagunwa, Daniel Olorunsemi (1895–1963), Nigerian novelist. A Yoruba chief, his work is being translated into English, notably by Wole Soyinka. Periodical extracts—for example from *The Brave Hunter in the Jungle of the Four Hundred Gods*—reveal the same rich folk vein exploited in his own style by Tutuola. C. P.

Fairbairn, Arthur Rex Dugard (1904–57), New Zealand poet and essayist, was associated with the short-lived but ambitious literary magazine of the thirties, *Phoenix*. In his poetry, as in his articles and essays, he sought to to drive out the apologetic and derivative approach of New Zealand writing. His own vigorous and lyrical poems, dealing with subjects as elemental as love and death, are published in *Strange Rendezvous* and *Three Poems* (both 1952). S. R.

Farjeon, Eleanor (1881–1965), English writer, is known chiefly for her fantasies and children's stories. She collaborated with her playwright brother Herbert in *Kings and Queens* (1932), and her memoirs appeared in the same year. Later titles include *The Little Book Room* (1955). P. E.

Farjeon, Herbert (1887–1946), English actor, playwright and critic, brother of Eleanor Farjeon, was the writer and producer of witty intimate revues as well as a notable editor of Shakespeare. P. E.

Farnol, Jeffrey (1878–1952), English novelist, went to America in 1900; but his first novel *Broad Highway* was published in England in 1910 after being turned down by a number of American publishers. This picaresque novel set in rural England was an immediate success, and having established himself as a writer, Jeffrey Farnol was able to return to England. He now wrote about one novel a year, swashbuckling romances written in an easy if undistinguished style. *The Times* described him as a 'full flavoured romantic novelist who entertained and endeared himself to a happily more innocent younger generation than the present'. His many books include *The Amateur Gentleman* (1913), *Crooked Furrow* (1937) and *Glad Summer* (1951). K. M. H.

Farrell, James T. (1904–), American novelist, is best known for the proletarian Studs Lonigan trilogy set in the Chicago of the twenties. This justly famed work, though undeniably his best, needs to be set in the perspective of its author's vast and varied output if its full significance is to be appreciated; and the ill-starred Lonigan should ideally be taken in conjunction with Danny O'Neill, the materially successful hero of a subsequent pentalogy (and a self-portrait), as well as the later figure of Bernard Carr who embodies a way of life beyond material success or failure.

The chronicle of the short life of Studs Lonigan—begun unpropitiously in *Young Lonigan* (1932), decisively frustrated in the slender opportunities of escaping disaster provided in *The Young Manhood of Studs Lonigan* (1934), and inexorably concluded in *Judgment Day* (1935)—is the story of a life of above average potential that is corrupted and ultimately ruined through the false values of a depraved culture. By nature sensitive and capable of a pure and romantic love, we see Studs become progressively brutalised as he schools himself to be tough and tells himself that 'a big tough guy should only want to jump a girl'. Being tough involves a premature assumption of adulthood (as expressed in the gambling, drinking and brawling of the pool-room) and a corresponding contempt for the 'punks' who are still at school: and Studs's chronic truancy from school is followed by a period in which his life is so dominated by the crude pool-room mores that his eventual key dating of his childhood sweetheart Lucy misfires hopelessly, because of their resultant incompatibility. The cleaner, smoother world that he encounters at the dance (in which his own sisters are involved), apparently contrasting so strongly with his own clap-ridden drink-dissipated set, is phoney in its sophisticated politeness, which masks values of materialistic self-advancement and sexual fulfilment not essentially superior to those of Lonigan's own more blatantly futile existence. Other escape routes that he explores in vain are the cult of physical fitness (an inevitable cul-de-sac) and a revivalistic Catholicism whose only lasting effect is the reinforcement of his existing prejudices against Negroes, freethinkers and radicals. It is left to the 'punk' Danny O'Neill to see that radical politics could provide the solution that Studs is never to find; for the latter—who has already seen one of his companions drink himself to death—the end is already foreshadowed when, with Lucy (on whom he has pinned all his hopes) married, he decides that he 'might as well get a girl and marry. What the hell else was there to do?' K. R. R.

Fast, Howard (1914–), American historical novelist whose books reveal an experience of, and sympathy for, revolutionary politics. *Spartacus* (1958), for example, portrays the Roman slave rebel. Later titles include *Torquemada* (1967), a tale of the Spanish Inquisition. K. R. R.

Faulkner, William (1897–1962), American novelist, is generally accepted as one of the major figures of twentieth-century literature. Superficially he is one of the most markedly regional writers, since the bulk of his work is set in the American deep south, drawing its inspiration from southern myths and traditions and the profound agonies of the southern racial and national predicament. But it is precisely through exploiting this peculiar predicament, with its capacity to generate the extremes of human behaviour, that Faulkner is able to lay bare the universal condition of man. If the gloomy picture he paints of human nature seemed exaggerated in the early 1930s, the experience of subsequent generations has been such as to confirm it.

From the point of view of style and technique, many of Faulkner's novels do not make easy reading. As with James Joyce, whose 'stream-of-consciousness' technique Faulkner adopted on a number of occasions, the complexities of human life are mirrored in the complexities of his writing. It is a measure of the satisfaction to be gained by readers who persevere that he is among the most widely read of American novelists, especially in France and England.

His first novel was *Soldiers' Pay* (1926), which breathes the disillusionment characteristic of the period following the first world war (in which Faulkner himself had served with the R.A.F. in Canada). Critics have detected traces of the spirit and style of his English contemporaries Eliot and Huxley, and the influence of the latter is very evident in *Mosquitoes*

(1927), a novel full of the bright talk of the New Orleans art world. When Faulkner wrote these early works, he had already been living and working (chiefly as university postmaster) for some years in Oxford, Mississippi, seat of Lafayette county—that 'little postage stamp of native soil' which was to provide the material for the great series of novels that began with *Sartoris* (1929). Here we encounter his mythical Yoknapatawpha county, with Jefferson its county seat, and the family of the legendary Colonel John Sartoris, a character based on a colourful ancestor of Faulkner's. Here, too, we find his preoccupation with ancestry and tradition, and with time itself: the past living on and dominating the present (a characteristic of southern life), the present showing only the decay and dissolution of families and a society for whom the clock has stopped generations ago.

In the same year Faulkner published his first masterpiece, *The Sound and the Fury* (1929). It is also one of the most difficult of twentieth-century novels—which is scarcely surprising insofar as it represents life as 'a tale told by an idiot, full of sound and fury, signifying nothing'. The first of its four sections is literally a tale told by an idiot, the thirty-three-year-old Benjy Compson: and in it the reader encounters, as in a mist, some of the other members of the now degenerate Compson family and their household. The time dimension is non-existent, with events that occurred eighteen years ago appearing side by side with those taking place in the present; and additional complications stem from the fact that there are two characters called Quentin. Not till much later in the book do the relationships and the chronology become clear. However, images are developed of two people who are central to Benjy's life—the one a girl called Quentin, who serves to remind him (as also do the cries of the golfers on the nearby course) of the other, a girl called Candace or Caddy. Caddy, we gather, was the only person who had responded to Benjy's need for affection but she is now married and he no longer sees her.

The second section, set eighteen years earlier, is told in stream-of-consciousness by the other Quentin, brother to Benjy and Caddy, and uncle to the first Quentin whom we now learn to be Caddy's daughter. He, too, is obsessed with Caddy: not, like Benjy, as someone who can give him the love that his selfish father and hypochondriac mother have denied him but as the embodiment, in her virginity, of what remains of the family honour. To preserve the latter, he wishes it to be believed that he has committed incest with her, so that the world will withdraw in horror from the two of them and leave them inviolable. His suicide, which is the climax of this section, is a similar piece of perverted idealism: he, at least, will bring no more children into the world to degrade the Compson honour yet further.

The third section is narrated by Jason, Caddy's older brother, and the only member of the family to function on the plane of everyday normality. He it is who shoulders the burden of the family's affairs and saves them from total ruin. It is precisely because of his normality that he of all the family exhibits most clearly the besetting failure of the Compsons, and the ultimate cause of their downfall: the failure of love. Also it is in his straightforward narrative, set on the day after Benjy's, that we at last see emerging the clear outlines of the central story: the desperate, near-nymphomaniac rebellions first of Caddy and then her daughter Quentin, against a loveless environment.

The book is completed by a section which centres on the enduring rôles of the Negro servants of the household, especially the aging Dilsey who alone has offered Caddy and subsequently her daughter the kind of affection that her self-centred parents and demanding brothers have denied her. Here in the servant quarters, in contrast with the decaying Compsons, is a pattern of living which has not been sapped by involution and inbreeding, with their trail of alcoholism and idiocy: and there is a quasi-religious flavour of redemption in the unfailing love with which Dilsey embraces the whole fabric of the Compson tragedy.

This was followed by *As I Lay Dying* (1930), a book that Faulkner wrote in a prodigious burst of nocturnal creativity. It is a comic-macabre account of a family taking its dead mother to Jefferson to be buried, a journey in the course of which her relationships with her husband and children are explored. The issues of love and selfishness (here seen as a self-containment that needs to be violated) are again uppermost. Although one of Faulkner's least pretentious works, it is one of his most effective. However, by this time the difficulties of his technique had alienated many readers; and Faulkner's next book, *Sanctuary* (1931), was ostensibly intended to restore its author's failing finances. It is regarded by some as a crude piece of popular sensationalism. Popular it has certainly proved owing to its comparative simplicity and readability, but it is arguable whether it is appreciably more sensational than some of his other works; certainly it is a major work.

Here the theme of southern degeneracy is only a contributory motif, playing its part in the triumph of evil and injustice which is the central theme of the book. Temple Drake, a fatally innocent southern belle (a characteristic southern type), is exposed to a singularly perverted violation at a bootlegger's hideout as a result of the liquor-craving of her escort Gowan Stevens, a degenerate alumnus of the University of Virginia. Detected in raping her with the husk of a corn cob, the impotent psychopath Popeye shoots his observer, the innocent Tommy, and abducts the bleeding girl to a Memphis brothel, leaving the bootlegger Lee Goodwin to be charged with the murder. Goodwin's wife enlists the services of the well-meaning but mediocre Jefferson lawyer Horace Benbow, whom we have already seen (as the enfeebled embodiment of goodness) stumbling into Popeye in the opening pages. But such is the spiritual domination that Popeye now establishes over Temple, that Benbow loses his case through her perjury and Goodwin is duly executed. The book's final irony is the arrest and sentencing of Popeye for a crime that he has not committed.

Sanctuary proclaims the triumph of evil, in a world where the old sanctities are in decay and such goodness as remains is impotent. *Light in August* (1932), its successor, explores more fully the nature of evil. In the light and dark races into which mankind is split Faulkner sees a mirror image of the dichotomy that can exist in a human personality—especially when polarised by a Calvinistic obsession with God and the devil, by a real or imaginary racial ambivalence, or by that hopeless contradiction that lies at the core of any liberal or Christian southerner. And although the almost schizophrenic behaviour of most of the characters is clearly seen as the product of their religious and historical conditioning there is no doubting the universality of their predicament, and the need for a sacrificial catharsis.

The protagonist and chief victim, who believes himself to have some Negro blood, is significantly named Christmas. The task of establishing and coming to terms with his own identity is increased by his being placed in an orphanage soon after birth; and when the pattern of punishments and rewards imposed by the orphanage authorities, and later by a pitiless Presbyterian foster-father, is confused through a series of unfortunate experiences involving women—first the orphanage dietician whom he surprises with her lover and who bribes him when he expects retribution; then his emotionally deprived foster-mother whose love he cannot accept because of his hatred for her husband; and finally the café prostitute who is his first love and who in sheer self-protection deserts him after he has half-killed his foster-father, and robbed his foster-mother, in order to be with her—he becomes as incapable of having a normal relationship and of making the appropriate emotional responses, as he is of identifying himself with black or white. For years he walks in the country in search of his own identity, eventually coming to rest on the estate of a New England hermit, a woman as much divided against herself as he is. A battle of wills develops in which he will only accept what she offers him—first food and shelter, then a place in her bed—when he can take them by force instead of receiving them as gifts. Her daemonic sexual liberation is matched by a mounting desire to make him pray, and when she finally tries to force him to do so at gunpoint he overpowers and murders her. Thus is set in motion the chain of events that culminate in the customary lynching, catalysed by the morally bankrupt Judas-figure of Brown who has been Christmas's assistant in his bootlegging business. The positive qualities of patience and fidelity are represented in the book by Lena Grove, whom we meet at the beginning of the book travelling in search of one Lucas Burch (*alias* Brown), the father of the child she is carrying; and by the lonely bachelor Byron Bunch who protects her. The death of Christmas (a Christ-like figure only in his rôle as victim) is counterpointed by the birth of Lena's child, a child of hope: and both events serve to liberate the dispossessed minister Hightower from the paralysis caused by his own inner conflict (southern patriotism and Christian values), by forcibly involving him first on an errand of mercy and then as midwife. After the sacrifice, there is new life —a different verdict from that of *Sanctuary*.

Pylon (1935), a heavily symbolic story about a family of aviators, was one of Faulkner's failures: but *Absalom, Absalom* (1936), the climax of a phenomenally productive seven-year period, is another of his best works. This, perhaps of all his novels, is the one that is most directly concerned with the essence of the southern agony, as embodied in the history of the house of Sutpen. It also represents a high-water mark in the writer's technique, the events themselves emerging with all the enigmatic ambiguity of history from a three-dimensional narrative. Two of the narrators are already familiar—the suicide Quentin Compson and his father, the latter being the son of the General Compson who was Sutpen's friend and contemporary. Quentin's reconstruction of the story, in the course of discussions with his Harvard room-mate Shreve, focuses on the theme of incest in the Sutpen family relationships—a theme already familiar from his version of the Compson tragedy, and one which may be taken to symbolise the fatal inbreeding of the southern tradition. The central relationship is that between Sutpen and his son Charles, who has inherited his mother's taint of Negro blood and is consequently rejected by his father. The denial of his passionate plea for acceptance, culminating in his desire to marry his half-sister Judith, provoke a conflict with his half-brother Henry that ends with the latter shooting him. More important, however, than the story itself is its capacity to illuminate the experience of the narrators, and their own relationship to the southern tragedy.

During this seven-year period, Faulkner had produced a large number of short stories and in the next six years he was to make new use of his expertise in this field, by combining groups of loosely related stories (some old, some new) to form an artistic unity. The first of these groupings was *The Unvanquished* (1938), a book whose unity derives from the person of the narrator, the same Bayard Sartoris that we have met in the first of the Yoknapatawpha novels. This was followed by *The Wild Palms* (1939), a double-narrative whose two components are unrelated in subject matter but thematically contrapuntal. But perhaps the most celebrated of Faulkner's works in this genre is *Go Down Moses* (1942), a book that is equally notable for its profound understanding of white-Negro relations and for the technique of its multi-dimensional narrative through which they are illuminated (for example, the story of a young Negro who goes berserk with grief at the death of his wife, as told from both the Negro and white viewpoints). During this period also Faulkner wrote the novel *The Hamlet* (1940), later to be seen as the first part of a trilogy. But from 1942 some six years were to elapse before he began to publish the novels of his last period. These fall into two groups: the remaining works of the 'Snopes trilogy' (of which *The Hamlet* had been the first part), and a group of what have been called 'committed' novels—ones in which the story appears to have been composed to embody his explicit views on the civil rights question. The trilogy—completed by *The Town* (1957) and *The Mansion* (1959)—focuses on the lives of a type of southern family previously accorded only peripheral interest. Sartorises, Compsons and Sutpens, for all their latter-day degradation, have a tragic stature: but the Snopeses are mean, ignoble bourgeois, battening like insects on the ruins of the old south. The squalor of their private and public lives spreads like a canker through southern society, so that even incest and idiocy take on a dark splendour in contrast. The south may be doomed, says Faulkner, but heaven preserve it from the ravages of the Snopeses.

The plague of Snopeses is a forewarning of what can be expected if the south be forced to submit to the rootless bourgeois of the north—a fate to be avoided at all costs. This—reinforced by the view that only the south can sort out its troubles, that only from the white southerners can the Negroes receive their rights and the south's redemption finally come—is the philosophy expressed in the other novels of the period. These include the famous civil rights novel *Intruder in the Dust* (1948), and the Temple Drake sequel *Requiem for a Nun* (1951). In the former, a small white boy, together with his Negro friend and a frail spinster, sets out to save the life of the half-Negro Lucas Beauchamp (previously encountered in *Go Down, Moses*), whose pride has led him into a situation where he is exposed to arrest and a probable lynching for a murder he has not committed. Innocence, in Faulkner's previous novels, has most frequently been either impotent or irresponsible: but this young intruder proves potent enough to see justice done. However, the story has another dimension. It is Lucas's intransigent refusal to accept the status of a Negro that has landed him in trouble: and his rescuer is possessed with precisely the same sense of outrage that makes the townspeople eager to see him lynched. As a child he has been the recipient of an act of kindness from Lucas, kindness for which he tried to pay with money. Now, in the course of his own heroic act of kindness, in which it is Lucas who insists on paying for the aid that he receives, he eventually learns to accept Lucas as an equal. Here, then, is not merely an affirmation of the positive qualities of innocence, but a statement of the need for, and the possibility of, adjustment of attitudes. Another such statement is made in *Requiem for a Nun* where Temple and Gowan Stevens finally recognise their responsibility for the disasters they have precipitated, and set out together to redeem the society that has produced them. A more generalised version of Faulkner's philosophy in this period—corresponding to the remarks in his Nobel Prize speech about the need for sacrifice—is found in the ponderous Christian allegory *A Fable* (1954), set in France during the first world war. But it is doubtful whether the explicit messages of these later novels add anything significant to the cumulative effect of the great works of the period 1929–36, and it is on these that his reputation rests.

K. R. R.

Fedin, Konstantin Alexandrovich (1892–), Soviet novelist whose work covers the whole time span of Soviet literature. His first story was published in 1920 after he had met Gorky and joined a literary group. In his early stories Fedin shows a strong desire to experiment with form and content. He also tried to be a truthful writer and this honest approach gives his work a lasting freshness. His first novel *Goroda i gody* [*Cities and Years*] (1924) portrays the effect of the revolution on an intellectual who loses his early enthusiasm for the cause. He is eventually killed by his former friend, a Bolshevik, because he spares an 'enemy of the people'. Fedin's works, not surprisingly, have had their share of official criticism: *Transvaal* [*Transvaal*] (1928) was said to idealise the Kulaks, while *Bratya* [*The Brothers*] (1928) was supposedly too sympathetic to the non-conformist intellectual; and his first trilogy *Gorky sredi nas* [*Gorky Among Us*] (1943–44) was bitterly attacked and never completed. During the black years after World War II Fedin published two parts of his second trilogy, *Perviye radosti* [*Early Joys*] (1945) and *Neobyknovennoye leto* [*Extraordinary Summer*] (1948), which depict a small town on the Volga before World War I and during the civil war; the author recollecting his own experiences in the person of Lieut. Dibich who returns home after having been interned in Germany. In the second part Fedin also had to contend with portraying Stalin as the hero of Tsaritsyn (Stalingrad/ Volgograd) instead of Trotsky whose name was taboo. He completed the trilogy in 1962 with *Kostyor* [*The Bonfire*]. His later career has been more straightforward, his production excelling in its psychological depth;

although not a great writer, he has shown himself remarkably capable of communicating from his own experiences the atmosphere of time and place. B. W.

Ferber, Edna (1887–), American novelist, was the author of *Showboat* (1926) on which the famous Kern and Hammerstein musical was based. Her works also include *So Big* (1924), which won the 1925 Pulitzer prize; *Cimarron* (1930), a tale of the Oklahoma land rush of the 1880s; *Giant* (1952), portraying the effect of an oil-strike and subsequent affluence on a Texan community; and the much praised *Ice Palace* (1958). K. R. R.

Ferlinghetti, Lawrence (1919–), American beat poet and novelist. The origins of the beat movement centred in New York, Los Angeles and San Francisco, and Ferlinghetti used his own San Francisco City Lights Bookshop as a base for encouraging young writers to meet and also for publishing small paperback editions of their work; Ginsberg and Corso (qq.v.) being first published in this way. Ferlinghetti also issued a mimeographed magazine of beat poetry called *Beatitude*. The 'beat' title derives not only from the sense of weariness with conventional society but (with a clever pun) also from the beatification that may come through dissociation from contemporary mores and a voluntary taking on of poverty. Beat fulfilment comes from an increase in intensity at one point in the individual's contact with reality. The beat equivalents of Aldous Huxley's mescalin and Coleridge's opium are such disparates as drunkenness, sexual ecstasy, drugs and Zen Buddhism.

Ferlinghetti's own work, in contrast with that of many of the 'beats', is conscious of political attitudes and is concerned, too, that poetry should be relevant to a large reading public and not merely the possession of an esoteric group. It does possess, however, the spontaneity and colloquial wit of the 'beats'; the individual poems stand up well to public reading, especially when this is given by the poet himself, often to a jazz accompaniment. His poetry can be both over-clever and over-pitched in its protest, but at its best can have either the absurd irreverence of Cummings or a really powerful and serious anger in face of the pretentious and the unjust in society. Published volumes of poetry include *Pictures of the Gone World* (1955), *A Coney Island of the Mind* (1958) and *Starting from San Francisco* (1961). *Her* (1960) is a novel. D. L. P.

Fermor, Patrick Leigh (1915–), English writer whose pre-war travels in the hellenic world were followed by wartime action on the Greek mainland and in Crete (where he lived disguised as a shepherd organising the island's resistance) and who in the 1950s emerged as an outstanding travel writer. *The Traveller's Tree* (1950), dealing with the Caribbean, and *A Time to Keep Silence* (1953), were succeeded by *Mani* (1958) which is concerned with a remote community of the southern Peloponnese, a feudal people characterised by a centuries-old code of hospitality, chivalry and retribution. Other titles include *The Violins of St Jacques* (1953), a novel; and *Roumeli* (1966), a successor to *Mani* and the second in what is to be a series of volumes exploring the remoter parts of the Greek world.

K. R. R.

Ferreira de Castro, José Maria (1898–), Portuguese novelist. The formative years of his teens were spent working in Brazil, first in the rubber plantations and later in journalism. Though seeking to live by his pen he did not achieve success until his publication of *Emigrantes* [*Emigrants*] (1928), nine years after his return to Portugal. His country's first great social novel, it drew heavily on personal experience to produce a diffuse though vigorous account of the privations of emigrants to Brazil. *A Selva* [*Jungle*] (1930) won international acclaim and earned translation into seventeen languages through its bitter condemnation of working conditions in the Brazilian rubber plantations. His deep concern for the underprivileged informed the next four novels, *Eternidade* ['Eternity'] (1933), *Terra Fria* ['Cold Earth'] (1934), *Tempestade* ['Tempest'] (1940) and *A Lã e a Neve* ['The Wool and the Snow'] (1947), the latter being the most effective in its close examination of the harsh lives of Portuguese shepherds and textile operatives. A change of approach is evident in his later fiction *A Curva da Estrada* ['The Bend in the Road'] (1950) and the *novella* entitled *A Missão* [*The Mission*] (1954), which are set respectively in Republican Spain and the France of 1940. Here the themes are complicated by the characters' need to make agonising decisions in the face of conflicting political pressures. Since 1937 Ferreira de Castro has also dedicated himself to non-fictional works and has published three monumental and highly informative studies born of his extensive travels and interest in the arts. Characteristically, he has constantly refused to allow his candidature for the Nobel Prize.

R. C. W.

Feydeau, Georges (1862–1921), French playwright who became known in Paris before the first world war as a follower of Labiche and a writer of boulevard farces. His plays became famous for the excellence of their plots and the effervescent charm and unreality of his characters. Feydeau's theatre is the archetype of the bedroom farce, and professional productions have obtained great success with them as repeated revivals have shown.

His best-known plays include *Tailleur pour dames* ['Ladies' tailor'] (1894), *Monsieur chasse* ['The master's hunting'] (1892), *Feu la mère de Madame* ['Madam's late mother'] (1908), *Occupe-toi d'Amélie* [*Look after Lulu*] (1908), *Mais ne t' promène donc pas toute nue* ['Don't walk about naked'] (1912), *La Dame de chez Maxim* [*The Lady in Maxim's*] (1914) and in conjunction with Desvallières, *L'Hôtel du libre échange* [*Hôtel Paradiso*] (1894). D. E. A.

Field, Rachel (1894–1942), American novelist, wrote the best-seller *All This and Heaven Too* (1938), based on a French murder trial, in which a woman who has been unjustly implicated in the murder of the wife of the man she loves is rescued by an American clergyman, who enables her to start a new life in the United States and becomes her husband. She also wrote *Time Out of Mind* (1935) and an assortment of children's literature. K. R. R.

Firbank, [Arthur Annesley] Ronald (1886–1926), English novelist and aesthete, very much a writer's writer and one who frequently finds place in critical studies of the literature of 1910–30 for his strikingly original and impressionist style. His short novels have little in the way of conventional plot development but consist mainly of fragments of conversation that sketch in a situation (the baptism of a dog opens *The Eccentricities of Cardinal Pirelli*, 1926), and indicate the resultant ripples that touch all levels of the social hierarchy. Firbank, who entered the Catholic church at twenty, returns again and again to mock the hypocrisy and confusion of thought and motive among rich Catholics and especially the clergy. His fertile wit, his outrageous statements and occasional startling sexual innuendo, and above all his unerring ear for words and languages, give great vigour to his writing, with its lists of bizarre and exotic names and invented foreign phrases, its outlandish snippets of imagined history, and the longer songs and poems that Firbank includes to give verisimilitude to the fantastic confections he has conjured up. The close, hot-house impression left by the pervasive sexual depravity and perversion of his characters is sometimes relieved by the freshness and beauty of the natural setting (as in rural *Valmouth*, 1918) and sometimes further inflamed by the warm scented tropical background (as in *Prancing Nigger*, 1925). Most of his works were originally published at his own expense, but now seem certain to endure as wry, delicate *fleurs du mal*. The earlier titles include two short stories, *Odette d'Antrevernes* and *A Study in Temperament*, published in one volume in 1905; *Inclinations* (1916); *Caprice* (1917), a play; *The Princess Zoubaroff* (1920); *Santal* (1921); and *The*

Flower Beneath the Foot (1923). *Valmouth* was turned into a musical by Sandy Wilson in the 1950s, and this did much to kindle interest in Firbank among a new generation. S. R.

Fitzgerald, Francis Scott (1896–1940), American novelist of the twenties and thirties, was a lone romantic among the leading writers of his time. And at a time when the majority of American writers were more concerned with those who were suffering most from social and economic evils, he was also unique in writing almost entirely about the very rich.

On the appearance of his first novel *This Side of Paradise* (1920), tracing the adolescence of a sensitive intelligent egoist, he was immediately hailed by the bright young things of the 'jazz age' as their authentic spokesman. But although he had shared the gay Princeton life he describes so tenderly—he went there as an undergraduate in 1913—his romanticisation is that of an outsider, of a midwesterner not himself born to such affluence.

As an outsider he could see the other side of the picture, and the increasing ambivalence of his attitude to the rich is very evident in his second novel *The Beautiful and the Damned* (1922); the lives they lead still have an irresistible glamour, but they nonetheless stand judged by Fitzgerald the moralist. This trend—which had already begun to alienate his original readers, without winning him any corresponding respect from the devotees of either the 'hard-boiled' style or the proletarian school—was to culminate in *The Great Gatsby* (1925), generally regarded today as his best book. The story of Jay Gatsby, who as a poor young man has lost the rich girl he loved to a man of her own class, has subsequently become rich himself, and has come to live in a nearby mansion where he throws extravagant and spectacular parties with the sole aim of impressing her, is a strangely poignant one. And although the mysterious and glamorous façade of his life is to collapse, and his dream is to be shattered, he is a romantic figure to the end. Not so the congenitally rich Tom Buchanan, the man whom the girl Daisy has married: his unsought wealth has made him hard, self-centred and purposeless.

When Gatsby's dream founders on the naked reality of the sordid and crooked life he has been living in order to become one of the rich, it is not just his personal tragedy but that of a whole society. Not only does he pursue wealth as the key to happiness (in his case, love); he also lets himself believe that appearances are more important than realities (in the early part, for instance, nobody knows who and what Gatsby is: all they see is the façade). The latter point is seen in its full horror when he and Daisy (at the wheel) kill Tom's mistress in a car accident: what matters to them is not the death of a human being, but the need to conceal Daisy's responsibility.

During the 1920s Fitzgerald published several volumes of short stories, including *Flappers and Philosophers* (1922), *Tales of the Jazz Age* (1926) and *All the Sad Young Men* (1926). Perhaps the most famous of these stories are 'The Rich Boy' and 'The Diamond as Big as the Ritz', the latter being a fantasy which postulates the consequences of being infinitely rich and at the same time neatly expresses Fitzgerald's theme of inevitable disillusion following the dream of youth. Fitzgerald was now spending much of his time in Europe, in the company of well-to-do American exiles; and this is the setting for his next novel, *Tender is the Night* (1934). Here we meet a different kind of personal tragedy. Dick Diver, a distinguished nerve specialist working in Switzerland, might have shared with Jay Gatsby the epitaph 'all for love'; but in his case the 'all' is composed of fine talents, a sense of purpose, and great generosity, while the love is something he must give to save the sanity of a rich young girl patient, to the extent of sacrificing everything else. When he has sacrificed everything, he has destroyed himself: and he becomes one of the idle rich.

At first, the all-consuming love of Dick and Nicole is in itself a thing of great beauty and tenderness; and their wealth enables them to enjoy an earthly paradise. But following Dick's inner death, corruption sets in: he drinks ever more heavily, and eventually becomes unfaithful to Nicole. She in turn shows that she can now manage without him—that maybe the sacrifice was in vain. One might argue that it is Nicole and her psychological needs that destroy Dick: but Nicole and her wealth are inseparable. She is a representative of a class that lives off the vitality of the creative and the productive, sapping it till it dries up completely. And yet . . . even here, there is the characteristic ambivalence: for all the pathos of the destruction of Dick, there lingers the ineffable sweetness of countless tender nights.

Fitzgerald spent his last years in Hollywood, and saw at first hand the effects of the great crash. If it is true that there is in both Jay Gatsby and Dick Diver a partial identification with his own experience of wealth, it is even more marked in his last hero, Monroe Stahr in the unfinished novel *The Last Tycoon* (1941)—who, like his creator, was driving himself to a premature death. Stahr, a film magnate, is the perfect example of the creative use of wealth—both in the films he makes and in the care he has for his employees' welfare. His willingness to lose money on a film, and his reluctance to accept the inevitable crystallisation of his world into employers' alliances and labour unions, characterise him as the true tycoon. Like Fitzgerald's earlier heroes, Stahr destroys himself for love. There is nothing in the world he cannot have for the asking—until in the wake of an earthquake he glimpses an unknown girl who reminds him of his wife. After a brief affair with Stahr, the girl Katherine goes through with the marriage she had already consented to: and the rest of the book (much of it only existing in outline) centres on his disastrous efforts to recapture her. He sacrifices everything, including his own character: and by the end he has degenerated into a crude gangster.

Fitzgerald died in 1940, believing himself to be a failure. His notebooks and letters were published in 1945, entitled *The Crack-Up*. K. R. R.

Fitzgerald, Robert David (1902–), Australian poet, author of the prize-winning 'Essay on Memory', printed in *Moonlight Acre* (1938), has always been concerned with the philosophical aspects of time and of memory, and these themes recur in his volumes *To Meet the Sun* (1929), *Between Two Tides* (1952), *This Night's Orbit* (1953), *The Wind at Your Door* (1959) and *Southmost Twelve* (1963). S. R.

Fitzpatrick, Percy (1862–1931), South African writer, best known for his *Jock of the Bushveld* (1907), the South African equivalent of Jack London's *White Fang*. His *Transvaal from Within* (1899) had immense political moment just before the Boer war. C. P.

Flecker, James Elroy (1884–1915), English poet and dramatist, is most widely known for his posthumous verse-play *Hassan* (1922), an exotic romance of the near east where Flecker himself had worked as a diplomat. It celebrates the doomed ecstasy of two lovers in Baghdad who have chosen a night of consummation and a violent death at the hands of the caliph in the morning, rather than a lifetime apart: but its hero is the caliph's confectioner Hassan who, despite his protests at their execution, prefers to continue life's journey and 'take the golden road to Samarkand'. The play contains some of Flecker's richest poetry.

Flecker's verse is heavily under the influence of the French Parnassians, especially the Cuban-born poet Hérédia. Like that of the latter, it is lush in imagery and sonorous in effect. The Parnassians in general, including Baudelaire and Verlaine, rejected subjectivism and romantic emotionalism for detachment and precise technique: and Flecker, despite his gorgeousness of metaphor, likewise pursued perfection of technique and form. His published verse includes *Collected Poems* (1916) and *Selected Poems* (1918). K. R. R.; D. L. P.

Fleming, Ian (1908–64), English novelist. Fleming more than any other author established the cult of the spy story in the 1950s and 1960s. Having been an intelligence officer of some seniority in the war, Fleming created an escapist hero, James Bond, whose ethic and function in life are contained in the word skill. Bond is skilful at making love, skilful at playing cards, at shooting, at killing, at driving, at skiing, at avoiding deep emotional involvements. His world is a world of pleasure in experience and action. In the later novels, written shortly before Fleming's death, Bond's skills both as a spy and as a man begin to disintegrate with age and over-use and he has no firm values on which to fall back. But perhaps even this is reading too much into what are essentially exciting, hard, brittle, well constructed, quietly sadistic adventure tales appealing to the arm-chair hero—and unequivocally commercial in intention. The best of them include *Casino Royale* (1953), *From Russia With Love* (1957), *Dr No* (1958), *Goldfinger* (1959) and *Thunderball* (1961). D. L. P.

Fleming, Peter (1907–), English travel writer and novelist, the brother of Ian Fleming. Among his books are *Brazilian Adventure* (1933) and *News from Tartary* (1936); *Siege at Peking* (1959), on the subject of the Boxer Rebellion; and *Bayonets to Lhasa* (1961), an account of the 1904 British invasion of Tibet. P. E.

Ford, Ford Madox (born F. M. Hueffer; 1873–1939), English novelist, grandson of the pre-Raphaelite painter Ford Madox Brown, collaborated with Conrad on two early novels before writing *The Fifth Queen* (1906), the story of Henry VIII and Katherine Howard and *The Good Soldier* (1915), 'a tale of passion'. He served in the first world war and subsequently produced a number of books once highly esteemed as war novels: titles include *No More Parades* (1925), the second volume in a tetralogy eventually published as *Parade's End* (1950).

However, if Ford's depiction of the first world war does not in itself seem specially remarkable today, the broader themes of the tetralogy—personified in the semi-autobiographical character of Christopher Tietjens, a scion of the English landed gentry whose attitudes to the imminent eclipse of his class may instructively be compared and contrasted with those of Guy Crouchback in Evelyn Waugh's World War II trilogy—make this a major work of art when seen as a whole. The overall title *Parade's End* implies an end to all that is ordered, controlled, dignified, ceremonious and seemly both in public and private life. (In *No More Parades* the context is specifically that of military life as degraded by the years of chaotic trench warfare.) In personal life 'parade' involves, for example, self-control in the face of emotional upheaval, and upheld standards of marital behaviour in face of a wife's infidelity. These traits in Christopher Tietjens, the 'last English tory' (in the eighteenth-century sense of the word), goad his beautiful but amoral Catholic wife Sylvia, a metropolitan and cosmopolitan aristocrat of the twentieth century, into increasingly outrageous and cruel behaviour to provoke in him a loss of composure, an admission of pain, and a breakdown of his 'not in front of the servants' principle.

But Christopher is more than just an eighteenth-century country gentleman: he is also a Christian. And what drives the ostensibly devout Sylvia into her most diabolical treacheries is his persistently Christ-like behaviour—forgiving her adulteries and protecting her from the ensuing notoriety, giving his money to anyone who asks for it (particularly to his lowly-born friend Macmaster), and refusing to defend himself when this unworldly behaviour is misconstrued by those who cannot conceive of anything but a cynical motive for it. Thus his clemency to Sylvia is taken to mean that he himself is really the guilty party; or that if he is wronging her in no other way, he preserves the marriage solely to live off her money. When he does not reclaim his money from Macmaster, it is assumed that this means that the latter's wife is his mistress. Malicious gossip is relayed to his father, who dies believing his son a scoundrel; and his bank returns a cheque made out to his club, thereby obliging him to resign and thus be publicly dishonoured.

The latter incident, engineered by a young man with designs on Sylvia, evokes from Christopher the opinion that it is the war that has made quite 'decent' people behave like 'squits'. This is a not particularly convincing judgment: at other times Tietjens clearly considers the rot to have set in during the previous century, with the self-conscious, 'circumspect' highmindedness of the progressive Victorian intelligentsia—whose duplicity is epitomised for him in the 'spiritual adulteries' of the pre-Raphaelite poet-painter Rossetti, hero of Macmaster and of the latter's mistress/wife Edith Ethel. It is significant that whereas the title words of the opening volume *Some Do Not* (1924)—from Pope's 'Some enter at the portals, some do not'—seem likely at first to be applied to the self-made, opportunist Macmaster, it is the latter who achieves every kind of success and is publicly honoured by an establishment long-since perverted in its values. It is Tietjens, then, who proves to be one of those who 'do not'—doubly so, in that it is precisely because he scrupulously refrains from (for example) assisting the government that employs him in perpetrating a fraud, and from defending his own reputation at the expense of those who have wronged him, that he is denied Macmaster's success. At the same time he denies himself the happiness of consummating his love for Valentine Wannop, the daughter of his father's oldest friend, on the eve of his departure for France: of the countless tommies who find themselves in a position to spend their last night with their girl with little need for worrying about the consequences, 'some do, and some do not', and Christopher is one of the latter.

However, if the war finally sees to it that there will be 'no more parades' of such an outworn code of behaviour, it at the same time creates for this truly Christian gentleman a climate in which he feels that he can abdicate from his responsibilities as heir to Groby, the family estate. In the third volume *A Man Could Stand Up* (1926) the men who finally stand up from the trenches see a world irrevocably altered, one in which even a Tietjens can find a corner for himself and his mistress to be happy in.

Their happiness is portrayed in a fourth volume *The Last Post* (1928), of doubtful merit: a subsequent collection of Ford's works omitting it, as a postscript which Ford himself later regretted. The trilogy that remains must rank among the outstanding creations of the period. K. R. R.

Forester, Cecil Scott (1899–1966), English novelist, best known as the creator of Hornblower, an English naval captain of the Napoleonic wars who has justly joined the ranks of romantic British heroes. *The Happy Return* (1937) began a series which covered Hornblower's career from midshipman to admiral and in a succession of best-selling novels gave a fascinating accurate picture of the navy of the time. Hornblower's complex character is made powerful by his self-discipline and skill, and these characteristics, with their application by the individual to his own circumstances, are the motif in all Forester's work. *The General* (1936), one of the best World War I novels and probably his own finest, shows a cavalryman, without any imagination, in a situation that he never anticipated; the impression is made of a brave and admirable man, even though his effect is nearly disastrous.

Forester's first book, the crime novel *Payment Deferred* (1923), a brilliant study of the disintegration of the mind of a murderer, was filmed; as were *The African Queen* (1935) and Hornblower's adventures under the title *Captain Horatio Hornblower*. Other titles include the pre-Hornblower *The Gun* (1933), a story set at the time of the Peninsular War; *A Ship of the Line* (1939), awarded the James Tait Black Memorial Prize, *The Commodore* (1944) and *Hornblower and the Hotspur* (1962); the posthumous autobiographical work *Long Before Forty* (1967); and a play *Nurse Cavell* with C. E. Bechofer Roberts (produced in 1934).

H. C.; K. M. H.

Forster, E. M. (Edward Morgan Forster; 1879–   ), one of the major English novelists of the twentieth century, is in many ways the outstanding literary spokesman for humanist values. The meaning of the term 'humanist' has undergone some separation of meanings over the past fifty years, so that it may be used today to denote either a classical scholar (its original meaning) or an agnostic who finds life's ultimate reality in personal relationships; but in Forster's humanism these two meanings coalesce. It would not be enough to say of him that a classical education engendered humane values and a rational—and therefore sceptical—approach to organised Christianity: for there can be found in some of his novels and stories a positive belief, however humorously expressed, that the ancient Greek gods accurately represented spiritual realities, and that a knowledge of these realities is a prerequisite for an honest human relationship.

Not only the Christian religion, but also our civilisation's conventions of thought, feeling and behaviour—sanctioned and strengthened, in the case of the English upper-middle class, by public-school education—are blamed for unreal attitudes to human nature and to individual people. These attitudes are thrown into relief by being contrasted with the spontaneity and directness of contemporary Italy, a country whose 'naturalness' combined with a rich humanist heritage makes it a powerful symbol. Two kinds of hero recur in Forster's first three novels—the 'natural' man in whom good and evil are integrated, and who has been unspoilt by this social conditioning (e.g. Gino in *Where Angels Fear to Tread*, 1905, and Wonham in *The Longest Journey*, 1907); and the person who through a humanist education has come through to a knowledge of the truth (e.g. Ansell in *The Longest Journey*). The 'natural' man requires no 'salvation': on a trial-and-error basis he will acquire wisdom, and he will progress to spiritual maturity. But for those who inhabit the civilised world there will be 'symbolic moments' of challenge: only if they will expose themselves unflinchingly to the truth, and obey the dictates of the heart, will they 'live'. Similarly the villains exhibit a common pattern: in rejecting the challenge and conforming to the world's conventions they have become 'benighted' and have ceased to be real living people (e.g. Pembroke in *The Longest Journey* and Charlotte in *A Room with a View*, 1908). This humanist doctrine of salvation shows a remarkable analogy to that of the Christianity that Forster had rejected. And when we find the resurrection theme presented in terms of genetic continuity, the parallel is even more striking.

Together with the positive values of Forster's humanism, there is a strong vein of tragedy. In our society the 'saved' will inevitably be few, and the world will dictate the failure of many who have genuinely tried to create life and meaning amidst its emptiness. One of the most tragic figures is Ricky Elliott in *The Longest Journey*. The delicate child of a disastrous marriage, he has survived public school and arrived at Cambridge with his ideals intact but with a deep need for companionship. This need is partly filled by the friends he acquires—these including the philosopher Ansell, whose arguments about metaphysical reality are the starting-point of the book. But Ricky needs love, and falls a prey to the first girl who offers it to him—a girl whose first appearance is ignored by Ansell on the ground that she does not exist. Ansell later convicts her of lying and of lack of seriousness, thereby confirming his initial judgment that she represents a spiritual vacuum.

Agnes Pembroke is, in fact, on the rebound from a previous and real love. And her relationship with Ricky is at the outset a thing of some beauty, a beauty which it would be unthinkable to reject. Thereafter the compromises begin: in order to secure the kind of living that his writing will not earn he becomes a schoolmaster at Sawston, a minor public school where his brother-in-law Herbert is a housemaster, and gradually succumbs to the false values purveyed there. The measure of his deterioration is his behaviour towards his Wiltshire aunt's uncouth and illegitimate protégé, Stephen Wonham, whom he discovers to be his half-brother. Initially, despite protests, he accepts Agnes's view of Stephen as an embarrassment, and is persuaded to withhold this information from him: the climax comes when Stephen, having learnt the truth and come to greet his brother, encounters him with chequebook in hand prepared to buy off someone who has become a threat to his respectability. Even when brought to an awareness of his spiritual peril following a spectacular denunciation by Ansell, Ricky is still unable to respond to Stephen simply as a person: where formerly he was an embarrassment or a threat, he now appears as the son and image of his dead mother. However, there is still time for him to realise Stephen's power to save, and he dies in the act of rescuing him from the path of an oncoming train. After Ricky's death, the true worth of the short stories he had written before going to Sawston is established; and Stephen has learned how to live in a world of railway trains and Victorian schoolmasters.

Forster's fourth novel *Howard's End* (1910), his second most important book, integrates all that he has previously expressed about the state of England. The development of large-scale industry and commerce has produced depersonalisation and desecration, and has given birth to insensitive men of property like the Wilcoxes, who inhabit 'the outer world of telegrams and anger'; it has also produced Bloomsbury humanists like the Schlegels, who parade their reaction against it in terms of 'the inner life', but whose comfortable liberalism is only made possible through the inheritance of some of its capital; and thirdly there are its victims, represented by the mean and purposeless existence of the impoverished office-worker Leonard Bast. But the fine old Hertfordshire house that gives the book its title embodies—as does Ruth Wilcox, its keeper—the traditional sanctities of an older England, now fast disappearing: an England peopled with spirits that we have already experienced in the native Wiltshire of Stephen Wonham, an England of semi-personalised, semi-instinctive living rooted in the untamed vitality of a natural landscape.

The centrepiece of the novel is the marriage of Henry Wilcox, after the death of his first wife Ruth, to Margaret Schlegel. 'Only connect' is the oft-quoted motto of the book, and we may find its highest expression in this marital connection between people embodying aspects of England that Forster has hitherto represented as being in deadly enmity. Somehow, he is saying, these two worlds must be reconciled: just as 'the passion and the prose' inside a Henry Wilcox, and the dual standards of public and private life, must be made to connect. For Margaret, the union means the acquiring of roots; and the reconciliation works sufficiently in the end for her to take on the guardianship of Howard's End, a rôle for which Ruth had designated her before she died.

Being childless, the question remains: to whom shall she herself bequeath it? Symbolically and prophetically, an heir has been provided by a liaison between Leonard Bast and Margaret's younger sister Helen, who has realised that while she cannot make a man of Leonard by giving him the money he so urgently needs, she can do so by offering herself. We have met Helen, the more passionate and intransigent of the sisters, earlier in the book, where her abortive relationship with Henry's son Charles has underlined the incompatibility of their two worlds: and it is Charles who finally kills the 'seducer' of his stepmother's sister (Henry having previously ruined him financially) by giving him the conventional 'thrashing'. But the inheritance of Howard's End, and by extension of England, passes securely to the child of humanity and need.

The theme of reconciliation is taken up again, and given its final statement, in Forster's fifth and most famous novel, *Passage to India* (1924). On one level it is a tragedy of the failure of humanism in the face of one of its greatest challenges—the bridging of racial divisions; and the book ends with its original heroes, Aziz the young Indian doctor and Fielding the non-conforming English teacher, forced asunder by influences greater than themselves. Yet against their divisive power is set the unifying influence of an all-embracing religion of total acceptance, in which the importance of the individual and of his personal relationships is much diminished. In Forster's depiction of Hinduism we meet again that 'knowledge of good-and-evil'—as opposed to good and evil—which was a mark of enlightenment in the early novels: what that religion is shown to reject is the separation of the enlightened from those who walk in darkness, the truly living from the virtually non-existent, the apostles of the inner life from the denizens of the outer world. Insofar as men surrender to the power of such an inclusive religion, there is total reconciliation: when that power recedes, there is division.

The 'outer world'—here seen at its most unpleasant—is represented by Anglo-Indian officialdom: the faith in personal relationships, by the elderly Mrs Moore, who has arrived to visit her son Ronnie, the city magistrate, accompanied by her prospective daughter-in-law, Adela Quested. The action begins in a mosque, the sanctuary of Aziz's Muslim India: the latter's passionate belief in the possibility of personal relationships between English and Indian belonging naturally with a religion which, like Christianity and Forster's earlier humanism, has a philosophy of division. The story ends in a temple, with the all-embracing Hindu India of Professor Godbole, who has replaced Aziz as the focal point. The crucial middle section centres on a moment of truth in the celebrated Marabar caves—caves whose echoing emptiness gives back to those who enter them the hollowness of their own pretensions. For Mrs Moore, who retires in a state of near-collapse after the first cave, it is the realisation that 'everything exists, nothing has value': her spiritual passage to India, already half-accomplished (as Aziz has recognised), is nearing completion, and though she cannot long survive the experience, she is to live on as a spirit in the popular Hindu pantheism. For Adela, who goes on to the next cave, the revelation is of the emptiness of her loveless relationship with Ronnie: and in her panic she experiences what has been generally thought a hallucination, imagining that she is being sexually assaulted by her companion. What actually happens is left deliberately ambiguous—ambiguity being of the very nature of India—but the succeeding trial, in which her sudden withdrawal of the charge ensures Aziz's acquittal, does for him what the caves have already done for the two women. From now on, Fielding cannot be his friend unless he will wholeheartedly espouse the cause of Indian nationalism: he must be either for or against.

When the book ends, Fielding has married Mrs Moore's daughter Stella, and has been reconciled with Aziz: but after the great Hindu festival which is the climax of the book, the pathways of the two friends diverge again. This final statement, of both the value and the limitations of personal relationships, of both the possibilities of union and the inevitability of division, is the last word of Forster the novelist. In the forty years and more that have elapsed since its publication—years that have seen the final disintegration of the world he portrayed—he has produced only a miscellany of shorter pieces, chiefly short stories and fragments, essays and criticism. His critical work *Aspects of the Novel* (1927) is outstanding in its genre. K. R. R.

Fowles, John (1927–), English novelist. With the publication of his ambitious second novel *The Magus* (1966), it appeared likely that he would escape the fate of being, as seemed possible, imprisoned, and for ever identified, by the instant success of his first novel *The Collector* (1963). The latter is about a young pools-winner keeping a girl captive in an isolated house: Fowles uses this framework to go quite deeply into the psychology and social conditioning of his characters. It is a better novel than the insensitive screen version would suggest. He has also published a philosophical work, *The Aristos* (1965). C. B.

Fox, John (1863–1919), American novelist, wrote two immensely sentimental best-selling novels: *The Little Shepherd of Kingdom Come* (1903), about a shepherd lad of the Cumberland mountains who goes off to fight in the civil war; and *The Trail of the Lonesome Pine* (1908), about an engineer who comes to help develop the primitive state of Kentucky and becomes involved in the life of its inhabitants, one of whom—a beautiful, illiterate girl—he marries. K. R. R.

Frame, Janet (1924–), New Zealand author now living in England. Her work explores the territory of madness, its fantasies and delusions, and finds in it a truth to reality that shames what passes for sanity; while sometimes on a deeper level these imaginings stand as a symbol of the fictitious 'real' world invented by the novelist, as in the strikingly original *Scented Gardens for the Blind* (1963).

Janet Frame has herself undergone the experiences that pervade her novels and a knowledge of her background is vital to an appreciation of her work. Her autobiographical piece 'Beginnings' in the New Zealand periodical *Landfall* (March 1965) describes her childhood in a family of antipodean Brontës, a virtual 'pocket of poetry' in the provincial wilderness; her own growing inability to communicate or conform to the outside world; her periods in mental hospitals, and her re-emergence through the therapy of writing down the words, the patterns, the thoughts that plagued her so.

Her first publication was *The Lagoon* (1951), a volume of short stories, slight in comparison with her later work but promising enough to win her a grant. She achieved full stature and immediate recognition with her first full-length novel *Owls do Cry* (1957) concerning a family of children, the sisters Francie, Daphne and Chicks Withers and their epileptic brother Toby, a family in many points closely resembling her own. The extreme poverty of the Withers in material things is contrasted with their richness in things of the imagination—the children finding their 'treasure', for example, in the town rubbish dump. As the children grow up, it is those with physical or mental abnormalities and shunned by society that either develop a defiant inner life and resourcefulness—Toby both in his miserly saving and in his career as a demolition expert—or achieve what is ultimately revealed to be the clearest vision—Daphne in her mental asylum dwelling daily in the abyss that the others fear. And when we read the inner life of Chicks, so emphatically the average housewife and mother, in all its barrenness and banality, the fabric of her day-to-day existence is revealed as a precarious structure, built (like the new brick house she plans to build over the top of their childhood rubbish dump) to camouflage the extent of her dread. Toby's life in the twilight zone of physical and mental stress in which his epilepsy places him was to be further explored in *The Edge of the Alphabet* (1962).

In *Faces in the Water* (1961), through the fictitious character of Istina Mavet, Janet Frame was able to recreate some of what she observed during her own period in the various wards of mental hospitals; and this book, almost documentary in the flavour of its first-person narrative, is remarkable for the beauty of its prose, and the unfolding and developing shape of what could have been a formless narrative. This beauty is enhanced by the sense of indignation aroused by the conditions in the hospitals and the pity at the tragic waste of human material.

Her later novels deal with subjects and backgrounds far removed from the complex and painful personal events that drove her initially to write. *The Adaptable Man* (1965), which may be seen as an ironic attack on progress and is set in East Anglia, was followed by a collection of stories *The Reservoir* (1966) and a further novel *A State of Siege* (1967).

S. R.

France, Anatole (Anatole Thibault; 1844–1924), French writer, born in Paris, was son of a bookseller on the Quai Malaquais and thus loved books and documents, and classical antiquity, from childhood. His first published work was poetry: *Poèmes dorés* ['Golden poems'] (1873) and *Les Noces corinthiennes* ['Corinthian wedding'] (1876). Appointed Senate librarian, he discovered his true vocation with *Le Crime de Sylvestre Bonnard* [*The Crime of Sylvestre Bonnard*], published in 1881. This is an ironic novel, with a colouring of humanism and sceptical philosophy. It was followed by *Le Livre de mon ami* [*My Friend's Book*], a book of childhood memories, in 1885; the historical novel *Thaïs* (1889); and the philosophical tales *La Rôtisserie de la Reine Pédauque* [*The Queen Pédauque Eating-House*] (1892) and *Les Opinions de Jérôme Coignard* [*The Opinions of Jérôme Coignard*] (1893). Next came a disillusioned love story *Le Lys rouge* [*Red Lily*] (1894), based on his affair with Mme de Caillavet, and a volume of sceptical reflections and maxims *Le Jardin d'Epicure* [*The Garden of Epicurus*] (1894). Then he went back to his first love, the ironical tale, with *L'Orme du mail* [*The Elmtree on the Mall*] (1897) and *Le Mannequin d'osier* [*The Wicket Puppet*] (1897). These two are the first volumes of France's *Histoire contemporaine* [*Contemporary History*] and are a light but implacable satire on the religious intrigues and foibles of a small country town.

The year 1897 was a turning-point in France's life. He joined Emile Zola in his campaign for justice for Captain Dreyfus, and from then on played an active part in republican and socialist politics. He redoubled his political activity in connection with the Russian revolution of 1905 and the approach of the first world war. But he was deeply disappointed by the failure of the Russian revolutionaries and the anti-trade union activities of Republican government ministers. This pessimism is reflected in *L'Ile des pingouins* [*Penguin Island*] (1908), *La Révolte des anges* [*Revolt of the Angels*] (1914) and even in *Les Dieux ont soif* [*The Gods are Athirst*] (1912). These three social fictions are perhaps his best-known works, especially *Penguin Island*, a mature and diverting satire based on a simple idea: a humorous interpretation of history in a series of episodes illustrating the origins and development of laws and customs, with penguins standing in for human beings. Here France reveals himself as a sceptical but urbane student of history who questions the idea that progress is irreversible.

In 1914 France retired to his property 'La Béchellerie' in Touraine, and —heartbroken at the outbreak of war, horrified and discouraged by human folly—devoted his last years to reliving his childhood memories in *Le Petit Pierre* [*Little Peter*] (1918) and *La Vie en fleur* [*Life in Bloom*] (1922). He was awarded a Nobel Prize in 1921. His thought had evolved from sceptical rationalism through socialist militancy to the despair of human moral progress displayed in *Penguin Island*. His writing was classical in its purity and simplicity, its subtle irony and comedy. But it was also tender and coloured by pity for humankind. Irony and pity are the two keys to Anatole France's art. A. L. W.

Frank, Anne (1929–44), German-Jewish writer (in Dutch) of *Het Achterhus* [*The Diary of a Young Girl*] (1944) subsequently dramatised as *The Diary of Anne Frank*. This reflects the growing to a remarkable emotional maturity of a young Jewish adolescent in hiding during the war confined with other refugees from the Germans in a small attic and subject to all the external pressures of the confined and the hunted. Anne Frank records simply and movingly an individual finding unembittered positive values while subject to these intense and continual strains. She was eventually captured and executed by the Nazis. D. L. P.

Frankau, Pamela (1908–67), English novelist. Daughter of the novelist Gilbert Frankau, she began her literary career at eighteen when she joined the staff of *Woman's Journal* and wrote her first novel while travelling to and from work by train. The novel *Marriage of Harlequin* appeared in

1927 and was followed by a number of competently written short stories. Her earliest novels although well written were rather inconsequential, but her reputation has grown with each successive novel. The roundly praised *The Devil We Know* (1939), a study of a young Jewish scenario writer, was followed by *A Democrat Dies* (1940), a political satire; but her first big success was *Willow Cabin* (1949), a sensitively written love story. In much of her writing, critics have detected the influence of Michael Arlen.

Other titles include an autobiography *I Find Four People* (1935); the novels *Wreath for the Enemy* (1954) and *Slaves of the Lamp* (1965); and *Pen to Paper* (1961), a study on the art of writing novels. K. M. H.

Franklin, Miles (1879–1954), Australian writer and woman of letters, wrote her first book before she was twenty—*My Brilliant Career* (published 1901). Despite its popularity, she produced nothing further until *Old Blastus of Bandicoot* (1932) and *Bring the Monkey* (1933), neither of which was particularly remarkable; but in 1936 *All That Swagger*, a prize-winning historical novel, restored her public and confirmed the critics' early predictions of her assured place in Australian literature as an author noted for her humour and feminine insight. She followed this with several works in collaboration with others—a biography of Joseph Furphy, a satire, a children's book—and after her death her reputation soared yet again with the posthumous publication of *Laughter, Not for a Cage* (1956), a review of Australian literature so outspoken and original that it reminded readers of the precocity of *My Brilliant Career* and its sequel *My Career Goes Bung* (publication delayed until 1946). In addition to these many and varied writings, and to her energetic provision of encouragement and advice to young writers, it now seems that she may be the author hidden behind the *nom-de-plume* of 'Brent of Bin Bin' (q.v.). S. R.

Freeling, Nicolas (1927–), English detective novelist, who uses the detective story as a medium in which to demonstrate the subtleties of human relationships which are invaded rather than dominated by crime and violence. His Dutch detective Van der Valk, who first appeared in *Love in Amsterdam* (1962), is a kindly man and a professional, and his methods are only unorthodox in a professional ambit. Freeling's character studies are varied and perceptive, and his descriptions highly evocative.

Other titles include *The King of the Rainy Country* (1966), *The Dresden Green* (1966) and *Strike Out Where Not Applicable* (1967). H. C.

Freud, Sigmund (1856–1939), Austrian psychologist, the founder of modern psycho-analysis, is not so much important as a literary figure himself, but rather of immense significance as an influence on modern writers, for example Wedekind. The results of his psychological research were published at the end of the century in *Untersuchungen über die Traumdeutungen* [*Investigation into the Interpretation of Dreams*] (1900). This destroyed many of the older psychological theories based on mechanistic ideas of physical science, all the more completely since Alfred Einstein was at that time undermining accepted scientific systems with his enunciation of the principles of relativity. Freud rapidly became the leader of an important Viennese school of psycho-analysts who emphasised the rôle of the subconscious as a determinant of behaviour and action, and especially that of subconscious determinants of a sexual character. Sex had largely been a taboo subject in the nineteenth century; the growing insistence upon its scientific importance made it possible for all writers after Freud to explore this largely unexplored territory. G. W.

Freyre, Gilberto (1900–   ), Brazilian sociologist and social historian born in Recife (Pernambuco), has had an immense influence in Brazilian literature. He made contact with *modernista* poets and writers in Rio de Janeiro and São Paulo during the twenties and shared their interest in Luso-Brazilian folklore. Freyre himself became the leader of the traditionalist regional movement which sprang up in the north-eastern states. In 1933 he published his best-known work *Casa-grande e senzala* [*The Masters and the Slaves*] which provoked fierce discussion and provided a scientific basis for the 'novel of the north-east'. *Casa-grande e senzala* studies the origins and evolution of Brazilian society, based on the great patriarchal slave-owning families and their sugar plantations in the north-eastern regions. His interpretation of the social history of the plantation manor reveals the distinctive civilisation of Brazil. On the important issue of miscegenation Freyre disagrees with earlier theories. He firmly opposes the pessimism of Euclydes da Cunha who saw the *mestizo* as degenerate in *Os sertões* [*Rebellion in the Backlands*] and accuses Euclydes of 'ethnocentric exaggerations rigidly based on 19th century theories'. In 1936, Freyre published a companion work *Sobrados e mucambos* [*The Mansions and The Shanties*] which studies the breakdown of the patriarchal system. Subsequent works develop related aspects of Brazil's social history and formation under the triple force of immigration, industrialisation and urbanisation. These include *Nordeste* ['North-east'] (1937), *O mundo que o Português criou* [*The World that the Portuguese Created*] (1940), *Região e tradição* ['Region and tradition'] (1941) and *Ordem e progresso* ['Order and progress'] (1959). Founder and director of the Instituto Joaquim Nabuco in his native Recife where much important sociological research is carried out, Freyre has also travelled and lectured extensively in Europe and the United States. G. P.

Frisch, Max (1911–), Swiss-German dramatist and prose-writer, born in Zurich. His first play, *Stahl* ['Steel'], was written at the age of sixteen; but it was never produced, and he pursued first journalism and subsequently architecture as a profession. Only in 1955 did he become a full-time writer.

Before this, however, he had established himself as a dramatist with what he described as 'an attempt towards a requiem', namely *Nun singen sie wieder* ['Now they sing again'] (1945). This describes the encounter between hostages who have been shot, and their executioners. In 1946 he published *Die chinesische Mauer* [*The Chinese Wall*], a satirical study of the dangers of dictatorship, featuring amongst others Huang Ti, Napoleon, Pontius Pilate, Brutus, Philip of Spain and Cleopatra. A challenging theme emerged in *Als Der Krieg zur Ende War* ['When the war was over'] (1949), the question of war guilt. This deals with the wife of a German officer who, in order to protect a German hidden in her cellar, has an affair with a Russian officer. Then she realises that she is in love with the Russian; but when her husband is found guilty of war crimes, her lover abandons her and she commits suicide. *Graf Olderland* ['Count Olderland'] (1956) was described by Frisch as a 'morality story'; a lawyer rejects the orthodox patterns of social life and as the leader of a gangster group creates a new pattern of society which is more terrifying than the one which he rejected.

Major dramatic successes in the years that followed were *Don Juan oder die Liebe zur Geometrie* [*Don Juan or Love for Geometry*] (1962), a parody of the traditional Don Juan theme in which the hero, after trying to be true to himself as an individual by withdrawing from the world to study geometry in a monastery, ends up a married man; the splendid comedy *Herr Biedermann und die Brandstifter* [*The Fire-Raisers*] (1958); and the play with which his world reputation was established, one with the much more serious theme of life under political pressure, *Andorra* [*Andorra*] (published 1962).

His prose work *Jürg Reinhart* (1934), *Die Schwierigen oder J'adore ce qui me brûle* ['The difficult ones or J'adore ce qui me brûle'] and *Bin oder die Reise nach Peking* ['Am or the Journey to Peking'] (1945) led finally to *Stiller* [*I'm not Stiller*] (1954) which won international acclaim. Indeed, his linguistic virtuosity, his wealth of imagination, his irony and his knowledge of man in all his aspects have led critics to compare him with Proust, Joyce, Mann and Musil. His works have been translated into sixteen languages. G. W.

Frost, Robert (1875–1963), American poet. Superficially Frost can be categorised as a poet of nature, especially of rural New England. He appears a kind of emasculated Wordsworth, concerned to find truth and beauty in nature but lacking the latter's transcendentalism. He is not uninfluenced by the main literary movements of the early twentieth century; the symbolism that lies under the surface description of his poetry is sophisticated and the tensions of thought and feeling are maturely expressed. But in general Frost can be said to be in reaction against the cultural trends of a developing industrial society.

Frost was born in San Francisco. His father died when he was ten and he went to live in Lawrence, Massachusetts. He changed schools a number of times before attending Dartmouth College which he left after a few months. He worked in a textile mill before going to Harvard in 1897. He left in 1899 without a degree, worked at various odd jobs and then on a farm for eleven years before going to England in 1912. Up to this time no American publisher had accepted his work but he made his name in England with two books of verse: *A Boy's Will* (1913) and *North of Boston* (1914). He returned, famous, to the United States in 1915. In 1916 he was made Professor of English at Amherst College where he remained until 1938.

Frost became one of the best known of American poets both in his own country and certainly in England, perhaps because his work is cast more into a classical than a modern idiom. Volumes continued to appear regularly for almost half a century, including *Mountain Interval* (1916), *New Hampshire* (1923), *West Running Brook* (1928), *Selected Poems* (1936), *Collected Poems* (1939), *A Witness Tree* (1943), *Steeple Bush* (1947), *Complete Poems* (1949) and *In the Clearing* (1962). He won numerous medals and honours including four Pulitzer prizes; and in 1961 he was asked to compose and read a poem at John Kennedy's inauguration as President of the United States.

The reality with which Frost's poetry is concerned is inside the everyday world of men and not outside it in any kind of metaphysical way. Wallace Stevens categorises the nature of Frost's involvements in the following extract:

> And it is he, in the substance of his region,
> Wood of his forests and stone out of his fields
> or from under his mountains.

Frost seeks identity for the individuality of man in a context where men play meaningful rôles; in other words there is no point in being an individual without being possessed of a secure background and environment. For him, this security is to be found in the permanence of a small rural community, even in the particular vocational skill with which a man is endowed. In the poem 'The Axe Helve' from the *New Hampshire* volume the only criterion for assessing Baptiste, a foreigner among a particularly insular Yankee group, is his capacity for craftsmanship. He gets his human rating in terms of his natural skill:

> Where I must judge if what he knew about an axe
> That not everybody else knew was to count
> For nothing in the measure of a neighbour.
> Hard if, though cast away for life with Yankees,
> A Frenchman couldn't get his human rating.

Frost is always concerned to capture the exact physical details of the environment around him. He is a symbolist, however, in the sense that there is more than surface meaning to his descriptions: thus in evoking an individual in a particular natural setting, he is often referring the world of nature to that of man. In 'Birches' from *Mountain Interval* the two worlds come together but never finally fuse. There is nothing of the reverie of Wordsworth in the latter's 'Intimations of Immortality' ode: in Frost's poem the swinging on the birches, the interaction between the boy and the tree, are merely a compensation for the failure to get to heaven:

> I'd like to go by climbing a birch tree,
> And climb black branches up a snow-white trunk
> Toward heaven, till the tree could bear no more,
> That would be good both going and coming back
> One could do worse than be a swinger of birches.

The world of the New England countryside is often tough and hostile and certainly never more than neutral to man's presence. Frost is not an affirmative poet; he seems, rather, to build a series of defences against malevolent forces. In 'Mending a Wall' from *North of Boston* he not only establishes a careful sense of craftsmanship as the farmer erects a traditional dry structure of stone upon stone, but evokes for the reader a feeling that protection is necessary to ward off some kind of evil encroachment. The encroachment is more openly dealt with when it involves the inroads of technical civilisation that threaten the serenity of the closely knit rural group: the unity and integration of such groups being the centre of the poet's moral attitudes. In 'The Egg and the Machine' from *West Running Brook* Frost takes up an apparently silly defensive attitude by threatening to hurl an egg at a train. He does not appear to be facing up to reality. Conceivably this is not a failure of realisation but an awareness that co-operation with the forces of contemporary society is impossible and that any gesture, however ironic, is justifiable:

> He told the distance, 'I am armed for war.
> The next machine that has the power to pass
> Will get this plasm in its goggle glass.'

There is no need to criticise Frost for failing to integrate with contemporary American society. There is a possible failure, however, to establish positive values. It is not that everything is chaos for him in the way that the universe is meaningless to Henry Adams: but his self-limitation to the reality of the rural world—craft, courage, friendship, an ironic acceptance of one's lot—seems often to preclude any soaring of the intellect or of the intuitive faculties into, let us say, religious affirmation. But can Frost really be criticised for not having a transcendent vision? In a poem like 'The Wilful Homecoming' from *A Witness Tree* it should be enough that there is a full appreciation of the toughness and will that is part of a man's character and that the reader's sympathies are fully extended to the subject of the verse. The words round off the sensation: 'exerting', 'astride', 'imprint', 'peer against', 'calmly consider', 'shrewd'; can one demand more of poetry than this hard realisation of the particular?

> The snow blows on him and off him, exerting force
> Downward to make him sit astride a drift,
> Imprint a saddle and calmly consider a course.
> He peers out shrewdly into the thick and swift.

D. L. P.

Fry, Christopher (1907–), English playwright who introduced in the late forties a revival of poetic drama, strongly influenced by T. S. Eliot as well as by the French dramatist Anouilh whose play *L'Invitation au château* he translated as *Ring Round the Moon.* His play *A Phoenix too Frequent* (1948) showed promise of a return to the verbal excitement of the Elizabethan theatre—verse packed with conceits and exuberant wit, engaging if at times overwrought. This promise appeared to be realised in *The Lady's Not for Burning* (1949), an allegory set in the fifteenth century where a soldier with a death-wish is persuaded to go on living by a young suspected witch who is condemned to death. The irony and comedy of the situation are realised in the atmosphere created by the writing rather than in spectacle, and this gives the play much of its charm; but this is a source of potential dramatic weakness, which is evident in other plays where Fry's natural skill and sense of stagecraft become subordinated to the poetry. In *The Light is Dark Enough* (1954), for instance, action is almost entirely lost to a form of poetic monologue.

Other plays which enjoyed a certain vogue for a time were *A Sleep of Prisoners* (1951), a passion play, seriously conceived and with a complex method of presentation in which four soldiers sleeping in a bombed church enact their allegorical dreams in commentary upon each other; and *Venus Observed* (1950), where the problems of youth and maturity are discussed in a welter of images and comic situations. Later plays such as *Curtmantle* (1961) failed to revive Fry's waning reputation. R. A. K.

Fuentes, Carlos (1929–), Mexican novelist, who has lived and studied in several European and Latin American countries and in the U.S.A., and is probably best known to English readers as the author of *The Death of Artemio Cruz*.

His early surrealistic short stories remain unpublished but with *La región más transparente* [*Where The Air Is Clear*] (1958), his first novel, which together with Rulfo's *Pedro Páramo* ended the patronised quarantine of Mexican fiction, we hear the authentic, strident voice of urban Mexico. An iconoclastic protest against the institutionalisation of the Mexican revolution exemplified in the career of Federico Robles, this ambitious literary mural exploits the full historical and social palette in an attempt to shock us into comprehension of the Mexican actuality—its Manichean duality, 'always two, the impeached eagle, the nocturnal sun', its contingent exorcism, 'Quetzalcoátls and Corteses and Iturbides and Juarezes and Porfirios and Zapatas, all lumps in our throats. What is the true image? Which of the many?'

Near the end of the novel Jaime Ceballos, a young Guanajuato lawyer, arrives in Mexico City; *Las buenas conciencias* [*The Good Conscience*] (1959) recalls his former short-lived tumescent piety and adolescent idealism, conventional bourgeois compromise, and cosseted provincial aspirations. By December 1955 he is trying to ingratiate himself with the national figure whose life we review in *La muerte de Artemio Cruz* [*The Death of Artemio Cruz*] (1962). Here, notwithstanding an evident indebtedness to Proust, Joyce, Faulkner and Dos Passos, Fuentes' dictum that Spanish-American novelists should leaven Balzac with Butor, that is, blend the public and the personal, fuse the social and the psychological, marry technical innovation to poetic intuition, is boldly implemented in an irregular series of cinematographic recapitulations and interior monologues. Cruz is Mexico. His mixed blood, uneasy marriage, jejune revolutionary ardour and mature rapacity are an analogue of contemporary Mexican society. Is it too on its deathbed? M. D. E.

Fugard, Athol (1933–), foremost South African dramatist. His two published plays, *The Bloodknot* (1963) and *Hello and Goodbye* (1966), are intensely theatrical and modern, not least in both the compactness and the width achieved by their being 'two-people' plays. The former examines the personalities and attitudes of a dark- and a light-skinned brother in a shanty-town, and is vast in both its subjective and socio-political overtones; the latter exposes the greeds and animosities in a brother-sister relationship in a fight for a patrimony. C. P.

Fuller, Roy (1912–), English writer, has achieved a solid if minor literary reputation. He has published several volumes of poetry but he is more distinguished as a novelist, his major titles being *Image of a Society* (1956), *The Ruined Boys* (1959), *The Fathers Comedy* (1961) and *My Child, My Sister* (1965). His favourite themes are concerned with the corrosive values and convention of middle-class society and he asserts that:

What determines human fate
Is the class structure of the state.

In *Image of a Society*, his best-known work, the middle-class writer hero finds himself in an ambiguous position towards the building society for which he works. He hates the ruthless calculation of the business world, yet derives his own security from its stability. This conflict forms the crux of Fuller's thought. Confessing that 'The dreams of tremendous statements fade', he establishes for us the tone of his writing.

Fuller's poetry develops from the 1930s when he was occupied with those same social themes that involved Auden and Spender. He contributed to *New Verse* and *Twentieth Century Verse*. In *Epitaphs and Occasions* (1949) he becomes a satirist of the post-war world. His later, mature poetry has the perspective of a writer who has learned to handle universal themes, especially the dichotomy between the order of art and the chaos of humanity. In 'The Final Period' from *Brutus's Orchard* (1957) he asserts a measure of positiveness, howbeit melancholy:

To some utopia of forgiving
And of acceptance I have come.
But still rebellious, still living.

Collected Poems (*1936–61*) was published in 1962. M. T.; D. L. P.

Furmanov, Dmitri Andreyevich (1891–1926), Soviet novelist of the twenties and creator of a major Soviet classic *Chapayev* [*Chapayev*] (1923). Born in the Ivanovo-Voznesensk region of peasant stock, he read much and studied hard to escape his depressing surroundings. He was sent to the Turkish front in 1915 with the Medical Corps. After the revolution he became first an anarchist and then a Communist Party member. The novel draws a sharp contrast between the picturesque revolutionary hero Chapayev and the Bolshevik commissar Klychkov (a self-portrait), the latter having been sent to direct Chapayev's undisciplined emotional revolutionary fervour into pre-calculated, disciplined channels—that is, to be a snooping watchdog over his own band. The book recounts Chapayev's activities and death, and reveals the commissar's scant respect for the legendary hero while at the same time sympathetically portraying Chapayev's concern for his men. B. W.

Furphy, Joseph (1843–1912), Australian writer (under the pen-name of Tom Collins) of *Such is Life* (1903), a rambling, voluminous work in comic vein. The book is given some thread of continuity by the presence of the first-person narrator, Tom Collins himself, and by the way in which its setting in the Riverina district is used to provide an impressionistic picture of an area and its people. Almost every type of humour is to be found in it—farce, ludicrous exaggeration, tongue-in-cheek anecdotes, unacknowledged classical quotation embedded in the prose to surprise the reader like a private joke. At other times, he writes with great pathos, for example in the section dealing with the child lost in the bush. *Rigby's Romance* (shortened version 1921; complete 1946), originally intended as part of *Such is Life* but omitted to make the book more manageable, has a different and political emphasis in that it examines the Australian way of life in terms of the basic conflict between the squatter and the teamster, with Furphy taking the part of the teamster, and in doing so attempting a theory of socialism. S. R.

G

Gadda, Carlo Emilio (1893–   ), Italian writer. A volunteer during the first world war, he has also worked abroad as an engineer. An author of extraordinary talent and limitless resources, Gadda has exerted a lively imagination and remarkable versatility in adopting a mixture of language and dialect, high-flown style and technical jargon, slang and humorous terms in conjunction with linguistic gimmicks and unconventional syntax to increase literary effectiveness. His best-known work is *Quer pasticciaccio brutto de Via Merulana* [*That Awful Mess on Via Merulana*] (1947), which in a style reminiscent of detective stories offers an account of the high-handed way in which a robbery with murder, committed in a Rome tenement, is investigated, and of the historic climate and social environment behind the story, set during the years of the fascist régime. Gadda's rôle is often that of a satirist caricaturing bourgeois conventions: his good-humoured onslaughts on middle-class mentality go hand in hand with his attacks on the niceties of conventional writing. D. B.

Gaiser, Gerd (1908–   ), German novelist, at first devoted himself to painting and the history of art. He served in the Luftwaffe during the war, and did not reveal himself as a major writer until after the war was over. Like Böll he was deeply influenced by his wartime experiences, and like Böll he submitted his experiences and his idealism to the test of religious conformity. A Lutheran, his approach to God is more direct and personal than is Böll's and it may be this which makes his undoubtedly deep religious convictions difficult to discern. His best work *Die strebende Jagd* ['The zealous hunt'] (1953) is one of the most sensitive of all German novels about the war; dealing with the Luftwaffe, its hero is something of an 'anti-hero' conscious of his own inadequacies within the bigger realisation that the war is lost no matter what the Luftwaffe might do. However, it is difficult to see precisely where Gaiser finds the real tragedy; and this opaque quality in his work may explain the fact that his international reputation is as yet small. G. W.

Gale, Zona (1874–1938), American novelist and short-story writer, was preoccupied with the theme of frustration and repression in the stifling social climate of her native Wisconsin. She won the 1921 Pulitzer prize for the stage adaptation of her novel *Miss Lulu Bett* (1920), the story of a frustrated Wisconsin spinster who is tormented by her sister and brother-in-law but surprises them by marrying the latter's brother. However, when her husband admits he has committed bigamy in marrying her, she returns to her sister's household, where she is forced to humiliate herself by telling the neighbours that she herself had failed as a wife, in order that the family should be protected from the scandal. K. R. R.

Gallegos, Rómulo (1884–), Venezuelan novelist, a prominent professional figure who has held a university chair and been president of Venezuela. He excels in his depiction of the life of the plainsman, showing powers of vivid realistic description, though frequently attaching insufficient importance to his plot. In 1929 his novel *Doña Bárbara* [*Doña Bárbara*] earned him an international reputation. A major example of the regional novel, it depicts a symbolic struggle. Santos Luzardo, a young man educated in the city, inherits an estate on the plains and sets out to bring to it the developments of civilisation. But he must first overcome the savage lawlessness of this territory ruled by Doña Bárbara. Fully interwoven in this epic plot—with its crude framework of sharp antithesis—is a love triangle involving the two chief protagonists and the daughter of Doña Bárbara. *Cantaclaro* ['Cantaclaro'] (1934) is valuable as a picture of local customs on the Venezuelan plains, while *Canaimá* ['Canaimá'] (1934) depicts man's virile struggle against the dark forces of the jungle in the valley of the Orinoco. Still on the basic theme of barbarity in opposition to civilisation, though from a political angle, is *El forastero* ['The stranger'] (1942). A stranger's arrival in a provincial town brings hope that the prevailing corruption and terrorism will cease. In all his works, Gallegos' general thesis seems to be that only the triumph of civilisation can bring peace and progress to his country. P. R. B.

Gallico, Paul William (1897–), American writer, began his literary career as a sportswriter, and by 1936 was one of the highest-paid sports columnists in New York. His first book was a book of reminiscences *Farewell to Sport* (1938). Then came a complete change with *Snow Goose* (1941), a short piece widely regarded as a *tour-de-force*. This story of a hunchback, the girl he loved and the white goose which flew over his rescue craft at Dunkirk is told with delicacy and an absence of sentimentality. It probably remains one of Gallico's best works.

His flair for writing about animals is demonstrated in two novels about cats, *Jennie* (1950) and *Thomasina* (1957), in which he captures the essence of being a cat. Most of his writings possess a fairy-tale quality and he contrives to wrap up a sermon in the kind of story which despite its improbability holds the reader's interest. As might be expected, he has written several successful children's books including *The Day Jean-Pierre Went Round the World* (1965).

His other works include *The Small Miracle* (1952), *Flowers for Mrs Harris* (1958), *The Hand of Mary Constable* (1964), *Mrs Harris M.P.* (1965) and *The Man Who was Magic* (1966). K. M. H.

Galsworthy, John (1867–1933), English novelist and dramatist. Galsworthy was born at Kingston Hill, Surrey, the son of a wealthy solicitor. He was educated at Harrow and Oxford. He read law but after being called to the bar he journeyed by ship to the far east, where he met Conrad who became a close friend and influenced him in deciding to take up writing as a career. Galsworthy has been described by Conrad as a humanitarian moralist. His plays and novels satirise the world of the upper and middle classes and question the materialistic and self-centred values at the base of the solid prosperity resulting from the Victorian business ethos. He is concerned, like Thackeray before him, to expose the hypocrisy underlying the surface morality and to demonstrate quite simply that there is one law for the rich and another for the poor.

Galsworthy's early novels and short stories, showing the influence of Turgenev and written under the pen-name of John Sinjohn, were not remarkably successful. They included *Four Winds* (short stories, 1897); the novels *Jocelyn* (1898) and *Villa Rubein* (1900); and another volume of stories, *A Man of Devon* (1901). But in 1906 he made his reputation with the novel *The Man of Property* and the play *The Silver Box*. The former is the first part of the long *Forsyte Saga* which also includes *In Chancery* (1920) and *To Let* (1921). The whole saga including two short pieces *The Indian Summer of a Forsyte* and *The Awakening* was published in 1922.

The trilogy is an examination of an influential and dominant family in Victorian England. Soames Forsyte, the epitome of the desire for possession, whether of people or of property, is contrasted with the younger, sensitive Jolyon. Life catches up with Soames when his wife Irene, an almost mysteriously feminine woman, falls in love with a young architect Phillip Bossiney, whom Soames hounds until his accidental death. The house which Bossiney has built for Soames remains a symbolic and central possession. Irene is divorced by Soames, who is prepared to stand the scandal only because his family rationalise revenge into righteousness. Irene subsequently marries Jolyon. Throughout the book she represents a compelling concept of fundamental womanhood, both sexually and maternally. (It is worth remarking that Galsworthy himself married the wife of his cousin after a love affair lasting ten years.) The final book deals with the relations between Fleur, Soames's daughter by his second marriage, and the son of Irene and Jolyon. In this saga, Galsworthy champions social justice, sensitivity and insight against the conventional, the materialistic and the philistine, which are not merely weapons against the former, but self-destructive elements in their possessors. However, it is not merely propaganda; it is a literary work of importance.

A second trilogy about the Forsytes, *A Modern Comedy* (1929), is concerned with Fleur and her family and shows Galsworthy in conservative reaction against what he regards as the lack of principles and anarchy of the post-war world of the twenties. Again, it is interesting to note that in these later volumes Galsworthy's attitude to Soames's traditional conservatism becomes increasingly sympathetic. Yet another, rather less meritable trilogy was published about the Forsytes, *End of the Chapter* (1933); while a volume of short stories *On Forsyte Change* was issued in 1930. Other novels written since the beginning of the Forsyte series included *The Patrician* (1911) and *The Dark Flower* (1913).

Galsworthy's plays, in contrast with the stylistic sophistication and verbal virtuosity of Shaw and Wilde, have the simplicity of craftsmanship. *The Silver Box* (1906) examines the injustice of law as it is applied to the petty crime of a servant when seen alongside the major criminal irresponsibility of a member of the family by whom she is employed. This theme is taken up again in *Justice* (1910) where a clerk, William Falder, commits a small crime to secure money for essentially humanitarian reasons and is savagely persecuted by his employers, by the officers of the prison to which he is committed and by society when he is released. The playwright stresses the retribution that follows an invasion of the materialistic rights of property at the expense of common human feelings. Winston Churchill, then Home Secretary, was invited to the première and a reform of solitary confinement conditions in prisons followed. *Strife* (1909) examines the the conflict of management and labour in a strike. Interest concentrates on the unyielding personalities of the leaders of each side, with human problems being swallowed under the name of principle. The strike ends only when the leader of the strikers has his wife dead through malnutrition.

Galsworthy's plays have a tendency to be didactic. He tends to be an intellectual rather than a passionate reformer. He is possessed of sympathy with, rather than depth of understanding of the working-class lives with which he deals. The novels, however, despite the conservatism of his later years, show a fine sensitivity to the shallowness of middle-class values and a profound awareness of the nature of man. D. L. P.

Galvão, Henrique (1895–), Portuguese dramatist. A former supporter of the Salazar government, he was successively Director of the National Radio, governor of the port of Angola and High Inspector of Colonial Administration. His adverse colonial reports estranged him from Salazar, foreshadowing seven years' imprisonment until in 1959 he escaped to

South America to mount the sensational hi-jacking of the liner *Santa Maria* in 1961 in unsuccessful support of the ill-fated General Humberto Delgado. His literary work is mainly of an Africanist nature and includes six plays, three novels and several collections of essays. Best known are two Africanist plays *O Velo de Oiro* ['The golden fleece'] (1936) and *Colonos* ['Settlers'] (1939), and two social comedies *Espada de Fogo* ['Fiery sword'] (1949) and *Farsa do Amor* ['Farce of love'] (1951), the latter in collaboration. Available only in English is his *Santa Maria: My Crusade for Portugal* (1961), a vitriolic and detailed attack on Salazar, with proposals for the gradual self-determination of the overseas territories. R. C. W.

Gálvez, Manuel (1882–1962), Argentinian novelist. Several journeys to Europe enabled him to form important contacts with its literature. A realist writer with wide interests—social and psychological—he has analysed a great variety of aspects of Argentinian life, seeking the essential truths of his country. Of his many novels the following are the most important. *La maestra normal* ['The normal school teacher'] (1914), which assured his reputation, describes the advent of a young man and a young woman to a provincial town, the relationship that forms between them and then breaks, and the inner problems which both seem unable to solve and which ultimately set their fate. Buenos Aires is the setting of *El mal metafísico* ['The metaphysical sickness'] (1916), a novel that relates the aspirations, failures and ruin of a sensitive, romantic youth who abandons his studies to become a writer, mixing with bohemian literary circles in the city. Gálvez's best-known work is *Nacha Regules* [*Nacha Regules*] (1922), a vivid, stark picture of life in the brothels and low quarters of the metropolis. *Miércoles Santo* [*Holy Wednesday*] (1934) depicts a further aspect of society: the daily life of a confessor. 'My task as a novelist', wrote Gálvez, 'is to reflect reality'. P. R. B.

Gann, Ernest (born Ernest Kellogg; 1910–   ), American novelist, whose adventure stories have gripping plots and racy dialogue. Many of them, probably as a result of his experiences during the second world war, are centred on flying, for example *Island in the Sky* (1944) which describes an air crash in the uncharted wilds of north Canada, and *The Trouble With Lazy Ethel* (1958) where the title derives from the name of a hurricane which blows up around a hydrogen bomb test area on a tiny Pacific island. In *Of Good and Evil* (1963) Gann departed from his usual formula to tell a story of the violence in society, the action taking place at police headquarters in a single day and night.

Other titles include *Blaze at Noon* (1947), *The High and the Mighty* (1953), and *Soldier of Fortune* (1955). K. M. H.

García Hortelano, Juan (1928–), Spanish novelist. His first novel *Nuevas amistades* ['New friendships'] was awarded the Premio Biblioteca Breve in 1959 and he went on to receive international attention when in 1961 he won the first-ever Formentor Prize with the manuscript of his second novel *Tormenta de verano* [*Summer Storm*] (1962), which constituted a vigorous attack on the insularity of the *dolce vita* of the rich beach-dwelling society of Spain. The discovery of a naked female corpse on the seashore of a smart, exclusive resort temporarily jerks the inhabitants out of their complacency, but after some superficial soul-searching and investigation all reverts to normal. The futility and boredom of such an existence is painstakingly probed in a manner recalling the technique of Flaubert in the first half of *L'Education sentimentale*.

R. C. W.

García Lorca, Federico (1898–1936), Spanish poet and playwright. The son of a landowner in the province of Granada, Lorca at first seems the archetypal Andalusian—writing of blood, lust and death—whose only appeal is to the literary tourist. Yet, especially in his poetry, Lorca's themes rise from local to universal significance. Like most of the young poets who emerged during the 1920s—the so-called 1927 Generation—he extols those life-enhancing values that transcend the ephemeral experiences of everyday life. His heroes are local—gypsies, bandits, women seeking fulfilment—but they represent universal longings in an age of crisis and constraint. His first book *Impresiones y paisajes* ['Impressions and landscapes'] (1918) is the prose account of a student's travels through Spain, but he was already writing poetry. Moving to Madrid in 1919 he found a focus for his activities in the Residencia de Estudiantes, a hostel run on the lines of an English hall of residence, where he stayed for a number of years. His handsome features and personable manner, allied to an obvious talent for music, painting, poetry and drama, soon created a legend around him. The insect play *El maleficio de la mariposa* [*The Butterfly's Evil Spell*] (1920), produced by Martínez Sierra, was a failure but there are glimpses of the mature poet in *Libro de poemas* ['Book of poems'] (1921).

The living tradition of popular poetry in Spain provides the basis for Lorca's production during the twenties. In a sense he was a modern troubadour, for *Poema del cante jondo* ['Poem of cante jondo'] (1931), a lyrical representation of the 'deep song' of Andalusia, *Canciones* ['Songs'] (1927) and *Romancero gitano* [*Gypsy Ballads*] (1928), wherein the conflict between gypsies and organised society symbolises the contrast between affirmation and negation which is Lorca's central theme, were all widely known through recitals long before publication. He was also working in the theatre, collaborating with Falla on the production of the puppet-play *Los títeres de Cachiporra* [*The Billy-Club Puppets*] (1923) and with Dalí on *Mariana Pineda* [*Mariana Pineda*] (1926). Mariana, executed for helping her lover, the liberal patriot Pedro de Sotomayor, is the first of Lorca's great tragic heroines.

The tercentenary of the death of the baroque poet Góngora (1927) provided the focal point of the activities of the '1927 Generation', and Góngora's influence on Lorca is discernible in some monumental odes. But he soon reacted against the sterility of elegance: like Alberti, Lorca emerged from neo-Góngorism into a period of personal crisis. Experiencing a deep sense of suffering, and resentful at his reputation as no more than a 'gypsy' poet, he considered becoming a teacher. The sense of frustration informs the 'violent farce' *La zapatera prodigiosa* [*The Prodigious Shoemaker's Wife*] (1930), written as an antidote against the excessively abstract art of the time, and *Amor de Don Perlimplín con Belisa en el jardín* [*The Love of Don Perlimplín and Belisa in the Garden*] (1931), the lyrical and comic drama of an old man's marriage to a vital young woman. In May 1929 Lorca had left for New York and away from Spain he wrote *Poeta en Nueva York* [*Poet in New York*] (published posthumously), his most powerful and personal verse work, characterised by a horrified awareness of the limitations of modern society and of man's tragic situation. In writing it Lorca purged himself of bitterness and on his return to Spain in September 1930 entered a period of intense activity. He founded La Barraca, a mobile student theatre which presented plays all over Spain; he gave lectures, and readings from his work; and produced his tragedies of feminine frustration. In *Bodas de sangre* [*Blood Wedding*] (1933) the bride elopes on her wedding day with Leonardo, a former sweetheart, but the bridegroom pursues them and the men die in a knife-fight. *Yerma* [*Yerma*] (1934) is the tragedy of a childless woman who in despair murders her unresponsive husband and thus thwarts her one hope of bearing children; while *Doña Rosita la soltera* [*Doña Rosita the Spinster*] (1935) depicts the melancholy spinsterdom of Doña Rosita whose erotic urges have been diverted into a social vacuum.

In both poetry and drama Lorca's theme had always been conflict—life and death, fantasy and reality, fulfilment and sterility, vital female and inadequate male. Now there came an increased sense of commitment: in 1935 he again attacked the concept of de-humanised art and resolved to write 'human social dramas'. *La casa de Bernarda Alba* [*The House of Bernarda Alba*] (1936) is the most 'realistic' of his plays. The tragedy of Spanish women is symbolised in Bernarda's stultifying observance of social convention and Adela's need to escape, ending in her suicide.

Death is rarely absent from Lorca's work. The long poem *Llanto por*

Ignacio Sánchez Mejías [*Lament for the Death of a Bullfighter*] (1935) is a remarkable product of the Spanish elegiac tradition: its careful orchestration in no way mutes the poet's horror at his friend's death. The poignancy of the *Llanto* was increased by the death of Lorca himself, executed by Civil Guards in Granada in August 1936. He had never been a political poet but his treatment of the conflicts inside Spanish society made his work abhorrent to Franco's supporters. The manner of his death may subsequently have caused critics to exaggerate Lorca's stature. His theatre has obvious defects: it is often melodramatic and its language too dense, its effects too rapidly traced, to be effective. As a poet, however, Lorca's greatness seems beyond dispute. D. H. G.

Gardner, Erle Stanley (1889–), American detective novelist. Born in Massachusetts, he studied law and practised for over twenty years. He began writing in 1921 but it was the introduction of the lawyer-sleuth Perry Mason which made him famous and led to his becoming one of the most successful detective-story writers in the United States. The Perry Mason cases with their bizarre titles—*The Case of the Stuttering Bishop* (1936), *The Case of the Perjured Parrot* (1939), *The Case of the Drowsy Mosquito* (1943)—are all written to a singular formula which turns on a point of law. Gardner has also written another series of novels featuring Douglas Selby with similarly standardised titles, such as *The D.A. Calls it Murder* (1937) and *The D.A. Calls a Turn* (1954). He has written other thrillers under the name A. A. Fair. K. M. H.

Garner, Hugh (1913–), Canadian novelist and short-story writer. Representative of his work are *Storm Below* (1944), a realistic and powerful war novel of six days at sea for the men on a naval corvette; *Cabbagetown* (1951), the chronicle of life in a Toronto slum; and *The Yellow Sweater and Other Stories* (1952), a collection in which he concentrates on portraying simple people and the human weaknesses to which they are prone. S. R.

Garnett, David (1892–), English novelist, became famous almost overnight with the publication in 1922 of *Lady into Fox*, a short fantasy about a woman who changes into a vixen, narrated as a true story in a slightly old-fashioned style. It won the Hawthornden and Tait Black prizes in 1923 and remains one of his most engaging works. Another fantasy *A Man in the Zoo* (1924) followed. *The Sailor's Return* (1925), a tragedy about an ex-sailor who marries a Negress, has its brief moments of comedy and was translated into a moving ballet. In *A Rabbit in the Air* (1932) he gave a vivid description of learning to fly. He has also edited writings by T. E. Lawrence and Thomas Love Peacock. Other works include: *The Golden Echo* (1953) and *Flowers of the Forest* (1955), autobiography; also *Go She Must* (1927), *No Love* (1929), *The Grasshoppers Come* (1931), *Beany-eye* (1935), *Aspects of Love* (1955) and *Ulterior Motives* (1966). G. S.

Gary, Romain (1914–), French novelist, born in Moscow, was pilot and career diplomat before becoming an author in 1945 with *Education européenne* [*A European Education*], a story of the Polish resistance. Other novels—*Tulipe* ['Tulip'] (1946), *Le Grand Vestiaire* ['The huge cloakroom'] (1949), *Les Couleurs du jour* [*Colours of the Day*] (1952)—were followed by a Prix Goncourt novel, *Les Racines du ciel* [*The Roots of Heaven*] (1956). Gary's novels are notable, not for their style, which is often heavy and sometimes clumsy, but for the density of their subject matter. In *Les Racines du ciel* the subject is the defence of wild animals against man, and this theme is treated with intensity and much human interest. *La Promesse de l'aube* [*Promise at Dawn*] (1961) is an autobiographical essay; and in 1963 Gary wrote *Lady L* which has been made into a successful film. He has also written short stories and a play.

D. E. A.

Gascoyne, David (1916–), English poet. Gascoyne's poetry is heavily influenced by surrealism. His is a world of intensity, of mystery and of visionary force. He is both horrified and fascinated by the nature of existence and for him the human world is a compound of pain and terror. Like the American poet Robinson Jeffers he despises the reality of intellectual systems that purport to describe the nature of the physical universe, yet also like Jeffers cannot fall back on the romantic comfort of human relations in sex, which he finds meaningless. His world is one of violence and chaos:

> Turbulence, uproar, echo of a War
> Beyond our frontier: burning, blood and black
> Impenetrable smoke. . . .

Gascoyne's style is rhetorical, declamatory and over-rich. Its effectiveness is derived not from detailed excellence but from an overall compelling, if depressing, force. Published work includes *Man's Life is This Meat* (1936); *Poems 1937–1942* (with drawings by Graham Sutherland, 1943); *A Vagrant* (1950); *Night Thoughts* (1956); and *Selected Poems* (1965).

D. L. P.

Gaskin, Catherine (1929–), Australian author of popular romantic and historical novels, now living in the U.S.A. She made her name with her first novel *This Other Eden* (1946) written when she was fifteen. Her best-known work is the historical novel *Sarah Dane* (1955) set in the early period of Australian settlement. Her later titles include *Corporation Wife* (1960), *I Know My Love* (1962) and *The File on Devlin* (1965). S. R.

Gelber, Jack (1932–   ), American writer for the theatre, is known primarily for his depiction of drug-addiction in *The Connection* (1959), a sensational, semi-improvised play, punctuated by jazz. Many who saw the play in New York and London found the theatrical experience overwhelming, and some critics were moved to declare that it had a significance far beyond the limited world it portrayed. Gelber's next play *The Apple* (1962) received as much abuse as its predecessor, but rather less praise.

K. R. R.

Genet, Jean (1910–   ), French writer. Born in Paris he came late to literature. His early life, which resembles in some ways that of Villon, was that of a wanderer; abandoned by his mother and brought up by the state, he was early a juvenile delinquent whose youth was spent in prisons and reform schools. Thief, exhibitionist, homosexual, traitor, Jean Genet is the incarnation of the anti-social man. This refusal of society became for Jean-Paul Sartre an interesting example of his theories, particularly in regard to liberty, and Sartre has 'explained' the Genet phenomenon at length in *Saint Genet, comédien et martyr* [*Saint Genet, Actor and Martyr*]. Genet has written novels, drama and poetry. *Notre Dame des fleurs* [*Our Lady of the Flowers*] (1949), *Le Miracle de la rose* [*The Miracle of the Rose*] (1951) and *Haute Surveillance* [*Deathwatch*] (1949), his best-known novels, are directly inspired by his own experiences and thus tend to be repetitive; but it is not the subject-matter—although this is strange enough, being accounts of particular crimes, of the sensations which accompany them, and of the willing acceptance of a chosen life of evil-doing—which forms the quality of Genet's novels, but the poetic, complex, sublime (and often difficult to understand) language in which it is written. His aim is 'saintliness', but saintliness in the perfection of evil; and his language is that of the saint—ceremonious, solemn, magnificent, colloquial, raw. His poems show this even more clearly: 'Le condamnè à mort, ['The man condemned to death'] and 'Un chant d'amour' ['Love song'] are notable among others. Genet's plays are less autobiographical and show more clearly his concern with the unreality of society in the fact that most characters themselves play a rôle, are false figures. In *Les Bonnes* [*The Maids*] (1955) the servants play the rôles of their masters; in *Le Balcon* [*The Balcony*] (1957) a number of brothel clients play the rôles their fantasy dictates; while in *Les Nègres* [*The Blacks*] (1959) the Negroes disguise themselves as Whites. Among other plays one must mention *Les Paravents* [*The Screens*] (1961).

D. E. A.

George, Stefan (1868–1933), German poet, perhaps one of the most difficult of German literary figures for the English public. His poems have been translated and published in America in *Works* (ed. Marx and Morwitz,

1949) but for the English reader his value lies in his influence on such writers as Hofmannstal. The curious paradox remains that in his background George was one of the least Germanic of poets, in that he studied closely the work of the French symbolists, especially Baudelaire, studied Spanish in order to enter into the spirit of that country's poetry, learned Norwegian in order to approach Ibsen more directly, and even attracted the interest of young followers of the early Pre-Raphaelites from England. The very catholicism of George's taste added to his severe concept of the function of the poet makes him a difficult poet to translate. Until middle age he was a conscious poet of 'art for art's sake'; his first works appeared in *Blätter für die Kunst* [*Leaves for Art*], a privately circulated journal; and it was not until 1899 that he permitted the publication of his work for a wider audience. In this journal he claimed that his work was 'classical' in the purest sense of the word. Structurally it followed the most severe rules, but he used words purely for their aesthetic appeal; and he was completely opposed to the didactic method of writing, believing that words themselves should produce an intoxicating effect and heighten the sensibilities of the reader. Abstruse as was this approach, his work was rendered even more difficult for the general reader by being printed in a special type, without the benefit of capital letters and punctuation.

His earlier works, *Hymnen* [*Poems*] (1890–92), *Das Jahr der Seele* [*The Year of the Soul*] (1897), followed his rich yet austere principles; but during the first world war in *Der Stern des Bundes* [*The Star of the Covenant*] (1914) and *Der Krieg* [*The War*] (1915) he began to show signs of being more aware of the contemporary scene. His final work *Das neue Reich* [*The Kingdom to Come*] (1929) showed that he had gone beyond 'art for art's sake' and was much more concerned with the thought content of a poet's work. His influence on German poetry was great, revealing as he did the most lyrical possibilities in the German language; but his influence was and still remains very much a native German influence, despite the cosmopolitan quality of his early studies and travels.

G. W.

Gerhardi, William Alexander (1895–), English novelist who was brought up in St Petersburg and whose Russian experiences play an important part in his writing. His first work *Futility* (1922) published after it was taken up by Katherine Mansfield, earned him the reputation of a satirist. Set in revolutionary Russia it is the story told in retrospect —and therefore overlaid throughout with the knowledge of failure—of an Englishman's unsuccessful courtship over a period of years of the daughter of a large Russian family, with whose problems the young man becomes inextricably involved. The theme of futility is developed on many levels throughout the book: the futility of love, of progress (the interminable train journey), of change (the new alignments within the family that replace the old are no more successful) and indeed ultimately of writing, for the novel makes constant reference to its own unavoidably Chekovian flavour.

He wrote several others in similar vein: notably *The Polyglots* (1925) and *Resurrection* (1934). His later and more straightforward works include the novels *Of Mortal Love* (1936) and *My Wife's the Least of It* (1938); the plays *I Was a King in Babylon* (1948) and *Rasputin* (1960); and two historical biographies *The Romanoffs* (1940) and *The Life and Times of Lord Beaverbrook* (1963). S. R.

Ghelderode, Michel de (1898–), Belgian dramatist. Born in Brussels, he had written his first play by 1918; in the years 1927–30 he worked in conjunction with the Flemish Popular Theatre, though always writing in French. Since 1930 he has become almost a recluse. He was virtually unknown until his plays won him a *succès de scandale* in France in the 1940s; most notable was the first performance of *Fastes d'enfer* in Paris in 1949. His work reflects the early influence of Poe, embracing elements of Satanism, blasphemy and indecency.

His best-known plays are *Trois acteurs, un drame* [*Three Actors and their Drama*] (1926), *Les Femmes au tombeau* [*The Women at the Tomb*] (1928), *Barabbas* [*Barabbas*] (1928), *Pantagleize* [*Pantagleize*] (1929), *Fastes d'enfer* [*Chronicles of Hell*] (1929), *Les Aveugles* [*The Blind Men*] (1933) and *Sire Halewijn* [*Lord Halewyn*] (1934). Also of interest are the expository *Entretiens d'Ostende* [*The Ostend Interviews*] (1951). All the above works are available in English in *Seven Plays* (1960). Ghelderode has also written several short stories and essays. R. C. W.

Gheorghiu, C. Virgil (1905–), Rumanian émigré novelist. He sprang into prominence after the second world war with his grim novel *Ora 25* [*The Twenty-fifth hour*] (1947) which was very soon to appear in both French and English translation. Settling in France, he continued to publish a series of novels (thenceforth written in French) which, although enjoying a certain continental vogue, never recaptured the impact of *Ora* 25. The most prominent are *La Seconde Chance* ['The second chance'] (1949), *La Cravache* ['The riding-crop'] (1960) and *Les Immortelles d'Agapia* ['The immortal women of Agapia'] (1964). All his novels emphasise the decreasing rôle of the individual in a methodical, technological age, and none carries a more trenchant condemnation of mechanical and inhuman categorisation of mankind than does Gheorghiu's masterpiece, *Ora 25*. Falsely accused of being a Jew, Johann Moritz escapes from a Rumanian requisition camp only to be interned in Hungary and later in Germany, where he is selected as a pure Aryan and pressed into the S.S., whose work he sabotages. After the Allied victory he is treated as a hero, until his Rumanian nationality earns him the classification of 'enemy alien'. He is sentenced at Nuremberg as a minor war criminal. Gheorghiu's explicit thesis was that modern justice merely prescribes categories and that categories alone establish innocence or guilt.

R. C. W.

Gibbons, Stella (1902–   ), English novelist, is best known for her comic novel *Cold Comfort Farm* (1932), which won her the Femina Vie Heureuse prize, immortalised the expression 'something nasty in the woodshed', and effectively satirised both the rural idyll and the novel of rural pessimism. Later titles, none of which have enjoyed comparable popularity, include *The Charmers* (1965). K. R. R.

Gibbs, Philip (1877–1962), English journalist, essayist and novelist, who was knighted for his work as a war correspondent and whose writings about the first world war, as in *Realities of War* (1920), constitute his most durable literary achievement. A series of once popular political novels written in the thirties are now little read, though the romantic historical novel *The Golden Age* (1931), about Victorian England, has been frequently reprinted. His more consistently popular later books, many of them topical novels with a strong sense of actuality, include *The New Elizabethans* (1953). It is fair to say that Gibbs's talent was primarily journalistic, and that his prolific output kept the patrons of the lending libraries abreast of current events—telling them, it might almost be said, what to think about the issues of the day. K. R. R.; S. R.

Gide, André (1869–1951), French writer and 1947 Nobel prizewinner. His father was a professor of law from the south of France, while his mother was of upper-middle-class stock from the port of Le Havre in Normandy. Both sides of the family, however, were strictly Protestant, a fact sufficiently unusual in France to make it worth mentioning. It also had a profound influence on Gide's youth. Being wealthy, he had no need to work and so was able to devote himself entirely to writing without thought of material gain. The desire to write came to him very early and his first efforts were in the symbolist tradition, naturally enough since he was the friend of Pierre Louys and Paul Valéry, and was sponsored by that other famous symbolist poet Stephane Mallarmé. These early works are *Les Cahiers d'André Walter* [*The Notebooks of André Walter*] (1891) and *Les Poèmes d'André Walter* [*The Poems of André Walter*] (1892); *Le Traité du Narcisse* [*Treatise on Narcissus*] (1891); and *Le Voyage d'Urien* [*Urien's Travels*] (1893).

Gide's work, stretching over half a century, is extraordinarily diverse and rich, consisting as it does of some sixty titles in many different genres. They can be divided into a number of groups. First there are the lyrical works, which include those already mentioned together with one of his most famous books *Les Nourritures terrestres* [*Fruits of the Earth*] (1897). It tells, or rather sings, in a mixture of poetic prose and rather loose verses, of the great sensual liberation Gide underwent on a two-year visit to Tunisia in 1893 when he was seriously ill with tuberculosis and feared he might die. Having gone there chaste, full of the fear of sin as inculcated by his Protestant upbringing, and faithful to his love for his cousin Madeleine Rondeaux, he made the discovery that he was a homosexual. The contradiction between these two parts of his being was to be the source of all Gide's greatest writing, which deals essentially with the moral problems of life in the great French tradition of a Montaigne or a Jean-Jacques Rousseau. In his 1927 preface to the *Nourritures*, Gide describes it as the book of a convalescent 'who embraces life as something he had all but lost'. It becomes a duty to know all and sample all. 'The sole good is life', this dazzling miracle, and it must be lived to the full and with fervour. We recognise here one of the central themes of twentieth-century French literature, very reminiscent of the work of the post-World War II writer Albert Camus, for example.

For the next twenty or more years Gide devoted his talent to two kinds of prose work of a rather different kind: the '*sotie*' or intellectual farce, and the '*récit*' or psychological narration. Gide uses the *sotie*—which in many ways recalls Voltaire's '*contes philosophiques*' or philosophical tales—to present, in symbolical form and with much wit and irony, the main themes of his reflections on the human condition and the conduct of life. Two of the best-known *soties* are *Le Prométhée mal enchaîné* [*Prometheus Misbound*] (1899), and *Les Caves du Vatican* [*Vatican Cellars*] (1914). In the former, Prometheus sits at a Parisian café terrace and gives a public lecture on his fate to Damocles (still afraid of the sword) and Cocles, just blinded by the eagle which is now again clinging to Prometheus' side. The moral conclusion of Prometheus' tale is: 'The history of man is the history of eagles, gentlemen'. The eagle symbolises both the individual conscience and the feeling of human conquest. 'It is not men I love', says Prometheus, 'I love what devours them'—that is, their conscience. *Vatican Cellars* is a very amusing tale in which Gide uses a highly complex and quite ridiculous James Bond-like plot, as Voltaire used the adventure tale, to put over his ideas.

Gide's *récits*, on the other hand, are always relatively short and pure in line. They recount moral dramas or dramas of passion in which the dénouement has already happened. They are told either by one of the central figures or by a bystander either in the form of a long monologue or a diary: this consisting in a slow and detailed analysis of the feelings of the one or two central characters. The most famous of Gide's *récits* are *L'Immoraliste* [*The Immoralist*] (1902), largely autobiographical, as also is *Si le grain ne meurt* [*If it Die . . .*] (1926); *La Porte étroite* [*Strait is the gate*] (1909); and *La Symphonie pastorale* [*The Pastoral Symphony*] (1919).

Having innovated in so many fields Gide was to do it yet again with his sole novel *Les Faux-Monnayeurs* [*The Coiners*] (1925). This novel, which has had one or two imitators in English, flouted all conventional notions of what a novel should be. In fact, it is a novel about a novel being written by the novelist Bernard, who is one of the central characters. In it Gide abandons all linear chronology and attempts to convey the simultaneity of thought and action of characters who are far from each other.

Mention must be made of Gide's plays such as *Oedipe* [*Oedipus*] (1931), the stage version of *Vatican Cellars* (1948), and an adaptation of Kafka's *The Trial* in 1946; of his famous *Journal* [*Journals*] covering some fifty years of his life; and of his vast and invaluable contribution as a literary critic and director of the famous literary review *La Nouvelle Revue française*. Gide's life and work were in the great tradition of the French *homme de lettres* or man of letters. He ceaselessly examined his own soul in the manner of such great predecessors as Montaigne, Rousseau and Stendhal, thus greatly enriching that 'continual discourse on man' which is the heart of French literature. A. L. W.

Gilmore, Mary (1865–), prolific and popular Australian novelist and poet. In her work we can detect her passionate concern for the place of women in society and for the rights of the aborigine, as well as her own personal devout Christianity. The novels themselves are straightforward with a warm and sympathetic approach to the subject: representative titles are *The Passionate Heart* (1918), *The Wild Swan* (1930) and *Under the Wilgas* (1932). Her poetry can be found in *Selected Verse* (1948) and *Fourteen Men* (1954). S. R.

Ginsberg, Allen (1926–), American beat poet. Ginsberg marks a transitional stage in the development of American verse. Writers influenced by the seventeenth-century metaphysicals, like Richard Wilbur, traditionalists like Allen Tate, and those poets in the mainstream of the effect of the works of Eliot and Pound, all continue to produce work: but the momentum of these influences had to wane. When in the period following the second world war there appeared the generation of beat poets who totally rejected the structure of the society in which they lived, these consequently sought a new style to reflect the anarchy of their social and moral rejections. Ginsberg's *Howl and Other Poems* (1956) is a passionate denunciation of the effect of society upon the young men of his own era. The looseness of the style reflects the throwing off of these moral shackles. The book owes part of its popularity to a successfully defended lawsuit against obscenity. Other volumes to read include *Keddish and Other Poems* (1961) and *Empty Mirror: Early Poems* (1961).

D. L. P.

Giono, Jean (1895–), French novelist. Son of a poor family, he worked as an office-boy and messenger until the first world war, which he spent in the trenches. His pacifism and refusal to answer mobilisation in 1939 put him in prison, as did his 'Vichyite' sympathies later on. His early works celebrate the Mediterranean peasant culture and the region of Haute Provence, and novels such as *Colline* [*The Hill*] (1928), *Un de Baumugnes* [*Man of Baumugnes*] (1929), *Regain* [*Harvest*] (1930), *Le Grand Troupeau* ['The great flock'] (1931), *Jean le Bleu* [*The Blue Boy*] (1932) and *Le Chant du monde* ['Song of the world'] (1934) are tales of epic grandeur. After 1947, however, when he started publishing again, Giono's world had changed; the grandeur remains, but the heroes are men whose strong will and inner force can carry them to good or evil. Giono's tendency is toward classical tragedy and toward the sweep of history, but his awareness of the complexities of life lends depth to the post-war novels—*Le Hussard sur le toit* [*Hussar on the Roof*] (1951), *Le Moulin de Pologne* [*The Malediction*] (1952), *Le Bonheur fou* [*The Straw Man*] (1957), *Angelo* [*Angelo*] (1958), *Deux Cavaliers de l'orage* [*Two Riders of the Storm*] (1965). D. E. A.

Giraudoux, Jean (1882–1944), French novelist and playwright. Jean Giraudoux (Jean as in La Fontaine, he once said, in a humorously accurate description of his literary talent) was born at Bellac, a village in the Limousin, in the very heart of the French countryside. A brilliant scholar, he went to the Ecole Normale Supérieure, specialising in Germanic studies. After a brief period in journalism he entered the diplomatic service, rising to become Minister of Information at the beginning of the second world war.

Giraudoux in fact had two literary careers, first in the novel and then in the theatre. It is the latter that made him world famous, but a glance at his novels will give some idea of the unique Giraudoux style. He wrote them in the intervals of his diplomatic work, and indeed many were written in his office. His first published work was *Provinciales* ['Provincial stories'] appearing in 1909, and from then on until 1927 his novels came out regularly: *Simon le pathétique* ['Simon the sad'] (1918); *Elpénor* (1919), which recounts the Odyssey as seen by the least courageous and least intelligent of Ulysses' companions; *Suzanne et le Pacifique* [*Suzanne and the Pacific*] (1921), which tells the story of a beautiful, sensitive girl marooned on a desert island and ends with the famous comment, when she returns to France, 'I am the Inspector of Weights and Measures, Mademoiselle. Why weep?'; *Siegfried et le Limousin* [*My Friend from Limousin*] (1922), which is a poetic attempt at Franco-German reconciliation; *Juliette au pays des hommes* [*Juliette Visits the Land of Men*] (1924); *Bella* [*Bella*] (1925); and *Eglantine* [*Eglantine*] (1927).

Giraudoux's novels are impressionist, the equivalent of Manet or Debussy in literature. They are full of fantasy and whimsical invention, a flood of sometimes quite uncontrolled metaphor and poetry which frequently degenerates into preciosity and verbal affectation. At their best they can be deeply moving, as for example *Bella*, which combines the story of the political struggles between Philippe Berthelot and Raymond Poincaré with a sort of Parisian 'Romeo and Juliet'. The novels are highly idealised and reality is handled with the greatest nonchalance. The only English prose writer even remotely similar, though in a very different context, is Gwyn Thomas.

It was a meeting with the great French actor Louis Jouvet that helped Giraudoux to discover, rather late, his vocation as a dramatist. There can rarely, if ever, in the history of the theatre have been a closer and more fruitful collaboration between dramatist and actor-manager. Giraudoux's first play *Siegfried*, which was staged in 1928, was based on his novel *Siegfried et le Limousin* and was far superior. It was also a great success. The stern demands of dramatic unity disciplined Giraudoux's fantastically effervescent imagination, while his poetic humanism restored to the stage that heightened style that is present in the greatest dramatists: Shakespeare, Racine, Aeschylus. The thirties were the decade of Giraudoux on the Paris stage. Almost every year Jouvet brought out a new Giraudoux play: *Amphitryon 38* [*Amphitryon 38*] in 1929, *Judith* [*Judith*] in 1931, *Intermezzo* [*The Enchanted*] in 1933, *Tessa* [*Tessa*] (an adaptation of a play by Margaret Kennedy) in 1934, *La Guerre de Troie n'aura pas lieu* [*Tiger at the Gates*] in 1935, *Electre* ['Electra'] in 1937, *Ondine* [*Undine*] in 1939, and *La Folle de Chaillot* [*The Mad Woman of Chaillot*] posthumously in 1945, following Giraudoux's death the previous year.

Humour, diversity, fantasy—these are present in the plays as in the novels. They deal with classical Greek subjects, modern subjects, mingle comedy and tragedy. Even the style, of a limpid simplicity and beauty, mixes poetry and parody, elevation and gentle mockery. The plays breathe a spirit of cheerful humanism, of unaffected and civilised joy in the difficult, dangerous and delightful business of being a man . . . and especially a woman. As in the novels it is the female characters (Alcmena, Andromache, Isabelle) who seem to incarnate Giraudoux's philosophy of 'living life steadily and living it whole'. A. L. W.

Gironella, José María (1917–), Spanish novelist. After the cosmopolitan experiences of a restless youth—seminary, bank, the Republican Army, exile in France, a forgotten volume of poetry—Gironella returned to Spain and won the 1946 Nadal prize with *Un hombre* [*Where the Soil was Shallow*], the forceful if erratic study of Miguel Serra, an agnostic, sullenly Barojan creature. Already we find the ethical concern characteristic of Gironella and conspicuous in *La marea* ['The tide'] (1949) and *Los cipreses creen en Dios* [*The Cypresses Believe in God*] (1953). The latter, with which Gironella acquired an international reputation, is the lengthy first volume of a trilogy concerning the prelude to, the events and aftermath of the civil war. Its patently autobiographical hero Ignacio Alvear becomes a symbolic focus for the tensions of Spain during the thirties, and it heavily conveys the frustrations of that time. After its completion Gironella suffered a nervous breakdown, courageously described in *Los fantasmas de mi cerebro* [*Phantoms and Fugitives*] (1960). He emerged to write the second part of the trilogy, *Un millón de muertos* [*One Million Dead*] (1961), the least tightly written of his novels to date, and *Mujer, levántate y anda* ['Woman, rise and walk'] (1960) inspired by 'the eternal struggle between sin and grace'. The final volume of the trilogy, *Ha estallado la paz* ['Peace has broken out'], was published in 1967. D. H. G.

Gjellerup, Karl (1857–1919), Danish novelist who shared the 1917 Nobel Prize for Literature with his compatriot Henrik Pontoppidan; like the latter, he is primarily a nineteenth-century figure, but for the appearance of his best-known novel *Pilgrimen Kamanita* [*The Pilgrim Kamanita*] in 1906. An opponent of Georg Brandes, he rejected naturalism, introducing classical motifs into many of his novels. R. C. W.

Gladkov, Fyodor Vasilievich (1883–1958), Soviet novelist of the twenties whose novel *Tsement* [*Cement*] (1925) was very successful. His early childhood had not been too easy, his parents were strict, and they had to travel around to earn a livelihood. He began writing before the revolution but his work attracted little notice. *Cement* places a great emphasis on industrialisation and describes the reconditioning of a cement factory after the civil war by the hero Gleb Chumalov. The book also reveals the emancipation of Soviet womanhood, for Gleb's wife has acquired her independence; and while Gleb succeeds in reopening the factory he does not refind his pre-war happiness—his wife asserting her freedom to do as she likes and indulging in extra-marital relations, and his daughter dying from lack of parental affection. The work served as a model, despite its unpolished style, for later industrial novels. B. W.

Glasgow, Ellen (1874–1945), American novelist, born in Richmond, Virginia. Her first novel *The Descendant* (1897) began her life's work of critical evaluation of the southern society to which she belonged. Her novels fall into three groups. First there are those dealing with the social history of Virginia before, during and after the civil war, including *The Battleground* (1902), *The Romance of a Plain Man* (1909) and *Virginia* (1913). The second group consists of three comedies of manners about the Scotch-Irish families of Richmond before and after the first world war—*The Romantic Comedians* (1926), *They Stooped to Folly* (1929) and *The Sheltered Life* (1932). The last group, in which she fills out her characters more, contains some of her best work: *Barren Ground* (1925) and *Vein of Iron* (1935) both tell of the testing of indomitable character by adverse circumstances and of the decay into which the south had sunk. G. S.

Glazarová, Jarmila (1901–), Czech novelist. The wife of a country doctor, and after the second world war a cultural attaché in Moscow and a member of the Czechoslovak National Assembly, she writes about the social, personal and religious problems of modern woman. Her books include *Vlčí jáma* [*The Wolf Trap*] (1938). K. B.

Glover, Denis (1912–), New Zealand poet and founder of the Caxton Press (Christchurch). Early in his career he published *Enemies* (1937) in association with Allen Curnow, and thereafter continued to develop the epigrammatic and satirical side of his work already manifest in *Arraignment in Paris* (1937). Critics feel that his best work was done in the next two decades, published in *Sings Harry and Other Poems* (1951) and *Arawata Bill* (1952). S. R.

Glyn, Elinor (1864–1943), English novelist who enjoyed a great vogue at the beginning of the century. Writing from the inside, she produced a number of popular 'society' novels including *The Visits of Elizabeth*

(1900); but she was best known for her passionate romances, slightly tinged with eroticism. These included the very successful *Three Weeks* (1907) and a novel entitled *It* (1927) which introduced the popular term 'it' as a synonym for glamour or sex appeal. From 1920 to 1929 she worked as a script-writer in Hollywood. R. A. K.

Godden, Rumer (Mrs Rumer Haynes Dixon; 1907–), English novelist, particularly skilled at capturing the atmosphere of life in India before partition, as in *Black Narcissus* (1939) and the beautiful and moving *The River* (1946). In the latter novel she enters the imagination of children and adolescents, a feature also of *An Episode of Sparrows* (1955), set in the slums of post-war London, and of *The Greengage Summer* (1958). She writes with great sensitivity, only occasionally lapsing into sentimentality. Other titles include *Take Three Tenses* (1945), *Kingfishers Catch Fire* (1953), *The Battle of the Villa Fiorita* (1963), the children's book *Miss Happiness and Miss Flower* (1961), and the volume of memoirs *Two Under the Indian Sun* (with John Godden; 1966). S. R.

Goetel, Ferdynand (1890–1960), Polish writer. Goetel remains one of the more renowned of Polish contemporary novelists. Deported from Warsaw by the Russian authorities to Turkestan at the outbreak of the first world war he spent over five years there involved in road building and irrigation work until at the time of mobilisation into the Red Army in 1919 he managed to escape with a group of other Poles to Persia and then on to India. A year later he returned to Poland. His years in Turkestan and subsequent journeys in the middle east are reflected in most of his early writing, represented notably by the novel *Kar-chat* ['Kar-chat'] (1923) and *Z dnia na dzień* [*From Day to Day*] (1926), a novel in the form of a diary which progresses through two time sequences. To this same period belong several travel books and two dramas: and the years 1926–34 saw Goetel as president of the Polish P.E.N. club. After the second world war he arrived in England where among his publications there appeared *Czasy wojny* ['Times of war'] (1955), a volume of memoirs of the war years. His books have been translated into English, French and German. B. M.

Gogarty, Oliver St John (1878–1957), Irish poet and journalist, now chiefly remembered as a wit and personality. He was surgeon, senator (in the 1922 Irish Parliament), aviator, irrepressible mocker with a flair for the bawdy, and a man of generosity and physical courage. Joyce commemorated a friendship of opposites and their inevitable quarrels by putting him into *Ulysses* as Buck Mulligan. His own serious work (in

Collected Poetry, 1951) has much beauty, being classical in form and romantic in content. His memoirs include *As I Was Going Down Sackville Street* (1936), a vivid collection of Dublin scenes and individuals. H. C.

Gold, Herbert (1924–), American novelist whose works have often been labelled as existentialist—which they certainly are insofar as existentialism is concerned with man's capacity for creating values. The affirmative *Birth of a Hero* (1951) was followed by the equally optimistic *The Prospect Before Us* (1954); while *The Man Who Was Not With It* (1956), the story of a man who only half belongs with the group of travelling performers in whose company he journeys, has affinities with the more 'beatific' strain of beat writing. Gold's subsequent novels include the elaborate and impressive *The Optimist* (1959); *Therefore Be Bold* (1960), a study of the potentiality for human development experienced in adolescence; and *Fathers* (1967). K. R. R.

Golding, Louis (1895–1958), English novelist. He was born of Jewish parents, in Manchester which is recognisable as the Doomington of many of his novels. He first won acclaim with *Magnolia Street* (1931) although his first published work *Forward From Babylon* appeared in 1920. He was an ardent champion of the Jewish people and his strong feeling for race and family emerges in his Elsie Silver novels, *Five Silver Daughters* (1934), *Mr Emmanuel* (1939), *The Glory of Elsie Silver* (1945) and *To the Quayside* (1953). K. M. H.

Golding, William (1911–), English novelist, became well known with his first book, *Lord of the Flies* (1955), which established him as one of the most individual writers of his time. All his subsequent books share to a greater or lesser extent its preoccupation with the fall of man (or, in Christian terminology, original sin), as well as the fable-like quality of its narrative.

Lord of the Flies concerns a party of evacuated schoolboys who in some unspecified global war of the future are marooned on a desert island, and who by the time they are rescued have degenerated into murderous and superstitious savages. At first they behave in a rational, adult manner, electing a leader and assigning responsibilities. But it is not long before those whose job it is to hunt for food begin to feel the power of their own primitive hunting instincts; and when they learn to lose their individuality in a group ritual they surrender completely to blood lust and the desire to kill. (It is interesting that the main body of 'hunters' is composed of the school choir, who have already had experience of group activity.) Meanwhile, adult rationality is receding fast in another sphere: fear of the unknown (centring in this case on a mysterious moving object visible on the crest of the island) having already crystallised as the idea of a 'beast' on the island. Thus the hunters' rituals now culminate in an imaginary killing of the beast.

One boy, Simon, who is subject to fits, and who belongs to neither group, sets out to investigate the beast. He discovers that the mysterious moving object is the dead body of a parachutist (a grim comment on the world of adult rationality) and on the way down he encounters the pig's head that the hunters have set up on a stick, now surrounded by flies. The boy has a fit, and experiences a hallucination in which this 'lord of the flies' tells him: 'I'm the Beast. . . . I'm part of you. . . . I'm the reason it's no go.' Just how much 'The Lord of the Flies' (a literal translation of the name of Beelzebub, the Hebrew prince of devils) is part of them all, is dramatically seen when the now enlightened Simon arrives back at the shore at the moment when the hunters' 'kill-the-beast' ritual is reaching its climax, to become the first human victim of their depersonalised savagery. It is a short step from the ritual death of Simon to the intentionally murderous pursuit of Ralph, the original elected leader and the sole surviving opponent of the hunters; and only the arrival of a British naval officer brings them to their senses before it is too late.

The external projection of 'the beast within'—one of a number of features of the story which have led some readers to see it as a comment on the mass neurosis of Nazi Germany—also figures in Golding's second novel, *The Inheritors* (1955). In this strange book we witness the arrival of *Homo sapiens* on the evolutionary scene, as experienced by a doomed society of Neanderthal men. The new inheritors of the earth are characterised by the knowledge of good and evil—the accompaniment, in the Judaeo-Christian creation myth, of the fall of man. Divided against themselves, in their conscious minds they identify the submerged bestiality of their own nature in their unfortunate innocent predecessors. In the ensuing conflict, their superior mental equipment carries the day and innocence vanishes from the earth.

Golding's third novel *Pincher Martin* (1956) is concerned with the related issue of survival after death. At a superficial level, it apparently portrays the struggle for survival of the shipwrecked naval officer Christopher Martin marooned alone on Rockall. At this level, Martin is well equipped by his total self-seeking—illustrated by flashbacks of his earlier life, and focused in the image of a box of maggots which devour one another till only one is left; but it is precisely this complete egoism that guarantees spiritual extinction and we discover at the end that Martin's heroic struggle for survival has really been his death agony—that we have been witnessing his extended mental fantasies while on the point of drowning.

Free Fall (1959) is the only one of Golding's works that reads like a conventional novel: but here again we have the familiar theme. The title expresses neatly the ambivalence of the behaviour of its characters: are they truly free to behave as they wish, or do they behave as they do because of the fall of man (a state of affairs they are powerless to amend)? Golding's verdict is that both answers are correct. The analogy with the physical concept of 'free fall' is one that should not be pressed; more successful as a physical image is the all-pervading title-symbol of his fifth novel, *The Spire* (1964), where the spiritual significance of the human drama that surrounds the erection of the spire of (one presumes) Salisbury cathedral is given precise symbolic expression.

A further novel, *The Pyramid*, was published in 1967. K. R. R.

Golon, Sergeanne, is the combined name of the French novel-writing team Serge Golon (1903–), Russian-born, and his wife Anne Golon (1921–). Husband and wife have written between them a series of lusty, busty adventure stories of seventeenth-century France. The novels describe the career of Angélique de Sancé de Monteloup who marries Joffrey de Peyrac of Toulouse. On her husband's supposed death at the hand of King Louis XIV, Angélique becomes variously a member of the French underworld, a successful shopowner, an influential member of the king's court, a slave in Crete and then in turn the property of a masked buccaneer and an eastern sultan. Back in France she is held prisoner in her own château by Louis XIV, is raped by his dragoons, and has her son killed before her eyes. She leads her province in revolt against the king, is defeated, becomes a servant; and then with a group of Huguenots, together with her daughter, the product of the rape, she escapes to the West Indies on the boat of the same privateer who has once bought her as a slave. He finally sheds his mask and turns out to be her long-lost first husband. In the final novel of this group it takes over 400 pages to achieve their fulfilled reunion. The English versions include *Angélique I: The Marquise of the Angels* (1959), *Angélique II: The Road to Versailles* (1959), *Angélique and the King* (1960), *Angélique and the Sultan* (1961), *Angélique in Revolt* (1962) and *Angélique in Love* (1963). D. L. P.

Gombrowicz, Witold (1904–), Polish novelist, born in Małoszyce. Educated at Lwów and the University of Warsaw, he was perhaps the most original Polish prose writer of the 1930s. He began his literary career with a collection of tales under the general title *Memorial* (1933). A moralist and a patriot almost *à rebours*, his work reflects elements of irony, satire, the grotesque and the absurd. One of the most socially conscious of contemporary Polish émigré writers, he often violently, bitterly exposes the human decadence and spiritual contortions beneath the veneer of social façades. His greatest achievement lies in the novel *Ferdydurke* [*Ferdydurke*] (1937).

A play *Ślub* ['The Marriage'] (1947), another novel *Trans-Atlantyk* (1955) and subsequently *Pornografia* (1960) and *Kosmos* (1965) have rightly emphasised Gombrowicz's position as the leading Polish novelist of post-war years. His writing appears frequently in the Paris *Kultura* where he still continues his *Fragmenty z dziennika* ['Fragments from a Journal']. Free of any messianic inhibitions despite his patriotic tendencies, his relation to Poland's repeated tragedies is akin to that of Joyce's to Ireland. B. M.

Gorbatov, Boris Leontievich (1908–54), Soviet novelist, was born in the Donbas. He achieved recognition with his somewhat romantic novel *Nyepokoryenniye* [*The Taras Family*] (1943), which portrays the life and fate of a Kubán family during the German occupation of South Russia. In 1951 the first volume of his longer novel *Donbas* [*The Donets Basin*] appeared but Gorbatov died before the whole work could be completed. B. W.

Gordimer, Nadine (1923–), South African writer. She has written novels and short stories which are always concerned with her native country in its present state of political flux. Her collections of short stories *Six Feet in the Country* (1956) and *Not for Publication* explore the same path as her novels like *Occasion for Loving* (1963) and her novella *The Late Bourgeois World* (1966). She concerns herself with the inevitability of change in South Africa and with the certainty of being finally judged by colour whatever social viewpoint her characters hold. Hence, in her novella, she describes the crumbling of left-wing political thinking under pressure of mounting tension. The heroine's late husband had turned state evidence at a treason trial and she knows that, finally, she too will be forced to be associated with the present régime because of the colour of her skin. In her short story 'Happy Event' (1956), a trial about infanticide shows the prejudices of courts about black South Africans. A doctor testifies that 'a native woman' would be capable of returning to work immediately after the birth of a child, but that 'a European' would not. The African woman is sentenced to six months imprisonment, whilst her employers go on holiday. '. . . she did not go back to work for them again,' implies that judgment has been made elsewhere than in the courtroom but that the sentence has yet to be carried out.

Her style is always mild, lacking the polemic vein of most committed writers. Her concentration on the feelings of her characters indicates an insight lacking in more politically sophisticated writers. K. G. Y.

Gordon, Richard (1921–   ), English novelist, used his experiences in the medical profession as the basis for his immensely popular comic novel *Doctor in the House* (1952), to be followed by a sequence of progressively less stimulating sequels. K. R. R.

Gorky, Maxim (Alexei Maximovich Peshkov; 1868–1936), Russian writer, was an outstanding realist. He was born in Lower Novgorod and brought up by his grandparents. His childhood was a mixture of cruel beatings and stirring folk-tales before he set off to make his own way in the world. His experiences were many and varied. During his travels he began writing for local papers and in 1895 his story *Chelkash* [*Chelkash*] brought him national recognition. His first stories were mainly romantic in tone and very popular. After Gorky arrived in St Petersburg he joined the Social Democrats and gave a large amount of his income to this Marxist party. He took an active part in the 1905 revolution but was allowed to go abroad after his arrest. He made an unsatisfactory visit to the U.S.A. and then took up residence in Capri. His novel *Mat'* [*Mother*] (1907) is a rare blend of romanticism and realism and was hailed as a precursor of socialist realism in literature. This is Gorky's only truly revolutionary work, despite what may be read into his other works, especially those depicting that defiant spirit of the downtrodden and poor. For example, the play *Na dne* [*The Lower Depths*] (1902) is essentially an unresolved drama between two philosophies—those of a physically strong thief and a spiritually strong pilgrim—and between reality and illusion.

Gorky returned to Russia and produced the first part of his famous autobiographical trilogy, *Detstvo* [*Childhood*] (1913), followed by *V lyudakh* [*In the World*] (1916). Disillusioned by the Soviet régime he returned to Capri for a period in 1921 and completed his trilogy with *Moi Universitety* [*My Universities*] (1923). These three works contain a gallery of vivid portraits and reminiscences about his colourful but difficult early life. While abroad he also wrote *Delo Artamonovykh* [*The Artamonov Business*] (1925) about the decay of one of the merchant families which he disliked but which excited his curiosity. This is one of his most important works.

Heralded as the greatest Russian writer since Pushkin, Gorky was never a disciplined communist. His main concern was to keep literature free from restrictions and he used his influence to save many a writer and poet. He helped to found the concept of socialist realism but he never intended it to be the narrow, dull, restrictive formula that it became in the hands of party officials. In 1936 he died in hospital in circumstances which still have not been fully clarified. B. W.

Gosse, Edmund (1849–1928), English critic and poet. Gosse, who worked in the British Museum as a librarian and later as a lecturer at Cambridge, was a friend to such literary figures as Swinburne and Henry James. Among his critical books is a *Life of Ibsen* (1908) and his best-known work of scholarship, *Life and Letters of John Donne* (1899).

His *Collected Poems* was published in 1911. The verse has many qualities of the pre-1914 Georgian school: immersion in nature, thankfulness to God, a feeling for the innocence of young children, a dash of classical learning, and a touch of sexual love swiftly retrieved by a measure of emotional euphoria; the mixture being then stirred by a not very profound poetic talent. D. L. P.

Goudge, Elizabeth (1900–), English novelist, always had an ambition to write, and her first book *Island Magic* appeared in 1934. However, she did not achieve any substantial success until the appearance of her novel *Green Dolphin Country* (1944), a historical romance set in New Zealand in the last century. Since then she has written a number of best-selling novels, including *The Herb of Grace* (1948), *The Heart of the Family* (1953) and *The Rosemary Tree* (1956). Miss Goudge's novels with their fairy-tale plots are a mixture of enchantment and nostalgia leading some critics to object to 'her paraphernalia of sentimentality', but nevertheless there is a human warmth and insight into character in all her writing, and nowhere is this more apparent than in her highly successful children's books. She won a Carnegie Medal with *The Little White Horse* in 1947.

Her other works include *The Scent of Water* (1963) and a life of Christ, *God So Loved the World* (1951). K. M. H.

Goytisolo, Juan (1931–), the most prolific and cosmopolitan of the younger Spanish novelists. Born in Catalonia, Goytisolo has lived in France since 1957 and works for the publishing house Gallimard. His novels show a marked technical evolution, contrasting with their unchanging ideological basis. *Juegos de manos* [*The Young Assassins*] (1954) presents a group of 'angry young men' who plan an absurdly unsuccessful crime and commit a senseless murder. But the characters are mere types, with the received shibboleths of anti-bourgeois youth. Goytisolo is more successful in *Duelo en el Paraíso* [*The Children of Chaos*] (1955)—wherein a band of children, refugees from war, turn on one of their number and kill him—and in the three novels forming *El mañana efímero* ['The ephemeral morrow'] (1957–58)—set in the working-class suburbs of Barcelona. There emerges, especially in the first of the trilogy, *Fiestas* [*Fiestas*] (1958), a vision of Spain as empty and sterile, yet with terrible forces at work beneath the surface. Subsequently Goytisolo aimed at a more objective realism: *La isla* [*Island of Women*; also, *Sands of Torremolinos*] (1961) and *Fin de fiesta* [*The Party's Over*] (1962), written in the first person, lack a traditional plot-structure—*Fin de fiesta* consisting of four tales of bourgeois boredom told by the respective protagonists—as well as the explicit social comment of the earlier novels. *Señas de identidad* ['Signs of identity'] (1966) is a disillusioned analysis of the author's self, and of the society which formed him. It points the way to a new and distinct stage in Goytisolo's development. D. H. G.

Graham, Winston M. (1911–), English writer of intelligent suspense fiction. Best-known works include *Fortune is a Woman* (1953), *The Sleeping Partner* (1956) and *Marnie* (1961). Subsequent titles include *After the Act* (1965) and *The Walking Stick* (1967). R. A. K.

Grahame, Kenneth (1859–1932), Scottish-born essayist who became famous through his books for children. His first collection of essays *Pagan Papers* appeared in 1893 and was followed in 1895 by *Golden Age* and in 1898 by *Dream Days*. In these books he showed a delicate appreciation of a child's mind, but his best work was yet to come. *The Wind in the Willows* (published 1908), written to entertain his son Alistair who was to die so tragically at twenty. This animal story has become a classic, belonging to that select body of children's literature which has a timeless appeal to adults. His animals behave like human beings whilst still retaining their natural animal characteristics. Toad, who dominates the latter part of the book, and becomes the central character of *Toad of Toad Hall*, a dramatisation of the book by A. A. Milne, is the most human of all the animals, having rather less charm than the more animal Mole, Rat or Mr Badger. There is an evocative quality about Grahame's writing and an indefinable feeling of sadness particularly apparent in those parts of the *Wind in The Willows* dealing with the Wild Wood.

He did very little writing after 1908 apart from editing the Cambridge *Book of Poetry for Young People*. K. M. H.

Grant, Joan (Mrs Denys Kelsey; 1907–), English novelist. She attracted attention with her first novel *Winged Pharaoh* (1937), the story of a co-ruler of Egypt of the First Dynasty. It is written in the first person and as in many of her later novels, such as *Life as Carola* (1939), *Lord of the Horizon* (1943) and *Scarlet Feather* (1945), she employs a technique which she claims to be 'far memory' to recapture the past. She describes this faculty in greater detail in her autobiography *Time out of Mind* (1956). Whatever importance one attaches to this gift she claims to possess, she certainly succeeds in bringing the past to life very vividly. K. M. H.

Granville-Barker, Harley (1877–1946), English theatrical writer, though best known for his critical works (especially on Shakespeare), was also the author of two successful plays, *The Voysey Inheritance* (1905) and *The Madras House* (1910), both about moral problems in finance. The former was successfully revived in 1966. K. R. R.

Grass, Günter (1927–), German poet, playwright and novelist, was born in Danzig of mixed German-Polish parentage. The German element was the strongest, and he was first a member of the *Jungvolk*, later of the Hitler Youth, before becoming at seventeen a soldier. Captured by the Americans, he subsequently worked as agricultural labourer, coal-miner and jazz-band musician. By the late forties he had settled down to study sculpture, travelling first to Italy and later Spain. He began writing lyrical poetry during this period, and published anthologies of poems and drawings, notably *Die Vorzüge der Windhühner* ['The advantages of chickens'] in 1955, and *Gleisdreieck* ['The isosceles triangle'] in 1960. In 1956 he went to live in Paris before settling in West Berlin with his family in 1960; and this stay definitely marked his concentration on literature as a career, a concentration which was marked by the award of several literary prizes. His plays *Hochwasser* ['High water'], *Noch 10 Minuten bis Buffalo* ['Still 10 minutes to Buffalo'] and *Onkel* ['Uncle'] were produced in this period, but it was his novel *Die Blechtrommel* [*The Tin Drum*] (1959) which won him international acclaim. The 'anti-hero' of this work is both physically deformed and mentally retarded. Involved in a murder, he tells his life story in a mental asylum, beginning with the petit-bourgeois world of pre-war Danzig, experiences as a youthful gang-leader, the suicide of a friend in the famous 'Crystal Night' when Jewish shops and synagogues were sacked, then the war and the ravages of the post-war period. Most critics have regarded this as a masterpiece; even the obscenity and blasphemy used to heighten its stylistic effect have not detracted from its admiration. The same approach is featured in *Katz und Maus* [*Cat and Mouse*] (1961). Here a schoolboy with an inferiority complex steals a military decoration, only to be awarded one for his bravery at the front; yet, still influenced by his inability to excel before his school-mates, he deserts and disappears. The later novel *Hundejahre* [*The Dog Years*] (1963) has a strong autobiographical quality and is markedly critical of contemporary society.

Subsequent publications include *Selected Poems* (trans. Michael Hamburger and Christopher Middleton, 1965) and the tragedy *Die Plebejer proben den Aufstand* [*The Plebeians Rehearse the Uprising*] (1966), a modern *Coriolanus* based on the East German revolt of July 1953. G. W.

Graves, Robert (1895–   ), English poet and novelist. After service in the first world war (in the same regiment as the poet Siegfried Sassoon), and marriage to the sister of the painter Ben Nicholson, he went up to Oxford, studying first the classics and then English Language and Literature. Straitened financial circumstances induced him to accept the post of Professor of English Literature at the Royal Egyptian University, Cairo, in 1926, but he only remained there for a year and on his return to Britain gave his whole time to writing. After the failure of his marriage he settled in Majorca, and although forced to leave on the outbreak of the Spanish civil war, he returned there after the end of the second world war.

Robert Graves's work must be judged on more than one level. It is as a poet that he would wish to be remembered, though it is as a historical novelist that he is best known to the general reading public. His first volumes of poetry *Over the Brazier* (1916) and *Fairies and Fusiliers* (1917) were written during the war. There is no trace of foreign influence in his work despite his Irish and German ancestry; he is essentially an English poet. Nor has he ever been a member of any school or stream. His headmaster at Charterhouse once advised him that his best friend was the waste-paper basket; and certainly he has throughout his life pruned his poems, discarding those which no longer satisfy him. He is his own sternest critic and his poetic development is one of continuous rejection. Graves regards himself as a traditionalist insofar as he believes that there are certain principles of poetry that cannot be violated, namely the need for metre and the use of words primarily for their meaning; yet he is in many ways an innovator, and is never derivative of other poets. As a romantic poet, he put forth his plea for Romanticism in an essay *On English Poetry* (1922); then in 1925, with *Poetic Unreason*, he argued the case for classicism. At the present time he holds his position midway between the two points. Some critics maintain that he is the only true classic poet of our time whose words could be translated into Latin without any alteration of tone; whilst by others he is held to be the only lyric poet writing today.

From being a minor war poet, Graves has become in subsequent decades one of England's major contemporary poets, but like so many other poets he was forced into writing prose in order to make money. His first important prose work, the autobiographical account of his schooldays and the first world war *Goodbye to All That*, appeared in 1929 at a time when public interest in the war had been reawakened. In this book he writes about the horrors of life in the trenches with simplicity and a complete lack of emotion or bitterness. There is a directness and clarity about his prose writing, an economy of style, which results from his elimination of unnecessary phrases and the use wherever possible of verbs and nouns instead of adjectives and adverbs.

He made his first excursion into the field of novel writing with *I Claudius* and *Claudius the God* both written in 1934. Written in the first person, they tell the story of Claudius who became fourth Roman emperor. Feeling himself to be lacking in the gift for the construction of plots, Graves was able to use history for the framework of these brilliant if eccentric novels. In his next, *Count Belisarius* (1938), he took for his material the later period of the Byzantine empire under Justinian and his empress Theodora, with his central character the brilliant soldier Belisarius resembling Claudius as the only good man in a corrupt world. In each of his succeeding novels—*Wife to Mr Milton* (1943), an imaginative reconstruction of Milton's first marriage to Mary Powell; *King Jesus* (1946), a bold interpretation of the life of Jesus; and *Homer's Daughter* (1955)—Graves takes the characters of history and gives them the motives, beliefs and speech of the twentieth century. His *Collected Short Stories* was published in 1965.

Though his novels and stories have been widely acclaimed, his most ambitious prose work is undoubtedly *The White Goddess* (1946) in which he takes as his thesis the idea that the language of poetic myth anciently current in the Mediterranean and northern Europe was a magical language bound up with popular religious ceremonies in honour of the Moon Goddess or Muse. In many ways it is similar to Frazer's *Golden Bough*. Almost equally impressive is his two-volume encyclopaedia of Greek myths.

Nevertheless, with all he has achieved in the field of prose writing as novelist, critic and essayist, Robert Graves has remained true to his original calling as a poet. In his voluntary exile in Majorca, shared with his second wife, cut off from the main literary field except during his appointment as Professor of Poetry at Oxford in 1961, he has continued to devote much of his time to poetry. In his own words, 'poetry has been my ruling passion . . . prose has been my livelihood'. Although his output is small his *Collected Poems* have continued to appear at regular intervals, in 1926, 1939, 1947, 1959 and 1965, representing at each stage of his development only those poems by which he wishes to be judged.

K. M. H.

Green, A. S. (or Grin; Alexander Stepanovich Grinyevsky, 1880–1932) was a Soviet romantic, a writer of fantastic stories. He was born in Vyatka (Kirov) of Polish parents but his youth was so dreary that he ran away to sea. He was completely apolitical and lived in his own dream-world, which is reflected in his stories. Because of his style and his use of foreign-sounding names he was often mistaken for a foreign writer in translation. His tales of adventures in 'Grinland' have always been popular with the reading public if not with literary officialdom. His whimsical stories had a strong influence on later Soviet writers, although by the mid-1960s he had not been accorded official recognition. His best-known works outside the U.S.S.R. are the stories *Krysolov* [*The Ratcatcher*] (1924) and *Zolotaya tsep'* [*The Golden Chain*] (1925), and the novel *Doroga nikuda* [*The Road Nowhere*] (1929). B. W.

Green, Henry (Henry Vincent Yorke; 1905–), English novelist who over a period of thirty years produced a series of nine novels, each characterised by his distinctive and unusual style. The titles themselves deserve attention—for example *Living* (1929), *Party Going* (1939), *Loving* (1945), *Concluding* (1948), *Doting* (1952), *Caught* (1943), *Back* (1946)—consisting as they do of a single word, usually a participle or gerund. The grammatical features of these words are twofold—they have no subject, no person or number, and they focus attention on the activity itself rather than the doer; thus in any one novel we find many combinations of characters 'doting' or 'loving' or to whom the word 'caught' could apply. This is not all, for on another level Green is stating his concept of what the scope of the novel is—as he himself once expressed it, "to create 'life' which does not eat, procreate or drink, but which can live in people who are alive"; and for him this distilled essence of life is best conveyed by the cryptic verbal noun.

Among the distinctive features of his style is the way he avoids long passages of description as part of the narrative yet nevertheless selects the vivid and poetically exact detail that will make a lasting impression —the cavernous railway station, the grey densely packed faceless crowds, the drifting wreaths of fog of *Party Going*; the peacocks, the gallery and its statues, of the Irish castle in *Loving*; the lush natural vegetation and growth of *Concluding*. These visual images not only provide a background to the characters' actions but have a secondary rôle as symbols.

Green's dialogue, his chief method of revealing character, is perhaps at first glance similar to that of Ivy Compton-Burnett (q.v.) in its forthrightness, but in fact his characters speak in all the possible forms, from the trite or hypocritical public statement to the naked and self-revealing utterances made in private. Here Green excels, in his rapid cross-cutting from the pompous declamations of (say) Charlie Raunce in *Loving* (1945), a man secure in his position, to the same man's urgent and naked pleading in a sexual encounter, or his child-like sentimentality in a letter to his mother.

Green has been credited with extending and deepening the range of the social comedy, or comedy of manners. It is true that he usually describes a stratified society, including for example both the rich Mayfair travellers, with their chauffeurs and maids, and the ordinary London working people in *Party Going*, both factory-worker and factory-owner in *Living*; but his novels cover a much wider range of human activity than is suggested by such a categorisation. In spite of the quite evident process of selection, his characters are presented in the whole of their existence, working and playing, talking and dreaming, and by no means purely in their social rôles.

Other titles not mentioned above are *Blindness* (1926) and *Nothing* (1950). S. R.

Green, Julien (1900–), French-American writer. Born of American parents living in Paris, Julien Green writes in both English and French. His early novels *Mont-Cinère* [*Mont-Cinère*] (1926) and *Adrienne Mesurat* [*Adrienne Mesurat*] (1927) are perhaps his best-known works. The latter is the story of a young girl living at home, her mother dead, her sister ill, her father narrow-minded and insensitive. Lost in her inner life of dreams, she pushes her father and kills him. The loneliness of her subsequent existence drives her to insanity. Green's subsequent novels, *Léviathan* [*Leviathan*] (1929), *Minuit* [*Midnight*] (1936), *Varouna* [*Varouna*] (1940) and the post-war *Si j'étais vous* [*If I were you*] (1947) and *Moira* [*Moira*] (1950), reflect also the intense inner life of characters whose situation seems to make despairing prisoners of them. He conveys a strong sense of background and reminds one of Henry James, or of Swinburne in his reflective and introspective style, which is well suited to the writing of diaries. His intense inner religious life (he was converted to Catholicism in 1939) and concern with the eternal combat of sin and grace, his visionary quality and obsession with the problem of evil, mark him off from other writers of today, and are reflected even in the titles of recent novels—*Le Malfaiteur* [*The Transgressor*] (1956) and *Chaque homme dans sa nuit* [*Each in his darkness*] (1960).

Julien Green has also written plays: titles include *Sud* ['South'] (1953), *L'Ennemi* ['The enemy'] (1954) and *L'Ombre* ['The shadow'] (1956). His diary for the period since 1928 is being published in volumes, such as *Le Bel Aujourd'hui* [*Beautiful Today*] (1958), *Partir avant le jour* ['Leave before dawn'] (1963), *Mille chemins ouverts* ['A thousand ways open'] (1964) and *Vers L'invisible* ['Toward the invisible] (1967). He has also written a number of essays, particularly on English authors from Samuel Johnson to the Brontës and on Nathaniel Hawthorne. D. E. A.

Greene, [Henry] Graham (1904–), is generally regarded as the outstanding English Catholic novelist of our time—although 'outstanding Christian novelist' would be equally apt (and for many readers in America and on the Continent he is even the 'outstanding English novelist'). In Greene's major novels a man's relationship with God is portrayed as something in every way as real and vivid as his relationship with other people; while the writer's vision of humanity's inevitable corruption and consequent need for redemption is meaningful to many who do not share the Christian faith. More typically Catholic is the part played in his characters' lives by the ideas of mortal sin and the subsequent alternatives of sacramental confession or final damnation. It is true that many of Graham Greene's novels can be read as straightforward thrillers—irrespective of whether or not they fall into his category of 'entertainments' (i.e. books that he wrote with the conscious intention of making money, or which have no serious religious content). As an absorbing storyteller, and constructor of taut plots, he has few rivals; and his books are given additional colour by the great range of exotic backgrounds: Haiti, Mexico, Cuba, west Africa, Indo-China, the Brighton underworld. It should be emphasised, however, that the picture of the world to be found in the entertainments is substantially the same as that of the novels, with man's spiritual corruption generally matched by an atmosphere of purely physical decay. (The locations might almost have been chosen for the corrosiveness of their climates.) It is a consistent vision of hell on earth, of an all-pervading supernatural evil at work in the world.

In his mid-twenties Greene was converted to Roman Catholicism. Soon after, he published his first novel, a historical romance entitled *The Man Within* (1929); and from then on he worked mainly as a writer, though intermittently accepting assignments as a newspaper correspondent in various parts of the world. This was quickly followed by *The Name of Action* (1930) and *Rumour at Nightfall* (1931); but Greene now found it necessary to step up his earnings by writing an 'entertainment', the result being *Stamboul Train* (1932), which not only succeeded in its immediate aim but also seemed just as serious as the preceding 'novels'. Its themes of betrayal and arbitrary justice reappear in *It's A Battlefield* (1934) and *England Made Me* (1935), which were followed by the 'second entertainment', *A Gun for Sale* (1936). Two years later came the first of the religious novels on which his reputation today is largely based, *Brighton Rock* (1938). This, at first sight, is a straightforward crime thriller. It is a tale of the dual pursuit of a hardened juvenile delinquent (who leads a gang of adult criminals) by a woman whose lover he has had murdered and who is determined to bring him to justice; and by a girl who loves him and wants to redeem him. However, the story takes on a heightened significance when its theological implications are grasped. The Brighton underworld is an image of hell, its wickedness having a supernatural quality; while the boy Pinkie (who has had a Catholic upbringing) is a soul doomed to damnation, from which he would be saved if only he could respond to the girl Rose's love. There is also the implication (to a non-Catholic, curiously perverse) that the possibility of redemption is a reality for the damned Pinkie in a way that it is not for the good-hearted non-believer who is his other pursuer: even when he has leapt to his death, his flesh steaming with his own vitriol—a death intended for Rose—there is the hope that a record he has made for her will show that he really loved her, and is therefore not beyond hope. 'The worst horror of all' is her discovery of the truth: of his final perdition.

From now on the religious element becomes all important. It is just possible to read *The Power and the Glory* (1940) simply as a thriller—and it certainly is that—but to do so is to skate over the surface of the book. An account of the hunt of a militantly anti-clerical police lieutenant for the only practising priest left in a Mexican province after the banning of Christianity by the revolutionary laws, this is a certainly an exciting story set in an authentic background: but the real drama takes place inside the priest's soul. Before the revolution, when the church is comfortably established, he is already a 'whisky priest': the inevitable process of corruption has set in. This is mirrored here, not only by the general putrescence of the physical environment, but also by images such as tooth decay and dyspepsia—the book opening with the priest's encounter with Mr Tench, a dentist, and later depicting an English trader's wife surrounded by bottles of patent medicine. (The latter's teenage daughter, on the other hand—who gives the priest shelter—provides an image of the purity and innocence that precedes the corruption.) When the law is passed requiring priests to marry, and most of his fellow priests either escape or are shot, he finds himself the only practising priest left, and in consequence a hunted man. He is not, he feels, a likely candidate for the rôle of martyr (he is still drinking heavily, and in a moment of despair had added another sin, fathering a child in the process): the logical thing for a man in his circumstances is to make his getaway, find another priest to hear his confession, and resume parish duties in a province where these are still permissible. (The trouble is, he still loves his sins: though a return to a secure ecclesiastical environment will probably remedy that.) When we first meet him, in his encounter with Mr Tench, he is in fact waiting for the chance to get away by boat. But now as later he is prevented by a message that someone is sick and needs him. And throughout the province there are many others who want to confess, to have their children baptised, to receive the sacraments—at the risk of their own lives. So for a time he continues to bring God to them, aware that by not seeking absolution from his sins he is putting his own soul in jeopardy. Eventually he realises that if he takes God to a village he is also taking the danger of death or imprisonment. Finally he decides to make for the border.

He reaches safety, only to be called back once more. A Judas-like figure, a believer who has been coveting the reward the lieutenant has placed on the priest's head (and who had already narrowly failed to get it), brings him the dying summons of a murderer: the words 'Father, for Christ's sake' written on some paper belonging to the English trader's daughter, whom he has only recently killed. The call of a soul on the brink of damnation is one that the priest cannot ignore: and so he goes to his own death, and (he believes) damnation.

Greene's next book was an entertainment, *The Ministry of Fear* (1943), a melodrama about a fifth-column in wartime London; after which he returned to his preoccupation with religious themes. In *The Heart of the Matter* (1948) we again meet a man who, by the standards of Catholic orthodoxy, damns himself to save others. The guiding principle in the life of Scobie, an assistant commissioner of police in west Africa, is the responsibility he feels for securing the happiness of his wife, whom (in the nature of things) he has ceased to love. To do this he finds it necessary to borrow money from Yusuf, an unscrupulous Syrian trader, hereby putting himself in the man's power; in consequence he finds himself abetting smuggling, and eventually becoming morally responsible for the murder of his boy Ali. Worse is to follow: for while his wife is enjoying in South Africa the comfort and security that his deal with Yusuf paid for, he finds himself becoming responsible for a second person's well-being—that of the young widow Helen Rolt, a human wreck washed up by the tides of war. Only he, it seems, can nurse her back to life; and when, leaning on his support, she has recovered, he cannot take it away again. To save this second woman he has become an adulterer. Finally his wife returns, and his spiritual predicament is impossible. To confess his adultery would be a betrayal of Helen; to avoid going to mass would be to arouse his wife's suspicion and destroy her peace of mind. The only way out is to go, unconfessed, to mass and to receive the sacrament—to his own damnation. Even so, his situation *vis-à-vis* the two women is untenable: the final solution, the only one which does not involve a denial of either of them, is the final denial of God, a disguised suicide.

In *The Heart of the Matter*, God appears as one of the principal characters: when Scobie receives the sacrament with his sins unconfessed, it is a personal denial, a betrayal of a personal relationship. In Greene's next novel, *The End of the Affair* (1951), God is again one of the chief *dramatis personae*. When the resisting unbeliever Bendrix is taken for dead, his equally unbelieving mistress Sarah finds herself exclaiming 'Dear God . . . make me believe . . . Let him be alive and I *will* believe'; and when Bendrix recovers he finds that she has deserted him for another lover—God. Such a rival cannot but be real to him: in hating Him, Bendrix can no longer not believe in Him.

In *The Quiet American* (1955), a comparatively lightweight book set in war-racked Vietnam, the drama takes place on a more worldly plane. Innocence has previously figured in Greene's novels as an indication of the raw material on which life's corrupting forces work, or as a foil for the corruption. Here, in the person of the naïvely idealistic American Alden Pyle, it is seen to be a lethal liability: he is profoundly shocked by the old-world cynicism of his more realistic English friend, but his own faith in human nature only leads to people getting killed. In the comic-melodramatic spy story *Our Man in Havana* (1958), an entertainment set in Cuba during the early stages of the Castro rising, we are back with the familiar images of innocence and corruption, and a plot involving a man prepared to damn himself to save somebody else—though here, again, in a worldly sense. But after the physical realities of these two books Greene was to return to the spiritual dimension for his next major work, *A Burnt Out Case* (1960), set in a leper hospital in central Africa. Its hero, a white man who has had in wordly terms a highly successful career, is the victim of a spiritual disease which has run its course leaving him, like a man to whom leprosy has done its worst, 'cured' but also 'burnt-out', mutilated, unable any longer to desire or even to suffer: spiritually dead. The novel describes his slow spiritual regeneration and his end—ironically (but orthodoxly) at the hands of a 'good' Catholic whose conventional 'piety' has already been ruthlessly exposed to the reader.

The Comedians (1966), however—another major work, set in Haiti—confirmed Greene's returning tendency, already noticed in the 1950s, to embed his spiritual dramas in a this-worldly, social context. It is also remarkable for uniting almost all the strands previously found in his work, and for integrating the comic element (hitherto confined largely to the 'entertainments') with the religious. Significantly, its theme is of commitment and engagement in the social nexus, its positive values being carried by a Catholic who is also a communist as well as by the comic bogus petty-crook Jones who, like the whisky-priest before him, is carried by events to an unlikely martyrdom, in a political cause. The true 'comedians' are the irresponsibly indifferent: the exponents of that old-world cynicism which we have previously seen contrasted only with the dangerous innocence of the 'quiet Americans'. Greene's Haiti is still a hell on earth: but it is a hell to be redeemed by the kind of faith that issues in involvement.

Graham Greene's other works include a number of plays, notably *The*

Potting Shed (1957) in which a whisky-priest barters his most precious possession, his faith, for God's resurrection of a dead child, much to the embarrassment of the boy's humanist parents; and a volume of short stories entitled *May we Borrow your Husband?* (1967).

K. R. R.; J. T. M.

Greenwood, Walter (1903–), English novelist and playwright, best-known for the grim and angry novel *Love on the Dole* (1933), a landmark of the depression years in the north of England. Greenwood's later novels include *What Everybody Wants* (1954); his most popular play has probably been *The Cure for Love* (1945). *There Was a Time* (1967) is an autobiography.

K. R. R.

Gregory, Lady Isabella (1852–1932), Irish dramatist, worked with Yeats in the development of the Abbey Theatre. Her own best-known contributions are her one-act plays, such as *The Rising of the Moon* (1907).

K. R. R.

Grey, Zane (1875–1939), American novelist, wrote over fifty books, principally straightforward westerns with an implanted, simple moral code, of which the most popular has been *Riders of the Purple Sage* (1912).

K. R. R.

Grieg, Nordahl (1902–43), Norwegian poet, playwright and novelist. He was killed on a bombing raid over Berlin and is venerated as a great Norwegian patriot. His posthumous *War Poems*, published in England in 1944, show him to be a fervent and at times strident lyricist. Widely travelled, he reveals the influence of J. V. Jensen and Kipling in his early work, especially in the novel *Skipet gaar videre* [*The Ship Sails On*] (1927). After spending the years 1933–35 in Russia, Grieg showed marked communist leanings and those of his plays written in the thirties concentrate particularly on man's exploitation of man. Characteristic is *Nederlaget* [*Defeat*] (1937). Another important study is the novel *Ung må verden ennu vaere* ['The world may still be young'] (1939) which is based on his experiences in Russia and in the Spanish civil war. R. C. W.

Grossman, Edith Searle (1863–1931), New Zealand writer, university-educated and a zealous campaigner for feminism, which makes itself felt in her Australian novels *In Revolt* (1893) and its sequel *A Knight of the Holy Ghost* (1907). Her early works are often striking for their portrayal of sensitive emancipated heroines and the raw brutal husbands and men they are surrounded by—an interesting picture of the coarsening effect of colonial life. Her last work, *The Heart of the Bush* (1910), weighs the virtues of England against those of New Zealand with considerable insight and, in a mood of calm acceptance, finally decides on the merits of the latter. S. R.

Grove, Frederick Philip (1872–1942), Canadian novelist and essayist of east European origin, who remained in Canada from the age of twenty onward, was author of some dozen novels. His subject is most often prairie life (he had worked on arrival as a casual labourer on farms, and later acquired one in Ontario), and with his European background he was able to see it in a wider setting than most writers. Representative of his considerable volume of writing are the essays in *Over Prairie Trails* (1922); his absorbing autobiography *In Search of Myself* (1946); and his prairie novels *Our Daily Bread* (1928), *The Yoke of Life* (1930) and *The Fruits of the Earth* (1933). He has also written novels with other backgrounds, such as *The Master of the Mill* (1944), an experimental work ambitious in scope analysing the microcosm of a flour mill over a period of forty years; and *Consider Her Ways* (1947) in which the behaviour of an invading tribe of ants is the vehicle for satire of the besetting sins of North American society—pride and greed. S. R.

Guareschi, Giovanni (1908–1968), Italian writer and journalist. Having worked his way up in the world of journalism from an inconspicuous start, he became editor of the humorous weekly *Bertoldo* in 1936. After the second world war he was for several years editor of another humorous paper, *Candido*, which constantly indicted the shortcomings of Italian society and added a refreshing note to the bitter political atmosphere of post-war Italy. After publishing a series of humorous books, Guareschi sprang to world fame with his diverting collections of stories, the first of which was published in 1948, concerning the unconventional parish priest Don Camillo, who is engaged in a perpetual pinprick war with the 'red' mayor of the village, Peppone, and his henchmen. Guareschi's humour is sympathetic and devoid of bitterness, betraying a warm and charitable approach to people and their idiosyncrasies. His Don Camillo stories have appeared in English with the titles *The Little World of Don Camillo, Don Camillo and His Flock, Don Camillo and the Prodigal Son, Don Camillo's Dilemma, Don Camillo and the Devil* and *Comrade Don Camillo.* Among Guareschi's 'non-Camillo' works is *Diario clandestino: cronache di prigionia* [*My Secret Diary*] (1946), relating his experiences in a German concentration camp. A collection of amusing anecdotes on his family set-up has been published in English with the title *The House That Nino Built.* D. B.

Guedalla, Phillip (1889–), English man of letters, began with books of poetry and parody, but turned to the writing of brief historical essays from which were to develop the fuller biographies by which he is best known. These 'character sketches' appear in *Supers and Supermen* (1920) and *A Gallery* (1924). His full-length historical works include *The Second Empire* (1922) and *Palmerston* (1926), and his interest in South America is shown in *Conquistador* (1927) and *Argentine Tango* (1932). The book he is best known for is his biography of Wellington, *The Duke* (1931). Guedalla's work is largely in the tradition of Lytton Strachey, but his approach to Wellington is devoid of the customary debunking.

R. A. K.

Guillén, Jorge (1893–), Spanish poet. Born in Valladolid, Guillén spent much of his youth outside Spain and lectured at the Sorbonne from 1917 to 1923. While in France he began writing poetry and on his return to Spain his compositions appeared regularly in reviews. Long before the publication of *Cántico* [*Cántico*] (1928), Guillén was regarded as a poet of great promise. His translation of Valéry's *Le Cimetière marin* and subsequent editions of *Cántico* (1936, 1945, 1950) have confirmed this reputation. Professor of Spanish Literature at Seville from 1931 to 1938, he has lived in the United States since the civil war. During a visit to Spain in 1949 he began *Clamor* ['Clamour'], which consists of three books published separately: *Maremágnum* ['Pandemonium'] (1957), . . . *Que van a dar en la mar* ['. . . That flow into the sea'] (1960) and *A la altura de las circunstancias* ['To rise to the occasion'] (1963). He was subsequently working on *Homenaje* ['Homage'] with which to complete his poetic *opera. Cántico, Clamor* and *Homenaje* are complementary and form one work, to be entitled *Aire nuestro* ['Our air'].

Posterity is likely to accord the highest honours to *Cántico.* This remarkable work grew from 75 poems in 1928 to 334 in the 'First Complete Edition' (1950). It is the product of a specific literary milieu, the post-Jiménez world of essences and delight in the present moment, and the 'pure poetry' debate of the twenties. (Guillén in 1926 favoured a poetry that was 'fairly pure, *ma non troppo*'.) Like so many poets of his generation, Guillén is concerned with the genuineness of reality. Since 1945 the full title has been *Cántico, Fe de vida* [*Cántico, In Praise of Living*] because he sees the world as good and harmonious. He only begins to live when at dawn he perceives reality—'Reality invents me', he says in the opening poem—and the plenitude of experienced reality, the 'peak of delight', comes at midday. Guillén's vision, then, focusses on the world's harmonies and intensities. He flees cities, where only lovers experience true reality. He refuses to be preoccupied by death, which he accepts as 'law' not 'accident'. For he believes that the nobler sentiments—friendship, love—can overcome the frustrations of society and the human condition. *Cántico* is a uniquely dignified reaction to the twentieth-century crisis. An excellent selection in English, edited by N. T. di Giovanni, was published in 1965. In *Clamor* Guillén's poetic themes are no longer life and fulfilment: now he conveys the negative elements, evil and death, which he feels around him. It is a 'committed' poetry which lacks the intensity of *Cántico*. *Homenaje* contains homages to other writers and occasional verse. As a critic Guillén has published in English *Language and Poetry: Some Poets of Spain* (1961). D. H. G.

Güiraldes, Ricardo (1886–1927), Argentinian novelist and poet, divided his life mainly between Buenos Aires and the family ranch, though a number of visits to Paris enabled him to form a close acquaintance with young French writers. He was co-director of the abortive *avant-garde* literary periodical *Proa* ['Prow'] (Buenos Aires, 1924–25). He reveals a dual concern for indigenous themes of Argentina and for a style largely influenced by Flaubert and the French symbolist poets. Publications, of which all but the last met with little immediate success, include poems, short stories and four novels. His penultimate book, *Xaimaca* ['Jamaica'] (1923), is a novel in diary form describing in poetic prose a journey from Argentina to the Caribbean. Evocations of the landscape and reflections on eternal human problems form a framework in which he sets a simple love story. With his last completed work, the novel *Don Segundo Sombra* [*Don Segundo Sombra. Shadows on the Pampas*] (1927), he achieved international recognition. The narrator, Fabio Cáceres, attaches himself to the wandering gaucho, Don Segundo Sombra, and serves under his guidance an apprenticeship to the life of the pampas. First seen as a shadowy figure on horseback, Don Segundo retains an air of the mysterious and symbolic until he eventually rides away, leaving with Fabio the impression of one who is 'more an idea than a man'. Although sometimes episodic in structure, the novel acquires vigour, depth and colour as it moves from a scene of horsebreaking to one of meditation, from a local dance to a storm on the pampas. The style, while seeking—particularly in the dialogue—a simplicity to match the characters and scene, is nevertheless impressionistic and symbolic. P. R. B.

Gumilyov, Nikolay Stepanovich (1886–1921), married awhile to Anna Akhmatova, was an anti-Bolshevik acmeist poet. The acmeists, in reaction against the mysticism and vagueness that had characterised much Russian symbolist poetry, stressed the need for the precise and concrete in imagery. Gumilyov peopled his poems with heroes, and is almost the only Russian poet who wrote with great clarity about the exotic lands he had visited. He was eventually shot for his supposed participation in an anti-communist plot. His best work to be found in translation is in *Kostyor* [*The Pyre*] (1918) and *Ognenniy stolp* [*Pillar of Fire*] (1921). B. W.

Gunn, Mrs Aneas (1870–1961), Australian writer whose tales of the outback and of aboriginal life in northern Australia, *Little Black Princess* (1905) and *We of the Never-Never* (1908), are still popular today, despite the rather romantic oversimplification of the relationship between the white settlers and the natives. S. R.

Gunn, Thom (Thomson William Gunn; 1929–), English poet. Gunn, the son of a newspaper editor, was educated at University College School, London and Trinity College, Cambridge. He is one of the poets included in Conquest's anthology *New Lines* and regards himself as one of the National Service generation in terms of formative values.

Gunn is one of the many contemporary writers influenced by the quality of the seventeenth-century metaphysical poets. His poetry like theirs is remarkable for a sensibility formed by a union of intellectual clarity and deep emotion, and it contains a heavy spicing of wit and irony. However, the warmth and sensitivity of the metaphysicals is not always present, and a dominating theme of his verse is an aggressive desire for the individual to dominate his environment, in terms not only of imposing order on the flux of existence in an intellectual form but also of the heavy dominance of one personality over others. Gunn's concern to define will, to interpret responsibility, to create individual standards of value and define them within the aesthetic structure of verse have received a great deal of praise from critics and fellow poets alike with only cautious limiting adverse comment on the occasional cold-bloodedness of his aggression. Published work includes *Fighting Terms* (1954), *The Sense of Movement* (1957) and *My Sad Captains* (1961). D. L. P.

Gunnarsson, Gunnar (1889–), Icelandic novelist. Having received little formal education in Iceland, he went to Denmark at the age of eighteen, where he studied for two years at a folk high school. Moving to Copenhagen he struggled to become an accepted writer in Danish. He was prolific in many genres but made his reputation as a novelist who portrayed on vast canvases the rich panoply of Icelandic life, customs, history and tradition. Deeply patriotic, he analysed and even glorified the common people and their frequent heroic struggles against all manner of adversity. His literary renown was established by his monumental *Borgslaegtens Historie* [*Guest the One-eyed*] (1912–14), an evocative and nostalgic novel of Icelandic life, characterised by a curious brand of neo-romanticism. Later he turned his pen to a series of historical novels, among which *Edbrødre* [*The Sworn Brothers*] (1918) and *Salige er de Enfoldige* [*Seven Days' Darkness*] (1920) are the most prominent. His own rich and varied literary testament is presented in the five volumes of the autobiographical novel cycle entitled *Kirken paa Bjerget* [*Ships in the Sky* and *The Night and the Dream*] (1923–28). Gunnarsson finally re-settled in Iceland in 1939. R. C. W.

Guthrie-Smith, William Herbert (1861–1946), New Zealand writer. English born and bred, he came to New Zealand in the 1880s. In his first book *Tutura* (1921) he describes a locality (his sheep run) in such detail that it comes to represent a history in miniature of the whole country. Despite its formidable appearance—a geological, geographical and historical treatise—it is enlivened by accurate social observation and the kind of dry humour that describes man's acclimatisation to a new country as if he were merely one of the species of transplanted fauna. S. R.

H

H.D. These are the initials with which Hilda Doolittle (1886–1961), American poet, signed herself. She was one of the original imagist school of poets and possibly the purest. She continued, throughout her life, to write verse close to Pound's definition of the poetic image: 'an intellectual and emotional complex in an instant of time'.

Hilda Doolittle was born in Bethlehem, Pennsylvania, and attended Pennsylvania University where she made friends with Ezra Pound and William Carlos Williams. Her first encounter with the imagists was in Europe where she went in 1911 and where she married Richard Aldington in 1913. She was divorced in 1937 and subsequently made her home in Geneva.

Her early verse together with that of a large number of American imagists was published in the Chicago magazine *Poetry*. Subsequently she issued several volumes, *Collected Poems* (1925) going into six editions. Unlike William Carlos Williams, 'H.D.' did not allow her poetry to deviate far from the aim of focussing on concrete objects of attention. Her only concession from this purpose is the occasional personal and very simple statement of attitude:

I saw the first pear
as it fell—
the honey-seeking, golden banded,
the yellow swarm
was not more fleet than I,
(spare us from loveliness)
and I fell prostrate
crying:

'Orchard' from *Sea Garden* (1916).

'H.D.'s work is influenced by her scholarship, with a symbolism married to the Greek period. The poetry has clarity, sensitivity and a quality of lyricism but the strict adherence to the early imagist theories loses for it much of the richness of life and leaves it delicate but slight.

Other volumes of her verse include *Collected Poems*(1940) and *Helen in Egypt* (1961). She also published a quantity of fiction including *Bid Me to Live* (1960). D. L. P.

Haggard, William (1907–), pseudonym of an English novelist who sets his adventure stories in the world of international business and espionage. His character Colonel Charles Russell (*The Unquiet Sleep*,

1962; *The High Wire*, 1963; and others), who is 'head of the Security Executive' which employs a variety of skilfully portrayed people, combines professional ability with moral courage to a remarkable but convincing degree. Later titles include *The Hard Sell* (1965) and *The Power House* (1966). H. C.

Hall, Radclyffe (1886–1943), English novelist, wrote the sensational book *The Well of Loneliness* (1928), which outraged many readers by its uncritical treatment of female sexual deviation, and was banned.

K. R. R.

Hamilton, [Anthony Walter] Patrick (1904–1962), English novelist and playwright. Known chiefly as the author of two spine-chilling plays *Rope* (1929) and *Gaslight* (1939), his novels did not achieve the recognition they deserved. *The Midnight Bell* (1929), *The Siege of Pleasure* (1932) and *The Plains of Cement* (1934) collected as *Twenty Thousand Streets under the Sky* (1935) tell of the characters who frequent a small public house near Euston and authentically convey the bewilderment of inarticulate people adrift in the vastness of London. Other works include *Monday Morning* (1923), *Twopence Coloured* (1928), *Hangover Square* (1941), *The West Pier* (1951), *Mr Stimpson and Mr Gorse* (1953), *Unknown Assailant* (1955) and *The Duke in Darkness* (a play, 1942). G. S.

Hammett, [Samuel] Dashiell (1894–1960), an outstanding American crime novelist, best known for *The Maltese Falcon* (1930) and *The Thin Man* (1932), whose admirers have compared him to Hemingway. Resemblances, however, are scarcely more than stylistic, and in the context of the widespread imitation of Hemingway by his contemporaries they are not specially remarkable. Certainly Hammett (who was reputedly left-wing) sometimes implies comment on the social context of the crimes he deals with, and this is specially evident in his portrayal of political gangsterdom in *The Glass Key* (1931): but the creation of a suspense-laden detection narrative—the details of which carry no wider significance or implications—remained his prime objective. K. R. R.

Hamsun, Knut (1859–1952), Norwegian novelist and winner of the 1920 Nobel Prize for Literature. In his youth he worked as jack-of-all-trades in Norway and the United States, his occupations being so varied as to include those of teacher, tram-conductor, shop-assistant and deep-sea fisherman. His early attempts to write met with only moderate success; his literary reputation was not established until 1890 with the publication of his novel *Sult* [*Hunger*]. This work scrutinised the psychological effects of starvation on an introvert's mind, and shocked by its clear contempt for contemporary narrative techniques. Above all it underlined Hamsun's deep desire to use literature to draw attention to the rôle of the individual and to preserve his identity. The period 1890 to 1936 was for Hamsun one of intense and prolific literary activity, in which he wrote poetry, plays and above all twenty-four works of narrative fiction of which the vast majority are available in English. In all, Hamsun has been translated into twenty-five languages. Many varying strands are found in his novels: admiration for the wanderer, for the vagabond of life in all his manifestations, delight in nature, opposition to materialism and opposition to all conventions which sap individuality and independence of body and mind. Such ideas were diversely introduced into such prominent novels as *Pan* [*Pan*] (1894), *Victoria* [*Victoria*] (1898), *Konerne ved Vandposten* [*The Women at the Pump*] (1920) and *Sisste Kapitel* [*Chapter the Last*] (1924), and achieved their most satisfactory synthesis in *Markens Grøde* [*The Growth of the Soil*] (1917) which is regarded as his masterpiece. The admiration he had shown for Prussian militarism in the first world war became open sympathy for the Nazis in the second. His closing years were saddened by the consequent and practically total opprobrium of his compatriots. R. C. W.

Han Suyin (Mrs Elizabeth Comber, née Elizabeth K. Chow; 1917–), English-language novelist. Of Chinese and Belgian parentage, educated in Peking, Brussels and London, she graduated as a doctor in 1948 and has practised since that time. Her most famous work is *A Many Splendoured Thing* (1952), a semi-autobiographical and most moving account of a love affair between a Eurasian doctor and an American journalist which ends in tragedy with an untimely death. Also widely known are *Destination Chungking* (1942), again drawing on her own experiences, and *The Crippled Tree* (1965). S. R.

Hanley, Gerald (1916–), English novelist concerned primarily with stories of action against a natural background. His novels, leavened with a peculiar brand of humour, deal with the analysis of characters in tough situations. His titles include *Monsoon Victory* (1946), *The Year of the Lion* (1953), *Without Love* (1957) and *Gilligan's Last Elephant* (1962). R. A. K.

Hanley, James (1901–), English novelist and short-story writer, has used his experiences as a seaman as a basis for his tales of the sea. His books include *The Closed Harbour* (1952) and *Levine* (1955). K. R. R.

Hardy, Frank (1917–), Australian author of the book *Power Without Glory* that caused a public outcry when it was published in 1950. Although called a novel and supposedly fictitious, in its vitriolic attack on Australian society so many politicians and well-known people could be detected that a court case resulted—in which, however, Hardy was acquitted. He later published *The Four-Legged Lottery* (1958) but this did not reveal any real talent. His writing is at times two-dimensional, possibly because his primary concern is to convince readers of the decadence and corruption of the capitalist system rather than of the reality and sympathy of his characters. S. R.

Hardy, Thomas (1840–1928), English novelist and poet. Hardy's novels were all published in the nineteenth century, most of his poetry not until the twentieth century. The novels thus fall outside the scope of this work and will be discussed only insofar as they are related to the poetry by a common motivating philosophy and it is necessary to know something of the novelist before understanding fully the poet.

Hardy was born in Dorset the son of a stonemason. He was educated privately at Dorchester, mainly in classics and the romance languages. He later qualified as an architect before turning to literature. The best of the novels, which include *Far From the Madding Crowd* (1874), *The Return of the Native* (1878), *The Mayor of Casterbridge* (1886), *Tess of the D'Urbervilles* (1891) and *Jude the Obscure* (1895), express a vision of a tragic universe where man is inevitably overcome by the forces which surround him whether of society, of nature, of fate or from within himself. In a sense Hardy is a product of nineteenth-century determinism, but to say this is to limit the area of a tragic awareness which after all he shares not only with Thackeray in the nineteenth century and Hemingway in the twentieth but with the Greek tragedians: and his work certainly bears comparison with the latter. It is not enough, as some critics have done, to say that Hardy is a descriptive writer of the English countryside whose work has tragic overtones; he is much more than that. His 'Wessex' settings do catch at the heart of the Dorset countryside, and he does depict in detail the idiosyncratic characteristics of its inhabitants, and the country framework is certainly essential to his writing; but the centre of his vision, the force which makes him a great writer, is in the intensity of inevitable and overwhelming tragedy. This is nowhere more evident than in *Jude the Obscure*, a novel which aroused so much critical and moral animosity that Hardy henceforward published only verse. Jude is a man of intellectual capacity denied expression by a limited educational and social environment. He aspires to the glistening towers of Cambridge but achieves only the merits of solid craftsmanship as a stonemason. He is trapped into marriage by an insensitive and instinctive woman, whom he leaves to live with his cousin who has both sensitivity and intelligence and who has in turn left her husband. The guilt of both destroys their happiness and in a terrible climax Jude's son by his first marriage kills the children of the second relationship and then hangs himself.

The poetry Hardy had written from about 1860 was collected and published in 1898 as *Wessex Poems*. This and volumes subsequently issued were published as *Collected Poems* (1931). The verse like the prose is often intense, harsh and powerful rather than elegant, and Hardy's grim personality juts through the words in the fashion of Browning from whom he borrowed the technique of the dramatic monologue. But the harshness, the awkwardness, the heaviness of the language when combined with genuine lyricism and compassion lift the verse into an intensity and beauty that mark a major poet.

The Dynasts, published in sections between 1904 and 1908, is an epic drama in blank verse in nineteen acts. Its content is the Napoleonic wars, a subject which had interested Hardy from his boyhood. The wars are seen from the viewpoint of supernatural entities, bare intelligencies —almost gods—who chorus rather than intervene in man's futile struggle against forces that are at best indifferent to him.

Contrastingly, for instance in 'At Castle Boterel', Hardy could write poetry that recollected in old age the passion and tenderness of romantic love. Here he recalls a moment of emotional and physical ecstasy and relates the importance of that moment to his time past. The hill he looks at, marked by history, records for him only:

. . . that we two passed.

And to me, though Time's unflinching rigour,
In mindless rote, has ruled from sight
The substance now, one phantom figure
Remains on the slope, as when that night
Saw us alight.

I look and see it there, shrinking, shrinking,
I look back at it amid the rain
For the very last time; for my sand is sinking,
And I shall traverse old love's domain
Never again.

D. L. P.

Harraden, Beatrice (1864–1936), English novelist and suffragette, famous before the turn of the century for her *Ships That Pass in the Night* (1893), continued to write into her sixties and was the author of such books as *Interplay* (1908) and *Rachel* (1926). K. R. R.

Harris, Frank (1856–1914), English writer who was during his career editor of the *Fortnightly Review, Saturday Review* and *Vanity Fair*, and who by his eccentricity and his arrogance left a great trail of notoriety surrounding his life and his works. His fiction writing never really developed, and it was in his biographical works that he revealed a certain psychological insight, particularly in what is probably his best book *Oscar Wilde* (1920) and in his fiery approach to Shakespeare in *The Man Shakespeare* (1909) and *The Women of Shakespeare* (1911). It was in his autobiographical work *My Life and Loves* (1922) that Harris really established his reputation as a literary commentator and a human 'monster'. The work, banned in Britain for many years, is a panorama of social and literary life at the end of the nineteenth century and an insight into the sexual prowess of Harris and others. It is the product of a man who knew Oscar Wilde and G. B. Shaw, and who, as Wilde is reputed to have said, was invited to all the great houses—once. R. A. K.

Harris, Max (1921–), Australian poet, was for a time editor of the *avant-garde* literary periodical of the 1940s, *Angry Penguins*. This journal never recovered from the loss of face it sustained on exposure of the 'Ern Malley' hoax. Two young poets, critical of the obscurity and tendency towards surrealism of poetry associated with the journal, concocted a pastiche purporting to be the *oeuvre* of a young soldier, killed in action. The magazine acclaimed the discovery of a new poet and published all the 'poems' (and the police intervened to fine Harris £5 for publishing 'indecencies'); the trick was revealed and the journal deflated.

Harris in his own early work experimented with different verse forms, and his poetry is characterised by enigmatic private verbal associations; but he later developed a more vigorous and realistic style. His publications include *The Gift of Blood* (1940), *Dramas from the Sky* (1942) and a novel *Vegetative Eye* (1943). S. R.

Hartley, L. P. (Leslie Poles Hartley; 1895–), English novelist, short-story writer and critic. His first published works were short stories in a macabre vein (*Night Fears*, 1924), works already distinguished by imaginative insight into states of mind and by analyses that have considerable psychological validity. His first novel *Simonetta Perkins* appeared in 1925, but thereafter for nearly twenty years he published only one further book —another volume of short stories, *The Killing Bottle* (1932). However, during this time he was already working on the first book (*The Shrimp and the Anemone*, 1944) of a trilogy that was to be acclaimed by many as his greatest achievement. In this first section we meet the child Eustace and his sister Hilda, in whom we recognise respectively the 'shrimp' and the 'anemone' of the title. Eustace, a gentle, delicate little boy, worships Hilda and feels dimly that he must devote himself to her, even sacrifice himself for her, but never acknowledging to himself that he expects something from her in return—her love. In this novel, we are encountering for the first time a feature to be repeated in later works (*The Go-Between, The Brickfield*)—a child as the central character. This does not mean that Hartley excels as the painter of whimsical children; rather that he perfectly catches the embryo adult and that painful and sudden growth that is adolescence. In *The Sixth Heaven* (1946) Eustace is an undergraduate at Oxford, still dominated at a distance by Hilda, making some friends though choosing them more for their wealth and social status than from any close personal feeling. The accuracy and spirit of Hartley's description of this social group of the 1920s are such that this particular book can be appreciated on the level of a comedy of manners. The final part of the trilogy is called *Eustace and Hilda* (1947) and the title announces a relationship that in its embryonic form could only be expressed in symbols (the shrimp and the anemone) and later was seen as incapable of more than an imperfect realisation (the sixth heaven). It is in this third book that Eustace makes his most determined efforts to 'win' Hilda—for the lover he has chosen for her. Dick Stavely, their neighbour since childhood, is in every way different from Eustace, a cut above him socially, more dynamic, masculine, with a village reputation for ruining women. It is during the courtship of these two that Eustace experiences his most intense pleasure; and when it comes to nothing, he behaves with the desperation we would expect from Dick, the book ending with tragedy and the final sacrifice of the shrimp to the anemone.

Next came *The Boat* (1949) which analyses the conflict between the demands of the group—i.e. the state—and the right of the individual to act alone; and this was followed by *My Fellow Devils* (1951) where Hartley returns to the theme of the trilogy—expressed here in the story of the passionate and sensitive person of Margaret Pennefather who, like Eustace, can never quite follow her desires. But perhaps even better known than any of these previous works is *The Go-Between* (1953). This concerns a thirteen-year-old boy Leo who acts as messenger between his cousin Marian, for whom her parents have ambitious plans of marriage, and Ted, a local farmer. It is a stiflingly hot summer, Leo is the only child of the company, and alone he attempts to cope with both the sexual awakening of adolescence and the intensely romantic associations which accompany it. In a way that he only half understands, he thinks his cousin is beautiful, so beautiful that he is rather disappointed by the 'spooning' of the couple—which does not satisfy his craving for an ecstatic romantic exchange. Nevertheless he is tormented by the conflicting feeling of attraction/repulsion for the lovers and one day spies on them in the greenhouse and finds them in the act of making love. His hysterical screams precipitate the final tragedy—the love affair is abruptly ended by being discovered, Ted shoots himself and Marian is sent away.

L. P. Hartley's characters very often come to tragic ends though it is interesting to note that only those with some overpowering obsession, something which excludes every other element in their lives, meet death. The ones who compromise, who come to terms, survive. Leadbitter, in *The Hireling* (1957), is another of the former—entirely withdrawn, sour and disillusioned, he has a stony but respectful façade which, as private chauffeur of a hire car, he assumes before his clients. A young titled widow, tormenting herself for failing to communicate with her husband and practising an exercise recommended by her analyst of interesting herself in someone else, succeeds in penetrating his reserve. Leadbitter is so moved by the fantasy picture of his warm family life that he invents as something to tell her, that he falls in love with his listener who has become for him the only possible occupant of the phantom image of his 'wife'. Once again, this impossible situation can only be resolved in tragedy: Leadbitter drives himself and the young couple who have discovered his passion until the car crashes at high speed. However, something is salvaged from his disaster; the widow is told that he loved her and this knowledge enables her to pick up the threads of her life again. This is an interesting conclusion because it suggests that the only possible consummation of love is in the mind—Leadbitter being transformed by the secret love which irradiated his lonely life, but killing himself the minute it was revealed; the widow rejecting his one desperate physical advance, but accepting his dying declaration of love.

The fatality and beauty of love and desire has previously been summed up in the symbol of the belladonna plant of *The Go-Between*; and the failure of most people to recognise, comprehend and accept this is a recurring theme of this and other novels. This particular idea is taken up again in *The Brickfield* (1964), which like *The Go-Between* is a story of adolescent love—this time actually consummated, and because the passion has been expressed, and even more because it has been discovered (and by an unpleasant and unsympathetic person), ending in death. The importance of two other writers as models for L. P. Hartley has been noted by critics. Like Nathaniel Hawthorne he takes his symbols of deadly beauty from the natural world; and he is influenced by Henry James in his choice of subject, type of character and above all in his concern for the form of the novel. *The Brickfield* can be seen as a definite statement about the limits within which the author must inevitably work. It is an extended reminiscence of a perfect childhood love told by a dying man to his young male companion. The tragedy of the book lies in the gulf between the importance of the story in this its first telling for the speaker and its lack of impact on his selfish listener who, we realise with dawning horror, is planning his employer's death. Here is the kind of framework in which emotion can be 'recollected in tranquillity', and here too is the relationship between writer and reader shown in its most extremely unsatisfactory state.

L. P. Hartley's other works include *A Perfect Woman* (1955), *Facial Justice* (1960), *Two For the River* (1961), and *The Betrayal* (1966), a sequel to *The Brickfield.* S. R.

Hašek, Jaroslav (1883–1923), Czech writer. Forced to serve in the Austrian army during the first world war, Hašek eventually deserted and joined the Free Czechoslovak and later the Red Army where he became a political commissar. After his return to Czechoslovakia he wrote *Osudy dobrého vojáka Švejka za světové války* [*The Good Soldier Schweik*] (1920–23), an amorphous collection of anecdotes held together by the central figure of Schweik, a cunning egotist pretending idiocy in order to save his skin in the upheaval of the war. K. B.

Hassall, Christopher (1912–63), English poet, dramatist, librettist and biographer, characterised by the religious themes of much of his writing. His titles include *The Red Leaf: Poem* (1957) and a play for Westminster Abbey *Out of the Whirlwind* (1953). His verse drama *The Hidden King* (1956) was the theatrical centrepiece of the Edinburgh festival of that year, but has not been revived professionally. *Rupert Brooke: a Biography* was published in 1964. D. L. P.

Hauptmann, Gerhart (1862–1945), German dramatist, born in Silesia, studied sculpture in Breslau and Rome before settling in Berlin. Deeply influenced by the drama of Ibsen and Strindberg and the naturalism of the novels of Zola, his first play *Vor Sonnenaufgang* ['Before sunrise'] provoked violent scenes in the Berlin Freie Bühne when it was first produced in 1889. He became at once the leading dramatist of the naturalist movement with this stark picture of moral corruption in which the action is conditioned both by environment and heredity. Hauptmann, however, was to show more compassion in his work than was common in the naturalist movement. *Einsame Menschen* ['Lonely people'] (1891) portrayed a man torn between his love for two women: one young, ardent and intellectual, and the other plain, self-effacing and dull—his own wife. The compassion is revealed by the fact that the wife, not the girl, is clearly the heroine. By 1892, Hauptmann had introduced a new dramatic phenomenon, the collective hero; in that year *Die Weber* [*The Weavers*] was produced. It deals with the famous revolt of the Silesian weavers in 1844; but no one hero emerges. This work was closely followed by the historical play *Florian Geyer* (1896) which showed the beginnings of a new tendency towards the mingling of naturalism with romantic symbolism, this being maintained with the fantastic *Hanneles Himmelfahrt* [*Little Hanne's Journey to Heaven*] (1894). Hauptmann's social conscience, his questioning of the established political shibboleths, exactly suited the temper of his time; but he was also a gifted storyteller, and his output was enormous. His comedies *Der Biberpelz* [*The Beavercoat*] and *Der Rote Hahn* ['The red cock'] were later revived and produced by Brecht and the Berliner Ensemble in the 1950s.

In 1912, Hauptmann was awarded the Nobel prize and was regarded as the leading German man of letters. After the war he continued to turn out plays in his established vein, but he interjected *Die Insel der grossen Mutter* ['The isle of the great mother'] (1924), a novel with a piquant theme, the life of a number of women cast up on a desert island with only one man. A thinly disguised account of his own experiences in love and marriage followed in *Buch der Leidenschaft* ['Book of passion'] (1929), and in a straightforward autobiography *Das Abenteuer meiner Jugend* ['The adventure of my youth'] (1937). An old man by the time of the Nazi rise to power, Hauptmann made no criticism of the new régime and appeared at least outwardly to accept it. He was spared from having to give an account of himself by his death. G. W.

Hay, Ian (John Hay Beith; 1876–1952), Scottish-born playwright and novelist. He wrote both war stories and light humorous novels; but he is best remembered for two light comedies he wrote for the London theatre: *Tilly of Bloomsbury* (1919) and *Housemaster* (1936). R. A. K.

Heath-Stubbs, John (1918–   ), English poet. Heath-Stubbs's early poetry derives in form and subject matter from the art and culture of ancient Greece, Rome and Alexandria. It is literary and academic and removed at the farthest extreme from the immediate and the colloquial. Later poetry in volumes like *The Triumph of the Muse* (1958) and *The Blue-Fly in his Head* (1962) involves a more contemporary idiom mixed with wit and satire. Throughout his verse there is a concern with Christianity, whether more scholarly as in the early poetry or more felt in his later work. Volumes include *Beauty and the Beast* (1943), *The Swarming of the Bees* (1950) and *A Charm Against Toothache* (1954). D. L. P.

Heidegger, Martin (1889–   ), German existentialist philosopher, who was strongly influenced by the work of Kierkegaard, though lacking the latter's Christianity. His treatise *Sein und Zeit* [*Being and Time*] (1927–1935) had a powerful impact on international letters, most notably on Sartre. For Heidegger there were two types of being: *Dasein* (human existence) and *Vorhandensein* (the non-human presence of all other being, including physical objects). *Dasein* was characterised by personal consciousness and by *Angst*, a general dread of nothingness, of the void. 'Authentic' *Dasein* involved an acknowledgment of the challenge of the world and of death; 'unauthentic' *Dasein* was the state of those persons who became absorbed or submerged in a myopic, day-to-day involvement with the mundane. R. C. W.

Heinlein, Robert (1907–   ), American novelist, one of the most prolific and able writers of science fiction, both short stories and long. His main work forms a co-ordinated 'History of the Future', extrapolating from present conditions rather than creating a new world with new concepts: thus his characters are normal human beings facing problems mainly of organisation, as in *Starship Troopers* (1959). He also wrote the screenplay for one of the first space films, *Destination Moon* (1950).

A Robert Heinlein Omnibus was published in 1966. C. B.

Heller, Joseph (1923–   ), American novelist, leapt to fame with his widely praised and best-selling novel *Catch 22* (1961). At a time when the bulk of second-world-war fiction was still predominantly serious (whether heroic or horrific), Heller brought to it a lethal blend of farce and fantasy, sick humour and icy casualness; and as has been the case in several other outstanding war novels (e.g. Mailer's *The Naked and The Dead*), his treatment of war was such as to extend its significance well beyond the limits of actual warfare—in this case, primarily, to the American way of life and the free-enterprise economic system, and ultimately to the nature of man.

The scene of action centres on an American air-base in the Mediterranean in 1944; the principal character is a Captain Yossarian, a man with many of the characteristics of the classical anti-hero, and whose avowed aim is simply to stay alive. As he sees it, everyone is out to get him: his own colonel, with his repeated raising of the number of missions to be flown before a man could go on leave, as much as the enemy. There were various ruses to be adopted, but there were always catches: one might, for instance, feign insanity, only to come up against catch 22, which stated that anyone wishing to get out of flying combat missions was clearly sane and therefore had to fly them. A crazy logic and essential sanity emerges constantly from the near-lunatic anarchy which characterises the book—an anarchy reflected also in its loose and often haphazard structure, with the story sometimes moving outwards from individual characters taken as focal points (all the chapters being in fact named after characters), and with a generally cyclic pattern having superimposed on it a progressive extension of the reader's knowledge of certain key events.

Yossarian (and everybody else) is, indeed, menaced by the murderous potentialities inherent in the 'normal' careerism of his senior officers and in the equally 'normal' desire of the mess officer to make profits (leading him to elaborate trading operations and financial transactions across the lines); and the book is a savage indictment of the society in which such ambition and desire is the norm. By contrast, Yossarian with his intense love of life (embodied in a lavish celebration of a life-affirming sexuality) emerges as the bearer of the book's positive values. K. R. R.

Hemingway, Ernest Miller (1898–1961), American novelist, born in Oak Park, a respectable Chicago suburb, son of a doctor who was also a keen sportsman, twice ran away from home before becoming a reporter in Kansas City in 1917. Next year he was a volunteer ambulance driver on the Italian front; he was badly wounded, but returned to serve the last few weeks of the war with the Italian infantry. The war had a shattering effect on him, reproduced in the succession of characters he was to create with both physical and psychic wounds. The first of these is Nick Adams, hero of several of the stories in his first collection, *In Our Time* (1925). We observe Nick, like the young Hemingway himself, coming face to face with violence and pain and learning to live with it; and later we see him learning to cope with his own wounds.

Hemingway had married in 1921 and set off again for Europe the same year, where he worked as a roving reporter and met Gertrude Stein, James Joyce and Ezra Pound. Much of his life in the circle of expatriates in Paris is recorded in his memoirs, published after his death; it also provided the material for much of his writing. His first novel, *The Sun Also Rises* (1926; published in England as *Fiesta*), is a moving story of the 'lost generation'. In its central character, Jake Barnes, who has been rendered impotent by a war wound, we meet a typical Hemingway hero—sensitive, stoical, wanting to enjoy the good things of life and above all honest. Contrasted with him is the figure of Robert Cohn, who has not learned to live with the harsher realities of life.

The war's long-term effect on Hemingway, as on many of his contemporaries, was that total collapse of values which is represented in the meaningless, aimless lives of the characters in *The Sun Also Rises*. When good or bad, right or wrong, no longer had meaning it seemed to Hemingway that the only approach possible for the novelist lay in the bare reportage that is so characteristic of his writing. The writer's only virtue was absolute honesty, particularly in relation to the basic realities of human life—eating, drinking, physical love, death, and man's fighting and hunting instincts. Hemingway's affirmation of these two instincts is seen in his own active interest in boxing, bull-fighting and big-game hunting, and in stories such as 'Fifty Grand' and 'The Undefeated' in the collection *Men Without Women* (1927).

Beyond an affirmation of the desirability of these basic characteristics, he would not go: in the words of the hero of his war novel *A Farewell to Arms* (1929), 'There were many words that you could not stand to hear and finally only the names of places had dignity . . . Abstract words such as glory, honour, courage or hallow were obscene beside the concrete names of villages'. This widely hailed masterpiece was the fruit of ten years' digestion of his experiences in the first world war. It has an ending that is as pessimistic as anything written during this period: an ending which, despite its being a purely personal tragedy in no way resulting from the military operations, is symptomatic of the author's feelings about life in the aftermath of war. It is to be taken as a statement about the world we live in—a world that can produce horrors on the scale of the Great War. The central character is Frederick Henry, a young American who is in Italy when war breaks out and who enlists with an Italian ambulance unit. The war on this front is light-hearted enough at the outset with hostilities virtually suspended during the winter and ample time to enjoy eating and drinking and flirting with the nurses. The story deepens as Henry finds himself increasingly involved with a British nurse, Catherine Barclay, and at the same time is wounded in action. Their love affair during his convalescence is the high-water mark of the book. Soon after his return to the front—by which time Catherine is pregnant—Henry is involved in a chaotic retreat. At one moment he is shooting a deserting sergeant; not long after he himself is being arrested as a deserter. He is now totally sickened by the war and only interested in rejoining Catherine. He is oppressed by the feeling that everything worth caring for is being destroyed and by the fear that the world will soon catch up with him and Catherine. They do in fact meet up again and make a hazardous escape into Switzerland, where they wait for Catherine to have her baby. But 'the world' has the last word: not only is her child born dead, but Catherine herself bleeds to death in the process. As he has reflected earlier, 'If people bring so much courage to this world the world has to kill them to break them . . . It kills the very good and the very gentle and the very brave impartially.'

During the next decade Hemingway was to produce nothing on the same scale. There were two notable pieces of non-fiction, the study of bull-fighting entitled *Death in the Afternoon* (1932) and the big-game hunting travel-book *Green Hills of Africa* (1935)—books full of practical details of the skills involved as well as of the thoughts and feelings on life and art occasioned by the experiences. There were two outstanding short stories, both to become titles of volumes in subsequent collections—'The Short Happy Life of Francis Macomber' and 'The Snows of Kilimanjaro'; the latter using the details of an injured writer-sportsman's death from gangrene in the African safari, as images of the destruction of a writer who has betrayed himself and been corrupted. All these writings reflect Hemingway's absence from the American scene in particular and from the world social-economic-political scene in general. This dissociation was partly the continuance of his mood of the 1920s, his distrust of 'abstract words'; partly a sense that he had already discharged his responsibilities to 'serve time for society, democracy and the other things'; and partly a sense that in America, in particular, he was vulnerable to corruption, like Harry, the writer in 'Snows of Kilimanjaro'. But that he was nonetheless increasingly conscious of the miseries and injustices inflicted by the American economic system in times of depression is evident from his one novel of the period, *To Have and Have Not* (1937). Though hastily put together—two of the three parts had previously appeared in a magazine in 1934 and 1936—there is much that is compelling in the narrative of Harry Morgan, who, having lost his means of livelihood and become one of the 'have-nots', and finding himself faced with the problem of feeding his family, has to choose between 'going to dig sewers for the government for less money than will feed them' and becoming a law-breaker. He chooses the latter and takes to smuggling liquor, illegal immigrants, and finally Cuban revolutionaries. But if Harry is a 'have-not' in economic terms, he is a 'have' in others—for instance, in his marriage, one of the things in which he is contrasted strongly with Richard Gordon, the prosperous left-wing New York novelist who features in the sub-plot. The 'haves', in fact, cut an unattractive figure—their comparative wealth seeming an affront in the circumstances, while their means of acquiring it add up to a political indictment; and the various references to revolutionary agitation are not without significance. When Harry is found dying in his boat, with the bodies of the three Cuban revolutionaries whom he has killed in an attempt to forestall their killing him, he gasps out the lesson that his experiences have taught him: 'a man alone ain't got no bloody chance'.

The growing threat of fascism in the 1930s was chief among the factors that had engendered Hemingway's new values: here, at least, was something wholly evil, and the solidarity needed to defeat it acquired the status of a virtue. Hemingway himself was with the International Brigade in the Spanish civil war; and *For Whom the Bell Tolls* (1940), the story of one incident in that war, is a monument to his new faith. 'No man is an island . . .', 'never send to know for whom the bell tolls; it tolls for thee'. Where Frederick Henry had contracted out, Robert Jordan, an American lecturer in Spanish, is committed to the hilt. Though the book is extended in scope by lengthy flashbacks (in the form of conversations), the whole of its action centres on the blowing of a single bridge, occupying only four days. Much of the story is concerned with the development, in the course of the preparations, of Jordan's own attitude to the war, and of his feelings—in the face of likely death—about life and death. He has many reservations about what he is fighting for, and there is no attempt to gloss over the cruelty and fecklessness of some of those who fought on the Republican side; but as he lies wounded and awaiting death, he feels that 'the world is a fine place and worth the fighting for'. He is also quite ready to die, feeling that he has already packed a great deal into a short life: and large areas of the book are taken up with describing the quality of this life during his last four days—the well-seasoned food that the woman of Pablo cooks for the guerrillas to eat; the ample supplies of wine in the goat skin that hangs outside their cave; the courage and companionship in the face of danger; and the intensely physical love that he has with Maria, a girl who has been rescued from the fascists.

In the decade that followed before his next book, Hemingway was to participate in yet another war. He, like Robert Jordan, had found that the positive purposes of war and the opportunities it offered for human development could outweigh the horror and the sense of futility that had so deeply wounded him earlier. The wounds however remain, and fresh wounds are added with each experience. Colonel Cantwell in *Across the River and into the Trees* (1950), the last of Hemingway's soldier heroes, has been particularly badly battered by it all. But he has reached his last river. Whereas Robert Jordan, awaiting his death while in the fulness of life, was still largely concerned with coming to terms with life, Cantwell is preoccupied with the business of dying—though that also involves trying to make some sense of his own individual past life in order that he can cross the river calmly and finally come to rest in the trees. In *Across the River and into the Trees*, Hemingway experimented with various symbolic devices, and the book as a whole has seemed unsatisfactory to many readers.

Hemingway's last major work was *The Old Man and the Sea* (1952), which won him a Pulitzer prize and the 1954 Nobel prize. Here he achieves the success with symbolism which, with the rare exception such as in 'Snows of Kilimanjaro', he has not previously attempted with any satisfactory results. As a fishing narrative it has all the detailed realism of the earlier books; but it is also a parable of man's quest for the ideal. The old fisherman sets out to sea, and becomes engaged with a prodigious quarry that carries him out into the depths and tests his courage, skill and endurance to the utmost. He finally wins the battle and sets off home with the gigantic prize lashed alongside—only to find that there is nothing he can do to prevent the predators from eating away its flesh. When he reaches home exhausted there is only a useless skeleton left; and when laid out on the shore, it becomes an object of derision to the passers-by. Yet the reality and significance of his feat is not diminished. This short masterpiece may well be thought to include a reference to Hemingway's own life work. He died nine years later with a bullet from his own gun.

K. R. R.

Henry, O (William Sydney Porter; 1862–1909), American writer of short stories, characterised by a racy exaggerated manner. There are more than 12 volumes of stories, many dull and pointless but some of great wit and even tragic intensity. O. Henry was among the first to perfect the technique of the unexpected ending. He possessed a gift for observation and in such stories as 'The Pendulum' this gift is directed at one of his favourite topics —habit. His sense of the romantic and mysterious is shown vividly in such stories as 'The Green Door'. In common with Dickens he loved to write about ordinary people, and his skilful portrayal of the shop-girl is shown in 'A Lickpenny Lover' and 'Elsie in New York'. Collections include *The Four Million* (1906) and *Cabbages and Kings* (1905). R. A. K.

Henshaw, James Ene (1924–), Nigerian playwright, by profession a medical practitioner who qualified in Dublin. His plays—seven of which are published in *This is our Chance* (1956), *Children of the Goddess* (1964) and *Medicine for Love* (1964)—are conventionally sound, easy-developing though sometimes melodramatic reconciliations of the old to the new, or light sympathetic comedies that reveal the tribal past almost as exotica.

C. P.

Herbert, A. P. (Sir Alan Patrick Herbert; 1890–), English writer. He began writing for *Punch* in 1910 and joined its staff in 1924. From 1935 to 1950 an Independent M.P., he has campaigned for divorce law reform and author's rights as well as being a champion of waterways, particularly the Thames beside which he lives; and many of his 'good causes' have been used in his novels and humorous essays. His first publication *The Bomber Gipsy* (poems, 1918) was followed by a novel *The Secret Battle* (1919). Another novel *The Water Gipsies* (1930) was made into a musical play and he wrote many other librettos. *Misleading Cases in the Common Law*

(1927), *Holy Deadlock* (1934), *The Point of Parliament* (1946), *Topsy Omnibus* (1949), *The Right to Marry* (1954) and *The Silver Stream* (1962) are among his other titles. G. S.

Herbert, Xavier (1911–), Australian novelist who achieved fame with his long savage work *Capricornia* (1938) attacking the treatment of the aborigines in the Northern Territory. The satire apparent in this book was repeated but with less fervour and consequently more artificial results in *Seven Emus* (1959). However, his early vigour returned in the compelling *Soldiers' Women* (1961), recounting the gamut of sexual encounters experienced by a variety of women thrown into an unfamiliar situation by the war. S. R.

Hergesheimer, Joseph (1880–1954), American novelist and short-story writer, author in his early career of several once-esteemed historical novels. These included the three-part saga of a Pennsylvanian iron-founding family, *The Three Black Pennys* (1917); and *Java Head* (1919), which explores the China-trade origins of New England prosperity, centring on the fatal marriage of the son of a sea captain with a Chinese girl. His subsequent books, such as *Cytherea* (1922) and *The Party Dress* (1930), were more clearly designed for their popular appeal. K. R. R.

Hernández, Miguel (1910–42), Spanish poet. Of humble origins and with little time for formal education, Hernández spent most of his childhood tending goats. As a poet he was self-taught. By reading Golden Age poetry and, especially after visiting Madrid in 1931, the work of the twentieth-century masters, he prepared himself technically. The audodidact's concern for form is evident in the hard-packed, contorted syntax of *Perito en lunas* ['Expert in moons'] (1933). In 1934 he met Josefina, his muse for *El rayo que no cesa* ['The unceasing flash'] (1936). In this striking and energetic depiction of a poet's suffering in love, he displayed his complete mastery of the sonnet form. Increasingly concerned in radical politics through his friendship with Neruda and Alberti, Hernández volunteered for the republican forces in 1936; and he revealed himself as Spain's leading war poet in *Viento del pueblo* ['The people's wind'] (1937), incisive verse written in the trenches that brilliantly conveys the joys and bitterness of the struggle. Imprisoned after the civil war, he continued to write: *Cancionero y romancero de ausencias* ['Songs and ballads of absence'], published posthumously, passionately evokes his despair at separation from Josefina, at the death of their son, and at Spain's prostration. Hernández, who also wrote a number of plays, died of tuberculosis after three years' imprisonment and ill-treatment. D. H. G.

Herrick, Robert (1868–1938), American novelist, now largely remembered by his most widely read book *The Master of the Inn* (1908), in which a doctor who has found both physical and spiritual health in the New England countryside dispenses medicine to the bodies and souls of city-ravaged business and professional men. To the realistic portrayal of the corrupting influences of American city life, which characterises many of his other novels, is added a quasi-religious dimension which gives this book its distinctive quality.

Another common feature to be found in Herrick's novels is the intersection of private and public life, for example in *The Common Lot* (1904) and *Together* (1908). Notable amongst his later works is *The End of Desire* (1932), portraying an autumnal relationship between two aging professional people. K. R. R.

Hesse, Hermann (1877–1962), German novelist and poet, and 1946 Nobel prizewinner. The son of a missionary, he actually attended a theological college himself for a short time before settling in Basle and working as an antiquarian bookseller between 1895 and 1902. His first novel *Peter Camezind* appeared in 1904, and from that time he devoted himself to writing. His themes reflected strongly his own life and spiritual struggles; the appeal of religion, of art, of love and the clash of these in the characters of his heroes and heroines. His sensitivity made him adopt an ever increasingly psychoanalytic approach, as witnessed in *Rosshalde* (1914) which treats of a painter living near and yet apart from his wife, who remains close to her for the sake of his love for their second son; all the time the man is torn by his desire to go to the tropics to find themes for his painting and women for his appetite for love. The conflicting demands of different kinds of love are carefully and yet romantically described.

This analytic character of his work was sharply expanded with the onset of mental illness experienced as a direct result of the horrors of the 1914–18 war. Treated by a pupil of Jung, he produced *Knulp* (1915), the story of a vagabond and a lover of women; while in *Klein und Wagner* ['Klein and Wagner'] (1919) Klein finds himself approving of the murder by Wagner of the latter's wife and children. But in *Demian* (1919), the psycho-analytic study of incest is reached after a minute delineation of the changes in a boy's mind with the onset of adolescence and maturity. In *Der Steppenwolf* [*Steppenwolf*] (1927) the artistic dilemma is delineated; cut off by his very art from the normal world, and yet a part of the world, the artist is one in two, wolf and man, with the wolf snarling at the man. The duality of man's nature is again the theme of perhaps Hesse's greatest novel *Narziss und Goldmund* [*Death and the Lover*] (1930). Dealing with two novices in a mediaeval monastery, it traces the career of one to become the abbot, and of the other who leaves and enjoys woman after woman until women tire of him. Turning to art, Goldmund becomes a wood-carver; his first masterpiece being the image of Narziss as the apostle John, loved by him both as a man and an ascetic. At the end, Narziss is present at Goldmund's death and seals their friendship with a kiss.

Hesse's crowning achievement was the novel *Das Glasperlenspiel* [*Magister Ludi*] (1943), an intellectual exercise in which the ascetic Knecht evolves an educational system seeking to combine the best of western and oriental traditions. Other works include *Siddhartha* [*Siddhartha*] (1922), *Gedichte* ['Poems'] (1942), *Briefe* ['Letters'] (1951) and *Beschwörungen* ['Affirmation'] (1955). G. W.; R. C. W.

Hewlett, Maurice (1861–1923), English writer. Born in Kent, he studied law but although called to the bar in 1891 he never practised. He was both a poet and a novelist, though his first published work *Earthwork out of Tuscany* (1895) was a sketch of Italy. This was followed in 1898 by the novel *The Forest Lovers* which, like *Richard Yea-and-Nay* (1900) on Richard Coeur-de-Lion, captures the atmosphere of mediaeval romance and chivalry, and which won him fame and fortune. He has written other popular novels including *The Queen's Quair* (1904) and the trilogy comprising *Open Country* (1909), *Halfway House* (1908) and *Rest Harrow* (1910); but his poetry is deserving of much greater recognition, particularly *The Song of the Plough* (1916). K. M. H.

Heyer, Georgette (1902–), English novelist, author of more than 30 works including detective stories but best known for her light romantic novels set in the Regency period which derive much of their appeal from detailed description of the clothes, customs and manners of that time. Representative titles are *These Old Shades* (1926), *Regency Buck* (1935), *Friday's Child* (1946), *Arabella* (1949), *Bath Tangle* (1955) and *Frederica* (1965). S. R.

Heyerdahl, Thor (1914–), Norwegian explorer and writer who organised and led the Kon-Tiki expedition in 1947, a voyage by balsa raft from South America to Polynesia made in order to test his belief that the Polynesian people were not in fact Asiatic. The book describing this heroic and primitive undertaking was published in 1948 and has been translated into 63 languages. Other publications include *Aku-Aku: The Secrets of Easter Island* (1957). S. R.

Heyward, DuBose (1885–1940), American novelist of the South, best known as the author of the Negro novel *Porgy* (1925). His own stage version won a Pulitzer prize and formed the basis of Gershwin's opera

Porgy and Bess. Heyward had begun his literary career as a poet, and he and Hervey Allen had published a volume entitled *Carolina Chansons* (1922). K. R. R.

Hichens, Robert Smythe (1864–1950), English novelist, known before the turn of the century for his portrayal of Oscar Wilde in *The Green Carnation* (1894), was popular in the Edwardian period with books such as *The Garden of Allah* (1904), set in Muslim north Africa. K. R. R.

Hiebert, Paul (1892–   ), Canadian author, is known for his *Sarah Binks* (1947), a somewhat heavy-handed satire on the self-consciousness of the Canadian literary scene. S. R.

Hikmet, Nazim (1902–63), Turkish poet. Born in Salonika, he soon progressed beyond the fervent nationalism of the period towards an optimistic faith in international communism. During the late twenties and early thirties he worked as a film script-writer, wrote various plays, drafted plans for a huge poem in several volumes, *Memleketimden insan manzaraları* ['Human landscapes from my country'] (1966–7), and published freely: *835 satir* ['835 lines'] (1929), *Jokond ile Siyau* ['Gioconda and Si-a-u'] (1929), *1+1=Bir* ['1+1=One'] (1930), *Varan 3* ['One, two, three'] (1930), *Sesini kaybeden sehir* ['A city which lost its voice'] (1931), *Gece gelen telegraf* ['A telegram received at night'] (1932), *Portreler* ['Portraits'] (1935) and *Taranta,Babuya mektuplar* ['Letters to Taranta Babu'] (1935). In 1938 he was arrested as a suspected subversive and not released until 1951; shortly afterwards he went to live permanently in Russia. Throughout the long dispiriting years in prison he continued writing—*Rubailer* ['Rubais'] (1966)—always affirming his communism, his belief in the essential beauty of life, his sense of fellowship with all mankind and, especially in *Saat 21–22 şiirleri* ['Poems written between 9 and 10 at night'] (1965), his deep, sustaining love for Pirayé, his wife. Ironically, when he was at last set free, his poetry lapsed into banality. In Turkey, Hikmet is regarded as one of the few outstanding national poets, ancient or modern, a genius whose linguistic assurance and vitality rejuvenated the language; on the Continent—and not only behind the Iron Curtain where his *Seçilmiş şiirler* ['Selected poems'] (1954) were published, in Sofia—he has been likened to Lorca, Neruda or Eluard and honoured as yet another name on the melancholy roll-call of twentieth-century artists stultified, incarcerated, exiled or silenced by a faceless bureaucracy; in Britain, until Taner Baybars translated him, *Selected Poems of Nazim Hikmet* (1967), he has been ignored. M. D. E.

Hilton, James (1900–54), English novelist, best known for the extremely sentimental *Good-Bye, Mr Chips* (1934), about the life of a schoolmaster, and *Random Harvest* (1941), about a man suffering from loss of memory. Also popular but perhaps more durable—and certainly more full-bodied —was his earlier novel, the Hawthornden prizewinner *Lost Horizon* (1933) which immortalised 'shangri-la' (the name given to an imaginary pass in the Himalaya) as a term for an earthly paradise. K. R. R.

Hinde, Thomas (Sir Thomas Chitty; 1926–), English novelist. A realist with the gift of economy and understatement and the ability to satirise so quietly that one is almost deceived about his intention, he became known with his early novels *Mr Nicholas* (1952) and *Happy as Larry* (1957). His subsequent titles include *For the Good of the Company* (1961), on the subject of the demoralising effect of impersonal big-business; *The Day the Call Came* (1964), a compulsively readable story of a schizophrenic; *Games of Chance* (1965), a novel in two parts of which the first, 'The Interviewer', is the story of an interviewer who is insufficiently unscrupulous to be successful until he interviews a famous eccentric, while the second, 'The Invigilator', is concerned with a businessman in a toy-making firm who cannot accept society's dishonesty; and *The Village* (1966). P. E.

Hłasko, Marek (1934–), Polish writer. Hłasko began work when he was thirteen and tried his hand at a large variety of jobs, and the experience he gained at one of them he utilised in his tragic story *Nastepny do raju* [*Next One to Paradise*] (1958). This relates how lorry-drivers transporting timber in broken-down vehicles get killed one after the other. In 1955 Hłasko became literary editor of *Po Prostu* and shortly afterwards, in 1957, was awarded a prize for his very successful collection of short stories *Pierwsze kroki w chmurach* [*First Steps in the Clouds*]. His novel *Osmy dzién tygodnia* [*The Eighth Day of the Week*] (1957), about the need for an extra day when all men can be happy, depicts the lustreless life of disappointed and frustrated young Poland. It has been filmed. For publishing *Next One to Paradise* abroad (in France) Hłasko was severely criticised, and he subsequently left Poland.

Hochhuth, Rolf (1931–), German playwright, the whole of whose childhood and adolescence was overshadowed by the second world war and its aftermath. Though representative of the young German intelligentsia in that he shares their anxiety to understand and explain recent German history, he became very much an *avant-garde* figure with the production of *Der Stellvertreter* [*The Representative*] in 1963. This immediately caused a European furore; it was rapidly translated and produced abroad. In Rome it was banned; in London its first performance was followed by an on-stage debate between a leading theatre critic, a Jew and a prominent Jesuit. Its central theme is the tacit responsibility of Pope Pius XII for the 'Jewish solution' of Nazi Germany. The main character is a young Jesuit who is told of the extermination of the Jews by an S.S. officer; he has this information passed to the Pope, who refuses to act because of the danger of appearing to take sides and because of the need to keep Germany as the defence against bolshevism. An Italian Jewish family is seen being taken to Auschwitz, where the Jesuit has gone in place of a Jew; discovered for what he is, he is killed in attempting to prevent individual atrocities. Some critics have pointed out that the play is badly constructed, while others have said that it is an attempt by a German to find a scapegoat for German misdeeds, a scapegoat who furthermore cannot defend himself; but the play has tremendous value as a searching inquiry into one of the most horrifying modern experiences. Almost equally controversial was *Die Soldaten* [*The Soldiers*] (1967) with its portrayal of Churchill plotting the death of Sikorski. G. W.

Hochwälder, Fritz (1911–), Austrian dramatist. In wartime exile he wrote *Das heilige Experiment* [*The Strong are Lonely*] (1942) which may well rank amongst the major dramatic allegories of the use and abuse of power written this century. Completely classical in structure, it concerns the Provincial of the Jesuits in Paraguay where an almost utopian state had been established. The Spanish crown wishes to take over the state, which would entail the introduction of the worst features of colonial rule. The Provincial argues against this with his old university friend who has been sent to take over; but the blow comes when the Provincial is instructed by his General to relinquish his office and hand over the state. A searing and poignant treatment of politics, both religious and secular, and of principles both worldly and spiritual, it has been translated into many languages. In London it was expected to run for a few weeks at one of the smaller theatres when it was presented in the late fifties; it was such a success that it was transferred to the West End where it played to packed houses for months.

Hochwälder's next play *Hôtel du Commerce* ['Commercial Hotel'] (1945) was described by him as '*Kommödie in 5 Akten nach Maupassants Novelle* Boule de Suif' ['Comedy in 5 acts after Maupassant's *Boule de Suif*'] and is unusual in that it is the only one of his plays to have some slight love interest. *Meier Helmbrecht* (1946) was a dramatisation of the old German folk tale of the farmer's boy whose head is so crammed with tales of chivalry that he dons armour and proceeds to ravage the countryside. By 1949 Hochwälder had consolidated his powers once again on the theme of the use and abuse of power. He himself describes *Der öffentliche Ankläger* [*The Public Prosecutor*] (1948) as *Schauspiel* (straightforward play), but it is a classical tragedy set in the Conciergerie in Paris during the Terror. Fouquier-Tinville the Public Prosecutor is persuaded that the head of the government Tallien can be brought down in a trial provided that his name is not mentioned until the end. The climax of the trial is to be the opening of an envelope containing his name. In a brilliant speech, the Public Prosecutor who has sent hundreds to the guillotine pleads passionately for the death of the one who shall be the last victim of the Terror; the envelope is opened and the name inside is—his own! This masterly technical expertise continues to be the hallmark of Hochwälder's later plays and confirms his reputation as one of the leading European dramatists. G. W.

Hofmannsthal, Hugo von (1874–1929), Austrian poet and dramatist. A Viennese, born into a wealthy family which combined Jewish and Italian blood with its Austrian antecedents, he began life an orthodox Catholic, ceased to practise his faith and returned to it in the autumn of his life. All these factors could have made him the subject of one of his own poems. He attracted attention as a youth by his neo-romantic symbolic poems, such as *Der Tod des Tizian* [*The Death of Titian*] published when he was eighteen. One of the outstanding pieces of German symbolism, it is a panegyric of beauty, provoked by the death of the great painter. The same year appeared *Der Tor und der Tod* [*The Fool and Death*] (1892), romantic in the extreme. Death comes to call a young dilettante, not clad in a shroud and armed with a scythe, but elegantly clad; at the moment of death the young man calls out his despairing *Ich habe nicht gelebt!* ['I did not live!'].

By the turn of the century, however, Hofmannsthal abandoned poetry and turned to drama, treating the great classical themes in a way peculiarly his own. Thus his *Elektra* (1904) is a drama of sexual repression. Shortly before the first world war, he turned to the mediaeval morality play; and *Jedermann* ['Everyman'] (1912) was produced before the cathedral of Salzburg by Max Reinhardt. This foreshadowed a close association, for together with Reinhardt and Richard Strauss he was a moving force behind the Salzburg festivals after the war. By this time he had abandoned poetry, much to the disgust of his old patron Stefan George.

Hofmannsthal is perhaps best known to English audiences as the librettist for Strauss' operas *Der Rosenkavalier* (1911), *Ariadne auf Naxos* [*Ariadne on Naxos*] (1912) and *Die Frau ohne Schatten* [*The Woman without a Shadow*] (1920). He died before the Nazis' rise to power; they showed their opinion of his sensuous, feminine poetry by removing his statue from Salzburg. His works have been translated by

Michael Hamburger under the titles *Poems and Verse Plays of Hugo von Hofmannsthal* (1961) and *Selected Plays and Libretti by Hugo von Hofmannsthal* (1964). G. W.

Holcroft, Montague Henry (1902–), New Zealand writer, is the author of an extended reflective essay on the problems involved in the development of a creative and individual New Zealand literature. This essay became the first volume of the trilogy *Discovered Isles* (1950); the remaining volumes containing a great variety of articles on different writers and aspects of life in New Zealand, so that it becomes a valuable guide to the cultural scene. Other titles published since include *Dance of the Seasons* (1952) and *Eye of the Lizard* (1960). S. R.

Holtby, Winifred (1898–1935), English novelist and feminist who is chiefly remembered for her *South Riding* (1935), a novel set in an imaginary riding of Yorkshire. Dealing with the activities of the county council and their impact on the people subject to its authority, it centres on the conflict between an attractive but socially militant headmistress and an influential local gentleman farmer to whom she is both opposed and attracted. Winifred Holtby's other novels include *The Land of Green Ginger* (1927) and *Poor Caroline* (1931). She wrote also a study of Virginia Woolf (1932). P. E.

Holthusen, Hans Egon (1913–), German poet, now resident in New York, was the son of a Lutheran clergyman, and studied at Berlin, Tübingen and Munich universities. The influence of Rilke on him has been great—he published a biographical study of him in *R. M. Rilke in Selbstzeugnissen und Bilddokumenten* ['R. M. Rilke in his self-testimony and pictures'] in 1958—and a further influence has been T. S. Eliot. His first poems published after the war, in which he served as a private, had the title *Hier in der Zeit* ['Here in our time'[(1949) and they attempt to convey the impression of five years of war. The influence of Eliot's *Four Quartets* is apparent, especially in the identity of past, present and future.

Holthusen is an example of the way in which many modern Germans have rediscovered the value of religion as a means of comprehending and overcoming the tormented years beginning with the rise of National Socialism and ending with the defeat of Germany in the war. Without being specifically Lutheran or borrowing heavily on Catholic liturgy as a source of inspiration in poetry, their work can only be fully comprehended in a religious context. Holthusen has written several essays on his concepts, especially *Kritisches Verstehen* ['Critical understanding'] and *Avantgardismus* ['The cult of the *avant-garde*'] which appeared in the early sixties; his only novel *Das Schiff* ['The ship'] (1956) is generally regarded as being an unfortunate deviation from his main work. G. W.

Hope, A. D. (Alec Derwent Hope; 1907–), Australian poet and professor of English, whose poetry is characterised by harsh satire of modern civilisation, explicit sexual imagery ranging in attitude from tenderness and luxuriant sensuality to lust and disgust, and above all by an intelligence and power that rank him with the major English and American contemporary poets.

The opening lines of the title poem from the collection *The Wandering Islands* (1955) give some indication of his control, his music and his use of paradox:

> You cannot build bridges between the wandering islands,
> The Mind has no neighbours, and the unteachable heart
> Announces its armistice time after time, but spends
> Its love to draw them closer and closer apart.

and his description of the country that is a cultural desert, from his poem 'Australia', is an example of his savagery:

> And her five cities, like five teeming sores
> Each drains her, a vast parasite robber-state
> Where second-hand Europeans pullulate
> Timidly on the edge of alien shores.

But he is also capable of a delicacy and freshness in writing about love, as in 'Chorale' with its tentative opening stanza and its perfect poetic expression of the climax:

> Hear the shuddering cry begin,
> Feel the heart leap in her breast,
> And her moving loins within
> Clasp their strong, rejoicing guest.

Hope can also handle remarkable changes of mood within a poem. In 'Standardisation', after a vituperative list of the usual trite and affected voices raised against industrialisation, he catches the infinitely wise and slow tones of nature herself:

> She does not tire of the pattern of a rose.
> Her oldest tricks still catch us with surprise.
> She cannot recall how long ago she chose
> the streamlined hulls of fish, the snail's long eyes. . . .

In addition to poems appearing in magazines and anthologies, two further volumes of his work have been published, *Poems* (1960) and *The Cave and the Spring* (1966). S. R.

Hope, Anthony (Anthony Hope Hawkins; 1863–1933), English novelist much read in the early years of the twentieth century, is best known for his romantic adventure *The Prisoner of Zenda* (1894), which gave the word 'ruritanian' to the language. He was a master of the fast-moving story and, as in *The Dolly Dialogues* (1894), of sophisticated, witty dialogue. Later titles include *Lucinda* (1920). H. C.

Horia, Vintila (*c.* 1910–), Rumanian émigré novelist who lives in France and writes in French. Son of an agronomist, he was Rumanian press attaché in Rome in 1940 and in Vienna in 1942 but was in the latter year interned by the Germans. Rejecting communist Rumania after the war, he lingered indecisively in Italy, Argentina and Spain before ultimately settling in France as a writer. He has published four novels: *Dieu est né en exil* [*God was Born in Exile*] (1961), *Le Chevalier de la résignation* ['The knight of resignation'] (1961), *Les Impossibles* ['The impossible ones'] (1962) and *La Septième Lettre* ['The seventh letter'] (1964). For the first of these he was awarded the Prix Goncourt for 1961, which was subsequently and controversially withdrawn on the grounds that he had been a wartime collaborator with the Nazis. Nurtured by his own experiences, *Dieu est né en exil* was a reconstruction of Ovid's exile on the Black Sea; but contrary to the evidence of Ovid's epistles, in Horia's account the poet becomes resigned to his lot and from paganism gropes his way to recognition of the nascent religion of Christianity. Almost equally successful was *Le Chevalier de la résignation*, a novel set in seventeenth-century Transylvania, which, with a clear moral for the twentieth century, portrayed the desperate guerrilla warfare waged by the princeling Radu Negru against the Turkish oppression and the indifference of the Venetian republic to his appeals for its aid. R. C. W.

Hornung, Ernest William (1866–1921), English novelist, with an Australian background which is evident in his first two novels. He is best known, however, for his creation of the gentleman-crook Raffles who appeared first in *The Amateur Cracksman* (1899) and later in other stories, and who might be regarded as the urbane counterpart of Conan Doyle's Sherlock Holmes. Further collections include *Mr Justice Raffles* (1909).

R. A. K.

Hostovský, Egon (1908–), Czech writer, has lived in the west since 1948 when he resigned his post in the Czechoslovak diplomatic service. His novels have exciting plots and are concerned with the psychological and ethical problems of contemporary man. Titles include *Sedmkrát v hlavní úloze* [*Seven Times the Leading Man*] (1942), *Nezvěstný* [*Missing*] (1952), *Půlnoční pacient* [*The Midnight Patient*] (1954), *Dobročinný večírek* [*The Charity Ball*] (1957), *Tři noci* [*Three Nights*] (1964). K. B.

Houghton, William Stanley (1881–1914), English dramatist, known solely for his long-running play *Hindle Wakes* (1912), set in the Lancashire cotton industry in which he had himself worked. K. R. R.

Housman, A. E. (Alfred Edward Housman; 1859–1936), English scholar and poet, born on the borders of Worcestershire. In 1892 he was appointed Professor of Latin at University College, London; and in 1910 he became Kennedy Professor of Latin at Cambridge. In 1895 he wrote most of *A Shropshire Lad*, which was rejected by Macmillan's, was finally published by Kegan Paul at the author's expense in 1896, and after the first world war became one of the best-selling works of poetry by a living author. *Last Poems* (1922) contains poems written at various intervals between 1895 and 1910. Housman delivered the Leslie Stephen Lecture on 'The Name and Nature of Poetry' in 1933; thereafter his health began to fail and he died on 30 April 1936. *More Poems* was published posthumously in 1936.

Although more eminent as a classical scholar than as a poet, his major claim to popular fame rests on *A Shropshire Lad*. He believed that '... to transfuse emotion—not to transmit thought but to set up in the reader's sense a vibration corresponding to what was felt by the writer—is the function of poetry', and wrote in a letter to his sister that 'the function of poetry is to harmonise the sadness of the world'.

Houseman declared that his major conscious literary sources of inspiration were 'Shakespeare's songs, the Scottish Border Ballads and Heine'. To these it is important to add the *Barrack Room Ballads* of Kipling, together with the popular ballads of enlistment. It is worth noting the parallels in subject matter, theme and mood between his poetry and that of Hardy whose novels he had read at Oxford.

Housman described the production of poetry in himself as: 'a morbid secretion like the pearl in the oyster . . . I have seldom written poetry unless I was rather out of health'. This suggests a reason for the prevailing consciousness of mortality in his work where death is seen as an overhanging threat of annihilation to all transient moments of human happiness. Most of his poetry is dominated by a poeticised vision of the Shropshire hills landscape, similar in kind to Hardy's 'creation' of Wessex and peopled with figures from his own pastoral mythology—country lovers, soldiers, ploughmen and above all the 'Shropshire Lad' who provides Housman with his favourite persona, by turns cynical, resigned, bitter and nostalgic. His customary genre of poetry tends to be a cross between lyric and ballad and many of the poems are written in the quatrain form of the ballad.

In tone, they vary from moods of grim humour to those of the paradoxical fear of and desire for death. The image of the world in *A Shropshire Lad* and *Last Poems* is one characterised by betrayal of friendship, reversal of fortune, the transience of love and in particular the isolation of the individual in a hostile world:

I a stranger and afraid
In a world I never made.

The speaker frequently identifies with the outcast from the community; thus:

'They hang us now in Shrewsbury jail',

or:

'Fare you well for ill fare I:
Live, lads, and I will die.'

Poems containing the enlistment theme appear as grim attempts to gain a reluctant social acceptance:

I will go where I am wanted, for the Sergeant does not mind
He may be sick to see me but he treats me very kind.
He gives me beer and breakfast and a ribbon for my cap,
And I never knew a sweetheart spend her money on a chap.

Yet for all his jingoism, Housman expresses a fascinated anguish at the thought of mass slaughter of 'Lovely lads and dead and rotten'. Frequent use is made of the pathetic fallacy and nature emerges as a sympathetic or hostile presence, replacing human indifference:

The earth, because my heart was sore,
Sorrowed for the son she bore;

The melancholic lethargy is sometimes disrupted in a deliberate desire to shock the reader. A girl asks her lover:

'What is it falling on my lips,
My Lad that tastes of brine?'

The lover replies casually:

'O like enough 'tis blood, my dear,
For when the knife has slit
The throat across from ear to ear
'Twill bleed because of it.'

These shock tactics are the crudest form in which Housman's genuine gift for compression and precision appears. His peculiar talent is the ability to select the suggestive detail or unpredictable image within the terms of an increasingly predictable philosophical and metrical framework. Read in bulk, his poetry can appear both tedious and ridiculous just because of his easily recognisable personal idiom which is at once his strength and his weakness. Yet despite the overriding morbidity of theme we are compelled into an awareness of the curious vitality springing from his conflicting desire towards social conformity and derision of society's values. His verse is at its best in the rare moments when he appears reconciled to a spectator's rôle. M. T.

Howard, Elizabeth Jane (1923–), English novelist, is noted for her thoughtful and perceptive delineation of character, particularly of women, and for her subtle unfolding of delicate and complex plots—despite which, her subject matter can sometimes seem almost novelettish. In *The Sea Change* (1959), for example, the characters are a successful middle-aged Jewish Broadway playwright, his beautiful neurotic wife, his young manager—an orphan with a chip on his shoulder—and a naïve English secretary who receives the full Cinderella treatment. The action takes place in expensive hotels, apartments and aeroplanes and on the idyllic Greek island of Hydra. However, the form of this novel, in which each of the characters speaks in turn, is skilfully handled and the way in which each comes to terms with his inner conflict is essentially non-sentimental and realistic: the young encountering in their lives echoes of the crises that the older couple have faced, and giving an aging lover and a grieving mother new hope. Other titles include *The Beautiful Visit* (1950), *The Long View* (1956) and *After Julius* (1965). S. R.

Hoyle, Fred (1915–), English writer on science, and science-fiction novelist. This eminent astronomer is the author of two outstanding SF novels, *The Black Cloud* (1957) and *Ossian's Ride* (1959), and in collaboration with his son Geoffrey has also written *Fifth Planet* (1963). As might be expected, Hoyle's SF is deeply rooted in scientific theory, and in *The Black Cloud* he even resorts to the use of mathematical equations to substantiate the plot. *Ossian's Ride* might well be described as a very good spy story set against an SF background which does not really become important until the final chapters. As also with *The Black Cloud*, one has the strong impression that Hoyle is indulging in a certain amount of autobiographical fantasy: his disdain for Authority (especially in the world of politics), and the merciless way in which he exposes its stupidity, giving the actions of his 'heroes' a strong wish-fulfilment quality.

G. D. G.

Hudson, W. H. (William Henry Hudson; 1841–1922), English essayist and novelist, born near Buenos Aires. Although his parents were American,

Hudson had English ancestors and after growing up on the Argentine pampas he came to England in 1874. For most of his life he was poor and obscure. His first novel *The Purple Land* (1885), a romance of travel among the gauchos, was a failure. He was more successful with the long short-story, 'El Ombu' and 'Marta Riquelme' (both 1902) being among the best of his work. His last novel *Green Mansions* (1904) was popular and its royalties made his later years comfortable. He loved the English countryside and had a wonderful gift of observing and vividly describing birds, animals and the landscape; and his essays on them were his greatest achievement, particularly the volumes *A Shepherd's Life* (1910) and *Hampshire Days* (1903). Other works include *The Naturalist in La Plata* (1892), *Birds and Man* (1901), *Afoot in England* (1909), *Far Away and Long Ago* (autobiography, 1918) and *A Hind in Richmond Park* (1922).

G. S.

Hughes, Richard (1900–   ), English writer whose first novel, *A High Wind in Jamaica* (1928), set him apart as one writing about children from an uncommitted observer's point of view. The children in question are isolated from their normal environment, since they have been captured by some curious tenderhearted and decadent pirates while on their way from Jamaica to school in England. They are demonstrated to be living each in his or her own world, and Emily, the central figure, is exactly and delicately portrayed as a child as yet only half aware of her identity, of her responsibility for her actions. At the end of the book she still acts with the irresponsibility of a child, when her emotional breakdown in court hangs the pirate captain and mate for the murder of a captive killed by Emily herself in a panic when shut in alone with him. The inconsequential nature of children's thought and reactions and the apparent ease with which they drop the past is fully demonstrated. Emily's elder brother is killed in a fall soon after their capture and he is never again mentioned between them.

Hughes's other works include some poetry, *Confessio Juvenis* (1926), and further novels. *In Hazard* (1938) is about a steamer in a freak hurricane, with penetrating, sometimes humorous studies of the reactions of the officers and crew. *The Fox in the Attic* (1961), the first part of a long novel to be called *The Human Predicament*, is a broad-spectrum study of life between the two world wars. The scene ranges from the introverted sea-town community in Pembrokeshire, where the hero Augustine has inherited a large decaying property, and the manor house in Dorset of his brother-in-law, a member of parliament, to the castle of Augustine's Bavarian cousins. Here, hidden in the clock tower, is an anarchist fugitive,

Wolff, whose political fervour has become blood-lust, and who gives the book its title. Psychological, social, political and philosophical problems are discussed both implicitly and openly, yet a unity of vision is maintained.

G. C.

Hughes, Ted (1930–   ), English poet. Hughes is a Yorkshireman, educated at Mexborough Grammar School and Pembroke College, Cambridge. He has been accused of using his poetry to rape the attention of the reader with an aggressive involvement in the violence of the physical world expressed without subtlety or elegance. *The Hawk in the Rain* (1957) won the First Publication Award of the New York City Poetry Centre, judged by Auden, Spender and Marianne Moore. Hughes's aggression, passion and fierceness combined with his interest in violence and suffering lead one to compare his work with that of the seventeenth century—though not with the poetry of Donne and the metaphysicals so much as with the drama of Webster and Tourneur. The animal savagery of *The Hawk in the Rain* is bulwarked by a seemingly intuitive sympathy with the animal world which resolves itself in vivid imagery. Hughes, like so many of the writers of the generation before him, seems contemptuous of physical sex although fascinated by its implications. For the poet, romantic love is simply violence repressed. As one of his mythical characters remarks:

Whilst I am this muck of man in this
Muck of existence, I shall not seek more
Than a muck of a woman.

The later poetry contained in *Lupercal* (1960) continues the involvement with violence but in a more speculative and subdued mood.

D. L. P.

Huidobro, Vicente (1893–1948), Chilean poet and key figure of twentieth-century literature, claimed to be the originator of 'creationism'. Apart from his brief candidature for the presidency in 1925, his life was mainly one of letters. A large proportion of it was spent in Europe, first promulgating aspects of vanguard poetry, later as war correspondent. After an initiation in the traditional modes with *Ecos del alma* ['Echoes of the soul'] (1910), he soon announced his revolutionary aesthetics and embodied them in *El espejo de agua* ['The mirror of water'] (1916). Subsequently he continued to write 'creationist' poetry in both French and Spanish, published in numerous works, among them two anthologies: *Saisons choisies* ['Selected seasons'] (1922) in French, and *Antología* ['Anthology'] (1945) in Spanish.

Huidobro saw the poet as 'a little God', and his task as that of obliterating the real world and creating in its place a world of the imagination. 'A work of art,' he wrote, 'is a new cosmic reality that the artist adds to Nature.' 'When I say a bird's nest in a rainbow I say something you have not seen but would probably like to see.' His poetry therefore is pure metaphor—metaphor that has become not symbolic or representative of an objective reality, but is in itself the objective reality. In free verse, with chaotic enumerations, neologisms, capricious spelling, his poetry can be humorous, but it can also be anguished and personal. P. R. B.

Hunt, Violet (1860–1942), English novelist and biographer, was the daughter of the Pre-Raphaelite painter Holman Hunt and mistress of Ford Madox Ford, and her portraits of the personalities of the Pre-Raphaelite movement, for example in *The Wife of Rossetti* (1932), are more memorable than her highly coloured novels, such as *White Rose of Weary Leaf* (1908). K. R. R.

Hurst, Fannie (1889–), American novelist, became known with the publication of her volume of short stories of Jewish life in New York, *Humoresque* (1919). Her novels range from *Lummox* (1923), the story of a sensitive Scandinavian servant-girl working amidst squalid surroundings, and the less well-known *Stardust* (1921), to *God Must Be Sad* (1961).
K. R. R.

Hutchinson, Alfred (1924–), South African playwright and prose-writer, was one of the accused in the notorious 'treason trials' but escaped to Ghana—*Road to Ghana* (1960) being the vibrant and moving autobiographical account of that journey. *The Rainkillers* (1964) is a play set in Swaziland and concerned particularly with inter-tribal prejudice; its themes and philosophy closely parallel those of Achebe's novels.
C. P.

Hutchinson, A. S. M. (Arthur Stuart-Menteth Hutchinson; 1879–), English novelist, known almost entirely for his once highly-popular *If Winter Comes* (1920). The bleakest depths of the winter in the heart of its hero, the unhappily married businessman Mark Sabre, come when he incurs the suspicion of having fathered the child of an unmarried girl, whom he had befriended when pregnant—a suspicion which becomes well-nigh impossible to clear when the true father is killed. But, in the words of Shelley, 'If Winter comes, can Spring be far behind?', and spring comes for Sabre when his painful marriage is ended by divorce and he is able to wed another woman, the one he has always loved.

Hutchinson's later works include *He Looked for a City* (1940) and *Bring back the Days* (1958). K. R .R.

Hutchinson, R. C. (Ray Coryton Hutchinson; 1907–   ), English novelist. Born in London and educated at Oxford, he cut short a career in commerce in 1935 to devote his whole time to writing. His first book *Thou Hast a Devil* appeared in 1930, but he gained his first big success with *Testament* (1938) which won the *Sunday Times* gold medal for fiction. His most ambitious work to date *Elephant and Castle* (1949) was eight years in the writing and is a panoramic study of life in the London slums.

R. C. Hutchinson makes no apologies for the fact that he has not lived an adventurous life as have so many writers; to quote his own words he is 'simply a standard English bourgeois who has written a few books'. But his modesty cannot hide the fact that he is an expert craftsman. In *The Stepmother* (1955) where he studies the relationship of a second wife with her two grown-up stepchildren, he writes with remarkable delicacy and sensitivity about the problems facing the woman who takes the place of a dearly loved first wife. What must be said, however, is that, for all its fluency, his treatment of this classic problem tends to be a little stereotyped.

His other works include *Shining Scabbard* (1936), *The Fire and the Wood* (1940) and *A Child Possessed* (1964). K. M. H.

Huxley, Aldous (1894–1963), English novelist, although most widely known as the author of *Brave New World* (1932), is distinguished by the enormous variety of his literary output, ranging from the social satire of the twenties through the 'novels of ideas' of the thirties to the excursions into mysticism that dominated his last years. In all his works, however, the reader is reminded of his scientific background (his grandfather was T. H. Huxley, and his brother Julian Huxley): either, as in the early novels, by the recurrence of science as a topic of conversation and of scientists as characters, or, as in the later ones, by the scientific basis of many of his ideas.

Apart from scientists, the early novels, beginning with the scintillating *Crome Yellow* (1922), contain several other recurring figures. There is for instance the aesthete-cynic, such as the loquacious Mr Scogan in *Crome Yellow*, the poisonous Mr Mercaptan in *Antic Hay* (1923), or the dry Mr Cardan in *Those Barren Leaves* (1925); and the *femme fatale*, such as Myra Viveash in *Antic Hay* and Lucy Tantamount in *Point Counter Point* (1928). Steering their way between these destructive forces are a fourth series of figures—the 'heroes' if they may be so called. These are usually sensitive and earnest, sophisticated and idealistic; and they are generally impaled on the horns of monetary and/or sexual dilemmas of the kind that arise from the conflict between the ideal and the real, or (in the case of sex) between the spiritual and the sensual. In *Those Barren Leaves*, for instance, there are two such characters: the poet Chelifer who lives by editing the 'Rabbit Fanciers' Gazette', and the philanderer Calamy who withdraws to a mountain-top to engage in 'chaste meditation'.

These earlier novels abound in brilliant conversation, which is at its most glittering in *Crome Yellow*. But in many ways the most satisfying is *Antic Hay*, largely because of the extra dimension of pathos to be found in the experiences and situations of both Theodore Gumbril, its hero, and some of the minor characters. We first meet Gumbril as an impoverished schoolmaster, sitting on a hard chapel pew and planning to finance his entrée into cosmopolitan life by the patenting of pneumatic breeches. Once arrived in London, he becomes one of the lost, caught up in the endless to-ings and fro-ings of those who—like Mrs Viveash—dare not pause for fear of the emptiness within. Neither his economic nor his sexual dilemma is resolved. An escape route opens up in the person of Emily, a girl from another world, a world of semi-rural (yet not unsophisticated) innocence and security: with her it is possible to lie naked between the sheets in a cool night-long communion, and he gladly embraces the peace and security of the life she offers him in her country cottage with its ancient piano. At the last minute, he is delayed from joining her there by the importunity of the despairing Myra; and when he finally escapes her clutches, Emily has disappeared without a trace.

Music figures in various ways in Huxley's works, and in *Point Counter Point* he attempted to weave together a number of thematically contrapuntal narratives. It is sometimes argued that in this process his writing lost much of its vitality. This novel is also distinguished by a growing sense of the importance of politics, already seen by many of Huxley's contemporaries as the mode of action for dealing with the sicknesses of society; and the characters include both a fascist (based on the British fascist leader of that period) and a communist (in the rôle of assistant to the scientist Lord Edward Tantamount). Conflict between the forces represented by these two result in a violence not previously found in Huxley's writings, and the fascist Everard Webley is sensationally murdered. To this ominous appearance of totalitarianism and violence must be added a piece of pure and gratuitous evil, in the death through meningitis of the much-beloved child of the novelist Philip Quarles, a character whose detached observation of life has suggested a self-portrait of Huxley. The book's violence and pessimism is matched by the recurrence of physical disgust, particularly in relationship to sex: and while the marital infidelities of the tormented young Bidlake with Lucy Tantamount seem quite exceptionally cruel, and the latter's cold-blooded sensuality sends a shiver down the spine, it is the nausea engendered by the scene in which Burlap (based on John Middleton Murry) takes a pseudo-spiritual bath with his secretary, or expressed through the character of the perverted and sadistic Spandrell (a reincarnation of Baudelaire), that leaves the nastiest taste in the mouth. Through it all there wanders the unlikely figure of Mark Rampion (D. H. Lawrence), expressing, beneath only the gentlest of satire, the possibility that one may come to terms with sex and be happy.

The precocious salon talk of Mr Scogan on 'test-tube babies' and the scientist's growing awareness of the dangers of science in the hands of totalitarians led naturally to the nightmare of *Brave New World* (1932). In the era of Our Ford (alternatively known as Our Freud)—acknowledged with the sign of the T, and worshipped under the leadership of the Arch Community Songster of Canterbury—the techniques of mass production and applied psychology are used for the production of human beings of differing qualities, in the proportions required for future economic needs. Unforeseen originality, as manifested in Bernard Marx—an 'alpha' specimen whose freakish behaviour results from the upsetting of his decanting bottle during his embryo stage—only creates problems. He, for instance, wants the exclusive attentions of Lenina Crowne, a girl whose normality is manifested in her carefree, unemotional and plural sex-life, which is not only painless but socially cohesive; and when stress and strain occur, he is perverse enough to refuse to seek an escape from it by taking the 'soma' drug. The very existence of such individuality is embarrassing and his employers are glad to let him travel abroad on a visit to one of the remaining 'savage' regions that have not yet been civilised by science.

Here he finds the opposite extreme: a truly natural life where women wear themselves out with child-bearing, and malnutrition and disease combine to make life nasty, brutish and short. He meets a 'savage' who has read Shakespeare, and who, on hearing of the wonders of a scientific civilisation, is keen to visit the 'brave new world that hath such creatures in it'. Thus Bernard is able to bring him back as an exhibit; and there now develops the central story of the book—the gradual discovery by Mr Savage of his brave new world. Admiration turns progressively to distress and despair, and he eventually commits suicide.

Brave New World is intellectually stimulating, frequently very funny, and compelling in its pessimism. By contrast, the works that followed are increasingly unsatisfying. Perhaps the most readable is *Eyeless in Gaza* (1936), which to some extent recaptures the satirical brilliance of his twenties novels, but which reflects its period in its increased preoccupation with politics, particularly pacificism. The following year saw the publication of two political essays—one on pacificism, the other (particularly relevant in a time of totalitarian politics) on ends and means. Huxley's next novel of ideas was *After Many a Summer* (1939), again employing a science-fiction device: a biologist ingeniously experiments with the possibilities of extending the span of life, until he actually is confronted by a real-life bicentenarian. Even less satisfying is *Time Must Have a Stop* (1945), which investigates the thought processes of a man already dead. During this period, Huxley continued to write essays and travel books, and in particular to rethink the implications of *Brave New World*: one such postscript being the short novel *Ape and Essence* (1949).

Huxley's third period had already begun with an anthology of mysticism published shortly after the war. Destructive brilliance and pathetic hollowness in the twenties; perverted science and violent or dictatorial politics, in the thirties and early forties; now, at last, a more positive note appears. Significantly, he was to write only two more novels—one of which, *The Genius and the Goddess* (1955) has been very little read—in the last fifteen years of his life. During the 1950s his major writings were accounts of his exploration of mystical experience, particularly as induced by the drug mescalin, whose use he had encountered amongst the Mexican Indians. The titles *The Doors of Perception* (1954) and *Heaven and Hell* (1956) speak for themselves.

The novel which crowns his final period—and for which has been claimed an importance greater than for anything he had written for thirty years—is *Island* (1963). Although pessimistic in that the paradise he depicts is destroyed by a combination of power politics and personal cynicism—and despite a vein of humour that is deceptively reminiscent of *Brave New World*—it exhibits its author's new-found optimism in asserting that science, when complemented by a religious approach to life, can create such a paradise. The population of Huxley's island—significantly of mixed Scottish and Indian stock—has achieved the ultimate in human happiness through its ability to apply its scientific knowledge both rationally and with an awareness of the ultimate realities. Much of the book is taken up with a conducted tour of the island's way of life, for the benefit of the English journalist William Asquith Farnaby who has arrived precipitately in the course of a secret mission on behalf of the oil magnate Lord Aldehyde. Here, in contrast to the mass-produced humanity of *Brave New World*, individuality abounds; but the principles of eugenics are applied, making use of techniques such as 'artificial insemination and deep freeze' (i.e. of semen) to maximise the chances of happiness for each individual and for the community as a whole. In place of the psychological conditioning of the earlier work, we have an educational system designed to bring people to terms with the different levels of reality they will encounter, and to enable them to experience the fullness of life: rock-climbing, for instance, reminds them of the precariousness of life and the omnipresence of death, while the 'moksha medicine' initiates them into mystical experiences which include both the beatific vision and Huxley's 'essential horror'. The sceptical Farnaby, himself in flight from the latter, is completely won over; but not before he has betrayed his hosts and precipitated their destruction by the forces of greed, tyranny and decadence. K. R. R.

Huxley, Elspeth (1907–), English writer about Africa. She was the daughter of Kenya pioneers and her childhood experiences are retold with great imagination and clarity in *The Flame Trees of Thika* (1959) and *The Mottled Lizard* (1962). She and her husband, Gervas Huxley, have travelled extensively and her other books include travel stories such as *Four Guineas* (1954) and *The Sorcerer's Apprentice* (1948), biography, novels and detective fiction. She is well qualified in agriculture, and in *A New Earth* (1960) she makes an objective appraisal of the economy of East Africa.

G. C.

Huxley, Julian (1887–), English scientific writer, essayist and poet. He has produced numerous scientific papers, various articles and radio talks, and his literary skill has done much to help the spread of knowledge about scientific subjects. His works include *Essays of a Biologist* (1923), *Essays in Popular Science* (1926), *Religion without Revelation* (1927) and *Evolution in Action* (1953). *The Captive Shrew* (1932) is a collection of his poetry.

R. A. K.

Hyams, Edward (1910–), English writer. Apart from a number of books on gardening and horticulture, Hyams has written novels including *The Slaughterhouse Informer* (1955), *Into the Dream* (1957), *Taking It Easy* (1958) and *Cross Purposes* (1967). D. L. P.

Hyde, Robin (Iris Wilkinson; 1906–39), New Zealand poet, novelist and journalist who, despite constant ill-health that led to her early death, produced countless articles for periodicals in New Zealand and abroad, six prose works each completely different in kind from the others, and—her finest achievement—lyrical, carefully wrought and distinctive poems. In her early poetry (*The Desolate Star*, 1929) can be seen the influence of her English literary heritage; in later volumes (*The Conquerors*, 1935; *Persephone in Winter*, 1937) her own country became her muse. In the posthumous collection *Houses by the Sea* (1952) these conflicting influences are shown resolved and absorbed, and re-emerge in her successful marriage of style to subject. From this volume, her range is indicated by poems as diverse as the long philosophical 'Young Knowledge', the harsh and cryptic 'Isabel's Baby', and the compassionate and allusively autobiographical title poem 'Houses by the Sea'.

Her other books include *Journalese* (1934), a collection of her articles; *Passport to Hell* (1935), wartime and other experiences ostensibly related to her by a friend, and its sequel *Nor the Years Condemn* (1938); *Check to Your King* (1936), a historical reconstruction of the New Zealand figure Baron de Thierry; the fantasy *Wednesday's Children* (1937); a more conventional novel *The Godwits Fly* (1938); and her account of experiences in China in 1938, *Dragon Rampant* (1939). S. R.

I

Idriess, Ion (1890–   ), popular Australian novelist, wrote adventure stories, usually set in the little-known regions of the outback and in the most deserted regions of Australia and New Guinea. Representative titles are *Lasseter's Last Ride* (1931) and *Flynn of the Inland* (1932). However, perhaps his most interesting work is the autobiographical *Desert Column* (1932), a series of World War I diaries kept from the Gallipoli landings to his arrival in France in 1918. S. R.

Ilf, Ilya (Ilya Arnoldovich Fainzilburg; 1897–1937), Soviet writer, member of the 'Ilf and Petrov' partnership, was born of Jewish parents in Odessa. He worked on the local paper and eventually moved to Moscow where he met the Kataev brothers, with one of whom he formed the famous literary partnership that was to produce many devastating but uncriticised satirical sketches of Soviet life. Their best-known works are *Dvenadtsat' Stulyev* [*Twelve Chairs*] (1928) and its sequel *Zolotoi telyonok* [*Little Golden Calf*] (1931). These relate the picaresque activities of a notorious trickster, Ostap Bender. After travelling to America to collect material, they published their impressions in *Odnoetazhnaya Amerika* [*One Storey America*] (1936), but Ilf, weakened by the journey, contracted tuberculosis and died shortly afterwards. B. W.

Illyés, Gyula (1902–   ), Hungarian poet, novelist, playwright, critic and translator, comes from a family of estate servants in western Hungary. After years of hard and penniless study in Pest and Paris, he returned to draw deep and lasting inspiration from his home soil, although this does not prevent him from ranging the world in his verse. His lyric genius, which has gained international recognition for him, is rooted in the Hungarian classical tradition, but flavoured with the brevity, subtlety and precision of France. The reader is referred to *Hommage à Gyula Illyés* (ed. L. Gara; Paris, 1963).

His prose is terse and expressive, as typified particularly in his *Puszták népe* ['People of the Pusztas'] (1936), a sociological study based on his own childhood. Parts of this are translated in *The Plough and the Pen* (ed. Duczyńska and Polányi, 1963). His autobiography is continued in *Hunok Párizsban* ['Huns in Paris'] (1946), while *Ebéd a kastélyban* ['Lunch at the big house'] (1962) describes his encounter with the former owner of the estate where he spent his childhood. All these works prove him to be the finest stylist in modern Hungary. His feeling for language is also seen in his excellent translations. His studies include a classic portrait of the poet *Petőfi* (1936; revised, French version, 1962). After World War II he turned to drama, particularly historical plays, with less success. G. F. C.

Inber, Vera Mikhailovna (1890–), distinguished Soviet poetess, who was born in Odessa. At first she belonged to the group of poets known as the Constructivists and wrote numerous verses and tales, but her best work was not produced until 1942 when, during the terrible siege of Leningrad, she wrote *Pulkovskiy meridian* [*The Pulkovo Meridian*], an inspired war poem about the siege. It is complemented by her prose work *Pochti tri goda* [*Leningrad Diary*] written in 1945. She received a Stalin prize in 1946, and in 1948 published a poem *Put' vody* [*Path of Water*] which contrasts the backward imperialist east with the near-eastern countries flourishing under socialism. B. W.

Ingamells, Rex (1913–55), Australian poet who advocated the formulation of a distinctive Australian language and the jettisoning of traditional images and associations. To foster this aim, he founded the Jindyworobak Club (1938), the purposes of which were set down in *Conditional Culture* (1938). The 'Jindies' have not always been treated with respect, partly because in their efforts to find unassociative vocabulary they have turned to aboriginal words which sit oddly in the English sentence and render it incomprehensible. Ingamells's work can be found in *Selected Poems* (1944). S. R.

Inge, William (1913–), American playwright, became very popular with his emotionally powerful play *Come Back, Little Sheba* (1950), a study of a marriage threatened by the husband's alcoholism, reaching its climax in the latter's attempt to murder his wife and the subsequent brave attempts of both partners to come to terms with the situation thus produced. His next play *Picnic* (1953), less widely known, won a Pulitzer prize; and *Bus Stop* (1955) was made into a successful film featuring Marilyn Monroe. His more recent successes have included *The Dark at the Top of the Stairs* (1957), and the screenplay of the film *Splendour in the Grass* (1961). K. R. R.

Innes, Hammond (1913–), English novelist, worked first as a journalist. His first novels *Wreckers Must Breathe* (1940) and *Trojan Horse* (1940) passed almost unnoticed but with *White South* (1949) he established himself as a novelist and was able to devote his whole time to writing. His novels are adventure stories with nature and the elements playing a predominant part.

The Lonely Skier (1947), an action-packed novel of suspense and intrigue, is set in a ski lodge in the Dolomites. In *The Angry Mountain* (1950) there is a sense of atmosphere and a build-up of tension culminating in the eruption of Vesuvius. *Campbell's Kingdom* (1952) describes the search for a lost oil field and in *The Mary Deare* (1956) and *Atlantic Fury* (1962) the sea forms a background. His later novels include *The Strode Venturer* (1965), the story of a struggle for survival on the Indian Ocean; and *The Bloody Wood* (1966). K. M. H.

Innes, Michael (1906–), English detective novelist. 'Michael Innes' is a pen-name of John Innes Mackintosh Stewart, an academic who like so many scholars before him found relaxation in writing detective stories with a literary and intellectual flavour. His Inspector Appleby joined the ranks of famous detectives for the first time in 1936 in *Seven Suspects.* His stories are intellectual exercises with plots which are intricate, even on occasion tortuous. His many titles include *Hamlet, Revenge!* (1937), *Silence Observed* (1961), *A Connoisseur's Case* (1962) and *Money From Holme* (1964). K. M. H.

Ionesco, Eugène (1912–), French-Rumanian dramatist and one of the major figures of the European theatre in the twentieth century. Born in Rumania he was educated in France until he was 13 when he returned to Bucharest; he came back to Paris in 1938 to study for a doctorate and has remained there ever since. His first play, *La Cantatrice chauve* [*The Bald Prima-Donna*], was produced in 1949 to a very small audience; since then, although he has never become very popular, his audiences have generally increased.

La Cantatrice chauve presents an evening at the house of Mr and Mrs Smith, a middle-class English pair who converse in the unnatural phrases of a phrase-book (part of the dialogue having been inspired by a course of language-teaching records). Their clock strikes 17, and there is a generally surrealist atmosphere. Mr and Mrs Martin call and discover with surprise that they live in the same flat, share the same daughter and have lived together for some years. The Fire Chief calls and tells a long and complicated story about a cold. The dialogue becomes more and more heated and less and less meaningful until the Smiths and the Martins are shouting words to each other without regard to meaning. The play finishes with the Martins taking the place of the Smiths and repeating the same conversation as that which opened the play.

In *La Leçon* [*The Lesson*] (1951), a teacher is waiting for his pupil, a young girl whom he harangues, browbeats, brain-washes and finally kills.

His housekeeper points out that this is the fortieth today, and the play ends with the entry of the forty-first. *Les Chaises* [*The Chairs*] (1951) reinforces the lesson of the impossibility of communication, which is one of the conclusions to be drawn from the earlier plays; in it an old couple wish to make a declaration of their message to the power of the world. As the guests arrive to hear the message, the only two characters on stage, the original couple, mime their reception, put out chairs for them, chat of this and that, even start selling chocolates and ice-cream. The couple eventually commit suicide by jumping out of the windows in order to underline the importance of their message; whereupon the orator starts to deliver his speech, which is pure gibberish.

These early plays are about language, and the lack of communication which it really affords; words are mere things and Ionesco plays with them—associating them by sound, not sense, showing how many thoughts are really word-clichés, and how mechanical their production is. The physical world is also mechanical; matter (e.g. the chairs) tends to overwhelm man, who is thus reduced to a cipher. This theme is predominant also in *L'Avenir est dans les oeufs* [*The Future is in Eggs*] (1951) and in the play which made Ionesco famous—*Amédée ou Comment s'en débarasser* [*Amédée or How to Get Rid of It*] (1953), in which the central problem is how to get rid of a corpse, symbolising a love which is now dead, and which grows ever larger. *Victimes du devoir* [*Victims of duty*] (1952) illustrates another of Ionesco's preoccupations—a Kafka-like hatred mixed with fear of the workings of bureaucracy; and this becomes strikingly powerful in *Tueur sans gages* [*The Killer*] (1958), in which an entire town is terrorised by a mystery killer. Bérenger, a sort of hero figure who will recur in later plays, symbolises the individual surrounded by the unfeeling, inhuman forces of the Administration (symbolised by the Architect) and crushed by our mechanical society. *Le Rhinocéros* [*The Rhinoceros*] (1959) presents Bérenger as the only man who will resist the urge to become a rhinoceros, to lose his human individuality in a mass movement.

This play, which has been interpreted widely as an attack on Nazi Germany, follows the main preoccupations of Ionesco—as do his later plays *Le Roi se meurt* [*Exit the King*] (1962), *Le piéton de l'air* [*A Stroll in the Air*] (1962), *La Soif et la faim* [*Thirst and Hunger*] (1964)—with language, with bureaucracy, with matter and what is mechanical in life, with the individual opposed to any conformity, whether of ideology or word. These are presented in plays that are very funny, the later ones of which also show a depth of humanity absent from the earlier. As a critic and expounder of anti-theatre Ionesco is clear and intelligible; in *Notes et contre-notes* [*Notes and Counter-notes*] (1962) and in his play *L'Impromptu de l'Alma* [*The Alma Impromptu*] (1956) he explains and justifies his theatre, his refusal to accept ideologies or lend his plays to any positive 'propaganda', his criticisms of attempts at telling the creative artist—or the individual—what he should produce. D. E. A.

Irwin, Margaret (Mrs J. R. Monsell; 1889–1967), English historical novelist, achieved a minor success with her first novel *Still She Wished for Company* (1924), a ghost story combining the eighteenth century with the present, but it is for her Stuart and Elizabethan novels that she has become best known. The first in this series *Royal Flush* (1932) tells the story of Minette, a much loved sister of Charles II. Her books are remarkable for their feminine insight into character and their rapid witty style of writing. She also pays strict attention to historical detail, and there is a richness and colour in all her novels which matches the larger-than-life characters about whom she writes: Rupert of the Rhine in *Stranger Prince* (1937), Lord Montrose in *Proud Servant* (1934), and in *Gay Galliard* (1947) Bothwell the rascally Scot who became first the lover and then the husband of Mary, Queen of Scots. In 1944 came the first of the Elizabethan novels, *Young Bess*. This was followed in 1948 by *Elizabeth, Captive Princess* and in 1953 by *Elizabeth and the Prince of Spain*.

She has also written a life of Sir Walter Ralegh, *That Great Lucifer* (1960); and several short stories collected in *Bloodstock* (1953).

K. M. H.; G. C.

Isherwood, Christopher (1904–), English novelist, short-story writer and playwright. Isherwood was born at Disley, Cheshire, and educated at Repton and Corpus Christi College, Cambridge. He was a member of the Marxist group that included Auden and Spender and was a close friend of the former, collaborating with him on a number of plays in prose and verse (including *The Ascent of F*6, 1936) and travelling with him to China in 1939. They subsequently issued a joint account of the Japanese-Chinese War in *Journey to a War* (1939). Both Auden and Isherwood left Europe for America at the outbreak of war in Europe in 1939. *The Lion and the Shadows* (1938) is autobiographical.

Isherwood's best work is in his accounts of the social decay and moral decadence of pre-1939 Germany where he lived and taught English in Berlin. *Mr Norris Changes Trains* (1935), *Sally Bowles* (1937) and *Goodbye to Berlin* (1939) are unsparingly realistic in their portrayal of the underlying cancer beneath the surface hardness of the Nazi society. Mr Norris, outwardly a timid middle-aged, middle-class businessman, is revealed in a series of vividly drawn episodes as a degenerate pervert—a stripping to reality in which he epitomises the community in which he lives. *Sally Bowles*, the story of an apparently hard and brittle woman of the world, gradually pieces together the desperate plight of the Jew in the Germany of the 1930s. *The World in the Evening* (1954) is a study in individual salvation. Isherwood transfers from the corruption of pre-war Berlin to the American environment. His hero Stephen Monk, a socialite millionaire of Quaker origins, marries an intellectual English novelist twelve years older than himself who performs a maternal rôle until her death just before the outbreak of the second world war. Stephen marries again, this time a nubile American; but the marriage fails because Stephen has not acquired the ability to treat intimate relationships with sensitivity and understanding. He leaves his wife, and then in a period of convalesence following an accident he retraces his past, coming as he does so to a mature understanding of his present arrested development. Isherwood is concerned to demonstrate the necessity for harmonising physical passion, emotional maturity and intellectual perception before the individual can even begin to achieve spiritual fulfilment. There is also an interesting portrait in the book of Stephen's Quaker aunt, Sarah, who possesses semi-mystical qualities.

Isherwood's later books include *Down There on a Visit* (1962), *A Single Man* (1964), and *Exhumations* (1966), a mixture of stories, articles and verses which Isherwood has written over a period of forty years and which serve as a background to understanding his development as a man and as a writer. His early Marxism has been transformed, not like Auden's to Christianity, but to an involvement in mysticism in the manner of Aldous Huxley. D. L. P.

Istrati, Panaït (1884–1935), Rumanian novelist who wrote in French. The son of a Greek smuggler and a Rumanian peasant woman, he left home in his early teens and for twenty years wandered through the countries of the eastern Mediterranean, taking on a score of varied occupations and often enduring extreme trials and privation. On his return to Rumania in 1913 he was converted to Marxism by the Russian Rakovsky. Deserted by his wife and after an unsuccessful venture in pig-farming, he took to wandering again. In 1921 in Nice he attempted suicide. After his recovery he was befriended by Romain Rolland who urged him to write of his experiences. The result was the five volumes of the semi-autobiographical 'Adrien Zograffi cycle' of novels, of which the first, *Kyra Kyralina* [*Kyra my Sister*] (1925), won him instant fame. He spent the year 1927 working in Russia for Soviet institutions, but returned disillusioned to Paris to publish three volumes bitterly attacking the oppressive methods of Bolshevism. One of these, *La Russie nue* [*Russia Unveiled*] (1929), enjoyed a considerable vogue. Another highly effective work was *Le Pêcheur* *d'éponges* ['The sponge fisherman'] (1930), a series of autobiographical essays written after his return to his native village of Baldovinești-Braïla. All his work carries the stamp of a deep pessimism, an anguish at man's lack of liberty and at the grievous lot of the needy and the downtrodden. Although his style is trenchant and robust, writing in French did not come easily to him and he always submitted his manuscripts for grammatical checking before publication. Nevertheless, in the years 1925 to 1930 no less than a dozen major works came from his pen. Improvident and consumptive he died in 1935 leaving his second wife in penury. R. C. W.

Ivanov, Vsevolod Vyacheslavovich (1895–), is a Soviet novelist of the Ornamental school. He was born in the Semipalatinsk region but soon ran away to join the circus. His life and work have been compared with Gorky's, but Ivanov is a non-political writer, always appearing to be on two sides at once. His best-known work is *Bronepoyezd No. 14–69* [*Armoured train No. 14–69*] (1922) which deals with a group of poorly armed Siberian partisans who successfully seize a White armoured train full of munitions. Criticism led him to try to conform, but his work thus lost much of its power and originality. B. W.

Ivo, Lêdo (1924–), Brazilian poet, novelist and critic of the so-called '45 Generation'. His poetry fulfils the aesthetic canons of *neomodernismo* with its return to classical rhythms and formal perfection. His first volume of poems *As imaginações* ['Imaginations'] betrays the influence of earlier currents. *Ode e elegia* ['Ode and elegy'] (1945), however, already conveys the verbal power, intellectualism and respect for traditional forms which characterise subsequent collections. *Ode ao crepúsculo* ['Ode to twilight'] and *Acontecimento do sonêto* ['Birth of the sonnet'] both appeared in 1948. The latter exemplifies Ivo's mastery over his preferred form, and his sonnets provide ample evidence of the vigour of his lyricism and his novel use of adjectives. The process is continued in *Cântico* ['Canticle'] (1949) and *Linguagem* ['Language'] (1951).

The spirit of Ivo's poetry is often in harmony with that of his contemporaries, but elsewhere his poems echo the spirit of earlier generations. *Um brasileiro em Paris e o Rei da Europa* ['A Brazilian in Paris and the King of Europe'] (1955) is a striking example where the first part of the book gives evidence of his individual aestheticism, while the second part with its satire and immoderate vocabulary rich in proverbial wit recalls the excesses of the '22 Generation'.

Later poetry by Ivo includes *Magias* ['Witchcrafts'] (1960) and *Uma lira dos vinte anos* ['A lyre of twenty years'] (1962). In 1958 he published a regionalist novel *O caminho sem aventura* ['The road without adventure'], and in 1961 a collection of essays *Paraísos de papel* ['Paradises of paper'] and a book of short stories *Use a passagem subterrânea* ['Use the underground passage']. Ivo has also published several novels, some important critical studies on *modernista* poets, notably Mário de Andrade and Manuel Bandeira, and some remarkable translations of Rimbaud's works. A translation of his poetry appears in Leonard S. Downes's *Introduction to Modern Brazilian Poetry* (1954). G. P.

J

Jabavu, Noni (1921–   ), South African-born writer educated in England and married to an Englishman, has written two 'documentaries' based on return visits made to Africa as an adult, *Drawn in Colour* (1960) and *The Ochre People* (1963). Both portray with great insight the complex patterns of personal relationships that exist in Africa. C. P.

Jacks, L. P. (Lawrence Pearsall Jacks; 1860–1955), English unitarian philosopher and writer. In *Mad Shepherds* (1910), *The Legends of Smokeover* (1922) and many other volumes he presented an imaginary industrial city whose inhabitants express his own vigorous and charitable comments on life, and his idea of man integrated with his fellows, his past and his surroundings. H. C.

Jacob, Naomi (1884–1964), English novelist. The child of a Yorkshirewoman and a German Jew whose marriage failed, her early years were lonely and hard. She began as a pupil teacher and, educating herself, moved on to be secretary to a music-hall artist and met many stars of that time. In 1914 she became a Catholic. Overwork during the war caused an attack of tuberculosis deciding her to settle in Italy. Her first novel *Jacob Usher* (1926), based on a play by H. V. Esmond, revealed her as a good storyteller and after this she wrote about two novels a year including *Roots* (1931) and *The Gollantz Saga* (2 vols, 1952–53). In 1933 she wrote the first 'Me' book, *Me: a Chronicle about Other People*, followed by *Me in the Kitchen* (1935), *Me again* (1937), and several more. Sometimes repetitive, but usually lively and humorous, these tell more about her interests and friends than about herself. G. S.

Jacobs, W. W. (William Wymark Jacobs; 1863–1943), English writer, chiefly of short stories. He mainly took as his theme the Thames-side docks and the picturesque marine characters associated with them. Much of his work was written for periodicals and has the ephemeral atmosphere of that medium, but the strong eccentricity of his characters endures. In collections such as *Many Cargoes* (1896), *The Skipper's Wooing* (1897), *A Master of Craft* (1900) and *Night Watches* (1914) the reader is introduced to a world of intense individualism, the idiom of which Jacobs skilfully conveys, and the odd humours of which he reveals with intense understanding. The humour is sometimes laboured but the action is always lively.

Of a number of macabre stories that he wrote the best known is 'The Monkey's Paw' a neatly contrived tale woven around ordinary people confronted with a magic talisman which brings sudden hope, then equally sudden tragedy to the family. The dramatised version of this story became a strong feature of the amateur repertoire. R. A. K.

Jacobson, Dan (1929–), South African novelist, an expatriate and one of southern Africa's leading fiction-writers, made his debut with a striking, starkly exciting and finely symbolic novel *A Dance in the Sun* (1956), in which the shadowy background figure of an African is an ominous presence to the hiking white man, whose nervousness mounts sharply, explosively. *The Trap* (1955) and *The Price of Diamonds* (1957) are in the thriller-fable genre explored by Hemingway, Dürrenmatt and Simenon, with illicit diamond buying as a background. Jacobson's short stories *A Long Way from London* (1958) range over a wider geographical and psychological area, and in his next novel *The Evidence of Love* (1960) the experience of this exercise is brought to bear on a South African coloured-white relationship that has its climax in London. His later novel *The Beginners* (1966) traces the life of a Jewish family in South Africa, Israel and England. C. P.

James, Henry (1843–1916), American-born writer, is widely held to be one of the major novelists in the English language. During the last quarter of the nineteenth century he produced a spate of major works, and he crowned his achievement in the first decade of the twentieth with three towering masterpieces: (in order of composition) *The Ambassadors* (1903), *The Wings of a Dove* (1902) and *The Golden Bowl* (1904).

Henry James was born in New York, the younger brother of the philosopher William James. Much of his education took place in various parts of Europe, and his appreciation of the contrasting personalities and mores of Americans and Europeans was to provide him with an important source of material. His first novel of any importance, *Roderick Hudson* (1875), portrays an American artist transplanted to Rome in the hope (calamitously mistaken, as it turns out) that his talent will blossom in the richer cultural soil of Italy; and in the year of its publication—having already spent the greater part of the previous six years in Europe—James himself settled in France, which was to be the scene of much of his next novel *The American* (1877). Here we meet a more representative American, with all his country's most obvious and recognisable virtues and shortcomings, being introduced into French society by an expatriate fellow-countrywoman.

The situation is reversed in its successor, *The Europeans* (1878), where an expatriate brother and sister come to visit their Boston cousins. This exquisite little book, with its echoes of Jane Austen, has a gentleness and radiance that are to be found in much of his writing, and which might be thought to reflect both James's own innate capacity for happiness and the sunny, if not always untroubled, quality of his early years in America. In the novel, however, it is the appropriately named 'European' Felix who embodies this important Jamesian quality, and the Bostonian puritan Wentworths who, for all their gentleness and kindness, have lost it. They are initially no more able to come to terms with the spontaneous gaiety of Felix than they are with the mannered charm of his sophisticated baroness sister; but the result of the Europeans' continuing presence is to bring out the latent capacities of the young Gertrude Wentworth and to give a new assurance to her considerably travelled cousin Robert Acton—the latter maturing through his liaison with the baroness, while Gertrude is enabled to give a final no to the sombre young clergyman she has been expected to marry, and eventually to become the wife of the ardent Felix.

James had moved to London in 1876, and the next ten years saw the publication not only of *The American* and *The Europeans* but also of three more of his best-read works: the beautiful little New York novel *Washington Square* (1880), the large-scale masterpiece *The Portrait of a Lady* (1881) and the brilliant comedy of feminism *The Bostonians* (1886). *Washington Square*, a story of the repressive parental custody of an heiress daughter, has a universality, and its strong romanticism is an element that is seldom absent from James's writing. In *The Bostonians* one is rather more conscious of time and place, and at the same time of the originality of its principal character-creation, the charming and spontaneous Verena Tarrant, who in her eminent feminity has incongruously found herself espousing the cause of a crankish and aggressive feminism. But undoubtedly the most important of the three, and of all that James had written so far, is *Portrait of a Lady*. This is the story of a young woman who, though she is in fact American and may be thought to embody such characteristic American traits as an idealistic personal optimism and an innocence synonymous with inexperience, is nonetheless the incarnation of a universal human perfectionism to be found wherever there are young people with leisure to conceive it. Isabel Archer's perfectionism causes her to reject two eminently eligible suitors, the English artistocrat Lord Warburton and the American businessman Caspar Goodwood, partly because they are not good enough for her, but partly also out of a sense that her life's trajectory is still curving upward—that she has yet to reach the highest point, and is not yet ready to choose a husband.

What both suitors have indeed lacked is the superfine aestheticism and sophistication that is the magnetic opposite-pole to her own freshness and intellectual vigour; and at the high-point in her trajectory she encounters a man who has precisely these qualities. Only when she has been lured into marrying him does she learn that they are the qualities that are most likely to flourish in moribundity, and that her irritable aesthete husband is utterly sterile. After the most scrupulous guarding of her vital freedom she finds herself trapped in a life-destroying spiritual desert and totally unable to help herself.

From the mid-1880s (when James had already spent more than a decade in London) till the turn of the century, England and English life feature more substantially in his novels and stories. Much of his own social life had been spent in the company of the aristocracy and upper middle classes (there is his famous confession of having dined out 107 times during the winter of 1878–9); however, *The Princess Casamassima* (1886) is set in the other London, deprived and frustrated, sordid and shabby, and explores the fate of a person of Jamesian sensitivity of nature and fineness of mind who is born into it. *The Reverberator* (1888) takes us back to France and a modification of the American-European theme of his early novels; but in *The Tragic Muse* (1890), his second important work to have an artist as the principal character, there is a striking array of English character types of the kind that he met in English society. James's interest in the rôle of the artist at a time when his own works were enjoying only a very limited commercial success was also expressed in a number of short stories written at the time, for example 'The Death of the Lion' (1894); and some of the most enduring works of his second decade in London (a period during which he for some years abandoned the novel for an abortive attempt at writing for the stage) are in this form—notably 'The Aspern Papers' (1888) and 'The Turn of the Screw' (1898), which together with the earlier 'Daisy Miller' (1878) are among his best-known stories.

The first product of James's return to the novel was *The Other House* (1896), one of his least-read works; but this was followed by two of the most satisfying. *The Spoils of Poynton* (1897) and *What Maisie Knew* (1897). Both books are distinguished by the presentation of the narrative as it is experienced by one central character: the sensitive and scrupulous genteel-poor Fleda Vetch (who at times recalls Jane Austen's Fanny Price), and the buoyant ingenuous child Maisie. Both characters are centrally positioned in relation to the quarrels of the other principals (Fleda in virtue of her friendship and instinctive sympathy for the widowed Mrs Gereth, together with a growing love for the latter's estranged son Owen; Maisie simply as the child of divorced parents): the effect being that, within certain well-defined limits, they enjoy the kind of omniscience

—and more important, the all-embracing sympathy—that were invaluable to James at a time when, like those who were to follow him, he had become increasingly uneasy about the convention of the all-seeing author.

Mrs Gereth and her son Owen are in dispute over the 'spoils' of Poynton, the family home: lovingly and tastefully furnished with a lifetime's prudent and skilful collection of *objets d'art*, the fruits of a lifelong religion of beauty, duly bequeathed in its entirety by the late Mr Gereth to his good-natured but unappreciative son, and now soon to pass into the custody of the vulgar girl he is engaged to marry. When Mrs Gereth carries them off to the country cottage that has become her new home and her son is pressed by his fiancée Mona to demand their return under threat of litigation, it is to Fleda that she delegates the negotiations with Owen, thus creating a situation in which her young friend's moral fibre is put to the severest test. For the latter becomes aware that Owen is faltering in his own commitment in proportion as Mona shows herself unwilling to marry him before the spoils are returned; and that it is she herself who would be the most likely beneficiary if she failed to present Owen's case effectively to his mother. So scrupulous is she that even when Owen's love for her is manifest, she cannot encourage him to dishonour himself by breaking faith and contract with her rival; and when, inflamed by Mrs Gereth's own ardent desire to have her as a daughter-in-law and a worthy custodian of the sacred spoils, her emotions do eventually dictate her behaviour, it is too late. The wretched Mona, learning of her danger, has already coerced the malleable Owen into marriage, and has become the mistress of Poynton. But, as if some deity has presided over the spoils—which, in a moment of faith that Fleda was in fact to become their custodian, Mrs Gereth had returned to their proper home—they are consumed in a great fire before they can be possessed by her.

In 1898 James moved to Rye, in Sussex, which was to be his home for the rest of his life. The following year he published *The Awkward Age* (1899), a kind of English drawing-room comedy of manners in novel form in which the characters are only known (as on a stage) through their actions and words. This study of innocence and experience can prove tiresome to many readers with its disproportionately extensive treatment of some slender material. Its successor *The Sacred Fount* (1901) is another English society novel; but here the treatment of a country-house weekend has both a superimposed formal quality (in the intricate patterning of the kaleidoscope of relationships), and a substratum of mystery with a suggestion of the supernatural. The latter is not a new element in James, having been used very effectively in the haunting ghost-story 'The Turn of the Screw' (published some three years earlier), with its good-and-evil polarisation of the influence of the dead.

There was now to follow the great trio of mature masterpieces of the period 1902–4, and a return to the international theme: as if his departure from London, whose social life had provided him with the material for the best works of his middle years, allowed him to regain a wider perspective. In *The Ambassadors* and *The Golden Bowl* (particularly the former) the impingement of European values on a comparatively untutored American consciousness provides the mainspring of the plot; and in *The Wings of a Dove*, which centres on the ending (this time in premature death) of the career of a second tragic heroine with 'a great capacity for life', it is precisely her American freshness and receptivity that make hei aware of the potentialities for living that Europe offers. In all three, then, the international theme is employed to give a fresh, unstaled perspective on European life; and it is undoubtedly James's American background that enabled him to become in the twentieth century one of the outstanding figures of English and European literature.

The first 'ambassador' that Mrs Newsome of Woollett, Massachusetts, sends to France, to investigate the reasons for the delayed homecoming of her son Chad and to urge on the latter his responsibilities and benefits in relation to the family business, is her 60-year-old friend Lambert Strether. Unlike his friend Waymarsh, whom he meets on his arrival in England, he is himself constantly receptive to new experience; and when he finally tracks down his quarry he is not slow to perceive that the latter, far from being in any way endangered (as his mother fears) by his acquaintance with European life, has in fact become a more gracious and refined person. When he learns that Chad has acquired his style and sensitivity through his friendship with an older, married Frenchwoman, Mme de Vionnet, he is still sufficiently open-minded to realise that a relationship capable of such improvement in Chad must itself be beautiful; and he cannot bring himself to urge the discontinuing of the latter's emotional education in the interests of his business responsibilities. At the same time, he feels that he is himself discovering, before it is too late, new dimensions of living, of which Woollett, Mass., has kept him in ignorance; and even when he realises, in a chance meeting in the country, the intimate basis of Chad's beautiful friendship, he sustains the shock and finds that he can see no fault—finds, indeed, that he is ready to take the part of Chad's mistress in her fears of losing him.

If Strether blooms late in life, Milly in *The Wings of a Dove*—based on James's own cousin Minny, who had died of tuberculosis at 24—must bloom early or not at all. This knowledge lends an intensity to her experiences, and induces her friends to behave in ways which in other circumstances would seem fantastic—for instance in their active concern that Milly should enjoy a consummated relationship with the man to whom she has long been attracted (but who is emotionally committed to another woman), and thus die not totally unfulfilled as a woman.

Marriage is also the desideratum for a fuller life for Maggie in *The Golden Bowl,* a girl who on the surface is not totally unlike Milly; but here the treatment, initially at least, is comic, and a necessary corrective for the highly-charged tragic romanticism of its predecessor. Maggie—perhaps a little like the early Strether in his longstanding idealised feelings about France—is aware that marriage to an Italian prince could do something for her: as indeed it *could,* though in a way of which she in her unparticularised thinking is quite unaware. Her father, too, must marry; and it is sheer bad luck that Charlotte, the woman chosen for him, should be a former object of her prince's affections, and that these two should be thus provided with an opportunity for renewing their relationship. In her subsequent, more dramatic efforts to regain control of the situation she can become for many readers an increasingly unsympathetic figure: if Milly's friends can be said to want her to 'collect' the greatest experience life can offer before she dies, Maggie's collecting urge only brings her into the depths of emotional experience at the point where she is forced to fight for her principal exhibit.

After this great burst of creativity James's powers began to wane. *The Outcry* (1911) is a work of little interest, and the posthumous *The Ivory Tower* (1917) and *The Sense of the Past* (1917), though very readable, are unfinished. The most satisfying of his last works are generally thought to be the travel book *The American Scene* (1907) and his autobiographical writings (1913–17). He died in 1916, having become a British citizen the previous year and been awarded the Order of Merit. K. R. R.

James, M. R. (Montague Rhodes James; 1862–1936), English mediaeval scholar and writer who, apart from his palaeographical works and his translation of *The Apocryphal New Testament* (1924), wrote a number of spine-chilling and dreadfully plausible ghost-stories, published as *Ghost Stories of an Antiquary* (1905, 1911; collected in one volume 1931).

H. C.

Jameson, [Margaret] Storm (1897–), English novelist. *The Lovely Ship* (1927) was the first of three novels portraying the life of a Yorkshire shipbuilding family; *The Voyage Home* (1930) and *A Richer Dust* (1931) continued this theme, which is derived from her own family background. Her other works since 1926 have included *Cousin Honoré* (1940) and its sequel *Cloudless May* (1943), *The Hidden River* (1955), *A Ulysses Too Many* (1958), and a critical work on modern drama in Europe. R. A. K.

Jarrell, Randall (1914–65), American poet. Randall Jarrell is an academic and a war poet. He is capable both of delicate imagery and intellectual conceit and also of facing the universal problems of war with simplicity and directness.

Jarrell was born in Nashville, Tennessee, was educated at Vanderbilt University and has subsequently taught in a number of American universities. During the second world war he was on operational duties with the U.S. Air Force. His poetry derives valuable qualities from his background. Jarrell is steeped in American history and literature and consequently is capable of taking a historical perspective of the condition of modern man. In addition he possesses a fine control of words and imagery and a lightly directed sense of irony. The verse gains depth, sympathy and warmth from the poet's first-hand experience of war and death. He is capable of facing abstractions with reality.

'A Girl in a Library' (*Seven League Crutches*, 1951) employs delicate rhythm and a precise vocabulary to blend sympathetically a sense of cultural inheritance with the lightly humorous subject of a girl asleep in a college library. 'The Death of a Ball Turret Gunner' from *Little Friend, Little Friend* (1943) is written in an entirely different tone:

> From my mother's sleep I fell into the State,
> And I hunched in its belly till my wet fur froze.
> Six miles from earth, loosed from its dream of life,
> I woke to black flak and the nightmare fighters.
> When I died they washed me out of the turret with a hose.

Collections of Jarrell's verse include *Selected Poems* (1955), *The Woman at the Washington Zoo* (1960) and *The Lost World* (1966). He has also published volumes of critical essays *Poetry and the Age* (1953) and *A Sad Heart at the Supermarket* (1961), and a novel *Pictures from an Institution* (1954).

D. L. P.

Jaspers, Karl (1883–), German philosopher who, together with Heidegger, has defined and expounded the concepts of existentialism to the German public. Both are concerned with the real 'Being' (*Sein*) of self and things; both seek to eliminate any opposition between self and things. In art, the existentialist philosophy has had a negative effect, for the basic concept that man is cast unprotected into a world on which he is wholly dependent has led to the view that even art is no source of solace. The intensity of this feeling has led in Jaspers, however, to some feeling for transcendental values; where one outcome of existentialism could be nihilism, the other could be mysticism. Jaspers' main contribution to philosophy was expressed in *Allgemeine Psychopathologie* ['General psychopathology'] (1959). In the same way as Sartre and Simone de Beauvoir became more and more 'engaged' in political action, so also did Jaspers; first in the general sense, as in *Vom Ursprung und Ziel der Geschichte* [*The Origin and Goal of History*] (1950), and more specifically in *Wohn treibt die Bundesrepublik* ['Where drifts the Federal Republic'] (1966). G. W.

Jeffers, Robinson (1887–), American poet. Jeffers is an oppressive and fatalistic poet whose declamatory verse is the opposite of Whitman's affirmation in American man. He was born in Pittsburgh, Pennsylvania, the son of a professor of Classics. He was educated variously in Europe and America and included among his studies forestry and medicine. He married and settled as a recluse on the north Californian coast.

Jeffers's twenty or so books of verse interpret man as depraved and disgusting compared with the wild integrity of nature. It is certainly not a case of Byron's 'I love not man the less but nature more'. The poet seeks within the desirable order of nature 'being without consciousness'. His imagery records the repetitive theme of the bestiality of man in a Nietzschean struggle for power. Jeffers pursues a primal universal force and he despises scientific method as illusory in its pursuit of knowledge. In *Science* (1925) he makes reference to:

> A little knowledge, a pebble from the shingle,
> A drop from the oceans: who would have dreamed this
> infinitely little too much.

The poetry has a powerfully depressing world view and the imaginative force of the work makes it compelling rather than attractive reading. Volumes include *Selected Poetry of Robinson Jeffers* (1938); *The Double Axe* (1948); *Hungerfield and Other Poems* (1954). D. L. P.

Jellicoe, Ann (1928–), English playwright. The earlier plays of Ann Jellicoe (*The Sport of My Mad Mother*, 1956, new version 1964; and *The Knack*, 1961) can best be summed up by the author herself: 'When I write a play I am trying to communicate with the audience. I do this by every means in my power—I try to get at them through their eyes, by providing visual action; I try to get at them through their ears, for instance by noises and rhythm. These are not loose effects; they are introduced to communicate with the audience directly through their senses, to reinforce the total effect of the play . . . The theatre is a medium which works upon people's imagination and emotion—not merely upon their intellect.' (*New Theatre Magazine*, Bristol University.)

This is a clear statement of effort towards total effect—effect upon all the senses by means of mime, dancing, chant and ritual as integral parts of the text; and all of these are frequently visible in the plays. Examples are the painting of the wall and the carrier-bag episodes of *The Knack*;

in the scene in *My Mad Mother* where the unconscious Caldaro or Dean is wrapped in newspaper which is then ceremonially torn from him; in the two pages of pings and plongs of the imitation piano scene of *The Knack*. For these are not plays in which the text can be read and appreciated in isolation; these can only be seen and felt fully interpreted on the stage. They do not appeal to our intellects but bypass these to reach as directly as possible our emotions, for the author is reminding us of that part in us which is not reasoned and which controls our behaviour far more than we think. These are plays about incoherent, inarticulate people, real people, people acting as we ourselves do often act.

This is however pre-eminently director's theatre, for the bare text is only the score from which the final production has to be orchestrated. As Kenneth Tynan has said: 'It stands in the same relationship to conventional play-making as jazz does to conventional music.' But much of Ann Jellicoe's experience lies in the field of direction, so that the touch is sure. The inarticulate teddy-boys and the gang-quarrels, the destructive and violent forces of the incoherent of *The Sport of My Mad Mother*, the non-reasoning and therefore again incoherent forces at work in the realm of sex in *The Knack*, all these are painted in a way that we can immediately experience through our emotional impressions.

The author's later play *Shelley* (1965) broke new ground for her, and pleased the critics less. Possibly they were disconcerted by the fact that the words themselves had now become a vehicle of communication instead of forming mere sound-patterns. The play is an accurate and intelligent portrayal of the closing years of Shelley's life, a solid work but not one typical of what had hitherto been considered Ann Jellicoe's vein.

J. B. M.

Jennings, Elizabeth Joan (1926–), English Catholic poet whose first collected publications *A Way of Looking* (1955) and *A Sense of the World* (1958) established her as a writer of fresh, not obscure, but sometimes slightly overwrought poems. They express in a cool detached manner, in regular verse-forms, intensely personal experiences. Her sympathetic self-absorption into the life and history of a place or of a Christian event is remarkable; and places and people seem to lose their separateness from each other. Another common theme is the hidden but real relationship which may exist between strangers. *Collected Poems* appeared in 1967.

G. C.

Jensen, Johannes Vilhelm (1873–1950), Danish novelist, poet and essayist, and winner of the 1944 Nobel Prize for Literature. A North Jutlander, he achieved prominence at the close of the nineteenth century with his 'Himmerland Tales' or collections of short stories devoted to the folklore and scenery of his Jutland *Heimat*. In his thought he was inspired by Heine, Whitman, Kipling and especially Darwin, and he is particularly noted for his opposition to the principles of the eminent Danish critic Georg Brandes. His first major work was the novel *Kongens Fald* [*The Fall of the King*] (1900–01), a tragic historical study about Christian II of Denmark which presented the character of the Danes as being essentially indecisive yet captivating. By far his most successful work, however, was his six-volume *Den lange Rejse* [*The Long Journey*, reduced to three volumes: *Fire and Ice*, *The Cimbrians*, *Christopher Columbus*] (1909–22). This work generally treats of man's long journey from the time of the pre-glacial baboon to the discovery of America, and more particularly of the rise of the Cimbrians, a Teutonic race, culminating in the feats of Christopher Columbus whom Jensen quaintly claimed to be a Cimbrian. Jensen travelled widely, especially in the United States, and it was his travels and his Darwinism which informed his essays. All his prose work is characterised by his impressionist imagery, by his predilection for the rapid yet colourful vignette and the flashing picture. A useful selection of his verse is available bilingually in *The Jutland Wind* (ed. R. P. Keigwin, 1944). R. C. W.

Jerome, Jerome K. (1859–1927), English novelist and playwright best known for his *Three Men in a Boat* (1889), a thread of narrative of three young men who take a rowing boat on the Thames during an English summer. This thread is broken by a series of comic incidents relevant both to the river theme—mad capers in Hampton Court maze—and to the private lives of the three main characters. The story is also interspersed with light local history and is redolent of the boater and blazer age. Jerome K. Jerome's skill at climactic wit and the comedy of situation is at its best in this story; it was followed by *Three Men on a Bummell* (1900). His best-known play is *The Passing of the Third Floor Back* (1908).
R. A. K.

Jesenský, Janko (1874–1945), Slovak novelist, was a member of the Free Czechoslovak Army fighting for the liberation from Austria-Hungary during the first world war, and was later vice-president of the Slovak local administration. His novel *Demokrati* [*The Democrats*] (1st vol. 1934, 2nd vol. 1938) is a satire on political life in Slovakia during the thirties. K. B.

Jesus, Carolina Maria de (1921–), Brazilian diarist. Although she has written several short stories, the author's reputation rests entirely on her grim journal *Quarto de Despejo* [*Beyond all Pity*] (1960), the extensively edited version of a diary kept between 1955 and 1960. It presents a harrowing account of her life with her three illegitimate children in the appalling slum shacks of São Paulo. Though she had never known a decent environment, her descent to the slums was the final degradation. Her brutalised existence was eked out by collecting waste paper and her little remaining pride by her ability to write, her one form of escapism and a source of frenzied rage to her fellow slum-dwellers. This moving account of the techniques of survival on a human refuse-tip is told with a rare combination of outrage, detachment and courage. R. C. W.

Jhabvala, R. Prawer (1927–), English-language novelist of India. She was born in Germany of Polish parents, educated in England, married an Indian architect, and subsequently lived in Delhi. She describes with humour and tenderness the minutiae of urban social, political, commercial and intellectual life in modern India. A consistent feature of her writing is the gentle deflation of each of her characters' most cherished conceptions; but she wields her needle with surgical kindness and her portraits remain endearing. Her titles include *To Whom She Will* (1955), *The Nature of Passion* (1956), *Esmond in India* (1958), *The Householder* (1960), *Get Ready for Battle* (1962), the collection of short stories *Like Birds, Like Fishes* (1963), and the screenplay of the film *Shakespeare Wallah* (1964). S. R.

Jiménez, Juan Ramón (1881–1958), Spanish poet, was awarded the Nobel Prize for Literature in 1956. Juan Ramón Jiménez is with Antonio Machado the father of the Spanish poetic renaissance in the twentieth century. His importance lies less in his large production, his *Obra* ['Work'], than in his poetic ideals—the *depuración* ('purification') from the poem of all non-poetic elements, his care for the structure and presentation of his work, his tireless recasting of individual poems. His steadfast pursuit of these ideals made Juan Ramón a sort of high priest of poetry whose influence on the young poets who came to the forefront in the 1920s was decisive.

Born in Moguer on the coast of western Andalusia, Juan Ramón was delicate in health and artistic in temperament from his earliest youth. While studying law at Seville he was already writing and publishing poetry and in 1900 he met Darío in Madrid. That meeting was decisive: Juan Ramón was thenceforth completely involved in Madrid's literary life. His earliest verse, *Almas de violeta* ['Violet souls'] (1900) and *Ninfeas* ['Water-lilies'] (1900), is clearly modernist, but there is soon evidence of poetic evolution. The death of his father in 1900 affected Juan Ramón profoundly and he spent some years in a sanatorium. His poetry now takes on a more melancholy note and the *depuración* begins: there are simpler verse forms; the sensual lilt and emotive epithets of modernist lyric are excised; the anecdotic, narrative elements disappear. The result is a simpler, concise verse that concentrates on one aspect of reality. The poet focuses on 'peaks of delight', the present moment—not the passage of time, which is Machado's central preoccupation. By 1916, the year of his marriage, a distinctive lyric vein had emerged and Juan Ramón dated his poetic maturity from *Diario de un poeta reciencasado* ['Diary of a newly married poet'] (1917).

Thenceforward he devoted himself entirely to the *Obra*, publishing anthologies of his earlier verse in recast forms (1917, 1922, 1957) as well as new poems in reviews, *cahiers* and books. The twenties saw Juan Ramón at his most influential, but subsequently he lost contact with the main current of Spanish poetry. After he left Spain on the outbreak of the civil war his themes became increasingly ambitious and his language less polished and precise. In *La estación total* ['The total season'] (1946) the early motives of death and love are less effectively treated. *Animal de fondo* ['Deep animal'] (1949) describes his search through poetry for a God 'desired and desiring', but this aesthetic mysticism seems unsatisfactory to the Anglo-Saxon reader.

Juan Ramón was also a fine prose writer and *Platero y yo* [*Platero and I*] (1914), the life and adventures of an Andalusian donkey, is already a classic. There have been published several excellent anthologies of English translations from his work. D. H. G.

Johnson, B. S. (1933–), English novelist and poet whose work has shown the influence of an interest in the aesthetics and techniques of the cinema. In his first novel *Travelling People* (1963) he rang the changes on a variety of literary genres, with chapters in the form of diary entries, letters, conventional narrative, interior monologue as well as a film scenario. Other titles include *Albert Angelo* (1964). K. R. R.

Johnson, Louis (1924–), New Zealand poet, was founder (1951) and editor of the *New Zealand Poetry Yearbook*, which though it first promised to be the organ of young rebels has since printed a wide range of poetry. Johnson's own work at this time, as in *The Sun among the Ruins* (1951) and *Roughshod among the Lilies* (1952), is characterised by urban themes and by his distinctive treatment of sexual love. In his next work, *New Worlds for Old* (1957), he widens his scope to include a range of social and political subjects. This was followed by *Bread and a Pension* (1964). S. R.

Johnson, Pamela Hansford (1912–), English novelist. Her first novel *This Bed Thy Centre* was published in 1935, and she has grown in literary stature with each successive novel, achieving popular success and winning acclaim from the critics. Her earlier novels dealt with serious human problems as in *The Impossible Marriage* (1955) which explores the delicate relationship between two individuals facing the break-up of a marriage; but in her later writing she has developed a rich comic strain. This is exemplified in *The Unspeakable Skipton* (1959), with its slightly ridiculous pseudo-intellectual characters, many of whom appear again in *Night and Silence Who Is Here?* (1963), a satire on the eccentricities of American university life, and *Cork Street, Next to the Hatters* (1965), a merciless take-off of present-day trends in the theatre.

Pamela Hansford Johnson is married to novelist and politician C. P. Snow (Lord Snow) and is also well known as a Proustian scholar (*Six Proust Reconstructions*, 1958). K. M. H.

Johnson, Uwe (1934–), German writer, born in Pomerania, has been described as the novelist of divided Germany. After studying German at the universities of Leipzig and Rostock he spent three years without any regular employment. Moving to West Berlin, he published his first novel *Mutmassungen über Jakob* [*Speculations about Jacob*] (1959). Written in an extremely modern style, it is an investigation into politics and morality. When the novel opens, the central character is already dead, and the author uses the 'speculations' of those who knew him to recreate his story. Jakob is an enigmatic figure under the surveillance of the eastern security police who escapes to join his love (a secretary working for NATO) after the Hungarian rising but who returns after the Suez affair. His second novel *Das dritte Buch über Achim* [*The Third Book about Achim*] (1961) has as its central figure a champion cyclist and member of the *Volkskammer* ('People's chamber', the lower house of the East German parliament). The interest of this novel lies in its unusual approach, for it describes the inability of a West German writer to write a satisfactory book about this 'national sportsman' because he cannot accept the images put out by the state propaganda machine. A third novel, *Zwei Ansichten* [*Two Views*] (1965), relates the plight of two lovers separated, like a modern Pyramus and Thisbe, by the Berlin wall. Johnson's preoccupation with real-life political themes and his pessimistic verdict that the division of Germany is too wide to be repaired has been sharply criticised, but it has equally been praised as a masterly treatment of the major reality in modern Germany. G. W.

Jones, David (1895–), Anglo-Welsh water-colour artist and writer. His work is not easily categorised: it has been described, for example, as 'written as Picasso paints or like Malory rewritten by Joyce', and as 'a mixture of phantasmagoria and reality'. *In Parenthesis* (1937) deals with infantry life in World War I with a combination of realism, Celtic mythology, and Arthurian legend mixed with Christian symbolism. *The Anathemata* (1954), written like the former in a mixture of prose and verse, is a heroic record of British history employing appropriate, though individually rendered, languages for the periods through which it travels. The affinities with Joyce's *Ulysses* lie both in this use of language, and in its development of meaning through a pattern akin to a flow of consciousness rather than through a narrative thread. In sections the author has incorporated the sounds and meanings of the Welsh language.

David Jones has described his own work as follows: 'It is about one's own "thing", which *res* is unavoidably part and parcel of the western Christian *res* as inherited by a person whose perceptions are totally conditioned upon his being indigenous to this island.' *Epoch and Artist; Selected Writings* was published in 1959. D. L. P.

Jones, James (1921–), American novelist whose first book, the army novel *From Here to Eternity* (1951), won him both fame—it was chosen by the Book of the Month Club, received the National Book Award in 1952 and was filmed in 1953—and notoriety—it was criticised in some quarters for the obscenity of its language which recorded with complete frankness the sexual preoccupations of the enlisted men. Jones had spent several years writing the novel, drawing on his own experiences of army life in Hawaii for material, and on the works of Thomas Wolfe (something of whose style can be seen reflected in his own) for inspiration and encouragement to write. Jones's total involvement both with the writing of the book and with the army comes over extremely strongly and gives to the novel its almost overwhelming force and impact, but also inevitably some of its confusion. For Jones's attitude to the army would seem to be very much that of his main character, the bugler and boxer Prewitt, who is fundamentally a soldier but who is involved in a constant war, a love-hate relationship with the army as an institution. He loses everything that is dear to him, his bugling post and his stripes, when he tries to follow his own ethical code; he is turned into a killer by his experiences during his imprisonment in the Stockade. However, he is utterly lost when he is outside; and with dreadful irony, when he decides to return and give himself up after deserting, it is the army that kills him. The book at times reads like an exposé, a bitter condemnation, at others as a warm tribute to the comradeship and hardihood the army promotes. It is possible to compare this ambivalent and unresolved attitude with the development of the love affairs in the book. They begin in the exacerbation of sexual desire, become ideals of romantic love, and end ultimately in impermanence and fantasy—Alma's description of Prew's 'heroic' death, the Warden and Karen's mutual deception.

His later works, none of which equal *From Here to Eternity* in stature, include *Some Came Running* (1957), *The Pistol* (1959), *The Thin Red Line* (1962) and *Go to the Widow Maker* (1967). S. R.

Joseph, Michael Kennedy (1914–), New Zealand poet and novelist. His verse, which is characterised by an erudition and wit not common in his fellow poets, can be found in *The Imaginary Islands* (1950) and *The Living Countries* (1959). His prose work *I'll Soldier No More* (1958) has been praised as a most authentic and moving war novel. He has since published *A Pound of Saffron* (1962). S. R.

Joyce, James Augustine Aloysius (1882–1941), Irish-born novelist. 'No man . . . can be a lover of the true or the good unless he abhors the multitude; and the artist, though he may employ the crowd, is very careful to isolate himself.' This, written when Joyce was 20, is a key to his whole literary career, which exemplifies the difficulties as well as the ultimate impossibility of the search for perfection. To isolate himself from the crowd, in one sense, was simple: Joyce never even considered its existence, or tried to palliate the feelings of publisher, printer and public, though this meant delays in publishing almost every book he wrote. However, isolation in itself is not enough: the artistic detachment necessary for the stories in *Dubliners* (1914) brought a clarity of vision which is as clearly conveyed to the reader; but the almost total isolation of the author of *Finnegan's Wake* (1939), who had abandoned not only crowds and critics but the common forms and uses of language itself, results in an obscurity which is incomprehensible except to the dedicated expositor.

In early youth, in Dublin, Joyce was subjected to powerful influences: his magniloquent, feckless father dominated the household, driving it from modest affluence to penury; and from the age of six, for 14 years, Joyce underwent the full rigours of a Jesuit education. For a sensitive and physically fragile child with an introverted personality the effects of both must often have been terrifying, and from *A Portrait of the Artist as a Young Man* (published 1917) there emerges a pathetic picture of Joyce's love for his mother, a gentle artistic woman completely submerged by her husband, and a frightening one of the repressions and coercions of Irish Catholic schools.

But it cannot be denied that he had an excellent education of which he took full advantage. His flair for languages was soon apparent, together with his feeling for European literature. His contempt for a National Irish Theatre which excluded Hauptmann and Ibsen led to his pamphlet *The Day of the Rabblement* (1901). This was ignored by all the champions of the Celtic Twilight (Yeats *et al.*) against whom it was addressed, but it contains the above quotation and is significant in the light of what followed. He would not be contained in the parochialism of Irish culture, and his flight from Ireland was a positive rejection of the forces that stood between himself and a personal aesthetic. He went to Paris in 1902 to live a bohemian life and fill notebooks with observations on Aristotle and Aquinas, Catholicism, poetry and his own analyses of thought.

He was recalled to Dublin for his mother's last illness and death, and spent a year thereafter in the sort of bohemian life that Dublin provided. *Dubliners* was written in this period, and from direct observation. In this sense its stories are, so to speak, the sepia sketches from the album of a painter, and they have the same evenness of tone. They are not, however, sketches in the sense of being unfinished. Each story is an entity, perfectly contained, and each ends at the moment when the story reaches its significant culmination. There is no epigrammatic dismissal, or the lowering of a curtain upon uncertainty. And at the start, when the scene is set and the characters introduced, a subtle use of tense (varying between the imperfect and the perfect) and a deceptive hesitancy give the kind of impression that is long retained, although scarcely felt at the time. Only in the last story, 'The Dead', does Joyce allow himself to imply comment.

At this time his rejection of the influences upon his early life became painful, especially to himself. His chosen companions were the men with fewest illusions, and he lived for a few months with Oliver Gogarty, then a medical student. But in the midst of his attempted self-exile and its loneliness he met the girl who later became his wife, and with her, in 1904, he left Ireland. From then on he lived in Trieste, Paris and Zurich, teaching to keep himself and his family, writing, and waging a long war with publishers and printers to get his books accepted. By the time that *Dubliners* was given to the public, after a delay of ten years, *A Portrait of the Artist as a Young Man* was completed and *Ulysses* begun.

Joyce planned the former as a *magnum opus* which was to be longer than *War and Peace*. A version under its originally intended title *Stephen Hero* was published posthumously in 1944, and is of academic interest, to be compared with its shorter, final version which while not the greatest of Joyce's books is probably the most perfect. Its author's detachment makes it a novel rather than autobiography: though clearly Joyce projected himself in the character of Stephen Dedalus, whose career he depicts from infancy to the moment when he rejects his environment and leaves Ireland—'to forge in the smithy of my soul the uncreated conscience of my race'. Stephen, in Christian history, was the first martyr; Dedalus, in Greek mythology, was the prototype artist. To be an artist, Joyce's Dedalus must virtually martyr himself, and must embrace the three attributes of 'silence, exile and cunning'. The many memorable incidents are so well integrated that the narrative is never interrupted, while observation and imagination combine powerful style with an unsentimental tenderness. It is a book to stir the heart as well as intrigue the intellect. For Joyce the work was cathartic; by writing it he achieved his longed-for isolation. In his succeeding works, the reader too is not required to participate: he has simply to understand.

Ulysses, which was published in Paris in 1922 but not passed by the American censor until 1934 and the English until 1936, is a book with so many layers of meaning, so many dimensions of significance, that whole books have been written on it, and the reader who wishes to appreciate it to anything approaching the full must be referred to exegeses on this scale. However, it must be stated emphatically that for the general reader of moderate intelligence and liberal education it can be understood and enjoyed in good measure.

The title indicates that the book has for a model the Odyssey of Homer, the archetypal comic epic poem in which a wandering husband after many adventures is united first with the son who has set out to find him, and finally comes home to his wife whose fidelity like his own has been tested during their separation. Leopold Bloom, a Jewish advertising salesman, is Ulysses or Odysseus, and Dublin the world of his travels; his wife Marion or Molly is Penelope; and the young man he adopts as his spiritual son, the already familiar person of Stephen Dedalus, is Telemachus. The twenty years of Ulysses' journeying is represented by a period of twenty-four hours, referred to as 'Bloomsday', during which Bloom or Stephen or Molly have experiences which correspond to the twenty-four episodes that make up the books of the Odyssey.

This however is only a framework, a pattern (and there are several other coexistent patterns imposed on the twenty-four episodes): within it is represented, through a process of multiple association and the use of every conceivable literary technique (different for each episode), the totality of human history. Dublin is the world, *Irish history is the history of the human race*, and the characters of the story are mankind. No detail is left to the imagination: every scene, every character, is rendered subtly and precisely. (Bloom, it is often said, is the most complete character in literature.) No person, incident or sensation is redundant; apparently irrelevant parts are sooner or later found to be essential to the whole, while the ordinary and the jejune are invested with symbolic greatness. At the end of *Ulysses*, although the reader is left with a sense of wonder, it is wonder at the magnitude of the work. The exact significance of the 'yes yes yes' at the end of Molly Bloom's soliloquy which concludes the book, sometimes taken to be a passionate affirmation of life, sometimes nothing but lust for an animal form of life which Joyce himself affected to despise (and he had certainly rejected all other schemes of value), is much debated.

Joyce's attempts to indicate different things happening at once (and how else can microcosm be realised?) are attempts to use words (even the words he invented) for something they can scarcely be expected to do; but the measure of his success in conveying implications of one activity while he describes another on a different level (for instance, in the Sirens episode) justifies his use of language and exemplifies his skill. In communicating humanity's diversity he conveys also its defencelessness, which he demonstrates with a clarity that is occasionally painful (it was this that his adverse critics could not bear)—his other principal technique for creating this all-revealing multiplicity being the 'stream of consciousness' method which he used more often, and more profoundly, than any other writer. This method of presenting personality, whereby a continuity of conscious and subconscious thought is actually expressed, with all its non-sequiturs and ellipses, tries the capacity of the writer to the utmost: he runs a course between exposition and, simply, boredom—and Joyce is never boring.

In *Finnegan's Wake* the process repeats itself: the attempt at microcosm, to contain the universe in words, to express the innumerable simultaneously. Where in *Ulysses* the story is given different levels—the actual, the symbolic and the esoteric—here the long dream of a drunken Dubliner is expanded into history and mythology, humanity and the heroic. But here the levels are inseparable: one is contained in the other, so that time and space are given single expression. Unfortunately the expression, though single, is not and cannot by its nature be instantaneous, which was what Joyce strove for. *Finnegan's Wake* is a long book, and the language is compressed until it bears no resemblance to normal English. It is filled with double meanings, puns, references and portmanteau words, elisions of words and their significance, as well as words and phrases from many other languages; every word being charged with Joyce's own precise meaning or meanings. Again, all the reader has to do is comprehend. But he cannot do so without unremitting application, and this alone will not avail without resort to commentary and exegesis. Application is rewarded by certain passages which are, if not entirely comprehensible, appreciable as being of great beauty. Beyond that, the complexity of the pattern prohibits communication, without which art does not exist.

The only possible approach to *Finnegan's Wake* is through the rest of Joyce's work, for it developed from *Ulysses* just as *Ulysses* developed from *A Portrait* and *A Portrait* from *Dubliners*. His work is a monument to its period, one of the finest monuments to a transitional literature which experimented in an age of confusion. With other artists of the time Joyce sought the impossible, both by attempting to assume the rôle of God, which implies absolute solitude and omnipresence, and by subordinating the whole of existence to his medium, the written word; and in so doing he demonstrated the paradox of art, that the nearer it gets to perfection the more it defeats itself. That he should be judged by some to have fallen short of perfection is an indication of his proximity to it.

H. C.; K. R. R.

József, Attila (1905–37), one of the most remarkable poets of modern Hungary, was born in a Budapest slum and spent almost all his life in utter poverty. He published his first volume, characteristically entitled *Szépség koldusa* ['The beggar of beauty'] (1922), at the age of 17. Even then, his mature technique and skilful prosody won him wide recognition, although he was plainly following the earlier Hungarian tradition of Ady (q.v.) and his contemporaries. But his revolutionary spirit, which led him early to Marx, and his inquiring and restless mind, which took him to Freud, soon produced a unique synthesis of these idols of the age. His poem *Tiszta Szívvel* ['With a pure heart'] (1925), with its curt denial of traditional values, caused a furore and earned him dismissal from his studies. He became too revolutionary for the underground Communist Party which expelled him. Never mentally well balanced, he succeeded in committing suicide at the age of 32.

His poetry remains unique—a blend of classically strict form with language varying from the deceptively simple to the surrealist, expressing thoughts that astonish with their sheer beauty, terrifying reality, humanity and morbid introspection. Translations—e.g. *Poems* (ed. T. Kabdebo, 1966), or *Poèmes* (Budapest, 1960)—rarely reflect his creative genius adequately. A sympathetic portrait by Arthur Koestler appears in *Encounter* (May 1954).

G. F. C.

Jünger, Ernst (1895–), German novelist whose reputation rests on the pitiless, nationalistic war-novel *In Stahlgewittern* [*The Storm of Steel*] (1920) and on the *volte-face* of *Auf den Marmorklippen* [*On the Marble Cliffs*] (1939).

R. C. W.

K

Kafka, Franz (1883–1924), German-language writer from Czechoslovakia, was born in Prague of German-Jewish parents. To be a German amongst Czechs was difficult enough; to be Jewish was worse; to be as sensitive as Kafka proved to be in a family dominated by an extrovert father was to be the crowning burden of his tragically short life. His early studies were mainly in chemistry and German literature and language; he took a law degree in 1906, but his literary leanings were obvious. When in 1917 it was confirmed that he was tubercular, he abandoned everything to devote himself to writing in Berlin; but his condition rapidly became worse and he died in a Viennese sanatorium.

This sketch of Kafka's life is in fact the key to his work; his extraordinary sensitivity and his ability to transfer it to writing is apparent in all of his work, but perhaps most of all in the three fragmentary novels which he himself did not publish and the destruction of which he asked in his will. These were *Amerika* ['America'] written in 1912, *Der Prozess* [*The Trial*] in 1914 and *Das Schloss* [*The Castle*] in 1920. *The Trial* deals with a successful bank official who is arrested and put on trial for some offence which is never defined. He is released but lives under the continual threat of re-arrest and punishment, again of an undefined nature. The structure of his personal life disintegrates under pressure and he gradually accepts guilt. The guilt in question seems of a general symbolic kind and applicable to the whole of mankind. The symbolism is never made explicit but is effectively carried forward by Kafka's cold and impersonal language. Finally two shadowy and mysterious agents of the law take the victim to a deserted spot and he passively allows his throat to be cut. At the moment of death he sees a bright shaft of light cut through the night. Whether or not this is a symbol of hope is difficult to ascertain since the fragments of the book were ordered not by Kafka but by a friend.

The brilliance of Kafka's cold and impersonal style is even more apparent in *The Castle*. This is the nightmarish account of the appointment of the hero, K, as surveyor of a castle. When he arrives, however, no one wants him and he is denied admission; and all his attempts to gain entry fail. The book is an elaborate allegoric treatment of the life of man, poised between here and eternity. A significant feature of this novel and also of *The Trial* is the rôle performed by women; they move on a higher plane than man and act as mediators between him and higher things. The first of the novels, *Amerika*, is often considered to be the least satisfying because of its uncharacteristic optimism; but Kafka's friend and literary executor

Max Brod who saw to the publication of all three insisted that Kafka spoke of a tragic ending to *Amerika* when he had completed another novel *Der Heizer* [*The Boilerman*] in 1913.

The son-father conflict is the cardinal feature of *Das Urteil* [*The Verdict*] written in 1916, in which a boy in response to his father's orders drowns himself; and in *Die Verwandlung* [*The Metamorphosis*] written in 1915. This extraordinary long short-story concerns a commercial traveller who wakes up one morning to find that overnight he has been transformed into a gigantic insect, doomed to crawl along the walls and hang down from the ceiling. Yet he can still hear and understand his family, he can still think like a man, but he cannot communicate with them himself. Eating only filth, he becomes an object of horror to his family who leave him to his own devices; and so he spends the hours thinking about the past and especially about the lack of understanding shown by his family to his own yearning for art and beauty. The parallel with Kafka's own life is apparent, for it was his father who made him take up a salaried post at a time when he was actually devoting himself to writing though officially an unpaid lawyer at a law court.

Isolation, frustration, fear and the sense of being rejected are the recurring themes of the fourteen sketches or short stories *Ein Landarzt* [*Selected Short Stories*] published at the end of the first world war. They further dominated *Beim Bau der chinesischen Mauer* [*Great Wall of China*] published posthumously in 1931. In the story after which this collection is named, Kafka seems to argue that man can never know the secrets of his own existence in the world; we are so obsessed with our own experience that we cannot form a synthesis of the collective experience of mankind. Those building the great wall only see the stretch on which they work; they all wait for a message from the emperor in Peking, but it never comes. *Forschungen eines Hundes* ['Research of a dog'] shows flashes of humour; a dog starts to think on food and where it comes from, and tries to work out the relationship between food and his constant need to urinate. Here again, Kafka is probing into the mystery of why man exists in the world.

We are indebted to Max Brod who published Kafka's *Biographie* [*Biography*] in 1936 for much of what we know of his life, and especially his last few happy years living with Dora Dymant. But this love relationship did not alter the fact that Kafka's relations with his father dominated his life and work; indeed Kafka wrote to his father in 1919 'My writings are all about you'. His *Tagebücher* ['Diaries'] covering 1914–23, published posthumously, reveal this also, as well as his feeling of isolation and rejection. The story *In der Strafkolonie* [*In the Penal Settlement*] published in 1919 brought out again the theme of *The Trial*—that the very nature of the world makes it a place of punishment for those who innocently are born to live in it.

Despite the relatively small quantity of his work, and the fact that some of it has never yet been translated, Kafka's influence on the whole of modern European literature has been immense. His writings require a sympathetic approach, but such an approach is amply rewarded.

G. W.

Kantor, Mackinlay (1904–), American novelist, who after more than twenty years of writing achieved a major international success (and a Pulitzer prize) with the monumental *Andersonville* (1955), a story of prison camp life in the American civil war. Among his previous titles are *Long Remember* (1934) and *The Voice of Bugle Ann* (1935); later ones include *Spirit Lake* (1961). K. R. R.

Karlfeldt, Erik Axel (1864–1931), Swedish poet, who was posthumously awarded the 1931 Nobel Prize for Literature, having refused it in 1918. Most of his verse derives its themes from provincial sources and from folklore. Selected poems are available in English in *Arcadia Borealis*, tr. C. W. Stork (1938). R. C. W.

Kasprowicz, Jan (1860–1926), the first great Polish poet of peasant origin. Born in the village of Szymborze in Kuyavia he studied first in Germany, then completed his education himself and eventually gained a professorship in comparative literature at Lwów. There too appeared his first poems *Poezje* (1889), a rough realistic poetry of concrete diction. Subsequent years produced several volumes of verse in which features of realism, lyricism and symbolism revolve around themes drawn from everyday life. With *Ginącemu swiatu* ['To the perishing world'] (1902), his first cycle of hymns, Kasprowicz entered upon his major poetic work. Kasprowicz's symbolism, perhaps the most notable in Polish literature, found its best expression in *Ballada o słoneczniku* ['The ballad of the sunflower'] (1908) where the initial symbol of the sunflower becomes a consensus of associations and interpretations. The collections of poems enclosed in *Księga ubogich* ['The book of the poor'] (1916), a religious and poetic affirmation of everyday life, and in *Mój swiat* ['My world'] (1926), which to a certain degree manifests its continuation, conclude his poetic output. Reflecting a universality of interest in which sentiments and themes are superimposed on an ordered pattern of everyday life, Kasprowicz's poetry constantly exploits to advantage his own social experiences. Never hampered by any constrictions or patriotic inhibitions, it marks a transition from a social to a personal, religious doctrine. A poet and translator writing at the time of Polish neo-romanticism, or more popularly of *Młoda Polska* ('Young Poland'), his ultimate aim was to evolve a sincere poetry of everyday life.

B. M.

Kassil, Lev (1905–), Soviet Jewish writer, born in Pokrovsk (Engels). He is a stylist whose great talents are directed towards writing stories for children. His best-known works are *Dorogiye moi mal'chishki* [*My Dear Boys*] (1948) and *Ranniy voskhod* [*Early Dawn*] (1957). Using the genre of children's literature Kassil has been able to express himself in an especially telling fashion. B. W.

Katayev, Valentin Petrovich (1897–), is a successful Soviet novelist and playwright. He was born in Odessa, the son of a schoolmaster. His earliest literary activity was in the realm of poetry, but after the civil war he began to write prose. He gave some help and inspiration to his brother Yevgeni (see Petrov) and to Ilya Ilf but did not continue the collaboration. His first novel *Rastratchiki* [*The Embezzlers*] (1926) is a picaresque satire, based on the activities of two seemingly respectable Soviet bureaucrats whose elegant tastes require a lot of money, thus causing them to defraud the state. They have a merry trip around Russia, itemising their expenses, before they give themselves up to justice. Katayev's play *Kvadratura kruga* [*Squaring the Circle*] (1928) is a humorous satirical play about the housing shortage and about how two incompatible couples living together find conjugal bliss by exchanging spouses. *Vremya, vperyod* [*Forward, Time*] (1933) is a construction novel written to order, and it is very good. It describes the Soviet Union trying to catch up with the rest of the world by showing how workmen try to break the world record for pouring concrete. *Beleyet parus odinokiy* [*Lonely White Sail*] (1936) is a delightful story of two boys living in Odessa who witness the events of the 1905 revolution. This is the first novel of a tetralogy, the others being *Khutorok v stepi* ['A cottage on the steppes'] (1950), *Za vlast' sovetov* [*For the Power of the Soviets*] (1951) and *Zimniy vetyer* ['Winter wind'] (1960). B. W.

Kaufman, George S. (1889–1961), American playwright, was joint author of a large number of popular successes, his collaborators including Edna Ferber, Ring Lardner, Moss Hart and Alexander Woolcott. Among the best-known are three of his later plays, all with Hart as co-author: *You Can't Take it with You* (1936; Pulitzer prize), *The Man Who Came to Dinner* (1939) and *George Washington Slept Here* (1940). He also worked on the book for the Gershwin musical *Of Thee I Sing* (1931) which won another Pulitzer prize, and was co-author of *The Solid Gold Cadillac* (1952). K. R. R.

Kavanagh, Patrick (1905–67), Irish poet who wrote 'The Great Hunger' (1942), a long poem which tells of the longing of the poorer Irish farming people for life and land. A collection of his poems, *Come Dance with Kitty Stabling*, was published in 1960. P. E.

Kaverin, Venyamin (Venyamin Alexandrovich Zilberg; 1902–), is a Soviet writer who enjoys arbitrarily juggling with the narrative in his stories. In his early novels he dealt in fantasy and adventure and wrote about the dignity of the individual. Such a novel, perhaps his most original, is *Khudozhnik neizvesten* [*The Unknown Artist*] (1931). Afterwards he began to conform to the tenets of socialist realism and he describes an intellectual's adjustment to the new society in *Ispolneniye zhelaniy* [*The Larger View*] (1935). Subsequently, with his trilogy *Otkrytaya kniga—Yunost', poiski, nadezhdy* [*Open Book—Youth, Searches, Hopes*] (1956) Kaverin identifies himself with the modernising trend, consequently incurring sharp criticism for presenting a poor impression of Soviet medical work and research. His short story *Kusok stekla* [*A Piece of Glass*] (1960) explains that people are inadequate unless they have fully rounded personalities, and that the arts will help achieve this result. B. W.

Kaye-Smith, Sheila (1887–1956), English regional (Sussex) novelist and poet, among the best-known of whose novels are *Sussex Gorse* (1916), *Tamarisk Town* (1919), the dramatic *Joanna Godden* (1921) and the outstandingly successful *End of the House of Alard* (1923). P. E.

Kazakov, Yuri (1927–), is a prominent modern Soviet short-story writer who was born into a working-class family in Moscow. He studied at a Moscow music school and then played in jazz and symphony orchestras before attending the Gorky Literary Institute. His literary career began at this time, and despite several adverse criticisms he has remained unscathed and his deeply personal, apolitical short stories have continued to be in favour both in Russia and in the west. It would be difficult to choose any one of his many translated tales as representative, but *Arktur, gonchiy pyos* ['Arcturus—a hunting dog'] (1957), *Dom pod kruchey* ['A house over a precipice'] (1957) and *Goluboye i zelyonoye* ['Blue and green'] (1957) should provide a reasonable selection of work from this talented and colourful author who writes 'with a look into the heart'. A recent collection of his work can be found in *Po dorogye* [*Going to Town and Other Stories*] (1964). B. W.

Kazantzakis, Nikos (1883–1957), a Cretan, perhaps the greatest, certainly the most controversial of modern Greek authors, provocative of both the antagonism of linguists and the consternation of philosophers, studied in Paris under Bergson after graduating in law at Athens. Philosophically his works are all of a piece, all part of one integrated vision and should be read as such, allowing the one to illuminate the others. *Salvatores Dei, Askētikē* [*The Saviours of God, Spiritual Exercises*] (1925), a record of his fundamental attitude, discloses divergent, even antipathetic, borrowings from various sources but is at bottom a mixture of Bergson's ceaseless aspiring creation and Nietzschean tragic optimism. The study of Nietzsche confirmed an instinctive preference for Dionysian involvement yet paradoxically did little to dispel the rival attraction of Apollonian discipline; and everything written by Kazantzakis, the travel journals, the autobiography *Anaphora ston Gkreko* [*Report to Greco*] (1961), the fiction, the poetry and plays, as well as the philosophy, is a reflection of the conflict between these contrary modes of experience and a constant striving for that momentary harmony within a sudden insight, that reconciliation of east and west, that synthesis of incompatibles, of flesh and spirit, which he termed the 'Cretan glance'. In *Bios kai politeia tou Alexē Zormpa* [*Zorba the Greek*] (1946), Zorba, 'the living heart, the large voracious mouth, the great brute soul, not yet severed from mother earth', lives at the opposite pole psychologically to his admiring employer, the narrator, a bookish, withdrawn intellectual in whom the ingenuous desire of uniting two opposed sensibilities, 'of winning both the earthly life and the kingdom of the skies', is rekindled by their relationship.

In *Ho Christos Xanastaurōnetai* [*Christ Recrucified*] (1954) the participants in a Passion play, Greek villagers under Turkish domination, come to identify with their dramatic selves, Jewish victims of Roman oppression. Inevitably, the tragedy is repeated. In *Ho Kapetan Michales* [*Freedom and Death*] (1953), a story of Cretan resistance to Ottoman rule which symbolises the complexity of Turco-Greek relations by the blood-brotherhood of Captain Michales and Nuri Bey, the insurgents equate Crete with Christianity, liberation with the Resurrection; in his last novel *Aderphophades* [*The Fratricides*] (1963) archetypal antipathies adopt contemporary ideologies as Greek fights Greek in the royalist-communist civil war. *Ho phtōchoules tou Theou* [*God's Pauper—St Francis*] (1956), a masochistic realisation of the agony of conversion, the rigours of renunciation and abnegation in a materialistic society, subordinates hagiography to jeremiad. The spiritual tortures of this interpretation may be repellent if one subscribes to the conventional fable but, unlike the torments and transubstantiation of a crypto-Nietzschean Christ in *Ho teleutaios peirasmos* [*The Last Temptation*] (1963), they hardly smack of heresy. In the latter the spirit and the body of the Saviour achieve a synthesis which is apparently obnoxious to dogma and incompatible with Resurrection—yet obviously congenial to the author, for the flesh of Odysseus, too, dissolved and 'the great mind . . . soared high and freed itself from its last cage, its freedom'.

Kazantzakis is famous as a novelist, few people read his poetry. *Odysseia* [*The Odyssey: A Modern Sequel*] (1938), a 33,333-line epic, magnificently translated by Kimon Friar, is one of the glories of modern literature.

M. D. E.

Keesing, Nancy (1923–   ), Australian poet, has experimented with a wide range of verse forms and subject matter, and shows both considerable technical skill and an interesting ironic detachment. She has published *Imminent Summer* (1951) and *Three Men and Sydney* (1955). S. R.

Kemal, Yashar (1922–   ), Turkey's best-known writer. Born in Anatolia, a progressive, politically conscious intellectual well versed in the traditional peasant folk tales and beliefs, he exploits these interests in his novels. The first, *Ince Memed* [*Memed, My Hawk*] (1958), draws on the author's knowledge of Anatolian topography and custom. Slim Memed, the hero, runs away from his tyrannical village overlord, Abdi Agha. He is recaptured but vows to liberate his cowed fellow-villagers. Eventually he elopes with his sweetheart Hatché, the Agha's nephew's betrothed, fails to promote a village rebellion, becomes an outlaw and, Hatché dead, vanishes into legend. *Ortadirek* [*The Wind from the Plain*] (1960), his second novel, recounts the fortunes and adventures of Taurus mountaineers who every year go down to the plains for the cotton harvest in order to augment their meagre income. Kemal has adopted the form of the novel whereas his affinity is with the great sweep and verve of the folk epics, an oral tradition which still flourishes from Yugoslavia to Siberia. When judged by contemporary west European standards, his plots are simple, direct, conventional, the dialogue often stilted, the construction often flawed, but his heroes and their legendary exploits are firmly rooted in the living Turkey. These novels are as much history as fiction and *Ince Memed*, at least, can be read as political allegory. Their attraction lies in Kemal's ability to convey the atmosphere rather than the verisimilitude, their absorption and value in the variety and accuracy of observation, character and incident. M. D. E.

Kennedy, Margaret (Lady Davies; 1896–   ), English novelist, author of the best-seller *The Constant Nymph* (1924). Albert Sanger, *avant-garde* composer, dies in his Swiss mountain chalet, leaving a wild family (mistress and seven children). Florence Churchill, daughter of a Cambridge don, arrives to sort out their affairs, and meets and marries Lewis Dodd, a bohemian young composer. Their social attitudes prove incompatible and Lewis finally runs away with Theresa Sanger, whose love and sympathy has remained constant since childhood. The book's real theme is the clash between the idealistic single-minded artist and the humanist who for social reasons will compromise with such integrity.

Later novels include *Red Sky at Morning* (1927), *Troy Chimneys* (1953; James Tait Black Memorial Prize) and *Women at Work* (1966). G. C.

Kerouac, Jack (1922–   ), American beat writer, is primarily a novelist. His prose is best described as spontaneous in the sense that Cassavetes's film technique (as in the film *Shadows*) is spontaneous. To accuse Kerouac of making his characters amoral and selfish to the point of narcissism is to miss the point that he is focusing on the culminating issues of a society which amidst the stifling pressures of conformity remains dedicated to individualism, whether commercial or personal. Kerouac's prose echoes the long loose line of the beat poets, and he has often been accused of lack of organisation: but here one must bear in mind Henry Adams's prophecy, fifty years before, that art must be chaotic to reflect the chaos of life. Kerouac's books include *On the Road* (1957); *The Subterraneans* (1958); *The Dharma Bums* (1960); *Big Sur* (1962); and the retrospective *Desolation Angels* (1966). D. L. P.

Kessel, Martin (1901–   ), German writer, studied widely in literature, music and art at Berlin, Munich and Frankfurt before settling down in Berlin in 1923. Two years later his first published poems *Gebändigte Kurven* ['Smoothed curves'] (1925) won him critical acclaim. They revealed extraordinary linguistic skill and precision; within a year they were followed by the four short stories published under the title *Betreibsamkeit* ['Activity'] (1926) three of which later appeared under the title *Eine Frau ohne Reiz* ['A woman without charm'] (1929). These stories were ironic in treatment, a characteristic developed more fully in the novel *Herrn Brechers Fiasko* ['Herr Brecher's fiasco'] (1932) which appeared in the early thirties. Set in the advertising agency of a Berlin insurance company, it tells how one employee decides to obtain power in some field; he becomes the staff manager and succeeds in having a critical and intelligent colleague dismissed. Kessel's home town is also the scene of *Die Schwester des Don Quixote* ['The sister of Don Quixote'] (1938) completed just before the war, which deals with the way in which a painting is achieved, and at the same time describes in a masterly prose the love of a painter for his beautiful model. The high moral tone of Kessel's writing is in the best traditions of German literature, particularly exemplified in *Essays und Miniaturen* ['Essays and miniatures'] (1947) published shortly after the war. It is because of this that he has been awarded several highly prized German literary awards. G. W.

Keyes, Frances Parkinson (1885–   ), American novelist, had written stories ever since she was a child, but her first novel *The Old Grey Homestead* was not published until 1919. In 1920 she began the first of her articles from Washington, the forerunner of *Letters From a Senator's Wife* (1924), and since then she has written a succession of best-selling novels. Drawing on her experiences as a senator's wife her novels present a rich kaleidoscope of the American scene, as in *Senator Marlowe's Daughter* (1933) and *Joy Street* (1950). She has a gift for narrative, which makes all her novels eminently readable. Her other works include *All That Glitters* (1941), *The Royal Box* (1954) and *The Explorer* (1965).

K. M. H.

Keyes, Sidney (1922–43), English poet, who combined the symbolism of European poets such as Rilke with the English Romantic tradition. He had produced some remarkably fine mature work, entirely unobscure, by the time of his death at the age of 20. His *Collected Poems* were published in 1944. H. C.

King, Francis (1923–), English novelist, poet and travel writer. Among his titles are *So Hurt and Humiliated* (1959), a volume of short stories; *The Dividing Stream* (1951), a story set in contemporary Florence about the problem of human isolation in situations where the barriers are racial, intellectual, financial or temperamental; *The Man on the Rock* (1957), a novel of modern Greece, the central character of which is a parasitical but charming young man; and *The Last of the Pleasure Gardens* (1965), the tragic story of a mother's obsession with the mentally defective child of her middle age. P. E.

Kinsella, Thomas (1927–), Irish poet, whose publications *Another September* (1958) and *Downstream* (1962) show him to be an eloquent, serious, sometimes morbid writer, with a flair for violent and apocalyptic scenes and for the precise evocation of atmosphere. G. C.

Kipling, Rudyard (1865–1936), English poet and novelist. Kipling was born in India but educated in England as a young child. He returned to India when he was 17 and took a post on *The Civil and Military Gazette* of Lahore, subsequently becoming editor of *The Allahabad Pioneer.* He married and settled in Vermont, U.S.A., in 1892, returning to live in England in 1897. He turned down the post of poet laureate in 1895 but accepted the Nobel Prize for Literature in 1907.

During his time as a journalist he published numerous short stories, mainly of the impact of India on the English living there. These stories, if not profound, are shrewd and perceptive, and technically brilliant. Published volumes of them include *Plain Tales From the Hills* (1886) and *The Phantom Rickshaw* (1889). Their formal qualities in terms of character and drama can be judged from the ease with which they were turned into successful television playlets in 1965.

Kipling's popular poetry is very well known. The simple ballad style, the colloquial language, the catchy phrases, caught on both with the people he wrote about and with the English audience at home. It can be said that he made poetry available to the soldier and to the man in the street; that he conveyed a fairly realistic picture, if sometimes romantic, of an India remote to the English public and to all classes within that public. *Departmental Ditties* was published in 1886 and *Barrack Room Ballads* in 1892, the latter describing British army life throughout the empire and containing 'Gunga Din', 'Danny Deever' and 'Mandalay'. These were followed by *The Seven Seas* in 1896. There is another more traditional aspect of Kipling's poetry which complements the ballad form and is rich in a romantic sense of time past and of pastoral beauty. 'The Way through the Woods' from *Rewards and Fairies* (1910) illustrates this:

You will hear the beat of a horse's feet,
And the swish of a skirt in the dew,
Steadily cantering through the misty solitudes
As though they perfectly knew
The old lost road through the woods . . .
But there is no road through the woods.

A selection of Kipling's poetry with an introduction by T. S. Eliot was published in 1941.

Kipling's novels and stories, possessed of a forceful sense of adventure, appeal strongly to children. *Kim* (1901) is the story of Kimball O'Hara, an Irish orphan, who journeys all across India with a Tibetan lama, pursuing a mystic river. In his journeying, romantically and patriotically, he serves the British secret service. The two *Jungle Books* (1904 and 1905) contain delightful animal stories. *The Just So Stories* for children were published in 1902.

Kipling's popularity with children is partly a product of his simple patriotism, which makes for clear and unequivocal value judgments about the rôle of the English in the empire—and consequently about the heroes of the books. He is, of course, now recognised as a representative figure of an outmoded jingoism and of the doctrine of the Englishman's right to rule; and it can be argued that throughout his work he neither plumbs the depths of human personality nor, in the fullest sense, has genuine poetic insight. Eliot's view, however, is that the apparently precocious and superficial judgments that the writer makes, however lucidly, both in prose and verse may be related to the nature of short-story form and ballad form; and that what counts with Kipling is not the lack of oblique intellectual sophistication but his ability to catch at physical and emotional reality. What he indisputably has, in poetry and prose, is a combination of verbal craftsmanship and sharp perception which enable his writings to exude the real smell of the whole Indian sub-continent; and these, together with his eloquence, romantic sense of adventure and patriotism, give his writing its particular flavour. D. L. P.

Kirst, Hans Hellmut (1914–), German novelist, born in East Prussia, was caught up in the tide produced by the rise of national socialism and from 1934 was both a soldier and party member, having, in his own words, 'confused national socialism with Germany'. Interned for some time after the war, he later worked as a manual labourer before obtaining employment as a film critic. His first work *Wir nannten ihn Galgenstrick* ['We called him gallows bird'] (1950) was based on the officers' plot to assassinate Hitler in 1944; *Sagten Sie Gerechtigkeit Captain* ['Did you say justice, captain'], also published in 1950, describes the conflict between the demands of justice and of retribution in an American internment camp for high-ranking officers. *Aufruhr in einer kleinen Stadt* ['Riot in a small town'] appeared the following year, but it was *08/15 heute* [*8.15 Today*] (1955) which won him acclaim at home and abroad. A trilogy, its central character is Gunner Asch, and we trace the decline of the German army from immediate pre-war years because of the overimportance attributed to 'secret weapons'. This trilogy has been translated and published individually as *The Strange Mutiny of Gunner Asch*, *The Return of Gunner Asch* and *Gunner Asch goes to War*. Kirst finds his greatest strength in a fast-moving plot, and together with a keen and cool appraisal of the German military machine, this has made him extremely popular. *Fabrik der Offiziere* [*Officer Factory*] (1960), *Kameraden* [*Brothers in Arms*] (1961) and *Die Nacht der Generale* [*Night of the Generals*] (1962) have continued to support his popularity. G. W.

Klyuyev, Nikolai Alexeyevich (1887–1937), Russian peasant poet, the remarkably finished quality of whose verse had a strong influence on Sergei Yesenin. His best works are *Lenin* [*Lenin*] (1924) where he expresses his faith in the revolution; and *Derevnya* [*The Village*] (1927) and *Plach o Yeseninye* [*Lament for Yesenin*] (1927) where he shows his disappointment in its anti-peasant nature. After this none of his work was published in the U.S.S.R. B. W.

Knox, Ronald (1888–1957), English writer, was converted to Roman catholicism in 1917 and retired from a distinguished ecclesiastical career to make a new translation of the Vulgate. He has written many works of much theological significance and some in lighter vein such as *Essays in Satire* (1928) and *Let Dons Delight* (1939). He is also author of several detective stories of great ingenuity including *Footsteps at the Lock* (1928) and *The Body in the Silo* (1933). His *Barchester Pilgrimage*, a parody, continues the adventures of the Trollope characters as far as 1934.

P. E.

Koestler, Arthur (1905–), Hungarian-born writer, who became a British subject in 1945. Koestler was a journalist and popular science writer in the Germany of the twenties and thirties, during which time he lived in Palestine for a period, and became a communist (1931). *Arrow in Blue* (1952) is an autobiography covering his childhood and early life; *The Invisible Writing* (1954) deals with the seven years he spent as a communist. Koestler's experiences while held under sentence of death by the fascists in the Spanish civil war are recorded in *Spanish Testament* (1938); *Scum of the Earth* (1941) portrays a period of internment as a refugee in France at the beginning of the second world war.

The best-selling *Darkness at Noon* (1941) is a detailed study in fictional form of the fate of political prisoners during Stalin's savage purges and is based on Koestler's interpretation of the Moscow trials. The novel is concerned with the fate of Rubashov, an old Bolshevik commissar, who is forced to confess to treason of which he is innocent. His fate is treated by the author with a sympathy which contrasts with the harsh descriptions of Soviet bureaucracy. The prison scenes owe a great deal to Koestler's own incarceration at the hands of Franco's fascists. *Darkness at Noon* is in fact the middle volume of a trilogy, begun by *The Gladiators* (1939) and ending with *Arrival and Departure* (1943)—dealing with the ethics and ethos of revolution (and of politics in general) and focusing on the question of whether ends justify means. Rubashov drives with ruthlessness for the Ideal State of rational formation, but the route of singleminded ruthlessness fades the reality of the ideal; whereas in *The Gladiators* Spartacus has doomed his revolution because his retained ideals deny sufficient ruthlessness in action. Both attitudes end in tragedy. At the end of the latter book Fulvius, a lawyer henchman of Spartacus, has nothing left of dignity but to empty his bladder before crucifixion; similarly Rubashov empties his before being taken from his cell and beaten to death.

During the 1950s and 1960s Koestler's writing became predominantly philosophical and reflective. Capital punishment is examined in *Reflections on Hanging* (1957). *The Lotus and the Robot* (1961) is a comparative study of eastern and western thought which deals with the tensions created in India and Japan by their experiencing technological revolutions without the three centuries' change in spiritual and intellectual climate undergone in the west. *The Sleep Walkers* (1959) is concerned with man's creative processes and argues, especially in terms of the scientific revolution of the sixteenth and seventeenth centuries, that scientific discovery is an inexact and almost aesthetic process. After an introduction dealing with Greek and mediaeval European thought Koestler follows the sometimes accidental creative activities of Copernicus, Kepler, Tycho Brahe, Galileo and Newton. He indicates, for example, that many of Kepler's correct conclusions about the movement of the planets were based on a sequence of balancing mistakes and inaccurate assumptions. D. L. P.

Kohner, Frederick (1905–), Czech-born American writer of screen and stage plays, best-known for *Gidget* (1957) which inspired a wave of similar 'surfing' comedy-romances that became extremely popular in America and to a lesser extent in Europe. P. E.

Kops, Bernard (1926–), English playwright and novelist, became known with *The Hamlet of Stepney Green* (1956), which draws its inspiration from Kops's East End Jewish upbringing and environment, particularly in its treatment of the relationship between the Stepney 'Hamlet' David Levy and his mother and in its sentimental reversal of the catastrophe of the original. David's father's 'ghost' appears, revenge is mooted, and eventually a 'poison' is drunk: but the latter turns out to be a love potion, and all ends in human warmth and affirmation. Kops's novels include *The Dissent of Dominick Shapiro* (1966). K. R. R.

Kožík, František (1909–), Czech writer of biographical novels. His *Největší z pierot ů* [*Pierrot*] (1939) is about the French mime Jean-Baptiste-Gaspard Debureau (1796–1846), a native of Bohemia. K. B.

Krige, Uys (1910–), versatile South African Afrikaans-language writer: of poems, short stories, plays, reportage, essays, criticism, translations. He has rendered many of his own and other Afrikaans writers' poems into English as well as translating from Spanish and French into Afrikaans, and has published translations and adaptations from poems and songs in indigenous African languages. *The Dream and the Desert* (1953) contains, *inter alia*, stories culled from his wartime experiences. C. P.

Krleža, Miroslav (1893–), Yugoslav novelist, dramatist, short-story writer, essayist and poet, and with Ivo Andrić (q.v.) one of the outstanding figures of Yugoslav literature. His first published works were poems written during and immediately after the first world war. In the period between the two wars he was extremely active in all fields of literature, and identified himself with the aims of the revolution. He became a prominent personality in Tito's Yugoslavia, and his speech at a writers' congress in 1952 urging freedom of development for the arts had considerable influence on the cultural climate of the country. Essentially, Krleža's fictional works are devoted to portraying his native town Zagreb and its surroundings, analysing the conditions of Croatia from the beginning of the twentieth century to the present day. A series of ballads in the local dialect prove the extent of his involvement in the district of his birth. Krleža is an extremely prolific writer, a man of great erudition, and a bitter critic of the social injustices of pre-war Croatia, which he saw as decayed and corrupt. His ideas are vigorously expressed in the series of prose pieces and plays *Glembajevi* ['The Glembays'] (1936), describing the downfall of a family which bases its struggle for success and status on a crime. Members of the family achieve position as bankers, but their blood is tainted and they are drawn irresistibly to violent and immoral acts. The same theme of decay in civilisation is fundamental to Krleža's three novels: *Povratak Filipa Latinovicza* [*The Return of Philip Latinovicz*] (1932), a novel of alienation and wasted talent; *Na Rubu Pameti* ['On the edge of reason'] (1938), describing the revolt of a Zagreb lawyer against his corrupt and superficial surroundings; and *Banket u Blitva* ['Banquet in Blitva'] (1938–9), a portrait of Croatia set in the imaginary country of Blitva. Krleža has written numerous essays, critical works and prose pieces since the war. His style is torrential, forceful, linguistically rich, and contains passages of great lyricism. C. W.

Krog, Helge (1889–), Norwegian playwright. At first a dramatic critic, he produced his first successful play, a social satire, in 1919. Irony, wit and satire, sometimes tender, sometimes mordant, are the hallmarks of all his plays, of which several are available in English: *Three Plays* (trans. Roy Campbell, 1934) and *Break-Up and Two Other Plays* (trans. Margaret Linge, 1939). R. C. W.

Krymov, Yuri (Yuri Solomonovich Beklemishev; 1908–41), Soviet novelist who was killed during the second world war. His novel *Tanker Derbent* [*Tanker Derbent*] (1938), despite its apparently conforming to the stringent demands of socialist realism, actually utilises this method to describe the personal problems involved in the life and work on a Soviet oil tanker. It also encompasses the attitudes to socialist competition—Stakhanovism—in its account of the crew shipping oil on the Caspian Sea. B. W.

Krymov, Vladimir Pimenovich (1878–), is an émigré Russian writer whose work has been sympathetically received in English translation. In Russia Krymov had been the editor of an illustrated journal *Stolitsa i*

Usad'ba and was on a world cruise when the Russian revolution broke out. Unable to return home he eventually settled in Paris and produced many interesting novels. Among his most notable work is the trilogy *Za millionami* [*Out for a Million*] (1926) of which the first part *Sidorovo uchenye* ['Sidorov's apprenticeship', trans. as *Out for a Million*] is probably the best known. The other parts are *Khorosho zhili v Peterburgye* [*He's got a Million*] and *D'yavolyonok pod stolom* [*The End of the Imp*]. In 1940 he began to write an entertaining melodrama set in pre-revolutionary Russia, full of well-drawn characters though lacking a real villain; this eventually appeared as the novel *Fienka* [*Fienka*]. B. W.

Kuprin, Alexandr Ivanovich (1870–1938), Russian writer of the first two decades of this century. His education at a cadet school and his life as an officer in the imperial army left an indelible impression on him. His experiences provided material for his best novel, *Poyedinok* [*The Duel*] (1905), which exposes the senseless brutality and sadism of army life. The novel was enormously popular as were his shorter stories: these included *Shtabs-kapitan Rybnikov* [*Captain Rybnikov*] (1906), concerning the unmasking of a Japanese spy; *Granatoviy braslet* [*The Bracelet of Garnets*] (1911), a romantic tale about the love of a poor clerk for a lady of high society; and *Yama* [*The Pit*] (1915) which deals crudely yet sentimentally with prostitute life in Odessa. Kuprin's undoubted talent was generally dissipated in too many directions and he often did not possess sufficient stylistic ability to achieve his purpose. His émigré writings are of little importance. B. W.

L

La Capria, Raffaele (1922–   ), Italian novelist, columnist and translator. He combines novel-writing with diverse contributions to journals and newspapers and work in the field of broadcasting. His outstanding novel *Ferito a morte* [*The Mortal Wound*] (1961), which won him the Strega literary prize, depicts the conflicting emotions and reminiscences which overwhelm Massimo De Luca on the day of his leaving his home town, Naples, to take up a job in Rome. There is also an English translation of La Capria's earlier work *Un giorno d'impazienza* [*A Day of Impatience*] (1952). D. B.

Lacerda, Alberto de (1928–   ), Portuguese poet and the outstanding figure among the younger generation of poets in Portugal. Born and reared in Mozambique he migrated to Lisbon in 1946, where he studied French and English for five years. In 1947 his first collection, *Ponte Suspensa* [*Suspension Bridge*] was accepted by Pessoa's publisher, but the enterprise was frustrated by the latter's death. In 1951 Lacerda 'escaped' from Portugal to visit England, making a certain impact, and one of his poems was consequently published bilingually in *Encounter* in 1953. In Portugal again, he particularly impressed Roy Campbell who made an unfulfilled promise to translate his poems. At long last in 1955 there appeared in London Lacerda's first publication in book form, a bilingual edition entitled 77 *Poems*, with translations by Arthur Waley. This comprised both *Ponte Suspensa* and a second series entitled *Aventura* [*Adventure*]. The work was at once hailed as a remarkable success. Subsequent collection include *Palácio* ['Palace'] (1961) and *Exílio* ['Exile'] (1963); further series await publication. Lacerda's melodious verse is essentially mood poetry, few of his delicate compositions exceeding twenty lines, while many are far shorter. One consists of one line: 'Mastro suspenso sem mar e sem navio' ('Mast suspended without sea and without ship'). His imagery is always relevant, sharp and economically executed with a minimum of adjectives. Particularly effective in their evocation are the last sixteen poems of *Exílio* which were written on his return to Mozambique in 1963. R. C. W.

Ladipo, Duro (1920–   ), Nigerian playwright whose genre is the Yoruba folk opera. His *Three Yoruba Plays* (1964) are translations of poetic drama in the restrained classical mode, based on Yoruba mythology, legend and history. C. P.

Lagerkvist, Pär (1891–   ), Swedish novelist, playwright and poet. An Academician, he was awarded the 1951 Nobel Prize for Literature. His earliest literary attempts reveal the strong influence of the Fauvist and Cubist trends prevalent in French art in the second decade of the twentieth century, and his collection of poems *Angest* ['Anguish'] of 1916 is a typical example of the French reaction against naturalism. All his work reveals him as a profound humanist, an earnest champion of human ideals and endeavour and as one who rejected systematic metaphysics for a vague mysticism. These traits are evident both in his novels and in his plays, of which all the major works are available in English. His credo was first expressed in the semi-autobiographical novel *Gäst hos verkligheten* [*Guest of Reality*] (1925) and was magisterially proclaimed through his two most successful novels *Dvärgen* [*The Dwarf*] (1944) and *Barabbas* [*Barabbas*] (1950). The former presented the allegory of Renaissance Italy as seen through the eyes of an evil court dwarf, while the latter offered a realistic evocation of the early years of the Christian era, projected through the experiences of the hounded and hardened protagonist questing for a noble ideal. *Barabbas* was also the subject of a successful film. Three of Lagerkvist's plays are also available in English: *Mannen utan stjäl* [*The Man without a Soul*, in *Scandinavian Plays of the Twentieth Century*, series I] (1936), *Den befriade människan* [*Let man live* in *Scandinavian Plays of the Twentieth Century*, series III] (1939) and *Midsommerdröm på fattighuset* [*Midsummer Dream in the Poorhouse*] (1941). R. C. W.

Lagerlöf, Selma (1858–1940), Swedish author and Academician, winner of the 1909 Nobel Prize for Literature. A native of the Swedish province of Värmland, she was reared with a deep veneration for its folklore and traditions and came to reject the late nineteenth-century techniques of realism and naturalism. Her reputation was established by her first work, *Gösta Berlings saga* [*Gösta Berling's Saga*] (1890–94), which ran into many editions and has been widely translated. Marred only by the influence of the style of Carlyle, this saga based on Värmland legends known since her childhood won her a renown second only to that of Hans Andersen in this genre. Drawing her inspiration and plot from the past and writing with an essentially Romantic simplicity, she urged a return to the themes of atonement and reconciliation and sought an equation of happiness and goodness. In 1895, with financial aid from the monarchy, she made a prolonged visit to Italy to acquire new themes for her talents and at the turn of the century a second journey took her to Egypt and Palestine, the product of which, her two-volume novel *Jerusalem* [*Jerusalem*] (1901–2), brought her world renown, though many earlier collections of her tales and stories were already circulating widely in translation. A further highly successful work was a state-commissioned school reader, *Nils Holgerssons underbara resa genom Sverige* [*The Wonderful Adventures of Nils; Further Adventures of Nils*] (1906–07), which described the magical flight of a little boy through Sweden. In translation it was used as a school text as far away as the United States. The essential fact about Selma Lagerlöf is that as a teller of homely tales and stories which cherish traditional virtues her appeal extended not only to children but also to generations of adults.

R. C. W.

La Guma, Alex (1925?–   ), South African novelist and short-story writer who produced *And a Threefold Cord* (1965), an outspoken attack on *apartheid*, while he was under house arrest in Cape Town. He earlier published *A Walk in the Night* (1962), a brilliant cinematic anatomy of slum-life in Cape Town's District Six. S. R.

Lambert, Gavin (1924–   ), English novelist and writer of screenplays, including that for the film based on his own novel *Inside Daisy Clover* (1963). This is the touching and often wildly funny story told in the first person by a young girl who is built up to be a Hollywood star. His other books include *The Slide Area* (1959), a picture of the fantastic world-within-a-world that is Hollywood; and *Norman's Letter* (1966), a novel in letter-diary form portraying an English upper-class gentleman of uncertain parentage, eccentric connections and extraordinary circumstances.

P. E.

Lamming, George (1932–   ), Barbados novelist whose first two books, *In the Castle of my Skin* (1953) and *The Emigrants* (1954), seemingly trace the course of his own life. The former is set on or near Barbados and features U-boat and trade-union campaigns against the island's military and social establishment; while the latter follows the West Indians to London—Mecca and El Dorado in one. *Of Age and Innocence* (1958) and *Season of Adventure* (1960), both set on the fictitious San Cristobal, are simultaneously more overtly political and more introspectively personal and metaphysical. Lamming's works are characterised both by their passion, power and poetry and by their rich earthy humour and deep sympathies. C. P.

Lampedusa, Prince Giuseppe Tomasi di (1896–1957), Italian novelist and Sicilian nobleman whose literary reputation was established posthumously. His literary testament consists of two works, *Il Gattopardo* [*The Leopard*] (1959) and *Racconti* [partially translated as *Two Stories and a Memory*] (1961). The novel *Il Gattopardo* was a brilliant international success and carried off the 1959 Italian Premio Strega. Its impact was intensified in that it was published shortly after critical accounts of wretched social conditions in Sicily by Danilo Dolci and Carlo Levi. Particularly interesting is its highly sensual evocation of decadent nineteenth-century Sicily in its description of weird betrothals, of love affairs legitimate and illicit, of banquets and junketings, of Sicilian cuisine. The whole novel is deeply rooted in a Proustian world of death and decay. The most significant piece in *Racconti* is the first story, *Il Mattino di un mezzadro*, which was really intended to be the opening chapter of a second novel to be entitled *I Gattini ciechi* ['The blind kittens'], a modern sequel to *Il Gattopardo*, in which would be illustrated the passage from nineteenth-century decadence to twentieth-century destruction. R. C. W.

Lane, Jane, pseudonym of Elaine Kidner (1905–), English historical novelist and biographer. She wrote her first novel at the age of seventeen, but her first successes came with *Undaunted* (1934) and *Be Valiant Still* (1935). She is now an established writer, and is at her best when writing about the Stuarts and the turbulent times in Scotland during the seventeenth century, as in *Farewell to the White Cockade* (1961), the story of Bonnie Prince Charlie. She has also written several very popular children's books dealing with the same period, such as *Escape of the King* (1950) and *Trial of the King* (1963). Amongst her biographies, *Titus Oates* (1949) is the most scholarly and the best known. K. M. H.

Langfus, Anna, Franco-Polish novelist who received the Prix Goncourt in 1962 for *Les Bagages de sable* [*The Lost Shore*]. Marie, a young Polish refugee living in Paris, meets an older man who shares her feeling of loss, and they go together to the Riviera. Marie refuses his advances and associates instead with a group of adolescents. A member of the group, a young girl, commits suicide and the shock drives Marie closer to Michel Caron; but the latter finds he cannot sustain the emotional stress, writes to his wife, and Marie leaves, hoping that some day she will be able to escape time and human contact. Anna Langfus has also written *Le Sel et le soufre* [*The Whole Land Brimstone*] (1960). D. E. A.

Langley, Noel (1916–), South African-born novelist. His light, satirical novels include *Cage Me a Peacock* (1935), *There's a Porpoise Close Behind Us* (1936) and *Hocus Pocus* (1942). In similar vein are a number of plays and screen plays produced mainly in America.

R. A. K.

Larbaud, Valéry (1881–1957), French man of letters and literary xenophile, wrote much of his *Journal* ['Diary'] (1912–35) in English. He championed, among others, St John Perse, Svevo, Joyce, Faulkner, Borges, Güiraldes,

Alfonso Reyes, Azuela, Eça de Queiroz, and Ramón Gómez de la Serna. He claims a minor poet's fame, vicariously, through the addictive charm of his *alter ego* A. O. Barnabooth, especially in *Poèmes par un riche amateur* [*Poems of a Multimillionaire*] (1908) and *A. O. Barnabooth, son journal intime* [*A. O. Barnabooth, his diary*] (1913). M. D. E.

Lardner, Ring (1885–1933), American humorist. Lardner wrote his first really successful story for the *Saturday Evening Post:* it was about a baseball novice and called 'You Know Me Al; A Busker's Letter'. His style is cynical, colloquial, bitter and behind the humour lies disillusion with the characters portrayed—the ordinary people of America. Lardner's published work includes *Bib Ballads* (1915); *The Love Nest and Other Stories* (1926); and a play written with George Kaufman, *June Moon* (1929), which stingingly attacks the American song-writing business. D. L. P.

Larkin, Philip (1922–), English poet and novelist. Larkin's poetry relates to his own personal life in a provincial setting. For this reason he has been attacked by writers like Charles Tomlinson for ignoring the cultural heritage exploited by Eliot and Pound. Larkin was educated at the King Henry VIII School at Coventry and St John's College, Oxford. He is a librarian.

Larkin's concern is with life. Part of his reaction against the post-symbolist school of writing is in his rejection of the obscurity of much of the symbolism employed and his feeling that poetry should examine man and nature rather than turn inward to contemplate art itself. His work has been compared with that of Auden but in fact he has less intellectual breadth and greater sensitivity and formal technical elegance. He is closer to Hardy, if more compassionate, in his feeling of futility and melancholy at the pointless suffering in life. Larkin's language is skilfully controlled in its transitions from the colloquial to the speculative and meditative. The probing development of 'Church Going', published in Conquest's anthology *New Lines*, has been compared with the meditative weight of Wordsworth's 'Tintern Abbey'. In the poem 'Wants' Larkin sums up sadly and with resignation the substance of his philosophy:

> Despite the artful tensions of the calendar,
> The life insurance, the tabled fertility rites,
> The costly aversion of the eyes from death—
> Beneath it all, desire of oblivion runs.

Larkin's published work includes three volumes of verse, *The North Ship* (1945), *Poems* (1954) and *The Less Deceived* (1955); and two novels, *Jill* (1946) and *A Girl in Winter* (1947). D. L. P.

Lartéguy, Jean (1920–   ), French novelist, took a degree in history and became secretary to the historian Joseph Calmette. He enlisted in the army in 1939, escaped from France in 1942 and fought in the Free French forces, in Korea and in Indo-China. His novels are a mixture of fiction and reporting, many with the same background of the armed forces engaged in colonial wars: *Les Centurions* [*The Centurions*] (1960), *Les Mercenaires* [*The Mercenaries*] (1961) and *Les Prétoriens* [*The Praetorians*] (1961), his three best-known novels, being set against the wars in Indo-China, Korea and Algeria respectively. These novels are very popular, partly because of their topicality for the French, to whom they explain much of recent French history, and partly because of their easy-to-read semi-journalistic style, which is unpretentious and makes no attempt at 'literature'; the publication of *Les Centurions* being an especially great success. Lartéguy's other titles include *Du sang sur les collines de la Margeride* ['Blood on the hills of Margeride'] (1954), the original version of *Les Mercenaires*; and *Le Mal Jaune* [*The Yellow Peril*] (1962). D. E. A.

Lavrenyov, Boris Andreyevich (1891–   ), Soviet writer who began his career as a poet but soon began to publish romantic idealised war stories. He had a tendency to leave the tedium of everyday life for the realms of fantasy, yet he did sometimes deal with contemporary problems. This is evident in his tale about art, *Gravyura na deryevye* [*The Wood Engraving*] (1928), and in his play about radio propaganda *Golos Ameriki* [*Voice of America*] (1949). His best-known work is perhaps *Sorok perviy* [*The Forty-First*] (1958), which was filmed. B. W.

Lawler, Ray (1921–   ), Australian playwright who achieved an international reputation with his first play, *The Summer of the Seventeenth Doll* (1957). Two aging Queensland cane-cutters Barney and Roo come to town during the 'lay-off' to spend their earnings in a wild spree with their girl-friends, as they have done every summer for sixteen years. The play describes, with a sureness of touch that blends the raucous, the sad and the tired grey moments of reality, the failure of their romantic and escapist illusion (that they are heroically tireless in their labours, and timelessly happy in their leisure) to sustain the quartet this seventeenth summer. His next play *The Piccadilly Bushman* (1959), not so widely acclaimed, concerns an Australian actor who, after a period in England during which he eradicates his accent, returns to star in a film and suffers a very mixed reception. S. R.

Lawrence, D. H. (1885–1930), is widely accepted as one of the major novelists in the English language. It is ironic that his name became a household word largely on the strength of his least satisfactory novel *Lady Chatterley's Lover*, a book whose sensational career has tended to obscure the fact that his writings have long appeared in the English Literature syllabuses of British universities and have subsequently become recognised as school texts. Any apparent anomaly in this situation will disappear if it is realised that, amongst other things, Lawrence was a nature poet; and that his writings are full of an intense worship of nature in all her aspects—from the petals of a flower and the skin of a snake, to the highways and byways of the sexual instinct. It was his lot to burst on the scene at a time when human sexuality was more often repressed or debased than celebrated.

Like other nature poets, Lawrence was something of a seer; and like most seers, a preacher. In his early masterpieces his vision is embodied in human dramas that speak for themselves; later, the reader too often hears the voice of the preacher. It was not enough, he came to feel, to express in art his vision of the state of man: he had also, like Freud, to preach salvation—through self-knowledge, and the redemption of the repressed instincts.

David Herbert Lawrence was born into a Nottinghamshire collier's family, the fourth child of a mother who had earlier been a schoolteacher. From his writings we may picture the young D. H. Lawrence growing up in an industrial environment that was harsh and often de-humanising, and in a family where the miner's rough ways could inflict pain on his more sensitive wife and children. But we also find a childhood and youth enriched by the experience of a natural world not yet completely smothered, and by an increasingly close relationship with his mother.

He won a scholarship to the local grammar school, and later became a pupil teacher. In 1906 he entered University College, Nottingham, and in 1908 became a teacher in Croydon. At this time he was writing energetically, and mingling with a bohemian set in London; but he was already afflicted with ill-health, which led him to resign his post in 1911. The same year saw the publication of his first novel, *The White Peacock*, a lightweight pastoral distinguished by passages of much lyrical beauty. It was well received, and enabled Lawrence to earn his living as a writer thereafter.

Two years later he published the largely autobiographical *Sons and Lovers*, probably his most widely read book up to the time of the 'Lady Chatterley' controversy of 1960. It appeared in 1913, the year of his mother's death, and a year after he had met the woman who was to be his wife. The novel opens with the marriage of Arthur Morel, a miner whose physical vitality and spontaneity have captured the love of a sensitive woman from a higher social stratum. Both husband and wife are prototypes for a series of Lawrence characters—of men who are 'nature's aristocrats', and of women who (at least for a time) find fulfilment in relationships with them, a satisfaction that their bourgeois counterparts are unable to provide. The detailed treatment of the early lives of the Morels' first two children can make much of the first part of the book seem slow-moving; but the disintegration of the marriage—through the suffering inflicted on Mrs Morel by the coarser side of her husband's nature, and through the deterioration in his own character that results from his consequent growing sense of inferiority—is Lawrence at his best.

However, the main interest in the book is the growing-up of Paul, the youngest child, and his experiences as a son and a lover. His relationship with his mother is especially close, in proportion to her increasing estrangement from her husband, and it overshadows both of the love affairs of his adolescence. Miriam, his first love, is a dreamy romantic girl whose ethereal demanding ideals leave no room for physical sex. Harriet, his second, already embittered by an unsuccessful marriage, has built up a hard unsympathetic exterior, but when Paul breaks through it she is able to offer him a passionate physical relationship. In each case, however, Paul's mother, intensely jealous, is able to hold him and retain his love; and in her last illness we see the immense depths of his love for her.

If the death of his mother, like that of Paul Morel's in *Sons and Lovers*, was a key event in Lawrence's life, his marriage to Frieda Weekly, née Von Richthofen, was another. Time and time again we are reminded in his novels (and in poems such as 'Manifesto') that the finding of the right marital partner is of supreme importance; for Lawrence himself the 'one woman' happened already to be married, albeit unhappily. She, like the most famous of Lawrence's heroines, was unsatisfied by the intellectuality of the relationship with her husband, a Nottingham professor, and of the circle in which they moved: unlike Connie Chatterley (and others), she deserted him for a man whose completeness as a human being made life-long union possible. For this union they paid a price in social ostracism—reflected in the poem 'Look we have come through'—and for much of the two years before their marriage in 1914 they travelled abroad, beginning a series of migrations that were to furnish Lawrence with much material for his later novels, stories and poems.

His next two novels, however, *The Rainbow* (1915) and *Women in Love* (1920), which are generally regarded as his best work, are firmly rooted in England. They were originally conceived as one work, to be entitled 'The Sisters'; and in their final form they still have a superficial continuity, in the lives of the two young women Ursula and Gudrun Brangwen. But *The Rainbow* is concerned with three generations of the Brangwen family, beginning with the sisters' grandparents; while *Women in Love* centres on the two men with whom they are in love.

To the uninitiated, *The Rainbow* is the more readable. Its title may be taken to indicate a journey from the known to the unknown, with the overtones of promise that the symbol acquires from its Biblical associations. The journey, and the promise, relate as much to England as a whole as to the Brangwen family—the progressive broadening of human horizons (culminating in Ursula's entry into a teacher training college) being set against the evolution of a pastoral society into an industrial one. Indeed, purely as social history the book is outstanding. The idyllic early chapters invite comparison with Hardy; but Lawrence, for all his awareness of the dehumanising elements of industrial life, does not mourn the passing of rural England. Rather, he sees the industrial revolution as a liberating force, creating the potentialities for Will, in the second generation, to be an independent artisan, and for Ursula, in the third, to become a teacher.

If personal fulfilment is one of the chief themes of *The Rainbow*, a second is the need for a balance between independence and dependence in personal relationships; and this, with the idea of the need for 'otherness', becomes the principal theme of *Women in Love*. Total self-surrender, ecstatic though it may be, involves a destruction of the integrity of the individual; and the forging of a bond with another free person—implied in the union of the first-generation Tom Brangwen with the Polish widow Lydia (whose foreignness is a symbol of her 'otherness')—is seen as a higher achievement than the complete fusion of personalities in an ecstatic oneness.

Women in Love presents the long, and finally successful, struggle of Rupert Birkin, an itinerant school-inspector, to achieve such a balanced relationship with Ursula, counterpointed by the frenzied and disastrous affair between her sister Gudrun and Gerald Crich, a colliery owner. The occupations of the two men may be taken as symbols of detachment and domination respectively—the exertion of, and submission to, power being the key to the failure of Gerald and Gudrun, as well as to that of the domineering Hermione Roddice in her love for Rupert. In *Women in Love* Lawrence's technique is more intellectualised than in any other work; the themes being presented symbolically throughout, with the succeeding chapters consisting of a sequence of significant events rather than a continuous narrative. To many readers it is his finest book, though it is not one that is easy to read.

The Rainbow, which was banned, had evoked a storm of protests—'a monotonous wilderness of phallicism' was the *Daily Mail's*, verdict—and with the volume of persecution Lawrence was now encountering, both on the grounds of his elopement and of the supposed obscenity of his frank treatment of sex, he and Frieda chose to leave the country in 1919. The places they lived in are reflected in the novels that Lawrence wrote in the

1920s—*Aaron's Rod* (1922) is set partly in Italy, *Kangaroo* (1923) in Australia, and *The Plumed Serpent* (1926) in New Mexico. While adding little to his previous achievement, they explore more fully some of the themes of the earlier masterpieces. *Aaron's Rod* centres on the need to 'give oneself, but not give oneself away'—i.e. without violating one's own personality; *Kangaroo* takes up again the theme of power as something demonic (as in the Gerald-Gudrun relationship in *Women in Love*), and also the question of man-to-man relationships (as previously explored by Rupert and Gerald) and the wider field of political action; and in *The Plumed Serpent* we encounter again those 'dark gods', of unreason and self-annihilation, that Lawrence has so often been accused of worshipping (here embodied in the ancient Mexican gods), but whose 'mindless sensuality' he has already unequivocally rejected in *Women in Love*.

All these novels are marred by Lawrence's tendency to sermonise; and this becomes a major defect in his last novel, *Lady Chatterley's Lover* (1928). Here, maddened by the fate of his books at the hands of a false puritanism, still in exile, and sickening fast from tuberculosis, Lawrence to some extent set out deliberately to challenge and shock his contemporaries, to 'burn out' their shame; and the exquisitely beautiful descriptive passages (many of them expurgated in the only editions legally available for the next thirty years) must be taken in conjunction with much crude pulpitry. Also, the overall thesis of the novel is extreme and over-simplified: for all the aptness of the image of the waist-down paralysis of Clifford Chatterley as a symbol of the intellect-dominated life Lawrence deplored, it is scarcely credible that his highly intelligent wife should find lifelong fulfilment in a relationship with her gamekeeper that does not extend beyond the purely physical. (Perhaps it should be added that the famous four-letter words are of minimal importance, and belong to an abortive attempt to redeem their currency.)

More satisfying artistically than any of the novels since *Women in Love* are the short stories and poems. Tales like 'The Woman Who Rode Away', 'St Mawr', 'Sun', and poems like 'Snake' (and many other flower and animal poems), 'Fidelity' and 'Ship of Death', have an artistic purity that make them rank with his greatest works. Also very readable are his travel books—and, for those wishing to probe further, his letters. K. R. R.

Lawrence, T. E. (Thomas Edward Lawrence; 1888–1935), English writer. Lawrence was born at Tremadoc, Caernarvonshire, and educated at Oxford High School and Jesus College, Oxford. From 1912 to 1914 he worked in Egypt as an archaeologist.

The Seven Pillars of Wisdom (1926) is a massive testament to his organisation of the Arab guerrilla opposition to the Turks in the first world war. Quite apart from the exciting narrative there emerges a finely drawn picture both of the politics of the Arab world and of the macchiavellian activities of the Allies. Lawrence refused both a V.C. and a knighthood because he felt keenly that the British had broken their pledge to the Arabs for expedient motives. *The Seven Pillars of Wisdom* is given extra dimensions when seen in terms of Lawrence's own pervading personality; at one level he is acting out a consistent philosophy of life, at another he is manifesting a series of inwardly turned and almost masochistic psychological tendencies. An abridged version of the book, *The Revolt in the Desert*, was published in 1927.

Lawrence sought anonymity by enlisting in the ranks of the post-war Air Force under the name of Shaw. The diaries he wrote during this period are published under the title of *The Mint* (1955). He was killed in a motorcycle crash. D. L. P.

Lawson, Henry (1867–1922), Australian writer of bush ballads and of countless short stories, for many people the classics of the Australian bush. He is best known for his portrayal of that elusive quality, Australian mateship—a kind of unspoken, understated comradeship which illumines the rather gloomy struggle for survival. Most of his stories and poems concern the outback and its characters—the drover, the farmer on the small selection, the swagman and the gaunt bushwoman and her scrawny children. His most famous stories 'The Drover's Wife', 'The Loaded Dog' and 'Water Them Geraniums' illustrate perfectly his combination of farcical incident, lugubrious humour and vivid characterisation.

Most of his writings are now assembled in *The Prose Works of Henry Lawson* (1957) and *Poetical Works of Henry Lawson* (1947). S. R.

Laxness, Halldór Killjan (1902–), Icelandic author of six major novels and many minor works. He is a member of the wealthy Gudjónsson family but changed his name to Laxness after one of the family estates. Among his literary honours are the 1953 Stalin Prize for Literature and the 1955 Nobel Prize for Literature. He published his earliest work at the age of 17, before embarking on a ten years' tour of Europe and the United States. In 1923 a stay of several months in a Luxembourg monastery brought about his conversion to Roman Catholicism, with which, however, he gradually became disillusioned. More lasting in its effect was his meeting with Upton Sinclair in 1929, which caused him to adopt an ideology little short of communism. These intellectual struggles are sharply reflected in his early writings. In 1930 he returned to Iceland to pen the two volumes of his first major novel, *Þú vínviður hreini* (1931) and *Fuglinn í fjörunni* (1932), which are collectively available in English under the title of *Salka*

Valka. Much maturer than his earlier works, *Salka Valka* gained him national and international recognition as a major novelist. A detailed and markedly leftist study of an Icelandic fishing village, its folk, their hardships and privations, it has been widely translated. A further novel, *Sjálfstaett fólk* [*Independent People*] (1934–35), enhanced his reputation as Iceland's leading twentieth-century literary figure. Though this was sternly criticised in some quarters for its strong left-wing viewpoints, Laxness has continued to assert that he is 'a leftist socialist, not a communist'. *The Fish Can Sing* (1966), was his most recent novel to appear in English translation. R. C. W.

Laye, Camara (1924–), West African writer in the French language, was born in Upper Guinea but lived for a time in Paris before returning to Africa. He wrote *L'Enfant noir* [*The Dark Child*] (1955), a lyrical and fond account of his childhood. This was followed by *Le regard du roi* [*The Radiance of the King*] (1956), a symbolic story of a white man's adventure on his quest for a 'king' who would provide a solution to all his problems. S. R.

Leacock, Stephen (1869–1944), Canadian writer. Born in England but brought up in Canada, he combined a career as an immensely prolific and popular humorous writer with an equally successful life as an economic historian at McGill University. His writing, most of it in brief essays or anecdotes which reflect his popularity as a public lecturer in an age before radio or television, range over the whole spectrum of light humour. Included in such collections as *Literary Lapses* (1910), *Nonsense Novels* (1911), *Further Foolishness* (1916) and *The Garden of Folly* (1924) are literary spoofs, comic monologues, extended puns, tales of the simple man bemused and baffled by the world around him, and light verse. Sometimes he is seen as the descendant of the North American frontier wit deflating sophisticated pomposities, and at others as the forerunner of Thurber and Perelman. Much of his humour has come to seem dated and laboured, but *Sunshine Sketches of a Little Town* (1912), which pokes gentle fun at the small Ontario town in which he spent his summers, has remained popular. K. W.

Leavis, F. R. (Frank Raymond Leavis; 1885–), English critic. Leavis has probably left the most marked effect on English literature of any critic in this century. His editorship of *Scrutiny* (1932–53) evolved a completely new concept of literary criticism that influences, still, every university department of English in the country. It marked a swing away from the analysis of character in literature, marked by Bradley and attacked by

Leavis's colleague L. C. Knights in his essay 'How many children had Lady Macbeth'. Leavis is concerned with the close analytic study of texts, with the work itself and not with the personality or intentions of the author. He is involved with moral criteria and the moral effect of a work of art upon society. Consequently he has become the outspoken champion of novelists like George Eliot, Henry James and D. H. Lawrence.

With Leavis there is no room for compromise. His style is as tough as his mind. It is awkward rather than elegant but the awkwardness is a reflection of exactness. He gives no quarter to the mediocre: hence his attacks on some literary figures. There is no question but that his work is required reading by serious students of English literature, whatever their critical views. His publications include *New Bearings in English Poetry* (1932); *Revaluations* (1936); *The Great Tradition* (1948); *The Common Pursuit* (1952); and *D. H. Lawrence, Novelist* (1955). D. L. P.

Le Carré, John (David Cornwell; 1931–), English novelist, educated at Sherborne, Berne University and Lincoln College, Oxford. At one point in his career he taught at Eton and from 1960 to 1964 was in the foreign service. His thriller novels are noted for their depth of insight into real human personality and motivation as opposed to the slick superficiality of the run-of-the-mill, best-selling spy story. In Le Carré's best-known book *The Spy Who Came In from the Cold* (1963) the hero Leamas is sent to East Berlin on a mission throughout which he is continually deceived by his own employer, the British secret service. The latter is seen as ruthlessly manipulating real, living, breathing human beings to the advantage of some obscure and abstract policy. The novel sheds the glamour of the spy world and depicts it as extraordinary only in relation to the ordinariness, ugliness or squalor of its inhabitants. Leamas dies disillusioned with the players on both sides of a manipulative game which ignores the genuine needs of human individuals. Other novels include *Call for the Dead* (1961), *A Murder of Quality* (1962) and *The Looking Glass War* (1965). D. L. P.

Le Clézio, Jean-Marie Gustave (1931–), Anglo-French novelist who achieved fame in 1963 with the publication of *Le Procès-verbal* [*The Interrogation*], followed in 1965 by *La Fièvre* [*Fever*], a collection of eight short stories. His descriptions of the world are detailed and often horrifying, particularly in *La Fièvre*; the physical world is felt in an oppressive way as a very real component of his philosophy. He has also written the novels *Le Déluge* [*The Flood*] (1966) and *Terra amata* ['Terra amata'] (1967), and the theoretical essay on the novel *L'Extase matérielle* ['Material ecstasy'] (1967). D. E. A.

Lee, Harper (1926–), American writer, won a Pulitzer prize for her beautifully written novel *To Kill a Mockingbird* (1961). Set in the race-conscious South, it recounts the stand against injustice (and in particular the unsuccessful attempt to save a Negro from wrongful conviction for rape) of a white lawyer and his two small children. The book is made specially appealing through the part played by the children, who are themselves victimised by those who hate their father and who, despite his efforts to protect them, identify themselves completely with his stand.

K. R. R.

Lee, Laurie (1914–), English poet. Lee was born in the west country, and educated at Stroud Central School. Early in the second world war he helped to make films with the G.P.O. and the Crown Film Unit; during the latter part he was in the Ministry of Information. In 1951 he was involved with the Festival of Britain, and was awarded the M.B.E. in 1952.

Lee's poetry is ostensibly simple, lyrical and pastoral, possessed occasionally of rich imagery and always motivated by a traditional romanticism. The form is undeniably elegant but the lyrical is simple often only with the apparent simplicity of sophistication. There emerges a strong dramatic sense interfused with descriptive passages of nature which can border on sensation; as with the following extract:

> Blown bubble-film of blue, the sky wraps round
> Weeds of warm light whose every root and rod
> Splutters with soapy green, and all the world
> Sweats with the bead of summer in its bud.

Lee's verse publications are slim volumes containing only a limited number of fairly short poems. They include *The Sun my monument* (1944), *The Bloom of Candles* (1947) and *My Many Coated Man* (1955). A play written for the B.B.C. has been published—*The Voyage of the Magellen* (1948)—and to a wider audience he is known for the best-selling *Cider with Rosie* (1959), a volume of tales of rural life, based on his own childhood experiences—tales of intimacy with nature, of eccentricity, primitive violence, and 'the first bite of the apple'. D. L. P.

Lehmann, John (1907–), English man of letters, brother of the novelist Rosamund Lehmann, is best known as the editor of a succession of influential literary journals, including the left-wing *New Writing* in the late 1930s, and the contemporary *London Magazine*. His own writings include the autobiographical *The Whispering Gallery* (1955) and *I am my Brother* (1960). K. R. R.

Lehmann, Rosamund (1903–), English novelist, has occupied a minor but consistently distinctive position in the English literary scene for some forty years. A recurring theme in her early novels (e.g. *Dusty Answer*, 1927; *Invitation to the Waltz*, 1932) is the emotional and mental awakening of a young woman as she grows up and passes through various key events (e.g. college, love, first party etc.). The later novels, which are generally both weightier and technically more elaborate (e.g. *The Ballad and the Source*, 1945; *The Echoing Grove*, 1953), are more often concerned with the mature woman in love—though the events in the former (spanning three generations of a family) are recorded as they are experienced by a fourteen-year-old girl. K. R. R.

Lemelin, Roger (1919–), Canadian novelist, whose portrayals of French-Canadian working-class life, written with humour and tenderness but without false sentiment, have been equally popular in the original French and in English translations. Lemelin's first novel *Au Pied de la pente douce* [*The Town Below*] (1944) won France's Prix de la Langue Française, and *Pierre le magnifique* [*In Quest of Splendour*] (1952) was awarded the Prix de Paris. *Les Plouffe* [*The Plouffe Family*] (1948) became the basis for a weekly Canadian television serial, written in both French and English by Lemelin. K. W.

Leonov, Leonid Maximovich (1899–), is a Soviet novelist and poet of distinction. Born in Moscow of peasant stock, he later accompanied his self-taught poet father into exile in Archangel where the country produced an indelible impression on him. He left his studies at Moscow University uncompleted and later served for three years with the Red Army in the civil war. He began his literary career in the 1920s by writing some poetry and short stories, the latter being published and thereby determining Leonov's future path. He developed his considerable talent for prose and in 1924 he wrote his first novel *Barsuki* [*The Badgers*] in which he describes the problems of the early years of the revolution as they are faced by two brothers who find themselves on different sides. Leonov presents a sympathetic view of the 'Greens' who sided with neither the Reds nor the Whites.

Leonov was greatly influenced by Dostoyevsky. This can be seen in his novel *Vor* [*The Thief*] (1927) which is perhaps his best work. Set against the background of the New Economic Policy (NEP), it traces the degeneration of a Red Army officer into a gangster and the promise of his eventual reforming. Leonov painted a whole gallery of types who were taking advantage of the NEP period, which Leonov considered a betrayal of the revolution. Among his other works are *Sot* [*Soviet River*] (1929), a tale of industrialisation, and *Skutarevsky* [*Sabotage in the Electrical Industry*] (1932) which he wrote as his contribution to the five-year-plan. *Doroga na okean* [*Road to the Ocean*] (1936) is a not particularly successful novel dealing with Soviet idealism.

Leonov wrote a number of plays the best of which is perhaps *Nashestviye* [*The Invasion*] (1943), of interest because it has a non-communist for its hero. His subsequent short novel *Vzyatiye Velikoshumska* [*The Taking of Velikoshumsk*] (1944) evolves around the crew of a Russian tank, but is very bitty. During the 'thaw' Leonov produced his *Russkiy lyes* [*Russian Forest*] (1953) as well as a revised version of *The Thief* which removed much of the author's earlier sympathy for the hero. *Russian Forest* has an abundance of nature descriptions as well as a complicated plot. It is interesting to note that despite the literary demands of officialdom the villain's case is as well represented as the hero's. B. W.

Lera, Angel María de (1912–), Spanish novelist. He is the author of several major novels of which the second, *Los clarines del miedo* [*The Horns of Fear*] (1958), and the third, *La boda* [*The Wedding*] (1959), are available in English. *Los clarines del miedo,* which probed the problems of the minor bullfighter living amid rural society, established Lera as a major novelist with an unusually perceptive eye for sociological phenomena; it has subsequently been translated into seven languages.

More gripping, though less widely acclaimed, was *La boda,* the story of a traditional riotous hullabaloo accorded to a widower on the night of his second marriage; the climax is reached in the middle of the night with the unintended deaths of the widower and his former rival's brother. It was not until his sixth novel, *Hemos perdido el sol* ['We have lost the sun'] (1963), that Lera finally fulfilled his early promise by producing a great national novel. It deals with Spain's greatest contemporary social dilemma, the temporary emigration of hundreds of thousands annually to seek higher salaries abroad, their disillusionment on return and the danger that for many a second emigration would be permanent. R. C. W.

Lessing, Doris (1919–), Rhodesian novelist, based in England since the publication of her first book *The Grass is Singing* in 1949. She has since written more novels (including a sequence, begun with *Martha Quest,* 1965, that has the overall title *Children of Violence*), some volumes of short stories (of which *Five* won the Somerset Maugham award in 1953), two plays, and two factual reports on life in Rhodesia and Britain: *Going Home* (1959) and *In Pursuit of the English* (1960).

The Grass is Singing is set in Rhodesia and deals with a white farmer, his wife, and their African servant. It is a remarkable first novel—clearly using the author's experience, but without the common restrictions of this sort of first novel. It shows a strong social and political concern, but again without the limitations this might imply: the novel is primarily about individuals and their failings. In various ways it looks ahead to her later books and especially to *The Golden Notebook* (1962) which is her masterpiece and is a sort of digest of, and commentary on, all her work to date. It is about a woman writer, Anna, who is trying to sort out all of her experience into a novel: the book consists almost entirely of Anna's separate notebooks, in which she sets down her experience and thoughts under different headings. She fails in the end to create the novel: her life (and by implication modern life in general) is too complex, and to impose a pattern would be to falsify it. Anna meets a gradual frustration not only in her writing but in her relationships with men, her work for the Communist Party, the education of her daughter, all her social activities. There are long sections set in Africa, recalling *The Grass is Singing*, and many direct echoes of her intermediate work, while the last section of the book formed the material for her second play, *Play with a Tiger* (1960). *The Golden Notebook* is a comprehensive, honest, and in a way desperate book and one which marked a culminating point in the development of Miss Lessing's work.

Her short stories, whether of medium length as in *Five*, or shorter as in *The Habit of Loving* (1957), are perhaps the best by an English writer since D. H. Lawrence. C. B.

Levi, Carlo (1902–), Italian writer, journalist and painter. The son of a merchant and amateur painter, he was trained to become a medical practitioner, but soon gave up his career as a doctor to exhibit his paintings, often in one-man shows in Italy and abroad. Levi, whose painting is clearly connected with his human interests and reflects his experiences both of everyday life and of his writing, has also concerned himself with sociological and political issues, and found himself from the early 1920s on the side of those Italian intellectuals who, at home and abroad, opposed the newly-born fascist movement and subsequent régime. He was persecuted by the fascist authorities and interned for nearly a year in a small village in the south of Italy. Levi's existing concern for the social conditions and the backwardness of those areas was thus enhanced and he gave a detached, serene account of his experiences in his work *Cristo si è fermato a Eboli* [*Christ Stopped at Eboli: the Story of A Year*] which rapidly won him an international reputation. This book, which was written in 1944 but not published until the year after, presents a stark picture of the life of a Basilicata village which had constantly remained outside the influence of Christian civilisation (hence the title): its people bear the marks of centuries of indifference and neglect, and their resigned yet dignified behaviour arouses the sympathy of Levi who can detect the unspoilt charm of an ancient civilisation. The life and problems of the local population are viewed against the general background of the wider issues confronting the deprived areas of southern Italy. Since this success Levi has published several more books: *Paura della libertà* [*Of Fear and Freedom*] (1947), an ideological essay throbbing with unusual insights and unorthodox views, was followed in 1950 by *L'orologio* [*The Watch*], set in Rome in the uncertain period following the liberation, a remarkably lively book though somewhat obscure in its appraisal of post-war Italian politics. Levi's journeys to other parts of Italy and to foreign countries have inspired a series of books relating impressions of his travel: *Le parole sono pietre* [*Words are Stones: Impressions of Sicily*] (1955) was written after a visit to Sicily, *Il futuro ha un cuore antico* ['The heart of the future lies in the past'] (1956) after a visit to the Soviet Union and *La doppia notte dei tigli* [*The Two-fold Night: A Narrative of Travel in Germany*] (1959) after a visit to the booming Germany of the post-war period.

D. B.

Lewis, Alun (1915–44), Welsh-born poet and short-story writer, writing in English. His attitudes are very much a product of his Welsh environment. He grew up in a depressed mining area, becoming resentful of the destructive effects both of industrialisation and of the narrowing impact of puritanism on the old vigorous non-conformism. He became an uncertain pacifist, and equally uncertainly joined up in 1940, to be killed four years later in a shooting accident.

Lewis is a war poet of some stature. Whereas Owen, Rosenberg and Sassoon wrote savagely from the trenches of the first world war, Alun Lewis accurately recorded the weary rootlessness of army life and of soldiers who have not yet faced the enemy. In 'All Day it has Rained' from the volume *Raider's Dawn* (1942) he captures a weary emotion from a soldier's life, almost time out of life, as he considers people and events far removed in place from the training he is engaged on:

> . . . Yet thought softly, morosely of them, and as
> indifferently
> As of ourselves or those whom we
> For years have loved, and will again
> Tomorrow maybe love;

The reality of war breaks in at the end of the poem where he thinks of the poet Edward Thomas:

> . . . till a bullet stopped his
> song

Both his stories and poems develop from the expression of this rootlessness to an exploration of almost Platonic metaphysical values in the life beyond death. 'Almost a Gentleman', a short story in the volume *The Last Inspection* (1942), simply shows the army reflecting the class system in its rejection of a potential Jewish officer; but the poem 'The Jungle' from *Ha! Ha! Among the Trumpets* published only two years later in 1944 shows a very remarkable development in attitude and maturity, with Lewis searching here for universal human values and perhaps finding them in the consummation of death:

> Then would some unimportant death resound
> With the imprisoned music of the soul?
> And we become the world we could not change.

Other published work includes *Letters from India* (1946) and *Selected Poetry and Prose* (1966) introduced by Ian Hamilton. D. L. P.

Lewis, Cecil Day. See **Day-Lewis,** Cecil.

Lewis, C. S. (Clive Staples Lewis; 1898–1963), English critic, poet, Christian polemicist and science-fiction novelist. The greater part of his working life was spent as an Oxford don, apart from the last few years when he was professor of mediaeval and renaissance English literature at Cambridge. His conversion to Christianity in the early 1930s is described in *Surprised by Joy: The Shame of my Early Life* (1955) which relates the growth of his faith as a primarily intellectual process. Lewis is well known for his widely read essays on Christian problems and especially for *The Screwtape Letters* (1942) which represent the problems of sin from the point of view of a trainee devil. In literary criticism *The Allegory of Love* (1936), a study of the mediaeval courtly tradition, and *The Discarded Image: an Introduction to Mediaeval and Renaissance Literature* (1964) show him as a humane mediaevalist, and a critic feeling to the centre of the literature of that period.

Lewis also wrote brilliant science fiction which he used as the vehicle for allegories of good and evil. The trilogy consisting of *Out of the Silent Planet* (1938), *Perelandra* (1943) and *That Hideous Strength* (1945) is successful in that it develops a compelling narrative line without the use of the detailed technical material usually involved in the 'science' part of science fiction. Lewis makes no attempt to investigate the mechanical functioning of spacecraft or computer: rather his hero battles symbolically with the encroachment of evil on an unspoiled Venus. The climax of the trilogy coincides with the sinking of a whole northern university town into an earthquake brought about by the manifestation of the evil of misused scientific discovery.

Lewis wrote a number of imaginative books for children, the best known being concerned with the magic land of Narnia. These enclose a world of talking animals, magical events, friends bound together by adventure and above all allegory combined with a strong moral sense. Titles include *The Lion, The Witch and The Wardrobe* (1950) and *Prince Caspian: The Return to Narnia* (1951).

Lewis's poetry was usually published under the pseudonym of Nat Whilk (N.W.). *Poems* (1964) contains the bulk of the author's revised verse.

D. L. P.

Lewis, Norman (–   ), English novelist and travel writer. His close knowledge of Spain gives depth to *The Day of the Fox* (1955), a novel as formal and precise in its construction as the strict Catalan codes of behaviour that it depicts. The central figure, a strong and simple fisherman shunned by the villagers for his accidental 'heroism' during the civil war, is victim of a series of misunderstandings and ironies of fate, all of which are due to the villagers' avoidance of verbal communication in favour of a more primitive reliance on signs or the interpretation of appearances. So in a life already harsh, the tragedies multiply; these, Lewis shows, are the result of the great complexity and intractability of the so-called 'simple life'.

The success of this novel was echoed by that of his next, *The Volcanoes Above Us* (1957). Other titles include *Sand and Sea in Arabia* (1938), *Within the Labyrinth* (1950), *The Tenth Year of the Ship* (1962) and *A Small War Made to Order* (1966), this last being a witty spy story which serves as a devastating attack on the American Central Intelligence Agency and its handling of the abortive Bay of Pigs invasion of Cuba in 1961.

S. R.

Lewis, [Harry] Sinclair (1885–1951), American novelist. Lewis is one of the outstanding American novelists of the period after the first world war. In 1930 he won the Nobel Prize for Literature having previously turned down the American Pulitzer Prize for *Martin Arrowsmith* (1925). Lewis was born in Minnesota, in the mid-west. He was educated at Yale where his brilliance was eccentric but recognised.

Essentially his novels describe the small towns of the mid-west which he knew so well, but more than this they satirise the whole concept of the American way of life and indeed the materialism of western civilisation, Like the eighteenth-century English satirists Lewis attacks a set of attitudes from within. He is part of the world he depicts; not an outsider trying to tear down the whole framework but an insider trying to isolate the destructive elements in a structure with which he is in fundamental sympathy.

Lewis believed in progress; he was in sympathy with liberal individualism but like Coleridge he realised that economic and material individualism are not necessarily complementary to the organic growth of human personality. In *Main Street* (1920) Carol Kennecott has a superficial and undigested cultural ethos which is inadequate to cope with people who are more bourgeois than agrarian in their material concepts of the 'worth' of the countryside, who are vulgar in manner because of the one-sided materialism of their outlooks. She is a half-educated human being failing to impress the superficial on the gross.

The novel opens with Carol at college, coming for the first time into an awareness of the twin problems of marriage and career. With her liberal education she wishes to dedicate herself to some challenging and socially useful rôle; and after a period in a public library which fails to satisfy her aspirations, she settles for marrying a bluff doctor from the small mid-western town of Gopher Prairie, believing that her life's mission will be to bring her college-acquired liberal cultural ideals (civic improvement, semi-sophisticated social life, amateur involvement in the arts, and generally progressive social thinking) to its deprived inhabitants. Much of the novel is taken up with her fruitless endeavours in these various directions—with hopes momentarily raised only to be dashed again, as the complacent, inhibited, joyless townspeople retreat into their smug, self-frustrating mediocrity and narrowness. The result of this process is that Carol herself becomes increasingly like them (as she discovers to her horror when she visits the metropolitan background of her adolescence); and when, following a temporary escape in the form of an extended tour, she finally rebels and goes to live in Washington, it is only a matter of time before she realises that she does not belong there: that she has become at last a citizen of Gopher Prairie.

In *Babbitt* (1922) Lewis draws a figure who is basically likeable and potentially human but the essence of whose personality is lost in a commercial stereotype. Lewis feels that the rapid growth of science and industry have made size and material wealth the criteria which the mediocre man transforms into a sense of ultimate value. Babbitt lives in a world of illusion where he wishes to feel that the individual pursuit of money, of buying and selling, has some correlation with early American frontier independence. Individualism has become identified with some abstract economic code of jungle warfare which ignores personality to concentrate on size. Babbitt's tragedy is his total lack of self-knowledge. He identifies the profit motive with community service, and greed with doing good for one's neighbour.

In *Martin Arrowsmith* is to be found a translation, to some extent, of Lewis's own personality. It is an easy novel to read and contains a main character who does battle with the compromises and false values of the American medical profession. Arrowsmith wishes to attain a real ideal of service to the community; in Leona his first wife, is drawn in depth a picture of a truly feeling human being. For the novelist, Arrowsmith and his wife, both as human beings and as doctor and nurse, are concerned to harness science and technology to the real needs of man. The novel is in epic form, covering the development from youth to mature manhood.

These are three novels which seem to catch at the central problem of western civilisation: how to engage the impersonal economic and material growth of an industrial and scientific age with a real understanding of what individual human personalities are and need.

Other novels include *Elmer Gantry* (1927); *The Man Who Knew Coolidge* (1928); *Dodsworth* (1929); and a sequence of progressively less successful later titles including *Cass Timberlane* (1945), *Kingsblood Royal* (1947) and *World So Wide* (1951.) D. L. P.

Lewis, [Percy] Wyndham (1882–1957), English novelist, painter, essayist and poet. Lewis like Jean Cocteau was a man who spread his genius over a number of artistic occupations, slightly diluting his talents in the process. He was born in America, and educated at Rugby and the Slade School of Art. Before World War I he was chiefly known for his painting, and as a vorticist—a vague term applicable to a radical attitude to life and art in the days preceding such movements as cubism, expressionism and surrealism. A number of Lewis's paintings hang in the Tate Gallery. Between 1914 and 1915 he edited *Blast* with Ezra Pound and was associated with Pound, Eliot and Joyce in an anti-romantic movement. His first autobiographical work *Blasting and Bombardiering* (1937) describes both the latter period and his life in action in the second part of World War I. *Self-Condemned* (1954) describes in fictional form his life on emigration to Canada in 1939. *Rude Assignment* (1950) is a fuller autobiography.

As a novelist his work is aggressive and satirically devastating. The best-known novels are *Tarr, the Apes of God* (1918) and the trilogy *The Human Age* issued between 1928 and 1955. *Tarr* deals dramatically with a group of students of mixed nationalities in Paris. Lewis uses the book as a vehicle to attack German romanticism and militarism. The trilogy, consisting of *The Childermass* (1928), *Monstre Gai* (1955) and *Malign Fiesta* (1955), is a satiric epic written in a surrealistic and obscure style dealing with a journey through a fantastic and macabre heaven. Lewis's fascism, of which Roy Campbell was a disciple, comes out strongly in *Rotting Hill* (1951), a novel attacking a degenerate Britain under post-war socialism.

The poetry, notably *Poems* (1933), is cast in the same aggressive, satiric mould but is a less effective medium than the prose:

In any medium except that of verse
Forthwith I could enlighten you. Too terse,
And as it were compact, this form of art. . . .

So you will understand that argument,
Except in intent stylistic, or to invent
A certain pattern, is out of question here.

Lewis's critical essays include *The Demon of Progress in the Arts* (1954).

D. L. P.

Libedinsky, Yuri Nikolayevich (1898–1959), is a Soviet writer whose early works tried to portray sympathetically the workings of the Communist Party. His first novel, *Nedelya* [*The Week*] (1922), was hailed as a great work, although his best work *Rozhdeniya geroya* [*Birth of a Hero*] (1930) has gone unnoticed outside the USSR because of his admitted communist orthodoxy while being condemned for ideological deviation within it. Libedinsky used this story to say those things which he felt had been forgotten and needed to be restated. For his trouble he was expelled from the Writers' Union, but managed to survive the purge of 1938. His later writings are more of a reminiscent nature—for example *Sovremyeniki* [*Contemporaries*] (1958)—though they shed little light on the enigma of his own career.

B. W.

Lima, Jorge de (1895–1953), Brazilian poet, novelist and critic born in União (Alagoas). He graduated in medicine and practised in Alagoas and Rio de Janeiro. During the 1920s he actively participated in the *modernista* movement in the Brazilian northeast. In 1930 he settled in Rio de Janeiro and taught Luso-Brazilian literature at the Federal and National Universities.

A poet of many tendencies, Lima's first book of verse *XIV alexandrinos* ['XIV alexandrines'] reveals Parnassian and symbolist influences. The rapid development, however, of his individual lyricism is evident in the *modernista* innovations of his *Poemas* ['Poems'] which appeared in 1927. His early *negrista* poems show a profound humanity and understanding of the Negro race in Brazil and his much acclaimed *Essa negra Fulô* ['That nigger Fulô'] (1928) embodies the essence of Brazilian *negrista* poetry. However, he is best known as a religious poet: the meditations of his spiritual verse deepening in the *Poemas escolhidos* ['Selected poems'] (1932) where he rejects his epoch and deplores a civilisation void of spirituality. The same need for escape from encroaching injustice and materialism informs the religious verse of *Tempo e eternidade* ['Time and eternity'] (1935), a work which he shared with Murilo Mendes and which coincided with his conversion to Roman catholicism. Here, as in *A túnica inconsútil* ['The seamless tunic'] (1938), he conveys a sense of religious mission and incorporates the versicles of church psalms and the symbols of holy scripture into his poems.

Lima returned to *negrista* verse with *Poemas negros* ['Negro poems'] (1947), which celebrate the African deities and the life and passion of the Negroes in Brazil. In his *Livro de sonetos* ['Book of sonnets'] (1949) he showed his mastery of the shorter lyric. In these sonnets the verse is measured, although they are modern in expression. Often obscure in his later poetry, Lima retraces his meditations in the somnambulant atmosphere of a world in formation, which hovers between heaven and earth, spirit and matter, good and evil. His last important work *Invenção de Orfeu* ['The invention of Orpheus'] (1952), intended as an epic in ten cantos, is deficient in structure. Isolated sections of the poem, however, exemplify the eloquence and poignancy of Lima's lyricism despite the hermeticism and figurative language which he now favoured.

The themes and treatment of Lima's novels repeat unmistakably features of his poetry. Of particular note are *O anjo* ['The angel'] (1934), *Calunga* (1935) and *A mulher obscura* ['The mysterious woman'] (1939).

Translations of his poetry are available in the Dudley Fitts *Anthology of Contemporary Latin-American Poetry* (1942), in selections of *Modern Brazilian Poetry* edited by Leonard S. Downes (1954) and John Nist (1962) and in *The Poem Itself* edited by Stanley Burnshaw (Pelican, 1964).

G. P.

Lin Yutang (1895–), Chinese-born writer on a wide range of topics, perhaps best known for his popular philosophical writing exemplified in such works as *A Leaf in the Storm* (1941). Apart from these he has produced a number of short stories and novels, and has done much to interpret the Chinese way of thinking for western readers. R. A. K.

Lindsay, [Alfred William] Norman (1879–), Australian novelist and illustrator, member of a talented artistic family, and head of a successful literary one. His own writing is characterised by a boisterous sense of humour, a knockabout satire, such as in *A Curate in Bohemia* (1913), but of all his many publications he will be remembered best for a series set in his imaginary small town of Redheap, dealing with the childhood (*Saturdee*, 1933), adolescence (*Halfway to Anywhere*, 1947) and young manhood (*Redheap*, 1930) of a young Australian Huckleberry Finn, and for *The Cautious Amorist* (1934) on which was based the film *His Girl*

Friday. He also wrote the book now regarded as a classic among Australian children's stories, *The Magic Pudding* (1919), which he illustrated himself. His drawings and cartoons have appeared in many works by both English and Australian authors. S. R.

Lindsay, Jack (1900–), versatile Australian-born author who has published poetry (*Fauns and Ladies*, 1928), translations from the classics (*Lysistrata*, 1925), novels dealing with ancient history (*Last Days with Cleopatra*, 1935), novels dealing with English history (*Sue Verney*, 1937) and an ambitious series using his historian's approach to portray contemporary British life. The son of the artist Norman Lindsay (q.v.), he has also written art criticism and the autobiographical *The Roaring Twenties* (1960). S. R.

Lindsay, [Nicholas] Vachell (1879–1931), American poet who spent most of his life travelling the road, reading his poems. Most of his early verse is characterised either by being strongly in the modern jazz idiom—such as *The Daniel Jazz* (1920)—or by its urgently stressing the contrasts between the veneer of civilisation and what lies beneath—as in *The Congo* (1914) and *Santa Fe Trail* (1914). Later books of verse included *The Golden Whales of California* (1920) and *Every Soul is a Circus* (1929). R. A. K.

Linklater, Eric (1899–), prolific Scottish novelist noted mainly for his dry satire and a range of backgrounds for the picaresque characters in his novels. His best-known works include *Poet's Pub* (1929); *Juan in America* (1931), which combines elements of travel, satire and fantasy; *The Crusader's Key* (1933); *Judas* (1931); *Cornerstones* (1941); and *Private Angelo* (1946), a remarkable comic war novel, made into a successful film. Later titles include *Roll of Honour* (1961); *Husband of Delilah* (1962); and *A Terrible Freedom* (1966). The latter, his twenty-third novel, shows the same narrative skill and romantic atmosphere as his earlier books, combined with a degree of technical innovation. He has also produced historical and travel writing of distinction. R. A. K.

Lins do Rêgo, José (1901–57), Brazilian novelist born in Pilar (Paraíba) and the most representative author of the *romance nordestino* ('novel of the north-east').

The five novels of his 'sugar-cane cycle' draw heavily upon his own childhood experiences on his grandfather's plantation. The cycle opens with *Menino de engenho* ['Plantation lad'] which he published in 1932 at the age of thirty. Critics readily identified the adventures of Carlos de

Mello with those of Lins do Rêgo himself, and the developments in *Doidinho* ['Daffy boy'] (1933) and in *Bangüê* ['The old plantation'] provide further parallels between character and author. In these three novels the story of Carlos de Mello is dramatised against the changing social pattern in the north-east. The next two novels *O moleque Ricardo* ['Black boy Richard'] (1935) and *Usina* ['The sugar refinery'] (1936) close the cycle and trace the disappearance of the patriarchal system on the land as the co-operative *usina* ('sugar refinery') gradually absorbs the privately owned *engenho* ('sugar plantation'). The author's social preoccupations frequently betray the influence of Gilberto Freyre's writing. Lins do Rêgo, however, enriches the sociological dimension with his memorable portraits drawn from life which symbolise the psychological implications of human degeneration and social injustice.

Later novels show new directions in his work. *Pureza* [*Purity*] (1937) has a sexual theme. *Pedra bonita* ['Wondrous rock'] (1938) and *Os cangaceiros* ['The outlaws'] (1953) are set in the *sertão* ('backlands'). *Água-mãe* ['The water-mother'] (1941) explores regional superstitions, and *Eurídice* (1947) marks an attempt at the psychological novel. In *Fogo Morto* ['Dead fires'] (1943) there was a highly successful return to the setting of the 'sugar-cane cycle'. In these as in his earlier works Lins do Rêgo insists upon the physical life of man and nature. His characters are creatures of instinct rather than reflection—lyrical and sensual, innocent and brutal at the same time. His narrative abounds in animated descriptions of regional life, and his prose style is characterised by sparse dialogue and the simplicity and spontaneity of his vocabulary. G. P.

Livings, Henry (1929–), English playwright. Henry Livings's early training at Theatre Workshop as an actor has left something of an impress upon his work. Its most frequent theme is that of the humble and ignored at last receiving attention and justification, as in *Stop it, Whoever You Are* (1960) or *The Rise and Fall of a Nignog* (1960). In both these plays, as in *Big Soft Nellie* (1961) and *Nil Carborundum* (1962), what at first appears mere farce is found to be both forceful and profound, and the unexpectedness of the profundity is always heightened by the author's vital and colloquial style. J. B. M.

Llewellyn, Richard (Richard Llewellyn Lloyd; 1907–), Welsh novelist and playwright, who achieved a major success with his story of life in a Welsh mining village *How Green Was My Valley* (1939). *None but the Lonely Heart* (1943) was a less successful attempt to portray the Cockney character. He achieved some theatrical success with *Poison Pen* (1937) and *Noose* (1947). R. A. K.

Locke, William J. (1863–1930), English novelist, wrote the best-selling book *The Beloved Vagabond* (1906), about a travelling bohemian musician-philosopher. His later works include *The Great Pandolfo* (1925).

K. R. R.

London, Jack (John Griffith London; 1876–1916), American novelist, born in San Francisco, is now read in the English-speaking world chiefly for his extravert and often brutal adventure stories, such as *The Call of the Wild* (1903), the story of a Klondike sledge-dog; its successor *White Fang* (1905); and *The Sea-Wolf* (1904), the portrayal of a sea-captain as a Nietzschean superman. Much of the material for these stories was gathered during his own tough early life, which included an adventure in Alaska and a spell at sea.

In the communist world, however, he is regarded as one of the major writers of the west, on the strength of the socialistic novels *The Iron Heel* (1907) and *The Valley of the Moon* (1913), as well as his study of London's slums entitled *People of the Abyss* (1903) and ideological tracts such as *The War of the Classes* (1905). On the other hand, there is also a distinct streak of fascism to be found in his adventure stories, manifesting itself in a suggestion of the racial superiority of the Anglo-Saxon as well as in the cult of the brute and the superman.

A fictional account of his early struggles as writer and journalist is contained in *Martin Eden* (1909).

K. R. R.

Long, [Gabrielle] Margaret (1886–1952), English novelist, wrote prolifically under a variety of names, including her maiden name Margaret Campbell (*The Debate Continues*, 1939; her autobiography), and the pseudonyms Marjorie Bowen (historical romances such as *The Viper of Milan*, 1906); Joseph Shearing (generally historical crime stories such as *Angel of Assassination*, 1935); and George R. Preedy (light romantic novels such as *No Way Home*, 1950). She also wrote plays and biographies.

K. R. R.

Loos, Anita (1893–), American novelist, is best known for her best-selling portrait of the Hollywood gold-digger in *Gentlemen Prefer Blondes* (1925), which was subtitled 'The Illuminating Diary of a Professional Lady'. Its successor *But Gentlemen Marry Brunettes* (1928) was less successful.

K. R. R.

Lowell, Amy (1874–1925), American woman of letters. Amy Lowell's main contribution to American literature is as a propagandist rather than as a poet. Her vigorous campaign for the cause of imagism had a marked effect on the development of poetry between the wars. She was born, of a distinguished New England family, in Brookline, Massachusetts, and later divided her time between her home town and extensive travel abroad. She spent a good deal of energy rigorously preparing to be a poet and her first verse was published in the magazine *Atlantic Monthly* in 1910. Her first-issued volume, *A Dome of Mercy-colored Glass*, was undistinguished but in 1912 she met Pound and became converted to imagism. Subsequently Amy Lowell gave a dinner in London for the imagists, the result of which was the publication in 1913 of *Some Imagist Poets* which puts forward a blueprint for poetry: that verse should employ everyday language; that only the exact word must be employed; that cadence should be substituted for metre; that a free choice of subject matter is essential; that only definite and concrete images should be employed in verse written with the utmost concentration.

In 1914 Amy Lowell followed these precepts with the publication of *Sword Blades and Poppy Seed.* Her work tends to self-consciousness and is notable, with its flashing style, for a portrayal of surface impressions rather than felt emotional experiences. It has colour rather than depth and this is true of all her later volumes.

Amy Lowell's death in 1925 was brought on by the excessive strain of writing her massive biography of Keats (2 vols, 1928). The obituary notices tended to stress her eccentricity and strength of personality rather than her poetry. It is true that her chief claim to distinction is the favourable climate she created for young poets by her forceful propaganda; but this was no mean achievement. Her verse is collected in *Selected Poems* (1928) and *Complete Poetical Works* (1955). She also published a volume of essays, *Tendencies in Modern Poetry* (1917). D. L. P.

Lowell, Robert (1917–), American poet. Robert Lowell's distinguished work belongs to the more formal school of American poets publishing after the second world war. To describe his verse as academic or traditional is not to categorise it rigidly but to distinguish it from the less conventional poetry of writers like Kerouac, Ginsberg and Ferlinghetti whose work, however individually different, falls the other side of a line marking formal from beat.

Lowell (Amy Lowell's cousin) was born in Boston. He attended Harvard and Kenyon Universities, where he studied with John Crowe Ransom, and finished his education at Louisiana State University. As a writer he made his reputation early and for some time was a consultant in poetry to the Library of Congress. His work is strongly influenced by the tension between his Puritan New England background and his later conversion to Catholicism. This tension produces an introspective tortuousness in the poetry, reminiscent of Edward Arlington Robinson. Concerned with depravity, corruption and damnation, Lowell employs complex and condensed religious imagery. In one of his best-known poems, 'The Quaker Graveyard in Nantucket' (from *Lord Weary's Castle*; Pulitzer Prize, 1946), he balances, with a powerful rhythm, religious symbols and macabre imagery, using the sea as a background of death and immortality. In the same volume 'The Drunken Fisherman' again uses the symbolism of water as a backcloth in a search for Christ in a context of chaos, futility and the perversion of religious values:

The Fisher's sons must cast about
When shallow waters peter out.
I will catch Christ with a greased worm,
And when the Prince of Darkness stalks
My bloodstream to its Stygian term. . . .
On water the Man-Fisher walks.

For The Union Dead (1964) marks a natural extension of Lowell's areas of sensibility. He is concerned with the despairs of passion rather than with the delights of emotions such as love. While he shows compassion for the dispossessed of this life, he is nevertheless seized with horror by a life that imposes so much wretchedness on human beings. The poetry establishes meaning through the associations of its linked imagery rather than by developing a narrative form; while the pessimism, almost moroseness, of the poet makes him complement his sensuous symbolism with the sudden usage of coarse vocabulary.

The force and complexity of Lowell's poetry and his religious imagery have echoes of Blake and make him one of the most powerful of the post-war American poets. Other volumes include *Land of Unlikeness* (1944) and *The Mills of Kavanaughs* (1951); *Life Studies* (autobiography in verse and prose, 1951) and *Imitations* (translations and adaptations, 1961); and *Poem 1938–1949* (published in England, 1950). D. L. P.

Lowndes, Belloc (Marie Adelaide Lowndes, née Belloc; 1868–1947), English novelist, sister of Hilaire Belloc, is remembered for her murder story *The Lodger* (1913) based on Jack the Ripper. K. R. R.

Lowry, Malcolm (1909–57), English novelist, short-story writer and poet whose reputation—which underwent a remarkable reflation during the 1960s—probably owes as much to the exotic-tragic circumstances of his own life as to the merits of his writing. He is best known for a substantially autobiographical psychological novel *Under the Volcano* (1947) which is the account of the disintegration, through alcohol and mescalin, of a former British diplomat in Mexico. The symbolism with which Lowry has enriched the story, as a means of extending its significance, is not always convincing; the consul's half-brother Hugh, for example—a rebel who has rebelled against even the conventional modes of rebellion—can scarcely be labelled a Judas-figure on the strength of a liaison with the consul's wife Yvonne that followed rather than preceded his initial withdrawal into alcoholism. However, the concluding physical descent into the abyss—a rubbish dump into which he is thrown by some irregular police at the climax of an irrevocable return to mescal-drinking—is tellingly counterpointed by his imagined ascent of the adjacent volcano Popocatepetl; while on a purely naturalistic level Lowry's account of a man's self-destruction has few equals.

Lowry's other prose works include the experimental *Ultramarine* (1933) and the posthumous collection *Hear Us O Lord from Heaven Thy Dwelling Place* (1961); his *Selected Poems* were published in 1962. K. R. R.

Lubbock, Percy (1879–1965), English author of *The Craft of Fiction* (1921) which deals mainly with form in the novel through the detailed, unifying study of specific works. He also wrote *Earlham* (1922), a memoir of his kinsmen and a masterpiece of evocation of the best Victorian Quaker traditions. H. C.

Lucas, E. V. (Edward Verrall Lucas; 1868–1938), English essayist, travel writer, biographer and minor novelist, is remembered chiefly for his *Life of Charles Lamb* (1905) and his collection of essays *Adventures and Misgivings* (1938). K. R. R.

Lunts, Lev Natanovich (1901–24), was a brilliant young Russian playwright who considered that Russian literature should learn more from the west and rid itself of its excess of realism. In 1922 he wrote a fine article about the Serapion writers which became known as their manifesto. Of his four plays his last, *The City of Truth* (1924), was written when he was an émigré just before his death. B. W.

Lustig, Arnošt (1926–), Czech writer. During the period 1942–45 Lustig was imprisoned in various Nazi concentration camps and his novels and short stories deal with the life and the psychology of the prisoners. A notable work is *Démanty noci* [*Diamonds in the Night*] (1958). K. B.

Lytton, David (1927–), South African-born critic, radio playwright and novelist, who has produced a series of novels set in the Cape. *The Goddam White Man* (1960) attempts to depict the life of a Cape Coloured, its unrealistic melodrama cloaking a few true insights. *The Paradise People* (1962) is more successful in its portrayal of the Afrikaner in the post-Boer War era. However, Lytton's best published work is undoubtedly *The Freedom of the Cage* (1966), a simply written minor *tour-de-force*. Compelling narrative and sharp analysis are combined with true artistry in this movingly quiet and true examination of the shut-in mind of an Afrikaner who seeks release in a self-aborted attempt to 'assassinate' the republic's premier. C. P.

M

Macartney, Frederick T. (1887–   ), Australian poet who has produced a great many types of verse from his conventional, flowery and 'poetical' early work to his more polished and satirical later achievements. His long apprenticeship culminated when he produced the unusual *Tripod for Homeward Incense* (1947), a story-poem of an Australian captain torn between his love for a Chinese girl and his feeling for his native country —the two conflicting moods being echoed in the very different verse forms used for each. His work is collected in *Selected Poems* (1961). S. R.

Macaulay, Rose (1881–1958), English novelist, travel writer and critic, won acclaim for her first novel *Potterism* (1920), a satire on vulgarity, humbug and hypocrisy in public and private life, and continued to enjoy a reputation as a writer of distinction throughout her prolific career; but she achieved her greatest popularity towards the end of her life, with her last novel *Towers of Trebizond* (1956), and in the years that followed her death, with her posthumously published letters to a priest, *Letters to a Friend* (1961). In the year she died she was honoured with the D.B.E.

This last-named volume of personal letters illuminated a love affair that had occupied a large part of Rose Macaulay's adult life and had contributed to her long estrangement from her early religious beliefs and practices; and the need for the kind of religious certainty to which she was feeling her way in the course of this correspondence was something that had made itself felt in her novel *Told By an Idiot* (1923). More characteristic of her early novels, however, is a preoccupation—sometimes autobiographical, often humorous—with the changing rôle of woman in a rapidly changing society (e.g. *Dangerous Ages*, 1921) and with the ensuing possibility of conflict in the female personality (e.g. *Keeping Up Appearances*, 1928): perhaps her most characteristic creation being 'the wild girl' who finds herself at odds with civilisation itself (e.g. in *Crewe Train*, 1925). What might be taken as a more generalised expression of the latter idea (i.e. of nature reasserting itself) is the novel *Orphan Island* (1924), though here there are wider implications concerning the nature of man.

In the 1930s the varied settings of Rose Macaulay's books reflected more clearly the wide range of her sympathies and interests. *Staying with Relations* (1930) is set in the tropical forests of Guatemala; *They Were Defeated* (1932) in seventeenth-century England; and *Going Abroad* (1934) was the first of a number of books set in Spain, its easy-going humour at the expense of the Oxford Group (later renamed Moral Rearmament) giving way to a more sombre mood of disillusionment and crumbling faith in the post-Civil War *And No Man's Wit* (1940). In happier mood is the travel book *Fabled Shore* (1950), a pioneer work of Costa Brava tourism.

'The wild girl' makes another appearance in *And No Man's Wit* and her conflict with civilisation receives its fullest treatment in *The World My Wilderness* (1950). But it is the travel element in Rose Macaulay's later writing that becomes the ideal setting for the spiritual journeying of *Towers of Trebizond*. This much-celebrated book does in fact proceed much more like a Black Sea travel book than a novel for the greater part of its length, at the same time providing a superb vehicle (in the character of the eccentric camel-riding Dorothea ffoulkes-Corbett, the heroine's aunt) for the expression of many of its author's cherished convictions (on religion, women's rights etc.) and personal eccentricities; but the interest shifts from Aunt Dot, and her companion the high-church Anglican priest Father Chantrey-Pigg, to the narrator herself and her own spiritual journey. Eventually she is to keep a rendezvous with her cousin Vere, with whom she has a consuming but adulterous love affair; meanwhile she is haunted by the vision of the romantic towers of the last outpost of Byzantine Christendom, symbolising for her a faith to which she will always aspire but into which she will always be unable to enter. The book ends with a totally unexpected disaster, the death of Vere in a car crash.

K. R. R.

McAuley, James (1917–   ), Australian poet with strong Catholic beliefs which he expounds in his poetry. A superbly polished writer, his satirical verse is as effortlessly accomplished as that of Pope. His work can be seen in the volumes *Under Aldebaran* (1946), *A Vision of Ceremony* (1956) and *Selected Poems* (1963). S. R.

McBain, Ed (Evan Hunter; 1926–   ), American writer of detective stories, known for his witty and accurately observed novels of police investigation in the '87th precinct' of a fictitious New York-type city. Some of his titles are *King's Ransom* (1959), the story of a kidnapping; *Like Love* (1962), about an apparently obvious suicide; *Axe* (1964), in which the murder of an elderly janitor leads to some even more surprising discoveries; *He Who Hesitates* (1965); and *Doll* (1966). He also wrote, under his own name of Evan Hunter, a series of novels including *The Blackboard Jungle* (1954), a drama of the classroom with the familiar ingredients of unruly pupils and bullying headmaster intermingled with the hard-pressed teacher's domestic/romantic involvements. P. E.

McCarthy, Desmond (1877–1952), English critic, at one time literary editor of the *New Statesman* and later editor of *Life and Letters*. He gained a reputation as a speaker of verse. His critical works include *The Court Theatre* (1907), *Portraits* (1931) and *Drama* (1940), and he published studies of Leslie Stephen and George Bernard Shaw. R. A. K.

McCarthy, Mary (1912–), American writer, born in Seattle in the Pacific north-west and brought up as a Catholic, has maintained a high reputation in a wide range of literary genres. Her first book, the novel *The Company She Keeps* (1942), portrays the experiences of a Catholic girl from the north-west, from the divorce that ends her first marriage to the course of psychoanalysis which enables her to adjust to her second. It is also a series of portraits of 'the company she keeps' during this period; and while the girl, Margaret Sargent, is central to the first and last chapters, the chief characters in the other four are men—a feckless antique dealer who employs her as a secretary ('Rogues' Gallery'), a travelling business executive who makes love to her on a train ('The Man in the Brooks Brothers Shirt'), a social leech who includes her in his dinner parties ('The Genial Host'), and a professional middle-class radical who becomes her lover and is converted by her to Trotskyism ('Portrait of the Intellectual as a Yale Man').

At times Margaret Sargent is only in the background; but a picture builds up of a pattern in her life—of rejection of the men she has allowed to become fond of her. Also the reader becomes aware of the origins of this neurotic behaviour, in her non-Catholic father's effective withholding of his love in order to honour a pledge given to her dying mother that she be given a Catholic upbringing by her aunt. The pattern begins to dissolve only when she marries a husband who means much less to her than the various men she has begun to love; and, ironically, with the process of adjustment to marital normality there comes the sense that she is a poorer person for the change.

The behaviour of liberal intellectuals, which is a recurring theme in *The Company She Keeps*, becomes the main subject matter of *The Oasis* (1950), later published in England as *A Source of Embarrassment*, in which a group of intellectuals form a utopian community during the war. However, it is as much a study of life in a closed community; as also is *The Grove of Academe* (1952), where a college campus is the scene of a political drama. During the 1950s Mary McCarthy in addition published three notable pieces of non-fiction—*Venice Observed* (1956), *Memories of a Catholic Girlhood* (1957), and a collection of writings on the American theatre entitled *Sights and Spectacles 1937–1956* (1956).

But probably her most famous book is her novel *The Group* (1963). This traces the experiences of a group of eight girls from Vassar (the women's college in New York state of which the author was herself a graduate), from their graduation in 1933 in the New Deal era, to the early stages of the second world war. In an age of social change, we see what is predominantly an 'establishment' group trying out the ideas that have been generated by their progressive education—on careers and politics, love and marriage, contraception and child-rearing, cookery and interior design.

The central strand of the novel is the story of Kay, the only westerner in the group, whose marriage and funeral provide the opening and closing chapters. In her marriage to a self-styled theatre 'technician' (who in practice is chiefly a writer and producer) she is identifying herself with a new class; but at the same time she is transferring to him her unfulfilled artistic ambitions, and in so doing, at a time of economic uncertainty in the theatrical profession, she saddles him with an intolerable burden. Given his own psychological complexities—chiefly arising from social insecurity—this is more than the marriage will stand. After a nervous breakdown and their subsequent divorce, Kay retires to the west for a year before returning to New York to make a fresh start. When shortly afterwards she falls from a window during a bout of aircraft spotting, there is no certainty that it is not suicide.

When the spotlight is not on Kay it rests intermittently on the other members of the group. We see the churchgoer Dottie have her first sexual experience with a man she meets at Kay's wedding; afterwards she steels herself to visit one of the newly legalised birth-control clinics. What proves to have been a one-night affair leaves her profoundly affected, and on the rebound she marries a wealthy American businessman. Priss has married a doctor who wants her to breast-feed their child and together they struggle against the hospital staff's belief in the bottle; Polly, hitherto content for men to seek her out, has an affair with a married man who is undergoing daily psychoanalysis as a possible means of salvaging his marriage; while Elinor spends the years travelling Europe, returning finally as an unequivocal lesbian. The group is completed by the carefree society girl Pokey, who trains as a vet and marries an aviator; the neurotically virginal Libby, who despite inadequate talents pursues a literary career; and the apparently sexless Helena, their chronicler whose well-to-do parents successfully obstruct her plans for a career in social work. Though Kay acquires prominence as the member whose story provides a continuous narrative (and whose experiences thus occupy much of the book), it would be a mistake to consider these others as in any way subsidiary: it is the Group, not Kay, that constitutes the true subject of the narrative. It is their collective ideals that are doomed to be abandoned, or at least compromised, if life is to go on. K. R. R.

McCullers, Carson (1917–67), one of America's best-known women writers, has written some half-dozen full-length novels and plays in the course of twenty-five years, as well as a number of short stories. She was born in Georgia, and it is in the South that almost all her tales are set.

The theme of much of her writing is expressed in the title of her first novel, *The Heart is a Lonely Hunter* (1940). Many of her characters, in this as in subsequent books, are engaged in a quest of some kind—in some cases without knowing clearly what it is that they want. Their difficulties in communicating this quest to anyone else in the town serves to accentuate for them the loneliness that is fundamental to human life. A symbol for the isolation that comes from this inability to communicate may be found in the figures of the town's two deaf-mutes.

The lonely hunters of this book include a Negro doctor, whose mission is to educate his fellow Negroes to a greater self-respect and awareness of their rights, and arouse them from their inertia; an itinerant socialist preacher, similarly frustrated in his efforts to communicate his vision to the exploited masses; and Mick Kelly, an adolescent girl. Each finds himself drawn to the company of Mister Singer, one of the deaf-mutes, whose life centres on his friendship with his companion Antonopoulos (now in a mental hospital)—a relationship that has given Singer a serenity and sense of fulfilment that eludes all the others. But when Antonopoulos dies, Singer is totally alone, and takes his own life.

Mick Kelly's lonely hunt is the indefinable quest of the adolescent, and the nature of her experiences is recorded with great sensitivity. A fuller treatment of the experience of adolescence is found in *The Member of the Wedding* (1946), subsequently adapted as a successful stage play. For Frankie Addams its chief characteristics are a search for identity, the need to belong, and the incommunicability of what is happening to her. In her childhood she is Frankie, and by the end of the book she has become Frances; in between, she is F. Jasmine—the name she adopts so that she can share the same initial letters with her brother Jarvis and his fiancée Janice. Her passionate desire to be a 'member of the wedding', to be able to say 'we', provides the central theme of the book.

In between these two books, Miss McCullers had produced *Reflections in a Golden Eye* (1941), where the loneliness she portrays is that which stems from a real psychological freakishness. This tends to underline the fact that the freaks of her first novel are only social eccentrics—while Frankie Addams merely feels that she belongs with the freaks she sees at the fairground. In her next novel—published a full fifteen years after *The Member of the Wedding* (a period during which she wrote only a number of stories of which the best known is 'The Ballad of the Sad Café', and a play *The Square Root of Wonderful*, 1958)—we meet both biological and social eccentricity. The title of *Clock Without Hands* (1961) refers to the experience of a man with leukaemia who has been told that his days are numbered but does not know when his time will be up. The pharmacist J. T. Malone is the most ordinary of all Carson McCullers's characters, acquiring distinction only by the singular nature of his experience, and by the fact that in what remains of his life he is to perform an action whose significance stems from his very ordinariness.

The more characteristic freakish individuals in the racial drama in which Malone is to play a key part include the aging Southern politician Judge Clane, leader of the town's most reactionary elements; the latter's grandson Jester, a boy of ardently liberal ideas; and Sherman Pew, a parentless young Negro who feels himself a sensitive instrument for recording every injustice inflicted on his race, and who is employed by the judge as his servant. It transpires that before he was born the judge had passed an unjust sentence on Sherman's father, in a trial in which his own son—Jester's father—had been the defence lawyer; the latter having followed his failure to save his client by taking his own life. The judge's efforts to make some atonement cut no ice with Sherman once the truth is out, while Jester's earnest attempts to establish a friendly relationship have been equally unsuccessful; and the climax comes when in a gesture of suicidal defiance Sherman rents a house in a white area, thus provoking the judge and his fellow-extremists into a plan for violent retribution. Amongst those the judge conscripts is his old friend Malone, and when lots are cast to determine who shall throw the petrol bomb, it is to the latter that the assignment falls. In such a situation, this most ordinary of men finds that he cannot bring himself to perpetrate such violence; and thus is privileged to deliver a verdict on behalf of the millions of ordinary men—a verdict not invalidated when the planned action is duly carried out by one of the extremists. The book ends with Jester reaching a decision not to return evil for evil by avenging his friend. K. R. R.

McDiarmid, Hugh (Christopher Murray Grieve; 1892–), Scottish poet. McDiarmid is a leader of a revival in Scottish literature, writing a form of dialect known as 'Lallans'. His longer poems are remarkable for a gathering together of disparate themes, since he is both an ardent nationalist and a convinced Marxist with the resultant emergence in his work of the corresponding social and political themes and involvements. In addition he is inclined to merge the latter with philosophical meditation and savage satire. The shorter poems are concerned with the lyrical qualities of love and nature and are cast in a more traditional form—for example:

Your body derns
In its graces again
As the dreich grun' does
In the gowden grain.

McDiarmid has been rated by some of his poetic contemporaries as among the half-dozen worthwhile poets of the present era. *Collected Poems* was published in 1961 and an autobiography *Lucky Poet* in 1943. D. L. P.

MacDonagh, Thomas (1878–1916) and Donagh (1912–), father and son, Irish poets. Thomas was executed after the Easter rising and his *Poetical Works* (1916) provide a moving memorial. Donagh, who became a judge in the Irish republic, is better known for his ballad comedy *Happy as Larry* (1946). K. R. R.

MacDonell, Archibald (1895–1941), Scottish writer of the popular *England, their England* (1933), an extremely funny satirical novel on English life. MacDonell also wrote *The Autobiography of a Cad* (1939), and, under the pseudonym of Neil Gordon, detective stories such as *The Shakespeare Murders* (1933). K. R. R.

McFee, William (1881–), London-born American writer, is the author of numerous tales (sometimes reminiscences, sometimes fiction) of life at sea, including *Letters from an Ocean Tramp* (1908), the novel *Command* (1922), and the autobiographical *In The First Watch* (1946). His novels, which sometimes show the influence of Conrad, also include *Casuals of the Sea* (1916), set in a London suburb, and *The Harbourmaster* (1932), set in Salonika and South America. K. R. R.

MacGaig, Norman (1910–), Scottish poet. MacGaig's poetry is written under two main influences, a love of his native Scotland and the seventeenth-century metaphysical poet John Donne. His poems are elegant, sensitive and witty. They draw strength and integrity from a feeling for the land and the sea which is woven into a pattern of philosophical speculation and emotional intensity. As with Donne the love poems do not concentrate exclusively on sexuality in its physical form but are concerned to explore the metaphysical nature of a close human relationship. Published work includes *Riding Lights* (1955), *The Sinai Sort* (1957), *A Common Grace* (1960) and *A Round of Applause* (1962). D. L. P.

McGinley, Phyllis (1905–), Canadian author of the kind of deft and cryptic humorous verse associated with Ogden Nash. Her publications include *On the Contrary* (1934), *Pocketful of Wry* (1940), *The Love Letters of Phyllis McGinley* (1955) and children's books such as *The Horse who lived Upstairs* (1944). S. R.

Machado, Antonio (1875–1939), Spanish poet. Born into a family of radical intellectuals, Machado was educated at the Institución Libre de Enseñanza, the progressive day-school in Madrid whose influence on Spanish thought in the twentieth century has been decisive. There Machado acquired his love of the Castilian countryside, his concern with spiritual values and his sense of history—of progressive Spain kicking against the pricks of reaction. Together with his brother Manuel, also a poet, Machado moved in literary circles at the turn of the century and his first book *Soledades* ['Solitudes'] (1903) shows traces of modernism. These disappear, however, in *Soledades, galerías y otros poemas* ['Solitudes, galleries and other poems'] (1907), a work of poetic maturity full of honest sadness. Machado is perplexed by three central mysteries: the passage of time, the world of dreams and God. Yet this is not overtly metaphysical poetry. The anguish is evoked by symbols—fountains, trees, landscapes.

In 1907 Machado moved to Soria to teach French. There he met Leonor, his wife, and found in the austere Castilian countryside his great symbol, both national and personal, for the relentless passage of time. In *Campos de Castilla* ['Castilian countryside'] (1912) Machado evokes Spain as dead, just as he himself is dying. The sonorous meditations on Spain's tragedy end with Leonor's death in 1911, which pervades the augmented edition of *Campos de Castilla* (1917). In 1911 Machado had moved to Baeza, a decaying Andalusian town, and there two trends became more marked. After hearing Bergson and Bédier on a trip to Paris (1911), he was increasingly interested in philosophy, which he now studied in Madrid, and popular culture, which he experienced at first hand among the people. In his poetry death matures from a personal into a philosophical problem, whose solution he finds in popular wisdom, synthesised into brief snippets of verse which he calls *proverbios*. There is also a new political awareness: Spain's decadence is symbolised by representative figures of the provincial bourgeoisie, rotting away in casinos and clubs.

In 1919 Machado moved to Segovia and in his last twenty years the pace of his life quickened. All the themes of his previous work are present in *Nuevas canciones* ['New songs'] (1924). From popular tradition he distils not only the form but the matter of his verse: to his recurring symbols—rivers, mountains, landscapes—he adds the great myths and the ancient philosophies. He also attacks the premises of the new lyric of the twenties, with which he felt profoundly out of sympathy. His critique is largely made in prose writings through the apocryphal figures of Juan de Mairena and his master Abel Martín. *Juan de Mairena* [*Juan de Mairena*] (1936) contains the synthesis of Machado's philosophy and aesthetics. During the republic and the civil war, the poet completely identified himself (and Mairena) with radical forces. He died in Collioure, France, in February 1939. Since his death Machado's stature has been increasingly recognised in Spain and abroad. There have been published in English three selections from his poetry and a translation of *Juan de Mairena*. D. H. G.

Machen, Arthur (1863–1947), Welsh novelist and essayist, specialised in material with a supernatural flavour, such as *Strange Roads* (1923) and the novels *The Great God Pan* (1894) and *The Hill of Dreams* (1907). It was Machen who created the legend of 'the angels of Mons', in a short story. K. R. R.

McInnes, Colin (1914–), Australian-born novelist, essayist and journalist who settled in London, comes from a literary family: the novelist Angela Thirkell (q.v.) being his mother, while his brother Graham has also produced two autobiographical works. Colin McInnes has made a distinctive contribution to English literature in his chronicling of previously uncharted areas of London life and in capturing the flavour of each phase in a rapidly changing era in his series of fast-moving and tender novels. *City of Spades* (1957) gives a vivid impression of what it means to be coloured in London; *Absolute Beginners* (1959) depicts teenagers in London's Harrow Road emerging into the only kind of adulthood available to them; *Mr Love and Justice* (1960) sets in contrast the moral codes of a pimp and a policeman. Yet underlying the surface detail can be found the broad sweeping lines of allegory, perhaps hinted at in the names of his characters—Mr 'Love', Mr 'Justice', Inspector 'Purity', Johnny 'Fortune'—or, as in *All Day Saturday* (1966), which returns to the Australian setting of the early *June in Her Spring* (1952), emphasised by the formal poetic eloquence of the dialogue.

His other works include a collection of essays *England, Half England* (1961) and *London, City of any Dream* (1962). S. R.

Mackenzie, Compton (1883–), English writer. After coming down from Oxford in 1904 he began writing with a play *Gentleman in Grey* and *Poems* both published in 1907. His first novel, a picturesque eighteenth-century story *The Passionate Elopement* (1911), was warmly acclaimed. He then turned to novels based on his own experience describing the life of contemporary young people. *Carnival* (1912) about theatre life, was followed by *Sinister Street* (1913–14), a two-volume novel and probably his most enduring work, bringing vividly to mind the thoughts and experiences of the generation who were undergraduates just before the first world war. His service in the Dardanelles and the Aegean prompted

Gallipoli Memories (1929), *First Athenian Memories* (1931) and *Greek Memories* (1932). The author of about a hundred books, mainly popular novels, his most successful later works are his humorous stories such as *The Monarch of the Glen* (1941) and *Whisky Galore* (1947). His autobiographical volumes *My Life and Times, Octave One to Octave Five* (1963–66) are interesting chronicles of social history. Other titles include *Guy and Pauline* (1915), *The Four Winds of Love* (6 vols, 1937–45), *The Windsor Tapestry* (1938), *Thin Ice* (1956), *The Stolen Soprano* (1965) and *Paper Lives* (1966). G. S.

Mackenzie, Kenneth (1928–), South African-born novelist now settled in the U.K., an ex-teacher and husband of the author Myrna Bloomberg, wrote *A Dragon to Kill* (1963) which though apparently lop-sided in its depiction of the political motives and methods of anti-*apartheid* fighters in South Africa, gives insights into the personality and development of the average young white South African male. In many ways it is comparable to Nadine Gordimer's *Lying Days. The Deserter* (1965) is a compact, complex anatomy of the mind of a pacific young Boer in the South African War, its treatment of this atypical figure verging on the apocalyptic. C. P.

Mackenzie, Kenneth (1913–55), Australian poet who writes in celebration of the ripe, sensuous and productive aspect of nature, and of physical human love. His collections are *Our Earth* (1937) and *The Moonlit Doorway* (1944). He also wrote novels under the name of Seaforth Mackenzie, typical of which is *The Young Desire It* (1937), a gentle and perceptive account of a young country boy's encounter with a homosexual master when he goes to boarding school; other titles including *Chosen People* (1938) and *The Refuge* (1954). S. R.

Macleish, Archibald (1892–), American poet. Macleish's poetry reflects the trends of the post-World War I generation. It is a matter of critical dispute whether or not his individuality transcends the derivative qualities of his ideas and techniques.

Macleish was born in Illinois in 1892. Together with Thornton Wilder and Stephen Vincent Benét he was educated at Yale and Harvard. He practised law until 1923 after which he spent five years in Paris. He was appointed to the Library of Congress in 1939 and made Professor of Rhetoric at Harvard in 1949. In the 1914–18 war Macleish served in a hospital unit. During the Spanish civil war he worked with the Loyalists.

His earlier verse echoes the interest in the seventeenth-century metaphysicals and French symbolists evident in Eliot. The volume *Happy*

Marriage (1924) owes something to Conrad Aiken. *Pot of Earth* (1925) derives directly from Eliot's formal techniques. Macleish's first and highly successful long poem *Conquistador*, which won a Pulitzer prize in 1933, was started on the poet's return from France in 1928. It follows the route of Cortés' victories in Mexico. Even with this poem there can be found the influence of Pound's early 'cantos' but a rich and individual texture begins to emerge.

Macleish's pursuit of contemporary movements extends to social and intellectual issues; he found involvement with Einstein's relativity theories in *Einstein* (1929) and with the depression in *Mr Rockefeller's City* (1933). He became a chief spokesman for Roosevelt's New Deal with *Public Speech* (1936). He is concerned, too, for America's rôle in world history, in the same sense as Whitman and Sandburg. However, even if its closeness to the literary and intellectual concerns of the 1920s and 1930s make much of Macleish's work seem borrowed, it is interesting to read not only as a reflection of an era but because there does emerge in the later poetry an individual pattern in the handling of form and ideas. D. L. P.

MacLennan, Hugh (1907–), Canadian novelist, essayist and academic. His earnest, humourless works are concerned almost solely with Canadian themes and Canadian backgrounds. *Barometer Rising* (1941) deals in fictional terms with the 1917 munitions-ship explosion which devastated Halifax; *Two Solitudes* (1945) with Canada's French-English problems; and *The Watch that Ends the Night* (1959) with communism and Canadian intellectuals. His other novels include *The Precipice* (1948) and *Each Man's Son* (1951); and his essays have been published in *Thirty and Three* (1954) and *Scotchman's Return* (1960). Though highly respected in Canada, MacLennan's novels have received little attention elsewhere. K. W.

MacNeice, Louis (1907–63), Irish-born English poet. MacNeice was born in Belfast and educated at Marlborough and Merton College, Oxford. He was a lecturer in Classics at Birmingham and London universities, also teaching for a while in the U.S.A.; and in 1936 he published a verse translation of *The Agamemnon of Aeschylus* (1936). He has written and produced plays for the B.B.C. and was for a time director of the British Institute in Athens.

During the 1930s MacNeice was involved with Auden and the left-wing literary movement, contributing to *New Verse*. Like Spender he was involved more with the aesthetics of literature than with the politics of Marxism. It is true that his poetry is concerned with social change but as a phenomenon related to human beings or to art rather than necessarily to abstract political manipulation. For instance, in 'An Eclogue for

Christmas' MacNeice is concerned to satirise not only the rootlessness of life in a technically sophisticated age but also to indicate the effect of political and social materialism on people and on art:

> The excess sugar of a diabetic culture
> Rotting the nerve of life and literature;
>
> . . . I have not been allowed to be
> Myself in flesh or face, but abstracting and dissecting me
> They have made of me pure form, a symbol or a particle,
> Stylised profile, anything but soul or flesh.

The feeling of MacNeice's poetry is elegant and intellectual. One can apply varied adjectives: lyrical, satirical, graceful, stylish, perceptive, descriptive, self-assured, ironic, astringent, highly coloured. One has the impression of a sensitive, intellectual, modern man applying an essentially aesthetic sensibility to the human problems of his environment.

The Dark Tower, a volume of plays for radio which greatly enlarged the scope and potentialities of radio drama, was published in 1947. *Collected Poems* was published in 1949 and *Solstices* in 1961. Some notable posthumous volumes include the autobiographical prose work *The Strings are False* (1965). D. L. P.

Madariaga, Salvador de (1886–), Spanish writer. Born in Corunna, Madariaga trained in Paris as a mining engineer but went to London in 1916 as correspondent for several Madrid newspapers. Completely trilingual in Spanish, French and English, Madariaga writes with equal fluency in all three languages. On the international scene he is a widely respected liberal: an active supporter of the League of Nations and UNESCO, he was ambassador in Washington and Paris and minister of education under the republic, and opposes the Franco régime. *Disarmament* (1929), *Anarquía o jerarquía* [*Anarchy or Hierarchy*] (1936), *Portrait of Europe* (1952) and *Democracy Versus Liberty?* (1958) provide statements of his radical views on Spain and Europe. In the field of creative literature Madariaga has worked in various genres, but his theatre and poetry offer less interest than his novels and essays. His novels are diverse in theme. *La jirafa sagrada* [*The Sacred Giraffe*] (1925), set in a fictional African country of the future, is a satire on modern civilisation. The biography of its supposed author, Julio Arceval, appears in *Arceval y los ingleses* ['Arceval and the English'] (1925). *El enemigo de Dios* ['The enemy of God'] (1936) describes the redemption of Don Morabito, a militant atheist, while *Ramo de errores* [*Bunch of Errors*] (1952) is an essay in Ortegan perspectivism. It gives eleven differing accounts of a crime, one of them by a dog. *El corazón de piedra verde* [*The Heart of Jade*] (1942) and *Guerra en la sangre* [*War in the Blood*] (1957) are historical novels set in Mexico in the early colonial period. As an essayist, Madariaga displays a similar virtuosity. As well as his works on international relations, he has published critical studies of Don Quixote, Hamlet, the English Romantic poets and contemporary Spanish literature, and biographies of Columbus, Cortés and Bolívar. His most celebrated essay, however, is *Ingleses, franceses, españoles* [*Englishmen, Frenchmen, Spaniards*] (1929), a comparative study of the psychology of three peoples. D. H. G.

Maeterlinck, Maurice (1862–1949), Belgian writer and 1911 Nobel Prize-winner. His early poems and plays, for example *Pelléas et Mélisande* [*Pelleas and Melisande*] (1892), the inspiration for Debussy's work, reveal a symbolist influence and fondness of ambiguity. His early philosophy develops, in *La Sagesse et la destinée* [*Wisdom and Destiny*] (1898), to an exaltation of goodness, and in later works his happiness is reflected in sentimental treatises on detailed aspects of natural history: *La Vie des abeilles* [*The Life of the Bee*] (1901), *La Vie des termites* [*The Life of the White Ant*] (1926) and many others. His best-known work is *L'Oiseau Bleu* [*The Blue Bird*] (1909), a fairy play reflecting his discovery of happiness. His main interests were philosophy and natural history. D. E. A.

Mailer, Norman (1923–), is best-known for his lengthy best-selling novel of the second world war, *The Naked and the Dead* (1948). Superficially, it is the story of the American invasion of the Japanese-held island of Anopopei; and it has been publicised, in its popular editions, for its admittedly gruesome (though in fact infrequent) accounts of the horrors of the battlefield.

From the Allied viewpoint, the war was fought against fascism, in one form or another; and it is with fascism that Mailer's book is concerned. The American army (or any army), as seen by Mailer, is itself organised on fascist principles; and those members of it who are most effective are the natural fascists. Much emphasis is laid on the apparently natural division of human beings into those who nature it is to command and those whose instinct is to obey. Linked with the theme of fascism is the elaborate deterministic framework in which the story is set. It is only the rare natural leaders—Cummings the general, Croft the platoon sergeant—who can shape the pattern of events; the rest are entirely moulded by them. From time to time the narrative is interrupted with a passage headed 'The Time Machine', a series of flashbacks into the formative years of all the principal characters (chiefly the members of Croft's platoon): these being designed to emphasise that the part that each plays in the story is entirely predetermined. Even the apparent natural autocrats, we are led to feel, are themselves shaped by their previous experiences.

A common pattern runs through these flashbacks. Most of the men have shared the experience of growing up in the depression years; and with few exceptions (notably Hearn, the liberal intellectual lieutenant) the experience has been a bitter one. The implication is not that they were the victims of an unfortunate occurrence in world history: rather that the conditioning of all but a few socially fortunate individuals is such as to produce human beings who are cynical, self-preserving and foul-mouthed, and whose aspirations in life are pared down to the naked minimum of satisfying the sexual appetite.

Hearn's opposition to both the theory and practice of fascism as represented by Cummings provokes the latter into making him take Croft's platoon on a reconnaissance patrol with a near-impossible objective, involving a crippling trek to the other side of the enemy lines. The carrying out of this feat of endurance, culminating in the ascent of a precipitous mountain, becomes the main feature of the book; the seemingly summitless mountain symbolising Croft's boundless determination to drive his men on to achieve the impossible. Hearn's commonsense decision to call off the patrol, should the pass alongside it prove occupied, is a threat to Croft's determination to take the men over the mountain; Croft therefore arranges for him to be killed in an ambush. From that point, the survivors of the stricken platoon are completely at the mercy of Croft's naked will: as they struggle upward in obedience, they are gradually stripped of all personal attributes and reduced to the barest residue of human material.

The Deer Park (1956) is one of the more interesting of the spate of novels about Hollywood. But neither this nor any of Mailer's other novels have been widely esteemed, and several are marred by tendencies towards sensationalism and exhibitionism. Also, it is not always clear what he is trying to achieve; though some light is thrown on his aims and methods by the autobiographical work *The Presidential Papers* (1963). Critics were particularly perplexed over *The American Dream* (1965), many feeling that beyond its extravagant and sensational narrative there was little to be found in it. This novel concerns an amoral university professor and popular broadcaster in sociology. The centrepiece of the book is a scene worthy of Henry Miller in which, having just murdered his wife by ejecting her from a skyscraper window, he discovers the *au pair* girl in an act of sexual perversion and happily adds his own contribution to the sum total of perversions being practised. What has remained through most of Mailer's later writings, and might be thought to have reached a climax in this last-named novel, is a radical critique of the American way of life. The whole of *The American Dream* is concerned with a society geared to sensuality and consumption. The appetite for consumption swallows up human values and leaves merely appetites. K. R. R.; D. L. P.

Majerová, Marie (1882–1967), one of the most important Czech social novelists. Born of working-class stock in a mining area, she wrote several works about the life of the miners. *Havířská ballada* [*Ballad of a Miner*] (1938) is perhaps the best of them. K. B.

Malamud, Bernard (1914–), American novelist. Bernard Malamud was born in Brooklyn, N.Y. Of his novels, *The Natural* (1952) centres on a baseball hero; *The Assistant* (1957) is concerned with the ambiguous relationship of an Italian-American to a Russian-Jewish immigrant family in Manhattan; and *A New Life* (1961) deals with the life of a Jewish ex-alcoholic New Yorker, who joins the staff of the English Department of a minor agricultural college in a north-west state.

Although *The Assistant* has been praised for its poetic language and intense observation, *A New Life*, displaying a more highly developed comic and realistic awareness of social pressures, seems to be Malamud's most important novel. The hero enjoys a paradoxical success and failure in his attempts to liberalise the atrophied English curriculum of the college and in his efforts to emerge from his personal isolation into a meaningful relationship with the wife of one of his colleagues. Underestimating the ruthlessness of his academic opponents, he finds that though he makes some headway towards his reforming projects, he is driven from his post in the college. Moreover, although his relationship to the woman has proved an illusory ideal, at the end of the novel he finds himself forced to accept responsibility not only for her but for her two children as well. His impact on the college has been felt, and he has won a small but significant victory. In personal terms society has both imposed on and rejected him.

The tension produced by this situation is typical of Malamud's most acute ironic perception and is a good example of his preoccupation with the rôle of the Jew as an ambiguous social alien. A major strength of his work is his avoidance of the melodrama which James Baldwin brings to his novels dealing with the more pronounced group isolation of the American Negro. The absence of an element of paranoia allows Malamud a more searching and subtle appraisal of his characters' predicament.

A further novel *The Fixer* was published in 1967. M. T.

Malaparte, Curzio (Kurt Erich Suckert; 1898–1957), Italian novelist, playwright and journalist. An imaginative and versatile writer of chronicle and fiction and a keen observer and commentator of political events, he wrote in French, at an early stage, a study of political ambition and success, *Technique du coup d'état* [*Coup d'Etat, the Technique of Revolution*] (1931); but his international reputation began with the publication, during and after the second world war, of his sensational works based on his experiences as a war correspondent and liaison officer. To this stage in Malaparte's production belong *Il Volga nasce in Europa* [*The Volga Rises in Europe*] (1943), *Kaputt* [*Kaputt*] (1944) and *La pelle* [*The Skin*] (1949), which created much controversy with their unconventional crudeness and gruesome, often shocking, details. In *Maledetti Toscani* [*Those Cursed Tuscans*] (1956) he presented an impassioned analysis of his love-hate relationship with his own fellow-countrymen. Malaparte's writings are composed in a characteristically uninhibited style often rich with heavy sarcasm and paradoxical asides, betraying a searching intelligence yet frequently relying on the amateurish or gimmicky. D. B.

Mallea, Eduardo (1903–), one of the founders and leading exponents of the modern Argentinian novel. Son of a surgeon of Bahía Blanca, he has held important posts with literary periodicals and has been a diplomatic representative for his country. An existential philosophy characterises the thought of his work. The protagonists, lacking effective communication among themselves, suffer the anguish of a metaphysical solitude. Most of his novels are set in Argentina, though as they probe into the nature of life itself their basic implications are universal. *Historia de una pasión argentina* ['History of an Argentine passion'] (1937) is more an autobiographical essay than a novel; it examines the contemporary Argentinian's place in the world of the twentieth century, passionately voicing the author's anguish. In *Fiesta en noviembre* ['Fiesta in November'] (1938) Mallea builds a novel around the execution of Federico García Lorca. A lengthy novel with a significant title, *La bahía de silencio* [*The Bay of Silence*] (1940) traces the search for authentic qualities and beliefs in a world which has lost its traditional values. The first half of *Todo verdor perecerá* [*All Green Shall Perish*] (1941) takes place in a rocky barren setting, where a farmer and his wife struggle vainly against the elements. The sterility of their marriage and their hostile silence match the landscape, and accentuate the tedium of life. When the man dies, Agatha moves to Buenos Aires, where, despite the animation of the crowds, her solitude intensifies and her terror increases. A more recent publication was the important novel-trilogy *El resentimiento* ['Resentment'] (1966). In his novels Mallea poses more problems than he answers; yet he presents his crucial message with intensity and authenticity. P. R. B.

Mallet (later **Mallet-Joris**), Françoise (1930–), Belgian novelist. The rich visual details of her Flemish scenes evoke Bosch, Breughel and Vermeer, while the warp and weft of her social fabric supposedly suggest Balzac. Pre-eminently however she is the moralist who, in an autobiographical rumination *Lettre à moi-même* [*A Letter to Myself*] (1963), finds Cézanne picturesque, Gauguin merely hackneyed. She is fascinated by 'that damnation which consists of an intelligent man becoming voluntarily stupid, of a sensitive man in his turn becoming voluntarily hard, of a man who has been hurt becoming the one who in his turn inflicts pain, of a proud man humiliating himself to prevent himself being humiliated'. This predicament, made feminine, underlies her first two novels, the precocious *Le Rempart des Béguines* [*Into The Labyrinth*] (1951) and *La Chambre rouge* [*The Red Room*] (1955). *Le Rempart des Béguines* is also translated as *The Illusionist*. This is appropriate: for whether we are the varied characters of her embryonic novels *Cordélia* [*Cordelia*] (1956)—a patriarch's covetous heirs and dependants—and *Les Mensonges* [*House of Lies*] (1956), or second-rate musicians with a talent for bogus idealism as in *L'Empire céleste* [*Café Céleste*] (1958), or the intriguers at the court of Louis XIII depicted in *Les Personnages* [*The Favourite*] (1961), Mallet-Joris is concerned with our social carapace —'The Boss asserts himself as Boss, describes himself before he sets about existing'—the illusions, assumed personalities, acrobatic moralities, conditioned reflexes, alibis and lies which mask our nothingness and nonentity. This view of society also permeated the more recent novel *Les Signes et les prodigies* [*Signs and Wonders*] (1966). M. D. E.

Malraux, André (1901–), French novelist. Educated at the Lycée Condorcet, Malraux studied at the School of Oriental Languages in Paris before setting out for Indochina in search of temple sculptures. While in the area he took an active part in opposing the excesses of French colonial rule by his articles and exposés in an opposition newspaper; he also came into contact with Chinese revolutionary groups. A number of novels and essays were written after this experience—*La Tentation de l'occident* [*The Temptation of the West*] (1926), *Les Conquérants* [*The Conquerors*] (1928), *La Voie Royale* [*The Royal Way*] (1930), *La Condition humaine* [*Man's Fate*] (1933): works in which Malraux's basic setting is that of the east, of revolution and of violent, often bloodthirsty, action. His characters are revolutionaries, capitalists, prostitutes, gamblers; the whole range of humanity being examined, and depicted in ever broader canvases. But the setting is not all; Malraux's concern is with the point of existence. His starting point is the starting point of existentialism—the external world is hostile to man; God is dead, man must find a solution to the tragic inevitability of his own condition. Malraux depicts, in *Man's Fate*, some of the possible answers—Ferral's self-transcendence by eroticism, Clappique's by the intensity of the gambler's despair, Tcheng's by terrorism, Katow's and Kyo's by the fraternity of a common struggle for others.

In *L'Espoir* [*Man's Hope*] (1937), a novel of the Spanish civil war, in which Malraux took an active part, he shows that the lyrical illusion of revolt is not enough—to create, one must organise and discipline. His own personal answer to the problem of man's fate seems to have been in art—with *Les Noyers de l'Altenburg* [*The Walnut-trees of Altenburg*] (1943), a dialogue on the nature of man, foreshadowing *Les Voix du silence* [*The Voices of Silence*] (1951).

In this work Malraux's main thesis is that the proof of man's immortality, his noble refusal to accept his destiny, is given in the great works of art which have survived and which live in a world-wide 'museum' formed by the general awareness of their existence. These 'voices' speak for man's triumph over death, the great 'silence'. The book also reflects Malraux's striking and original views on many topics associated with art—for example, the influence of photography on present-day awareness of great art.

From his early revolutionary political activities Malraux emerged in 1945 at the side of General de Gaulle; and as Minister of Culture during de Gaulle's presidency his voice continued to be heard. But it is as a novelist of immense power and intelligence, who represented earlier than most the major intellectual preoccupations of the twentieth century, that Malraux will be remembered. The first volume of his penetrating *Antimémoires* appeared in 1967. D. E. A.

Mandelstam, Osip Emilievich (1892–1939), was a Russian acmeist poet (see under Gumilyov) and prose writer. He was deported in 1930 because of his anti-Soviet attitude; his work up to that time had been excellent though slight. His poems *Tristia* [*Tristia*] (1916) are classical in conception, balanced in execution, pessimistic in emotion. His collection of prose work is more cheerful, containing recollections of his youth and including his only known work of fiction *Yegipyetskaya marka* [*The Egyptian Stamp*] (1928), which has a flimsy plot to hold together the narrative, autobiography and criticism to be found in it. B. W.

Mander, Jane (1877–1949), New Zealand novelist, is not always able to avoid facile romanticism, but at her best she analyses perceptively the reaction of women to the colonial homestead existence and to the problem of emancipating themselves from the apron-strings of English ways of life. Her works include *The Story of a New Zealand River* (1920) and the popular *Allen Adair* (1925). S. R.

Mankowitz, Wolf (1924–), English short-story writer, novelist, playwright and writer for the cinema. Mankowitz writes with realism, humour and a touch of sentimentality usually about working-class (especially Jewish) Londoners of the East End; and he has been especially popular for his numerous shorter pieces, often written for evening newspapers or for television—the one-act play 'The Bespoke Overcoat', with its rich vein of Jewish sentimental humour, being a notable example of his work on this scale. *A Kid for Two Farthings* (1953) deals with the imaginative world of a small child from such a background, whose fantasy world translates a goat into a unicorn. The story effectively explores the mind and emotions of the child. The latter rather than the imagined unicorn work apparent magic on the real outside world. *Expresso Bongo* (1959), filmed in 1960, explores the distorted world surrounding the personalities who create popular music. Later titles include *The Biggest Pig in Barbados* (1965), in which he memorably captures the West Indian idiom. D. L. P.

Mann, Heinrich (1871–1950), German novelist, elder brother of Thomas. His best-known works are *Der Untertan* [*The Patrioteer*] (1918) and *Professor Unrat* [*The Blue Angel*] (1905), this latter being the subject of the celebrated Marlene Dietrich film. R. C. W.

Mann, Thomas (1875–1955), German novelist and critic, of distinguished Lübeck commercial stock. His father was a corn merchant; his mother, a talented musician, was not pure German, there being a mixture of both Portuguese and Creole blood in her background. The juxtaposition of the conservative business outlook and the artistic Latin temperament was to be extraordinarily fruitful in the case of Thomas; his early studies were, however, undistinguished. On the death of his father, the Mann family moved to Munich where Thomas worked for a while as a clerk before attending the university for a short time.

His first love story *Gefallen* ['Fallen'] (1894) appeared when Mann was 19; then followed a year in Italy with his family. At the end of the century, Mann returned to Munich, becoming proof reader for the satirical magazine *Simplicissimus* which published many of his short stories. Mann became famous when he published *Buddenbrooks* [*Buddenbrooks*] (1901), the chronicle of a family much like his own, tracing the interaction of art and business throughout four generations. He married the daughter of a university professor and on her account went to Davos in 1912, as she was suffering from consumption. Earlier he had returned to Italy, the setting for *Der Tod in Venedig* [*Death in Venice*] (1913) in which a homosexual encounter in Venice culminates in the death of an elderly German.

He escaped conscription during the war on health grounds, but he never concealed his militant German nationalism and a distrust for political ideologies, expressed especially in *Betrachtungen eines Unpolitischen*

['Meditations of a non-political person'] (1918). After the war he received many honours culminating in 1929 in the award of the Nobel Prize for *Der Zauberberg* [*The Magic Mountain*], inspired by visiting his wife in the sanatorium at Davos. While the book deals at one level with a patient in such a sanatorium, the sanatorium itself is made to symbolise Europe in decay before the Great War. Mann's keen interest in psychology was indicated in his short story *Unordnung und frühes Leid* [*Early Sorrow*] (1926) which deals with the experiences of a child who falls in love with a grown-up; ten years after its publication he was to deliver an address in honour of Freud's 80th birthday in 1936, and before that, influenced by the psycho-analyst's own interest in the personality of the biblical figure Joseph, had begun the cycle of novels about him, *Joseph und seine Brüder* [*Joseph and his Brethren*] (1933–44): *Die Geschichten Jaakobs* [*Tales of Jacob*], *Der junge Joseph* [*Young Joseph*], *Joseph in Ägypten* [*Joseph in Egypt*] and *Joseph als Ernährer* [*Joseph the Provider*]. These novels revealed once again the pervading themes of Mann's work: the idea that degeneration is closely connected with culture (which had been the feature of his early novel *Tonio Kröger* [*Tonio Kröger*] published in 1903), and the dualism of the sensual and aesthetic features of man (which he had described in his drama *Fiorenza*, 1905).

The early thirties were to be difficult for Mann; his strong opposition to national socialism at home and fascism abroad found its strongest expression in *Mario und der Zauberer* [*Mario and the Magician*] (1930). He left Germany in 1933; his property was confiscated and he was deprived of German citizenship in 1936. Nevertheless, British and American universities continued to hail him as the custodian of the German literary tradition, and shortly before the war he went to Princeton, New Jersey. He took American citizenship in 1944; and it was in America that *Lotte in Weimar* [*Lotte in Weimar*] (1939), dealing with an encounter between Goethe and his former love Charlotte Buff, was first published. In 1947 he published perhaps his greatest work *Doktor Faustus* [*Doctor Faustus*], a modern version of the old mediaeval myth; it treats both the life and tragic end of a musical composer, and the collapse of Germany as a result of two wars. An immediate favourite with English readers was the translation of *Bekenntnisse des Hochstaplers Felix Krull* [*The Confessions of Felix Krull*] (1955), written with astonishing wit and humour. These last works were written in Switzerland after the war; but Mann had the distinction of being honoured by both East and West Germany, and being hailed as the outstanding novelist of the century before his death in 1955.

Mann's output was vast; apart from his completely original work, he was one of the most important critics of the century. His essays on Schiller,

Goethe and Nietzsche were published posthumously, as was his study of the Russian novelist Chekhov. He had early shown his historical grasp in *Friedrich der Grosse* [*Frederick the Great*] published in 1915, and *Der Erwählte* [*The Holy Sinner*] on the life of the incestuous Pope Gregory appeared in 1951. Mann has been described as essentially a German conservative whose cultural landmarks were swept away by the Great War, a brilliant storyteller in the classical German tradition whose subject was, paradoxically, the end of that tradition. His own mixed background, artistic and commercial, made him ambivalent in his attitude towards the artist; at one and the same time he valued art and yet feared the degeneracy associated with the bohemian character of many artists. G. W.

Manning, Frederic (1882–1935), Australian-born writer who came to England at the age of 15. He published several volumes of verse including *The Vigil of Brunhilde* (1907) and *Poems* (1910), but he is now best known for his novel *Her Privates We* (1930) originally published anonymously under the pseudonym Private 19022, one of the most highly praised of all war novels. In it he describes with great frankness and realism the experiences of men in the lower ranks during the trench warfare of the first world war. S. R.

Manning, Olivia (–), English novelist and short-story writer. Amongst her novels are *School for Love* (1951) a tragi-comic story set in Jerusalem with an outrageous, repellent yet compelling central figure Miss Bohun; *The Doves of Venus* (1955), which gives a perceptive and gently mocking picture of the contemporary London social scene; and perhaps most important her Balkan trilogy. The first volume of this, *The Great Fortune* (1960), is set in Bucharest, a city of rumour and tension, at the beginning of the second world war, and is memorable for its witty and subtle characterisation—both of individuals and of a whole society—of a still-new nation of rich endowments. Narrative continuity centres on the new marriage of an English lecturer at the university, Guy Pringle, and Harriet, his wife, and on their changing situation as the European balance of power is seen to shift: the fall of Paris providing the climax of the novel. *The Spoilt City* (1962) shows the same characters against the background of the break-up of Rumania, with the city's elegance and gaiety turning sour and giving way to fascist violence and racialism. In fear of its safety the British colony dwindles, and the book ends with the city under German occupation—Guy alone remaining, loyal to a liberal cultural ideal that he has no longer any means of serving, while Harriet, driven to despair by his impersonal unselfishness, flees to Athens. *Friends and Heroes* (1965) begins with the entry of the German army into Bucharest, reunites Guy and Harriet, and ends during the last days of the Greek campaign and the retreat of the British forces.

A Romantic Hero (1967) is a volume of short stories remarkably perceptive in their treatment of relationships and attitudes.

P. E.; K. R. R.

Mansfield, Katherine (Kathleen Mansfield Beauchamp, later Katherine Mansfield Murry; 1888–1923), New Zealand short-story writer. She spent her childhood in Wellington, N.Z., but completed her education in England; returning home for several years, she was discontented until able to rejoin the London cultural scene that she had found so attractive. In 1911 her small volume of short stories *In a German Pension* appeared but did not attract much notice. These are to a certain extent autobiographical and reveal the bitterness she was feeling in the first years of her return to London—years that were not particularly happy or successful (she left her first husband days after they married and went to Germany in a kind of exile, there to bear another man's child, which was stillborn). She began contributing short stories regularly to *The New Age* and *Rhythm* and in 1912 met the man who was then editor of the latter, John Middleton Murry, whom she was later to marry.

The next significant event in her life was the death of her brother in 1915. This occurred only three weeks after his return to the front and after he had spent an extended convalescence with her, unlocking her childhood memories of New Zealand which were to provide the richest seam of material for her writing. The first story from this period, written in 1916, was 'Prelude' (later published in the collection *Bliss and Other Stories*, 1921), a long and evocative mosaic in twelve sections in which she enters the minds of various members of a family—the mother Linda Burnell, Stanley her husband, her sister Beryl, the grandmother and little Kezia—at the moment of their moving into a new house. In condensed and poetic prose, memories, thoughts and dreams are fused until the significance of the story has been extended far beyond the experiences of a few days. The names of the characters are worth remarking because subsequently they crop up again and again (as in 'At the Bay', published in *The Garden Party*, 1922), and each succeeding encounter enriches the portrait.

In the years that followed the writing of 'Prelude', until her untimely death seven years later, a diversity of stories that are clearly based on her own personal experiences continued to flow from Katherine Mansfield's pen: some set in Europe and London, as well as the New Zealand ones. Her style, which she herself once described as 'a special kind of prose' and which many critics have praised for possessing the same qualities as poetry, can convey the lyrical joy of a child's happiness, a summer morning, or the stirrings of a love too vague and too young to have discovered its object; or it can deal with sorrow and recreate in us with surprising economy of means the loss of a grandchild, the discovery of a betrayal, the mingled relief and despair at the death of a tyrannical father. Apart from her short stories, a further two volumes of which—*The Doves' Nest* (1923) and *Something Childish* (1924)—were published posthumously, some of her most interesting writing, including her views on style and on the form of the short story, is that contained in her letters (collected in *Katherine Mansfield's Letters*, 1928, and *Letters to J. Middleton Murry*, 1951) and above all in her journal (most complete edition, 1954). Here she gives extremely honest and perceptive accounts of her life, of her relationships within the literary circle she inhabited (e.g. with D. H. and Frieda Lawrence) and of her struggle to reconcile herself to approaching death—tuberculosis finally killing her, after a long illness, at the age of 34.

S. R.

Manson, Harley A. W. (–   ), English playwright domiciled in southern Africa. His poetic dramas are interesting (and by some highly regarded) attempts at integrating rhythmic fluency, conventional metre and rhyme, and personal idiom. His subjects are often distant—balladic, epic, legendary-heroic, as in *The Noose-Knot Ballad* (1963). C. P.

Maraini, Dacia (1937–   ), Italian novelist. Daughter of a Sicilian princess and an eminent orientalist she first sprang to prominence in 1962 when she was awarded the Premio Formentor for the manuscript of her second novel, *L'età del malessere* [*The Age of Discontent*] (1963). But for two years in a Japanese prison camp, her early years were uneventful. Married at 19 and soon separated, she became the intimate protégée of Alberto Moravia, sharing his leftist views and moral nihilism. Saganesque in conception (though this she denied), her prize-winning novel searingly portrayed a section of Italian student society, living an aimless, creedless *dolce vita* without the high-society gloss. Forlorn and confused, the seventeen-year-old Enrica clings desperately to her unfaithful blond god, Cesare, while rebuffing the advances and proposals of the ardent Carlo. Despite technical and cinematographic brilliance, this novel may be thought to concentrate too fully on dialogue and action at the expense of psychological motivation. More effective is *La vacanza* [*The Holiday*] (1962) which explores, with the same Saganesque neutrality, the effect of the sensual experiences of a seaside holiday on Anna, a fourteen-year-old receiving a convent education. Almost without reaction as her familiar world crumbles, she returns to her grim nunnery apparently unchanged. A third novel *A memoria* ['By heart'] appeared in 1967. R. C. W.

Marcel, Gabriel (1889–), French writer, born in Paris, is best known for his contributions to philosophy. With Sartre he is one of the foremost existentialist thinkers, who have had great influence, particularly since the second world war, on philosophy and also on literature. His *Journal métaphysique* [*Metaphysical Journal*] (1927) first clarifies his belief in the self in relationship with others and with God, and through his later works *L'Etre et l'avoir* ['Being and Having'] (1935), *Homo Viator* [*Homo Viator*] (1945), *Le Mystère de l'être* [*The Mystery of Being*] (1951) and *Les Hommes contre l'humain* [*Man against Mass Society*] (1951) the main themes of his reflection can be traced. These are: the existence of the self and of that of others; the idea of the existence of one's body; the idea of invocation and prayer; and that of the mystery into which the problems, particularly that of communication, resolve themselves. Marcel's existentialism is opposed to that of Sartre in that it is a Christian, Catholic thinker's philosophy; prayer is fundamental for Marcel in proving the existence of the other, and therefore in getting beyond Having to Being. This movement lies at the basis also of Marcel's attacks on technological society. Marcel is also a playwright and a literary critic; indeed for him philosophical problems first took shape in his plays, which have the same source and themes as his philosophy. *La Grâce* ['Grace'] (1911), *Un homme de Dieu* [*A Man of God*] (1922), *La Chapelle ardente* [*The Funeral Pyre*] (1925), *Le Monde cassé* ['Broken World'] (1932), *Le Dard* ['The Dart'] (1936), *La Soif* ['Thirst'] (1937), *L'Emissaire* ['The Emissary'] (1945) and *Rome n'est plus dans Rome* ['Rome is no longer in Rome'] (1951) are perhaps the most important of his numerous plays. D. E. A.

Marquand, John Phillips (1893–1960), American novelist, became well known with his Pulitzer prize novel *The Late George Apley* (1937), later a successful play. Like much of his best work, it portrays, at once lovingly and satirically, the puritan-aristocratic New England society of which he was a product, in its refusal to come to terms with the values of the new America that now threatens to engulf it. The peculiar combination of high-mindedness, plain living and respectable affluence is identifiable as the same Bostonian culture that the young Henry James had portrayed sixty years earlier. In similar vein is *Wickford Point* (1939), where we meet a family that is further advanced in its inevitable decline, and is now living on borrowed time. In *H. M. Pulham, Esq.* (1941), probably one of Marquand's most enduring works, we see the title-figure availing himself of the escape route provided by the first world war and a New York love affair with a girl from a different social milieu, only to be reclaimed by his family and married off to the girl of their choice. A similar dramatic opposition between the old values and the new (though here the latter are in the ascendant) gives distinction also to *Point of No Return* (1949).

Marquand's other works include the early biographical work *Lord Timothy Dexter* (1925), about an eighteenth-century Massachusetts tycoon, and the posthumous *Timothy Dexter Revisited* (1960); the notable army novel *Melville Goodwin, U.S.A.* (1951) and the business novel *Sincerely, Willis Wayde* (1955); and a number of popular detective stories featuring the Japanese sleuth Mr Moto, such as those collected in *Thank-You, Mr Moto* (1936). K. R. R.

Marquis, Don (1878–1937), American journalist, best known for his creation of 'archy', a philosophical cockroach, who used the author's typewriter to record his views on 'the underside of life', and of 'mehitabel', the alley cat, who sings the glories of a life on the razzle. The verses first appeared in the *New York Sun* and the *New York Herald-Tribune*. The collection *archy and mehitabel* was published in 1927 and *archy's life of mehitabel* in 1933. G. C.

Marsh, Ngaio (1899–), New Zealand detective novelist, came to London and wrote her first detective story *A Man Lay Dead* in 1934. Like most thriller writers she has created a popular detective, Chief Inspector Alleyn, and she has drawn on her experiences of the art world and the stage to provide the background to some of her most successful novels. In 1948 she was awarded an O.B.E. for services in connection with drama and literature in New Zealand. Amongst her best-known books are: *Surfeit of Lampreys* (1941), *Final Curtain* (1947), *Opening Night* (1951), *Hand in Glove* (1962) and *Dead Water* (1964). *Black Beech and Honeydew* (1966) is an autobiography. K. M. H.

Martín Descalzo, Ignacio (1930–), Spanish novelist. Educated at the Gregorian University in Rome, Descalzo is a priest and Professor of Literature at Valladolid Seminary. Highly influential among young Spanish Catholics, he won the Ínsula Prize in 1957 for his *Diálogos de cuatro muertos* ['Dialogues of four dead men'] and the 1958 Nadal Prize for *La frontera de Dios* [*God's Frontier*], a novel which rapidly earned international recognition. The setting is that of a small Spanish town in the grip of a merciless drought. Renato, a young railway signalman, discovers to his amazement and chagrin that he can perform miracles. He refuses to do so to order, though harried by good men and sinners, poor folk and mercenary local worthies, frustrated women and plotting cynics, and even by the local priests. His reluctance culminates in his murder, and with his death comes the rain and a head-on train crash is miraculously averted. This penetrating indictment of human turpitude, with its incisive moral portraits, deservedly ran into many editions. R. C. W.

Martin du Gard, Roger (1881–1958), French novelist, playwright and critic, 1937 Nobel prizewinner. He published his first novel in 1908, followed by the novel *Jean Barois* [*Jean Barois*] (1913) and a number of plays. From 1920 he devoted himself to a vast eight-part family novel *Les Thibault* [*The World of the Thibaults*] whose last volume was not published until 1940. His plays *Le Testament du père Leleu* ['Father Leleu's will'] (1914), *La Gonfle* ['The Swelling'] (1928) and *Un Taciturne* ['A silent man'] (1931) and a short story *Confidence africaine* ['African confidence'] were to prove less popular, and the last years of his life till his death in 1958 were spent in reflection, producing works such as *Notes sur André Gide* [*Notes on André Gide*] (1951). D. E. A.

Martínez Sierra, Gregorio (1881–1948), Spanish writer, best known as a dramatist. The plays, noteworthy for their delicate tone and feminine themes, were largely written in collaboration with his wife María. A close friend of Juan Ramón Jiménez and Benavente, Martínez Sierra soon turned from the *conte* to the theatre, achieving triumphs with *Canción de cuna* [*The Cradle Song*] (1911) set in a Dominican convent, its companion piece *Los pastores* [*The Two Shepherds*] (1913), and *El reino de Dios* [*The Kingdom of God*] (1916). As a director, introducing to Spain the modern revolution in stage lighting and design, his influence was unrivalled.
D. H. G.

Martinson, Harry (1904–), Swedish author. Of lowly origins, he spent his early years leading a nomadic life at sea; this harsh and constantly changing background informs all his work, his robust verse and forceful prose alike. His best-known volume is the verse collection *Aniara* [*Aniara*] (1956), 'a review of man in time and space', the English version being an adaptation by Hugh McDiarmid and E. H. Schubert. R. C. W.

Masefield, John (1878–1967), English poet and dramatist. Masefield was born at Ledbury, Hertfordshire, the son of a solicitor, and educated at King's School, Warwick, before training as a merchant navy cadet. At the age of 15 he became an apprentice before the mast. He then spent three years in odd jobs in New York before returning to England in 1897. There he worked on a number of journals including the *Manchester Guardian*.

Sea Water Poems and Ballads (1902) gave him the reputation of a sea-poet and included such individual and heavily anthologised pieces as 'Sea Fever' and 'Cargoes'. During the subsequent decades Masefield also wrote a series of action-packed novels, filled with romantic incidents, such as *Sard Harker* (1933); and a number of verse plays beautifully and ideomatically written but highly melodramatic in form. He served with the

Red Cross during the first world war, publishing *Gallipoli* (1916) and *The Battle of the Somme* (1919).

However, Masefield's best work is contained in his long narrative poems deliberately modelled on the realistic and earthy tales of Chaucer. Like his contemporary Kipling, Masefield wrote in a colloquial style, considered shocking at the time. What it lacks in technical skill is made up in vitality and narrative force. A representative poem is 'Dauber' which deals with the life and tragic death of a young painter who is derided and victimised by his fellow-sailors aboard a ship:

> This is a matter touching only me;
> My sketch may be a daub, for aught I care.
> You may be right. But even if you were,
> Your mocking should not stop this work of mine;
> Rot though it be, its prompting is divine.

Masefield was made poet laureate in 1930, though like so many laureates he was hardly the most profound writer of his times. He had the distinction, however, of creating a large reading public for his verse. *Collected Poems* (1923) sold nearly a quarter of a million copies and it is no mean feat to be a popular poet on that scale. D. L. P.

Mason, A. E. W. (Alfred Edward Woodley Mason; 1865–1948), English novelist, wrote adventure stories, often set in colourful places, sometimes with a strong patriotic flavour. Perhaps the best-known is *The Four Feathers* (1902), about an Englishman accused of cowardice who dramatically proves himself in the Sudan. Mason's later works included detective stories such as *At the Villa Rose* (1910) and *The House of the Arrow* (1924) in which he may be considered to have made a contribution to the development of that genre. K. R. R.

Mason, Ronald Alison Kels (1905–), New Zealand poet, was acclaimed for his competence before he reached twenty, and moved to a mature though pessimistic achievement in his collection *No New Thing* (1934). He subsequently tried to make his verse the outlet for his radical consciousness, but failed to retain its poetic quality. His later titles include *End of Day* (1936) and *This Dark will Lighten* (1941). His *Collected Poems* was published in 1962. S. R.

Masters, Edgar Lee (1869–1950), American poet. Masters's importance lies in the impact and influence of one book, *Spoon River Anthology* (1915), which, published in the same year as Robert Frost's *North of Boston*, depicts in detail the underlying sterility of life in the small villages and towns of the mid-west.

Masters was born in Kansas but moved in early childhood to Illinois where he grew up. He practised as a lawyer but continued to publish mediocre and largely unrecognised poetry until he was inspired, by reading a copy of Mackail's *Select Epigrams from the Greek Anthology*, to write a series of pen pictures of village inhabitants. The characterisation in each case is achieved by the contrast between the epitaph on a tomb and the reality of the dead person's own revelations of his former life. Originally publishing them as a series in a St Louis paper, Masters, given the encouragement of Harriet Monroe, the editor of *Poetry* (Chicago), issued the whole series as an anthology.

Stimulated by the successful form of Sandburg's early poetry, Masters describes his 'people' in free verse within a set of semi-philosophical sketches which show a keen insight into human nature. What Masters really achieved, in his account of the frustration and hypocrisy and barrenness in the lives of the Spoon River people, was to demonstrate that the corruption and spiritual malaise, which Americans had already discovered in the big cities, extended into the small towns and villages of the countryside. The way was paved for the novels of Sherwood Anderson and Sinclair Lewis.

Masters's subsequent work—novels, verse and biographies (including a savage attack on Lincoln, 1931)—never lived up to the standing of *Spoon River Anthology*. His autobiography is entitled *Across Spoon River* (1936). D. L. P.

Masters, John (1914–), English novelist. Masters, born in India, has been a professional soldier and describes his experiences in *Bugles and a Tiger* (1956) and *The Road Past Mandalay* (1961). The latter is a vivid account of the author's participation in Wingate's 'Chindit' campaign. The best known of his novels describe the fortunes of the Savage family in India from the seventeenth century through to the present. *The Deceivers* (1952) portrays William Savage and a long struggle with the Thugs, a secret society of bandits of the eighteenth and nineteenth centuries inspired by religious motives. *Nightrunners of Bengal* (1951) deals with Rodney Savage and the Indian mutiny. *Far, Far the Mountain Peak* (1957) concerns Peter Savage conquering himself and the mountains which challenge him. The context of the novel includes his participation in the 1914–18 war. *Bhowani Junction* (1954) deals with Colonel Savage and his love for an Anglo-Indian in the period of immediate Indian independence. These and other novels in the sequence do not merely present an exciting narrative but portray a background to India with sensitivity, sympathy and perception. Among other novels are *Fandango Rock* (1959) and *The Venus of Kanpara* (1960) and *The Breaking Strain* (1967). D. L. P.

Mathew, Ray (1929–), Australian poet, playwright and short-story writer who has experimented with sophisticated forms while retaining simple and local subjects for his work. His poetry is published in *With Cypress Pine* (1951) and *Song and Dance* (1956). S. R.

Matute, Ana María (1926–), Spanish novelist and short-story writer. She first received attention in her late teens for a number of stories published in *Destino*, a Spanish weekly. In 1947 her first novel *Los Abel* ['The Abels'] was the runner-up for the Premio Nadal, a prize which she ultimately won in 1959 with the manuscript of the novel *Primera memoria* [*Awakening*] (1960). This work, considered her supreme achievement so far, was the first part of a trilogy dedicated to the description of village life in Majorca during the Spanish civil war. The second part, *Los soldados lloran de noche* ['Soldiers cry at night'], appeared in 1964; part three, *La trampa* ['The trap'], was yet to be published. The first two parts both display the author's acknowledged talent for penetrating the thoughts and emotions of children and adolescents; both parts also illustrate the indirect manner in which civil war can disrupt a community, widening the feuds and rifts in and between families and generations, presenting thereby an ironic microcosm of the major conflict. Srta. Matute's work to date includes several collections of stories and over a dozen novels, one of which, *Los hijos muertos* [*The Lost Children*], was awarded the Premio Miguel Cervantes in 1959. R. C. W.

Maugham, William Somerset (1874–1965), English short-story writer, novelist, dramatist and essayist. Son of a solicitor in Paris, he lived there until his father's death in 1884. He had been deeply grieved by the death of his mother two years previously. He was sent to live with an uncle, the vicar of Whitstable, but he was lonely and unhappy there. Maugham later frankly (some would say unfairly) described this uncle in *Of Human Bondage* (1915) and in *Cakes and Ale* (1930). His years at King's School, Canterbury, were made wretched by his stammer and shyness. Although he had early decided to make a career as a writer his guardians insisted that he chose a profession. So he entered St Thomas's Hospital Medical School and qualified in 1897. His first novel *Liza of Lambeth* (1896) is an objective but vital account of the last year in the life of a young cockney girl. It uses the experience of character and life in the slums that Maugham had gained during his medical training. In 1908 came fame and financial success when four of his plays, comedies of manners, were performed in London. From 1912 to 1914 he wrote what has become his most widely read novel, *Of Human Bondage*. Long and largely autobiographical,

Maugham wrote it to try and free himself from the painful memories of his earlier life.

He spoke French, German, Spanish and Italian, and during the first world war did intelligence work on which he later based his Ashenden stories: for example *Ashenden* (1928). After the war Maugham travelled all over the world gathering material. In 1928 he bought a villa on the beautiful Cap Ferrat near Nice, where he lived between travels until his death, and filled it with a collection of famous paintings and *objets d'art*. *Cakes and Ale* published two years later is considered his best novel, and the character of Rosie, the barmaid, one of his finest creations—full of a warmth and kindness not usually attributed to women by Maugham. Its publication caused a scandal as many people thought the main characters were uncharitably based on Hardy and Hugh Walpole.

His short stories, which were influenced by Maupassant, are tightly constructed and often exciting. Although 'Red', a cruel love story, is probably the best, it is 'Rain', the tragedy of the repressed clergyman and the prostitute, that has become the most famous. Often charged with cynicism in his portrayals of human nature, he was not really devoid of human sympathy and understanding; this becomes clear on a reading of a representative cross-section of his *Complete Short Stories* (3 vols, 1951). However, he was an agnostic and convinced that life was essentially meaningless.

More widely acclaimed by the reading public than by the critics, Maugham was probably the most financially successful of all serious authors of his period. His imperfections—a lack of subtlety and of verbal freshness, a failure to develop his characters, and a tendency to reproduce stereotypes—have prevented him from attaining a place in the first rank; but his almost unique readability could well ensure the survival of his best writing.

Other successful works include *The Moon and Sixpence* (1919), *The Gentleman in the Parlour* (1930), *The Summing Up* (1938) and *The Razor's Edge* (1944). G. S.

Mauriac, Claude (1914–), French novelist, son of François Mauriac, was private secretary to de Gaulle, won the 1949 Prix Sainte-Beuve with a study of André Breton and is now one of France's leading film and literary critics. A peripheral association with the 'new novelists' is obvious from the technical gambits in *Toutes les femmes sont fatales* [*Femmes Fatales*] (1957) and *La Marquise sortit à cinq heures* [*The Marquise went out at Five*] (1961); but the narrative parsimony and concentration on voiced and unvoiced dialogue of *La Conversation* ['The conversation']

(1964) and *Le Dîner en ville* [*Dinner in Town*] (1959), a witty, ingenious, entertaining de Médicis prizewinner, suggest that he reserves a particular sympathy for the work of Nathalie Sarraute. This was further evidenced by *L'Oubli* ['Oblivion'] (1966). M. D. E.

Mauriac, François (1885–), French novelist. Born in Bordeaux, François Mauriac was of solid middle-class Catholic stock and was deeply attached to his origins. He devoted himself to writing immediately on leaving university. His first publication, in 1909, was a collection of verse *Les Mains jointes* ['Hands joined'] but it was in the novel that his poetic gifts were to flower. Already by 1914 *L'Enfant chargé de chaînes* [*Young Man in Chains*] marked out the Mauriac territory: man's soul, and the battle therein between flesh and spirit. *Le Baiser au lépreux* [*Kiss for the Leper*] (1922) revealed the true tone and style of Mauriac and the novels that followed, between 1923 and 1927, confirmed his talent and brought about his election to the French Academy in 1933. The best known of these is *Thérèse Desqueyroux* [*Thérèse Desqueyroux*] (1927) which is the story of an intelligent but withdrawn young woman who marries the farmer next door, quickly comes to detest him and tries to poison him. To avoid scandal she is acquitted and then lives in enforced solitude; she thinks of committing suicide, only the unexpected death of her aunt stopping her; and is in such a state of prostration that her husband finally takes her to Paris and decides to give her her freedom. Thérèse is a typical Mauriac character, torn between God and Satan.

Up till this point Mauriac's work was very sombre in its accents, but peace and hope showed themselves in such a work as *Ce qui était perdu* ['What was lost'] (1930). *Le Noeud de vipères* [*Vipers' Tangle*] (1932) was a return to the black mood. In 1933 there came *Le Mystère Frontenac* [*The Frontenac Mystery*] and in 1941 *La Pharisienne* [*Woman of the Pharisees*]. Through the decade 1928–38 Mauriac produced a number of non-fiction works including *La Vie de Jean Racine* ['Life of Jean Racine'] (1928)—in which the preoccupation with Jansenism and Catholic doctrine is clear. Mauriac also wrote a number of plays, among them *Asmodée* ['Asmodeus'] (1938) and *Les Mal Aimés* ['The ill-loved'] (1945). In 1952 he was awarded the Nobel Prize for Literature.

François Mauriac has claimed that he is not a Catholic novelist, but a Catholic who writes novels. His characters are fallen creatures, creatures of passion with a thirst for solitude, purity and love. He has great gifts of psychological observation, an unerring eye for the austere beauties of the dry pine-clad *Landes* in the Bordeaux region, and a beautifully melodious prose style. A. L. W.

Maurois, André (1885–1967), French writer. Born at Elbeuf he studied at Rouen under the philosopher Alain. During the first world war he was a liaison officer with the British forces, and on the publication of a novel based on this experience—*Les Silences du Colonel Bramble* [*Colonel Bramble's Silences*] (1918), whose success was immediate—he abandoned the family business for the world of literature. *Les Discours du Docteur O'Grady* [*Doctor O'Grady Says*] (1922), in the same vein of satire, was followed by a succession of elegant and subtle novels: *Bernard Quesnay* [*Bernard Quesnay*] (1926), *Climats* [*The Climates of Love*] (1928), *Le Cercle de famille* [*Family Circle*] (1932), *Terre promise* [*The Promised Land*] (1947), *Les Roses de Septembre* [*September Roses*] (1957). These are works of psychological analysis, skilfully written and reflecting little of the disturbing changes in society, much as the earlier works reflected little of the horror of the war in which their characters moved. In *Climats* the narrator recounts his love for Odile, his jealousy at her liaison, his despair at her death; in the second part of the novel the story of love is taken up by Isabelle, who has later married him, and who recounts in the same way her love and her despair, in an attempt to capture the true nature of this love. Maurois is also known for his short stories collected and published as *Pour piano seul* [*For Solo Piano*] (1958).

A very prolific writer, he is perhaps best known for his excellent biographies and histories—*Ariel ou la vie de Shelley* [*Ariel, the Life of Shelley*] (1923), *A la recherche de Marcel Proust* [*The Quest for Proust*] (1949), *Lélia ou la vie de George Sand* [*Lélia, the Life of George Sand*] (1952), *Olympio ou la vie de Victor Hugo* [*Olympio, the Life of Victor Hugo*] (1955), *Les trois Dumas* [*The Three Musketeers*] (1957), and histories of France, England and the U.S.A. D. E. A.

Maxwell, Gavin (1914–), Scottish writer, author of the best-seller *Ring of Bright Water* (1960), an account of his life and otters in his west highland seaboard cottage, Camusfeàrna, written with a sensitive awareness of fundamental values which almost amounts to a philosophy. *The Rocks Remain* (1963) continues the same story with exciting interludes in north Africa and Majorca. Since then *The House of Elrig* (1965) has appeared, telling the story of his childhood in a vein no less readable and enthralling.

Before the war Maxwell was a freelance journalist and had made ornithology a special interest; after it, he bought an island in the Hebrides, and tried commercial shark-fishing, the subject of his first book, *Harpoon at a Venture* (1952). *God Protect me from my Friends* (1956) is about the philanthropic bandit, Salvatore Giuliano, and *The Ten Pains of Death* (1959) arose from his experience of living in a peasant community in

Sicily. He won the Heinemann Award of The Royal Society of Literature for *A Reed Shaken by the Wind* (1958) about his travels in Iraq. He is also a professional portrait painter and poet. G. C.

Mayakovsky, Vladimir Vladimirovich (1893–1930), Soviet poet and playwright, was the foremost futurist Soviet poet of his generation. He was born in Bagdadi in Georgia where he had a restless childhood. Unmoved by the splendid Caucasus that had inspired Pushkin, Mayakovsky eventually discovered a cure for his boredom in the revolution of 1905. After he moved to Moscow he began to dabble in poetry and joined the futurist school. He enjoyed breaking literary traditions and making outrageous experiments. He rapturously accepted the 1917 revolution and devoted himself to the Bolshevik cause.

His early works include the fantastic poem *Oblako v shtanakh* [*Cloud in Trousers*] (1915), a story of unrequited love, and *Misteriya buff* [*Mystery Bouffe*] (1918), an allegorical play in verse which foretells the eventual defeat of capitalism by the revolution. In 1923 he helped found the Left Front of Art; his own works were written in a declamatory style and became very much in favour. On the death of Lenin in 1924 he wrote a sort of elegy, but his fervour for the Soviet régime was not entirely uncritical as his two satirical plays *Klop* [*The Bedbug*] (1928) and *Banya* [*The Bath-house*] (1929) show. *The Bedbug* consists of two parts—the first dealing with the unfortunate death of the 'hero' during the early revolutionary period, while the second part presents his resurrection at a time when communism has been achieved. A bedbug in his clothing also returns to life. The effect of the 'hero' on the virtuous communists is so bad that he is locked up in a cage for people to gape at. *The Bath-house* is a caricature of the workers in a government department. A delegate from a future communist society—the Phosphorescent woman—invites the Soviet people to return there with her. On the way home she gets rid of the unwelcome parasitic elements. The force of these two plays depends very much on caricature and parody, and Mayakovsky was never really forgiven for so clearly revealing Soviet shortcomings. He committed suicide on 14 April 1930. B. W.

Meireles, Cecília (1901–64), Brazilian poetess, born in Rio de Janeiro, began to write verse at the age of nine, and continued to study languages and music, specialising in folklore, educational methods and oriental civilisation.

In 1919 her first book of verse *Espectros* ['Spectres'] was favourably reviewed by the eminent Brazilian critic João Ribeiro. The seventeen sonnets recall Parnassian models with their eloquent evocation of historical personages. Four years later she published *Nunca mais . . . e poema dos poemas* ['Never more . . . and poem of poems'] (1923). The first part of this collection consists of poems with regular metrical rhythms, while the second part is devoted to short lyrics with free verse. Here as in *Baladas para el–Rei* ['Ballads for the king'] (1925) the themes and moods have their roots in symbolism, but the individual quality of Meireles' poignant lyricism and her mastery of technique are already evident.

In 1934 Meireles visited Portugal, where she lectured on Brazilian literature at the universities of Lisbon and Coimbra, and the following year became lecturer in Luso-Brazilian Literature in the new Federal University in Rio, where she also taught oriental history and philosophy. Her next book of verse, *Viagem* ['Voyage'] (1939), received a Brazilian Academy award and the importance of her poetic innovations attracted the attention of contemporary '*modernistas*'. *Vaga música* ['Vague music'] (1942) is characterised by a new virtuosity and the poems of *Mar Absoluto* ['Absolute sea'] (1945) draw their imagery from marine symbols; every manifestation, thought, life itself and even death all dissolve into the waters of the sea. Later in *Retrato natural* ['Natural portrait'] (1949) she begins to write poetry about external objects, sights and landscapes.

In 1940 Meireles accepted an invitation to lecture at the University of Texas and a period of intensive travels followed which took her to Mexico, Uruguay, Argentina, Europe, the Azores, India, Goa, Puerto Rico and Israel. Some of these experiences are captured in the poems of *Doze Noturnos da Holanda* ['Twelve nocturnes of Holland'] (1952) and *O Aeronauta* ['The Aeronaut'] (1952). Her *Romanceiro da Inconfidência* ['Romances of the Minas conspiracy'] (1953) revives her interest in history and legend and she relates in verse the fabulous wealth and glorious past of Minas. As in her *Pequeno Oratório de Santa Clara* ['Small oratory of St Clare'] (1955) these poems are appropriately modelled on the 'romance popular' of fifteenth-century Spain.

Subsequent collections, *Canções* ['Songs] (1956), *Romance de Santa Cecília* ['Romance of St Cecilia'] (1957) and *Poemas Inéditos* ['Unpublished poems'] (1958), reaffirm the constants of her poetry—her preference for abstractions, the cult of incorporeal beauty, her detachment from reality and the predominance of musical and pictorial themes. Meireles has traced the spiritual roots of her verse to the lyrics of ancient Greece, to the cultures of the classical orient, the middle ages, the English romantics and French and German symbolists. The edition of Meireles' *Obra poética* ['Collected poems'] was published in 1958 with the inclusion of her *Caderno de desenhos* ['Cahier of drawings']. Innumerable contributions to Brazilian periodicals and *carioca* newsapers, particularly the *Diário de*

Notícias and *A Manhã*, lectures, and translations of European and oriental classics represent other aspects of her remarkable output. Translations of her poetry are available in selections of *Modern Brazilian Poetry* edited by Leonard S. Downes (1954) and John Nist (1962), and in *The Poem Itself* edited by Stanley Burnshaw (Pelican, 1964). G. P.

Memmi, Albert (1920–), Tunisian novelist and philosopher who writes in French. A goy inside the ghetto, a Jew outside it, a north African in France and a Frenchman in north Africa, Memmi is a phenomenon appropriate to our time, a representative anomaly who says: 'If you recognise yourself in my mirror, so much the better!' His work is a continuing, demanding exercise in self-analysis; fascinated by his Jewishness, curious and even sceptical as to its connotations but always insistent on its relevance and eventually triumphant in its assertion, it is in considering how he is different and why he rejects himself that he discovers why he is the same and how he can respect himself. Two novels examine the problems of a young Jew intent on a career in Gentile society, *La Statue de sel* [*The Pillar of Salt*] (1953), and the difficulties inherent in a mixed marriage, *Agar* [*Strangers*] (1955); a masterly socio-philosophical treatise, *Portrait d'un juif* [*Portrait of a Jew*] (1962), asks what it means to be a Jew today; an equally impressive study, *La Libération du juif* [*The Liberation of The Jew*] (1966), answers another contemporary conundrum, *how* to be a Jew today? Hailed by Senghor as an indispensable investigation into the psychology of colonial exploitation, *Portrait d'un colonisé précédé du Portrait d'un colonisateur* [*The Colonizer and The Colonized*] (1957) corroborates and indeed often anticipates the findings of Frantz Fanon: for Memmi, although wholly absorbed by his personal dilemma, comes to realise that his deracination, his alienation, his sense of moral and mental amputation are the characteristics of subject people everywhere. His relentless, dispassionate sifting of himself through his existentialist sieve has saddened some people, infuriated many and stimulated a few: as Isaac Bashevis Singer said, 'Jews are people who can't sleep themselves and can't let anyone else.' M. D. E.

Mencken, H. L. (Henry Louis Mencken; 1880–1956), American journalist, writer and editor. Much of his vitriolic and iconoclastic journalism now seems ephemeral, but his six volumes of *Prejudices* (1919–27) can still make stimulating reading. More enduring, however, than the predominantly destructive essays on various aspects of American culture contained in these volumes, is his classic scholarly work *The American Language* (1919; supplements 1945 and 1948). K. R. R.

Metalious, Grace (1924–64), American novelist. Her best-known novel *Peyton Place* (1956) had sold 9,600,000 copies by 1965, to become the best-selling novel of all time. It is the story of an American small town—a supposed uncovering of skeletons in cupboards, notably in the form of sexual and other intrigues and of the generally harsh realities behind the apparent moral rectitude of a small ingrowing community. The novel's hold on the public imagination has led to an endless television series the main characters of which correspond roughly to those in the book. Grace Metalious's other novels include *Return to Peyton Place* (1959), *The Tight White Collar* (1960) and *No Adam in Eden* (1963). D. L. P.

Michaëlis, Karin (1872–1950), Danish novelist and short-story writer. She spent much of her life in the United States, Germany and Austria. Prolific and widely translated, she is noted chiefly for her profound feminism. It is this feature which characterises her best-known novel *Den farlige Alder* [*The Dangerous Age*] (1910) and the autobiographical work *Trold* [*Little Troll*] (1904). Perhaps the tenderest of all her works in the feminist vein is *Mor* ['Mother'] (1935). R. C. W.

Michaux, Henri (1899–), Belgian poet and essayist, wrote comments on his travels to South America and Asia in *Ecuador* [*Ecuador*] (1930) and *Un Barbare en Asie* [*A Barbarian in Asia*] (1932); and in *Epreuves, exorcismes* ['Tests, exorcisms'] (1945) he shows his objections to the modern world, by creating a world of fictitious beings and nightmare décor, half-way between the effects of madness and those of extreme abstraction. *L'Espace du dedans* [*The Space Within*] (1944) underlines this attitude, as do the other collections of poems and essays—*Liberté d'action* ['Freedom of action'] (1947), *Face aux verrous* ['Facing the bolts'] (1954). His view of life seems similar to that of the surrealists, and this view is supported by his paintings, which have also had a considerable influence over the younger generations. D. E. A.

Mihura, Miguel (1905–), Spanish dramatist and humorist. The son of an actor, Mihura has spent his life in the world of commercial entertainment—mainly in the cinema—yet, paradoxically and to his avowed surprise, has brought to the Spanish stage an irrational black comedy admired by Ionesco. During an illness in 1932 he wrote *Tres sombreros de copa* ['Three top hats'] but no management dared produce it. In 1941 he founded the satirical weekly *La Codorniz* ['The Quail'], which has since proved a lively feature of the Spanish scene. Finally, in 1952, *Tres sombreros de copa* was performed, being awarded the National Theatre Prize. Dionisio is trying on top hats in his hotel bedroom on the eve of his wedding when Paula, a dancer, bursts in pursued by her Negro lover.

From that moment the dialogue is strange, dense with innuendo. The play finishes as Dionisio leaves to be married, convinced that the strange people who have held a party in his bedroom were living a freer existence denied to him. Subsequently Mihura has written a number of plays in a similar vein. In *Ninette y un señor de Murcia* ['Ninette and a gentleman from Murcia'] (1964) and *La bella Dorotea* ['Fair Dorothy'] (1963) the odd humour cloaks the presentation of the theme of sexual frustration. Behind the irrational mask, Mihura is a very serious playwright. D. H. G.

Millay, Edna St Vincent (1892–1950), American poet. Edna St Vincent Millay is a lyricist of some charm and freshness. She was born in Maine, educated at Vassar and contributed to *Vanity Fair* for a time under the editorship of John Peale Bishop. She was married in 1923.

She published a number of volumes between 1920 and 1950. *Harp Weaver* won her a Pulitzer Prize in 1922 and in 1931 she published *Fatal Interview*, a collection of fifty-two love sonnets which at the time were compared with those of Shakespeare and Sir Philip Sidney.

Essentially however she is a minor lyrical poet with an intuitive gift not wholly at ease when she explores the world of thought and abstract concepts. *The Collected Poems* were issued in 1956. D. L. P.

Miller, Arthur (1915–), American dramatist, is probably the most celebrated American playwright of the two decades following the second world war. The core of his work, to date, is the group of four plays that received their first performances during the years 1947–55: *All My Sons* (1947), the world-famous *Death of a Salesman* (1949), *The Crucible* (1953) and *A View from the Bridge* (1955). The first three constitute some of the most devastating comment ever made on the American way of life; while the first two and the last have a tragic quality, in their portrayal of the catastrophic moral and physical downfall of a very ordinary rather than especially good individual, that is rare in twentieth-century theatre.

In *All My Sons* and *Death of a Salesman* the personal tragedy springs directly from the protagonists' fidelity to values that are inherent in the American way of life—values which Miller has always rejected with varying degrees of left-wing radicalism, once to the extent of associating himself with orthodox communists. The central obsession of both Joe Keller, the aero-engine manufacturer, and Willy Loman, the salesman, is that their own happiness and that of those they love is dependent first and foremost on their success in business. Both share also the twin delusion that success (in life or business) depends on appearances.

Keller's business has thrived during the war on government contracts. The day comes when a batch of urgently needed cylinder-heads develop cracks: failure to deliver the goods could mean the loss of contracts, and the ruin of the business that he has built up for his sons, so he gives instructions for them to be patched up. Soon the papers are full of the death-crashes of the pilots whose aircraft have been fitted with them. When the play opens, the cracks in Keller's life have been papered over just as effectively. Having evaded responsibility and seen his partner go to jail instead, he has won back his place in society; but forces are now acting that have the capacity to blow him asunder.

Keller's tragedy is that he is a man of average moral calibre, totally identified with the values of the society in which he lives, who has to meet a formidable moral challenge; faced with the likelihood of the collapse of his business, he would have had to be an exceptional person not to take a chance. (After all, he has persuaded himself, if the parts are unserviceable, someone will discover it in good time, and no-one's life will be endangered.) But if Keller is a representative American figure, so also is his idealistic son Chris, who by his proposal of marriage to Ann—the daughter of his father's jailed partner, and formerly the fiancée of his dead brother Larry—precipitates the action of the play. Chris, once he has become suspicious of his father's rôle, is determined to discover the truth, and learns that Larry had died in a suicide flight after hearing of the charges brought against his father. He drives the increasingly pathetic Joe relentlessly on to an admission of his guilt and a willingness to confess, and in so doing he becomes directly responsible for his father's suicide as the latter has been for the death of Larry.

Willy Loman, in *Death of a Salesman*, has not made any individual errors of similarly murderous proportions. The person who suffers most from his equally false ethos is himself, and we see him more as a victim imprisoned within a framework of false social values. Most of the play takes place inside his head, much of it consisting of memory and dream: most significant of the recurring images being that of his brother Ben, an Alaskan pioneer who embodies for Willy the concrete success that he has not achieved himself, and who might be taken to represent the pioneer spirit that was the antecedent of contemporary American values.

Willy's values recur in the career of his son Biff, who is a star on the football field but 'flunked maths'. Father and son are equally doomed to failure, not realising that even in the American business world a shoeshine and athletic prowess are not enough. When Willy loses his job and his situation becomes critical, he still believes that if only he can raise enough money all will be well for his family. The sickening logic of this monumental delusion culminates in his suicide—for if, alive, he can no longer help them, at least his death will benefit them by releasing his insurance.

In both these plays, much stress is laid on the failure of ordinary and essentially decent individuals to make any connection between their private and public rôles. Only when Joe Keller learns that he is morally responsible for his son Larry's death does he begin to see that the crashed pilots are all his sons. And only when Willy Loman is dead does the message sink in that the people whose decisions in the public sector have hastened his downfall are morally guilty of his death.

Miller's next play, *The Crucible*, which concerns witch-hunting in Salem, Massachusetts, in the seventeenth century, may be taken as a comment on the McCarthyite persecutions of the 1950s, of which he himself was shortly to become a victim. However, the play is notable for its sympathetic understanding of the characters of those who were concerned with the trials of the supposed witches, as well as for its sense of almost supernatural evil in the fanaticism that grips them. The agonies of most of the innocent are heightened by a sense of bewilderment as to what is happening to them—a sense of helplessness in the face of uncontrollable social forces which might well be compared to that of Willy Loman. But in the case of the exceptionally sane and intelligent John Procter and his wife, there is a greater individuality, an extra-ordinariness, which includes a capacity for heroism.

A View from the Bridge is perhaps the most classical of Miller's tragedies, the one most concerned with a personality and least with social forces. The fatal flaw in the life of the Italian-born docker Eddie Carbone lies in the nature of his affection for his niece Catherine, whose guardian he is. He fails to understand the character of his own fierce reaction when she is courted by the blond, tenor-voiced young Sicilian Rodolpho, who with his friend Marco, a relative of his wife's, has entered the country illegally and is being sheltered under their roof; and the force of his passion for her—which he still believes to be nothing more than a desire to protect her—sweeps him on to a course of action that culminates in his total moral destruction and violent death.

An index of Eddie's subsequent moral degeneration is provided at the start of the play when he talks with loathing about a man who had stooped so low as to inform on a family of illegal immigrants—and of the stool-pigeon's terrible fate. It is not long before we gather that all is not well with Eddie's marital relationship, and that his desire to 'protect' Catherine is excessive. He torments himself with the idea that Rodolpho is homosexual, and in an effort to demonstrate to Catherine what he has honestly persuaded himself to be the truth, he forcibly kissed him in front of her (a scene which caused the London banning of the play). The climax, which precipitates the final catastrophe, comes when he finally denounces Marco and Rodolpho to the police. This most terrible of Miller's endings acquires an extra dimension from its Sicilian context, and as seen through the eyes of the lawyer Alfieri, the play's narrator, it has the stark splendour of a vendetta. Nothing that Miller has written since is of comparable stature.

In 1956, the year in which he was investigated by the congressional committee, Miller astounded the world by his marriage to the film actress Marilyn Monroe, the sex symbol of a generation. The marriage lasted four years, and during this time Miller produced a short story, 'The Misfits' (1957), which he subsequently adapted as a film script, expanding it to provide a substantial rôle for his wife. The film disappointed most of his admirers, but it provides an interesting complement to the two plays that have shown how fatal it can be to conform to the prevailing American values. All Miller's previous heroes have been well integrated into the social fabric, but in this machine-age western we have the first suggestion that to be an economic and social misfit does offer some scope for integrity, even when the path taken is inevitably a cul-de-sac.

In 1960 Miller and Marilyn Monroe parted; in 1962 she committed suicide. When the theatre section of the Lincoln Center, New York's new arts centre, opened in 1964, the inaugural production was Miller's new play *After the Fall*. This met with no better reception that the film version of *The Misfits*, and its apparently autobiographical nature—especially the presumed portrayal of his late wife—caused a minor scandal. But with the appearance of *Incident at Vichy* (1965), it became clear that Miller had at last worked the experiences of the past decade out of his system and had returned to the preoccupation with private and public morality, responsibility and guilt, that had been a dominant feature of his first two major plays. The tentative searching for more positive, redeeming values, which can be traced in both *The Misfits* and *After the Fall*, here takes the form of a gentile's thoroughgoing declaration of personal responsibility for the welfare of a Jewish detainee in wartime Vichy: a commitment which is embodied in a preparedness to die in his place. This play, though not widely praised, was his first theatrical success for twelve years, and represents a return to the themes, form and style of his early masterpieces: succeeding as it does in containing some of the darkest deeds of which man is capable within the framework of a tightly-knit classical drama.

Miller's other works include *A Memory of Two Mondays* (1955), a one-act play double-billed with the original one-act version of *A View from the Bridge*; the early play *The Man Who Had All the Luck* (1944); two early novels; and a further play, *The Price* (1968). K. R. R.

Miller, Henry (1891–   ), American novelist. Miller was born in New York. He lived in Paris from 1930 to 1939. Most of his work is, at least, semi-autobiographical and his personal involvement in the central themes of the novels is almost total.

The books of this important novelist have been banned for obscenity but the defence would be that any subject he explores, he explores in complete detail and with complete honesty. Sex is simply an area in which these criteria apply. Miller's prose has been described as lusty and Rabelaisian but the focusing point of his work is a quest for intellectual and aesthetic truth. His best-known novel is *Tropic of Cancer* (1936) which was published in neither America nor England until the sixties. It describes life in Paris for a footloose, hungry and morally anarchic group who apparently degenerate both physically and spiritually. The sexual life of the protagonist is described in complete and perverse detail. The perversity, however, is abnormal only in the sense that abnormality is the normal extended under pressure. Miller's characters are involved with nothing more sensational than was later revealed in the Kinsey report. The novel is punctuated with passages of philosophical speculation and Miller is concerned that his hero should emerge if not from chaos into order then through suffering and abandon (not without humour) into a kind of realisation of truth about life.

Other works include *The Tropic of Capricorn* (1938) and *The Rosy Crucifixion*, a trilogy (*Sexus, Plexus, Nexus*) begun in 1949. D. L. P.

Millin, Sarah Gertrude (1889–), one of the most prolific South African authors of the 1920–50 era: as novelist, biographer and autobiographer. *God's Stepchildren* (1924) and *King of the Bastards* (1950) attempt to draw sympathetic attention to the position of the South African 'coloureds' (i.e. people of mixed descent). C. P.

Milne, A. A. (Alan Alexander Milne; 1882–1956), English playwright who became better known for his classic children's books (*Winnie the Pooh*, 1926; *The House at Pooh Corner*, 1928). His plays, generally rather sentimental, include *Mr Pim Passes By* (1920) and *The Dover Road* (1923). He also wrote a popular detective story, *The Red House Mystery* (1922). K. R. R.

Miró Ferrer, Gabriel (1879–1930), Spanish novelist, and a master of Castilian style. Born in Alicante, Miró spent his youth in eastern Spain, a region which left upon him an indelible imprint. After gaining a degree in law, he worked largely in public administration, never able to devote himself completely to writing. Miró's first real success came with *Nómada* ['Nomad'] (1908), the tragic account of the downfall of Don Diego, the mayor of Jijona. Thenceforth he produced a series of novels. After his move to Barcelona (1914), there appeared the first part of *Figuras de la pasión del Señor* [*Figures of the Passion of Our Lord*] (1916): intended to be the first of a series on biblical themes, it was not a life of Christ, but of the Jewish people of His time. Its lack of success affected Miró deeply, yet he was now entering the period of his finest work. This was to yield *Libro de Sigüenza* ['Sigüenza's book'] (1919), dealing with Miró's fictional *alter ego* Sigüenza; *El humo dormido* ['Slumbering smoke'] (1919), evocations of Miró's youth; and his twin masterpieces, the novels set in the cathedral town of Oleza, modelled on Orihuela where as a child Miró had attended a Jesuit school. The first of these, *Nuestro Padre San Daniel* [*Our Father, San Daniel*] (1921), depicts clerical life in an enclosed community and above all the struggles, political and social, surrounding the appointment of the new bishop. The resolution of these conflicts is seen in *El obispo leproso* ['The leprous bishop'] (1926), the tragedy of Don Francisco, too radical for Oleza. Miró died in 1930, at the peak of his powers. D. H. G.

Mistral, Frédéric (1830–1914), Provençal poet and 1904 Nobel Prize-winner, is best known for his work in forging a new literary language of Provençal in conjunction with a group of regionalist poets calling themselves collectively the Felibrige. He published in particular his dictionary of the language, *Lou Tresor dou Felibrige* ['The Felibrige thesaurus'] (1875–86); the *Pouemo dou Rose* ['Poem of the rose'] (1897); and his best-known work *Mirèio* [*Mireille*], a Provençal poem printed side by side with a French translation, in 1859. The Felibrige movement lost a great deal of its importance after his death; previously he had published *Mes Origines* [*My Origins*] (1906) and *Les Oliviades* ['The Oliviades'] (1912). D. E. A.

Mistral, Gabriela (1889–1957), Chilean poetess born in the Valley of Elqui (Coquimbo), received the Nobel Prize in 1945. She started her career as a teacher in the provinces and subsequently became director of elementary and secondary schools throughout Chile. In 1914 she was awarded first prize in the *Juegos Florales* of Santiago for her *Sonetos de la muerte* ['The sonnets of death']. Gabriela's first book of poems *Desolación* ['Desolation'] appeared in 1922. Under the separate titles of *Dolor* ['Anguish'] and *Naturaleza* ['Nature'] these poems tell of her love for a man who committed suicide. Influenced by *modernismo*, her poetry nevertheless rejects exoticism in favour of simplicity. Rather than the revolutionary techniques of Huidobro, Rokha and Neruda, she introduces provincial forms and biblical terms into her verse. Predominantly based on the theme of love, her poems express the jealousies, humiliations and frustrations of her loss. Later, purified in suffering, she progresses towards a spontaneous love for her fellow men in the poems of *Ternura* ['Tenderness'] (1924).

Tala (1938) marks a return to the religious themes of *Desolación*, but here the vision is more abstract. After the passion, deceptions and suffering expressed in her earlier verses, she now turns to symbols and dreams, and this process of stylisation is carried even further in her last book *Lagar* ['The wine press'] (1954) which continues to express her love of nature and man. Mistral has also written poems in prose, essays and letters, many of which remain unedited. In 1922 she was invited to collaborate in Mexico's educational reform programme. She represented Chile as a diplomat in Europe, Mexico, Brazil and the U.S.A. G. P.

Mitchell, Margaret (1900–49), American writer of the epic civil-war novel *Gone With the Wind* (1936), which by the time of her death had sold over eight million copies. Her only book, product of ten years' work, it sets a drama of romantic love against the poignant destruction of the old South, with its fatal pride and courage, gaiety and elegance. K. R. R.

Mitchell, William Ormond (1914–), Canadian novelist and short-story writer. *Who Has Seen the Wind* (1947) describes life on a Saskatchewan prairie farm as seen by a small boy and *Jake and the Kid* (1962), which was originally written as a series of radio plays, is a humorous, episodic treatment of farm and small town life in western Canada. K. W.

Mitford, Nancy (1904–), English writer of great wit, extravagance and skill, especially in dialogue, is best known for her novels *The Pursuit of Love* (1945), in which the earlier chapters are largely autobiographical, *Love in a Cold Climate* (1949), *The Blessing* (1951) and *Don't Tell Alfred* (1960). She has also written the biographies *Madame de Pompadour* (1954) and *Voltaire in Love* (1957) and translated *La Princesse de Clèves* (Madame de La Fayette); while *The Sun King* (1966) deals with Louis XIV. *The Little Hut*, a French play by André Roussin, was adapted by her and had a long run in the West End. She also edited *Noblesse Oblige* (1956, essays on U-usage) and two collections of letters, *The Ladies of Alderley* (1938) and *The Stanleys of Alderley* (1939). Her own delightful essays were collected in 1962 in *The Water Beetle*. G. C.

Mittelholzer, Edgar (1909–66), productive British Guiana novelist who depicts mainly the smug middle class, depraved or decadent. A tendency to draw characters who are mentally abnormal or sexually perverted, and an ability vividly to describe the Guianese landscape in sensuously rich and tropic detail, combine with the violence of action, and the recurrence of the Mittelholzer *Übermensch* who is heroically beyond good and evil, to inflate his novels, especially the historical ones such as *Children of*

Kaywana (1952) and *Kaywana Blood* (1958), into melodramatic exotica. When he denies himself the licence of event and person that the past offers, he can achieve a fine amalgam of the imaginative vision and the critical eye, e.g. *Of Trees and the Sea* (1956), or an exposé of class and race stratification in Trinidad and Guiana, e.g. *A Morning at the Office* (1950). Moreover, Mittelholzer has a wide range, which also covers tales of mystery such as *My Bones and My Flute* (1955); the account of the tension that political involvement can bring to a rural English county, in *Uncle Paul* (1963); and some interesting experiments, notably *Latticed Echoes* (1960), which is subtitled 'a novel in the leitmotiv manner'. C. P.

Mňačko, Ladislav (1919–), Slovak journalist and writer. His novel of the second world war *Smrť sa volá Engelchen* [*Death is Called Engelchen*] (19) is a partly autobiographical story of the punitive expedition of the SS units against the partisans in Slovakia, and reveals in an interesting way the relationship between the partisans and the population. Though a loyal supporter of the Stalinist régime, he later portrayed the excesses of that period in his novel *Ako chutí moc* [*The Taste of Power*] (1967). K. B.

Modisane, Bloke (William Modisane; 1923–), South African short-story writer, whose work has appeared widely in magazines and anthologies. His autobiography *Blame Me on History* (1963) is passionate, searing, frank, expressionistic. C. P.

Mofolo, Thomas (1875–1948), South African writer, born in Basutoland, was the first African Negro to become known as a writer. *The Pilgrim of the East* (1920) can be seen as an allegorical inquiry into the relevance of Christian ideas to the African. His next book available in English was *Chaka the Zulu* (1931), an account based on what he had heard and could learn about this legendary figure, whom he compares to European conquerors like Caesar and Napoleon. His careful reconstruction of Chaka's life and the influences that were acting on him make absorbing reading. S. R.

Monsarrat, Nicholas (1910–), English novelist, soon gave up his work in a solicitor's office in order to devote more time to writing. His first book *Think of Tomorrow* (1934) was a moderate success and by 1940 with the publication of *This is the Schoolroom* he had begun to establish himself as a writer. During the second world war he served in the navy, most of the time in command of frigates and corvettes, and as a result of his experiences he wrote a brilliant account of these little ships, *H.M. Corvette*, published in 1942. After the war he used the same material for his most successful novel *The Cruel Sea* (1951). Although the characterisation in the book is not memorable, he succeeded in capturing the atmosphere of life on a small ship in wartime to such an extent that one can almost smell the sea and the oil of the engines. Although he has written about a dozen novels since *The Cruel Sea*, it remains his finest work.

His later works include *The Story of Esther Costello* (1953), *The Tribe That Lost its Head* (1956), *Smith and Jones* (1963; based on the story of Burgess and Maclean) and *Something to Hide* (1965). K. M. H.

Montague, Charles Edward (1867–1928), English essayist, critic and novelist. *Disenchantment* (1922) deals with his experiences in the first world war; but perhaps of greater interest today are his remarks on style in the posthumous *A Writer's Notes on his Trade* (1930). K. R. R.

Montale, Eugenio (1896–), Italian poet born at Genoa. He interrupted his studies to learn *bel canto* and his lifelong interest in music is reflected both in his poetry and criticism. He took part in the first world war, fighting as an infantry lieutenant in Trentino. After the war he settled in Florence, working for a publisher, and eventually became director of Vieusseux until his dismissal for political reasons in 1938. His early poems appeared in numerous literary periodicals: *Primo Tempo, L'Esame, Fiera letteraria* and *Solaria* among others, where he also contributed critical reviews on poetry, music and drama. After the second world war, Montale settled in Milan and in 1948 he joined the editorial staff of the *Corriere della Sera.* Three important volumes trace his evolution as one of the most interesting and original exponents of *poesia pura*: these are *Ossi di seppia* [*Bones of the Cuttlefish*] (1925), *Le occasioni* [*Occasions*] (1939) and *La bufera e altro* [*The Storm and Other Poems*] 1956). In 1965 there appeared *Poesie-Poems*, a bilingual collected edition with facing versions by George Kay, and *Selected Poems*, an anthology of versions by various translators. Montale's own translations of verse include poems from T. S. Eliot and Jorge Guillén. G. P.

Montgomery, Lucy Maud (1874–1942), Canadian novelist who achieved wide success with her stories of the childhood and adolescence of a young girl in a natural Canadian setting. These were first written as a serial for a Sunday-school paper, but were published in book form under titles such as *Anne of Green Gables* (1908) and *Anne of Avonlea* (1909). S. R.

Montherlant, Henry de (1896–), French novelist and dramatist. He reintroduced into the French novel, along with Malraux and St Exupéry, the theme of human greatness, of (to quote Gide) 'that surpassing of oneself that is obtained by a taut will'. His youth was divided between service in the first world war, sport and the bullring. His early novels reflect this virile experience. His first, *La Relève du matin* ['Morning relief'] was followed by *Le Songe* [*The Dream*] (1922), considered to be one of the best war novels, which opened the cycle of novels entitled *La Jeunesse d'Alban de Bricoule* ['The youth of Alban de Bricoule']. This ended in 1926 with *Les Bestiaires* [*The Bullfighters*] in which bull-fighting, as in Hemingway, gives Alban a permanent opportunity to surpass himself.

For the next ten years he travelled in Spain, north Africa and Italy. Typical of this period are such works as *La Petite Infante de Castille* ['The little infanta of Castille'] (1929), and *Service Inutile* ['Useless service'] (1935), a volume of autobiography dealing with his youth. These last two volumes illustrate the two sides of Montherlant: the sensualist and the seeker after moral grandeur. The former is a kind of lyrical 'guide-book' to Spain, the latter a manual of ethics. Montherlant is blessed with a style of classical elegance and purity, but there is a fundamental cleavage, never resolved, between his Christian asceticism and love of the body, his hedonism and heroism, the stadium and the cloister, which causes the reader to suspect his sincerity.

Following two early plays, *L'Exil* ['Exile'], written in 1914 and published in 1929, and *Pasiphae* (1936), it was the forties which saw the flowering of Montherlant's dramatic genius as the thirties had seen that of Giraudoux. Between 1942 and 1960 he published twelve plays including *La Reine morte* [*Queen after Death*] (1942); *Malatesta* [*Malatesta*] (1946), in which Montherlant brilliantly recreates the half-pagan, half-Christian atmosphere of the Renaissance; *Le Maître de Santiago* [*Master of Santiago*] (1947), one of his 'Christian' plays, as was also *Port-Royal* [*Port-Royal*] (1954), dealing with Jansenism; and *Le Cardinal d'Espagne* ['The Cardinal of Spain'] (1960). Montherlant's plays can best be described in his own words: 'There is in my (dramatic) works a *Christian* vein and a *profane* vein, which I cultivate alternately—I was about to say simultaneously—as is right, since everything in this world deserves to be both attacked and defended'.

A. L. W.

Moore, Brian (1921–), Irish-born novelist, has since emigrating divided his time between Canada and the U.S.A. He writes with an ear for tough, authentic dialogue but with an instinctive tenderness for the agony the individual undergoes in finally committing himself—a theme which recurs in all his novels. *The Lonely Passion of Judith Hearne* (1955) deals with an alcoholic spinster, *The Feast of Lupercal* (1957) with a timid schoolmaster; but by far the best known of his books is *The Luck of Ginger Coffey* (1960), a picaresque tale of a cocky Irishman who is one by one bereft of his protective fantasies about himself. Ginger, an Irish immigrant in Canada, faces the triple problem of middle age, unemployment and loss of his wife to a younger, richer man, and finds himself sinking lower and lower in his search for work and his fight to reclaim his wife and daughter. The conclusion—in which a grey reality penetrates Ginger's façade of lies and self-deceit—is deeply moving. Subsequent titles include *Return from Limbo* (1963) and *The Emperor of Ice-Cream* (1966). S. R.

Moore, George Augustus (1852–1933), Irish novelist. Moore's first novel, *A Modern Lover* (1883), was a brash portrayal of artist life in London and Paris, the life which he had experienced as an acquaintance of the Impressionist painters. *A Mummer's Wife* (1885) is perhaps the first of the English 'realistic' novels in the French style; and his main work, the novel *Esther Waters* (1894), broke new ground with its presentation of 'lower-class realism'. Esther, a serving girl and an unmarried mother, faces a world of poverty and degradation against which she fights heroically and eventually finds a form of peace. The story is told objectively and unsentimentally, and caused some censorship problems in its depicting of a scene in a maternity hospital. In some ways even more sensational was his later work *The Brook Kerith* (1916), which is based on the life of Jesus but shows him alive after the crucifixion, having renounced his earlier claims to divinity.

Moore's creative imagination is also evident in the series of autobiographical works which he produced, beginning with *Confessions of a Young Man* (1887) which was largely an attack on English life, and continuing in *Memoirs of My Dead Life* (1906) and *Hail and Farewell* (1911–14). His later short stories included some in the manner of Turgenev, collected in *The Untilled Field* (1903). R. A. K.

Moore, Marianne Craig (1887–   ), American poet. Marianne Moore was born in St Louis and educated at Bryn Mawr. For some time she was editor of the poetry magazine *Dial*. Her published work includes *Collected Poems* (1951); *The Fables of La Fontaine* (translations, 1954); *Predilections* (essays, 1955); *Like a Bulwark* (1956); *O To Be a Dragon* (1959); and *The Arctic Ox* (1964).

Marianne Moore's translations of La Fontaine give a clue to the character of her poetry. If she herself does not write fables as such, she does write fairly short pieces of tightly controlled free verse which employ immense variety of content and which individually present moral attitudes towards man in his environment. If her precedent goes back beyond La Fontaine to Aesop, her technique is firmly planted in modern America; and though her aims are fundamentally those of La Fontaine, her field of reference is limited, by the flux of her milieu, to the idiosyncratic and the arbitrary. She takes the disparate aspects of her society—the results of horse-races, the speeches of politicians, clippings from newspapers—and joins them together to form worlds of their own, aesthetic mobiles which criticise the real world only by implication. There is an apparent spontaneity in her writing which is the result of her ability to harmonise apparently irreconcilable elements in the subject matter, so that the final values are a product of the internal relations of the poem. The moral, as such, is not conveyed by a tag on the poem ('look here this is what I mean to say') but is an aesthetic result of the verse as a whole. This quality of apparent spontaneity is possibly the central difference between Marianne Moore and La Fontaine. The latter illustrates a moral truth ostensively, the former allows the values she wishes to put forward to spring from the tensions implicit in the poem. This makes her poem an organic whole, not an illustration of the moral but the moral itself. The delicacy and accuracy with which she selects and balances the 'items' of her poetry, and the brevity of the individual pieces, preclude emotional depth and leave the reader not so much with moral feeling as with a moral awareness.

The poet is able to make her point by organising a relationship, for example by putting the statement of a contemporary politician against the remark of an elder statesman, against the impression of a painting, against the background of Greek mythology. Since the emotion generated is essentially dependent on an idiosyncratic form—a form virtually independent of a traditional or a conventional field of reference—it is turned in upon itself and becomes complete and atomised. This intention is made explicit in 'Like A Bulwark':

> Compressed; firmed by the thrust of the blast
> till compact, like a bulwark against fate.

and again in 'Then the Ermine':

> Foiled explosiveness is yet
> a kind of prophet,
> a perfector, and so a concealer . . .
> with the power of implosion.

D. L. P.

Moore, Thomas Sturge (1870–1944), English poet, dramatist and art critic. Moore left school at the age of fourteen and educated himself. His poetry and drama reflect an involvement with the classics. Volumes of verse include *The Vinedresser* (1899); *The Gazelles* (1904); *Mariamne* (1911); and *Judas* (1923). Plays include *Aphrodite Against Artemis* (1901) and *Absolem* (1903). D. L. P.

Moraes, Dom (1938–), Indian poet writing in English. Moraes won the Hawthornden Prize for Poetry in 1957 for the volume *A Beginning*. The latter was praised for its combination of force and tenderness, of compassion and religious intensity. *Poems* (1960) shows the poet to possess a genuine lyrical quality in short poems where melody seems able to co-exist with intellectual subtlety and fairly oblique symbolism. The poem 'Girl' in this collection has a mixture of erotic symbol and ironic wit that produces an interesting effect reminiscent of the seventeenth-century metaphysicals. The poem starts with a fairly conventional erotic image: the hero wishes to take the girl of the title and

> . . . climb
> Into her branches there to see
> The folded rose untouched by time.

Irony succeeds, with the poet having

> But dreamed for days of courtly love,
> And took more trouble with my clothes.

The climax of the poem is reached when the physical contact with the girl is broken off abruptly: and

> The rose had shrivelled in my hand.

Moraes's variations of tone and pace are quite remarkable for their subtlety. D. L. P.

Morante, Elsa (1915–), Italian novelist, wife of Alberto Moravia, has shown remarkable artistic gifts in *Menzogna e sortilegio* [*The House of Liars*] (1948), a dramatic mixture of chronicle and fiction against the background of a complex prism of family connections, and in *L'isola di Arturo* [*Arturo's Island*] (1957), the vivid account of the estrangement of a young boy from his own environment after the destruction of the mythical image he has built around his father and his sudden awaking to the complexity of human relationships. Elsa Morante's works are the fruit of a rich imagination and are pervaded by a subtle yet undisguised hankering for the fantasies of childhood. D. B.

Moravia, Alberto (Alberto Pincherle; 1907–), Italian writer and journalist, married to Elsa Morante. Much of his production is haunted by the theme of the decadence and moral indifference of certain sections of contemporary society, which are observed with a detached eye; and it is frequently permeated with a characteristic atmosphere of unsophisticated eroticism. His writings are composed in a colloquial, yet compelling prose, reminiscent of the writers of chronicles.

Moravia's literary reputation began with the novel *Gli indifferenti* [*The Time of Indifference*] (1929), a disturbing portrayal of the moral vacuum and lack of determination behind the façade of respectability of a middle-class family after Michele has discovered that Leo, the lover of his widowed mother, has seduced his sister Carla. The works which followed include *Le ambizioni sbagliate* [*Mistaken Ambitions*] (1935), a harrowing exposé of ill-placed ambitions and snobbishness against the background of a complex network of relationships, and *Agostino* [*Agostino*] (1944), centred on the figure of a young boy who becomes aware of sex during a seaside holiday. In *La romana* [*The Woman of Rome*] (1947), an unusual inroad into a working-class background not without political undertones, a young girl Adriana, having failed in her attempt to attain a respectable position in society, becomes a prostitute, without however losing her fundamental dignity and pride; in the course of her involvement with a succession of men she is made pregnant by the thug and murderer Sonzogno who is subsequently killed in an affray with the police. There followed a number of novels again portraying middle-class characters: these include *La disubbidienza* [*Disobedience*] (1948), the untrammelled account of the first sexual experiences of an adolescent in the cosy atmosphere of a middle-class family; and *Il conformista* [*The Conformist*] (1951), in which the unscrupulous opportunist Marcello symbolises the passive behaviour of the Italian bourgeoisie in the face of the fascist dictatorship.

With *La ciociara* [*Two Women*] (1957), Moravia points to the significance of human suffering as a redeeming feature through the account of the vicissitudes during and after the second world war of a Rome working-class family. A shopkeeper, Cesira, escapes with her daughter Rosetta from Rome threatened by the war. When they arrive in Cesira's native district they find that the horrors of the war are just as real there; and after Rosetta has been raped by occupation troops, the two women engage in theft and prostitution. Moravia's subsequent production includes *La noia* [*The Empty Canvas*] (1960), a compelling analysis of the emotions of a lackadaisical and amoral painter during his involvement with an unfeeling young girl; and *L'attenzione* [*The Lie*] (1965), the account of the progressive alienation of the journalist Francesco Merighi from his family, culminating in the realisation on his part of the existence of incestuous feelings towards his stepdaughter: the gradual collapse of his marriage being completed when Merighi's wife, Cora, becomes seriously ill and eventually dies of lung cancer.

Moravia has published several collections of short stories most of which are available in English translation, the best known being *Roman Tales*. He has written for the theatre, and has also published a collection of literary, social and political essays under the title *L'uomo come fine ed altri saggi* [*Man As An End*] (1964). D. B.

Morgan, Charles (1894–1958), English novelist and playwright, acquired a considerable reputation in Europe, especially in France where he was honoured with membership of the Legion of Honour and of the Academy. This contrasts with the very limited readership enjoyed by his books in England, where he reached his widest public with his writings for the theatre towards the end of his life, notably the stage version of *The River Line* (1949).

His novels are often characterised by their religio-philosophical, sometimes mystical content, and by their fineness of style. The Hawthornden prizewinner *The Fountain* (1932) portrays a man in a state of unsought asylum from the world of action—a captured English officer confined indefinitely to a stately 'prison' in demilitarised Holland during the first world war. The opportunities for study provided by a fine library enable him to devote much of his time to a long-cherished project of scholarship; and the mental discipline that this imposes, together with the calm of spirit that results from his suspension from the active life, prepare him for the emergence within of a fountain of new life. So profoundly joyous and fulfilling is this experience that when an opportunity for 'escape' occurs he has no wish to take it.

Essentially no less characteristic is the James Tait Black Memorial prizewinner *The Voyage* (1940), an intense and sensitive love story set in the France of the late nineteenth century. The lovers are Barbet, a reasonably prosperous vine-grower, and Thérèse Despreux, an orphan who leaves her country background to become a celebrated Parisian singer and courtesan. Her chief intimate is de Courcelet, an influential if aging man of affairs. The novel is remarkable for the depth of understanding that Charles Morgan achieves in his handling of finely perceived characters. Barbet is an individual essentially innocent in his individuality, whose conduct is internally regulated by his own organic moral development. He becomes a national hero when he releases prisoners under his charge simply because he feels it right to do so. Thérèse, too, has an understanding of life that is both intuitive and intelligent. Their sensitivity is such that the lovers are not prepared to cage each other but pursue their separate voyages in life, coming together with integrity in love only when the course of their lives meaningfully connects them. De Courcelet, also, is ready to love Thérèse on her own terms; and he gains happiness from helping Barbet to achieve a pardon from the French government when the latter escapes from a jail into which he has been put as the result of his own act of liberation. This remarkable novel goes to the very heart of how it is possible to exist in relationships which are both sexual and understanding, impassioned and sensitive, emotional and tolerant: in it Morgan achieves the genuinely romantic relationship of total involvement with complete understanding.

Morgan's other works, several of them developing his concept of the ideal of 'singleness of mind', are no less distinguished. Among the novels are *Portrait in a Mirror* (1929; Femina Vie Heureuse Prize) and *Sparkenbroke* (1934). His plays include the much-praised *The Flashing Stream* (1938), which is thematically related to the novels; *The River Line*, set in occupied France during World War II, which while not in its original form one of Morgan's best novels has proved a durable piece of theatre; and *The Burning Glass* (1954), a problem drama dealing with the scientist's responsibility for his discoveries and for the use to which they may be put: the play culminating in the decision of the man who has invented 'the burning glass', a device for harnessing the power of the sun's rays, to consign to oblivion the formula for its manufacture. K. R. R.; D. L. P.

Morris, Wright (1910–), American novelist, became known on the publication of *The Home Place* (1948), a novel set in the alfalfa lands of Nebraska, and complementing its gallery of weird characters with photographs. In *The Huge Season* (1954) the subject is the damaging magnetism of the rich young man. Morris's other works include *Field of Vision* (1957), set in Mexico City with another assemblage of weird personalities (including some more bizarre Nebraskans), and *Cause for Wonder* (1963).

K. R. R.

Mortimer, John (1923–), English playwright, a barrister by profession. Although he sees himself as a traditional playwright, he is often grouped with the 'new dramatists' as he deals mainly with people's failure to communicate, and their problems of living in and, in some cases, escaping from dream worlds. His characters are drawn usually from the declining middle classes—in courts, as in his one-act play *The Dock Brief* (Italia Prize; 1958); in dilapidated private schools, as in the television play *David and Broccoli* (1959); or in shabby-genteel suburbs, as in his first full-length play *The Wrong Side of the Park* (1960). *Two Stars for Comfort* (1962), another full-length play, is set in a Thameside hotel which the proprietor, the hedonistic Sam Turner, runs in a feckless manner dreaming always of Regatta Week, when he crowns the queen and claims of her his *droit de seigneur*. Later plays include *The Judge* (1967); he has also written novels which include *Men Betrayed* (1953) and *Three Winters* (1956).

P. E.

Mortimer, Penelope Ruth (–), English novelist. Her books include *The Bright Prison* (1956), *Daddy's Gone A-Hunting* (1958), *Saturday Lunch With the Brownings* (1960). Her best-known book *The Pumpkin Eater* (1962), which was made into a film, deals with a woman whose compulsive urge to bear children eventually isolates her from her successive husbands. The style of writing—the disjointed flow of her thoughts—exactly captures the atmosphere of neurosis. Later titles include *My Friend Says It's Bullet Proof* (1967). S. R.

Mottram, Ralph Hale (1883–), English novelist. His experience in Flanders during World War I inspired the novel *Spanish Farm* (1924), a short chronicle-cum-novel of French life and atmosphere in the war zone. It was an instant success and was followed by two other works—*Sixty-Four Ninety-Four* (1925) and *The Crime at Vanderlynden's* (1926)—to complete the *Spanish Farm* trilogy. Also popular were *Early Morning* (1925), *Miss Lavington* (1939) and *Over the Wall* (1955). R. A. K.

Mphahlele, Ezekiel (1919–), South African-born writer and critic, fled from his native country and spent a time in Nigeria before finally settling in East Africa. *Down Second Avenue* (1957) is his autobiography and describes the life led by himself and his mother in Pretoria: in it, he attempts to jolt the reader by placing raw and brutally realistic passages alongside those of almost lyrical beauty. He is also a critic of both Negro and white literature as in *The African Image* (1962) and *Modern African Stories* (1964). S. R.

Mucha, Jiří (1915–), Czech writer. The son of the famous *art nouveau* painter, Mucha was a member of the Free Czechoslovak Army in the west during the second world war. His short stories *Problémy nadporučíka Knapa* [*The Problems of Lieutenant Knap*] (1946) and his novel *Spálená setba* [*Scorched Crop*] (1948) are based on this experience. The autobiographical *Studené Svetlo* [Living and Partly Living] (1968) deals with his imprisonment during the Stalinist period. K. B.

Muir, Edwin (1887–1959), Scottish poet, was born and brought up the son of an Orkney farmer. He moved with his family to Glasgow in 1901, where he had various jobs that failed to satisfy him; in 1919 he married and moved to London. He began to write poetry at the age of 35, after the purging of his Glasgow experiences by psycho-analysis.

Muir's poetry is visionary in theme and is concerned with the great questions of existence: life, death, eternity, good and evil, choice, the loss of innocence, the non-fulfilment of the human potential. His attitude is finally Christian, but his thinking and images derive as much from Greek and other mythologies as from the New Testament. He writes of his own deeply lived convictions, without preaching and without inflating his vision. His forms are uncomplicated and his symbolic images and syntax are straightforward. If there is any difficulty in his expression, it comes from his habit of thinking on an archetypal plane and from his characteristic self-projection to a level of existence beyond the concept of time.

Most of the poems first published in such volumes as *The Voyage* (1946) and *The Labyrinth* (1949) were later included in *Collected Poems* (1952), which also contains a number of earlier poems; *One Foot in Eden* was published in 1956. His autobiography *The Story and the Fable* (1940) is illuminating in showing Orkney as the prime source of his imagination and his ability to cross almost without noticing from the ordinary to the fabulous experience and back again. Muir's single-minded search for the real truths of man's life is further revealed in his essays (*Essays on Literature and Society*, 1949, enlarged and revised 1965), especially in 'A View of Poetry' where he speaks of the imagination as the great bond between men:

> Imagination unites us with humanity in time and space; by means of it we understand Hector and Achilles in their distant world, and feel the remote emotion in a Chinese poem; in such things we are at one with universal mankind and with ourselves.

Throughout his work we are aware of his own strong, sympathetic and above all real reactions to people, places, events, books, poems; he never speaks of that which he has not himself experienced and considered with his own imagination and judgment. His literary credo has its counterpart in the socialism of his Glasgow years; and in his last years he was warden of a working-men's college in his native Scotland. G. C.

Munk, Kaj (1898–1944), Danish playwright, distinguished translator and Jutland parson. Author of more than twenty plays, he gradually emerged as Denmark's leading twentieth-century dramatist after the production of his first play *En Idealist* [*Herod the King*] in 1928. An early sympathy for fascism gradually gave way to stirring and trenchant opposition to Nazi occupation. His works came to be banned and Munk himself was finally silenced, earning a martyr's glory, when the Germans murdered him in a ditch. His theatre is varied, comprising full-length and one-act plays, historical and modern plays, plays in prose and plays in blank verse. *En Idealist*, *Cant* [*Cant*] (1931), *Ordet* [*The Word*] (1932), *Hans sidder ved Smeltediglen* [*He Sits at the Melting-Pot*] (1938) and *Før Cannae* [*Before Cannae*] (1941) are translated by R. P. Keigwin in *Five Plays by Kaj Munk* (1953). Other works have been translated, most noteworthy being

Keigwin's versions in the magazine *The Norseman.* One of his most outstanding achievements was the banned one-act dialogue *Før Cannae* between Hannibal (Hitler) and Fabius Cunctator (Churchill) on the night before the battle of Cannae. A powerful essay, likewise inspired by the occupation, *Ved Babylons Floder* [*By the Waters of Babylon*] (1941), is also available in English. R. C. W.

Munthe, Axel (1857–1949), Swedish author and physician who became a British subject during the first world war. After serving as physician to the Swedish royal family he retired to Capri where he wrote his best-known work, the semi-autobiographical *Story of San Michele* (1930), subsequently translated in forty-four languages. During the second world war he withdrew to Sweden, though he later spent a few years in Anacapri. He died in Stockholm. His minor works include a number of travelogues and autobiographical essays rich in experience (real or imaginary): *Red Cross and Iron Cross* (1917), *Memories and Vagaries* (1908; 3rd enlarged ed. 1930), *En gammal bok om människor och djur* ['An old book about men and animals'] (1931). R. C. W.

Murdoch, Iris (1919–), English novelist, perhaps the most remarkable of those that emerged after the second world war. By profession an academic philosopher, and with a special interest in the existential philosophy of the French novelist-playwright Jean-Paul Sartre that she was subsequently to express in a distinguished monograph, she might reasonably have been expected to write philosophical novels. Given the 'anti-hero' qualities of her first creation, Jake Donoghue, and his affinities with the characters created by the 'angry young men' of the 1950s, it is also not altogether surprising that *Under the Net* (1950) was once talked of in the same breath as Amis's *Lucky Jim* and Wain's *Hurry on Down.* Her subsequent novels, however, have shown that—*Under the Net* and possibly *An Unofficial Rose* apart—she is not primarily a philosophical novelist in any special sense; and that her interest in the outsider or anti-hero is only one, and not necessarily the most important, of her preoccupations.

Even with her first novel, it is doubtful whether the appreciation of the myth-content of its exuberant fantasy is aided by a detailed analysis. It is probably enough to say that 'the net' from which it is Jake's concern to be free—a concern which when carried to an extreme produces total disengagement and effective sterility—is at once the socio-politico-economic nexus which threatens a man with physical constriction, and the mesh of falsehoods (including practically any form of expression in art or philosophy) which entraps the mind of anyone who seeks the truth.

When his refusal to commit himself has lost him the possession of Madge, the woman he has been living with, he reacts by committing himself up to the hilt in love for the singer Anna Quentin (whom he idealises in the process of his quest), only to become enslaved to his passion; but when his falsification of his friend Hugo's philosophy through giving it literary expression loses him the latter's friendship he embarks on a second quest which is the embodiment of precisely the kind of single-minded idealism that lost him Madge in the first place. When the book ends he has learned to be free from his enslavement without being disengaged: he has learned to be involved (in love, in his social rôle, and now finally as a creative writer) without losing himself in the net.

For all its special qualities *Under the Net* also contains much that is more generally characteristic of Iris Murdoch—a feeling for the fantastic and the tragi-comic, both in personal and public events. Her handling of personal relationships—always distinguished by an acute and often agonising sensitivity which is perhaps her outstanding quality—is predominantly romantic in almost all her subsequent novels from *Flight from the Enchanter* (1956) onwards; though the romanticism is often tempered by an element of the bizarre (either in the nature of the relationship, or in the circumstances in which it occurs), which in her fifth novel *A Severed Head* (1961) erupts in outright comedy. That the personal problems (spiritual/psychological/philosophical) of her characters and the situations in which they find themselves may be analysed in terms of (say) internal and external freedom is true enough; but from now on the human experiences are antecedent to the ideas they express. The bizarre and the tragi-comic exist in their own right, and fantasy, after all, is of the stuff of most human lives.

The tragi-comic ambivalence in *The Sandcastle* (1957) is well expressed in its title. However, the comedy inherent in the story is thereafter entirely subordinated to its romantic treatment, and it is hard not to enter into the experience of the public-school housemaster Bill Mor—for whom, though it is indeed washed away without visible trace by the tides of circumstance, the castle he builds is certainly real enough. Mor is married with two children; his wife Nan is fractious and overbearing, and holds him prisoner —her opposition to his ambition to branch out into politics being very nearly strong enough to contain it. Despite the strain in their marriage and some difficulties with their children, their life is a matter of routine. When the artist Rain Carter, recently bereaved of her father, appears on the scene, she gropes towards Mor as a father figure; this, and Mor's deprivation of real love, make it likely that when other circumstances throw them together they will be drawn to one another. When this happens, Mor is nonplussed: it is a preposterous situation to find himself in. All the circumstances are against the development of a love relationship between them.

And yet, with infinite beauty, such a relationship does develop. Mor becomes prepared to sacrifice everything—even his political ambitions. But he has reckoned without the ruthlessness and cunning that Nan is able to summon to her self-preservation: on the occasion of the presentation of the portrait, she makes a speech announcing her husband's forthcoming entry into politics. Wielding publicly the full force of his circumstances, of everything in his life that is threatened by his affair with Rain, she effectively imprisons him; and when Mor and Rain meet again, they know that the affair is over, the sandcastle has been swept away. Through the book there has been a debate—conducted in snatches of conversation, lectures, sermons—on the nature of freedom: and with the disappearance of Mor's sandcastle of fantasy (the idea of abandoning all for a new life with Rain) through the power of hard everyday reality, we see just how illusory was the moral freedom he has believed that he had.

Iris Murdoch's comic genius is again muted in *The Bell* (1958), another highly romantic tale dealing with an Anglican lay community. There is an ambivalence towards the idea of the community in the initial viewpoint of Dora, the frivolous wife of an ill-tempered over-earnest scholar (with whom she is a guest of the community): she becomes involved in the attempted practical joke of substituting the rediscovered mediaeval bell for the completely new bell that is about to be installed in the adjacent abbey with great ceremony, but abandons her prank when she herself succumbs to the supernatural atmosphere that surrounds the abbey. Such an ambivalence characterises Miss Murdoch's whole approach to the ideals of the community, and in particular to its attempt—personified by the central character Michael Meade—to achieve inner freedom through external restraint: and it is precisely this that makes the tragic *dénouement* so moving. It is triggered off by an act of sabotage not dissimilar from the practical joke in which Dora was involved—this time on the part of Nick Fawley, a drunken homosexual who like Dora has failed to respond to the influence of the community and whose sister Catherine is on the point of becoming a nun. Nick plays the rôle of a kind of devil's advocate; and when by weakening the structure of a bridge across which the new bell must pass on its ceremonial journey to the abbey, he engineers a repeat version of the mediaeval 'curse', he completes the chain of events that will destroy the community. Catherine attempts suicide, but is saved and promptly declares a passion for Michael: her own inner conflict having finally erupted when the second bell appears to have been cursed on her account. Michael is 'betrayed' by Nick, who is party to his homosexual leanings: for him, too, the community's life does not seem possible. And

Nick himself, who has always been beyond its pale, commits suicide. When the community is duly dissolved, its life taking on in retrospect the nature of a fantasy, Michael, Catherine and Dora have each found, the hard way, the prospect of a new freedom in the acceptance of the realities of their own natures.

A Severed Head (1961)—the stage version of which was once described as a 'sexual square-dance'—marks a turning-point. It is infinitely more comic than either of the preceding novels; it also packs more harrowing emotional experiences into the story than any other, moving from one to another with such rapidity as almost to strain belief. It is here that we can see for the first time those tendencies to romantic excess, almost to melodrama, and sometimes the frankly incredible, of which Iris Murdoch has been accused in her later books; and yet it remains an undoubted *tour-de-force*, rich in psychological significance. The title includes a reference to the head of Medusa, which in Greek mythology had the power to petrify anyone who looked at it, and which in Freudian psychology is associated with the castration complex—the fear of punishment (in the appropriate form of castration) experienced by the male as a result of his sexual desire for his mother. In the myth, the hero Perseus liberates man from such fears when he decapitates Medusa; in the novel, the narrator-hero is eventually liberated from his own crippling self-ignorance in relation to his subconscious primal desires, and is enabled to progress from a 'civilised' way of living (expressed first in a commonsense acceptance of a situation in which he loves both a wife and a mistress; then in an equally polite acceptance of his wife's leaving him to live with her analyst) to one in which he is capable of a more profound, mysterious, essentially primitive and therefore more truthful and free relationship.

Miss Murdoch's less satisfactory later novels include *An Unofficial Rose* (1962), which combines a suggestion of the existentialist ideas of her first novel with a plot structure not dissimilar from that of its predecessor; *The Unicorn* (1963), in which there are echoes of *The Bell*; *The Italian Girl* (1964), subsequently adapted as a successful play; *The Red and the Green* (1965), which is set in Ireland on the eve of the Easter rising; *The Time of the Angles* (1966); and *The Nice and the Good* (1968), in which some critics found a return to her best form. K. R. R.

Murry, John Middleton (1889–1957), English essayist and critic, was the husband of the New Zealand-born novelist Katherine Mansfield and the friend of many of the leading literary figures of his time. His autobiographical *Between Two Worlds* (1924) makes stimulating reading.

K. R. R.

Musil, Robert (1880–1942), Austrian writer. Of the lower nobility, he attended the same military academy as Rilke, his favourite poet, decided to study civil engineering and eventually graduated in philosophy and experimental psychology. Variously librarian, editor, dramatic critic, army officer, government official and, from 1922 onwards, freelance writer, he fled the Nazis in 1938, failed (despite the efforts of Mann and Einstein) to obtain the sponsorship necessary for his emigration to the U.S.A., settled in Switzerland and died in Geneva. Notebooks and journals apart, his reputation as one of the most important of modern authors rests on a comparatively slight *oeuvre*: two novels, two stories, three *novelle*, one play *Die Schwärmer* ['The visionaries'] (1921) and a farce in three acts *Vinzenz und die Freundin bedeutender Männer* ['Vinzenz and the girl-friend of important men'] (1924).

Set in a fashionable boarding school, *Die Verwirrungen des Zöglings Törless* [*Young Törless*] (1906) examines the reactions of a sensitive youth who falls temporarily under the influence of two older students and, as a result, finds himself implicated in a sadistic ritual, the systematic humiliation of a classmate. Superficially a story of homosexuality and cruelty told by a dispassionate observer, the novel's serious concern is with problems peculiarly interesting to a young writer of Musil's academic background: the confusions of adolescence, the apperception of the 'dark loam of our innermost being', the uncertain development of self-awareness and emotional maturity. The two short stories of *Vereinigungen* [*Unions*] (1911) and the three *novelle* of *Drei Frauen* [*Three Women*] (1924), perfect in their form, detailed and delicate in their observation, may well prove to be the most completely realised of all Musil's studies of human relations. Available in a single volume as *Tonka and Other Stories*, five analyses of the psychology of love, they argue dissimilar, perceptive solutions to difficult questions of social and sexual behaviour, indicate different possibilities of human nature, suggest constant motives for inconstant actions. In the variety of experience depicted and the subtlety of the technique employed, they look forward, beyond the confines of contemporary fiction and convention; in the cast of mind and quality of temperament revealed, they look back, to Stendhal, the writer whom Musil most admired.

This admiration or affinity is evidenced most clearly and appropriately by his masterpiece, *Der Mann ohne Eigenschaften* [*The Man Without Qualities*] (parts one and two 1930; part three 1932), in its wit, irony, scepticism and detachment, fondness for schemata and leisurely digressions, intrusive essays, generalisations and commentaries. Quizzable, encyclopaedic, extraordinarily ambitious, his great novel is both the investigation of an individual consciousness and, simultaneously, an inquisition of imperial Austrian society. Inspired by suspicion of modern man's ability to comprehend his environment and curiosity as to the perfectibility of love, it attempts a synthesis of inner and outer reality and the formulation of a new morality. But it does not achieve its ambition—'exactitude and soul do not fuse', and Musil left the fourth, final part of the work unfinished. Many critics believe he was unable to complete it; others, less dogmatic, merely observe that Musil and Ulrich, his hero, were, pre-eminently, *Möglichkeitmenschen*, men of possibility. M. D. E.

Myers, L. H. (Leopold Hamilton Myers; 1881–1944), English novelist. His first novel *The Orissers* (1922) and the subsequent four-novel sequence *The Near and the Far* (1943)—the latter combining the trilogy *The Root and the Flower* (1935) with *The Pool of Vishnu* (1940)—are set in ancient India, and oppose in their conflicting groups of personalities the 'fastidious' (i.e. serious to the last detail) to the 'trivial' (such as the aesthete), the spiritual to the material, the affirmation of life (and the possibility of goodness and perfection) to the denial of it. In the early novels Myers is concerned to establish the opposition; later he attempts some reconciliation between, for example, a spirituality that is impotent through being withdrawn and a worldliness that at least has the merit of being involved.

K. R. R.

Mykle, Agnar (*c.* 1925–), Norwegian novelist. He studied drama in France, England and America (where he was a Fulbright scholar) and is the author of a celebrated trilogy of novels, *Hotelværelset* [*The Hotel Room*] (1951), *Lasso rundt fru luna* [*Lasso Round the Moon*] (1954) and *Sangen am den røde rubin* [*The Song of the Red Ruby*] (1955). From the narrative standpoint *Hotelværelset* is chronologically the third. The central character of the trilogy is Ash Burlefoot (or Ash Grande in *Hotelværelset*), a man in his early twenties whose psyche is mercilessly harassed by a series of sexual encounters and torrid liaisons which are related with monotonous frankness. In *Lasso rundt fru luna* Ash is a young teacher hovering on the brink of maturity, caught between love and lust and rebelling against his dreary background. He has progressed little in *Sangen am den røde rubin* other than to dabble in socialist thought and to develop a cynical streak, concluding that by its apparent inaccessibility 'love is loneliness'. The setting of *Hotelværelset* is basically a court-room where Ash is charged with assault and battery of a hotel night porter who had used his passkey to interrupt Ash's latest bout of love-making. In a manner reminiscent of D. H. Lawrence, Mykle lards his narrative with abundant psychological introspection which both links with and muffles the stark eroticism, though the latter, nevertheless, provided the grounds in 1956 for a much-reported court-case with regard to *Sangen am den røde rubin*. Such character-penetration also informed his more recent novel *Rubikon* [*Rubicon*] (1966) which was hailed as his masterpiece. R. C. W.

N

Nabokov, Vladimir (1889–   ), Russian-born novelist and poet. Nabokov was educated in England and lived in Europe until moving permanently to live in America in 1940. Nabokov's early work, written under the pen-name of Vladimir Sirin, tends towards expressionism and a certain grotesqueness of style and subject matter which carries over into his later writing. Since 1940 he has written entirely in English rather than Russian. The early novels that have been translated include *Invitation to an Execution* (1938) and *The Luzhin Defense* (1930).

Nabokov is principally known for *Lolita* (1959), a satirical novel which aroused controversy because it deals with the perverse lust of a middle-aged university teacher, Professor Humbert Humbert, for a twelve-year-old 'nymphet'. To achieve possession of the girl Humbert is prepared to go to any lengths including murdering her mother whom he makes his mistress in order to get near the daughter. The apparently sensational nature of the subject matter should not obscure the sensitive psychological and social probings of the book, which is certainly a serious piece of literature. Other books include *Laughter in the Dark* (1938), *Bend Sinister* (1947), *Invitation to a Beheading* (1959), *Nabokov's Dozen* (short stories, 1958), *Poems* (1959), *Pale Fire* (1962), *Despair* (1966) and *Nabokov's Quartet* (1967). Of these, the most remarkable is perhaps *Pale Fire*, 'a sort of do-it-yourself detective story' in the form of a critical edition of a poem by a recently murdered poet, the text of which is accompanied by an editor's preface, an extensive commentary, and an index. D. L. P.

Nagibin, Yuri Markovich (1920–   ), Soviet short-story writer. Born in Moscow into an educated family, he studied at the Institute of Cinematography before joining the army in 1941. He later worked as a war correspondent before deciding to become a professional writer. His stories fall into four main groups: his war stories, of which the collection *Chelovyek s fronta* [*A Man from the Front*] (1943) is a good example; his post-war stories about how people reacted to the changes the war had created; his stories about children, well represented by *Zimniy dub* [*Winter Oak*] (1943) and *Chistiye Prudi* ['Clear ponds'] (1961), the latter being a collection of childhood reminiscences; and finally his stories of brief encounters and chance meetings which are of interest because they attempt no didacticism whatsoever. Nagibin does not try to force his views on to his readers: the tale *Na tramvaye* [*On the Tram*], for example, relates without any moral comment how a girl sets off to live with an older man. These writings show a passionate concern for people and their emotions, especially love. B. W.

Naidu, Sarojini (1879–1949), Indian poet who had an active career in welfare work, as lecturer and as politician. Her lyrical poetry, written in English, earned her the title 'nightingale of India', and was published in the volumes *The Golden Threshold* (1905), *The Bird of Time* (1914) and *The Broken Wing* (1917). S. R.

Naipaul, Vidiadhar Surajpsasad (1932–), West Indian novelist, born in Trinidad of a Hindu family. His first book was *The Mystic Masseur* (1957) and in 1959 he won the Somerset Maugham Award for *Miguel Street*, a loosely-strung series of tales about the bizarre inhabitants of a street in Port of Spain. These, and the novels that followed, many of them written in colourful West Indian dialect, are full of comic invention and rich characterisation. There may be satire in these books, but it is the gentle satire of a man who looks kindly on his fellow men.

In *A House for Mr Biswas* (1961) Naipaul achieved a wider significance in his account of a man who enters, without a single asset, a life which apparently offers no opportunity for him to realise an identity. The heavily mortgaged tumbledown house that he leaves behind him becomes a symbol for the spiritual niche that he ultimately carves out for himself in the bare rock of an underdeveloped human existence, for the identity he finally acquires in the cultural vacuum of a post-colonial society.

Other titles include *Mr Stone and The Knights Companion* (1963; Hawthornden Prize), his first with an English background; *An Area of Darkness* (1964); and *The Mimic Men* (1967). K. M. H.; K. R. R.

Nash, Ogden (1902–), American poet. Ogden Nash was born in Rye, New York, into a rather less iconoclastic family than one might suspect. His great-great-grandfather was Governor of North Carolina and the latter's brother, General Francis Nash, gave his name to Nashville, Tennessee. Ogden Nash left Harvard after a year, and was a teacher, editor, advertiser and writer of Hollywood scenarios before the success of his verse made him financially independent.

The apparent simplicity of his verse is deceiving. It is in fact concerned with social satire on man in Western society—though it is clearly best known for its high spirits, mild insanity and the refreshing liberties it takes with the conventions of diction:

How does a person get to be a capable liar?
That is something that I respectfully inquiar,
Because I don't believe a person will ever set the world on fire
Unless they are a capable lire.

Verses from 1929 on was published in 1959. D. L. P.

Nekrasov, Viktor Platonovich (1911–), Soviet writer, was born in Paris of émigré parents who returned to Russia before the outbreak of World War I. He studied architecture and tried to become an actor but on the outbreak of the second world war he was mobilised and served in the battle of Stalingrad. His experiences were utilised to the full in his popular war novel *V okopakh Stalingrada* [*Front-line Stalingrad*] (1946). Nekrasov wrote with great feeling and produced some marvellous characterisations. The battle is seen through the eyes of one of the soldiers and is related with such stark truth that it met with some official disapproval. Nekrasov's later novels *V rodnom gorode* [*In the Native City*] (1954), dealing with the return of soldiers from the front and the problems of post-war resettlement, and *Kira Georgievna* [*Kira Georgievna*] (1961), which states the inner conflicts of people who have suffered from separation because of political persecution, continue his sincere and uncompromising attitude towards everyday Soviet life. After travelling abroad in 1962 to a Congress of Writers, he wrote *Obye storony okeana* [*Both Sides*] (1962), for which he was roundly attacked. B. W.

Németh, László (1901–), Hungarian critic, novelist and playwright, was trained as a doctor, but abandoned his medical career to become a writer. Immensely erudite, he edited and wrote a periodical *Tanú* ['Witness'] during the thirties, in which his social philosophy, based on the urgent need for reform, both displayed his versatility and gained for him a wide following. His cultivated, ascetic prose is best seen in his studies, whose subjects range from history to art, medicine to literature, and particularly include the problems of Hungary.

As a creative novelist, he is best known for his lengthy psychological studies, of which one, *Iszony* [*Revulsion*] (1947), has appeared in English. It is a slow-moving, minutely detailed study of a woman's reactions to her badly matched husband. As in his *Egető Eszter* ['Egető Eszter'] (1956), he shows astonishing ability to analyse and penetrate the female character.

His dramas, both historical—*Történelmi drámák* (1956)—and social—*Társadalmi drámák* (1958)—are too static and crowded with ideas for stage performance, but make interesting reading. G. F. C.

Neruda, Pablo (Neftalí Ricardo Reyes; 1904–   ), Chilean poet of high international repute. He has been literary editor of a newspaper; consul in the far east, Buenos Aires, Madrid and Mexico; and member of the Chilean senate, where he lost his seat through strong Marxist views. His poetry has been translated into over twenty languages. In English it is available in four selections: *Residence on Earth and Other Poems* (tr. Angel Flores; 1946), *The Elementary Odes of Pablo Neruda* (tr. Carlos Lozano; 1961), *Selected Poems* (tr. Ben Belitt; 1964), and *Three Spanish American Poets* (tr. L. Mallan, M. and C. V. Wicker, and J. L. Grucci; 1942).

Neruda's poetic production is characterised by a pronounced development from 'modernism' through surrealism, obscurity and political didacticism, to a new simplicity. After the modernism of *Crepusculario* ['Crepusculary'] (1923)—his first important work—a more personal form of expression was arrived at in *Veinte poemas de amor y una canción desesperada* ['Twenty poems of love and one desperate song'] (1924). This is lyrical poetry, addressed to the loved woman, now happy, now sorrowful, always warm. The poems are short and simple, the imagery clear and logical. Conceiving of the universe as a unity, Neruda writes about love, woman; earth, sea, rivers; birds; day, night, sun, moon, and storms. But a radical contrast is apparent in *Residencia en la tierra* [*Residence on Earth*] (1925–45); his poetry is now complex in structure and meaning, its imagery is illogical and automatic: it has become surrealistic. Neruda continues to write about cosmic forces and phenomena, but these are now suggestive of conflict and confusion, death, decay and destruction. The next stage of development is that of the communist didacticism which inspired *Canto general* ['General song'] (1950), a work of epic dimensions portraying America: its geography, history and politics. These poems are more easily comprehensible, but less lyrical. Finally, he has entered a phase of realism with *Odas elementales* [*The Elementary Odes of Pablo Neruda*] (1954–57), seeking to penetrate to the simple, elemental nature of man. P. R. B.

Neverov, Alexandr (Alexandr Sergeyevich Skobelev; 1886–1923), Russian writer, had a promising career curtailed by his premature death. His stories deal mainly with peasant life, and his best work *Tashkent, gorod khlyebniy* [*Tashkent, City of Bread*] (1923) sympathetically relates how, during the famine of the twenties in the Volga region, a peasant boy leaves home to go to Tashkent for food, which he gets after many disappointments only to find on his return home that his mother has died.

B. W.

Newby, P. H. (Percy Howard Newby; 1918–   ), English novelist. He was seconded from the army to lecture in English Literature in Cairo from 1942 to 1946, an experience that he found very valuable for his writing later. He joined the B.B.C. in 1949 and became Controller of the Third Programme in 1958. His first novel was *A Journey in the Interior* (1945). He won the Atlantic Award in 1946 and the Somerset Maugham Prize in 1948. One of the most impressive of the post-war English novelists, he has the gift of evoking atmosphere and is a sensitive observer of character. Other works include *Agents and Witnesses* (1947), *Mariner Dances* (1948), *The Young May Moon* (1950), *A Guest and his Going* (1959), *The Barbary Light* (1962) and *One of the Founders* (1965). G. S.

Nexø, Martin Andersen (1869–1954), Danish novelist and short-story writer. Of humble origins and a socialist background he was a dedicated interpreter of the proletariat and came to embrace communism after the Russian revolution. His works have been widely translated, particularly in the communist countries, where he spent much of his later life until his death in Dresden in 1954. His best-known works are his two great novel cycles, the four-volume *Pelle Erobreren* [*Pelle the Conqueror*] (1906–10) and the five-volume *Ditte* [*Ditte*] (1917–21). The former is a semi-autobiographical study devoted to the rise of the Danish labour movement, while the latter is a more particularised life-history of a proletarian woman from childhood to old age. R. C. W.

Ngugi, James T. (1938–   ), Kenya writer. A Kikuyu who has studied in England, he has produced some short stories and two novels, *Weep Not Child* (1964) and *The River Between* (1965). His simple and unaffected English prose explores the tensions created in and between individuals as well as in society by political (Mau-Mau) and cultural conflicts.

A Grain of Wheat (1967) covers, with sensitive objectivity, the post-Mau-Mau period and the independence era in Kenya. The social scene is refracted chiefly through the experiences of an erstwhile freedom fighter and those of a settler. This novel has an interesting companion in Oginga Odinga's *Not Yet Uhuru* (1967). S. R.; C. P.

Nichols, Anne (–   ), American author of *Abie's Irish Rose* (1922), a long-running comedy of a Jewish boy and a Catholic girl who are secretly married by a Methodist minister. She also wrote *Just Married* (1923).
K. R. R.

Nichols, Beverley (1899–   ), English writer of a succession of sentimental and highly personal books that have made his houses, gardens and cats famous. Titles include *Down the Garden Path* (1932), *A Thatched Roof*

(1933), *Merry Hall* (1951) and *Laughter on the Stairs* (1954). He has also written mystery stories such as *Death to Slow Music* (1956) and a controversially critical and unsympathetic study of Somerset Maugham entitled *A Case of Human Bondage* (1966). K. M. H.

Nicol, Abioseh D. (1920–   ), west African poet, critic and short-story writer, born in Sierra Leone, was educated in Nigeria and at Cambridge. His stories have appeared in anthologies such as *An African Treasury* (ed. Langston Hughes, 1960) and his work has been broadcast on the B.B.C. S. R.

Nicolson, Harold (1886–1961), English biographer and historian, who was married to Victoria Sackville-West, and crowned a long and distinguished career with a sequence of celebrated books including *King George V* (1952), *The Evolution of Diplomatic Method* (1954) and *The Age of Reason* (1960). The products of his earlier life, when he had himself participated in public affairs in a left-wing rôle, included *Tennyson* (1923), *The Development of English Biography* (1928) and *The Congress of Vienna* (1946). K. R. R.

Nikitin, Nikolai Nikolayevich (1897–   ), Soviet writer whose early stories about the civil war, violence and sex—*Rvotniy Fort* [*Fort Vomit*] (1922), *Bunt* [*Bunt*] (1923) and *Prestuplyeniye Kirika Rudenko* [*Kirik Rudenko's Crime*] (1928)—were written with complete detachment. He shows Pilnyak's influence in his ornamental style and in his unprecedented use of words. He managed to adjust himself to the requirements of socialist realism and his later work is quite conventional. *Sevyernaya Avrora* [*Aurora Borealis*] (1950) is about the British intervention in north Russia in 1917 and gained him renown; he also wrote an essay on the inseparability of Formosa from the Chinese mainland in 1958. B. W.

Niland, D'Arcy (1920), Australian novelist, short-story writer and television playwright, whose first novel *The Shiralee* (1955) was extremely successful and later made into a film. It concerns an itinerant worker in the Australian outback who, having salvaged his very young daughter from the wreck of his marriage, takes her with him as he drifts from job to job. Gradually, and rather to his surprise, he comes to love her and to realise that this entails responsibility and commitment. Niland's interest in the man who walks alone—his physical courage, his pride, his moral code, the mateship for which he will break his solitude, all peculiar products of the harsh Australian rural life—is seen again in a collection of short stories such as *Pairs and Loners* (1966).

Other titles include *The Drums Go Bang* (1956), an autobiographical work written in conjunction with his wife Ruth Park (q.v.); *Call Me When the Cross Turns Over* (1957); and *Dadda Jumped over Two Elephants* (1963).
S. R.

Nilin, Pavel (1908–), Soviet writer who came to the fore in 1957 during the writers' struggle for the right to express their own thoughts. In that year he published his novel *Zhestokost'* [*Comrade Venka*] which portrays in an absorbing manner the determined hunting down of a gang of bandits in Siberia just after the civil war. Venka, the idealistic communist policeman who believes in justice and humanity, cannot reconcile his ideas with the cynical authority which he serves, especially after making friends with one of the bandits; so he shoots himself rather than continue serving it. B. W.

Nkosi, Lewis (1935–), South African journalist, playwright and short-story writer now living in London, has written *The Rhythm of Violence* (1964), a complex and moving play dealing with the events of a night in Johannesburg that surround a bomb attack on supporters of apartheid gathered in the City Hall. His *Home and Exile* (1965) is a collection of incisively written, intense autobiographical and critical essays. S. R.

Norris, Frank (Benjamin Franklin Norris; 1870–1902), American novelist, first attracted attention with *McTeague* (1899), the romantic and violent story of a professionally discredited San Francisco dentist who, after sinking into penury, murders his wife for her hoarded money and flees into the desert. Pursued by the man who had originally denounced his lack of qualifications, McTeague kills the latter too; but not before his dying victim has clapped handcuffs on him, thus fettering him to a corpse and dooming him to a slow death in the desert.

However, it is with the unfinished trilogy that followed—only two-thirds of which had been completed at the time of his premature death—that Norris's reputation rests most securely. This 'Epic of the Wheat', though imbued with some of the romantic and sensational qualities of *McTeague*, is more akin to the social fiction of Dreiser, and its two extant parts *The Octopus* (1901) and *The Pit* (1903) are among the outstanding novels of the business world written in America in the early years of the twentieth century. The wheat may be taken as a symbol of the life force, and of precisely that vitality that Norris found in the lives of those who dealt in it. 'The octopus' is the railroad whose stranglehold on the industry makes its captains fight like the warriors of old; 'the pit' is the arena of the speculators, the Chicago wheat exchange. K. R. R.

Norris, Kathleen Thompson (1880–), American novelist and short-story writer, the sister-in-law of Frank Norris. Her many popular sentimental novels include *Mother* (1911) and *Certain People of Importance* (1922). *Bakers' Dozen* (1938) is a volume of stories. K. R. R.

Nossack, Hans Erich (1901–), German novelist, born in Hamburg. He studied law and philology at Jena for a short time, and then had a variety of jobs such as commercial traveller and factory hand before going into his father's business in 1933. In his spare time he wrote plays and novels which he could not publish under the Nazi régime; all this work was literally burnt to ashes in a disastrous fire raid on Hamburg in 1943. This event had a profound effect on him; he became 'a man without a past'. His first published work *Nekyia*, appearing in 1947, dealt in fact with psychological strains imposed on the modern survivor of such traumatic experiences. He returned to this theme of the precarious situation in a war-ravaged world in an *Interview mit dem Tode* ['Interview with death'] (1948), published under the title *Dorothea* in 1950.

A shorter novel *Spätestens im November* ['At the latest in November'] appeared in 1955 and brought him notice outside Germany. It describes how the wife of a big industrialist gives up her senseless 'drifting and waiting', abandons her husband and child and finds happiness with a writer. Returning to her family, she escapes once more to find happiness, but also to meet death in a car accident. More recent novels and stories include *Der jüngere Bruder* ['The younger brother'] (1958), *Unmögliche Beweisaufnahme* ['Inadmissible evidence'] (1959) and *Begegnung im Vorraum* ['Meeting in the ante-room'] (1963). G. W.

Nott, Kathleen (–), English philosopher, poet and novelist, whose fiction includes *Mile End* (1938), *The Dry Deluge* (1947) and *Private Fires* (1960). Her poetry has been published in *Landscape and Departures* (1947) and *Poems from the North* (1956). Her literary criticism includes the celebrated volume *The Emperor's Clothes* (1953). Her fourth novel *An Elderly Retired Man* (1963) deals perceptively and sympathetically with the post-mortem that a man conducts on his own life. D. L. P.

Novello, Ivor (1893–1951), Welsh writer for the stage, was born David Davies, the son of Dame Clara Novello Davies, a singing teacher and choral conductor. Best known for his romantic musicals such as *Glamorous Night* (1935), *The Dancing Years* (1939) and *King's Rhapsody* (1949), he was also a straight dramatist of considerable skill and *The Rat* (1924) which he wrote with Constance Collier was an immediate success. Equally successful were *The Truth Game* (1928), *Symphony in Two Flats* (1929) and *Fresh Fields* (1934). K. M. H.

Noyes, Alfred (1880–   ), English poet. His verse has a certain tuneful and pictorial quality, and he has tended to follow traditional patterns particularly in such works as *The Loom of the Years* (1903), *Drake, an English Epic* (1906–08) and *Tales of the Mermaid Tavern* (1913). His major work *The Torch Bearer* (1922–30) deals with achievements in discovery and invention. R. A. K.

Nzekwu, Onuora (1928–   ), Nigerian novelist, whose works have the same general theme (old versus new) and setting (Iboland) as Achebe's. *Wand of Noble Wood* (1961) opposes romantic ideals and traditional pressures in the matter of marrying; while *Blade among the Boys* (1962) confronts Christianity with paganism and its ethic. *Highlife for Lizards* (1965) was Nzekwu's most original and organic work to date—an expression of Ibo life rather than an exposition. C. P.

O'Brien, Edna (–), Irish novelist of style and verve. Her books, memorable for a Celtic charm which, at her best, she preserves from excessive naïvety or sentimentality, include *Country Girls* (1960) and *Girls in their Married Bliss* (1964), its highly successful sequel. In *August is a Wicked Month* (1965) she takes her recurring Irish-innocent heroine to the big bad Riviera with its population of tycoons, movie stars and sexual misfits. This was followed by *Casualties of Peace* (1966), which showed a greater range coupled with signs of a deepening maturity. K. R. R.

O'Brien, Flann (pseudonym of Brian O'Nolan, 1911–66), Irish novelist, was almost unknown until *At Swim-Two-Birds* (1939) was republished in 1960. One of the funniest novels ever written, it combines different levels of action and significance, and contains folklore, heroic legend and broad comedy with lyrical poetry and farce. The narration is deliberately flat and ironic, the story is never obscure, and while the book is wildly comic it is basically serious, dealing not simply with brilliantly portrayed individuals but with the Irish people, made great, and as often made wretched, by their imagination. *The Hard Life* (1961) and *The Dalkey Archive* (1964) are as funny though their structure is smaller. Both reveal the author as a Catholic, and the Church is often represented as absurd but never contemptible. They also show an elegiac melancholy behind the rampaging, and *The Third Policeman* (1967) has its characters in a weird and comic situation which is recognisable in the *dénouement* as hell.

Under the name of Myles na Gopaleen, O'Nolan wrote a satirical column in the *Irish Times* for many years, with all his accustomed wit, fantastic inventions, terrible puns and mad wisdom. H. C.

O'Casey, Sean (1880–1964), Irish dramatist, brought up in the slums of Dublin, whose inspiration was the strife of the Easter rising of 1916, the rebellion against the English in 1920–21 and the later civil war in Ireland during 1922–23. He wrote about the people most involved in the 'troubles', the Irish townspeople, who suffered a great destruction of personal and political relationships, apart from actual personal loss by death.

The first three plays, *Juno and the Paycock* (1925), *The Shadow of a Gunman* (1923) and *The Plough and the Stars* (1926), are all concerned with that period and demonstrate the full extent and depth of O'Casey's peculiarly limited range. He contrasts the feminine and the masculine reactions in a way that is always sympathetic to women: they are the heroes, it is they who have a vision of the matters of the heart which are important to Ireland. The men, who are the fighters, the apparent heroes of patriotism, are seen as idealists acting half under a delusion. These plays have a realism which is effectively tragic, because the characters, although very ordinary recognisable types, are in the grip of moral problems which are universal. O'Casey's language comes from his own experience and is neither forced nor over-poetic; nor is it self-consciously Irish. It does sometimes verge on sentimentality and hysteria but only when that is consonant with the character who is speaking, for instance Mrs Boyle in *Juno and the Paycock*:

> 'What was the pain I suffered, Johnny, bringin' you into the world to carry you to your cradle to the pains I'll suffer carryin' you out o' the world to bring you to your grave! Mother o' God, Mother o' God, have pity on us all! Blessed Virgin, where were you when me darlin' son was riddled with bullets, when me darlin' son was riddled with bullets? . . .'

Throughout his writings, the virtues and vices of Ireland are shown typically and inevitably intermingled, beauty with ugliness, vision with egocentricity, idealism with profanity.

In 1926 O'Casey went to live in England. In 1928 the Abbey Theatre rejected his play about the 1914–18 war, *The Silver Tassie*, on the grounds that it was too abstract; *Within the Gates* followed in 1933. These plays show a movement away from realism to a kind of expressionism involving a drama of symbolic types rather than of individual characters. O'Casey's aim was ardently propagandist, intending to reveal the hypocrisy of society.

Later plays include *Red Roses for Me* (1942), *Cock-a-doodle Dandy* (1949) and *The Drums of Father Ned* (1958). These are concerned with the need of the youth of Ireland to shake off the repression of materialists, petty politicians, priests and puritans. In them O'Casey has returned to an apt theatrical style involving humorous dialogue, strongly dramatic situations and fast action. *Cock-a-doodle Dandy* is a satire in the form of a fantasy. The Cock, whose dance opens the play, represents life, all the creative urges and the joys of love and the arts. The characters are measured by their reaction to the Cock. The play is founded on several actual incidents of repression, and a good introduction to it is the article 'O'Casey's Lively Credo' in the *New York Times* of 9 November 1958. In scene two, Father Domineer comes to stop a dance, full of vicious anger, tries to get a lorry driver dismissed for living with a woman in sin, fails, tries to get him to promise to give her up, fails, strikes him on the head in an ungovernable burst of fury and kills him. Michael, the embodiment of the man willingly repressed by the priest, is left deserted by all at the end of the play. He asks the Messenger where he is going:

Messenger: 'To a place where life resembles life more than it does here.'
Michael: 'What, Messenger, would you advise me to do?'
Messenger: 'Die. There is little else left useful for the likes of you to do.'

O'Casey has written six books of a complete autobiography (*I Knock at the Door* etc.), published between 1939 and 1954 and now available as a two-volume paperback (1963). G. C.

O'Connor, Flannery (1925–64), American writer whose tales of the South are distinguished by her weird and sometimes fantastic characters and by a streak of violence, the latter usually related to their primitive religious obsessions. Her novels include *Wise Blood* (1952), and *The Violent Bear it Away* (1960). *A Good Man is Hard to Find* (1955) and the posthumous *Everything that Rises Must Converge* (1966) are volumes of short stories. K. R. R.

Odets, Clifford (1906–63), American playwright, was a notable contributor to the proletarian theatre of the thirties. *Waiting for Lefty* (1935) deals with a taxi-drivers' strike, and the murder of one of their leaders. *Awake and Sing* (1935) portrays a poor Bronx Jewish family, in which the heroic efforts of the mother place an intolerable strain on those for whom she feels responsible. In a society that no longer ferments with notions of the class struggle, even these minor classics are apt to seem ephemeral; ironically, it is a play such as *Golden Boy* (1937)—written deliberately for the commercial theatre following the Broadway successes of plays originally commissioned by a proletarian theatre group—that has a more timeless quality. Here, in the drama of a violinist who turns boxer in order to get rich, kills an opponent, and then commits suicide, Odets emancipated himself from the propagandist tendencies of a committed art.

It could be said that he also destroyed himself as an artist in the process; and his later work, such as *The Country Girl* (1950), was altogether of a slighter character. K. R. R.

O'Dowd, Bernard (1866–1953), Australian poet who believed passionately that the poet must lead his audience in a search for the truth. He himself was widely read and informed, and was influenced particularly by Walt Whitman in formulating his philosophy. His vocabulary contains hosts of *recherché* words culled from his extensive reading; and he has an apostrophising tone of address that is emphasised by his most frequent poetic convention, personification. His work is collected in *The Poems of Bernard O'Dowd* (1941). S. R.

O'Faolain, Sean (1900–), Irish novelist and short-story writer. His first collection of stories, *Midsummer Night's Madness* (1932), showed his wide range of style and approach in handling the theme of Irish life. *A Purse of Coppers* (1937) contains a number of stories in direct, dramatic style that indicate a sensitive observation of the Irish instinct for life. His novel *Bird Alone* (1936) is dominated by Grandfather Crone, a disreputable delight of a character among a bookful of memorable personalities. His other works include a biography of *The Great O'Neill* (1943); a percipient little travel book *An Irish Journey* (1942); and *The Heat of the Sun* (1966), another volume of stories. R. A. K.

O'Flaherty, Liam (1897–), Irish novelist, best known for *The Assassin* (1928), set in Dublin during the Irish troubles, after the 1923 treaty with England. Michael McDara is a fanatic with philosophical reasons for killing the head of government. He succeeds at the cost of personal disintegration and disillusionment. He has two accomplices, Gutty Fetch, a revolutionary professional thug, and Tumulty, an insurrectionist who would use assassination as an incitement to rebellion. McDara, on the contrary, regards assassination as an aesthetic mysterious necessity, which would only be obscured by a consequent revolt. Also of interest is *The Informer* (1925), made in 1935 into a film which became a classic.

G. C.

Ognyov, N. (Mikhail Grigorievich Rozanov; 1888–1938), Russian writer of a rather morbid nature despite his varied and interesting life. His two stories of the post-revolutionary years, with their forceful descriptions of academic life and methods, are notable: they are *Dnyevnik Kosti Ryabtseva* [*Diary of a Communist Schoolboy*] (1927) and its sequel *Iskhod Nikpetozha* [*Diary of a Communist Undergraduate*] (1930). B. W.

O'Hara, John (1905–), American novelist and short-story writer, is a prolific writer who since the second world war has generally been represented in the bookshops by the paperback editions of his most recent works —usually massive products and often bearing deceptively sensational titles. Critics generally agree however that his best works are the early books *Appointment in Samarra* (1934) and *Butterfield 8* (1935), particularly the former.

Much of his writing consists of a pedestrian account of the everyday lives of the inhabitants of a small American town. But in *Appointment in Samarra*, while conveying a strong sense of the fabric of life in Gibbsville, Pennsylvania, he so isolates the events of the last forty-eight hours in the central character's life that he is able to achieve a near-poetic intensity.

The story is of the meteoric fall of Julian English from a secure and carefree enjoyment of the life of the social upper-crust of Gibbsville, to a debtor's suicide. It all begins with his yielding to the temptation to throw a drink in the face of the Catholic *nouveau riche* Harry Reilly, a fellow club-member whose vulgarity nauseates him: that he should do such a thing being in itself an indication of his own sense of security. It quickly becomes clear that he has made an enemy of a powerful man capable equally of lending financial stability to English's car-sales business in a time of economic difficulty, or of wrecking it completely by his influence over potential customers; and his wife Caroline's resulting anxiety leads to a marital quarrel. When they next set off for the club he has agreed to try to put matters right, promising at the same time that he will be sure not to drink too much. As they arrive they make a date with each other for later in the evening. After some banter from his friends about the previous night's incident he decides to await his chance to sound out the Catholic priest, and lays on some whisky; but the priest is delayed, and in a mixture of embarrassment and resentment he drinks his way through a large part of the whisky. When he meets Caroline again, she is distressed that he has drunk so much, and their date fizzles out. His reaction to this is to get really drunk, and he moves on to a roadhouse where he courts danger by dancing with the mistress of the powerful local bootlegger. From now on he plunges deeper and deeper into trouble, getting into a fight at his own club and bringing total social ostracism on himself. The effect of this on both his business and his marriage is disastrous, and he finally takes his own life. Each stage in his downfall has had an apparently accidental quality; and yet it is as if Death has had an appointment with him.

Butterfield 8 is set in New York, a city with the power to destroy the innocent. The tragic heroine, Gloria Wandrous, is a new character; but there are references to some of the Gibbsville people, as if to underline the cardinal importance of the changed environment, with its scope for sexual freedom and social anonymity.

In O'Hara's later novels we find the same awareness of the social context of each personal drama, but none of these personal dramas are as powerful as those to be found in the first two novels. Instead there is a massive documentation of every detail of the story, as if to make up for loss of poetic power with a sense of historicity. In *Ten North Frederick* (1955), for instance, a study of the failure of Joe Chapin, a Gibbsville lawyer, to do anything with his life after having started with practically every personal asset, the story is diluted rather than strengthened by the lengthy flashbacks. The pattern that emerges of the devouring wife or mother who destroys two generations of Chapin males and threatens a third is weakened by consideration of other causes for Joe's failure: for instance, his unwillingness, at a time when his wife is backing his political aspirations, to dirty his hands by dealing with the Irishman Mike Slattery, the tough local party organiser.

O'Hara's volumes of short stories include *The Doctor's Son* (1935), *Files on Parade* (1939), *Pipe Night* (1945) and *Hellbox* (1947). Other titles are *Pal Joey* (1940), *Rage to Live* (1949) and *The Lockwood Concern* (1966) and *The Instrument* (1968). K. R. R.

Okara, Gabriel (1921–), Nigerian poet whose novel *The Voice* (1964) is an interesting attempt to inject the rhythms, grammar and syntax of the writer's own language (Ijaw) into the medium of English. It expresses the artist's rôle as revolutionary seer; and in Okara's own poems—mystical, delicate, muted—there can be heard the voice of the sensitive visionary. C. P.

Okigbo, Christopher (1932–), Nigerian poet, combines the brilliance of Clark with the power of Soyinka and the sensitivity of Achebe, while fusing, thematically, Babylonian myth, classical legend, Christian religion and African philosophy and life. His techniques are drawn from sources equally wide—including Eliot and Pound—but blend into a characteristically individual, fascinatingly manifold style. His early *oeuvre*—consisting of *Heavensgate* (1962), *Limits* (1964) and various poems in magazines ('Silences', 'Distances', 'Lament of the Drums' and others)—seem part of a vast epic, mythopoeic work-in-progress based on the theme of the individual's extinction through total, universal experience, psychical and physical: the deluge and the quest from which come social regeneration and true self-realisation. C. P.

Olbracht, Ivan (1882–1952), Czech writer, drew the themes for several of his novels and short stories from the Carpathian Ukraine, a poor and neglected region which was the most eastern part of Czechoslovakia before the war. His pre-war stories *Golet v údolí* [*Valley of Exile*] (1937) are about the unusual milieu of the poor Orthodox Jews of the region. His best novel is *Nikola Šuhaj Loupežník* [*Nikola Šuhaj Loupežník*] (1933), the story of a legendary robber fighting single-handed against the authorities and the established order. K. B.

Oldenbourg, Zoë (1916–), French novelist, who obtained the Prix Goncourt in 1953 for *La Pierre angulaire* [*Corner Stone*]. She has produced many works of popular appeal since, including *Les Brûlés* [*Destiny of Fire*] (1960), *Les Cités charnelles* [*Cities of the Flesh*] (1961) and *Massacre à Montségur* [*Massacre at Montségur*] (1963). Her favourite field is the historical novel, a genre in which she excels. *La Pierre angulaire* and *Argile* [*The World is not Enough*] (1962) bring to life the twelfth-century third crusade with remarkable fidelity and interest, and the author is able to combine a high level of historical accuracy with a sensitive portrayal of characters and emotions. The story of the papal crusades against the Albigensian heretics is combined with the life and feelings of Roger de Montbrun, of the Counts of Toulouse, in *Les Cités charnelles.* Her novels in modern settings have generally been less well received. D. E. A.

Olyesha, Yuri Karlovich (1899–1960), Soviet writer, was an important figure although his literary output was small. He voiced in nearly all his works the problems facing the intellectuals who could not fit into the prosaic Soviet system because of the frequent attacks on individuality and the numerous contradictions they could not fail to observe. Olyesha was born in Yelisavetgrad (Kirovgrad) and began writing after World War I. His first novel, *Zavist'* [*Envy*] (1927), portraying the Superfluous man of the Soviet state, was at first well received until Soviet critics condemned it for its apparent lack of enthusiasm for the new state. Olyesha also wrote a fantasy for children *Tri tolstyaka* [*Three Fat Men*] (1928), a volume of short stories *Vishnyovaya kostochka* [*The Cherry Stone*] (1931) and some plays. Forced into silence in the early 1930s he was rehabilitated in 1956.

After his death the sections of a new novel he had been working on were put together to produce his last work, *Ni dnya byez strochki* ['Not a day without a new line'] (1960). B. W.

O'Neill, Eugene (1888–1953), American playwright, has claims to be regarded as the founding father of a serious American drama, and has certainly been amongst the most influential figures in the contemporary theatre. Many of his epoch-making early plays—such as his first two Pulitzer prizewinners *Beyond the Horizon* (1920) and *Anna Christie* (1922) —are now seldom seen; and he is best known today by two groups of mammoth works which received their first performances in the periods 1928–31 and 1946–55—the former including *Strange Interlude* (1928; his third Pulitzer prize) and *Mourning Becomes Electra* (1931); the latter, *The Iceman Cometh* (1946) and *Long Day's Journey into Night* (1955; his fourth Pulitzer prize). In the intervening period he received a Nobel prize.

O'Neill was a restless dramatic experimenter and thinker, ranging from a straightforward realism to a universalised expressionism, from outlandish all-reconciling romances to Greek-style tragedies of human conflict. The strength of his first group of enduring works derives from his synthesis of the particular and the universal, the realistic and the symbolic, in a mode of tragedy suitable for a post-Freudian age. *Desire Under the*

Elms (1923) was the first to achieve this; but it was a few years before he was to follow this up with the gigantic nine-act analyst's-casebook *Strange Interlude*, in which he pioneered the theatrical use of the interior monologue, and the trilogy *Mourning Becomes Electra*, the latter based on the *Oresteia* trilogy of Aeschylus. What gives both of these, and also their forerunner, their tragic splendour is the sense of inevitable calamity, of the explosive potential present in the most fundamental human relationships (husband-wife, parent-child, brother-sister, lover-mistress) and which only requires the appropriate stresses to detonate it. The most destructive relationships in these plays are those in which circumstances compel a woman to combine the rôles of mother and lover, or to embrace infidelity to fill the vacuum created by a husband's prolonged absence. The end, if not always violent, is at least a living death of spiritual withdrawal or exhaustion.

The major plays of O'Neill's last decade (following a period when he again produced little of merit beyond the lightweight but popular *Ah! Wilderness*, 1933) are characterised by his final feeling that, despite its tragic potentialities, human life was predominantly comic—often painful and sordid, but generally not heroic and catastrophic; the prime reason for this being what Ibsen had called the 'life-lie', and which he himself called the 'pipe-dream'. It is possible to feel that the case is overstated in *The Iceman Cometh*, that it is not a universal experience for life to be made tolerable and non-tragic only through some cardinal personal delusion. This could be the result of the sheer size of the play and of the repeated emphasis on the fact that every character in it lives by a pipe-dream; or it could be simply that the derelict inmates of Harry Hope's bar (based on those of a bar that O'Neill had himself frequented at one time in his youth) do not convince as a representative microcosm, are no more the embodiment of a universal condition than the literally drug-addicted characters of some more recent theatrical pieces. With these important qualifications, it can readily be said that the play is one of O'Neill's most powerful, lucid and theatrically satisfying: the lengthy expositions of the life-saving self-deceptions (about past behaviour, present state, and likely future) of ex-soldiers and ex-radicals, bartenders and whores, ex-policemen and ex-students, being fitted neatly into a pattern of action in which all are eventually converted by the travelling salesman Hickey to the idea of making a break-out from their dreams. A new arrival —a radical who has betrayed his movement and seen his mother imprisoned—falls to his death; for the others the strain is too great, and Hickey himself (whose own delusion turns out to be the worst of all) takes refuge in madness. Of comparable power is the autobiographical *Long Day's Journey into Night*, dramatically portraying the searing relationships and crippling illnesses of O'Neill's own family: here, for much of the time, truth is not masked, but only in the narcotic anaesthesia and fantasies of the night does the painful intercourse of the long day find an end. K. R. R.

Onions, [George] Oliver (1873–1961), English novelist, trained as an artist, whose early work included a number of uncanny stories collected in *Widdershins* (1911), but whose real success came with a trilogy of novels —*In Accordance with the Evidence* (1912), *The Debit Account* (1913) and *The Story of Louie* (1913). Of these the first remains his finest work. It began as a short story and developed into a grim murder novel, uncompromising and vigorous. His other novels tend to lack this vigour. Later titles include *Poor Man's Tapestry* (1946; James Tait Black Memorial Prize) and *Arras of Youth* (1949). R. A. K.

Oppenheim, Edward Phillips (1866–1946), English novelist who wrote more than a hundred highly romantic thrillers dealing with international diplomacy, secret documents and seductive female spies. The series began with *The Mysterious Mr Sabin* (1901) and included *Anna the Adventuress* (1904), *The Great Impersonation* (1920), *The Ostrakoff Jewels* (1932) and *Envoy Extraordinary* (1937). R. A. K.

Orczy, Baroness (1865–1947), Hungarian-born novelist. Her family settled in London when she was fifteen. She became famous by the publication in 1905 of *The Scarlet Pimpernel*, an exciting romance of the French revolution which is still popular. It was followed by a long series of almost equally popular romantic historical novels including *I Will Repay* (1906), *Beau Brocade* (1908), *The Elusive Pimpernel* (1908), *The First Sir Percy* (1920), *Child of the Revolution* (1932) and *The Way of the Scarlet Pimpernel* (1933). Several of her stories were dramatised and *The Scarlet Pimpernel* was a very successful film. G. S.

O'Riordan, Conal (Norreys Connell; 1874–1948), was an Irish novelist (*Adam of Dublin*, 1920) and playwright. He was a director of the Abbey Theatre. K. R. R.

Ortega y Gasset, José (1883–1955), Spanish philosopher and essayist, one of the major influences on twentieth-century Spanish culture. From a Jesuit school Ortega went to Madrid University, obtaining his doctorate in 1904. During two years spent in Germany (1905–07), the neo-Kantian philosophy of Hermann Cohen made a deep and lasting imprint upon Ortega's thought and he returned to Spain determined to create media, similar to those he had admired in Germany, for the diffusion of the latest European ideas. Such was to be the *Revista de Occidente* ['Western Review'], Spain's most authoritative journal and publishing house, which he founded in 1923. Professor of metaphysics at Madrid from 1910 to 1936 and a frequent lecturer after his return to Spain in 1945, Ortega never published a systematic presentation of his philosophy—which has been deduced by various Platos from lectures, books and articles. Ortega's critique of physico-mathematical reason led him not to irrationalism but to 'vital' or 'living' reason: this vitalism, condensed into the formula 'I am myself and my circumstances', saw values in terms of human experience and, in his later work (influenced by Dilthey), of human history. Reason is thus relative, and this relativity leads to a number of Ortegan notions which have become commonplaces of Spanish criticism: perspectivism, the importance of fashion, the theory of generations. This latter principle —that men born in a certain milieu and within a certain period of time possess a 'common physiognomy' and display a 'real union of interest'— has especially bedevilled post-Ortegan accounts of Spanish literature and history.

Yet Ortega's individual works are disappointing. *Meditaciones del Quijote* [*Meditations on Quixote*] (1914), comparing 'profound' German culture with the 'surface' culture of the Mediterranean, contains the germs of his philosophy, which is more coherently stated in *El tema de nuestro tiempo* [*The Modern Theme*] (1923). Here Ortega's debt to the differing relativities of Einstein and Spengler becomes apparent. The latter's influence is marked in both *España invertebrada* [*Invertebrate Spain*] (1921), wherein Spain's prostration is attributed to 'the absence of an élite', and *La rebelión de las masas* [*The Revolt of the Masses*] (1930). Both works, with their pessimistic prognostications regarding the triumph of the masses, written in a style more brilliant than precise, were seized upon by the theoreticians of the Falange. Equally provocative is *La deshumanización del arte* [*The Dehumanisation of Art*] (1925), an apology for the modern movement, whose evident errors now seem as stimulating as its insights. In the long term, Ortega's importance seems likely to be as a stimulus and diffuser of ideas rather than as an original thinker.

D. H. G.

Orwell, George (Eric Hugh Blair; 1903–50), is best known as the man who in his last years wrote *Animal Farm* and *1984*, satirising respectively Soviet communism and left-wing totalitarianism in general; but for most of his life he was a vigorous fighter against poverty and injustice, in particular as they arose from the capitalist-imperialist system.

He was born of English middle-class parents in India, and was educated at Eton. In his schooldays he was already showing an independence of outlook with a specially ambivalent attitude to imperialism; and when he took a job with the Indian police in Burma it was as much a rejection of the idea of going on to Oxford or Cambridge. His mixture of Kiplingesque sentiment and sense of responsibility with radical opposition to the very idea of empire is reproduced in two essays written in the 1930s after his return to Europe (in the collection *Shooting an Elephant*, 1950), as well as his first novel *Burmese Days* (1937).

He left Burma in 1927 and went to live in Paris, intending to write. When his money ran out, he chose not to seek aid from friends in England, preferring to embrace the experience of poverty. In Paris, and subsequently in London, he identified himself with working-class people, and continued to develop a left-wing political creed that owed more to his knowledge of real working-class needs and aspirations than to socialist dogma. *Down and Out in Paris and London* (1935) is a record of these experiences.

About the same time, he published two novels, *The Clergyman's Daughter* (1935) and *Keep the Aspidistra Flying* (1936), neither being particularly successful. Both reflect his strong class-consciousness, as well as containing many passages that illustrate his love for England—particularly the working-class England of *Down and Out*, the England of which he was to accuse the middle-class socialist intellectuals of knowing so little. Orwell, now married and keeping a village shop in Hertfordshire, made this charge in his next book, *The Road to Wigan Pier* (1937), ostensibly an account of the conditions in the unemployed areas of the north (which he was commissioned to visit by Victor Gollancz on behalf of the Left Book Club). In its implications and conclusions this book made a devastating attack on English socialism—for instance, for its intellectual crankishness, a source of ridicule to the ordinary man; for its dishonesty about the true depth of class prejudice; and chiefly for its willingness to let ordinary humane values and a respect for truth be overridden (as in Russia) by the machine-like application of an ideology.

By the time that *Wigan Pier* made its explosive appearance, Orwell was already putting his own political principles into practice by fighting against fascism in Spain. He admitted that there were things happening that he did not like; but it was enough that the Republican government, which seemed to him to represent the true interests of the working class, was under attack from an authoritarian, reactionary movement. However, he was soon to be shocked and disillusioned at the manipulation of the situation by the communists, whom he saw discrediting genuine working-class groups (and imprisoning or executing their members fresh from the battlefields) in order to secure undivided control for themselves. It was this bitter experience—his own organisation P.O.U.M., affiliated to the

English I.L.P., was one such group—that was to provide the motivation for the two works by which he is best known; meanwhile, he dedicated himself to recording the agonies of Spain in *Homage to Catalonia* (1938).

Back in England, and disengaged from political activity, Orwell now produced one of his most balanced works, the comic novel *Coming Up for Air* (1939). Its central character, George Bowling, is a typical Orwellian working-class figure—with no illusions about the economic and social injustices that he has to put up with but equally unwilling to assist in any violent reorganisation of the system. The narrative consists basically of a trip that he makes to the village where he grew up, and of his sad reaction at its growth into a modern town. The story provided opportunities for Orwell to indulge in nostalgic evocations of an England that he saw disappearing with the advance of the machine age—a working-class England that had more to fear from the Hitlers and Stalins and the brave new world of applied science and mass production than from the inequities of a conservative and class-ridden capitalist society. There is also a universality in his jaded suburban-commuter hero's attempt to escape from his imprisonment in time and place, and come up for air. Bowling's predicament—the drabness and meaninglessness of his treadmill existence, by comparison with the freedom and potential richness of childhood—is common enough. And the attempt to escape, Orwell implies, is almost universally doomed to the same failure—first, because the clock cannot be turned back, and secondly because even if it could it would not help. Bowling's breath of air does not alter anything.

When the fight against Nazism started, Orwell was keen to contribute to the war effort and produced the pamphlet *The Lion and the Unicorn* (1940). The first section, the patriotic 'England, Your England', contains some of his most vivid descriptive writing; the remainder centring on the thesis that not only did the war provide the great opportunity for the economic and social reorganisation of England that he had never ceased to believe in, but that without it the war itself could not be won. The true patriot, he implied, had to be a socialist—a conviction to which he had clung unswervingly despite his criticisms of English socialists and his experience of the left in Spain. It is against this background that the biting satire of the classic *Animal Farm* (1945) must be viewed.

In the years when the Soviet Union was the great ally in the war against Hitler one did not need to be a socialist to want to turn a blind eye to the less humane side of Soviet communism; and in 1944 Orwell was unable to find a publisher for a book which made Stalinism look as much the enemy of justice and liberty as Nazism itself. Whatever the reasons, there is no doubt that *Animal Farm* is a far more powerful indictment of revolutionary communism than any of his previous works were of the capitalist *status quo*. It could be argued that this was because his experiences in Spain were more traumatic than anything that befell him in Paris or London; it could equally well be said that it was because he had only now found the right literary form for his type of writing. It is certainly true that an animal fable provided an ideal medium for a writer who had always wanted to create a self-contained work of art, while at the same time forging an effective political weapon. The story of a community of animals overthrowing their human master, only to find their own natural leaders (the pigs) eventually becoming as tyrannical as the farmer they have expelled, is as timeless as a fable of Aesop. Yet those readers who were Orwell's contemporaries could not fail to see the specific allusions to the events and personalities of the Soviet revolution—the early halcyon days of farmyard democracy and equality, the emergence of the intelligent pigs as leaders, the privileges that the pigs appropriate for themselves and their growing lust for power, the cult of personality on the part of the pig named Napoleon (Stalin) and the expulsion of his rival Snowball (Trotsky), the increasing need for lies, distortions and the rule of terror in order to maintain power, the slaughter of the innocent and loyal, and the final vision of the pigs aping Jones the farmer by learning to walk on two legs. The use of animals enables Orwell to make the most of the essential humour of the story; but it does not prevent him from evoking pathos as well—as for instance in the despatch to the slaughterhouse of the most noble and heroic of all the revolutionaries, the loyal carthorse Boxer.

Orwell's health had been poor for some years, and he was eventually found to be suffering from tuberculosis. It seems likely that his illness contributed towards the pessimism and the nightmarish quality of his last work, *Nineteen Eighty-Four* (1949). However, it is also clear that in his last years—years in which the Stalinist terror seemed at its most menacing—he was haunted by a fear of totalitarianism. *Nineteen Eighty-Four* may give an exaggerated picture of anything known in Stalinist Russia; the relevant point is that it portrays a situation in which the authorities do have total control. Each day, past history is rewritten to fit the current party-line and there is no such thing as absolute truth; while even a heretical thought is detected by a telepathic organisation known as the thought police. Total control is only achieved when the traitorous thought has been forcibly eradicated from the brain, and replaced with the appropriate set of conditioned reflexes.

The story is concerned with the inner rebellion of Winston Smith who works at 'the ministry of truth'. It consists partly in the affair that develops between him and a fellow worker called Julia (an exclusive personal relationship being in itself a threat to the monolithic solidarity required by the party); and partly in their belief in, and search for, objective truth.

But their rebellion is doomed to failure; and the book ends with their brainwashing at the 'ministry of love', where Winston finally learns to drool with love for the arch-dictator Big Brother. Many of the terms coined by Orwell have passed into the English language—such as 'double-think', a process whereby black is seen to be white, and two plus two make five (if the party says so).

Orwell had entered a sanatorium earlier in 1949, but recovered well enough to leave it. He married again, and settled down; but the following year he relapsed and died. K. R. R.

Osborne, John (1929–), burst upon the London theatrical scene in 1956 with his epoch-making play *Look Back in Anger*, which sounded a clarion-call to many of his contemporaries and established a vogue for theatre of protest and 'kitchen-sink' drama. At the time of the first performance, Osborne was in his late twenties. Like Jimmy Porter, the play's hero, he had come from a working-class background; like Helena, Jimmy's wife's friend, he had been working as an actor in a provincial repertory company. His first marriage had broken up, and he was shortly to marry Mary Ure, a professional actress; and he had already written seven other plays—one of which, *Epitaph for George Dillon*, composed in collaboration, was performed in London in 1958.

In all of Osborne's plays there is a central protagonist, in whose speeches is to be heard the voice of Osborne himself. Jimmy's anger is substantially Osborne's anger—anger that, amongst other things, England's much vaunted social revolution of 1945–51 had changed so little. In the play it is vented on Jimmy's wife, Alison, whose upper-middle-class origins make her embody for Jimmy everything that is wrong with England. Her mother is an arrogant member of the breed that had lorded it over India; she herself, despite her marriage to Jimmy, is conditioned to be polite and conventional. When he attacks her, she will not fight back: where he protests, she accepts. What maddens him most is the sight of Alison at the ironing-table on Sunday afternoon, failing to respond to his *cris-de-coeur* and meekly enduring his insults.

All of this serves to drive Jimmy into a rage—a rage that is extended to include Helena when she arrives to stay with them. Helena represents one of the things that Jimmy hates most—hypocrisy. Not only does she act in phoney, drawing-room plays: worse, she goes to church. This, for Jimmy, is more than just hypocritical: it is yet another retreat from reason, a betrayal of the rational approach to human problems.

Despite all this, Jimmy loves Alison, and she him. And when he has finally driven her to desperation and she leaves him, Helena takes her place. It is precisely because Jimmy is emotionally involved with first Alison, then

Helena, then Alison again, that he cannot tolerate their failure to measure up to his expectations and to respond to his needs.

Since *Look Back in Anger*, Osborne has written a number of successful plays, without making the same impact. *The Entertainer* (1957) reflected the extent to which he had been influenced by the music-hall tradition, and his feelings about the rôle of the professional entertainer. There is something of Archie Rice in all his protagonists, and something of them in him: to communicate and to entertain are opposite sides of the same coin.

If most of Osborne's leading characters are conscious of playing to an audience they are also aware of a uselessness in their lone protest and rebellion. After an abortive musical, *The World of Paul Slickey* (1960), centring on the life of a gossip-columnist, Osborne turned to a portrayal of a rebel who had decisively changed the pattern of history, the arch-protestant, Martin Luther. For all the licence it takes with history, *Luther* (1961) re-established its author as a highly professional craftsman of the theatre—albeit one whose message was substantially the same—and it had a long run in the West End.

Osborne's next major play was *Inadmissible Evidence* (1965), which was widely hailed as his best play since his original success. Bill Maitland, its hero, a man who was clearly not much older than Osborne himself, has been described as 'an angry middle-aged man' and the play obviously harks back to *Look Back in Anger*. Where the young Jimmy Porter was angry at the world his elders had fashioned, Bill Maitland is desperately defending himself against the charge that he has done no better—and turning in anger against the new generation for their failure to sympathise with his predicament. The mess that he has made of his life is symptomised by his chaotic sex-life: the inadequacies of each relationship making him turn to yet another, while his inability willingly to inflict pain makes him unable to act decisively in any of them.

This play too was a commercial hit. Its author—whose second marriage had been dissolved (he had subsequently married Penelope Gilliatt, the film and theatre critic)—was now approaching forty; and with a decade of experimentation in various types of subject matter having culminated in a genuine artistic success only with a subject strongly connected to that of his first play, the question arose of where he would go next. His second historical play *A Patriot for Me* (1965) was a failure; but his 'translation' of an obscure work by the renaissance Spanish playwright Lope de Vega, *A Bond Honoured* (1966), a religious (or anti-religious) drama of incest, murder and crucifixion, created a great sensation when it was presented by the National Theatre. The impression it gave was of a versatility and fertility of mind at the service of a fundamentally unchanged preoccupation.

Further plays include *Time Present* (1968). K. R. R.

Ossorgin, Mikhail (Mikhail Andreyevich Ilyin; 1878–), Russian novelist. Born into a noble family at Perm, he nevertheless played an active part in the first revolutions, but was exiled for his pains; during World War I he returned to Russia, to be exiled again in 1922. His literary output contains several fine short stories, but he is best known in English for two novels, *Sivtsev Vrazhek* [*A Quiet Street*] (1929) and *Povyest' o Syestrye* [*My Sister's Story*] (1931). B. W.

Ostrovsky, Nikolai Alexeyevich (1904–36), Soviet novelist, born in the Ukraine, was a remarkable writer in that his major novel was written while he was blind, bed-ridden and partially paralysed as a result of injuries sustained during the civil war. So great was his desire to make the most of his shattered life that he decided to write. His novel *Kak zakalyalas' stal'* [*How the Steel was Tempered*] (1934) is mostly autobiographical and tells how a poor youth joins the underground, conquers crippling obstacles and eventually becomes a writer and teacher. Even allowing for the fact that the novel was tidied up to satisfy the rules of socialist realism, thereby losing much of the suffering and tense home atmosphere of the original, it is not a well constructed work: but it burns with a strong enthusiasm for living and a refusal to accept defeat. Many people came to help him with his second novel *Rozhdyonniye buryey* [*Born of the Storm*] (1936), after he had found fame. It was published on the day of his funeral. B. W.

Otčenášek, Jan (1924–), Czech writer, worked in a factory during the Nazi occupation of Czechoslovakia and portrayed this tragic period in *Romeo, Julie a tma* [*Romeo and Juliet and the Darkness*] (1958), a sensitive story of the love of a student for a Jewish girl whom he hides from the Gestapo. K. B.

Otero, Blas de (1916–), Spanish poet. Belonging to what he has called 'an uprooted generation', Otero is a deeply human, anguished poet. His early verse is metaphysical in its concerns. *Angel fieramente humano* ['A fiercely human angel'] (1950) and *Redoble de conciencia* ['Drumbeat of conscience'] (1951) evoke man in a vacuum, tragically separated from divine and human love. Otero's frustrated searching induces a forlorn agnosticism and a rapid evolution towards political commitment. In *Pido la paz y la palabra* ['I ask for peace and a chance to speak'] (1955), *En castellano* ['In Castilian'] (1960) and *Que trata de España* ['Dealing with Spain'] (1963) he addresses the majority of men, not the 'immense minority' who formed Jiménez's audience, and attempts to convey their political and social tragedy. A selection in English appears in *Twenty Poems of Blas de Otero* (1965). D. H. G.

Ovechkin, Valentin Vladimirovich (1904–), Soviet writer, born in Taganrog. He has tended to restrict himself to tales of village life and has been one of the more outspoken writers in the struggle for the right to express one's own opinions. Of his early work, *Byez rodu, byez plemyeni* [*Without Kith and Kin*] (1939) is perhaps his most characteristic. It portrays the various people encountered by a roving journalist who divides them into two categories, the first consisting of avaricious tradesmen and the second of reliable *kolkhoz* members. At the end of the war Ovechkin won his greatest success with *S frontovym privyetom* [*October*] (1945). In 1952 he began a new stage in his development with *Rayonniye budni* [*District Workadays*] which deals with life in an average district in the U.S.S.R. Later novels in the same vein but with increasingly outspoken comment have been *Svoimi rukami* [*With One's Own Hands*] (1954) and *Trudnaya vyesna* [*A Difficult Spring*] (1956), in which the central character, Martynov, echoes much of Ovechkin's philosophy. B. W.

Owen, Alun (1926–), Welsh dramatist and novelist. Owen started his career as a repertory actor before graduating through the Old Vic to films and television. He started writing for radio and television in 1957. His plays include *Two Sons* (1957), *Progress to the Park* (1958), *The Rough and Ready Lot* (1958), *No Trams to Lime Street* (1959), *You Can't Win 'Em All* (1962) and *A Local Boy* (1963). Published in book form are *Three T.V. Plays* (1961), *Progress to the Park* (1962) and *A Little Winter Love* (1964). His work is usually characterised by its insight into the rougher tougher characteristics of the especially Welsh seedier city areas. Owen has a remarkably acute ear for dialogue. D. L. P.

Owen, Wilfred (1893–1918), English poet. Owen is the most formidable of the poets writing about the first world war. He was born at Oswestry, Shropshire, and educated at London University. He was to some extent influenced by Siegfried Sassoon whom he met in a military hospital. Sassoon collected and published Owen's *Poems* (1920). The style of this poetry, which uses alliteration and assonance rather than conventional rhyme, influenced the poets of the 1920s and 1930s, especially Auden and Spender. (The style of the few poems published before 1914 is romantic and heavily influenced by Keats.) What makes Owen's war poetry so memorable is the depth of pity and compassion in it: its realism, even a certain sensuousness, acquiring added poignancy from the poet's refusal to allow his feelings to be frozen into attitudes by the sheer horror of what is going on.

Owen's poetry came to an astonishing maturity under the pressures to which he was subject in the trenches. The bulk of what are probably the major war poems in the English language was written between August 1917 and his death in the autumn of 1918. However small in quantity, the quality of the poet's work gives him a position of importance in the development of English literature: though Owen himself, characteristically, says:

Above all I am not concerned with Poetry.
My subject is War, and the pity of War.
The Poetry is in the pity.

D. L. P.

P

Packer, Joy (1905–   ), South African writer married to an admiral. This and her considerable journalistic experience has led her to write a series of light-hearted accounts of the trials and tribulations of a naval wife forever on the move. Representative titles are *Pack and Follow* (1945) and *Grey Mistress* (1949). Her later titles include *The World is a Proud Place* (1966), her personal account of a trip round the world, and in particular of the flying doctor service. S. R.

Paço D'Arcos, Joaquim (1908–   ), literary pseudonym of Joaquim Corrêa da Silva, Portuguese author. The formative years of his life were spent in Angola, Mozambique, Macao and Brazil, except for the years 1922 to 1925 when he worked at the English Bank in Lisbon. Largely self-taught, he eventually adopted the family profession of overseas administration, ultimately rising to high civil service posts in shipping, railways and the foreign ministry. As a writer he has been successful primarily as a novelist, yet his considerable output involves many genres. He was president of the Portuguese Society of Writers in 1960.

Although his works have been widely translated into several languages, those available in English—*Poemas Imperfeitos* [*Nostalgia*, tr. Roy Campbell, 1960] and a biography of Churchill—are not truly representative. His most effective achievements are probably the six novels of the *Crónica da Vida Lisboeta* ['Chronicles of Lisbon life'] (1938–56); the aforementioned *Poemas Imperfeitos* (1952); his penetrating study of the U.S.A., *Floresta de Cimento* ['Cement forest'] (1953); and the whimsical novel *Memórias duma Nota de Banco* ['Memoirs of a banknote'] (1962). As a writer of prose fiction Paço d'Arcos avoids the pretentious and offers an objective and clinical examination of the human condition. By contrast, his twenty-nine modestly entitled 'imperfect' poems constitute an anguished and often moving personal testament which is especially characterised by a yearning for true religious conviction. R. C. W.

Pagnol, Marcel (1895–   ), French playwright, novelist and film-maker. Born at Aubagne, he became a teacher of English in Marseilles. In 1925 he wrote *Les Marchands de gloire* ['Merchants in glory'], a satire of those civilians who capitalised on the heroism of the soldiers of the first world war. He continued with the vein of satire and obtained success with

Topaze [*Topaze*] (1928), a play based on the transformation of a downtrodden schoolmaster into a business tycoon by cynicism and an abandonment of his moral principles. *Marius* [*Marius*] (1929), *Fanny* [*Fanny*] (1932) and *César* [*César*] (1931), a trilogy of life in Marseilles, were adapted for the cinema and produced by Pagnol himself, who then continued as film producer, making such films as *La Femme du boulanger* ['The baker's wife'], *La Fille du puisatier* ['The well-digger's daughter'] and many others. Subsequently Pagnol has produced several volumes of memoirs—*La Gloire de mon père* ['My father's glory'] (1957), *Le Château de ma mère* ['My mother's castle'] (1958), *Le Temps des secrets* [*Time of Secrets*] (1960)—and a novel *L'Eau des collines* ['Water from the hills'] (1962), in two parts entitled *Jean de Florette* and *Manon des sources*.

D. E. A.

Palle, Albert (1916–), French novelist. Born in Le Havre, a philosophy graduate and a journalist by profession, he has written for *Combat*, *Le Figaro* and *Elle* magazine. He has published three novels: *L'Expérience* [*Experience*] (1959), *Les Marches* ['The steps'] (1962) and *Les Chaudières et la lune* ['Boilers and the moon'] (1965). This last, which is set against the topical background of a sit-in strike of metalworkers whose factory, threatened with bankruptcy, had laid off some workers, poses the problem, for the new director of the works, of the aims of industrial civilisation. Though the factory fails, personal truth triumphs in the shape of the hope and happiness of family life. *L'Expérience* (Prix Renaudot) is the strange account of a reporter's investigation of a seaport suicide. D. E. A.

Palmer, Vance (1885–), popular Australian novelist and short-story writer, who gives a flat, accurate rendition of life in Queensland, but has been criticised by some for his lack of drama and of development of plot. Others defend him with the answer that it is this very un-sensational and un-glib style that endow such works as *The Passage* (1930), *The Swayne Family* (1936) and *Golconda* (1948) with realism. This criticism cannot in any case be levelled at his earlier works *Cronulla* (1924) and *The Man Hamilton* (1928); nor at his short stories, in which he abandons the limitations of narrative and plot and concentrates on character delineation—a trend of significance to later writers, who have been influenced by him in this respect. S. R.

Panfyorov, Fyodor Ivanovich (1896–1961), a Soviet writer who devoted his energies to illustrating the problems of the peasant and the kolkhoz. His first novel *Bruski* [*And Then the Harvest*] (1928–37), for which he is mainly remembered, traces the history of a village from the end of the civil war to the period of land collectivisation under the first five-year plan. His outline is very frank, even crude, and for his lack of artistry he was strongly attacked. He wrote a sensational war novel, *Bor'ba za mir* ['The battle for peace'] (1945), and then in 1953 caused a mild stir with his novel *Volga—matushka reka* [*Mother Volga*] which deals with the period of de-Stalinisation. B. W.

Panova, Vera Fyodorovna (1905–), Russian novelist whose work bears the strong imprint of her warm and honest personality. She was born in Rostov-on-Don where, because her father was drowned when she was only five, she spent a very poor childhood. Her formal education was scanty but she avidly read anything she could obtain. She started work with a newspaper and by 1933 had begun her literary career with some plays. However, the scope offered by drama was too limiting and Panova felt she could express herself better in a novel. Her best-known story is *Sputniki* [*Travelling Companions* or *The Train*] (1946), which describes life on a hospital train during World War II. The hero, Danilov, is described with deep sympathy, as are some of the lesser characters. Panova has been criticised for ignoring the rôle of the party in everyday life. Her novel *Kruzhilikha* (1947) saw the start of this criticism, which has continued over her subsequent works *Vremena goda* [*Seasons of the Year*] (1953) and *Sentimental'niy roman* [*Sentimental Story*] (1958). The former touches on the unmentionable idea that many respectable Soviet families produce a law-breaker, while the second is a semi-autobiographical account of the 1920s. B. W.

Papini, Giovanni (1881–1956), Italian writer, was literary critic, poet and philosopher. An insatiable reader, despite constantly declining eyesight, of Italian and foreign literature and philosophical works, his interests covered diverse and apparently irreconcilable fields. His first major work, *Un uomo finito* [*A Man—Finished*] (1912), an autobiography of the spiritual events of his youth, was published nine years after Papini had founded the Florence review *Il Leonardo* which contributed to the reaction of young writers to nineteenth-century positivism, and was the vehicle for the transmission in Italy of the pragmatist theories of W. James and C. S. Peirce. A writer of unrelenting activity and a contributor to several literary periodicals, Papini underwent a sensational conversion to Roman catholicism after the first world war, and as a result became increasingly preoccupied with religious issues, this preoccupation being reflected in works ranging from *Storia di Cristo* [*Life of Christ*] (1921) and *Gli operai della vigna* [*The Laborers in the Vineyard*] (1929) to *Sant'Agostino* [*Saint Augustine*] (1929) and *Il diavolo* [*The Devil: Notes for a Future Diabology*]

(1953), of which the last sparked off heated controversy. The colourful representative of a generation of abstract thinkers, Papini was often led by his cultural restlessness to facile generalisations and theological inaccuracies. None the less, he helped to give fresh impetus to the cultural trends of the early twentieth century in Italy, and remains conspicuous for the polemical nature of his writings. Among the many other works of Papini are *Gog* [*Gog*] (1931), containing a pessimistic appraisal of present-day civilisation; *Lettere agli uomini di Papa Celestino VI* [*Letters of Pope Celestine VI To All Mankind*] (1946), a collection of letters by a fictitious pope pointing to the plight of mankind; and the powerful and imaginative *Vita di Michelangelo nella vita del suo tempo* [*Michelangelo: His Life and His Era*] (1949). There is also an English translation of *Le memorie d'Iddio* [*Memoirs of God*] (1912) as well as a selection of critical essays collected under the title *Four and Twenty Minds* (1923). D. B.

Park, Ruth (–), New Zealand-born popular novelist now living in Australia. She is the author of *The Witch's Thorn* (1952) dealing with the racial problems of Maori and white in New Zealand, and the prize-winning *Harp in the South* (1948) which describes the urban working class in comedy with a Dickensian flavour. Other works, characteristically robust, are *Poor Man's Orange* (1949), *One-a-Pecker, Two-a-Pecker* (1959) and *The Hole in the Hill* (1962). S. R.

Parker, Dorothy (1893–), American writer of caustic, witty criticism, and of collections of satirical verse (*Enough Rope*, 1926) and short stories (*After Such Pleasures*, 1933; *Here Lies*, 1939). Her most characteristic subject is the crippling and distorting effect of convention on human behaviour, the psychological mechanics of which she sometimes probes with surgical skill. The sources of her humour are akin to those of her close friend Robert Benchley's, who was much influenced by her.

K. R. R.

Parrish, Anne (1888–1957), American novelist, whose most popular work is *The Perennial Bachelor* (1925). Her later works include *And Have Not Love* (1954). K. R. R.

Pascoli, Giovanni (1855–1912), Italian poet. For all his life he followed the teaching profession, first as a schoolmaster and later as a university lecturer, his career culminating in his appointment to succeed Carducci as Professor of Italian Literature in the University of Bologna. A delicate and often morbidly sensitive poet, much of his personal life was affected by the murder of his father, which was committed when he was 12 years old.

Dominant themes in Pascoli's production are a longing for the simplicity of rural life and a sense of awe before the mystery of the universe. Pascoli's poetry frequently relies on verbal contrasts, the use of rare or far-fetched stylistic features and also on alliteration and onomatopoeia, and presents a curious mixture of grandiose lyrical heights coupled with trite and often sloppily sentimental language. Pascoli's classical scholarship won him several times the Amsterdam Prize for Latin verse. His poetical works include *Myricae* ['Tamarisks': a reference to Virgil's '*humiles myricae*'] (1891), *Canti di Castelvecchio* ['Castelvecchio cantos'] (1903) and *Odi e inni* ['Odes and hymns'] (1906). English anthologies of his verse have been published by E. Stein in 1923 and A. M. Abbott in 1927, both with the title *Poems*, and by G. S. Purkis in 1935 with the title *Selected Poems of Giovanni Pascoli.*

D. B.

Pasinetti, Pier-Maria (1913–), Italian novelist. Born in Venice, educated in Italy, Germany, England and the U.S.A., he spent the war years lecturing in Sweden and is now a professor at U.C.L.A., California. As a film scriptwriter he has worked with Antonioni and Franco Rossi and for nearly forty years he has been a regular contributor to and editor of various reviews and journals; but by the late 1960s he had published only three books. The first was a collection of three *novelle*, *L'ira di Dio* ['The wrath of God'] (1942), one of which had previously appeared in English in *The Southern Review* (1939) and again in E. J. O'Brien's anthology *The Best Short Stories* (1940) under the title 'Family History'; the second was a memorable novel, *Rosso Veneziano* [*Venetian Red*] (1959); the third, *La confusione* [*The Smile on the Face of the Tiger*] (1964), in which certain of the earlier characters reappear, was something of a disappointment, enjoyable but unexceptional. Subsequently Pasinetti was working on his *magnum opus*, a third novel provisionally entitled *Il ponte dell'Accademia* ['From the Academy bridge']. All literary works in a Venetian ambience invite evaluation by comparison with those by James, Corvo, Mann and other distinguished foreigners; such is the ambition, intelligence, lucidity and artistic elegance of *Venetian Red*, qualities in no way obscured in the author's splendid English translation, that the more stringent the critical standards applied the more clearly its excellence is perceived. Two families, the waning, talented, impractical Partibons and the waxing, sensible, opportunist Fassolas, struggle for survival in a historic provincial backwater. Both are doomed, the one by the priority of their values, the other by the value of their priorities; but there are ways of losing, and in the outcome of their potentially trivial contest there is written a parable of civilisation. Infinitely mysterious marvellously sympathetic, the Partibons are equal to their mythological obligations.

M. D. E.

Pasolini, Pier Paolo (1922–   ), Italian writer of prose and poetry, actor and film director. An arts graduate, he belongs to the more genuinely Marxist fringe of Italian left-wing intellectuals and has endeavoured in several of his works to sublimate the dialect of the less privileged strata of Italian society in polemical opposition to the 'language' of the educated. The slang of suburban Rome has found its way into *Ragazzi di vita* ['The action boys'] (1955) and *Una vita violenta* ['Tough living'] (1959) which are a kaleidoscope of violence and crime amidst certain sections of Rome's youth. Among his 'Italian' works the verse collections *Le ceneri di Gramsci* ['Gramsci's ashes'] (1957) and *L'usignolo della Chiesa Cattolica* ['The nightingale of the Catholic Church'] (1958) reflect the author's preoccupation with sociological, historical and political issues. Pasolini has also edited collections of folk and dialect poems and songs. D. B.

Pasternak, Boris Leonidovich (1890–1960), winner of the 1957 Nobel Prize (which subsequently, under pressure, he refused), was an outstanding Russian poet and prose-writer. He was born in Moscow into a very talented family and at an early age developed an intense love of music. He was also greatly influenced by the poems of Rilke, but before deciding to become a poet himself he travelled to Marburg to study philosophy. Returning to Russia in 1914 he published his first book of poems *Bliznyets v tuchakh* [*The Twin in the Clouds*] and followed it with *Povyerkh bar'yerov* [*Above Barriers*] (1917). The same year he wrote *Syestra moya zhizn'* [*My Sister, Life*] but it was not published until 1922. This poem won him the reputation of an outstanding poet. His work, which is lyrical and very personal, has always been considered difficult yet it is rewarding to the diligent. Both in the sparkling, technically exciting verse of his early years and his mellower later work there is a luminous awareness of the Russian landscape and of the fragile beauty of human relationships. During the 'thaw' of World War II he published *Na rannikh poyezdakh* [*On Early Trains*] (1943) and *Zemnoy prostor* [*The Terrestrial Expanse*] (1945), which are not so complex as his early poetry.

Pasternak had also felt himself drawn towards prose. This proved to be an extension of his poetry, as poetry was an extension of his music. In 1925 he had written some short stories, including *Dyetstvo Lyuvers* [*Childhood of Luvers*] and *Pis'ma iz Tuly* [*Letters from Tula*], followed in 1931 with an autobiographical account of his childhood and youth in *Okhrannaya gramota* [*Safe Conduct*]. During the periods when he was out of favour he would not relinquish his principle of being true to himself and his art. He translated many foreign writers and produced some unsurpassed versions of Shakespeare's works.

But Pasternak today is world-renowned for his Nobel Prize-winning novel, *Doktor Zhivago* [*Doctor Zhivago*] (1957), which ten years later had yet to be published in the Soviet Union. In spirit this great novel is autobiographical, for the ideas and anguish of Pasternak and Zhivago are essentially the same. The story deals with the lives of pre-revolutionary characters, swept along by the world war, revolution and civil war, who try to retain their individuality and be true to themselves. The novel is apolitical, it preaches no Soviet moral, and has been roundly condemned for this omission. In portraying the destiny of Yuri Zhivago, the doctor and poet, Pasternak reveals how hard the last fifty years have been for a member of the intelligentsia. By describing his initial sympathy for the revolution—typical of many progressive Russians—and the inhumanity and brutality that followed in its wake, and by interweaving all this with Yuri's personal emotional conflict of love for Tanya his wife and Lara his mistress, Pasternak shows in beautiful poetical language his deep concern for the fundamental values and standards of life in the country he loves. B. W.

Paterson, 'Banjo' (Andrew Barton Paterson; 1864–1941), prolific Australian writer of bush ballads, the most famous of which are 'The Man from Snowy River' and 'Waltzing Matilda'. Their great popularity can be attributed to the vigorous rhythm and their romantic and adventurous outlook. Paterson's nostalgia for what he saw as Australia's heroic and pioneering past has meant that he has in his verse virtually created a national folklore. His work is assembled in *The Collected Verse of A. B. Paterson* (1923). S. R.

Paton, Alan (1903–), South African novelist, author of *Cry, the Beloved Country* (1948), *Too Late the Phalarope* (1953) and several short stories collected in *Debbie Go Home* (1961), has a lively understanding of his country's racial problems and a great breadth of vision and tact in his manner of expressing these which is far more effective than if it were openly propagandist. He states the fact of the dual community with a simplicity and directness which is unchallengeable. He does not openly offer criticism, but it is implicit in every page. *Cry, the Beloved Country*, written in a simple biblical prose which also tries to capture the idiom of the Bantu languages, tells the story of a rural Zulu churchman's search for his son in Johannesburg; its successor employs the voice of an Afrikaner to tell of her policeman-nephew's 'criminal' involvement with an African girl. In 1960 Paton received the Freedom Award in New York and on his return to South Africa was deprived of his passport. In 1965 he published a history (*Hofmeyr*) of Jan Hendrik Hofmeyr the younger, who so effectively supported the policy of education for the Bantus under Smuts.

G. C.; C. P.

Paustovsky, Konstantin Georgievich (1892–), popular Soviet Romantic writer with pronounced liberal views. He was born in Moscow but educated in Kiev where his first story appeared in 1911 in a Kiev magazine. The war interrupted his university studies and he never settled for very long after that, taking many varied jobs, from tram-driver to schoolteacher, before he finally took up journalism. His literary talent attracted Gorky's attention and in 1932 his novel *Kara-Bugaz* [*The Black Gulf*] made Paustovsky's name as a writer. His extensive travels have enabled him to write *Kolkhida* [*Colchis*] (1934), *Sevyernaya povyest'* [*Tale of the North*] (1939) and *Povyest' o lyesakh* [*Tale of the Forests*] (1948). Paustovsky has also written some stories for children and embarked on an autobiography *Povyest' o zhizni* [*The Story of my Life*] of which several volumes have appeared, *Dalyokiye gody* [*Distant Years*] (1945) beginning the series.

Paustovsky has a clear and gentle style which makes his stories delightful reading. He enjoys joining apparently separate portions of his stories together with a common theme or link between the characters. He frequently uses this device. Despite his being a firm supporter of the Soviet government, Paustovsky has stoutly defended a writer's need to express himself truthfully and artistically.

B. W.

Pavese, Cesare (1908–50), Italian writer, literary critic and translator. His reputation began with the novel *Paesi tuoi* [*The Harvesters*] (1941), in which the antithesis between town and country life is brought forth in the story of the relationship between Berto, a Turin mechanic, and the country villager Talino when they go to live in the latter's village after having met in prison; and *La spiaggia* [*The Beach*] (1942), in which the theme of escapism is viewed through the emotional experiences of a drifting marriage. But much of Pavese's production reveals the crisis of a generation preoccupied with the problems of communication and yet engaged in a programme of social reforms. Thus *Il compagno* [*The Comrade*] (1947) describes the political development of Pablo, who from his beginnings as a guitar-player in Turin evolves into an active participant in the underground anti-fascist movement in Rome, parallel with his evolution from his love for Linda, a wordly creature without any intellectual horizons, into his liaison with the more mature Gina. The theme of nature's attractiveness and the *leitmotiv* of sex are recaptured in *La bella estate* [*The*

Beautiful Summer] (1949), which in the Italian edition also includes *Il diavolo sulle colline* [*The Devil in the Hills*] and *Tra donne sole* [*Among Women Only*]. In the same year Pavese also published *La casa in collina* [*The House on the Hill*] describing the experiences of a Turin intellectual, Corrado, during his involvement with the resistance movement and eventual disillusionment.

Among his further works are: *La luna e i falò* [*The Moon and the Bonfires*] (1950), in which realism and symbolism become subtly intermingled in the story of the return home of Anguilla from America and his relationship with his old friend Nuto, with the tragedies of two local families in which death by fire plays a prominent part; *Il mestiere di vivere* [*This Business of Living*] (1952), Pavese's autobiography from 1935 to 1950 and an attempt to seek an internal metre and the meaning of life; and *Il carcere* [*The Political Prisoner*] (1955), an account of the experiences of internment of a Piedmontese intellectual, Stefano, in the stagnant atmosphere of a southern Italian village. A special place in Pavese's writings is occupied by *Dialoghi con Leucò* [*Dialogues With Leucò*] (1947), a series of meditations on ancient myths. A collection of short stories is also available in English with the title *Festival Night and Other Stories*, as well as his unfinished work *Fuoco Grande* [*A Great Fire*] (1959), written in co-operation with Bianca Garufi. Pavese's *Weltanschauung*, in which the problems of love and sex played a major rôle, emerged through a spiritual evolution which led him from a constructive attitude by various steps to a realisation of the futility of a moral code and a feeling of boredom and despair, culminating in his suicide in a Turin hotel in 1950. D. B.

Pavlenko, Pyotr Andreyevich (1899–1951), Soviet novelist whose highly praised yet not particularly distinguished novel *Schast'ye* [*Happiness*] (1947) was one of the first to herald a rebirth of anti-western sentiment after the second world war. The hero settles in the Crimea at the end of the war in order to find happiness. He takes part in post-war reconstruction as well as doing some interpreting at the Yalta conference, the latter providing the occasion for the author's anti-western remarks. B. W.

Paz, Octavio (1914–), Mexican poet and social philosopher, whose writings, above all, explore the question: what is a Mexican? *El laberinto de la soledad* [*The Labyrinth of Solitude*] (1950), probably the best of all essays on the Mexican personality, attempts to isolate the quiddity of the national experience, to define the existential Being within the being. To whom does the Mexican pray? Of what and in which language do the children of Sánchez dream? How do they see their Spanish father and

Indian mother? Does the intellectual still, in Fuentes' words, 'wear clothing cut by Auguste Comte, live in a mansion designed by Haussmann'? Or did the revolution, in giving the Mexican a past as well as a present and a future, put the indigenous cat among the post-colonial pigeons? All Paz's work is a step into the welter of his own and, by extension, the national psyche, an existential anabasis. His poetry, a probing of reality, a search for cultural identity and with it an ontology, a metaphysic, comes over well in Muriel Rukeyser's translations, some fifty poems taken from *Libertad bajo palabra, Obra poética (1935–58)* [*Selected Poems*] (1960) and, his finest achievement, *Piedra de sol* [*Sun Stone*] (1957). Steeped in the poetry and belief of the pre-conquest Indians, a Mexican Asturias, Paz is perceptively appreciative of Mexico's Spanish poetry, especially that of Tablada and López Velarde—see his excellent *Anthologie de la poésie mexicaine* [*An Anthology of Mexican Poetry*] (1952), translated by Samuel Beckett. Intimately conversant with Latin American literature and deeply familiar with its Spanish tradition, he is yet fully conscious of and indebted to the European heritage. Furthermore, this greatest living Spanish American writer is also a translator of the celebrated Japanese poet Bashō (1644–94) and, as his apologia *El arco y la lira* ['The bow and the lyre'] (1956) suggests, an initiate of oriental philosophy and mysticism, a student of eastern, particularly Hindu, culture and religion. Extraordinarily eclectic, he is intensely personal; hermetic, he is intelligible and accessible to all; immersed in Mexico and her Náhuatl myths, his imagery is universal.

In 1937 Paz went to Spain. There he met Neruda, Vallejo, Hernández, Alberti, Cernuda and Buñuel and made those early contacts with the surrealists which later, in Paris, Mexico and elsewhere, led to friendship with Breton and Péret, and to poetic and psychological maturity. However, for Paz, surrealism has never been an ideology. Although he accepts the orthodox genealogy of Hölderlin, Novalis, Nerval, Lautréamont and Rimbaud, although he admires Breton, his proper interests in the surrealist context are the means of access, without benefit of reason, to the Freudian and Jungian unconscious, to the cosmic archetypes and harmonies of primitive mythology, the means of participation in the racial union of Cortés and La Malinche, in the rhythmic, primeval, Zorbatic copulation of day and night, earth and the elements. In myth he seeks reality, in dream awareness. Acknowledging his own personality, he apprehends the Mexican identity. The poetry of *négritude*, Sartre observes, is Orpheus in search of Eurydice, an exorcism of the demon of European cultural hegemony with Césaire as sorcerer. Paz, in the mid-1960s the Mexican ambassador in New Delhi, and one of the finest lyric poets of the twentieth century, is the shaman of *mexicanidad*.

M. D. E.

Penn Warren, Robert (1905–), American novelist, critic, essayist, short-story writer and teacher. The spreading of his energies over such a wide area has probably meant the dilution of his creative abilities but nevertheless those abilities are considerable. Penn Warren was born in Kentucky and although his education extends to California, Yale and Oxford his preoccupation is with the Southern states of America. Through his work run several common characteristics and themes. His writings are generally concerned with the land and with the social condition of the people; while his fiction is specially concerned with the politics of the South, its code and history, as in the historical novel, *The Wilderness* (1961). There are, too, philosophical and metaphysical involvements which impose a pattern on his work.

The heroes of Penn Warren's novels have a superficial resemblance to those of Shakespeare; they possess tragic flaws which lead to breakdown in their relations with the world. For example, Bogan Murdoch in *At Heaven's Gate* (1943) is consumed with a destructive desire for economic power. Penn Warren's driving philosophy seems to depend like Thackeray's on the tragic inability of man to retain his innocence in face of the demands of the world. His heroes sail forth with firmly held principles only to founder on the realities that consciousness of power brings and the savage means they employ to achieve once-worthwhile ends. The best known of the novels is the symbolic and virile *All the King's Men* (1946), based on the life of the Louisiana Governor Huey Long. Here, the politician Willie Stark, once in power, allows himself to translate a simple political creed into a rationalisation of his actions as being for the general good. It is difficult for those with only a knowledge of English political life to conceive of politics as violent and as vicious as they appear in the latter novel; but Penn Warren's experience of the territory, when a lecturer at Louisiana State University, is not misleading. *The Cave* (1959) extends the novelist's technique into philosophical and psychological investigation. The hero, Jasper Harrak, is trapped in a cave surrounded not only by physical barriers but the hullaballoo of the mass media. His gradual revelation of self in these circumstances takes on the form of the allegory of Plato's cave.

Dating from the period of his contributions to *Fugitive* (1922–25) Penn Warren's poetry has been packed with content and imagery both related to the Southern condition and with a developing metaphysical sense. A curious mixture of fantasy and imagery is developed in 'The Ballad of Billie Potts' from *Selected Poems 1922–1943* (1944), where the poet's concern with the agrarian South is juxtaposed with long philosophical passages in a classic but macabre story of parents unknowingly murdering their rich son. It is however in the later verse that Penn Warren realises a fusion between his intellectual and descriptive abilities.

Penn Warren's contribution to criticism includes the editorship of *Southern Review* between 1935 and 1942; and his contribution to teaching includes the publication with Cleanth Brooks in 1938 of *Understanding Poetry*, a book seminal to the teaching of English in America. Despite this and the publication of a collection of often remarkably good short stories, Penn Warren must be seen primarily as a novelist and a poet of the South.

Other works of interest include a biography, *John Brown, the Making of a Martyr* (1929); two volumes of essays, *Selected Essays* (1958) and *The Legacy of the Civil War* (1961); and a volume of short stories, *The Circus in the Attic* (1948). Collections of his poetry include *Thirty-Six Poems* (1935); *Eleven Poems on the Same Theme* (1942); *Selected Poems* (1944); *Brother to Dragons* (1953); and *Promises, Poems 1954–1956* (1957). Novels not mentioned in this article include *Night Rider* (1939) and *World Enough and Time* (1950). D. L. P.

Penton, Brian (1904–51), Australian author of two volumes of a monumental and violent saga—*Landtakers* (1934) and *Inheritors* (1936). The main figure is a settler in the Queensland of 1844, Cabell, whom we meet in the first book as a young man in conflict with the rough and brutal pioneers, a conflict that brings about his own toughening and eventual degradation. The second book takes up the tale much later when Cabell has become a domineering, powerful and grotesque figure, surpassing in these respects all those with whom he had to contend previously. These vivid and sometimes horrifying books can be taken as an attack on the school of writing that saw the settlers and the pioneer days through a golden haze of romanticism and portrayed the struggle as one fundamentally strengthening to the character. S. R.

Perelman, S. J. (Sidney Joseph Perelman; 1904–   ), American humorist, probably second in repute only to Thurber. Much of his satirical writing—dealing with wide-ranging aspects of the American scene but most memorably with advertising, public relations and the world of show business—first appeared in *The New Yorker*; some of his best occasional pieces being preserved in *The Most of S. J. Perelman* (1958). His books include *Dawn Ginsbergh's Revenge* (1929), *Westward Ho! or, Around the World in* 80 *Clichés* (1948), *The Swiss Family Perelman* (1950) and *The Road to Miltown, or Under the Spreading Atrophy* (1957). He also wrote scripts for the Marx brothers' films. K. R. R.

Pérez de Ayala, Ramón (1880–1962), Spanish writer. Although he published poetry, essays and excellent drama criticism, Pérez de Ayala is mainly important as a novelist. The early novels are satirical and realistic: *A.M.D.G.* (1910)—*Ad majorem Dei gloriam*, the motto of the Jesuits—is a bitter attack on his Jesuit schoolmasters, while *Tinieblas en las cumbres*

['Darkness on the mountain tops'] (1907), *La pata de la raposa* [*The Fox's Paw*] (1912) and *Troteras y danzaderas* ['Bawds and dancers'] (1913) trace the sentimental education of Alberto Díaz de Guzmán, the author himself thinly disguised. The stylistic purification apparent in *Prometeo* [*Prometheus*], *La caída de los Limones* [*The Fall of the House of Limón*] and *Luz de domingo* [*Sunday Sunlight*], published in 1916, paves the way for the brilliantly orchestrated novels of his maturity. *Belarmino y Apolonio* ['Belarmino and Apolonio'] (1921) is a tragicomic dialectical novel of considerable complexity with layers of superimposed meaning. *Tigre Juan* [*Tiger Juan*] (1925) and *El curandero de su honra* ['The medicaster of his honour'] (1925) give a highly individual treatment of Don Juan and the theme of honour. D. H. G.

Perse, Saint-John (1887–), literary pseudonym of Alexis Saint-Léger Léger, French poet and winner of the 1960 Nobel Prize for Literature. Born on Saint-Léger-les-Feuilles near Guadeloupe in the West Indies, he was educated in France and served in the *corps diplomatique* from 1914 till the fall of France in 1940, when he moved to Washington. Only after many years did he return to France, settling in Toulon. His distinguished diplomatic career involved him in frequent and wide travels in the east, on which he became an expert. He was *chef de cabinet* to the foreign minister Aristide Briand in 1925, and in 1933 became secretary-general at the foreign ministry with ambassadorial rank. His earliest literary work dates back to 1911 with the collection *Eloges* [*Eloges*, i.e. 'Eulogies'], but his first notable volume was that of 1924, *Anabase* [*Anabasis*, tr. T. S. Eliot, 1930]. The product of a journey on a pony across the Gobi desert while on service in Peking, this study, expressed in sonorous and visually opulent poetic prose, effectively portrays the observations and historical musings of that experience.

From 1924 to 1940 he published nothing, though continuing to write, but his manuscripts were unfortunately destroyed by the Germans during the occupation. Once free of diplomatic commitments he was able to publish a series of volumes of which the most successful were *Exil* [*Exile*] (1942), *Vents* [*Winds*] (1947) and *Amers* [*Seamarks*] (1953), all of which assert his exceptional taste. His boyhood impressions of the sunny and colourful Caribbean have played a constant and important rôle in his verse. His imagery and cultured eloquence exalt the mighty manifestations of natural forces (winds, deserts, seas), his view of which is essentially cosmic and frequently transmitted by means of the *verset*. His Swedish translator, Dag Hammarskjöld, was influential in the awarding to Perse of the Nobel Prize, forcefully urging that his imagery 'in visionary fashion reflects the conditions of our time'. R. C. W.

Pessoa, Fernando Nogueira (1888–1935), Portuguese poet who is increasingly recognised as one of the outstanding literary figures of the twentieth century. Though born in Lisbon he spent the years 1896 to 1905 in Durban where his stepfather was Portuguese consul and where Pessoa received a British education; the Anglo-Saxon factor was to be a constant feature of his work. On his return to Lisbon he studied for a spell at the university before abandoning his course to set up a short-lived printing business. Thereafter he earned a steady though meagre living working obscurely as a commercial translator in English and French.

His first poems were written in English, between 1905 and 1908, at a time when his principal reading was the work of Milton, Shelley, Keats and Poe. Gradually he interested himself in *saudosismo*, a Portuguese brand of nationalistic symbolism, of which he became an earnest apologist in literary reviews. By 1914 he was profoundly under the influence of the writings of the Italian prophet of futurism, Marinetti, and of the American poet Walt Whitman. In that year occurred the birth of the first of Pessoa's 'heteronyms' to whom he gave the name of Alberto Caeiro. Two others, Álvaro de Campos and Ricardo Reis, soon followed. The mainspring of Pessoa's genius was, as he himself declared, dramatic, though in a special sense. These heteronyms or 'characters' wrote poetry and their poetry he published in Portuguese reviews along with verse written under his own name. So real were they to Pessoa, that like a novelist he provided each with a biography, a background and a complete physical and intellectual personality. Each was a totally individual poet with a totally individual philosophy.

When writing under his own name Pessoa was essentially a metaphysical poet, a poet of subjective and introverted idealism who saw himself as an occultist medium seeking to penetrate the labyrinth of the individual consciousness and indulging frequently in childhood reminiscence. Like Jiménez in Spain he popularised in Portugal the short poem which sought to capture the fleeting moment, the passing sensation, the sudden emotion, especially when it struck a deeper, more intimate chord within him.

Alberto Caeiro, the first heteronym, was diametrically opposed to Pessoa's often confused complexities and served as a form of purge. He represented for Pessoa the 'apprenticeship of unlearning'. In a manner which recalls Gertrude Stein, Jorge Guillén and logical positivism he refused, Occam-like, to multiply entities. Any thing, any object was merely what it appeared to be; the only world to be trusted was that of externals as registered by the senses. Abstract vocabulary was merely a guide, not a reality; adjectives he shunned since they tended to fuse one idea with another; there was 'metaphysics enough in not thinking about anything'. The Whitmanesque and futurist Campos was closer to Pessoa; in his noisy and tumultuous verse there was room for anything. His early verse thundered with the enthusiastic desire to identify the poet with the whole of creation but he ended pessimistically in isolationism. This contrasted sharply with the Hellenic calm of Ricardo Reis, with his moods of stoic acceptance, Promethean defiance and epicurean self-indulgence. Yet Reis' odes were essentially humanistic rather than coldly classical.

The bulk of Pessoa's considerable output was in his lifetime published only in reviews. Two short English collections appeared, however: *Antinous* (Lisbon, 1916) and *35 Sonnets* (London, 1918), the latter written in the manner of the Elizabethans Wyatt and Surrey. In 1934 Pessoa contributed a Portuguese collection, *Mensagem* ['Message'], to a national propaganda competition and so baffled the awarding committee that to its eternal shame it could only grant it a 'second category' prize. While alive Pessoa remained a nebulous and little-recognised literary figure; like Apollinaire and Mayakovsky he was ahead of his period. Translations of individual poems are to be found in Roy Campbell, *Portugal* (1957), J. M. Parker, *Three Twentieth-Century Portuguese Poets* (1961) and Stanley Burnshaw (ed.), *The Poem Itself* (Pelican Books, 1964). R. C. W.

Peterkiewicz, Jerzy (1916–), Polish-born writer, married to the English novelist Christine Brooke-Rose. He attended the universities of Warsaw and St Andrews and King's College, London, before becoming Reader in Polish Language and Literature at the University of London. His first poetry written at the age of nineteen was initially published in Warsaw—*Prowincja* (1936), *Wiersze i poematy* ['Poems and verse'] (1938)—and subsequently in London as *Pogrzeb Europy* ['The funeral of Europe'] (1946). He steadily gained for himself both respect and popularity, changing too from verse to prose. A novel *The Knotted Cord* (1953) marks the beginning of his writing in English. Since then he has written almost continuously both in Polish and English as novelist, critic and translator, a series of strikingly personal contributions to English fiction serving to establish him as an important English-language writer. *The Quick and the Dead* (1961) and *That Angel Burning at My Left Side* (1963), strange and seemingly unclassifiable novels written in a rather short sharp elliptical fashion where elements of the thriller and the picaresque adventure mingle fascinatingly and disturbingly with fantasy and the supernatural, are at once the most characteristic and the best of his work. His collection of earlier poetry *Poematy londyńskie i wiersze przedwojenne* ['London poems and pre-war verse'] (1965) was published in Paris. B. M.

Peters, Lenrie (1932–), Gambian-born writer who has also lived and studied in Sierra Leone and England. A surgeon by profession, his *Poems* (1964) and novel *The Second Round* (1965) attest to a clinical mind, strong physical awareness of the anatomy of things, burning social conscience and impressive imaginative control. Peters's poetry and prose carry the distinction of vividly re-embodied experience, whether they deal with a parachute-jump, returning home, cities or the life of a doctor who after qualifying in England goes back to practise in his native Sierra Leone.

C. P.

Petersen, Nis (1897–1943), Danish novelist and poet. His international reputation rests on two best-selling novels, *Sandalmagernes Gade* [*The Street of the Sandalmakers*] (1931), which is set in Rome, and *Spildt Maelk* [*Spilt Milk*] (1934) which deals with the Irish civil war. In Denmark, however, his repute derived rather from his steady output of lyric verse and witty short stories. R. C. W.

Petrov, Yevgeni (Yevgeni Petrovich Katayev; 1903–42), Soviet humorist and satirist who collaborated with Ilya Ilf (q.v.) until the latter's death. He then wrote film scripts and plays; and during the war he edited *Ogonyok* ['Little flame'] and sent despatches from the front at Sebastopol where he was eventually killed. His *Frontovoy dnyevnik* [*Diary at the Front*] was published after his death. B. W.

Peyrefitte, Roger (1907–), French novelist. Born at Castres he was a career diplomat from 1937 to 1944. His first novel, *Les Amitiés particulières* [*Special Friendships*] (1944), had a *succès de scandale* due to its describing a homosexual relationship; none the less the spirit of the book is a characteristic mixture of humour and gravity. After some less successful works, Peyrefitte published *Les Ambassades* [*Diplomatic Diversions*] (1951), an account of his experiences on a mission to Athens; and this novel, half-autobiography, half-exposé of the world of diplomacy, was followed by *La Fin des ambassades* [*Diplomatic Conclusions*] (1953), in the same vein, a humorous yet revealing confession and condemnation. *Les Clés de Saint-Pierre* [*The Keys of Saint Peter*] (1955) is an exposé in similar style of papal society, while *Les Chevaliers de Malte* ['Knights of Malta'] (1957) does the same for that order and *Les Fils de la lumière* ['The sons of light'] (1961) for the freemasons.

Peyrefitte has also written more intensely autobiographical works—such as *La Mort d'une mère* ['Death of a mother'] (1950); a travel book—*Du Vésuve à l'Etna* [*South from Naples*] (1951); and further novels—*Jeunes Proies* ['Young prey'] (1956), *La Nature du prince* [*The Prince's Person*] (1963), *Les Juifs* [*The Jews*] (1965) and *Notre Amour* ['Our love'] (1967). D. E. A.

Phillpotts, Eden (1862–1960), English novelist and playwright, made his home in Devon and drew on his knowledge of this beautiful county for most of his novels. Amongst the 250 books he wrote during his long life, the best known are the Dartmoor series, including *Secret Woman* (1905) and *Widdecombe Fair* (1913). His plays include *Farmer's Wife* (1916) which was revived by the National Theatre company at Chichester in the 1960s, and *Yellow Sands* (1926). K. M. H.

Pieyre de Mandiargues, André (1909–), French writer, born in Paris. Although his carefully written works are by no means examples of automatic writing, he has none the less been described as a surrealist. His favoured vehicle is the short story, particularly of an exotic, erotic or fantastic type, carefully and poetically suggestive of German romanticism, sometimes even in its most perverse forms. His first collection, *Dans les années sordides* ['In the sordid years'] (1943), was followed by others—*Le Musée noir* ['Black museum'] (1946), *Les Incongruités monumentales* [*Monumental Incongruities*] (1948), *Le Lis de mer* ['Sea lily'] (1956), *Le Cadran lunaire* ['Moondial'] (1958); and by the novels *La Motocyclette* [*The Motorcycle*] (1964) and *La Marge* ['The margin'] (1967), the latter winning the 1967 Prix Goncourt. D. E. A.

Pilnyak, Boris (Boris Andreyevich Vogau; 1894–1937?), Soviet novelist, was an important anti-western, almost anti-communist Russian writer who saw in the revolution a rebirth of a new Slavic pre-Petrine Russia. His unorthodox views were to bring him much tribulation in the thirties, but his first works were greeted with enthusiasm. He was acknowledged as a stylist and became the model for many other authors. To him is attributed the first Soviet novel—*Golyi God* [*The Naked Year*] (1922)—which is really a collection of varied stories using the revolution as its linking theme; underlying the whole is the Slavophil idea of deep-rooted, purely Slavonic traditions. With his remarkable *Povyest' nyenogashennoy-luny* [*The Tale of the Unextinguished Moon*] (1926) Pilnyak found himself in trouble because Stalin identified himself with the character of the mysterious party chief who orders a Red Army Hero to undergo an operation, an operation to which the man though rightly fearing for his life nevertheless submits. The previous year a famous Red Army officer had died on the operating table. In 1929 Pilnyak's story *Krasnoye derevo* [*Mahogany*] was printed in Germany, but not in Russia. This work was criticised for its harking back to the good old revolutionary times, and Pilnyak was expelled from the Writers' Union. His recantation gave him a few years' grace and he produced an enlarged and modified version of *Mahogany* called *Volga vpadayet v kaspiiskoye morye* [*The Volga flows to* *the Caspian Sea*] (1930) where he still maintains his sympathy for traditional Russian culture, despite his being superficially attracted to the new constructors. He wrote of his American impressions in *O.K.* [*O.K.*] (1931) and then was suppressed and arrested during one of the great purges about 1937. He is presumed to have died in prison. B. W.

Pinget, Robert (1919–), Swiss-French novelist. Born in Geneva, he has practised as a barrister, worked as a journalist, painted and exhibited in Paris and taught in England. His first novel *Mahu, ou le matériau* [*Mahu or the Material*] (1952), together with several plays and radio scripts *Lettre morte* [*Dead Letter*] (1960), *La Manivelle* [*The Old Tune*] (1960; trans. by Beckett), *Clope au dossier* [*Clope*] (1961), *L'Hypothèse* [*Hypothesis*] (1961), *Architruc* [*Architruc*] (1961) and *Autour de Mortin* [*Around Mortin*] (1963), earned him consideration as an interesting, if minor and perhaps derivative, talent; but his subsequent work has sustained and developed—within the context and under the collective aegis of the 'new novel', Samuel Beckett and the theatre of the absurd—the evident individuality of M. Levert's elusive letter to his son, *Le Fiston* [*No Answer*] (1959). The botanist in the Fémina prizewinner *Quelqu'un* ['Someone'] (1965) will never find the paper vital to his treatise; nor will the elderly manservant ever contribute any information of value to the detective of *L'Inquisitoire* [*The Inquisitory*] (1962); yet, inviolate in their private worlds, Pinget's characters immediately engage our attention by the comic poetry of their heightened vernacular, our sympathy by the frailty of their pretence and the paucity of their triumphs. Senescence starts at birth. M. D. E.

Pinter, Harold (1930–), English writer, is best known as a playwright although he has written for media other than the theatre. His rise in critical acclaim was meteoric following the success of his second full-length play *The Caretaker* (1960) which like *The Homecoming* (1965) caused critical controversy, being interpreted both as farce and serious horror piece. His best works contain elements of both and have an affinity with those of Samuel Beckett. Only the irrational is manifest in his plays, which tend to consist of duologues where one person tries implicitly to assert power over the other. His work achieves the effect of being casually written, but it hides a considered style which creates a feeling of tension between the characters, unequalled by any other contemporary playwright. It is also capable of a deeper symbolic meaning as can be seen when one considers that the anxieties which the characters feel are connected to fantasies about power, expressed in their seeming to adopt a pecking order. The ultimate power is often unknown and outside the play itself.

In *A Night Out* (1961) a stupid and overwhelming mother appears in what is both a funny and tragic situation, persecuting her son with questions which are delivered like threats. The questions are unanswerable for they concern themselves with whether he is leading 'a clean life'. In his turn he allows himself to be picked up by a refined but stupid prostitute whom he substitutes for his mother. Here he can retaliate and he applies the same treatment to her as he has received from his mother. He is unable to follow the sexual side of the relationship through but forces her to put his shoes on his feet and in this way satisfies both his Adlerian need for power and his incestuous desire for his mother.

Often Pinter's plays have a hackneyed structure, the end being totally predictable, but their strength lies in his ability to capture the way people actually speak when in situations where some of the factors are unknown. *The Birthday Party* (1959) and *A Slight Ache* (1961) follow this pattern. Implicit in his work is a criticism of the well-rounded drama with no loose ends. Characters in his plays lie and are unveiled by reference to someone else who in turn may not be telling the truth. But as in Kafka, the lie becomes the reality.

He has also written revue sketches, and screenplays for *The Servant* (1963) and *The Pumpkin Eater* (1964). K. G.-Y.

Piontek, Heinz (1925–), German writer, was born in Silesia, and the Silesian landscape with its Slav associations figures prominently in his verse and prose. He served in the army as a youth, later continuing his studies; since 1948 he has been a freelance writer, critic, poet and radio dramatist. His first verse volume *Die Furt* ['The ford'] appeared in 1952; the title poem being based on the recollection of the poet as a soldier. His lyric poetry is characterised by impressionistically coloured treatment of landscape; the last line is often the *pièce de résistance*. Perfectly classical verse is interspersed with lines of odd length, and brutally realistic language is often used to heighten the overall effect. *Vor Augen* ['Before the eyes'] (1955) is an attempt to create a new type of short story, one where the narrative breaks off and leaves the reader to finish the story for himself. Individual poems are translated in anthologies. G. W.

Pirandello, Luigi (1867–1936), Italian poet, novelist and playwright, winner of the 1934 Nobel Prize for Literature. After an indifferent start as a writer of verse, he turned to prose-writing and published short stories as well as literary criticism and his first novels. It was not until the early 1920s that he achieved his world-wide success.

After *L'esclusa* [*The Outcast*] (1901), a comparatively unsophisticated novel with melodramatic undertones on jealousy and misunderstanding in a middle-class marriage, Pirandello wrote a series of novels of which the most successful was *Il fu Mattia Pascal* [*The Late Mattia Pascal*] (1904). Mattia Pascal is mistakenly believed dead, decides to take advantage of this and changes his name and place of residence. When he realises that he has become entangled in a mesh of social relationships and tries to return home and resume his previous place in society, he finds that it is too late as his wife has remarried, and he remains an incongruous figure who occasionally visits his own grave. After the digression of *I vecchi e i giovani* [*The Old and the Young*] (1909), a study of the contrasts between two generations in Sicily towards the turn of the century, Pirandello wrote *Si gira . . .* [*Shoot! The Notebooks of Serafino Gubbio Cinematograph Operator*] (1915), which symbolises the conflict between the eternity of art and the fickleness of human existence through the story of the successful shooting by Gubbio of a sensational scene by which he attains what he regards as artistic climax.

With *Uno, nessuno e centomila* [*One, None and a Hundred Thousand*] (1926) Pirandello highlighted in novel form one of the main themes in his philosophy of life. When Vitangelo Moscarda discovers the many-sidedness of his personality, of which everybody else sees a different facet, he rejects the more binding social conventions and obligations and withdraws into a contented state of 'being everybody without being anybody'. The theatre was naturally a more suitable vehicle for the transmission of Pirandello's theories on the relativity, therefore non-existence, of truth, the lack of objectiveness in our knowledge of the outside world, and the continuous 'creation' of reality. Together with the belief that man is not truly free and that his multi-faceted personality is ultimately not 'real' goes his theory of the autonomy of characters whose existence becomes dissociated from the mind of an author upon their creation. A significant manifestation of his theories came with his first major play *Cosí è (se vi pare)* [*It Is So (If You Think So)*] (1916). The little town of Valdana is bemused by the unclear set-up of the Ponza family, as Mr Ponza and his mother-in-law give contradictory versions of the identity and indeed existence of the former's wife. During a public confrontation between the two, enter the veiled Mrs Ponza who states that she is 'what she is thought to be'.

To this fertile phase in Pirandello's production belong a number of three-act plays which, with the exception of *Liolà* [*Liolà*] (1917) which is a light-hearted vaudeville on the antics of a Sicilian womaniser, contain an indictment of the conventional code of middle-class morality. In *Il piacere dell'onestà* [*The Pleasure of Honesty*] (1917) Angelo Baldovino agrees to marry Marquis Colli's mistress Agata who is expecting the latter's baby. When the Marquis attempts a come-back Agata preserves her loyalty to her husband. A similar theme is that of *Il giuoco delle parti* [*The Rules of the Game*] (1918). Leone Gala's wife, exasperated by her husband's permissive attitude to her lover Guido, tries to make him take part in a duel. Leone however refuses and Guido, who has to take his place, is killed on the field. This critical view of bourgeois conventions found a further outlet in *Tutto per bene* [*All for the Best*] (1920): when Martino Lori learns that he is not the father of Palma, daughter of his dead wife, he has to give up his desire to take revenge as too much time has elapsed since the offence took place.

The year 1921 saw the controversial performance of *Sei personaggi in cerca d'autore* [*Six Characters In Search of An Author*] which, with *Ciascuno a suo modo* [*Each in His Own Way*] (1924) and *Questa sera si recita a soggetto* [*Tonight We Improvise*] (1930), constitutes a trilogy of plays known as 'theatre within the theatre' by which Pirandello intended to find artistic expression for his own theories on the fictitiousness of reality and its relationship with the true autonomy enjoyed by theatrical characters. Among the works that followed are the plays *Enrico IV* [*Henry IV*] (1922), *Vestire gli ignudi* [*To Clothe the Naked*] (1923) and *Come tu mi vuoi* [*As You Desire Me*] (1930). In the first, a young aristocrat becomes mentally unbalanced and spends twelve years believing himself to be the Emperor Henry IV. When he regains sanity he is driven by events to kill his erstwhile rival and is forced again to accept madness as a form of catharsis. In the second play Ersilia Drei, a governess in the service of an Italian diplomat, goes through two unhappy love affairs and, after a fatal accident and further disillusionment, takes her life. With *Come tu mi vuoi* Pirandello reverts to the theme of the relativity of existence: the wife of the Italian officer Bruno Pieri mysteriously disappears during the war, and when he tries to recreate her personality in a woman found in Berlin by a friend, this proves impossible and he loses her again.

All of Pirandello's short stories, of which several formed a basis for theatrical works, were collected under the title *Novelle per un anno* ['Stories for a year']: there are partial collections in English of these under various titles. Translations are also available of minor plays, among which are *Lumie di Sicilia* [*Sicilian Limes*] (1911), *La giara* [*The Jar*] (1925) and *L'uomo dal fiore in bocca* [*The Man With A Flower in His Mouth*] (1926).

D. B.

Pirro, Ugo (1920–   ), Italian novelist and playwright. He took part in the second world war and has recalled in his works wartime episodes, writing in a colloquial style and with an apparent lack of involvement. With *Le soldatesse* [*The Camp-followers*] (1956) he has given a haunting account of the vicissitudes of a group of Greek girls destined for the entertainment of the occupying fascist troops. In *Mille tradimenti* [*A Thousand Betrayals*] (1959), an Italian officer describes the conflicting emotions and fears besetting him during his bid to leave Sardinia for the mainland of Italy after his desertion from the army in the confused period following the 1943 armistice. Pirro's subsequent novel *Jovanka e le altre* [*Five Branded Women*] (1960) relates the attempt by a group of Yugoslav girls, ostracised for associating with enemy soldiers, to redeem themselves by joining the partisan forces. D. B.

Pitter, Ruth (1897–), English poet. A minor writer who cannot accurately be said to belong to any school, she has written some extremely pleasing, often lyrical verses on traditional themes—of which it is perhaps those of a religious nature that yield her most distinctive (if not always her best) writing. A memorable volume is *Urania* (1951); later titles include *Still by Choice* (1966). K. R. R.

Plaatje, Sol. T. (1890–), South African author, known for his pioneering translations of Shakespeare into Bechuana and famed for his classic *Mhudi* (1930), 'An Epic of South African Native Life a Hundred Years Ago'. A direct, unaffected (occasionally near-simplissistic) unfolding of the momentous confrontations between the tribes of central southern Africa and their meeting with the *Voortrekker* Boers, this early novel survives comparison with the work of Peter Abrahams and of Stuart Cloete covering the same epoch. C. P.

Plaidy, Jean (Eleanor Alice Burford Hibbert; 1906–), English historical novelist. Her first novel, *Beyond the Blue Mountains*, a colourful story set in the eighteenth and early nineteenth century in Newgate prison and Australia, was published in 1948. Most of her stories are woven around the lives of well-known characters, as in her trilogy on Catherine de Medici, *Madame Serpent* (1951), *Italian Woman* (1952) and *Queen Jezebel* (1953). Other titles include *Flaunting Extravagant Queen* (1957) about Marie Antoinette, *Louis the Well Beloved* (1959), *Evergreen Gallant* (1965) and *The Haunted Sisters* (1966). She has seventeen other pseudonyms including Kathleen Kellow, Ellalice Tate, Elbur Ford, and Victoria Holt, the name under which she has written a series of gothic romances including *Mistress of Mellyn* (1961). K. M. H.

Plath, Sylvia (1932–64), American poet. Plath, who was married to the English poet Ted Hughes, wrote in an elegant and controlled style quite in contrast to the toughness and violence of her husband's writing. *Colossus* (1960) contains poems which individually build up a structure of meaning through the careful use of image and metaphor, and give the impression of a refined and pleasing minor poet. The poetry of the last years of her short life shows an increasing preoccupation with, and fascination for, death. *Ariel* (1965) is a posthumous volume. *The Bell Jar* (1963) is a novel. D. L. P.

Plomer, William (1903–), South African-born author who farmed and traded in his native land, lived for periods in Japan and Greece, and subsequently settled in England. Plomer founded and edited, with Roy Campbell, the short-lived but influential literary magazine *Voorslag*. A passionately sympathetic artist, he is most versatile and is a polished writer of novels, short stories, verse, biographies, autobiography and criticism. Africa's most urbane writer, he is also the author of what is perhaps the strongest and truest depiction to date of the African in modern South Africa, the explosive *Turbott Wolfe* (1925). By contrast with this novel, Paton's *Cry, the Beloved Country* and F. A. Venter's *Dark Pilgrim* give altogether milder and more slanted pictures. His later fiction has included *Museum Pieces* (1950), which blends humour and humanity in its incisive portrayal of the mid-twentieth-century Englishman.

The range of Plomer's poetic style and subject-matter, the breadth of his intellect and the depth of his humanity are constantly in evidence in *Selected Poems* (1940); in *The Dorking Thigh* (1945), a collection of mordantly satirical verse spanning two decades; and in *Taste and Remember* (1966), where the sharp-eyed satire of a latter-day Pope (minus the embittering acid) is to be found alongside the deeply felt lyric or the passionate elegy.

As librettist for Benjamin Britten's *Curlew River* (1964) and *The Burning Fiery Furnace* (1966), Plomer reveals new dimensions of poetic drama. Stark, economic writing of a hieratic, stylised quality characterises these works. C. P.

Popa, Vasko (1922–), Yugoslav poet. Attracted by French surrealism before he began to publish, he has evolved his own style which has not changed essentially although its range is constantly growing. Popa is a controversial poet. He is concerned with the present in the light of the past and uses the language and imagery of the rich Serbian folk tradition, combined with universal symbols and colloquial idiom. His poems are concise and arranged in cycles, covering with great concentration the broad themes of existence, death, the cosmos—conveyed in a tense hermetic symbolism. There is a representative selection from the three small volumes of his poems in English translation, *The Poems of Vasko Popa* (1966). C. W.

Porter, Eleanor H. (1868–1920), American author of *Pollyanna* (1913) whose child-heroine is characterised by her unfailing optimism through the trials and tribulations of life. *Pollyanna Grows Up* (1915) is the sequel.

K. R. R.

Porter, Gene Stratton (1886–1924), American novelist and nature writer, brought up in Indiana, settled with her husband in a cabin on the edge of a swamp called 'the Limberlost', which was to provide the setting of many of her books. *Freckles* appeared in 1904 and was an immediate success, and in 1909 was followed by another best seller *Girl of the Limberlost*. These, and the novels that came after, are frankly sentimental; but her nature writings which include *Homing with the Birds* (1919), although less widely read, have a more enduring quality. Her other titles include *Laddie* (1913), an idealised portrait of her brother who was drowned at eighteen; *Michael O'Halloran* (1915); and *Daughter of the Land* (1918).

K. M. H.

Porter, Hal (1917–), Australian writer of plays, poetry, novels, short stories, autobiography and biography. His early life was spent in the country town of Bairnsdale, Victoria, and he has since lived in Melbourne, Japan, Europe and England before returning to his home town as librarian. Since childhood a voracious and eclectic reader, he brings to his work a rich and esoteric vocabulary, an acute eye for detail and ear for nuance, and one of the most exotic and surrealistic imaginations to be found in Australian writing. For his material he draws on his extended family and incidents from its past and present, and on the countless fragments of drama, melodrama and tragedy he has witnessed in his travels. Essential reading for an appreciation of Porter's work is his autobiography *The Watcher on the Cast-Iron Balcony* (1963) which reveals with merciless frankness both his own personal 'un-innocent' development and the gradual evolution of his detachment as an artist. In addition to his volume of poetry *The Hexagon* (1957), the novels *A Handful of Pennies* (1957) and *The Tilted Cross* (1961) and the play *The Tower* (1962), he has published three volumes of short stories. In the third of these, *The Cats of Venice* (1965), he demonstrates his ability to handle a variety of moods ranging from comedy and satire to tenderness and disillusion. The particularly notable title story, with its oblique style and cryptic distillation of a situation, shows his close connection with the main currents of modern and experimental writing.

S. R.

Porter, Katherine Anne (1894–), American writer, is most widely known for her best-selling novel *Ship of Fools* (1962). Begun some thirty years earlier and published when she was nearly seventy, this compelling and monumental book—her first full-length novel—has tended to eclipse its author's previous achievements as a short-story writer and essayist, achievements which had earned her many honours and a position of great respect in American letters.

Katherine Anne Porter's ship is both a very real vessel, whose day-to-day life is instantly recognisable to anyone who has travelled by sea, and at the same time a true microcosm. As individuals, passengers and crew exhibit a representative variety of race, class and age, of religious faith and political passion, and of emotional and sexual fulfilment and deprivation. As a miniature society, they reflect familiar patterns: in the authoritarian Junker captain and the anti-Semitic *petit-bourgeois* Herr Rieber, we have the seeds of Nazism; in the rabble-rousing demagogue of the steerage, a hint of communism. In the steerage passengers—counted in numbers rather than as individuals with names—we see the lot of the great mass of humanity. Transported in bulk, cramped, ragged and diseased, they have limited room for manoeuvre. Men and women copulate; a child is born; fights break out; and on Sunday the priest arrives to hear confessions. The demagogue abuses their superstitions, and is set upon; while the captain, fearing a disturbance, has had them all searched for possible weapons.

It might appear that the first-class passengers by contrast have every opportunity to live as they please, but they can only move within the limits of their personal circumstances. An ill-matched pair of young lovers ring the changes interminably on their tormented relationship. Two widows, a divorcee, a plain girl, and three frustrated men are all chronically unable to escape their plight, despite recourse to the young males of the ship's crew and the women of a Spanish dance company. Three married couples live constantly under the shadows of continuing problems—alcoholism, business failure and childlessness. Outside these personal problems, their freedom is more real; and wherever this freedom exists its use inevitably produces distress. The poison of anti-Semitism that distils from Herr Rieber gradually infects the whole of the captain's table: its malice is quite gratuitous and is concentrated on tormenting a German passenger whose wife (not with him) is Jewish. The shameless commercial greed of the professional dancers is all the time in evidence as they exploit the passengers and defraud the shopkeepers in the ports. Even the scrupulous ship's doctor, attending the sick-bed of an exiled drug-addicted countess, cannot escape the trap that is set for him, and ends up exploiting her addiction for his own perverted satisfaction.

By the end of the voyage, Miss Porter's microcosm of humanity presents a pretty sorry spectacle. The childless husband, a professor, clings almost stoically to his belief in the goodness of man; ironically it is his pathetic dog, which he and his wife dote on, that is thrown overboard by the diabolical seven-year-old twins of one of the dancers—a pair in whose nature is crystallised all the evil in the world. The professor consistently refuses to see the squalor around him as inevitable; his wife, who knows better, must submerge her knowledge out of the loyalty demanded by her husband. The picture is only redeemed by the erratic idealism of the young lovers and the extravagant self-sacrifice of the solitary craftsman from the steerage who is drowned in saving the professor's dog.

Katherine Anne Porter's southern, Catholic background, with its traditions and myths, provided material for many of the short stories contained in her three earlier publications—*Flowering Judas* (1930), *Pale Horse, Pale Rider* (1939) and *The Leaning Tower* (1944). The most frequently recurring theme in these stories is the quest for truth in the traditions and myths that have surrounded the childhood and adolescence of a girl called Miranda. During these years Miss Porter wrote numerous critical articles and travelled widely as a lecturer. She also voyaged from Mexico to Germany, a journey which clearly provided her with the basic material for her great novel. The commercial success of the latter enabled her to devote all her time to writing; and at the age of seventy she announced that she had 'three more books' to write.

K. R. R.

Postgate, Raymond William (1896–), English sociologist, historian and novelist, probably most widely known for his *Good Food Guide*. His books include *A History of the British Workers* (1926), *Karl Marx* (1933) and *The Common People* (1938; with G. D. H. Cole). *Verdict of Twelve* (1940) and *Somebody at the Door* (1943) were two successive detective novels.

R. A. K.

Potter, Stephen (1900–), English humorist and critic. He has had a varied career, having been secretary, lecturer, journalist, BBC producer and editor of *The Leader*. His first book in 1929 was a novel *The Young Man* but he turned to literary criticism with *D. H. Lawrence, a First Study* (1930) and *Coleridge and S.T.C.* (1935), and in 1934 he edited the Nonesuch edition of Coleridge and Mrs Coleridge's letters. He is chiefly known however for his clever, humorous writing describing how to establish personal superiority on all sorts of occasions. Some of the titles, *Gamesmanship* (1947), *Lifemanship* (1950), *One-upmanship* (1952), have become standard expressions. Other works include *Potter on America* (1956), *Supermanship* (1958), *Steps of Immaturity* (early autobiography, 1959) and *Anti-woo* (1965).

G. S.

Pound, Ezra Loomis (1885–), American poet, born at Hailey, Idaho, and educated at Pennsylvania University and Hamilton College, whence he later received an honorary doctorate. He went to Europe in 1907, staying initially in Italy and then living in England from 1908 to 1920. His first published works included *A Lume Spento* (1908), *Exultations* (1909), *Personae* (1910) and *Ripostes* (1912); which together put him at the forefront of the imagist movement in poetry. He was present in 1913 at the celebrated imagist dinner called by Amy Lowell and helped edit the first imagist anthology. He also assisted the founding of the vorticist magazine *Blast* and for a time was foreign editor of *Poetry*. During his lifetime Pound published a mass of critical material. A selection of this work includes *The Spirit of Romance* (1910), which was revised in 1953; *A.B.C. of Reading* (1934); and *The Literary Essays of Ezra Pound* with an introduction by T. S. Eliot (1954). Pound's influence was not only creative and critical but also, at times, quite practical. He assisted in the publication of the early work of Eliot, Joyce, Wyndham Lewis and many others.

Pound is one of the most important writers of the early twentieth century. He regarded himself as a poet-hero with the self-imposed task of employing his own cultural enlightenment for the salvation of western civilisation. His dissatisfaction with his environment, especially that of England, manifests itself in *Hugh Selwyn Mauberley* (1920) which bids a goodbye to a London that he had basically been unable to alter. He feels it to be corrupted by war and by the commercialisation of the arts. In the poem's opening section, written with a deliberate linguistic archaism and entitled 'E. P. Ode Pour l'Election de Son Sepulchre', the central figure of the poem prepares himself for a symbolic death:

> Unaffected by 'the march of events',
> He passed from men's memories in l'an trentiesme
> De son eage;

Later in the poem he writes:

> The age demanded an image
> Of its accelerated grimace,
> Something for the modern stage,
> Not, at any rate, an Attic grace.

Pound's central work is the *Cantos*, a massive production spanning nearly forty years including: *Cantos I–XVI* (1925); *A Draft of XXX Cantos* (1930); *Eleven New Cantos XXXI–XLI* (1934); *Fifth Decad of Cantos* (1937); *Cantos LII–LXXL* (1940); *Pisan Cantos* (1948); *Section: Rock Drill 85–95 De Los Cantares* (1956); and *Thrones: 96–109 De Los Cantares* (1959). The whole concept is a patchwork quilt the shape of which Pound claimed would only fully emerge when the planned 100 cantos were complete. Yeats, to whom Pound once acted as secretary, and who was with him at Rapallo in the 1930s, maintained a pose of total non-understanding. The epic has a loose structure with Pound as a kind of Odysseus seeking culture in his journeying through time and a multiplicity of events. It is a kind of Divine Comedy, a poetic survey of humanity dealing historically with such diverse cultural phenomena as the Italian renaissance, American constitutional history in the period of Jefferson and Adams, and the contemporary scene. Each group of cantos is a centre round which play all the universal themes. Essentially Pound is convinced that history should illuminate and evalute the present; that it should inculcate in the individual a moral awareness, and push society into humanitarianism through a knowledge of its economic basis. What he seeks, then, is an individual and cultural transformation in terms of the interpenetrating moral themes of his epic.

Pound's interest in Chinese poetry, which evolved with the production of *Cathay* (1915), an adaptation of Fenollosa's translations of Li Tai Po, and in Japanese drama, marked by his edition of *Noh or Accomplishment* (1916), emerges in the early Cantos as a sympathy with the cultural past modifying and developing the sensibilities of the present. Pound employs actual quotations from Provençal and Anglo-Saxon poetry as well as references to oriental literature. Later, his economic ideas translate into a horror of usury and a desire for state control of money and credit. The latter led to sympathy with fascism, to the point of broadcasting on the Italian radio during the second world war. His resulting incarceration by American troops in 1945 at a camp in Pisa led to the *Pisan Cantos*, ten sections which describe the physical surroundings of imprisonment, the guards and prisoners, as well as an emotional stability regained by turning back to nature. Pound was awarded the Bollingen Prize for this particular piece of work, a decision which when related to the context of the work not unnaturally caused a political storm. He was brought back to the United States to stand trial, but was judged mentally incompetent to submit a defence and in 1946 was committed to a Washington hospital. He was released only in 1958 when pressure from American poets, led by Robert Frost, caused the indictment for treason to be withdrawn. Two years previously he had published *Section: Rock Drill 85–95 De Los Cantares*, which after the purgatory of Pisa rediscovers a paradise for man in terms of the ultimate intellectual and emotional purity of which he is capable.

Pound's scholarship and points of reference are often obscure and his style intense; but the breadth in concept of his work is gigantic and despite that breadth his imagistic power of description and ability to seize sharply the focus, both intellectual and emotional, of an individual subject remain unimpaired. Pound is perhaps the most representative figure in that vast opening-out of new cultural forces that occurred in the early twentieth century. There is no doubt that he is a poet of immense stature.

D. L. P.

Powell, Anthony (1905–), English novelist. Powell's early novels, such as *Afternoon Men* (1931), *Venusberg* (1932) and *From a View to a Death* (1933), established their writer as a serious social satirist in the sphere of high comedy. They are chiefly concerned to explore private and public morality in the bored town and country lives of the English upper classes; though *Venusberg* is set in the diplomatic circles of a mythical Baltic capital.

But it is with a group of later novels that Powell's reputation has been consolidated. *A Dance to the Music of Time* is a sequence of books written with an underlying melancholy and developing the interconnecting patterns created by a series of characters from their early childhood to late middle age. Fifteen years after the publication of its first title the sequence had not yet been completed; it includes *A Question of Upbringing* (1951), *A Buyer's Market* (1952), *The Acceptance World* (1955), *At Lady Molly's* (1957), *Casanova's Chinese Restaurant* (1960), *The Kindly Ones* (1962) and *The Soldier's Art* (1966). The central commentator, Jenkins, is educated at public school and Oxbridge and becomes himself a minor novelist; he is possessed therefore of the qualities which enable Powell to develop him as a persona to reflect, and comment upon, the maturity of his contemporaries. Jenkins's school companions, Templer, Stringham, Widmerpool, enable him in adult life to enter the varied worlds of industry, politics and house parties that are part of the structure of the 1920s and 1930s. Characters like the eccentric painter Deacon and the left-wing writer Quiggin illustrate the quasi-bohemian, quasi-respectable world of arts and letters. Jenkins's own Uncle Giles counterpoints the action of the novels by intruding the values of a past era on the present with which the novelist deals. The last two books in the series take the central characters into the war where, though their characteristics remain the same, the rôles they play in relation to each other are often reversed. The intertwining of their lives is partly a reflection of Powell's sense of fate, and partly an opportunity to present a panoramic view of the world in which he has lived. Essentially, although the sense of time is almost Proustian, the work has an intensely English atmosphere which is only partly a product of its subject matter. The style is elegant, the comedy is severe and the intellect behind it is sharp. *A Dance to the Music of Time* seems to possess as much depth as, and perhaps greater breadth than, any comparable work of social fiction of the twentieth century. D. L. P.

Powys, John Cowper (1892–), English novelist and essayist. A lecturer who became the author of some dozen voluminous novels, he was born and raised in the west of England and always retained a powerful feeling for the countryside, towns and people he came to know. Later he travelled frequently to America on lecture tours and eventually settled there for a period. During this time he wrote the first of the group of fictional works that were to bring him fame, his fourth novel *Wolf Solent* (1929); this being followed in rapid succession by *A Glastonbury Romance* (1932) and *Weymouth Sands* (1934). These last two, praised by many as the work of a genius with vast imaginative breadth of vision, are typical of his work. An incredible variety of local eccentrics, most of them harbouring some secret obsession, are described by Powys with fond satirical touches. Almost to a man, his heroes are sensitive, mystical, philosophical, and romantic in their responses to nature. Most characteristically, they imbue sea, wind and stone with a palpable spirit. The sense of cosmic significance which attaches to the descriptive passages is often impressive; but on occasions the more slender observations are unequal to the weight they are expected to bear. At such times a heavy, overemphatic tone may deaden the narrative. S. R.

Powys, Llewelyn (1884–1939), English essayist and novelist, youngest son of the productive Dorset literary family which included his elder brothers John Cowper and Theodore Francis (q.v.), and whose feeling of communion with nature he shares. He lived abroad in America and Kenya, and visited the middle east and the West Indies, and his descriptive pieces, essays and novels are culled from his varied experiences. Representative titles are *Ebony and Ivory* (1922), *Black Laughter* (1924), *Dorset Essays* (1936) and the novel *Apples Be Ripe* (1930). Also noteworthy are the autobiography written with his brother John Cowper *Confessions of Two Brothers* (1916), and *Skin for Skin* (1925) based on his experiences in the Swiss sanatorium where he finally died of tuberculosis. S. R.

Powys, T. F. (Theodore Francis Powys; 1875–1953), English author of essays ('meditations'), short stories and novels, the second brother of John Cowper Powys, and thought by many to be a writer of greater distinction. Though he could not at first find the literary form that was most suited to his recurring thesis, nor publishers willing to handle his work, his humorous allegorical novel *Mr Weston's Good Wine* (1927) and some of his later short stories did bring him wide recognition during his lifetime. His main preoccupation is a kind of pantheism, illustrated by the recurring figure of God disguised perhaps as a tinker, a fisherman, a salesman or a squire. In each case, the blindness of simple people to goodness unless it is prominently labelled as such is the theme, which is developed with humour and charm, though also for a time with deep pessimism as in *Mr Tasker's Gods* (1925). However, in later works this despair lightens and a profound conclusion is reached on the nature of God; with the apparently irreconcilable concepts of love and death becoming acceptable at last in the story 'The Only Penitent' (1931). S. R.

Pratolini, Vasco (1913–), Italian writer. Of working-class origin, he lived in poor districts, was self-taught and held a variety of different jobs. His copious production, which includes *Il quartiere* [*A Tale of Santa Croce*] (1945), *Cronache di poveri amanti* [*A Tale of Poor Lovers*] (1947), *Un eroe del nostro tempo* [*A Hero of Today*] (1949), *Le ragazze di Sanfrediano* ['Girls of Sanfrediano'] (1955), *La costanza della ragione* [*Bruno Santini*] (1963), and the trilogy consisting of *Metello* ['Metello'] (1955), *Lo Scialo* [*The waste*] (1960) and *Allegoria e derisione* ['Allegory and derision'] (1966), constitutes a modern epic of the recent history of the city and people of Florence, and has given literary expression to the drudgery of the latter's workaday existence and their feelings of human solidarity. These themes are often intermingled with idyllic reminiscences of an autobiographical nature. Pratolini has attempted to portray more intimate emotions in *Cronaca familiare* [*Two Brothers*] (1947), a study of the relationship between himself and his dead brother. D. B.

Preedy, George R. See **Long,** [Gabrielle] Margaret.

Prévert, Jacques (1900–), French poet. Born at Neuilly, Prévert was a member of the surrealist group of poets in the years 1927 to 1930, and published his poems in reviews and journals. After the war he became well known owing to his songs and film dialogues. His first collection, *Paroles* ['Words'] (1945), made him famous and contains his best-known poems. He has also published *Histoires* ['Stories'] (1946) and *Spectacle* ['Spectacle'] (1951). His film scenarios include *Drôle de drame* ['Strange drama'] (1937), *Quai des brumes* ['Quay of mists'] (1938), *Le Jour se lève* ['Daybreak'] (1939) and *Les Enfants du paradis* [*Children of the Gods*] (1944).
D. E. A.

Prichard, Katherine Susannah (1884–), Australian novelist who has described in great detail a variety of aspects and periods of Australian life. Her first novel *The Pioneers* (1915) is set in Victoria in the early nineteenth century; *Black Opal* (1921) is a love story of an idealistic young girl who marries a young miner; *Working Bullocks* (1926) moves to Western Australia and relies more on description of landscape than on story for its success. *Coonardoo* (1929) is thought to be her best novel, perhaps because in entering the mind of an aboriginal girl Miss Prichard found the most suitable subject for her natural simplicity of style. In her later novels she abandons the pastoral convention for a more psychological analysis of character (*Intimate Strangers*, 1937), and finally concentrates on political content—social reform and championship of the underprivileged —in the trilogy *The Roaring Nineties* (1946), *Golden Miles* (1948) and *Winged Seeds* (1950). S. R.

Priestley, J. B. (John Boynton Priestley; 1894–), English novelist, playwright and critic. Priestley was born at Bradford, educated at Trinity Hall, Cambridge, and served in World War I. He became a critic and reviewer in London, publishing two novels before the advent of the immensely successful *The Good Companions* in 1929. This novel deals with the fortunes of a small theatrical group in a popular sentimental style which manages to depict human relations without becoming cloying. Priestley describes the characters in his novels in a good-hearted, unpretentious fashion which when combined with a compelling narrative line appeals strongly to a middle-class middle-brow audience. *Festival at Farbridge* (1951) is a similar kind of book, presenting as a microcosm a small group of likeable people who are setting up a small-town festival, in face of the mild adversities of fate and human nature, in order to participate in the national celebrations of the hundredth anniversary of the Great Exhibition of 1851. Later novels of note include *Lost Empires* (1965).

Priestley's plays are generally domestic dramas with a touch of social comment, for example *Laburnum Grove* (1933). More distinctive is *An Inspector Calls* (1936), which explores the underlying guilt of a family group exposed to a tragedy in which they deny involvement but for which they share responsibility. He also experimented with intellectual concepts of time in plays such as *I Have Been Here Before* (1937); these experiments, which are interesting rather than profound, resulting from the influence of J. W. Dunne's concept of serialism—which involves a belief that, while the individual human being lives through an apparent time sequence, all other times and places coexist simultaneously. In *Time and the Conways* (1937) Priestley gives the Conway family a glimpse of a future happening as they continue to live in the present. In *Johnson over Jordan* (1939) the pilot Johnson is involved in a crash and re-experiences episodes in his past.

Priestley's critical works include studies of Meredith (1926) and of Peacock (1927), and the massive *Literature and Western Man* (1960). He also acquired a wide public for his radio talks, notably during the second world war when he emerged as a national figure. *Midnight on the Desert* (1937) is an autobiography. D. L. P.

Prince, Frank Templeton (1912–), South African-born English poet. Prince is an academic poet, largely influenced by the seventeenth-century metaphysicals. In 1957 he became Professor of English at Southampton University. His early poetry is marked by severely controlled emotional force, strength of expression and use of language, and a richness of image and sound comparable to Yeats. *Soldiers Bathing* (1954) contains a group of love poems based on those of John Donne which have all the variations of mood, elaborateness of intellectual conceit and skilful argument of the latter. The overall emotional effect of intellect and passion combined does not equal that of Donne only because one is constantly aware of the original model. The title poem of the volume is a war poem of the second world war which bears comparison with the best of Wilfred Owen. The earlier *Poems* was published in 1938. D. L. P.

Prishvin, Mikhail Mikhailovich (1873–1954), Russian writer whose literary career began long before the revolution. He had studied agronomy before he started writing rather later in life; his works consist mainly of his impressions of meetings with people and glimpses from his own life. He tells a good story, but it was not until his long autobiographical novel *Kashcheyeva tsep'* [*The Chain of Kashchey*] (1923–28) was published that he became well known. Prior to this, his *V krayu nyepugannykh ptits* [*In the Land of the Frightened Birds*] (1905), a masterful collection of ethnographical and natural material from the Archangelsk region, had occasioned considerable interest.

Prishvin's personal diary furnished him with material for many stories, most of them lyrics about freedom of thought and word. He also added a second part to *The Chain of Kashchey*, and was working on a third when he died. B. W.

Pritchett, V. S. (Victor Sawdon Pritchett; 1900–), English novelist and critic. In his novels and short stories he reveals a Dickensian sense of humour but a greater detachment of style. His titles include *The Spanish Virgin* (1932), short stories; *Nothing Like Leather* (1935), a novel; *It May Never Happen* (1947), short stories; his best-known critical work, *The Living Novel* (1947); and *The Key to My Heart* (1963), containing three related stories. R. A. K.

Proust, Marcel (1871–1922), French novelist. Proust's father was a doctor, his mother of Jewish origin and of a wealthy family; his early life was therefore that of the comfortable middle-classes at the turn of the century. He suffered from asthma from the age of five and was carefully nursed by his mother; this early dependence on her developed into a strong feeling of devotion which continued until her death in 1907. This feeling combined with a guilt feeling and his homosexuality and deteriorating health were to make of Proust a semi-recluse; but first there was an early period of social life in which he frequented the salons of society, diverted himself as did his contemporaries, even publishing a slim volume—*Les Plaisirs et les jours* [*Pleasures and Regrets*] (1896)—of short stories, poems and character sketches. In this period he wrote articles for *Le Figaro* and translated and commented on Ruskin's works. His health deteriorated greatly about 1905 and he was then forced into a life of reclusion; the elegant dilettante became the intense writer, analyst and satirist. After a first attempt at writing a novel which was discarded and not published till 1952 —*Jean Santeuil* [*Jean Santeuil*]—Proust seems to have conceived the idea of his great seven-part novel about 1907, and it was published over the period 1913 to 1927: *Du côté de chez Swann* [*Swann's Way*] (1913), *A l'ombre des jeunes filles en fleurs* [*Within a Budding Grove*] (1919), *Le Côté de Guermantes* [*The Guermantes Way*] (1920), *Sodome et Gomorrhe* [*Cities of the Plain*] (1922), *La Prisonnière* [*The Captive*] (1923), *Albertine disparue* [*Sweet Cheat Gone*] (1925) and *Le Temps retrouvé* [*Time Regained*] (1927). Some of his critical writings and essays were assembled and published in *Chroniques* ['Chronicles'] (1927) and *Contre Sainte-Beuve* [*Against Sainte-Beuve*] (1954); and many collections of his letters have been published since his death.

The seven parts of his novel have the general title *A la recherche du temps perdu* [*Remembrance of Things Past*]. The setting of the novel is the bourgeois society Proust had frequented at the turn of the century and the whole is an invaluable picture of the world of this group. Half-fascinated, half-repelled by it, Proust gives a strongly satirical picture which widens in parts to include a large cross-section of characters, narrowing again to concentrate on the narrator and his life with Albertine. The central story is that of Marcel, the narrator, and Albertine, the central situation that of a cultivated middle-aged man looking back over his life—remembering incidents of his childhood at Combray, the ordered stable world he had known; remembering then the break-up of this order and stability, his adolescence and manhood; remembering the two temptations, the two 'ways' of society he had come to know—Swann's way, the way of the cultivated dilettante, of art and love, and Guermantes' way, the way of society, history, the aristocracy; remembering and discovering, in the last pages of the whole, a new organisation, a new order for his life, an order created by the knowledge that he holds his whole life in his own memory, that his remembrance of things past orders the present. This movement from order to chaos and back to order is the essence of the novel; but in it there are innumerable recurring themes. Human beings seem to act according to 'laws'—those which recur in the depiction of Swann's love for Odette, the narrator's for Gilberte or the Duchess of Guermantes or

Albertine; those which recur in the rise and fall of social cliques, those which control the merging of social milieux. But within these laws there is the constantly changing pattern of human contacts and feelings; and Proust's analysis of feeling, an intense, deep analysis which reminds us that Bergson, Freud and Jung were establishing at the same time the new science of psychological analysis, is accurate and sometimes even painful. Allied with this gift for analysis is his gift for creating living characters, people whose reality we cannot doubt. Proust's is a 'real' novel whose fascination for the reader is enormous; the intention of much of the description of society may be satirical, but the people are none the less authentic. His sensibility to art in all its forms, and the descriptions in particular of cathedrals, music and paintings and the reactions they evoke, are notable; it is also worth remarking that for Proust these forms of art may well symbolise his view of the relationship between man and time—the cathedral representing the human being, at once an entity in time and an embodiment of the time that has passed; the sonata or symphony representing the intense inner life, the subjective consciousness so closely analysed; the paintings representing the privileged moments, the moments of ecstatic union with the outer world which form the highlights of memory and the great moments of existence. Proust's conclusion, that human beings carry their own time with them and both shape and are shaped by time, leads him to create a novel in which our conception of time is fundamental—pure chronology has disappeared, some characters are described in their old age before we see them in their youth, some are depicted several times as the narrator remembers them at different stages of the novel.

Proustian concepts such as that of time have exercised a powerful influence on following generations of writers; but even more fundamental to Proust's novel is the style in which it is written. Proust writes in long meandering sentences, complex in their syntax and involved in the ideas they convey; his style is unmistakable and gives an enveloping, sometimes stifling, atmosphere to his novel, without being unclear or incomprehensible. The novel as a whole is much more than a novel; it is an attempt at a complete record of the world as seen by Proust, in addition to being an attempt to answer a number of problems of a crucial nature for any intelligent person—what is one's personality? what are the relationships which link us to others, and to time? in what way can we organise the chaos of experience so that our lives can be lived with some point and purpose? The novel is, in fact, Proust; and it is the fascination of the man's personality that has led to the present-day realisation that his answers, and his formulation of the questions, are crucial to twentieth-century man.

D. E. A.

Purdy, James (1923–   ), American novelist and short-story writer, became known through his short novel *63: Dream Palace* (1956), subsequently included together with some short stories in a volume entitled *Color of Darkness* (1957). This was followed by two novels, *Malcolm* (1959) and *The Nephew* (1960), the latter a subtle and moving story of the gradual revelation of the true character and feelings of a young man towards his aunt and uncle who idolised him. His writings are sometimes characterised by a weird and even macabre quality, giving them an affinity with the early work of Truman Capote. Later titles include *Children is All* (1963), a volume of short stories, and the novel *Cabot Wright Begins* (1965), and *Eustace Chisholm and the Works* (1968)—the latter, with its violent and tormented (and often homosexual) relationships, comparing in power with the novels of Faulkner. K. R. R.

Q

Quasimodo, Salvatore (1901–1968), Italian poet, winner of the Nobel Prize for Literature, 1959. Born in Syracuse, Sicily, he received a technical education before turning to literary studies. After teaching literature in Milan he was later appointed to the chair of Italian literature at Rome University. In his early poems, as exemplified in such collections as *Acque e terre* ['Water and land'] (1930), *Oboe sommerso* ['Submerged oboe'] (1932) and *Odore di Eucalyptus* ['The scent of eucalyptus'] (1933), he reflected the desire of young contemporary poets to break away from the classical and academic verse of which Carducci had been the last and greatest exponent. Despite his claim that his early verse could not be classed with the 'Hermetic' poetry of such as Montale and Ungaretti, there exists a certain analogy in those poems which present deep states of mind and intimate moods and which convey an element of dissatisfaction with human life in a way typical of the poetry of the inter-war years. His poetry is distinguished from that of his contemporaries by a nostalgic awareness of the mythological associations of the Mediterranean setting. It is this feature that makes his translations from the Greek poets and Virgil's *Georgics* more than purely formal experiences. After the second world war in collections such as *Giorno dopo giorno* ['Day after day'] (1953), *Il falso e vero verde* ['Green both true and false'] (1956), *La terra impareggiabile* ['The incomparable land'] (1958) and *Dare e avere* ['To give and to have'] (1960) he deliberately sought to banish all traces of effusiveness from his verse and to express a maturer, more confident sense of life, though without diminishing his basic poetic intensity. While not actively engaged in politics, Quasimodo belongs to the left-wing of Italian intellectuals, alongside Moravia and Silone. Two anthologies of his work are available in English: *Selected Writings* (tr. Allen Mandelbaum, 1961) and *The Poet and the Politician* (tr. T. G. Bergin and S. Pacifici, 1964).

R. C. W.

Queen, Ellery, is the pseudonym used by Frederic Dannay (1905–), American writer of detective stories, in a series of novels and short stories written in collaboration with Manfred B. Lee, in which the central figure, who also bears the name Ellery Queen, became almost the stereotype of the sophisticated detective during a period when this genre was at its peak of popularity.

R. A. K.

Queiroz, Rachel de (1910–), Brazilian novelist and journalist. Born, reared and educated in Fortaleza, Ceará, she later settled in Rio. Her main output belongs to the 1930s when she helped to pioneer Brazil's remarkable 'novel of the north-east' with *O Quinze* ['1915'] (1930), *João Miguel* ['João Miguel'] (1932), *Caminho de Pedras* ['Stony road'] (1937) and *As Três Marias* [*The Three Marias*] (1939). The first three—republished as *Três Romances* ['Three novels'] (1943)—examined the themes of backlands privation and the anguish of womanly love; the longer *As Três Marias* probed the adolescent psyche in a Fortaleza convent boarding-school and focused on the subsequent destinies of three of its inmates. R. C. W.

Queneau, Raymond (1903–), French writer. Born at Le Havre, and a member of the surrealist group, he has published both poems and novels. Little known before the war, he became celebrated after the publication of *Exercices de style* [*Exercises in Style*] (1947), superficially a linguistic game but enlivened by the humorous quality of his imagination ; and again with *Zazie dans le métro* [*Zazie*] (1959). The success of this latter was due partly to the situation ('innocent' young girl abroad in the wicked city) and partly to the language, a hilarious mixture of slang and worse. Queneau's other works—*Chiendent* ['Couchgrass'] (1933), *Les Derniers Jours* ['The last days'] (1936), *Odile* (1937), *Un Rude Hiver* ['A hard winter'] (1939), *Pierrot mon ami* ['My friend Pierrot'] (1942), *Loin de Rueil* ['Far from Rueil'] (1944), *Le Dimanche de la vie* ['The Sunday of life'] (1951)—show that his main concerns have always been philosophy, the laughable side of life, and language. *Courir les rues* ['Along the streets'] (1967) was a very successful verse collection. D. E. A.

Quennell, Peter Courtney (1905–), English poet, critic and biographer. Quennell is best known as an expert on Byron, having published *Byron, The Years of Fame* (1935), *Byron in Italy* (1941) and a volume of correspondence and diaries entitled *Byron: A Self-Portrait* in 1950. His other biographical and critical works include a biography of John Ruskin (1941), *Baudelaire and The Symbolists* (1929), and the very well known anthology of the metaphysical poets, *Aspects of 17th century Verse* (1933).

Quennell's own poetry derives a great deal from these latter involvements. While being technically and formally free it is elegant and witty. *Poems* was published in 1926. His prose work—notably a novel *The Phoenix Kind* (1931) and a volume of short stories *Sympathy and Other Stories* (1933)—is less heavy in symbolism but equally elegant. D. L. P.

Quiller-Couch, Sir Arthur Thomas (1863–1944), English man of letters, published a number of short stories and novels under the pseudonym Q (*Troy Town*, 1888; *The Splendid Spur*, 1889; etc.) which are Stevensonian, romantic and charming, often dealing with his native Cornwall, and thoroughly sentimental. His literary reputation rests on his published lectures, given as professor of English at Cambridge, *The Art of Writing* (1916) and *The Art of Reading* (1920), in which his geniality combines with his critical ability. In *Shakespeare's Workmanship* (1918) he examines some of the plays in an enjoyable, unpedagogic manner; and among other admirable anthologies in the Oxford Book series his monument for posterity is *The Oxford Book of English Verse* (1900, 1939). H. C.

R

Rabéarivelo, Jean-Joseph (1901–39), west African poet in the French language, has been acclaimed by critics as the most profound and original African poet and his work is often chosen for inclusion in anthologies. Of his seven volumes, only the selection *24 Poems* (1962) is available in English. S. R.

Raddall, Thomas Head (1903–), Canadian novelist who was born in England but grew up in Canada. Raddall is a prolific writer whose mainly historical novels are set in Nova Scotia, the Atlantic coast province in which he lives. They have enjoyed considerable popularity in Canada and, to a lesser extent, the United States. His titles include *His Majesty's Yankees* (1942), *Roger Sudden* (1944), *Tambour* (1945), *Pride's Fancy* (1946), *The Nymph and the Lamp* (1950), *Tidefall* (1953), *A Muster of Arms* (1954), *The Wings of Night* (1956), *The Path of Destiny* (1957), *The Rover* (1958) and *The Governor's Lady* (1959). K. W.

Raine, Kathleen (1908–), English poet, writes characteristically on 'great' themes such as birth and death, incarnation and eternity, held in a vision of urgency and precision. Her poetry is of a jewel-like clarity, and is self-sufficient in that it uses symbols so universal (blood, flower, rose, sea, rocks, bird, child) that they allow each poem to make its main impact at once on first reading, without a complicated analysis. She writes with an overpowering sense of the perpetuity of the natural world and its transcendence over merely human, temporary relationships and incidents; and she is strongly aware of her own individual being immersed and actively participating in the universal. Her attitude is not escapist, however; for she is not submerged in the world as the animals, rocks, plants are, but remains always a distinct being, capable of an objective view of herself and other people alive in time in relation to the timeless universe. In her introduction to *Collected Poems* (1956) she says: 'The ever-recurring forms of nature mirror eternal reality; the never-recurring productions of human history reflect only fallen man, and are therefore not suitable to become a symbolic vocabulary for the kind of poetry I have attempted to write'. Among her previously published titles are *Stone and Flower* (1943), *Living in Time* (1946), *The Pythoness and Other Poems* (1949) and *The Year One* (1952); subsequent ones include *The Hollow Hill* (1965). G. C.

Ramos, Graciliano (1892–1953), Brazilian novelist, and with Jorge Amado and José Lins do Rêgo one of the great masters of the Brazilian 'novel of the north-east'. His youth was spent both on the coastal strip and in the backlands of the depressed states of north-eastern Brazil. Although his formal education ended in his early teens, he was an avid reader and his youthful mind was nourished on the works of Balzac, of Dostoyevsky and particularly of Eça de Queiroz. After a comparatively undistinguished career in journalism, commerce, local politics and educational administration, he entered the world of letters relatively late in life with the publication of his first novel *Caetés* ['Caetés'] in 1933, a work which he had diffidently withheld since its completion in 1926. Pleased at its success he went on to publish three further novels, *São Bernardo* ['St Bernard'] (1934), *Angústia* [*Anguish*] (1936) and *Vidas Sêcas* [*Barren Lives*] (1938). Under suspicion of extreme left-wing views he was imprisoned on a penal isle near Rio de Janeiro from 1936 to 1937 in a period of political repression, during which time he wrote *Angústia.* After imprisonment he worked as a proofreader in Rio and came eventually to abandon his practice of writing sociological novels owing to the dangerous political climate under the Vargas régime, turning his pen to the composition of articles, short stories and autobiographical studies.

His first novel, ironically named after an extinct cannibalistic Indian tribe, is of a traditional, nineteenth-century flavour and is the least representative of his works. The resort to regionalisms and the strong sociological themes which inform his later novels are both comparatively suppressed. João Valério, the protagonist, seduces the wife of his employer and benefactor, Adrião, denies his guilt and drives Adrião to suicide and to a death-bed apology for having doubted his wife's fidelity. The materialism and cynicism of this study of life in the backlands township of Palmeira (of which Ramos was mayor in 1928) was intensified in *São Bernardo*, a penetrating sociological and psychological study of ruthless self-advancement in the cane plantations of the littoral of the state of Alagoas. Rising from obscure parentage, Paulo Honório cheats, schemes and murders his way to the ownership of a vast ancestral estate. His narrow egotism makes him insanely jealous of his wife, who, though innocent of infidelity, finds life so unbearable that she commits suicide. Later disabused, with his world collapsing around him, Paulo, though unrepentant, is driven to the brink of madness and despair. *Angústia*, with its Joycean 'stream-of-consciousness' is a harrowing narrative of a mind in flight. Luís Silva, the memory of whose nightmare upbringing in the backlands merges ever increasingly with the bewildering pace of life in the coastal city of Maceió, is incensed to the point of delirious and ineluctable homicidal rage when his girl-friend is made pregnant by a sophisticated playboy. His mind unhinged by the undistinguishable brutishness of the past and anguish of the present, he strangles his rival. Ramos' last novel, *Vidas Sêcas*, was born of a short story and has been the one to win the greatest acclaim. In 1963 it was both the subject of a successful film and in English translation the novel to win the prize of the William Faulkner Foundation. Its central figure, the almost totally inarticulate halfbreed Fabiano, is presented in a series of masterly vignettes as the helpless victim of recurrent drought, privation, ignorance and harsh exploitation in the backlands. Like pathetic and dejected animals (the analogy is a recurrent *Leitmotiv* in this work), Fabiano and his small family can only subsist from one crisis to the next, nourishing the faint hope that the ensuing generation may enjoy better things.

All four novels are characterised by a Flaubertian precision of style and by a deep pessimism. Although suspected of communism and widely translated in the countries of the Soviet bloc, Ramos is never doctrinaire; he offers no solution to the sociological problems he poses because he can foresee no satisfactory remedy, as is made plain by his posthumous four-volume *Memórias do Cárcere* ['Prison memoirs'] (1953), which some critics have regarded as his most successful achievement. Among Ramos' other works the most important are the autobiographical sketches of *Infância* ['Childhood'] (1945) and the collection of short stories entitled *Insônia* ['Insomnia'] (1947). R. C. W.

Ramuz, Charles Ferdinand (1878–1947), Swiss regionalist novelist, short-story writer and poet. After twelve years' study in Paris he returned to settle in Vaud, his native canton. His works faithfully reproduce the rough and ready speech of the Vaudois peasant; and their vital blend of lyrical and starkly tragic strains made of him a controversial figure. His best-known novels are *Le Règne de l'esprit malin* [*The Reign of the Evil One*] (1922), *Présence de la mort* [*The End of All Men*, also *The Triumph of Death*] (1922), *Beauté sur la terre* [*Beauty on Earth*] (1927) and *Derborence* [*When the Mountain Fell*] (1934). R. C. W.

Ransom, John Crowe (1888–), American poet. Ransom is a major critic and a minor poet of distinction. He was born in Tennessee, the son of a minister, educated at Vanderbilt University and was a Rhodes scholar at Oxford. He taught at Vanderbilt and later at Kenyon where he founded the world-famous *Kenyon Review* and became head of the English department. He was one of the southern 'Fugitive' group of writers which included Robert Penn Warren.

Ransom's combination of wit and grace owes much to the seventeenth century but is nevertheless independent of T. S. Eliot's influence. However,

Eliot's stated problem of the 'dissociation of sensibility' occupies his verse in the tensions between emotion and reason, science and faith. The poet's work is stiffened by biblical imagery and a southern idiom. He is caught, like many academic poets, between the romantic and the intellectual.

Ransom's main contribution to criticism is contained in *The New Criticism* (1941) which introduced into America the seminal techniques of I. A. Richards and F. R. Leavis. His published work includes *Grace after Meat* (1924), which is a selection from two American publications *Poems About God* (1919) and *Chills and Fever* (1924); and *Selected Poems* (1945). D. L. P.

Rattigan, Terence Mervyn (1911–), English playwright. Rattigan was born in London and educated at Harrow and Oxford. His plays, popular both in England and the United States, are remarkable for their technical skill, and he derives his critical acclaim as a craftsman rather than as a revealer of profound human truths. *Separate Tables* (1954) is the best-known play, dividing into two acts, where the leading characters change but the background and minor personalities of a resort hotel remain the same in each act. The theme of the play is the frustration and isolation caused to human individuals by the pressures of social convention; hence the symbolic title. Other plays include *French Without Tears* (1936); *The Winslow Boy* (1947); *The Browning Version* (1948); *The Deep Blue Sea* (1952); and *Ross* (1960), a version of the life of Lawrence of Arabia.

D. L. P.

Rau, Santha Rama (1923–), Indian writer, educated in England and America and who has also travelled extensively in Europe and Asia. Among her work is included the well-known dramatised version of E. M. Forster's *Passage to India.* Her own titles include *Remember the House* (1956), *My Russian Journey* (1959) and her autobiography *Gifts of Passage* (1961). S. R.

Raven, Simon (1927–), English novelist, also a journalist and television playwright (*Royal Foundation and Other Plays,* 1966). His first novel *The Feathers of Death* (1959) dealt with army officers, gambling, and homosexual love, and his subsequent work reveals a continuing preoccupation with élites of different kinds (social and intellectual) and with varieties of sexual activity. All his novels are intensely readable, superficially 'immoral' but in fact serious, expressing a confessedly old-fashioned faith in tradition and in personal honour. This is made explicit in his extended essay *The English Gentleman* (1961). In the mid-1960s he was working on a ten-novel sequence *Alms for Oblivion*; *Friends in Low Places* being published in 1965 and *Sabre Squadron* in 1966. C. B.

Rawlings, Marjorie Kinnan (1896–1953), American novelist. Her short story 'Gal Young Un' won the O. Henry Memorial Award in 1933 and this was followed by a novel *South Moon Under* (1933), but there is no doubt that *The Yearling* (1938) was her most successful novel. This delightful story describes the adventures of a boy and his pet fawn. It is set in the backwoods of Florida where Marjorie Rawlings had made her home, and is reminiscent of *Huckleberry Finn*. Her other works include *Golden Apples* (1935), *Cross Creek* (1942), and her last book *Sojourner* (1953), a good solid novel but lacking the fire of *The Yearling*.

K. M. H.

Raymond, Ernest (1888–   ), English novelist, best known for his *Tell England* (1922), a war novel of the Gallipoli campaign and its effect on the lives of young soldiers. In 1958 he published a sequel *The Quiet Shore* which is the story of a pilgrimage to the scene of the battle made by a veteran forty years later; and *Late in the Day* (1964) is the often highly amusing story of a survivor of Passchendaele who in his sixties revisits the scene of his most glorious moment and begins to discover himself. Raymond has also written *The London Gallery*, a sixteen-novel sequence portraying London life over half a century, culminating in *The City and the Dream* (1958), a novel of the City of London itself. P. E.

Read, Herbert (1893–1968), English poet and critic. Read's poetry is carefully constructed in free verse. His early work was influenced by the imagists and then by the cult of the seventeenth-century metaphysicals that had been introduced by Eliot. He is essentially, however, a romantic, influenced by Coleridge and the latter's belief that art as well as life must develop an organic form of its own. This view is fully expounded in Read's literary criticism which includes *Reason and Romanticism* (1926) and *Form in Modern Poetry* (1932); *Collected Poems* were published in 1946 and 1953.

Read initially supported surrealism in art and communism in politics. Eventually he decided that communism was an imposed political creed rather than a developing organic growth: at which point he became an anarchist, thus—it could be said—indulging in a form of political romanticism. As an art critic Read has upheld the view that art can be a seminal force in education, in industry and in society at large. *A Concise History of Modern Painting* was published in 1959. D. L. P.

Rebreanu, Liviu (1885–1944), Rumanian novelist. Born in Transylvania, the son of a village schoolmaster, he studied in Budapest and Vienna, gained a commission in the Austrian army and, in later life, was prominent in Rumanian literary, educational and theatrical circles. Though he was initially a short-story writer, his first novel, *Ion* [*Ion*] (1920), was a landmark in the history of the Rumanian novel. 'Only an unflinching singleness of mind gives life any real value!' muses the irresolute Titu, without irony, contrasting his vacillations with the peasant Ion's monomaniacal lust for land, which is gratified by seducing Ana the daughter of a comparatively wealthy smallholder. Unloved, Ana hangs herself, their son dies and Ion, attempting to revive an earlier, sincere attachment, is killed by a suspicious husband. Within this sordid narrative frame Rebreanu sketches rural Transylvania, under Hungarian domination, at the turn of the century: its village traditions and rivalries, its judicial and political shortcomings, social, racial and cultural antagonisms, moral and physical subjugation. *Pădurea spânzuratilor* [*The Forest of the Hanged*] (1922) was translated in 1930 but in Britain Rebreanu is probably best known by *Răscoala* [*The Uprising*] (1932). Grigore Iuga, heir to the authoritarian old boyar Miron Iuga, invites his protégé, Titu again, to visit the family estates where, in the early 1900s, Miron's intransigence, the reckless self-indulgence of Nadina, Grigore's wife, and the hungry desperation of the peasants precipitate a minor massacre, an incident representative of Rumania's bloody resolution of her ideological problems. M. D. E.

Reeves, William Pember (1857–1932), New Zealand man of letters, who assumed the rôle of cultural spokesman for the new nation at the dawn of the century. His works include *State Experiments in Australia and New Zealand* (1902) and *The Long White Cloud* (1898). S. R.

Remarque, Erich Maria (1897–), German novelist, born in Osnabrück of French extraction. He studied at Munster before being conscripted into the army early in the first world war; he was wounded several times. After the war he worked as a teacher, then became a racing motorist before turning to journalism. Suddenly his first novel *Im Westen nichts Neues* [*All Quiet on the Western Front*] (1929) rocketed him to fame with its brutal realistic treatment of horrors of war. It was filmed, and the film itself became a classic. A sequel *Der Weg zurück* [*The Road Back*] (1931) recounted the collapse of the German army and the efforts of the soldiers to adjust to civilian life. He became a productive and successful writer, but his brutal sensationalism and faulty composition have won him popular rather than critical applause. A Catholic suspected (rightly) of pacifism, he left Germany in 1932 and was deprived of his nationality. He divided his time between Switzerland and the United States before finally settling in the latter country in 1939, becoming an American citizen. *Drei Kameraden* [*Three Comrades*] (1937) traced the career of war veterans trying to make a living in the years of depression and political violence.

Arc de triomphe [*Arc de Triomphe*] (1946) gave Remarque his second great success. Dealing with German refugees from Hitler's Germany leading a shady existence in the Paris underworld, its central character is a gynaecologist who performs illegal but highly skilled operations; he finally meets a violent end. *Der Funke Leben* [*Spark of Life*] (1951) again had a violent theme; set in a concentration camp, it depicts a prisoner who attempts to measure the amount of pain a man can tolerate, only to break down himself. His later work includes a novel of political intrigue *Die Nacht von Lissabon* ['The night in Lisbon'] 1962). G. W.

Remizov, Alexei Mikhailovich (1877–1957), Russian writer, was born in Moscow where he eventually attended the university. His radical thirsting mind took him on religious pilgrimages and led him to hope for a renaissance of Russia purified by the revolution. His hopes were dashed and he emigrated to France. Remizov began writing his stories at the turn of the century. He was a follower of Gogol in his use of fantasy and of Leskov in his creating new words in his prose designed to give the effect of popular speech and folklore traditions. Dostoyevskian influence is also seen in Remizov's attitude to suffering. His style approaches that of the symbolists, though it is so varied that it is almost impossible to categorise it. His early stories *Prud* [*The Pond*] (1907) and *Krestoviye sestry* [*The Sisters of the Cross*] (1910) are horrific descriptions of town life, while his émigré novel *V polye blakitnom* [*On a Field Azure*] (1922) is a charming portrait of a girl who becomes a socialist revolutionary. Remizov was more a respected writer's writer than one popular with the readers. His writing abroad continued to have a considerable influence on Soviet authors even though much of it consisted of fairy tales and religious stories, such as the *Prichi sv. Nikolaya* [*Parables of St Nicholas*] (1924) and *Zga* [*Zga*] (1925). B. W.

Renault, Mary (Mary Challans; 1905–), English novelist, best known for three later novels based on the re-creation of Greek history and legend: *The Last of the Wine* (1956), *The King Must Die* (1958), *The Bull from the Sea* (1962). Subsequent titles include *The Mask of Apollo* (1966).

K. R. R.

Reyes, Alfonso (1889–1959), Mexican scholar, poet, essayist, humanist and diplomat, was born in Monterrey and graduated in law from the University of Mexico. His earliest verses date from around 1906. Collected under the title *Constancia poética* ['Poetic constancy'] his poems trace a rich and varied evolution from Parnassian and symbolist influences into the rhythms and imagery of *modernismo*.

Reyes lived in Spain from 1914 until 1924 apart from a brief period in France. This was probably his most productive period, during which he published innumerable learned articles, short stories, chronicles sketches, and critical reviews. Prose works like *Visión de Anáhuac* ['Vision of Anáhuac'] (1917), *El plano oblicuo* ['The oblique plane'] (1920), *Retratos reales e imaginarios* ['real and imaginary portraits'] (1920) and the five-volume series of *Simpatías y diferencias* ['Sympathies and differences'] (1921–26) attest to his wide erudition and his remarkable versatility of theme and style. A selection of these writings can be found in *The Position of America, and Other Essays* (1950). From 1925 until 1938 he travelled extensively throughout Spanish America and made several visits to France before returning to settle in Mexico in 1939. His steady output of essays covered a wide range of subjects from Anáhuac to Goethe. These are collected in his major works, *El testimonio de Juan Peña* ['The testimony of Juan Peña'] (1930), *Los siete sobre Deva* ['The seven above Deva'] (1942), *La experiencia literaria* ['The literary experience'] (1952) and *Quince presencias* ['Fifteen presences'] (1955), and give further evidence of his extensive knowledge and highly subjective prose style.

An original and resourceful writer, Reyes pursues lyricism and refinement in preference to mere extravagance. His classical serenity, depth of thought and versatility make him one of Spanish America's most representative and widely respected men of letters. Together with Pedro Henríquez Ureña (1884–1946) he founded the famous Ateneo de la Juventud (1910–40) and during the final years of his life he became the director and guiding spirit of the Colegio de México. Translations of his poetry are available in the Dudley Fitts *Anthology of Contemporary Latin-American Poetry* (1942). G. P.

Reymont, Władyslaw Stanisław (1867–1925), Polish novelist, the son of a village organist, was an ideal novelist as far as social experience is concerned. A man of little formal education, a travelling actor, railway official, even a novice in the monastery at Jasna Góra, his only qualification was that of a tailor. One of his earlier works *Pielgrzmka do Jasnej Góry* ['Pilgrimage to Jasna Góra'] (1895), an account of a pilgrimage to the shrine at Częstochowa, employs the reportage technique based on direct experience which served him with greater success in *Ziemia obiecana* [*The Promised Land*] (1899), a novel about the urbanisation of Łódź. The same year brought a peasant novel in the form of a moral comment, *Sprawiedliwie* ['Justly']. His monumental *Chlopi* [*The Peasants*] (1904–9), originally serialised but later expanded and elaborated into a peasant epic of four volumes, which correspond to the four seasons giving thus a natural unity to his work, is one of the greatest achievements in Polish literature.

Reymont had a perfect knowledge of rural society; his stylised narrative and dialogue evoke an atmosphere which is all-embracing; and a series of psychological conflicts sustain interest throughout, holding the novel together without obscuring the complex growth of an impressive plot. The 1924 Nobel Prize for Literature acknowledged this splendid contribution to Polish and European literature. An involved spiritualist and medium, his later book *Wampir* (1911) is of little literary value. B. M.

Řezáč, Václav (1901–56), Czech novelist. His early novels, such as *Dark Corner* [*Černé světlo*] (1940), were concerned with the artistically gifted individual struggling with corrupted materialist society. After the second world war he became one of the chief exponents of socialist realism in Czech literature, describing in his optimistic and didactic novels the economic and social changes under the Communist régime. K. B.

Ribeiro, Aquilino (1885–1963), Portuguese author of more than seventy publications, most notable as a novelist. A contant rebel against authority and champion of lost causes during his earlier years, he studied at the Sorbonne while in exile. Latterly he supported the presidential campaigns of opposition candidates Norton de Matos (1949) and Humberto Delgado (1958). Decorated by the Brazilian government, belatedly elected to the Portuguese Academy and first President of the Portuguese Society of Writers, he was in his last years a leading contender for the Nobel Prize. His early narrative fiction was primarily of regionalist flavour, but after he settled in Lisbon in 1932 following his return from France, city life predominated in his novels. His works frequently challenged the exploitation, tyranny and insincerity he claimed to find at all levels of Portuguese life, and none more so than his last major work *Quando os Lobos Uivam* [*When the Wolves Howl*] (1958), his only work available in English. Peasants' opposition to a government afforestation scheme leads to bloodshed despite the moderate counsels of their spokesman Manuel Louvadeus who is subsequently imprisoned. His father enacts a terrible revenge upon the informer. A savage attack on petty bureaucracy, suspect justice and secret-police methods, the novel was welcomed as a masterpiece. Ribeiro was at once arrested, being released only after strenuous protests by distinguished Portuguese, Brazilian and French intellectuals. The work is still allegedly 'out of print' in Portugal. R. C. W.

Rice, Alice Hegan (1870–1942), American novelist who wrote *Mrs Wiggs of the Cabbage Patch* (1901) and its sequel *Lovey Mary* (1903). The cabbage patch is a shanty settlement by a Kentucky railroad, and Mrs Wiggs is characterised by her indomitable optimism. K. R. R.

Rice, Elmer (1892–1967), American playwright, gained a reputation in the 1920s as an *avant-garde*, experimental playwright. In his expressionist fantasy *The Adding Machine* (1923) a man commits a murder because he is made redundant by a machine. More in keeping with the deterministic naturalism of the period is his *Street Scene* (1929; Pulitzer Prize), of which an operatic version was made by Kurt Weill (1947). Rice's novels (e.g. *A Voyage to Purilia*, 1930) and his later plays (e.g. *Dream Girl*, 1945) have failed to make the same impact. K. R. R.

Richards, I. A. (Ivor Armstrong Richards; 1893–), English literary critic and poet. He collaborated with C. K. Ogden in *The Meaning of Meaning* (1923), a classic work on the relation between language and thought. His *Principles of Literary Criticism* (1924) and the subsequent *Practical Criticism* (1929) had a profound influence on critical theories. Other works include *Coleridge on Imagination* (1934), *Interpretation in Teaching* (1938) and *Speculative Instruments* (1955). His poetry is collected in *Goodbye Earth & Other Poems* (1958) and *The Screens and Other Poems* (1960). R. A. K.

Richardson, Dorothy (1873–1957), English novelist, characterised by her adoption of the simple 'stream of consciousness' method with which her contemporary Virginia Woolf was later to be identified. The bulk of her work, which is not widely read today, is contained in her nine-novel series bearing the overall title of *Pilgrimage*, beginning with *Pointed Roofs* (1915) and ending with *Dimple Hill* (1938). The early volumes, depicting a fine awareness of the world as experienced by an evolving feminine mind, retain something of their freshness; but the later ones, with the intelligent and sensitive heroine Miriam Henderson failing to develop very significantly as a person (and, the Freudian might add, failing to plumb the depths of her own personality), proved to have little to offer to a world long grown familiar with the more substantial works of Virginia Woolf and James Joyce. K. R. R.

Richardson, Henry Handel (Ethel Florence Richardson; 1870–1946), is often regarded as the greatest Australian novelist, though definitely writing within the European tradition. She was born and educated in Melbourne but, except for a period in 1912, lived the rest of her life abroad. Though published second, *The Getting of Wisdom* (1910) was probably her first novel: it deals with a girl at boarding school and is almost certainly autobiographical. *Maurice Guest* (1908) is set in Leipzig, where the author had herself studied music, and is a powerful romantic novel exploring the boundaries of infatuation, love and possessive jealousy. An even more remarkable achievement is the trilogy, *The Fortunes of Richard Mahony*, in which the main character bears a strong resemblance to her father. In the first volume, which originally bore the title of the trilogy and appeared in 1917 but is now known as *Australia Felix*, a doctor comes out to Ballarat during the gold rush, and later remains in Australia to start a practice. Despite his success, he feels persistently critical of his new environment and returns for a time to his beloved England. *The Way Home* (1925) and *Ultima Thule* (1929) show his restlessness and dissatisfaction constantly increasing until eventually, with his health broken and his frequent journeys between England and Australia thus ended, his struggles cease to take place between these two worlds, his failing body and mind becoming their sole battleground until he finally dies.

The Young Cosima (1934), perhaps because it is not based on personal experience but re-enacts the story of Cosima Liszt and Wagner, reads stiffly like a history book and is her least successful work. S. R.

Richler, Mordecai (1931–), Canadian novelist whose writing reflects his urban-Jewish upbringing in Montreal and his residence in England for much of his adult life. Richler's first novel *The Acrobats* (1954) is set in Spain and reveals chiefly his youth and his lack of familiarity with his material; but his second, *Son of a Smaller Hero* (1955), with its deeply felt description of life and family relationships in the Montreal 'ghetto', is much more representative of his talents. This was followed by *A Choice of Enemies* (1957), which shows English left-wing intellectuals seen through the eyes of an east European exile.

The Apprenticeship of Duddy Kravitz (1959), written with great pace and *élan*, is the picaresque tale of an ambitious young Montreal Jew driven by the hunger to own his own land. As in Richler's second novel, it is the tangle of Jewish family affections and jealousies which give this book an extra dimension of pathos. *The Incomparable Atuk* (1963) is a wildly comic satire of an Eskimo poet's success with self-consciously Canadian intellectuals in Toronto and represents a departure in both style and content from Richler's earlier work. Later titles include *Cocksure* (1968), 'a serio-comic novel in 35 acts'. K. W.

Rilke, Rainer Maria (1875–1926), German poet born in Prague, the son of a railway official who had married the daughter of an imperial councillor. He studied at a school of commerce in Linz, and almost at once began to write: *Leben und Lieder* ['Life and songs'] appearing in 1894, and *Der Apostel* ['The apostle'], *Larenopfer* ['Offering to the gods'] and *Wegwarten* ['Waiting'] in 1896.

He now travelled extensively. In Italy Rilke thought he had found his spiritual fatherland; but his experiences in Russia, which included meeting Tolstoy, made him realise that this country was to be a vital influence—'the country where people are lonely, everybody full of darkness like a mountain; everybody deep in his devotions, without fear of humiliating himself and in consequence pious'. Rilke had turned away from orthodox Christianity in early youth—so far as to consider Christ an impediment rather than an aid in the search for God—but his Russian experience convinced him that only by constantly striving to know and love God would he become of any value himself. Consequently, the spiritual melancholy of his earlier verse developed into a mystical quest of the deity expressed in such works as *Geschichten vom lieben Gott* [*Stories of God*] (1900), and the three-part *Das Stundenbuch* [*The Book of Hours*] (1905) by which he achieved fame. The former deals with an abandoned and feeble God who is seeking man; whereas in the latter man is desperately searching for a God of strength.

Visiting Bremen, Rilke met a young sculptress and pupil of Rodin, Clara Westhoff. They were married the following year; and through this connection, Rilke became the great sculptor's secretary in Paris. Rodin's influence was immense; not only did he inspire *Das Rodinbuch* [*The Book of Rodin*] (1907) but he led Rilke to abandon his cult of religious mysticism in favour of the quest for purely aesthetic ideals, as illustrated in *Gedichte* [*Poems*] (1907–8).

However strong Rodin's influence was, it was not based on a very long association, for within a year Rilke left his wife and once again began travelling, especially in Scandinavia. The year 1908 saw him again in Paris, where he wrote *Aufzeichnungen des Malte Laurids Brigge* [*The Notebooks of Malte Laurids Brigge*]. Here we see Rilke himself in retrospect as a very young, poor and ill youth, near to mental derangement. The book reveals his conception of death, and his attitude to the great city, described as a nightmare world of noise, disease and lechery in which the poet dwells in isolation.

In 1912 he spent four months touring Spain before proceeding to Duino on the Adriatic coast. Here it was that he produced the first two of the celebrated *Duino Elegies*, the work he rated his best and loved most. He left Germany for ever in 1919, travelling in Switzerland and Italy before settling down to spend the last years of his life in an old tower in the Rhône valley in France. In 1923 his two masterpieces, *Die Sonnette an Orpheus* [*Sonnets to Orpheus*] and the ten *Duineser Elegien* [*Duino Elegies*], were published. Here the poet is hailed as the only arbiter between the roughness of the natural world and the aesthetic ideals of pure art. The subjects of the elegies include the confrontation of man and angel (1st and 2nd elegies), Rilke's anything but romantic gospel of sex

(3rd elegy), the drama of life as played in the consciousness of death's presence (4th elegy), the hero who rushes to death (6th elegy), and the idea that animals have unity of being (8th elegy). The 7th glorifies existence and the 9th is a hymn of life, but in the 10th the poet accepts pain and sorrow—for life is the city, death the land, of pain. In *Sonnets to Orpheus*, however, we encounter an entirely new theme: all existence is rhythms—being arises from the juxtaposition and alternation of these mathematical contraries.

Even today, when foreign travel is no longer the prerogative of the rich, the cosmopolitan quality of Rilke's life would be remarkable; yet he was a distinctively German writer, and has come to be ranked as the greatest of all the German lyric poets. It has been said that there is little variety of theme, not only in the elegies, but in his work as a whole; but Rilke's great strength was his ability to view the whole of creation as a divinely ordered whole, harmonious and rhythmic. He himself confessed that it was not until late in life that he began to understand the greatness of Beethoven, but his own poetry is superbly musical in verbal form, and revealed a range of expression and a subtlety of language which was and remains unique in German literature. G. W.

Rinehart, Mary Roberts (1876–1958), American detective novelist, wrote *The Circular Staircase* (1908) and *The Man in Lower Ten* (1909), the latter subsequently dramatised as *The Bat* (1920). Her later writings include horror stories, and a series of humorous novels including *Letitia Carberry* (1911) and *Tish* (1916). K. R. R.

Rinser, Luise (1911–), German novelist and short-story writer, born in Upper Bavaria; has twice married musicians. Her first husband, a pupil of Hindemith, was killed in the war; she now lives in Rome after being divorced from her second husband Carl Orff. The appearance of *Die gläsernen Ringe* [*Rings of Glass*] in 1949 brought her fame; it deals with a determined young girl who longs for freedom and wealth, but who comes to realise that in her case only the intellect will bring happiness. Another notable early work was *Jan Lobel aus Warschau* ['Jan Lobel from Warsaw'] (1948), which treats of a young Polish Jew and his tragic end; it is a brilliant short story which is contained in the anthology *Ein Bündel weisser Narzissen* ['A bunch of white narcissi'] (1956).

Much of her writing, including the novels *Die Stärkeren* ['Those who are stronger'] (1948) and *Mitte des Lebens* ['In the middle of life'] (1950), deals with the problems of the modern world; her later work *Geh fort, wenn du kannst* ['Go away if you can'] (1959), dealing with the conversion of a communist partisan into a nun, being especially significant. G. W.

Rive, Richard (1931–   ), South African short-story writer. His *African Songs* (1963) includes tales of sustained excitement and a vividness which springs from economy, which, with Rive's powerful ear for dialogue, tellingly re-create the life and tensions of the south-western Cape Province, in particular of Cape Town and its 'coloured' (i.e. mixed-blood) District Six. Rive is essentially the short-story writer even in his novel *Emergency* (1964) where he delineates, often strikingly, the character of a 'coloured' teacher-politico during the March 1960 South African political emergency —a drama previously depicted through Afrikaner eyes in Anna M. Louw's *Twenty Days that Autumn* (1963). Rive also collected, and contributed a story to, the volume *Quartet* (1963), in which the other items were by La Guma (q.v.), Alf Wannenberg and James Matthews: illustrating a thought-provoking diversity of style and treatment bearing on the same basic material. C. P.

Robbe-Grillet, Alain (1922–   ), French novelist, has incurred virulent criticism as the theoretician of a heterogeneous group of new or anti-novelists. *Pour un nouveau roman* [*Towards a New Novel*] (1964) posits a puritanical objectivity, rejects the 'pathetic fallacy', extirpates vestigial anthropomorphism: 'The world is neither significant nor absurd. It just is.' Accepted literary canons, characterisation, symbolism, psychology, plot, emotive language, all are anathema. Superficial, phenomenological, anti-depth, concerned with time, recollection, mensuration and topographical exactitude, the new imaginative reality puts many questions, provides few clues, fewer answers. Was the travelling salesman a criminal or was he merely *Le Voyeur* [*The Voyeur*] (1955)? Had they met *L'Année dernière à Marienbad* [*Last Year at Marienbad*] (1962)? Vilified as a triumph of technique over life, a sterile geometry bereft of relevance or humanity, the new dogma is certainly ascetic, yet some human traits survive. The setting of *La Jalousie* [*Jealousy*] (1957), a tropical banana plantation, perhaps reflects the author's experience of Martinique. Similarly, its characteristic, scrupulous attention to siting and terrain may stem from his training as an agricultural engineer and statistician. The pun in '*jalousie*'—jealousy or a Venetian blind—is a rare example of Robbe-Grillet's remote humour; but the latent sexuality (disturbingly suggested by references to the wife's hair), the claustrophobic tension, and the submerged violence, which erupts into murder in *Les Gommes* [*The Erasers*] (1953), murder and rape in *The Voyeur* and a pointless shooting in *Dans le labyrinthe* [*In the Labyrinth*] (1959), together with the hallucinatory obsession with details and the maddening unreliability of memory, recur throughout his work, from *The Erasers* to the film scenario *L'Immortelle* ['The everlasting flower'] (1963) and the significantly entitled *Instantanés* [*Snapshots*]

(1962). Nevertheless, critical exegesis and mitigating revelations of late-Romantic overtones, classical myth and Tarot parallelism apart, the extremity of Robbe-Grillet's position continues to provoke a polarity of extreme reaction. M. D. E.

Robbins, Harold (Harold Rubin; 1912–), American novelist whose books offer the sure-fire best-seller combination of sex (in every possible permutation), violence and sordid incident, and an exposé of both very high and very low life. Thus *The Carpetbaggers* (1961) uncovers the machinations of the Hollywood motion-picture industry, while *A Stone for Danny Fisher* (1952) deals with boxing and concomitant racketeering in the New York East Side slums. Other titles include *Never Love a Stranger* (1948) and *The Adventurers* (1966). S. R.

Roberts, Kenneth (1885–1957), American historical novelist, whose tales of the colonial and revolutionary era were based on a thorough-going investigation of the facts. *Arundel* (1930) centres on an American expedition against Quebec; and in *Rabble in Arms* (1933) we see the defeat of General Burgoyne. Also of interest is *North-West Passage* (1937).
K. R. R.

Robins, Denise (–), English novelist, is a prolific writer of the glamorous fiction of escapism which has delighted two generations of 6d. circulating-library members. Characteristic of her work are *Were I thy Bride* (1961), *Unlit Fires* (1963), *Fever of Love* (1964) and *Stranger than Fiction* (1965). P. E.

Robinson, Edwin Arlington (1869–1935), American poet. Robinson is a poet curiously neglected in England, especially since his writing derives more from late nineteenth-century English literature than from the experimental schools in America during the early years of the twentieth century.

Born in Maine, Robinson later went to Harvard which he left, on the death of his father, without taking a degree. His verse was produced in uncompromising conditions of poverty until Theodore Roosevelt, impressed by his long narrative poem 'Craig' (1902), offered him a job in the Customs House. From 1911 until his death in 1935 the poet divided his time between the MacDowell Colony for artists in New Hampshire and New York. During this period he won three Pulitzer Prizes: for *Collected Poems* (1921), *The Man Who Died Twice* (1925) and *Tristram* (1928).

Robinson's poetry divides roughly into three categories: the long narrative, the dramatic monologue and the lyrical. Owing little to the experimental world of the American literary renaissance it is not easy to characterise. The shorter poetry owes something to Hardy's clipped lyricism, the dramatic monologue to Browning's metaphysical turn of phrase, the Arthurian Legends to Tennyson and the reflective meditation to Arnold. Nevertheless Robinson retains a highly individual form of expression. He appeals to many American critics and to a large audience (*Tristram* sold sixty thousand copies) partly because his more traditional verse is not difficult, superficially at least, to understand. But he offers no concession to popular taste as for example does the later Frost, and despite his melancholia and alcoholism he is a writer and a man of profound integrity.

Perhaps his most characteristic mood is a deeply felt pessimism mellowed by the reflectiveness of the romantic. 'Children of the Night' (1897) contains dramatic studies of lives in an indifferent universe. 'The Man Against The Sky', the title poem of the volume that established the poet's reputation in 1916, possesses the meditative melancholy of Arnold's 'Dover Beach' or Wallace Stevens's 'Sunday Morning':

'Twere sure but weaklings' vain distress
To suffer dungeons where so many doors
Will open on the cold eternal shores
That look sheer down
To the dark tideless floods of Nothingness
Where all who know may drown.

The Arthurian Legends, *Merlin* (1917), *Lancelot* (1926) and *Tristram* (1927), are examinations in depth of the hopelessness of romantic love. In this trilogy, however, Robinson is working towards a point of spiritual fulfilment, a life-view. Throughout his work there pervades an air of hopelessness in the sense that man must employ his intellectual force to be a man but that it is this very force which leads him to recognise the futility of his temporary position in the universe. In *Tristram* he begins to work towards a positive feeling that intense spiritual experience may elevate man beyond the merely temporal.

Robinson's lyrical poetry is his most acclaimed work but his longer verse, despite its often tedious psychological investigation, possesses the strength and integrity of the poet's lonely attitudes to man's place in the universe which give his work a universality denied to many of his contemporaries.

In addition to the titles mentioned, editions of *Collected Poems* were published in 1921, 1929 and 1937. Also of interest is the posthumous *Tilbury Town* (1953). D. L. P.

Rochefort, Christiane (–), French novelist. *Le Repos du guerrier* [*Warrior's Rest*] (1958), told in the first person by a young woman, relates the story of a trip to the town in which her aunt has just died, of her meeting there a man whom she saves from suicide, and of her violent passion for this man, who is an alcoholic suffering from a strong sense of the purposelessness of existence. The account of this passion is full, and the book was a best-seller from publication; it is none the less a work of quality in which the characters come effectively to life. *Les Petits Enfants du siècle* [*Josyane and the Welfare*] (1960) shows Christiane Rochefort as a moralist and an accurate and revealing observer; while *Les Stances à Sophie* ['Verses for Sophie'] (1963) recounts the jealous thoughts of a woman whose lesbian relationship with another is ended by the latter's husband, who is responsible for a car accident in which she dies. The intensity of feeling involved is well caught in this introspective, lyrical novel. D. E. A.

Rodó, José Enrique (1872–1917), Uruguayan humanist and essayist and the most prominent modernist after Rubén Darío. He was educated in Montevideo where in 1895 he helped to found *La revista nacional de literatura y ciencia sociales* ('National review of literature and social science') for which he wrote numerous essays. He became Professor of Literature at the National University, director of the National Library in 1900, and a member of the Chamber of Deputies (1902–05 and 1908–11). Rodó's most famous work *Ariel* [*Ariel*] appeared in 1900 and became the ethical bible of his generation. The book discusses the moral formation of Spanish American youth and advocates an intellectual aristocracy to withstand the evils of a materialistic age. *Ariel* extols the eternal values of goodness, truth, justice and beauty which are to be derived from the dynamic and creative life.

The same tone of spiritual elevation prevails in *El mirador de Próspero* ['The watchtower of Prospero'] (1913) where he analyses the crisis of positivism. Subsequent essays develop the related themes of human personality and vocation and the all-important harmony between the complex interior unity of man and the complex exterior unity of the universe. Rodó's treatment of philosophical themes betrays his spiritual roots: the writings of the ancient Greeks and Romans, Plato, Marcus Aurelius, Montaigne, Renan and the nineteenth-century positivists Comte and Spencer. Lucidity of thought is carefully matched by elegance of phrase.

The fragments collected in the *Motivos de Proteo* ['Motifs of Proteus'] (1909) are presented in a variety of forms, often by means of parable, prose poem, anecdote or theoretical speculation. Each theme is developed with its own key symbol, and phrases are skilfully constructed to create a harmonious pattern of Parnassian perfection. Long considered the great essayist of the modernist group, Rodó's imaginative yet disciplined prose style exerted a profound influence over younger writers. G. P.

Roethke, Theodore (1908–), American poet. Roethke was born in Michigan and educated at Michigan University and Harvard. He became Professor of English at Washington. His poetic recognition came after the publication of his second book *The Lost Son* (1949). His style is intense and curiously fragmented in the effort to disperse meaningfulness as he believes it to be dispersed in life. This intention carries an echo of Henry Adams's dictum that art must be chaotic to express the chaos of life. However Roethke's poetry is solid and tangible. He seems to take the view of the eighteenth-century philosopher Berkeley, that abstractions are only bundles of particular observations. It is the particular heard, seen or felt thing that corresponds to truth:

> Take the skin of a cat
> And the back of an eel
> Then roll them in grease—
> That's the way it would feel.
> (from 'The Flight' in *The Lost Son*)

Other published work includes *The Waking* (1953) which won a Pulitzer prize; *Poems 1933–1953* (1954); *Words for the Wind* (1957); and *The Far Field* (1965). D. L. P.

Rohmer, Sax (Arthur Sarsfield Wade; 1886–), English popular novelist whose thrillers excited readers between the wars. The most successful were the sequels to *Dr Fu Manchu* (1913), which introduced a sinister arch-villain whose activities are recounted against an exotic oriental background. R. A. K.

Rolfe, Frederick (pen name Baron Corvo; 1860–1913), English novelist and historian and a man of great wit, learning and eccentricity. His work is related in thought to that of the chiefly French 'decadent' group whose work was characterised by the emphasis on creative self-expression in their pursuit of the ideal of pure art. Converted to Roman catholicism and unsuccessful in his aim to be selected for the priesthood, he wrote his revengeful novel *Hadrian the Seventh* (1904) in which he himself, in the person of George Arthur Rose, a shabby London outcast, becomes pope.

He remained passionately Romanist but detested his co-religionists, and his posthumous novel *The Desire and Pursuit of the Whole* (1934) is in the same retaliative vein. *Don Renato* (written 1909, published 1963), an intriguing and witty novel written in a particularly convoluted style, is composed mainly of the diary of a sixteenth-century Roman, physician to a patrician family. His other novels are *Chronicles of the House of Borgia* (1901) and *Nicholas Crabbe* (published 1958), the latter a thinly disguised account of Rolfe's own early literary struggles which, in its mixture of fantasy, wishfulfilment and harsh self-analysis, is characteristic of his work.

The interest being shown in Rolfe a half-century after his death, following a period of almost complete eclipse, owes much to the outstanding biography by A. J. A. Symons, *The Quest for Corvo*. P. E.

Rolland, Romain (1866–1944), French playwright and novelist, and 1915 Nobel prize-winner. Born the son of a notary in the small town of Clamecy in the Nièvre department in the centre of France, Romain Rolland led the life of the typical literary intellectual of his time. His first literary works were plays, including a play cycle on the French revolution, and a series of *Vies des hommes illustres* ['Lives of famous men']: *Beethoven* (1903), *Michelangelo* (1906), *Handel* (1910) and *Tolstoi* (1911).

But Rolland's greatest claim to fame lies in his famous *Jean-Christophe* [*John Christopher*], the first of the '*romans fleuves*', i.e. multi-volume novels, in France. *Jean-Christophe* is in ten volumes: *L'Aube* [*The Dawn*] (1904), *Le Matin* [*The Morning*] (1904), *L'Adolescent* [*Youth*] (1905), *La Révolte* [*Revolt*] (1907), *La Foire sur la place* [*The Fair in the Square*] (1908), *Antoinette* (1908), *Dans la maison* [*In the Home*] (1909), *Les Amies* [*Love and Friendship*] (1910), *Le Buisson ardent* [*The Burning Bush*] (1911) and *La Nouvelle Journée* [*The New Dawn*] (1912). It is the life story of a German musician of genius, 'Beethoven in the world today': a life full of trials, passion and energy set against the background of a whole period in the history of several European countries—Germany, France and Italy. This inspiring epic, full of poetry and idealism, is a monument to music (reminding us that Rolland wrote the greatest of all books on Beethoven) and also to heroism and generosity of spirit. Its militant humanism later found concrete expression in Rolland's condemnation of the first world war, in which he joined Bertrand Russell; and on the strength of it he won his Nobel Prize. A. L. W.

Rölvaag, Ole (1876–1931), Norwegian-born American novelist, best known for a trilogy centring on the settlement of the Dakotas by Norwegian immigrants: the first volume, subtitled 'A Saga of the Prairie', being

Giants in the Earth (1927). As with so many frontier novels, religious fanaticism looms large, and much of the remaining volumes—*Peder Victorious* (1929) and *Their Fathers' God* (1931)—is taken up with religious dissensions such as those that stem from a Norwegian Lutheran's desire to emancipate himself from the influence of the church, and from his subsequent marriage to an Irish Catholic girl. K. R. R.

Romains, Jules (1885–), French writer, was educated at the Ecole Normale Supérieure and became one of the founder-members of the 'Abbaye' group. The poem *La Vie unanime* ['Life in unison'] (1908) was the manifesto of the group and led to the use of the word '*unanimisme*' to describe their aims of mystical union with others. The beliefs of this group and particularly its concern with moral behaviour and group action have inspired Romains' other works, either directly or indirectly. Apart from poetry—he has published various collections, *Europe* (1916), *L'Homme blanc* ['The white man'] (1937) and *Pierres levées* ['Lifted stones'] (1957)—he has written plays, of which the best known are the comedy *Knock ou le triomphe de la médecine* [*Dr Knock*] (1924) and *Donogoo* [*Donogoo*] (1930), and novels. The latter include the trilogy *Psyche* [*Psyche*] (1922–30) consisting of *Lucienne, Le Dieu des corps* [*The Body's Rapture*] and *Quand le navire* ['When the boat']; and such later novels as *Violation de frontières* [*Tussle with Time*] (1951) and *Une Femme singulière* [*The Adventuress*] (1957). However, from 1932 to 1946 he was principally concerned with publishing a 27-volume series of novels called *Les Hommes de bonne volonté* [*Men of Good Will*], covering a wide range of characters and *milieux*, and which reveal his gifts as a storyteller, and as a man of wide interests and sympathies whose main aim in life is that of the '*unanimistes*'—for men to live in peace and goodwill with each other. D. E. A.

Rooke, Daphne (1914–), South African novelist, accomplished, productive but strangely neglected. *Mittee* (1951) well-nigh inaugurated the 'disguised voice' which has become something of a trend in South African fiction, especially when, as in this case, it contains an element of what has been called the South African gothic (i.e. politico-racial) melodrama. Miss Rooke makes a 'coloured' Afrikaans-speaking servant tell the compelling tale of her young white mistress's life. *Wizard's Country* (1957) shifts attention to Zulu magic, while *Beti* (1959) carries the novelist's ballad-like skill into the folk-fairy tale of India. C. P.

Rosenberg, Isaac (1890–1918), English poet. Rosenberg, killed in action in the first world war, is an outspoken and passionate writer and one of the major poets produced by that war. Like Owen's, his compassion for suffering and vivid descriptions of the brutalities of trench warfare mark out a sensitive but forceful poetic talent. The poem 'Break of Day in the Trenches' also indicates a mordant meditative quality; the poet contemplates the one live creature in a world of desolation between the opposing trenches and reflects on the mindless hostilities of men:

> Droll rat, they would shoot you if they knew
> Your cosmopolitan sympathies.
> (And God knows what antipathies.)

Rosenberg's *Collected Works* were published in 1937. D. L. P.

Ross, Sinclair (1908–), Canadian novelist and short-story writer, deals with the need for an individual Canadian creative imagination. In *As for Me and My House* (1941), he depicts the desperate life of a young clergyman and his wife in a small prairie town and ends on only a very qualified note of hope. This book is interesting for the style he has developed to convey and underline his characters' frustration, boredom and loneliness. His next novel, *The Well* (1958), which probes into the mind of a young criminal, was not quite so highly praised. S. R.

Roth, Philip (1933–), American short-story writer specialising in tales of Jewish life. His most famous collection is *Goodbye, Columbus* (1959). K. R. R.

Roy, Gabrielle (1909–), Canadian novelist who, though she writes in French, is available and much read in English translation. In *Bonheur d'occasion* [*The Tin Flute*] (1947) she traces the problems of existence for a slum family in Montreal, suggesting that progress for Canada has brought urban squalor—debasement, not growth. She has also written *The Cashier* (1955), the story of a bank teller, his teller's cage being a symbol of the constraints imposed by the mechanics of progress.

S. R.

Rozov, Victor (1916–), Soviet playwright whose major interests are the conflict between generations and the attitudes of modern youth. He is perhaps best known abroad for his script to the prize-winning film *Letyat zhuravli* [*The Cranes are Flying*] (1957) based on one of his own plays. Two typical plays available in English translation are *V poiskakh radosti* [*In Search of Happiness*] (1956) and *A.B.V.G.D.* [*ABC*] (1961).

B. W.

Ruck, Berta (1878–), English writer of light romantic fiction, wife of Oliver Onions (q.v.). Her titles include *His Official Fiancée* (1914) and *Fantastic Holiday* (1953). P. E.

Rudd, Steele (Arthur Hoey Davis; 1868–1935), is the Australian creator of the famous characters Dad and Dave, described in an inexhaustible series of sketches. The setting is southern Queensland, and the bush-farmers are the poorest and most primitive of any described in Australian literature. His work is collected in *On Our Selection* (1903), *Sandy's Selection* (1904) and *Back at our Selection* (1906). S. R.

Rukeyser, Muriel (1913–), American poet, was born in New York and educated at Vassar and at Columbia University. Occasionally a romantic lyricism emerges from the weighty emotional content of her verse but generally it combines social and political involvement with mysticism and a heavy symbolism. This is seen most clearly in *The Soul and the Body of John Brown* (1940) where the Old Testament world of Ezekiel is symbolically juxtaposed with the economic and national struggles of America. Other books include *Theory of Flight* (1935); *Beast in View* (1944); *Elegies* (1949); and the novel *The Orgy* (1966). D. L. P.

Rulfo, Juan (1918–), Mexican writer, has published one volume of short stories, *El llano en llamas* ['The plain in flames'] (1953), and a much translated novel, *Pedro Páramo* [*Pedro Páramo*] (1955), which have greatly influenced the subsequent development of Latin American fiction. Comala, a small mountain village once dominated by Páramo, is now literally a ghost town, an eternally troubled conscience endlessly resonant of its collective, inglorious misdemeanours. Implicitly the feudal Mexico of inequality, violence and oppression banished but not redeemed by the revolution, this squalid, timeless community is resurrected in poetic, oneiric fragments whose undoubted technical virtuosity and social commitment are subordinate to an indigenous, reflective fatalism.

M. D. E.

Runyon, [Alfred] Damon (1884–1946), American writer, chiefly of short stories, is characterised by the individuality of his racy, startlingly-metaphored style and his ability to capture the slang and idiom of the spoken word, particularly that of the half-world brotherhood of a New York small crook and his associates. His most famous book is *Guys and Dolls* (1932). K. R. R.; D. L. P.

Russell, Bertrand (1872–), English philosopher and writer. Russell is one of the foremost British philosophers of the century, his most famous work being *Principia Mathematica* (1910–13) written in collaboration with A. N. Whitehead. As a committed mind Russell has taken a number of philosophical stances during his long career but essentially has taken the commonsense view that for philosophy to deal with real problems it must adopt the attitude that the mind can apprehend external reality, as it is, in terms of sense data. In general he takes a materialistic attitude towards the nature of the existing universe. Russell has published an enormous amount of material during his long lifetime including many popular books on philosophy which can be read by student and layman alike, such as *The Problems of Philosophy* (essays, 1912); *Mysticism and Logic* (1918); *An Outline of Philosophy* (1927); *The A.B.C. of Relativity* (1926); *Religion and Science* (1935); and the enormously readable and much revised *History of Western Philosophy* (1945). Russell's other work varies from his classic study of *Leibniz* (1900, rev. 1937) to popular sociological volumes such as *Marriage and Morals* (1929) and *Education and the Social Order* (1932). He has even written a volume of imaginative short stories *Satan in the Suburbs* (1953). In his later years, despite his age, Russell's intellectual faculties have remained acute and he has given his support to movements campaigning against nuclear armaments, publishing *Common Sense and Nuclear Warfare* (1958); *Has Man a Future?* (1961); and *Unarmed Victory* (1963). In the first world war he had survived the unpopularity of his anti-jingoist sentiments and in the generation of the 1950s and 1960s he founded the Committee of 100 to use civil disobedience as a weapon for nuclear disarmament and international morality. Russell was awarded the O.M. in 1944 and the Nobel Prize for Literature in 1950. He succeeded to the family earldom in 1931. D. L. P.

Russell, Elizabeth Mary, Countess (1866–1941), Australian-born English novelist and a cousin of Katherine Mansfield. She married a Count von Arnim and lived in East Prussia where she produced a series of sketches on family life under the title of *Elizabeth and Her German Garden* (1898). Her husband died and she subsequently married Earl Russell, brother of Bertrand Russell the philosopher, in 1916. Other books include *The Enchanted April* (1923) and *Mr Skeffington* (1940). An autobiography *All the Days of My Life* was published in 1936. D. L. P.

S

Sabatini, Rafael (1875–1950), Italian-born English novelist. Sabatini was born at Jesi, Italy, and educated in Switzerland and Portugal before marrying an Englishwoman and settling down in Herefordshire in 1905. His novels are light, romantic tales of adventure, usually involving a gentleman-rogue as hero. *Scaramouche* (1921) concerns a charming vagabond during the French revolution. *Captain Blood* (1922), *The Chronicles of Captain Blood* (1931) and *The Fortunes of Captain Blood* (1936) deal with a gentlemanly and essentially noble pirate, the kind of character that Errol Flynn delighted to play in his early film career. Other novels include *The Sea Hawk* (1915) and *The Gamester* (1949). D. L. P.

Sachs, Nelly (1891–), German poetess and dramatist and joint winner of the 1966 Nobel Prize. Of a liberal Jewish family of manufacturers she was born and educated in Berlin and made her literary début in 1921 with a collection of short stories. In the inter-war years she devoted herself principally to writing expressionist lyrics and plays. Hounded by the Nazis she fled in 1940 to Stockholm where she settled permanently. Her most impressive verse was not published until the post-war era, the best-known collections being *Wohnungen des Todes* ['The house of death'] (1947), *Sternverdunkelung* ['The stars go dark'] (1949), *Und Niemand weiss weiter* ['And that is all we know'] (1957) and *Flucht und Verwandlung* ['Escape and transformation'] (1959); the first-named was probably the most successful. These poems are concerned with the Jewish tragedy and most especially with the ordeal and sufferings at the hands of the Nazis. Their anguished lyricism provides the basis for Nelly Sachs' reputation and the grounds for her several Swedish and German literary awards. Most notably she received the German book trade's 1965 Peace Prize in Frankfurt, on which occasion she declared her faith in Germany's new generation. She has translated Swedish verse and her collected *Werke* were published in 1966. English translations of her poems have appeared in the *Jewish Quarterly*. R. C. W.

Sackville-West, Edward Charles (1901–65), English novelist, cousin of Victoria Sackville-West, wrote a number of lightly satiric novels including *Piano Quintet* (1925) and *The Sun in Capricorn* (1934). D. L. P.

Sackville-West, Victoria (1892–1962), English poet and novelist, and an outstanding writer on gardens and gardening. In *Orchard and Vineyard*

(1921) and *The Land* (1926) she showed her strong feeling for the life of the soil in her native Kent; the latter, a long descriptive poem recording the exacting toil of the farmer through the year, won the Hawthornden Prize. Her novels include *The Heritage* (1910), *The Edwardians* (1930) and *All Passion Spent* (1931). She married Sir Harold Nicolson, the diplomat, and recalled their years in Persia in *Passenger to Tehran* (1926). Other works include: *Knole and the Sackvilles* (1922); *St Joan of Arc* (1936); *Sissinghurst* (1933); *The Eagle and the Dove* (1943); and *The Garden* (1946).

G. S.

Sadleir, Michael (1888–1957), English novelist whose most successful work was the period novel *Fanny by Gaslight* (1940). He produced studies of Sheridan and Trollope and wrote a number of bibliographical works.

R. A. K.

Sadoveanu, Mihail (1880–1961), prolific Rumanian writer, active in the theatre, the Senate and the Academy. Much of his work, like that of Ion Creangă, whose tales are also available in English, extols the natural beauty of Rumania, the rural activities and historic exploits of his countrymen. His fame, abroad, resides mainly in *Baltagul* [*The Hatchet*] (1930), an account of peasant murder and revenge which has entered the Rumanian consciousness, a novel become myth. Other novels and short stories have been translated, however, including *Povestiri din răsboiu* [*Tales of War*] (1905), *Povestiri de seara* [*Evening Tales*] (1910), *Bordeienii* [*The Mudhut Dwellers*] (1912), *Venea o moară pe Siret* [*The Mill that Came with the Floods*] (1925), *Hanul Ancuței* [*Ancuta's Inn*] (1928), *Zodia cancerului sau Vremea Ducăi Vodă* [*Under the Sign of the Crab*] (1929) and *Mitrea Cocor* [*Mitrea Cocor*] (1950). M. D. E.

Sagan, Françoise (1936–), French novelist and playwright. She first received attention at the age of eighteen through the publication of her first novel *Bonjour tristesse* [*Bonjour Tristesse*, i.e. 'Hello Sadness'] (1954), a startling analysis of promiscuous behaviour involving a middle-class family, in which the jealous teenager Cécile persuades her boy friend to pose as the lover of her father's former mistress—with tragic consequences. This work evinced a remarkably mature cynicism coupled with the psychological insight of a Stendhal. Her honest observation of the youthful mind was balanced by her almost equally successful understanding of the motivation of those in early middle age, characteristics which are the hallmark of almost all her work.

Three succeeding novels, *Un Certain Sourire* [*A Certain Smile*] (1956), *Dans un mois, dans un an* [*Those Without Shadows*] (1957) and *Aimez-vous*

Brahms . . . [*Aimez-vous Brahms . . .*, i.e. 'Do you like Brahms'] (1959) all won further though decreasing acclaim, as the vein of similar themes became gradually exhausted. In *Un Certain Sourire* the student Dominique is torn between affection for her youthful lover and ardent infatuation for his wealthy uncle. Chastened when the latter's enthusiasm wilts, she is able to return to his magnanimous nephew. *Dans un mois, dans un an* is a neatly executed study of a group of young Parisian intellectuals, the criss-cross of their amorous entanglements and their lack of emotional and moral purpose. By contrast, Paule and Roger, the central figures of *Aimez-vous Brahms . . .*, are two lovers of long standing, now on the brink of middle age, who struggle hopelessly to maintain their mutual fidelity in the face of youthful counter-attractions.

Subsequent works—the novel *Les Merveilleux Nuages* ['The marvellous clouds'] (1961) and sundry theatrical compositions—met with only moderate success. The later novel *La Chamade* [*La Chamade*, i.e. 'The parley'] (1965) attracted a little more attention with its elegant and sophisticated portrayal of the self-indulgent thirty-year-old Lucile who ultimately realises that she prefers to be the mistress of a rich older man rather than of a poorly paid man of her own age. R. C. W.

Saint-Exupéry, Antoine de (1900–44), French novelist and essayist. Born in Lyon into an aristocratic family, St Exupéry became a qualified pilot in 1922. He took part in the early postal service to South America, becoming later a journalist and travelling representative for Air-France. He was presumed shot down in 1944.

His early novels *Courrier-sud* [*Southern Mail*] (1928) and *Vol de nuit* [*Night Flight*] (1931) have become famous as epics of the early days of flying, epics of a new élite. In 1939 he published *Terre des hommes* [*Wind, Sand and Stars*], part novel, part essay, followed in 1943 by *Pilote de Guerre* [*Flight to Arras*]. *Le Petit Prince* [*The Little Prince*] (1943), a children's book but one in which all the key themes to St Exupéry's philosophy are expressed, was followed by the posthumous publication of *Citadelle* [*The Wisdom of the Sands*] (1948) and *Les Carnets* ['Notes'] (1953).

St Exupéry's answer to the problem of man's fate is one in which man transcends his individuality by work in common with others, work which will enable a man to give sense to his life and exchange his perishable existence for immortality in what he has created. St Exupéry examines the 'myths' which will enable man to do this, the cathedrals of which individual men can be the stones. In work in common, man finds friendship, the bonds which bind him to other men. The myth itself must lead to action, and St Exupéry is fascinated by the rôle of the man of action and of the leader.

But by contrast with the revolutionaries, he believes that man is formed by his childhood and that he should not reject all formative influences in order to 'start again'. D. E. A.

Saki was the pen-name of Hector Hugh Munro (1870–1916), Scottish short-story writer. Munro was a newspaper correspondent before turning to story writing. He was killed during the course of the first world war. His stories are humorous, satirical, sometimes savage and occasionally macabre. He takes apart, with very considerable skill, the silly world of society life in the pre-1914 period. Underlying the surface satire of manners is a more penetrating understanding of the human condition, which explains why his stories have survived the fifty-year period that George Bernard Shaw laid down as the necessary indication of more than transitory literary merit.

The tensions between the conventions of society that Saki satirises and the reality of some of the terrible underlying passions of nature is underlined by the use he makes of animals. In the contact between them and the human world, some kind of primitive force emerges—often issuing in terror and even death. With the celebrated story 'Tobermory', however (from *The Chronicles of Clovis*, 1911), the relation between animal and man is less fundamental, merely serving to expose what lies beneath conventional morality—Tobermory the talking cat is less a wonder of the world than a threat to the society he lives in because of what he knows of its sexual mores and social indiscretions.

Saki wrote one novel *The Unbearable Bassington* (1912). His stories were issued in complete collected form in 1963. D. L. P.

Salinas, Pedro (1891–1951), Spanish poet and critic. The senior member of the '1927 Generation' of young poets who emerged during the twenties, Salinas graduated from Madrid University in 1913 and after three years at the Sorbonne was appointed Professor of Spanish Literature at Seville. Subsequently, as well as poetry, novels and drama, he produced an outstanding body of literary criticism. His studies of Manrique and Darío, and above all *Reality and the Poet in Spanish Literature* (1940; unpublished in Spanish), are classics which provide a key to the appreciation of Salinas' own verse. He sees poetry as 'the aggregate of relations' between two distinct realities, an inner psychological reality ('the poetic soul') and ordinary external reality. It is this changing relationship which he explores in his own works of criticism and poetry. In *Presagios* ['Foreboding'] (1923), *Seguro azar* ['Reliable chance'] (1929), *Fábula y signo* ['Fable and sign'] (1931), his attitude is ambivalent. At times he delights in external reality, like Alberti in *Cal y canto* or Guillén in *Cántico*: yet elsewhere he offers a critique of the external and resolves to pursue his inner vocation. The tragedy of this decision is seen in *La voz a ti debida* ['The voice I owe to thee'] (1933) and *Razón de amor* ['Love's reason'] (1936), jointly translated as *Truth of Two*. In this severely metaphysical love poetry, Salinas tries to conquer the mortality of sensual experience by stripping the woman and her love of all human connotations. Like the mystics Salinas pursues an inner reality, but he is a mystic in a godless age—alone he cannot eternalise the transience of sensual love. The inner aspiration continues in his later poetry, written after he left Spain in 1936. In *El contemplado* [*Sea of San Juan*] (1940), not woman but the ocean becomes the symbol of his inward search, while *Todo más claro* ['Everything more clearly'] (1949) is filled with disillusion at a world doomed to strife and injustice.

D. H. G.

Salinger, J. D. (Jerome David Salinger; 1919–), American short-story writer and author of the novel *The Catcher in the Rye* (1953). In this widely acclaimed book Salinger presents the thoughts and reactions of the adolescent Holden Caulfield as he decides to run away from his exclusive private boarding school and bums his way to and for several days around New York. The style of this interior monologue is remarkable for its rich colloquial imagery and for its capturing of the awkwardness, the bravado and cowardice, the lapses into self-pity and the idealism of youth. A significant feature of the book is the strength of feeling that Holden has for his young sister Phoebe, symbolised in his image of himself as protector, as a 'catcher in the rye', catching children before they fall over the cliff.

It is Salinger's short stories, many of which appeared first in the *New Yorker*, that show most clearly his singular treatment of the art of fiction—a retreat from the author's position of omniscience to one allowing the character to reveal himself through his own statements, letters, telephone conversations, diaries, lengthy monologues (however contradictory such evidence may appear) and letting stand the lacunae that such a method stubbornly refuses to fill. Salinger is meant to be read as much between as along the lines. Where his character's attempts to communicate fail, Salinger turns to the minutiae of his behaviour as if no clue were too small in the persistent search for understanding another human being. This method generates in the reader the genuine excitement of getting to know a real person.

His first collection *Nine Stories* (1953), published in England as *For Esme—with Love and Squalor* (1953), takes as subjects the child, the adolescent and the neurotic adult, usually set in the brash successful world of the American middle class—satirising unerringly the latter's intellectual and social pretensions, its jargon, its clutter of possessions, its compulsive smoking and drinking, and indicating the diverse national origins of a people trapped beneath an awful veneer of conformity. Salinger's major creation and central preoccupation is the Glass family, seven precocious children of one-time vaudeville parents, three of whom are introduced in stories that were included in this volume. Seymour, the eldest, commits suicide in the opening story 'A Perfect Day for Banana-fish'; the twin Walt's death in a pointless accident behind the lines in Korea is described in 'Uncle Wiggily in Connecticut'; and Boo Boo appears in 'Down at the Dinghy'. The connection between these three, and further clues to the reconstruction of their complex family saga, were first revealed in two long stories eventually published together as *Franny and Zooey* (1962): 'Zooey' about the youngest son, and 'Franny' which deals with the youngest daughter, the actual origins of whose nervous breakdown remain obscure though her spiritual journey is clearly charted. These two stories and two more that followed, 'Seymour: an Introduction' and 'Raise High the Roofbeam, Carpenters' (published together in 1963) are concerned with explaining the beliefs worked out by the Glass children in their constant and omnivorous study of the world's religions and literature. From this they derive a positive belief in humanity which must override their scorn for society and the crass members of it with whom they come into contact—Franny, whose breakdown has occurred when she comes to despise the pompous and superficial college man she loved, emerging into a mood of acceptance after a passionate exposition from Zooey; while the death of Seymour, whom we see married to the archetypal American girl, though it takes on some of the quality of a martyrdom is now felt to be a failure of love, and continues to haunt the family. Salinger's position is contrapuntal to that of the beat generation: he sees the same horrible flaws in a materialist society, but he postulates humility rather than withdrawal. His message, delivered increasingly strongly through his *alter ego* in the Glass family, the writer brother Buddy who like Salinger is a college English teacher, is that, however difficult it is to do so, one must love—for 'Christ is the fat lady in the third row' of any audience.

S. R.

Sánchez Ferlosio, Rafael (1927–), Spanish novelist. Born in Rome the son of a Spanish journalist, Sánchez Ferlosio possesses a remarkable linguistic ability, abundantly displayed in his two published works *Industrias y andanzas de Alfanhuí* ['The travels and industries of Alfanhuí'] (1951) and *El Jarama* [*The One Day of the Week*], the Nadal prizewinner for 1955. *Alfanhuí* is a unique literary creation—in the author's words a 'story full of true falsehoods'—the Castilian counterpart of James Purdy's *Malcolm*. It recounts in magical detail the adventures of a young boy and the weather-cock who initiates him into life. *El Jarama* lies at the opposite extreme of the novelistic spectrum, the author having subjected his imagination to a rigorous discipline in order to convey an impression of stultifying inaction. Eleven young Madrid office-workers spend a summer Sunday bathing in the Jarama and one of them, Lucia, drowns. From the opening pointless discussion between Lucio and Mauricio, the owner of the bar, as to whether the doorway curtain should be drawn or not, very little happens. Yet *El Jarama* seems the most impressive and compelling novel, and its author the most richly enigmatic novelist, to have appeared in post-war Spain. D. H. G.

Sandburg, Carl (1878–1967), American poet. Sandburg is a poet of the people: essentially his verse stems from the same kind of involvement in America, as a nation, that possessed Whitman. From his experience of American life he draws an almost brutal energy. Born in 1878, the son of Swedish immigrants, he has spent the rest of his life plunged in the American experience. His work is an expression of submergence in that experience and derives strength from it. He travelled the mid-west working in a variety of odd jobs; in Puerto Rico he fought in the Spanish-American War; a socialist, he was at one time the District Organiser for the Wisconsin Social Democratic Party; and in Chicago he became a journalist. From this rich early material comes his faith in the people.

Sandburg is one of a large group of American poets who found recognition in Hariette Monroe's Chicago-based publication *Poetry*—though this made no difference to his lack of concession to the reader in *Chicago Poems* (1916):

> Hog Butcher for the World,
> Tool maker, Stacker of Wheat,
> Player with Railroads and the Nation's Freight
> Handler;
> Stormy, Husky, Brawling,
> City of the Big Shoulders . . .

His early volumes, including *Cornhuskers* (1918), *Smoke and Steel* (1920), *Slabs of the Sunburnt West* (1922) and *Selected Poems* (1926), which possess an underlying sympathy and understanding, even at times a lyrical quality, reflect nevertheless the vigour and vulgarity of American life. Sandburg himself defines poetry as giving music and softness, beauty and direction, to the coarseness of life. The coarseness he is concerned with is that of the steel mill and the city street. A more pessimistic mood emerges in *Good Morning America* (1928), with the uncertain symbolism of fog and mist.

The People, Yes (1936) is an American classic. Sandburg here is concerned with the reality of 'the people' as a concept, opposed to the fading oppression of the boss, the demagogue, the big-shot. The memorials to the people are the mill, the railroad, the skyscraper, which they have built with the labour of their hands. The lack of metre and form in the verse is compensated by its compelling emotional force.

The writer's concern with and for America manifests itself in other than poetic works. His contribution to folk-lore includes *The American Songbag* (1927) and *The New American Songbag* (1950). Apart from varied novels (such as *Remembrance Rock*, 1948) and biographies Sandburg's closeness to the preoccupations of Whitman reflects in the massive six-volume biography of the greatest American representative of the people, Lincoln, for which he won a Pulitzer prize in 1939 (*Abraham Lincoln: The Prairie Years*, 2 vols, 1926; *Abraham Lincoln: The War Years*, 4 vols, 1939). But Sandburg's second Pulitzer prize, for his *Complete Poems* (1950), recognises that he is, primarily, a poet; and, as such, perhaps the most representative spokesman of the emerging America of the twenties and thirties:

Who shall speak for the people?
who has the answers?
Who is the sure interpreter?
who knows what to say?

D. L. P.

Sansom, William (1912–), English novelist whose works contain a close analysis of the mechanism of suburban existence. They include *The Body* (1949), *The Face of Innocence* (1951) and *The Loving Eye* (1956). The characteristic Sansom blend of pungency and pathos is maintained in later volumes, notably in the short stories of *The Ulcerated Milkman* (1966) and the novel *Goodbye* (1966). R. A. K.

Santayana, George (1863–1952), American philosopher, novelist and poet. Santayana is primarily a philosopher concerned with aesthetics; he wrote however one outstanding novel and some memorable verse. He was born in Avila, Spain, where he spent his early childhood. He studied at Cambridge, Massachusetts, and Boston, took his Ph.D. at Harvard and subsequently taught there until in middle age a legacy enabled him to retire and live permanently in Europe. Santayana taught in the same department as William James and Royce and numbered Conrad Aiken, T. S. Eliot and Walter Lippmann among his students.

Santayana's mixed European and New England background seems to be reflected in the tension in his work. Permanently at war with what he regarded as the joylessness of puritan New England, he was fundamentally a determinist; he saw intellect and emotion as merely by-products of the mechanics of nature, and art he conceived as a kind of bonus lyricism to set against the main stream of animalistic dominance. Religion he regarded as poetry, and free moral choice as illusory. These deterministic views are contained in *The Life of Reason* (1905), a five-volume review of reason in common sense, society, religion, art and science.

Santayana is in the curious position of embracing a determinism against which he seems in permanent reaction, with an involvement in aesthetics and poetry which he apparently feels are peripheral. In his one novel *The Last Puritan* (1935), he allows the hero Oliver to be destroyed by his perfection and by his conscience whereas the romantic Mario is entangled in a hedonist existence where responsibility is thrown on to God. However, Santayana while rejecting New England puritanism develops a respect for the puritan hero far in excess of that for the joyful Mario.

Santayana expresses the tensions in the pull of romanticism against mechanical determinism. In *Realms of Being* (1927–46) he shows a leaning towards Platonic idealism while rejecting the same idealism as irrelevant to the world of causal events. Similarly he writes stylistically perfect sonnets while denying poetry importance in life.

Volumes not mentioned above include *The Sense of Beauty* (1896) and *Collected Poems* (1923). D. L. P.

Sapper (Herman Cyril McNeile; 1888–1937), English novelist, first attained fame with *Bulldog Drummond* (1920), featuring an ex-officer character who became famous for his tough adventures. Six of these novels appeared between 1922 and 1935 and helped to develop the type of the moral hero with a yearning for excitement. R. A. K.

Sargeson, Frank (1903–), New Zealand author of short stories with a flavour all their own, the most characteristic of which is perhaps the title story of the volume *Conversations with My Uncle* (1936). Usually extremely short, sometimes in the form of a monologue or a dialogue, sometimes narrated by a bland, wide-eyed observer, these stories have a radical political slant and display a sardonic view of the human race. Some strike a note of black comedy, as when a startling and callous killing is seen as the natural conclusion of what began as mere irritation or incipient rivalry. With the long stories 'A Man and his Wife' (1940) and 'That Summer' (1946), later published together with his earlier writings in *Collected Stories* (1964), Sargeson successfully extended his style from his former cryptic and pungent anecdotes to stories in a more leisurely, even picaresque, framework. This development culminated in his long *Memoirs of a Peon* (1965), in which his anti-hero John Newhouse (the

English version of the name Casanova) vainly attempts to prove his intellectual worth, seduce the women he desires and raise himself from poverty to affluence. His rake's progress is set against the poverty of New Zealand during the depression, and the novel is remarkable for managing to be both a moving and accurate social document as well as an ironic and humorous tale. S. R.

Saroyan, William (1908–), American writer of Armenian extraction. Saroyan is most famous as a writer of short stories although he has written plays and novels. The quality of his work was immediately noticeable in his first collection of short stories which was published in 1934 with the title *The Daring Young Man on the Flying Trapeze*. It is a romantic, sentimental and rambling book, full of good-natured characters who are inflated to heroic proportions. The impressionistic style leads to charming but somewhat empty works which peter out in a single sentence, leaving them unresolved. A good example is the short story 'The Man with his Heart in the Highlands' in which an old man, Jasper McGregor, sponges off a poor family. He charms them all especially the child, who is also the narrator, but leaves suddenly at a request to help in the annual show at an old people's home. This turns the tale full circle and the situation at the end is identical to that at the beginning. The action is an intrusion into an idyllic existence and is by its nature only a temporary condition.

The same pattern can be found in almost all his work. *Inhale and Exhale* (1936), *The Trouble with Tigers* (1938), *The Adventures of Wesley Jackson* (1946) which is about a soldier's experiences during the war, all contain the same rich characters of whom he can criticise none. Basically the joy which he finds in people of various kinds and nationalities reflects his attitude to America where he is both an alien and a native. He is overwhelmed by the wonder of it all. For all the monotony of its content, his work is skilfully written, sometimes developing into pastiches of other writers. His plays are less successful, exaggerating his weaknesses of construction, but *The Time of Your Life* (1939), *Jim Dandy* (1947) and *The Cave Dwellers* (1958), which are fairly representative, have all enjoyed some popularity.

Later titles include the novel *One Day in the Afternoon of the World* (1965). K. G.–Y.

Sarraute, Nathalie (1902–), French novelist. Winner of the International Publishers' Prize, 1964, an admirer of Kafka, Dostoyevsky and Ivy Compton-Burnett, she was born in Russia and attended various European universities, including Oxford, before graduating in law. Sartre designated her an anti-novelist, resuscitating the term in his introduction to her *Portrait d'un inconnu* [*Portrait of a Man Unknown*] (1948). But her own critical writings, *L'Ere du soupçon* [*The Age of Suspicion*] (1956), although fundamental to the new theory, when taken together with texts by Robbe-Grillet, Raymond Roussel and Valéry Larbaud suggest the casual adherence of a potential heresiarch, the fortuitous association of an independent development.

She had already revealed, in *Tropismes* [*Tropisms*] (1939), the course and substance of her mature inquiry. Tropisms—spontaneous, involuntary, mental responses to the stimuli of people and objects—hide beneath every gesture and feeling, the most commonplace conversations, behind the discussions on interior decoration of *Le Planétarium* [*The Planetarium*] (1959), the snobbery and sharp practice of *Martereau* [*Martereau*] (1953), the aesthetic appreciation of *Les Fruits d'or* [*The Golden Fruits*] (1963). Virtually incommunicable, their complex subtlety can best be rendered by involving the disorientated reader in the confused, multivalent immediacy of images which evoke analogous sensations. To this end, the opaque conventions of plot, character and psychology, such excrescences as 'he said' (and its variants) and characters' names, such vanities as novelistic omniscience and the resolution of perplexities, are jettisoned, and time expands into the hugely amplified present of the interstices of conversation and sub-conversation, 'the secret source of our existence, in what might be called its nascent state'. M. D. E.

Sartre, Jean-Paul (1905–), French philosopher and writer. Born in Paris, a student at the Ecole Normale Supérieure (1924–28), Jean-Paul Sartre taught philosophy in the *lycées* of Le Havre, Laon and finally Paris for some fifteen years until 1945. But from then on he became increasingly famous, both in France and internationally, as a great man of letters, pledged to commitment in the social and political fields. When Sartre refuses the Nobel Prize for Literature or rejects an invitation to the United States because of American policy in Vietnam he has an impact on public opinion which hardly any other writer in the world can achieve. Iconoclast, idealist, muckraker, playwright, novelist, philosopher, amateur politician, perhaps the one quality he is rather lacking in is wit.

It was as a philosopher that he began his literary career. In 1936 he published an essay on *L'Imagination* [*Imagination*], supplemented by *L'Imaginaire* [*Psychology of Imagination*] (1940) and *Esquisse d'une théorie des émotions* [*Sketch for a Theory of the Emotions*] (1939). But his two major philosophic works are *L'Etre et le Néant* [*Being and Nothingness*] (1943) and *Critique de la raison dialectique* [*Critique of Dialectical Reason*] (1960). The philosophical doctrine embodied in these writings is that of which Sartre was and is the principal exponent, existentialism. In the years following the war this completely dominated French thinking, the French novel, the theatre, and even tended to play a political rôle. It had a great influence on literature, especially since by its very nature it tended to be expressed in works of art as much as in treatises. The doctrine of existentialism puts the accent on existence as opposed to essence, the latter being illusory and problematical, the end rather than the starting-point of philosophical speculation. The immediately perceptible fact is existence, and it is perceived in anguish. In the words of Sartre, '*l'existence précède l'Essence*' (existence precedes Essence'). French existentialists claim descent from the Dane Sören Kierkegaard (1813–55) and owe a great deal to the German philosophers Heidegger, Jaspers and Husserl. Sartre was deeply impressed by Husserl who, by a return to the concrete, seeks to 'overcome the opposition between idealism and realism, affirm both the sovereignty of the mind and the presence of the world, as it gives itself to us', as Simone de Beauvoir puts it. While these abstract works of his make difficult reading, Sartre has nonetheless won a wide public for existentialism because he has the knack of coining striking formulas, and because he both illustrates his philosophy in novels and plays and translates it into action through his political commitment.

The basic postulate of Sartre's philosophy is that the existence of a man precludes the existence of God. There can be no such thing as a pre-existing human nature. Man is the picture of man, man is what he makes himself. It is in this sense that Sartre can declare that existentialism is humanism. Man is therefore 'responsible'; he is 'condemned to be free'. Freedom can never be abstract, we are always in a given situation, we must always choose, and choose in action in the real world. We are judged by our acts alone, not by our good intentions; and our acts are irreversible. Sartre's philosophy is then a philosophy of action. The experience of the 'absurd' as in Sartre's novel *La Nausée* [*Nausea*] (1938), that is the anguish felt by the mind becoming aware of the contingency of existence, is an essential critical step but must be transcended. Man must use his freedom to create, to act. But on what criterion? Sartre rejects traditional values of good and evil considered as absolute. For him freedom takes 'itself as a value inasmuch as it is the source of all values'. 'The work of art is a value because it is a call.' In fact, for Sartre evil lies in poverty and oppression; he opposes fascism, capitalism and bourgeois morality.

All Sartre's literary work and social and political action are an implementation of this philosophy. His output is enormous. As a novelist he began with *Nausea* in 1938, followed by *Le Mur* ['The wall'], a collection of short stories, in 1939. Both made a powerful impact. After the war—during which he was a prisoner, escaped and joined a resistance group—Sartre tried to set up a left-wing political movement, the R.D.R., and founded a review *Les Temps modernes* ('Modern times') which has specialised in documentation and reportage and has exercised a profound influence on French thinking during the past twenty years. In 1945 he published the first two volumes of his four-volume novel *Les Chemins de la liberté* [*The Roads to Freedom*]: *L'Age de raison* [*Age of Reason*] and *Le Sursis* [*Reprieve*]; a third volume *La Mort dans l'âme* [*Iron in the Soul*] followed in 1951. The fourth is hanging fire, though some chapters have been published in *Les Temps modernes*. In his early plays *Les Mouches* [*The Flies*] (1943) and *Huis clos* [*No Exit*] (1944), Sartre finds again the hard-hitting intensity of style of *Le Mur*. *No Exit* is considered by many to be his masterpiece. Other plays are *Morts sans sépulture* [*The Victors*] (1946), a drama of the resistance; *La P—— respectueuse* [*The Respectful Prostitute*] (1946), on the racial problem in the U.S.A.; *Les Mains sales* [*Crime Passionel*] (1948), on the intellectual in political action; and *Le Diable et le Bon Dieu* [*The Devil and the Good Lord*] (1951). In 1955 the violent satire *Nekrassov* [*Nekrassov*] stirred up a deal of polemic, while *Les Séquestrés d'Altona* [*The Condemned of Altona*] (1959) tended to drown its important theme in a flood of words. Sartre has also written a vast quantity of essays of philosophical, literary, political and social criticism of an extraordinarily high overall quality. His incisive mind and brilliant dialectic are a fine stimulant to thought. Examples are the six volumes of *Situations* [*Literary and Philosophical Essays*] published since 1947, especially the second and sixth volumes, on the nature of literature and the peace movement respectively; *L'Existentialisme est un humanisme* [*Existentialism and Humanism*] (1946); his study on *Baudelaire* (1947); and *Réflexions sur la question juive* [*Anti-Semite and Jew*] (1947).

A. L. W.

Sassoon, Siegfried (1886–1967), English poet and writer of memoirs. Sassoon was educated at Marlborough and Clare College, Cambridge. He served in France and Palestine in the first world war and was awarded the M.C. He was honoured with the C.B.E. in 1951.

His early poetry is lyrical, pastoral and not far distant from the Georgian school. The war changed his style and attitudes from lyric to satire, and from pastoral inclinations to savage bitterness towards the unnecessary horrors of trench warfare. Like that of Wilfred Owen, with whom he was in hospital for a time, his work is completely opposed to the sentimentality of a poet like Brooke. Sassoon's patriotism is not marred by jingoism and false heroics; he had sufficient reason and courage to turn to pacifism:

'Good-morning, good-morning!' the General said
When we met him last week on our way to the line.
Now the soldiers he smiled at are most of 'em dead,

And we're cursing his staff for incompetent swine.
'He's a cheery old card,' grunted Harry to Jack
As they slogged up to Arras with rifle and pack.
But he did for them both with his plan of attack.

Sassoon's qualities of romanticism, light satire, grace and nostalgia abound in his later poetry but are continually reinforced by the brutal experience in depth of his war years. His *Collected Poems* was published in 1946, and a volume entitled *Sequences* in 1956.

Sassoon's prose writings are also of considerable interest. *The Memoirs of George Sherston* published in three volumes between 1928 and 1936 are comparable in quality with Robert Graves's memoirs *Goodbye To All That*. The first volume, *Memoirs of a Fox-Hunting Man*, deals with wit and grace with pre-1914 England and takes Sassoon from the early youth of public school and cricket matches and village fêtes to the romance of training to be a soldier. The remaining volumes are hard with the bitterness of war—though there is less here of the fierce protest and savage realism to be found in the war poems, the tone being rather one of icily controlled irony at remembered events. A subsequent three-volume sequence of memoirs, *Siegfried's Journey*, was published in 1945.

Sassoon's interesting biography of *Meredith* (1948) treats the man with sympathy and understanding but reveals more of its author's own attitudes to verse than it uncovers about Meredith's poetry. D. L. P.

Satchell, William (1860–1942), New Zealand novelist, is the chronicler of a region, an antipodean Thomas Hardy, at his most successful in *The Toll of the Bush* (1905). In this, and in *The Land of the Lost* (1902), the country north of Auckland and the people who have settled there are brought vividly before us. In *The Elixir of Life* (1907) the setting is a ship and its New Zealand passengers, but its concentration on characters set outside their usual environment reveals the weakness of his portrayal of humans when isolated from his strong feeling for landscape. *The Greenstone Door* (1914) is his most ambitious work, a detailed historical novel designed to recapture a past era; but it is somewhat stiff and humourless in its portrayal of famous figures, and naïve in its oversimplification of the Maori character. S. R.

Sayers, Dorothy (1893–1957), English detective novelist and Christian polemicist. Dorothy Sayers is known for her excellent translations of Dante, issued between 1949 and 1955, and for her religious drama, especially *The Man Born to be King* (1942). A very wide cross-section of the public reads her sophisticated detective novels, especially those concerning her most famous hero, Lord Peter Wimsey. The characters and situations in her stories date rather easily into caricature but the ingenious plots, with the villain never revealed until the last few pages of the book, ensure a large and continued audience. Her titles include *Lord Peter Views the Body* (1928), *Gaudy Night* (1938) and *Busman's Honeymoon* (1937). Notable collections are *The New Sayers Omnibus* (1956) and *A Treasury of Sayers's Stories* (1958). D. L. P.

Schreiner, Olive (1855–1920), South African writer, famed as the founder of the South African English novel largely on the basis of her classic *The Story of an African Farm* (1883) and the less well-known but typical *Trooper Peter Halket of Mashonaland* (1897). Olive Schreiner's rôle in South African—and English—letters might be said to be that of a female Bernard Shaw. A complex personality, she was passionate of temperament, and deeply and widely sympathetic towards the oppressed and the lonely; yet she was also a rational, analytical philosopher who sought to solve the universal mysteries of inequality, sex, pain and death. These themes recur in her best-known works as well as in *Stories, Dreams and Allegories* (1920) and in *Undine* (published 1929), the story of a girl whose only apparent happiness is in her constant death-wish. C. P.

Schröder, Rudolf Alexander (1878–1962), German poet, essayist, writer, architect, theologian, was possibly the last of the Hofmannsthal-Rilke generation of humanists (in the sense of representatives of a unified western cultural tradition). He produced translations not only of the Greek and Latin classics, but also of modern and classical French, English and Dutch writers. He himself wrote much original lyric verse, and in the early thirties issued his autobiographical studies *Der Wanderer und die Heimat* ['The wanderer and the homeland'] and *Aus Kindheit und Jugend* ['Childhood and youth']. G. W.

Schwartz, Delmore (1913–), American poet, belongs to the mid-twentieth-century school of academic poets. He is a teacher, an editor and a reviewer as well as a writer of poetry, plays and short stories.

Born in Brooklyn he read philosophy at Wisconsin, New York and Harvard, later lecturing at a number of American universities including Harvard. He has been concerned with the editing both of *Partisan Review* and the *New Republic*. Schwartz's reputation was established in 1938 with the publication of *In Dreams Begin Responsibilities*, which contains a mixture of poetry, prose and drama. The writer is concerned with relating his philosophical training to the social problems of an environment against which he reacts strongly. The style is fluent but in the later plays and verse rather overfilled with academic symbolism. Schwartz's sense of irony is at its best in the volume of mainly Jewish short stories, *The World is a Wedding* (1948).

A characteristic poem is 'In the Naked Bed in Plato's Cave' (*In Dreams Begin Responsibilities*) which successfully blends specific references to the cave in Plato's *Republic* with the sleepy images of early morning and ties both down to a generalisation about the nature of man:

> . . . So, so,
> O son of man, the ignorant night, the travail
> Of early morning, the mystery of beginning
> Again and again,
> while History is unforgiven.

Delmore Schwartz is a much anthologised American poet who has not yet achieved the very first rank. His later published verse includes *Vaudeville for a Princess* (1950) and *Summer Knowledge* (1960); and amongst his dramatic works are *Shenandoah* (1941) and *Genesis* (1943). Also of interest are his translation from Rimbaud, *A Season in Hell* (1948); and a volume of essays, *The Imitation of Life* (1941). D. L. P.

Schwarz-Bart, André (1928–), French novelist. A French Jew of Polish extraction, he won international recognition and the Prix Goncourt with his first book, *Le Dernier des justes* [*The Last of the Just*] (1959). The title recalls the Jewish legend of the *Lamed-waf*, the thirty-six Just Men, indistinguishable from ordinary mortals, who function as humanity's whipping boys, 'the hearts of the world multiplied, into which all our griefs are poured, as into one receptacle'. One Just Man to each generation, for if he were lacking mankind would suffocate, they stem from Solomon Levy, the only survivor of the massacre at York in 1185, when the Rabbi, his father, slit the throats of his besieged flock rather than they should apostate. The first third of the novel follows the subsequent Just Men through centuries of pogrom and bigotry in France, England, Russia and Poland until Ernie Levy is born, in the Rhineland, the Last of the Just. With the rise of the Nazis, Ernie's family escape to France where he renounces his Jewish faith and enlists in the army in a futile attempt to protect his relatives. France is defeated and Ernie, essentially unassuming, and with none of the characteristics of his illustrious lineage, is comfortably installed in the Free Zone, until his destiny calls him to Paris and a love affair. Never mawkish, often ironical, comic even, the novel's gentle passion is superbly complemented by the flat, unemotional description of the closing scenes, as Ernie voluntarily accompanies Golda into the gas chambers.

In 1967, in conjunction with his wife Simone, a West Indian from

Martinique, Schwarz-Bart published *Un Plat de porc aux bananes vertes* ['A dish of pork and green bananas'], the first of a cycle of seven novels to be devoted to the social and racial implications of *négritude*.

M. D. E.

Schweitzer, Albert (1875–1965), German scholar and philanthropist born in Alsace when that province was part of the German empire, was naturally bilingual. It has often been said that he could have made a world reputation as a theologian, music critic, organist or doctor in tropical medicine. His university studies in Strasbourg were brilliant; both as a theologian and critic of Bach he achieved eminence, but from 1913 he chose to live and work as a medical missionary in Lambaréné, central Africa. The tremendously romantic appeal of such a scholar devoting himself to such work made *Zwischen Wasser und Urwald* [*On the Edge of the Primeval Forest*] (1921) and *Aus meinem Leben und Denken* [*My Life and Thought*] (1933) extremely popular best-sellers; but his real reputation as a writer rests on his philosophical works and his studies on St Paul. *Geschichte der paulinischen Forschung* [*Paul and his Interpreters*] (1911) and *Geschichte der Leben Jesu—Forschung* [*The Quest of the Historical Jesus*] (1913) revealed his intellectual range; and the philosophical aspects of Protestantism were fully examined in *Verfall und Wiederaufbau der Kultur* [*The Decay and Restoration of Civilisation*] (1923) and also in *Kultur und Ethik* [*Civilisation and Ethics*] (1923). A curious fact could be said to suggest a family leaning towards philosophy; for the French existentialist Jean-Paul Sartre is a relative of Schweitzer. He received the Nobel Peace Prize in 1952.

G. W.

Seeger, Alan (1888–1916), American poet. Seeger was born in New York, educated at Harvard and went to Paris in 1913. At the outbreak of war he joined the French Foreign Legion in 1914, winning the Croix de Guerre and the Médaille Militaire before being killed in action in 1916. His romantic style was transposed into war poems the most notable of which is 'I Have a Rendezvous with Death'. His *Collected Poems* were published in 1916 as were his *Letters and Diaries*.

D. L. P.

Seferis, Giorgos (1900–), Greek poet, winner of the 1963 Nobel Prize for Literature. 'Giorgos Seferis' is the literary pseudonym of Giorgos Seferiades, until 1963 the Greek ambassador to the Court of St James. His principal verse-collections are *Kichle* ['The Thrush'] (1947) and *Poiemata* ['Poems'] (1950 and 1951). Two anthologies of his poems are available, translated into English verse: *The King of Asine* (1948) by Bernard Spencer, Nanos Valaoritis and Lawrence Durrell, and *Poems*

(1960) by Rex Warner. His poems, though modernist in technique, reveal a profound consciousness of the eternal presence of the Greek past and owe a particular debt to the *Odyssey*, Aeschylus and Greek myth. The fundamental themes are the journey of the soul and the survival of a past which is repeatedly evoked. The imagery employed, essentially simple, is most frequently drawn from the sea, but also involves flowers, birds, stones, broken statues and ruins. Seferis' language is of a deceptive simplicity, being a vehicle for symbolist and surrealist devices, yet is occasionally complicated by use of the transferred epithet. Characteristic is a marked shortage of adjectives and an economical style which produce crisp and stark impressions and enhance his basic mood of gentle melancholy and stoic calm. Ideologically, Seferis grinds few axes; his poetry is pagan but without cults, evolves no metaphysic, shuns the political and is too classical and detached to be humanistic. A selection of essays in English translation, *On the Greek Style*, appeared in 1967.

R. C. W.

Segal, Ronald (1932–), South African author, founded and edited *Africa South* (later *Africa South in Exile*) 1956–62, and subsequently edited the Penguin Africa Series. *The Tokolosh* (1960), a satirical novel, is a cunning subversion of South Africa's pigmentocracy by an inversion of its order. *Into Exile* (1963), an autobiography, combines intellectual sharpness with political honesty, moral inquiry with sensitivity and well-wrought prose. C. P.

Semprún, Jorge (c. 1920–), Spanish émigré novelist who lives in France and writes in French. He won the 1963 Premio Formentor with the manuscript of his novel *Le Grand Voyage* [*The Long Voyage*] (1963). He fought for the Republicans in the Spanish civil war and later in the French resistance before his ultimate capture by the Gestapo and imprisonment in Auschwitz. Somewhat begrudgingly re-admitted into France after 1945 he has not always and everywhere been *persona grata*, owing to his extreme leftist politics. Partly autobiographical, his prize-winning novel deftly interweaves past, present and future in its compelling analysis of the anguish of exile, betrayal and the bestiality of man to man. Human beings crammed for days and nights in a cattle truck, brutish Nazi guards, the scornful or indifferent German civilians, the arrogant and smug liberators, all intermingle in a series of robust impressions related with a riveting realism. R. C. W.

Sender, Ramón (1902–), considered by many critics the finest novelist currently writing in Spanish. An Aragonese, displaying the harsh realism of his race, Sender's ability was clearly shown in *Imán* [*Earmarked for*

Hell] (1929), a virulent denunciation of the Moroccan war which he had experienced on national service. Rejecting the dehumanised art of the twenties, Sender embarked on a series of novels which probed the social problems of pre-civil war Spain. *Siete domingos rojos* [*Seven Red Sundays*] (1932) examines not anarchism but anarchists, and the strike that tragically fails because leaders like Gisbert refuse to play politics. Such an exploration of human motivations in concrete circumstances is masterfully effected in *Mister Witt en el cantón* [*Mr Witt Among the Rebels*] (1935), which marks Sender's maturity as a novelist. Against the historical background of the 1873 federalist movement are set the opposed characters of Mr Witt, middle-aged, anchylosed in his prejudices, and his wife Milagritos, youthful, identifying with the radical masses.

During the civil war Sender fought with the republicans, moving subsequently to America where he has continued to write prolifically. This later production divides into three main groups. Firstly, there are the novels set in America: the masterpiece of which is *Epitalamio del prieto Trinidad* [*Dark Wedding*] (1942), set on a penal island in the Caribbean, whose Mexican convicts mutiny on the wedding night of Trinidad, the chief warder. His murder and the pursuit of Niña Lucha, his bride, are conveyed with consummate technique and tension. Secondly, there are novels—such as *El rey y la reina* [*The King and the Queen*] (1948)—set in Spain's immediate past: these are not apologies for a view of the civil war but psychological studies of growing self-awareness, an exception being the polemical *Contraataque* [*Counter-attack in Spain*] (1937). Finally, there is the lyrical evocation of Sender's own past in the series of three trilogies *Crónica del alba* [the first trans. as *Before Dawn*] (1942–67). Here Sender's desire to discover a sense to man's existence, and to that of the autobiographical character of Pepe Garcés, is more naïvely obvious than elsewhere. Sender, now a citizen of the United States, has also published *El bandido adolescente* ['The adolescent bandit'] (1965), based on the life of Billy the Kid.

D. H. G.

Senghor, Léopold Sédar (1906–), Senegalese poet and politician, who became the first president of his country after independence. With Aimé Césaire, the Caribbean writer Léon Damas and others, he formulated, advocated and practised the widely polemicised concept of *négritude*. Evidently in part the *évolué's* violent reaction to 'assimilation', *négritude* postulates Europe and its civilisation as alien, dehumanised, dying; Africa and Africanness, blackness, as vital, nourishing, alive. It is the awakened African's antithesis to the imperialist thesis of a dark, savage continent and the pre-eminence of western ideas and ideals. Senghor's proud and resonant poetry, splendidly figurative, richly rhetorical and dazzling in its neo-surrealist traditions, achieves a synthesis of externals so that in thought, tone, form and feeling his verse often tensely bridges the gap that *négritude* seems to create between man and man. Whether this happens in the very stuff and being of his poetry is an open question; that his poetry, a substantial body of work in French, is very highly esteemed, not least in France, is a fact—attested to directly by Sartre, indirectly by Genet (for example in *The Blacks*), and critically by Gerald Moore (in *Seven African Writers*, 1962) who has made available the first representative anthology of Senghor's work in translation. C. P.

Serafimovich, Alexandr S. (Alexandr Serafimovich Popov; 1863–1949), Russian writer, was an established literary figure before the 1917 revolution. He was born in the Don region and began writing while in exile in northern Russia. His stories deal with the lower classes but he is primarily remembered for his novel *Zheleznyi potok* [*The Iron Flood*] (1924), which is regarded as a classic of socialist realism. The individual hero of the book, which is bloodthirsty and quite honest in its representation of the Red-White struggle, is a peasant officer who moulds a fighting body out of rebellious soldiers and leads them out of a White encirclement; but it is the mass of the people who emerge as true hero of the work. It was Serafimovich who helped Sholokhov have his *Silent Don* published. B. W.

Service, Robert William (1874–1958), English-born Canadian poet and novelist. Service wrote popular ballad verse of a sentimental character, and possessing a strong narrative line as in his best-known piece 'The Shooting of Dan McGrew'. His material was derived from extensive travel and a life of varied adventures. As an ambulance driver in the 1914–18 war he gained the background for *Rhymes of a Red Cross Man* (1916). The novel *Trail of '98* (1910) comes straight from his own involvement in the Klondike. Experience of life in Paris produced *Ballads of a Bohemian* (1920), and in Monte Carlo yielded the novel *Poisoned Paradise* (1922). *Bar Room Ballads* was written in 1940; and *Ploughman of the Moon* (1943) is an interesting and selective autobiography. D. L. P.

Seton, Ernest Thompson (1860–1946), English-born nature writer brought up in Canada who was a founder of the Boy Scouts of America and author of *Scouting for Boys* (1910). He is best remembered for his animal stories which he himself illustrated, titles including *Animal Heroes* (1905), *Woodland Tales* (1921) and *The Biography of an Arctic Fox* (1937). His autobiography is *The Trail of an Artist Naturalist* (1940). P. E.

Seymour, Alan (1927–), Australian playwright, author of *The One Day of the Year* (1962) which deals with a clash both between generations and between social classes. The occasion for conflict is the great Australian national holiday, Anzac day, which a working-class undergraduate and his society girl-friend plan to debunk in an article exposing its hypocrisy and sham and laying bare its finale of mindless drunkenness—much to the consternation of the boy's uneducated father and his Gallipoli-veteran friend whose confused emotions they have totally failed to understand.

S. R.

Shadbolt, Maurice (1932–), New Zealand writer, author of two volumes of short stories *The New Zealanders* (1959) and *Summer Fires, Winter Country* (1963). Shadbolt writes with a combination of freshness and assurance that gives new life to themes that in other hands have remained provincial or been rendered stale. He most frequently explores the conflict in the New Zealander between that part of him which acknowledges the power of the landscape and its rightful inheritors the Maoris, and that part which seeks refuge in a derivative urban sophistication. At other times he depicts the difficulties of the artist of real stature in a society unable even to recognise his talent. Particularly remarkable is his unstressed portrayal of the complete spectrum of human love, from intense emotional sublimation to the desperate extremes of sexual deviation. He has also published a novel *Among the Cinders* (1965) recounting the adventures of a teenage delinquent, and a collection of three *novelle*, *The Presence of Music* (1967). S. R.

Shaffer, Peter (1926–), English playwright, wrote plays for television and was a literary critic before his first stage success in 1958.

Until *The Royal Hunt of the Sun* (1964) Shaffer was highly impersonal. He was as withdrawn and enigmatic as is Walter Langer, hero of his *Five Finger Exercise* (1958). Walter, a young German, is the teenage daughter's tutor in what could so easily have been a typical Dodie Smith family, but Shaffer's greater psychological insight gradually removes the successive skins of pretence to reveal the family for what it really is beneath its own imagined attitudes. Walter is the catalyst which enables them to react upon one another and so reveal themselves, but unlike the catalyst he is himself finally destroyed.

Black Comedy (1965) shows this writer's versatility in a different art-form, a farce in which the actors all move around the stage in imagined pitch darkness while the audience watch every move. Undoubtedly, however, the play which to date has done most to enhance his reputation is *The Royal Hunt of the Sun*. This is a play which very forcefully and with great pageantry portrays a conflict between two civilisations, the Spanish and the Inca, 'hope and hopelessness, faithlessness and faith' as Shaffer expresses it, and at the same time examines in depth the personal clash between Pizarro and Atahualpa and their tortured search for common ground, finally discovered in their common humanity. There is some conventionality in the theme of the play, in the attitudes of the protagonists, propounding the normal liberal solutions to the problems involved, and Shaffer does not always preserve his former detachment, but nonetheless the agony of soul portrayed is very real. The play is an enormous spectacle painted on an enormous canvas, and uses every resource the theatre offers in such scenes as the ascent of the Andes, the entry of the Incas and the mime of the great massacre. It is true total theatre, and has considerable significance. J. B. M.

Shapiro, Karl (1913–), American man of letters, falls simultaneously into several categories of American writing: he is an intellectual, a teacher, a critic, a satirist, an editor and a poet of the generation of the second world war.

Shapiro privately published a volume of his own work in 1935 and was then taken up by *New Directions* with the issue of their *Five Young American Poets* in 1941. In *Person Place and Thing* (1942) he consciously dissociates himself from concern in an abstract conception of America such as occupied Hart Crane or even Carl Sandburg; he claims involvement only with himself and his immediate environment. However, wartime service in the Pacific made him a war poet, though he does not like the description; and *V-letter and Other Poems* (1944), containing many war poems, won him a Pulitzer prize.

Shapiro's verse is tightly controlled and seldom oblique in terms of obscurity of meaning. His poems are often sharply satirical of the American social scene and can verge momentarily on slickness. They do possess the quality of careful craftsmanship; and intellect and craft are complemented by what might be described as a gentle eroticism. The poetry can border on the obscene but more often mellows into the tender and the lyrical.

As the controlled form of his work might indicate Shapiro is concerned with the techniques of writing verse and with aesthetics in general. *Essay on Rime* (1945) and *Beyond Criticism* (1953) are examples of this involvement as is his long editorship of the magazine *Poetry*. All this might indicate that Shapiro is a slight and academic poet, but his upbringing during the depression and his war service have given his work an underlying strength and an involvement in the universal problems of the post-1945 period:

. . . Well might the soldier kissing the hot beach
Erupting in his face damn all your kind.
Yet you who saved neither yourselves nor us
Are equally with those who shed the blood
The heroes of our cause. Your conscience is
What we come back to in the armistice.
(from 'The Conscientious Objector' in *Trial of a Poet*, 1947)

Other volumes of Shapiro's verse include *The Place for Love* (1943); *Poems 1940–1953* (1953); and *Poems of a Jew* (1958). D. L. P.

Shaw, George Bernard (1856–1950), Irish-born dramatist. Shaw was born in Dublin and educated at the Wesleyan school. He worked for a while in Dublin before, in 1876, joining his mother in London where she earned her living as a singer and music teacher. He underwent a process of self-education while she maintained him financially. During the period up to 1885 he wrote a number of unsuccessful novels, became a socialist and a Fabian, and forced himself to overcome shyness to become a proficient platform speaker. In 1885 he became music critic for the *Star* and later for the *World*. In 1895 he was appointed dramatic critic for the *Saturday Review*. Shaw's criticism was witty, biting, savage although the humour, pointed as it might be, often caused his views not to be taken seriously. Hesketh Pearson remarks that Shaw's writing is unusual because he simply said what he thought. Shaw also gave vent to semi-serious disparaging remarks on Shakespeare's plays, which he compared unfavourably with his own. His attacks were made more pointed by his being more familiar with Shakespearian drama than many of the shocked and protesting critics. Among collections of Shaw's reviews is *Dramatic Opinions and Essays* (1907).

Shaw's early plays were rejected for performance because they were thought unactable or because they were banned for their controversial subject matter. Consequently he published a reader's volume of six *Plays Pleasant and Unpleasant* in 1898 with prefaces that pithily drove home the intellectual substance of the drama. The latter marked the precedent in a tradition of prefaces, to the published plays, that were often longer than the plays themselves. 'Plays Unpleasant' contained *Widowers' Houses*, an attack on housing conditions; *The Philanderer*, dealing with a concept of the developing rôle of women in society; and *Mrs Warren's Profession*, which is about prostitution. 'Plays Pleasant' included a satire on the military world, *Arms and the Man*; a farce, *You Never Can Tell*; and *Candida*, the story of a vicar's wife and her love for a young artist. *Three*

Plays for Puritans (*The Devil's Disciple*, *Caesar and Cleopatra* and *Captain Brassbound's Conversion*) was published in 1901; *Caesar and Cleopatra* broke new ground by treating historical characters in a contemporary fashion and idiom. *John Bull's Other Island* (1900) was written at the request of Yeats for the Irish National Theatre. It treats home rule not in a strict political context but as a conflict between two central characters, Irish and English, who are both treated sympathetically but whose characteristics epitomise the problems of Anglo-Irish relations. *Pygmalion* (1912) portrays Professor Henry Higgins evolving a society lady from Eliza Doolittle, a flower girl, by means of the science of phonetics. The play caused a social sensation when the well-schooled Eliza, in a moment of stress, reverted to the expressive use of the phrase 'not bloody likely'.

For all his involvement with social and political issues, Shaw was aware that these alone did not represent the ultimate problems; and amidst a torrent of social plays, he also sought to express his evolving religio-philosophical ideas. *Man and Superman* (1903) is a massive work which at one level deals with the pursuit and capture of a man, John Tanner, by an intelligent, scheming, cunning and typically Shavian woman, Ann Whitefield. At another level it describes Shaw's view of a life-force which is central to the evolution of man. In Act Three, Tanner dreams a dialogue between Don Juan and the Devil which describes this force as an emanation from God, which men may will themselves to develop, thus becoming the instrument of the will of God himself. Shaw develops the theme in *Back to Methuselah* (1921) in a progressive series of sketches from the Garden of Eden through the present and into the future. He wishes to demonstrate that man can achieve intellectual evolution to perfection through an effort of creative will.

Shaw's best-known plays from his middle years are *Heartbreak House* (1917) and *Saint Joan* (1924). Both are twentieth-century masterpieces. In the latter, which he himself described as an historical tragi-comedy, Shaw is concerned to illustrate his theme of Joan as an early symbol and example of nationalism and even of protestantism. She challenges not only the Church and the English occupation of France but the international aristocracy represented in the play by the worldly-wise Warwick. Intellectually the most effective and dramatic speech is that of the Inquisitor in the trial scene who is represented as a highly intelligent sympathetic man with a rational approach to the necessity of maintaining the structures of Catholic Christendom and the existing social systems—by the use of the Inquisition only if necessary. Joan needs to be saved or eliminated or destroyed only because she is a disturbing and therefore dangerous eccentric. Rationality is seen, too, in the character of the archbishop who quite sensibly describes miracles as those events, of no matter what nature, which create faith. However, it would be a mistake to think of the play only at the intellectual level: the play is certainly both tragic and comic, and Saint Joan is a historical character with whom Shaw seems to discover a genuine depth of understanding. He also endows her with lyrical qualities that border on prose-poetry:

> . . . if only I could still hear the wind in the trees, the larks in the sunshine, the young lambs crying through the healthy frost, and the blessed, blessed church bells that send my angel voices floating to me on the wind. But without these things I cannot live . . .

In the epilogue there is a last ironic comment when the characters of the play come together with a modern figure of the Catholic church and are prepared to eulogise her as a saint but not to endure the difficulties of her possible return to earth.

Well after he had achieved success with his plays, Shaw continued to be a prolific writer on political and economic subjects, especially on socialism. He was one of the best-known of the Fabian group, and his political publications included the celebrated volume entitled *The Intelligent Woman's Guide to Socialism* (1928). His attacks on British policy during the first world war led to temporary unpopularity which his immense international reputation enabled him to ignore and survive.

This reputation was maintained through the thirties and forties as much by his own personality as by the merit of his later plays. Shaw as a person was admittedly an eccentric, not only politically and socially iconoclastic but branching out to involvements in idiosyncratic causes such as vegetarianism, anti-vivisection, spelling reform and woollen clothing. But as a dramatist he is outstanding. The long intellectual dialogues once thought unactable are effective drama simply because the writer always has something interesting or tantalising or moving to say. It is true that he uses the stage as a vehicle for propaganda, social reform and as a method of presentation for the ideas already expressed in the prefaces. But the conflict of personalities and of ideologies or concepts in the plays is carried into a new dimension where understanding in the intellectual sense is bulwarked by sensitivity and sensibility. D. L. P.

Shaw, Irwin (1913–), American novelist and dramatist, first became known with his play *Bury the Dead* (1936), a one-act pacifist fantasy in which a group of dead soldiers refuse to be buried. However, it was his first novel, *The Young Lions* (1948), one of the most widely read novels of World War II, that established his reputation as a challenging if somewhat sensational writer on topical themes. In this novel he goes beyond the war itself to a consideration of its origins, selecting as his chief characters a Nazi sportsman, a displaced Jew and an irresponsible American.

Shaw continued in this genre, among his subsequent works being *The Troubled Air* (1950) which examined the sickness of American society by focusing attention on the virtually untenable position of the *bona fide* liberal.

Later titles include *Voices of a Summer Day* (1965). K. R. R.

Shaw, Robert (1928–), English novelist and actor, whose novels include *The Hiding Place* (1959), in which two British airmen kept captive and in ignorance of the war's ending by a fearful but kindly German who saved them from the Gestapo get the opportunity to escape when their captor becomes ill; *The Sun Doctor* (1961), the story of a British doctor in Africa who becomes a kind of Schweitzer-figure and featuring the extraordinary so-called Whitaker Negroes, putative descendants of a freakish tribe supposedly obtained as slaves for an eighteenth-century planter; and *The Flag* (1965), the first volume of a trilogy to be called *The Cure for Souls* and which tells of a vicar who arrives in a small town in East Anglia with a revolutionary new form of Christian socialism. *The Man in the Glass Booth* (1967) was a successful play. P. E.

Shearing, Joseph. See **Long,** [Gabrielle] Margaret.

Sheldon, Edward B. (1886–1946), American playwright whose drama *The Boss* (1911), featuring a crooked contractor-politician based on a then well-known real-life figure, was among the most notable of the 'serious' social plays that preceded the great development of American theatre in the 1920s. Sheldon had earlier written the sensational play *The Nigger* (1909) about a white man with Negro blood who has become a state governor. K. R. R.

Sherriff, R. C. (Robert Cedric Sheriff; 1896–), English playwright. He began writing plays for an amateur dramatic society; his first play for a professional cast, *Journey's End* (1928), ran for 594 performances. Called by James Agate 'a work of extraordinary quality and interest' it was an honest and moving portrayal of life in a dugout on the western front in 1918. He has since written other plays, film scripts and novels including *St Helena* (1934), *Miss Mabel* (1948) and *Home at Seven* (1950). G. S.

Sherwood, Robert (1896–1955), prolific American dramatist who was Franklin Roosevelt's speechwriter and biographer. His works include *Abe Lincoln in Illinois* (1938), based on the patriarch's early life and including passages taken from his actual speeches and writings. This won a Pulitzer prize, as also did *Idiot's Delight* (1936) and *There Shall Be No*

Night (1940) which like several of his other writings of the period portray the behaviour of widely differing personalities under the approaching cloud of European war. K. R. R.

Shklovski, Victor Borisovich (1893–), Soviet writer, is first and foremost a literary theoretician. His formalist ideas influenced Kaverin, Olyesha and Zamyatin and can be seen in his important paper *Literatura i kino* [*Literature and Cinema*] (1923). His own literary style is somewhat difficult to read. He tries to make people stop reacting automatically to the outside world. His autobiography *Sentimental'noye putyeshestviye* [*A Sentimental Journey*] (1923)—after Sterne—is an interesting collection of literary devices designed to keep the reader aware of the author's presence. B. W.

Sholokhov, Mikhail Alexandrovich (1905–), Soviet novelist, is one of the most widely known Soviet writers. He was born and grew up among the Don Cossacks with whose way of life he closely identified himself, and his literary output evolves around them. His first work of importance, *Donskiye rasskazy* [*Tales of the Don*] (1925), attracted little attention, and the first volume (1928) of his epic *Tikhii Don* [*Silent Don*; first part also trans. as *And Quiet Flows the Don*] might not have been published had not the writer Serafimovich realised the novel's potential as a great work.

The turbulent and bloody years of the first world war and the civil war are vividly described in this and the three subsequent volumes, the last of which appeared in 1940. The hero, Grigory Melekhov, personifies the desires of men for a home and peaceful life. The plot traces the aspirations of the Cossacks for independence and their failure to achieve it. The narrative describes the bitter fighting, the hatred between Red, White and 'Green', the atrocities committed, the apparent hypocrisy of the 'justice' of each cause, and the disillusionment and frustration the hero eventually feels towards it all. The silent Don is the unifying factor that has been and will remain the permanent feature when this seemingly world-shattering epoch is over. Sholokhov sympathetically portrays the violent emotions of the period. His realism jerks the reader into conscious awareness of the bitterness engendered by the civil war. The character descriptions are vividly done, especially Grigory's. The novel has been enormously popular in Russia because so many people identified themselves and sympathised with the hero who was much more convincingly drawn than any of the Bolshevik heroes.

Podnyataya tselina [*Virgin Soil Upturned*] (1930), and its later continuation [*Harvest of the Don*] (1955–59), detail the terrible suffering of the peasantry during the enforced collectivisation of the land. Not as well written as *Silent Don*, these are nevertheless important documents about the period, for Sholokhov once again does not allow his overt Marxist sympathies to cloud his eyes to the realities of the situation. Both these and *Silent Don* caused quite a stir because they did not openly advocate the Bolshevik cause as necessarily being the correct one. Parts of them have been altered occasionally to satisfy contemporary official criticism, but even these changes do not damage the remarkable qualities of the novels. A notable later work is *Sud'ba chelovyeka* [*One Man's Destiny*] (1958), a powerful short story about an ordinary Russian soldier during World War II and how he faces up to the misfortunes the war brings him. The ending of this story offers real hope for a better future. During the post-Stalinist era, Sholokhov's international reputation again expanded, and in 1965 he was awarded the Nobel prize. B. W.

Shute, Nevil (Nevil Shute Norway; 1899–1960), English-born novelist who settled in Australia. His first book *Marazan* was published in 1926 and from then on until the end of the second world war he divided his time between writing and engineering. He worked as managing director of an aircraft factory, and his autobiography *Slide Rule* (1954) illustrates very clearly the conflict between his two careers. In one of his best novels *No Highway* (1948) he drew on his knowledge of aircraft design to tell a compelling story about the effect of metal fatigue on the safety of an aeroplane. After the second world war he settled in Australia and many of his later novels such as *A Town Like Alice* (1950) and *The Far Country* (1952) were set there; but towards the end of his life a feeling of despair crept into his writing, culminating in *On the Beach* (1957) dealing with the effect of atomic war and the final destruction of the human race. However, in his last novel *Trustee from the Toolroom* (1960) he returned to something like his old style. K. M. H.

Sigerson, Dora (1866–1918), Irish poet. Sigerson wrote vivid poetry of a narrative and ballad form. Her work is influenced by her Catholicism, her involvement with the cause of a free Ireland and by her friendship with Katherine Tynan. Her published verse includes *Ballads and Poems* (1898); *Love of Ireland* (1916); and *Sixteen Dead Men and Other Ballads of Easter Week* (1919). D. L. P.

Sillanpää, Frans Eemil (1888–), Finnish novelist and winner of the 1939 Nobel Prize for Literature. A stylist and idealist yet never detached from reality, he introduces a strong vein of naturalism into his work which manages not to clash with the frequent poetic texture of his prose.

His best-known novels are *Hurskas Kurjuus* [*Meek Heritage*] (1919), *Nuorena nukkunut* [*Fallen Asleep While Young*] (1931) and *Ihmiset suviyössä* [*People in the Summer Night*, 1966] (1934). R. C. W.

Sillitoe, Alan (1928–), English novelist and short-story writer, whose first novel *Saturday Night and Sunday Morning* (1958) was greeted as an authentic picture of the anarchic rebelliousness aroused in the industrial working class of today by the pressures of 'the world' (other people's cynical self-interest coupled with stale and hypocritical conventions of behaviour) on the limited areas of personal freedom. Arthur Seaton, young, tough and vigorous, day-dreams away his week at the lathe, earning as much as he dare with the minimum of effort, until he can surface at the weekend: Saturday night being the occasion for aggressive, devil-may-care self-assertion—for putting on his best clothes and throwing his money around, for getting obstreperously (and ultimately nauseously) drunk, and ending up in bed with the wife of his stodgy workmate Jack. For every Saturday night, however, there is a Sunday morning of reckoning and reconciliation; and the long 'Saturday night' of Arthur's years of rebellion, culminating in his being savagely beaten up by two soldier-friends of Jack's, gives way to a 'Sunday morning' in which he finds a measure of peace and contentment in his love for, and half-willing domestication by, a nubile though virginal girl of conventional ideas. The novel conveys vividly the sordid realities that accompany his adventures, notably the gin-and-hot-bath abortion when he has made Jack's wife pregnant.

If Arthur Seaton may be said to sell out by settling down, the borstal boy in the title story of the volume *The Loneliness of the Long Distance Runner* (1959) finally refuses to come to terms with the world which for a time has very nearly won him over to its standards. This long short-story is the most perfectly realised of Sillitoe's work in its concentration on the thought processes that occur in the boy's mind. He battles shrewdly with the governor who, discerning in him the makings of an athlete and thinking to use him to vindicate his own ideas of reintegrating the delinquent into a competitive society, treats him preferentially, like a prize racehorse to be fed and trained for his capacity to win the long-distance race against a local public school. During the long race the boy evolves his own morality—that the only honest thing to do is to lose the race deliberately, thus showing that he will never accept the governor's terms.

Sillitoe subsequently published *The General* (1960), an ambitious symbolic novel, not entirely successful, about a general who, having captured an entire orchestra, allows them to give one final concert. On hearing the music he is undermined as a strategist and soldier, and begins to lose his war. He has also published some highly praised (and prize-winning) poetry; a volume of short stories, returning to the delinquent anarchic world of the petty criminal, *The Ragman's Daughter* (1963); and two further novels, the picaresque *The Death of William Posters* (1965) and *A Tree on Fire* (1967). S. R.

Silone, Ignazio (Secondo Tranquilli; 1900–), Italian writer and politician. Born in an underdeveloped district of central Italy, he made an early start in politics and took part in the foundation of the Italian Communist Party which he left however in 1930 to join the Socialist Party in exile. After his return to Italy at the end of the second world war he again took an interest in active politics but has remained somewhat on the autonomous fringe of Italian socialism.

He published, while in exile, *Fontamara* [*Fontamara*] (1930), a searing exposé of the exploitation of the peasants of an Abruzzi village under the fascist régime. This was followed by *Pane e vino* [*Bread and Wine*] (1937) and its sequel *Il seme sotto la neve* [*The Seed Beneath the Snow*] (1940), on the subject of the underground activities of a young anti-fascist, Pietro Spina, in his bid to fight the dictatorship. The long political essay *La scuola dei dittatori* [*The School for Dictators*] (1938, revised edition 1962) is essentially an attempt to define the meaning of democracy and an indictment of fascism and nazism.

To Silone's post-war production belongs *Una manciata di more* [*A Handful of Blackberries*] (1956) in which he defines the conflict between Marxism and Christianity in the light of the story of Rocco who becomes estranged from the Communist Party; *Il segreto di Luca* [*The Secret of Luca*] (1956), on the moral issues connected with a grave miscarriage of justice affecting a young peasant; and *La volpe e le camelie* [*The Fox and the Camellias*] (1960), in which Silone again deals with the issue of the struggle against the fascist dictatorship. Other works include the play *Ed Egli si nascose* [*And He Did Hide Himself*] (1944), based on *Pane e vino*, and a revised version of the latter entitled *Vino e pane* ['Wine and bread'] (1955). A collection of short stories is also available in English under the title *Mr Aristotle*. A prominent part in Silone's work is played by the countryside, along with his belief in the values of humanity. He married in 1944 the Irish writer Darina Laracy who has translated some of his works. His autobiography *Uscita di sicurezza* ['Safety exit'] appeared in 1965. D. B.

Simenon, Georges (1903–), Belgian novelist. Born in Liège of French and Dutch parents, Simenon joined the *Gazette de Liège* at the age of sixteen. Three years reporting court proceedings and local politics, military service, and seven years writing pulp fiction in Paris served to form and inform the novelist. In 1930 he began to publish his 'semi-literary' works, the Maigret novels. Closely based on police methods, they presented in Maigret one of the most complete figures in modern fiction, and differed from most examples of the genre in their concern to illumine human motives. (Simenon does not write 'thrillers': the reader is invited to deduce not who committed the crime, but why it was committed.) The success of the Maigret novels persuaded Simenon that he was now ready to write 'serious' works. Since the thirties some two hundred of these 'plain' novels have appeared, several set in the United States where Simenon lived for ten years; and in the years that followed the second world war, this author of the potboilers of the twenties, and of the early Maigret novels, was to produce—side by side with the later Maigret books such as *La Première Enquête de Maigret* [*Maigret's First Case*] (1949) —such excellent serious novels as *L'Aîné des Ferchaux* [*Magnet of Doom*] (1945), *Lettre à mon juge* [*Act of Passion*] (1947), *Feux rouges* [*Red Lights*] (1953), and *L'Horloger d'Everton* [*The Watchmaker of Everton*] (1954). Most are brief, densely written analyses of a weak or obsessional character facing a crisis, in which he either perishes or rises above his tragic flaw. Simenon often succeeds in his aim of 'depicting man stripped of his pretensions' and his austere prose seldom fails as a perfect vehicle for creation of atmosphere and swift delineation of character. D. H. G.

Simon, Claude (1913–), French novelist. Born in Tananarive, he lives in Perpignan and has studied in Paris, Oxford and Cambridge. After the war he published his novel *Le Tricheur* ['The cheat'] (1946), followed by *La Corde raide* ['The taut rope'] (1948), *Gulliver* (1954) and *Le Sacre du printemps* [*Seed Shall Serve*] (1954). *Le Vent* [*Wind*] (1957) and *L'Herbe* [*The Grass*] (1958), however, are the novels which first made him well known. In neither is there a clear 'story'; *Le Vent* relates the revolt against the world by an 'innocent' (in the Dostoyevskian sense of the word), while *L'Herbe* is the story of an old woman dying, her niece and the niece's husband and lover. In both the originality lies in Simon's style, a barrier to comprehension which hypnotises the reader. *La Route des Flandres* [*The Flanders Road*] (1960) is as complex. The hero, Georges, is mobilised in 1940 and his regiment, commanded by a cousin of his mother, de Reixach, is defeated and wiped out. In the prison camp he tries to recreate, as an antidote to his position, the legend of the Reixach, in company with his orderly, Iglésia. *Le Palace* [*The Palace*] (1962) is apparently the story of an episode of the war in Spain, but like several of its predecessors attempts to convey the total reality of the time. In 1967 Simon won the Prix Médicis with his *Histoire* ['Story']. D. E. A.

Simonov, Konstantin Mikhailovich (1915–   ), Soviet poet, novelist and playwright. Though he began his literary career by writing intimate verse, and gained popularity with his war-time lyrics, it is perhaps his novel about the fight for Stalingrad, *Dni i nochi* [*Days and Nights*] (1944), on which his reputation stands. This is largely accepted as the best and most objective of Soviet works not only about Stalingrad but about the whole war, despite its conventional love-plot. His plays are weaker than his novels, but *Russkiye Lyudi* [*The Russians*] (1942) about civilian war-time heroism is worthy of note. Simonov subsequently moved closer to the liberal camp, enunciating after his attack on Ehrenburg's *Thaw* that a writer must have the opportunity to answer his critics; and he incurred censure for helping to publish Dudintsev's *Not By Bread Alone*. His novel *Dim otyechestva* ['Smoke of the fatherland'] (1947) was anti-war and appeared even to promote peaceful co-existence. He later followed the trilogy trend with his fictionalised war memoirs: *Tovarischi po oruzhiyu* ['Comrades in arms'] (1953), *Zhiviye i myortviye* [*The Living and the Dead*] (1960) and *Soldatami nye rozhdayutsya* ['Soldiers are not born'] (1963.)

B. W.

Simpson, Helen (1897–1940), Australian-born novelist who has lived abroad for most of her adult life. She is best known for *Under Capricorn* (1937), a historical novel set in the Sydney of the 1830s. It is written with a restraint which contrasts strongly with the emphatic exaggeration of most of the novels involving convicts, transportation and exploration.

S. R.

Simpson, N. F. (Norman Frederick Simpson; 1919–   ), English playwright. His first play, *A Resounding Tinkle*, won third prize in the *Observer* play competition of 1956 and was produced at the Royal Court Theatre in the following year. Like his other plays it lacks continuity, relying on twists of phrasing and *double entendre* for its effect. 'What about the platoon sergeant who sent his men into a wood to take care and when they got there, said: you can take it easy, now, lads, we're out of the wood' asks one of his characters. This is a typical example of his humour, which stems from apparent paradoxes in language. 'I want to go on record' says another and soon he is speaking as if the needle has caught in the groove. The limits of this kind of writing, which owes something both to Lewis Carroll and Edward Lear, are immediately obvious and his plays are somewhat arid. *One Way Pendulum* (1959) was his most successful work to date. Here he tries to achieve continuity through content rather than its form. Apparently trivial objects begin to take over the lives of people. By building himself a model of the Old Bailey, a man finds himself in the dock; a young man with speak-your-weight weighing machines has them singing in chorus. Like the rest of his work it lacks drama and functions through a structure of *reductio ad absurdum.*

Later plays include *The Cresta Run* (1965). K. G.-Y.

Sinclair, May (1865–1946), English novelist, whose books reflect her own distinctive feminism and anti-Victorianism as well as her absorption of the psychology of Freud, the social ideas of Shaw and Wells, and the literary technique of Joyce. *Mary Olivier* (1919) involves most of these in its account of a girl's escape from the damaging effects of a repressive upbringing. May Sinclair drew considerably on the experiences of herself and of people she knew or knew about: *Three Sisters* (1914), another account of a Victorian upbringing, being based on that of the Brontë sisters. K. R. R.

Sinclair, Upton (1878–1968), American novelist, whose passionate and thoroughly documented attacks on the manifold evils of American capitalist society in the first quarter of the century have had a great and manifest social impact (for example in leading to prompt reform of food laws) while at the same time marring the quality of his purely literary achievement.

The Jungle (1906), probably his best-known book, records the career of the Lithuanian immigrant stockyard-worker Jurgis Rudkis from youth, health, innate happiness and optimism, with a beautiful wife and a bonny child, to being an unemployed, destitute physical wreck with his wife and baby dead; and thence via tramping, crime, political graft and further destitution to the espousal of socialism. A similar end is reserved for Bunny Ross, a plutocratic oil-magnate's son, in *Oil!* (1927). These and other novels of the period, in addition to the distortions of polemic and overdocumentation, suffer from oversimplification of character and issues; but they are books of great and compulsive power.

Sinclair continued to write prolifically through a further four decades, *World's End* (1940) being the first of an extensive series known by their central figure Lanny Budd. K. R. R.

Singer, Isaac Bashevis (1904–), American novelist and short-story writer, born into a Polish Rabbinical family, the younger brother of Israel Joshua Singer who wrote *Di Brider Ashkenazi* [*The Brothers Ashkenazi*] (1936). Singer first wrote in Hebrew, then turned permanently to Yiddish. In 1935 he emigrated to America and since that date has been a regular contributor to the New York *Jewish Daily Forward*, the paper in which many of his novels and stories have been serialised prior to publication. Indeed, bibliographically, he is something of a curiosity; some of his books are still unobtainable in Yiddish though available already in English translation, such as *Der Kunzenmacher Fun Lublin* [*The Magician of Lublin*] (1960), *Der Kurzer Freitog* [*Short Friday*] (1964) and *Der Hoif* [*The Manor*] (1967); some, like *Der Knecht* [*The Slave*] (1967), appeared first in translation then in the original; others, such as *Gimpel Tam* [*Gimpel The Fool*] (1964) and *Der Spinozist* [*The Spinoza of Market Street*] (1964) are published as one book in Yiddish and two in English; finally, as in the autobiographical *In Mein Tatn's Beis Din* [*In My Father's Court*] (1956), there are translations of collected pieces that differ in their contents from the Yiddish version. Singer's best-known works in English are probably *Der Soton in Goray* [*Satan in Goray*] (1953), published in Warsaw, a novel set in seventeenth-century Poland during the confused years of Messianic expectation consequent upon the Chmielnicki massacres, a period which gave birth not only to the Chassidic sect but to many more transitory and less reputable manifestations of religious fervour; and his masterpiece *Di Familie Mushkat* [*The Family Moskat*] (1950), an epic narrative of modern Warsaw Jewry before the holocaust, perhaps most succinctly described as a Yiddish *Buddenbrooks*. Many American authors have claimed Singer for their spiritual father, which is one reason for reading him; another is Bernard Malamud's *dictum* that today we are all Jews, and Singer, like Chaim Potok, is a mine of information on our traditions. M. D. E.

Sinyavsky, Andrei D. (1926–), Soviet writer and critic who, together with Daniel, was arrested in 1965 for pseudonymously publishing abroad (as 'Abram Tertz') works allegedly critical of the Soviet Union. His first short-novel, the nightmarish *Sud idyot* [*The Trial Begins*] (1959), written in stimulating but slightly unpolished style, was followed at intervals by the other stories. 'Tertz' was introduced as a young writer, although his knowledge of the twenties suggested he was a much older person. His writing reveals a high standard of culture and awareness of other literatures which he utilised in his attack on the tenets of socialist realism for their distortion of the purpose of literature in his essay *On Socialist Realism* (1959). B. W.

Sitwell, Edith (1887–1964), English poet and critic. Edith Sitwell does not easily categorise into any literary movement of the twentieth century. Like her brothers, Sacheverell and Osbert, she is a highly gifted eccentric. She was born at Scarborough into the pre-1914 world of the English landed aristocracy and her popular reputation owes much to the British reverence for a combination of nobility and singularity.

Edith Sitwell's early poetry is alternately experimental, light, imagistic, macabre, wistful—making for a spectrum of highly coloured qualities. During the first world war she edited *Wheels*, an annual magazine to which both she and her brothers contributed a great deal of work. Her style undergoes constant change and development: *Sleeping Beauty* (1918) takes on the surface fantasy of a fairy story, *Façade* (1922) is light, evocative and rich in imagery, while *Gold Coast Customs* (1929) is a macabre satire. After 1940 the poetry begins to change in texture, surface delicacy giving way to deep-rooted passion and religious involvement; and she was converted to Roman catholicism in 1954. However the overall impression that her work gives, as does that of Marianne Moore in a very different context, is of a series of aesthetic mobiles—a reaction of sensibility to the phenomena of beauty, the expression being sometimes elegant, sometimes flippant, sometimes fantastic but always melodious. She creates her own internally consistent world from particles stolen from the world outside, which she transforms and weaves like a spider into a fragile web:

> I always was a little outside life—
> And so the things we touch could comfort me;
> I loved the shy dreams we could hear and see—
> For I was like one dead, like a small ghost,
> A little cold air wandering and lost.

Editions of her *Collected Poems* were published in 1930 and 1957. Her critical works include *Alexander Pope* (1932) and a book on Swift, *I Live Under a Black Sun* (1937). A later volume of verse, *Music and Ceremonies*, was published in 1963, and an autobiography *Taken Care Of* was issued posthumously in 1965. D. L. P.

Sitwell, Sir Osbert (1892–), English poet, novelist and man of letters. Sitwell's background is that of the landed aristocracy. He succeeded as baronet to his father in 1943 having been schooled at Eton and served in the Grenadier Guards. Despite the satire and humour of his writing a deal of arrogance, howbeit intellectual, shows through. His poetry, *Argonaut and Juggonaut* (1919), is concerned with war but also catalogues English personality types in an essentially satirical manner. However the main body of his work lies in a five-volume survey of his family history which includes his personal development from childhood in a series of nostalgic reminiscences of an England in the period before 1914—possibly the most pleasant period to live in ever for the English upper classes. The volumes were titled: *Left Hand! Right Hand* (1944); *The Scarlet Tree* (1945); *Great Morning* (1947); *Laughter in the Next Room* (1948); and

Noble Essences (1950). *Tales My Father Taught Me* (1962) delightfully retails incidents in the life of the author's interesting and eccentric father Sir George Sitwell, whose characterisation in the family history is one of its most memorable features. D. L. P.

Sitwell, Sacheverell (1897–), English poet, critic and travel writer. Sitwell's poetry, like that of his sister Edith, is rich, imaginative and aesthetic. He is possessed of a descriptive love of beauty focused on the artifacts of artistic creativity and on the past. *Collected Poems* were published in 1936 and a book of *Selected Poems* in 1948.

As an art critic he published a number of volumes including *Canons of Great Art* (1933), and as a serious student of music, studies of *Mozart* (1932) and *Liszt* (1934). His travel books, which include a volume on *Portugal and Madeira* (1954) and one on Peru entitled *Golden Wall and Mirador* (1961), often involve substantial elements of art criticism; while the earlier critical volume *Spanish Baroque Art, with Buildings in Portugal, Mexico and other Colonies* (1931) may also be read as a travel book.

D. L. P.

Skinner, Cornelia Otis (1901–), American humorist, who has produced several volumes of light essays including *Tiny Garments* (1932), *Soap Behind the Ears* (1941) and *Nuts in May* (1950). But perhaps the most enduring of her works, written in collaboration with Emily Kimborough, is the autobiographical *Our Hearts Were Young and Gay* (1944), a wry and amusing chronicle of the experiences of two naïve but resourceful young girls on their first trip to Europe. S. R.

Slater, Francis Carey (1875–1958), was the first important English-language South African poet. Of his eight books of verse, three especially stand out for the qualities of empathy, utterance and evocation that together make them encompassingly South African: *Drought* (1929), *Dark Folk* (1935) and *The Trek* (1938). *Drought* contains moving poems of deep compassion, marred only by unintegrated tropes that vitiate the starkness of the otherwise profound imagery; *Dark Folk* often touches the heights of Vilakazi's visions, with subtly organised rhythms, images, metaphors and elements of vernacular, lacking only social context, as *The Trek* lacks historical perspective, to give them lasting excellence. C. P.

Slessor, Kenneth (1901–), Australian poet whose excited and fanciful youthful poetry later found a more suitable theme in the sea and ships. However, it is in the work of his third phase—characterised by reflection on time and memory—that he produced his greatest achievement. These three phases can be clearly seen in the three sections of *One Hundred Poems 1919–1939* (1944), later made available with additional material as *Poems* (1957). S. R.

Smith, Logan Pearsall (1865–1946), American-born essayist. His early collections, such as *Trivia* (1902), are now little read; but his autobiography *Unforgotten Years* (1938) can still make absorbing reading. K. R. R.

Smith, Pauline (1884–1957), South African novelist and short-story writer whose volumes *The Little Karroo* (1925) and *The Beadle* (1926) are minor classics. The former contains sensitive sympathetic re-enactments of the sufferings of the simple primitive people of Aangenaam ('Pleasant') valley in the arid Karroo. The complete wedding of style and theme in the englished Afrikaans of *The Beadle*—which evokes the poetic simplicity of the remote Boer community's existence, and has for its theme the innocent love of an Afrikaaner girl for an irresponsible young Englishman, whose sins are repeated in the child and eventually visited on the father—no doubt suggested themes and modes to, amongst others, Paton and Daphne Rooke. C. P.

Snow, C. P. (Charles Percy Snow; 1905–), scientist, novelist and administrator, born—like Lewis Eliot, the central character of nine of his first twelve novels—into a lower-middle-class family in provincial England. Lewis Eliot studied law, whereas Snow himself was a scientist, but both became fellows of a Cambridge college, and both entered the civil service. Snow gave up his research to write novels; was knighted for his public service in 1957; delivered a famous lecture at Cambridge in 1959 on 'The Two Cultures' and was subsequently reviled by the don and critic F. R. Leavis; and became Parliamentary Secretary to the new Ministry of Technology in the Labour administration of 1964, entering the upper house as Lord Snow. In 1950 he married Pamela Hansford Johnson, a fellow novelist. For his novels, Snow has drawn on his wide experience of public life, filling their pages with meticulous portraits of dons, civil servants, politicians, businessmen and industrialists—and above all (since few novelists have enjoyed similar first-hand experience) of scientists. *The Search* (1934), his third novel, depicts some of the human factors involved in scientific research; while in those later novels that portray dramas within a Cambridge college, an atomic energy research establishment, and a government department, we see scientists concerned not only with science but with moral and political issues as well. Snow's understanding of scientists as people qualified him for his various appointments concerned with the direction of scientific personnel, with the Royal Society (1939), the Ministry of Labour (1942) and the English Electric Company (1944); and it was widely recognised that whatever criticisms might be levelled at the profundity of his conclusions, or the cogency of their statement, there were few people better qualified than Snow to talk about the division of twentieth-century society into two cultures, the humanistic and the scientific, as he did in his published lecture *Two Cultures and the Scientific Revolution* (1959).

After *The Search*, Snow did no more research of his own; and the following year he conceived the idea of the sequence of Lewis Eliot novels—to which he eventually assigned the title of the first book of the series, *Strangers and Brothers*. These novels—eleven planned, nine published by the late 1960s—are about man in society. Taken together they form a remarkably comprehensive picture of our times; but Snow's purpose in portraying a complete society is to exhibit the forces it exerts on its individual members together with the impact that those individuals make in their attempts to shape it. It is also to show that in the social nexus we are all inevitably brothers; but that each individual is eternally himself and himself alone, and in the last resort is a stranger to all others.

The series is arranged in three cycles: in each cycle there are two or three novels of what Snow calls 'observed experience', in which Lewis Eliot is primarily an onlooker, together with one of 'direct experience' with Eliot as the central figure linking the narrative by telling his own story. The experiences of 'strangers' can never register in the same way as one's own: and Snow makes Eliot experience some of the things that he has witnessed, or will subsequently witness, in the lives of his friends, so as to achieve a dual perspective.

The first cycle covers the period of Eliot's early life, and is mainly set either in his native provincial town or in London. In *Strangers and Brothers* (1940) which covers the period 1925–33, Eliot tells the story of George Passant, a dedicated lecturer at the night school in his home town; and in *The Conscience of the Rich* (1958) set in London from 1927 to 1936, that of Charles Marsh, a wealthy fellow-student. Eliot's own narrative, covering the years 1914–33, is *Time of Hope* (1949). George Passant is an idealist, whose method of changing the world is to stir up his students to free themselves from restricting conventions of thought and behaviour. He is perhaps the most vivid of a number of Snow's characters who, though not strictly politicians, nonetheless find themselves involved in a political situation through their attempts to change society. Reactionary forces are set in motion; malicious gossip flows freely, while pressures are exerted behind the scenes; and the protagonist finds himself exploited at his point of weakness and is all but destroyed. In the story of the Marsh family we find another recurring problem, the effect of possessive love: the embarrassment of wealth driving Charles to a renunciation which increases the disharmony already existing between himself and his father. Eliot's own story during this period is largely concerned with his relationship with his mother, and his first marriage. It traces also his career as a lawyer, and his involvement in left-wing politics. His inability to respond to his mother's possessive love—echoing Charles Marsh's experience with his father—finds its counterpoint in his tragic love for a girl who is incapable of returning it: it is precisely because she is incapable that he is able to love her. Thus is stated the central theme in Eliot's own story: 'the pride or vanity which . . . prevented me going into the deepest human relation on equal terms'.

The second cycle starts in the mid-thirties and extends to the end of the war and the dropping of the atomic bomb. Much of it is set in Cambridge, where Eliot has become a fellow of the college. *The Light and the Dark* (1947) is about the brilliant young scholar Roy Calvert, cousin of Eliot's wife, who has appeared as a boy in *Strangers and Brothers*; *TheMasters* (1951) deals with the election of a new Master of the college; and *The New Men* (1954) is about a group of British scientists—including Eliot's younger brother Martin, and Walter Luke, already familiar from the Cambridge novels—engaged in research into nuclear fission during the war years. In all three there is the background of events in Europe. Eliot's own narrative is *Homecomings* (1957), covering a ten-year period from 1938. Eliot's interest in Roy Calvert, who is a manic-depressive, stems from his own knowledge of the havoc that can arise from some fundamental flaw in a person's character—Roy's career being threatened by scandal arising out of the depraved behaviour through which he escapes from his melancholia. In despair he looks for an authority outside himself, turning first to religion, then flirting with nazism; finally he becomes a bomber pilot, deliberately courting death. Equally dramatic, though in a quite different way, is the story of the election of a new Master, with the complexity of the intrigue and the constant fluctuation of the candidates' fortunes making it seem representative of the political struggles of a whole society. In the end it is the wider political issues that tip the balance, in favour of the man whose political sympathies are with the left. Now the spotlight falls on the scientists—'the new men', men endowed as never before with the power to make history: on their personal hopes and fears as they work on such a challenging project, the problem of their moral responsibility for the use to which it will be put, and the temptation to refuse to make their knowledge known. Threading through the book there is the uneasy relationship between Lewis Eliot, now a civil servant, and his brother Martin, who gains a position of administrative importance: a relationship vitiated by Lewis's acting out of his own hopes and fears for his brother's well-being. We are back with his own fundamental flaw: and when he takes up his story again, it is to tell how he has at last begun, in his second marriage, to come to terms with it.

Of the third cycle, only two books had been published by the late 1960s: *The Affair* (1960), set in Cambridge in 1953–54, and *Corridors of Power* (1964) dealing with the career of a Tory minister in the period 1955–58. 'The affair' is a scientific fraud allegedly perpetrated by a young physicist of the college, a man devoid of social graces and possessing extreme left-wing political views at a time when these have become unfashionable. He is twice judged to be guilty by the senior members of the college, before a legal investigation—in which Eliot is called in to act for him—transfers the blame to a colleague now dead. When the scene shifts to the corridors of Whitehall, we are back with the by now very familiar older generation of civil servants and scientists, involved this time in the evolution of a new defence policy by a Tory minister of unorthodox ideas. And in this the most political of all Snow's novels there are repeated references back to the 'politics' of the college—and suggestions, perhaps, of the 'politics' of Eliot's native town, of the scientific world, and of any other society within a society. But the central figure this time is a professional politician, a man with a real if limited opportunity to influence the pattern of events. As with George Passant, the forces of reaction and cynical self-interest come into play; again they are able to play on a weakness—this time a marital infidelity. But Roger Quaife, the minister, is himself a determined and skilful manipulator: and the issue is uncertain almost to the end.

Only as the sequence has progressed towards completion has its pattern become apparent. What has not altered is the way in which each book is sufficiently self-contained to be read in detachment. There is such a considerable variety that it is tempting to think that many of the books were conceived as separate entities: some gain power from being more dramatic, or less detailed, or less far-ranging; while others seem open to F. R. Leavis's criticism that the reader, instead of seeing an event actually occurring, merely hears about it from the discursive narrator.

Other titles include *Varieties of Men* (1967), a collection of portraits of some of Snow's contemporaries. K. R. R.

Soldati, Mario (1906–), Italian writer, journalist and film director. His intense literary activity has brought forth a number of works of which the best-known is *A cena col commendatore* [*Dinner with the Commendatore*, also translated as *The Commander Comes to Dine*] (1950), consisting of three diverting anecdotes told by a disillusioned theatrical impresario. In *Le lettere da Capri* [*The Capri Letters*] (1954) Soldati attempts, through the experiences of an American couple living in Italy, to capture the dilemma of the puritanical mind brought into contact with a Latin environment. With *La confessione* [*The Confession*] (1955) he explores the psychological reactions of a young boy to the morbid preoccupation with sin—identified with woman—obtaining in the unhealthy atmosphere of a seminary where religious education is carried to a one-sided extreme. *Il vero Silvestri* [*The Real Silvestri*] (1957) deals with the theme of the shocking discovery, through a chance encounter, of the evil side of Gustavo Silvestri's personality by one of his friends, the Turin lawyer Peyrani. Soldati's writing, which is rich with invention and captivating detail and occasionally borders on surrealism, often contains elements of surprise and an analysis of the devious paths of the human mind.

D. B.

Sologub, Fyodor (Fyodor Kuzmich Teternikov; 1863–1927), Russian writer, characterised as a symbolist. He was born in St Petersburg and though poor, received a good education which eventually enabled him to become first a schoolteacher and later a school inspector. He hated his job and sought relief in writing verse and prose but it met with little enthusiasm upon its eventual publication. However in 1907 after a false start he published what has become recognised as one of the best examples of Russian symbolist prose. This novel, *Mel'ki Bes* [*Little Demon*], is a remarkable description of life in a provincial town and in particular a perspicacious portrayal of the degeneration of a petty paranoid called Peredonov, who is a schoolmaster by profession and a sadist by inclination. No evil is beyond him but eventually so obsessed does he become with the demoniac symbol of his own wickedness that he goes mad. Sologub attempts to counteract the wickedness with his symbol of good in the person of a young schoolboy, but fails. Nevertheless the book was welcomed warmly into the realms of symbolist literature. In a way it is autobiographical, as was his first novel *Tyazholiye sny* ['Bad dreams'] (1896), but this cannot be said of his later work *Tvorimaya legenda* ['The created legend'] (1908–12). The fantastic stories and exquisite verse of these volumes are excursions into the world of the occult, where he shows superficial reality to be but an illusion, and death appears as the great liberator. Sologub, condemned as a decadent, was hostile to the revolution but was not allowed to leave the country. He stopped writing in 1922; his talented wife committed suicide, and Sologub died shortly afterwards.

B. W.

Solzhenitsyn, Alexandr Isayevich (1918–), Soviet novelist who sprang into prominence in 1962 with his descriptive novel about life in a prison camp. He was born in Rostov-on-Don and served in the army after completing his university studies. At the end of the war he spent eight years in concentration camps for passing unfavourable remarks about Stalin. After his release he submitted his novel *Odin den' Ivana Denisovicha* [*One Day in the Life of Ivan Denisovich*] (1962) for publication, and it is reliably reported that Khrushchev was instrumental in getting it published. The novel is extremely controversial for its theme had scarcely been touched in preceding Soviet literature. As its title implies, it details for just one out of nearly four thousand days the activities of one prisoner in the camp whose 'crime' was to have been captured by the Germans. Among his fellow-prisoners are many who have done similarly 'criminal' acts. The rule of life is to look after oneself in the most basic way, yet despite everything some human values still manage to hold good and increase the stature of the prisoners. The tiniest details of camp life, and the most marginal personal ups and downs, become almost fantastically magnified and acquire the status of major human events. In *Matryonin dvor* [*Matriona's House*] (1963) in relating how he refound work after his imprisonment and exile Solzhenitsyn describes Matriona in whose house he found lodgings. This meek, good person, misunderstood by the selfish collective-farm workers, lives her life to help others in need. B. W.

Soutar, William (1898–1943), Scottish poet. Born in Perth, the son of a carpenter, Soutar was one of the more important figures in the Scottish renaissance. He wrote both in Scots and English in a style combining delicacy with wit. *Collected Poems* was published in 1948; *Diaries of a Dying Man* in 1954. D. L. P.

Soya, Carl Erik Martin (1896–), Danish short-story writer, playwright and novelist. Soya's earliest reputation was established by a constant stream of witty and satirical short stories and by one relatively important novel *Min Farmers Hus* ['My farmer's house'] (1943). Despite his passionate desire to become a prominent dramatist he was for many years never more than moderately successful in his productions. Ultimately he succeeded with an impressive tetralogy: *Brudstykker af et Mønster* ['Fragments of a pattern'] (1940), *To Traade* [*Two Threads*] (1943), *30 Aars Henstand* ['Thirty years' respite'] (1944) and *Frit Valg* ['Free choice'] (1948). Written in the Ibsenian manner these plays further imitated the theatre of Ibsen by posing problems which Soya himself did not care to resolve. In the context of the theme of retributive justice they illustrate the ambiguity of the laws and accidents of human existence. In the comedy

Frit Valg justice is stood on its head; the honesty of the protagonist brings suffering to others, while his dishonesty is the source of their contentment. The translation of *To Traade* is available in Elias Bredsdorff's *Contemporary Danish Plays* (1955). R. C. W.

Soyinka, Wole (1935–), Nigerian writer, prolific, brilliant and versatile. He has produced outstanding work as a poet ('Idanre' in *Verse and Voice*, 1965, and other anthologised pieces) and as a novelist (his book *The Interpreters*, 1965, which received wide critical acclaim); but he is best known as a playwright. *Five Plays* (1965) brings together *The Strong Breed* (1962), technically and thematically interesting for its use of flashback to examine the function of a 'carrier'—the annual scapegoat of a remote Nigerian village; *The Swamp Dwellers* (1962); *The Trials of Brother Jero* (1962), a sharp but humorous satire centred on a revivalist 'prophet'; *The Lion and the Jewel* (1963); and *A Dance of the Forests* (1963) which exposes chauvinistic myth-making. *The Road* (1965) is a profound amalgam of African and European thought and dramatic modes. C. P.

Spark, Muriel (1918–), Scottish-born novelist, one of the most consistently successful writers of English fiction to emerge after the second world war. Her early reputation was based on a series of gently humorous tales, mainly set in London, and featuring characters of an unusual nature or in unusual circumstances. At its most lightweight—as in *The Ballad of Peckham Rye* (1960), recounting the impact on Peckham life and commerce of a genially diabolical 'arts man' from Edinburgh—her early fiction gives little hint of the stature to be achieved by her later works; but in *The Bachelors*, whose main character is not only a London bedsitter bachelor but also an epileptic and a Roman catholic, and in *Memento Mori* (1959), all of whose principal characters are in varying stages of senescence, there are penetrating studies of what it is to belong to these particular minority groups with patterns of living quite distinct from that of the healthy married couples in their prime who make up the bulk of the population. It is from groups such as these that are drawn the chief characters of her later, more weighty novels.

The first of these was *The Prime of Miss Jean Brodie* (1962), the story of a remarkable Edinburgh schoolmistress whose unorthodox educational theories include the initiation of her girls into her own experiences of life and love. Despite her avowed sympathy for the dictators of the thirties, it only gradually becomes clear to her adoring pupils that in her ideal of education as a process of leadership she is herself a born fascist. But the book in which she most dramatically enlarged her scope was the much-praised *The Mandelbaum Gate* (1965). Set in the Holy Land, with personal relationships becoming inevitably entangled in the mesh of religious and political ones, it centres on three characteristically singular personalities: Barbara Vaughan, a half-Jewish English Catholic spinster engaged in a pilgrimage, to whom love has come late in life in the person of a divorced protestant; the English diplomat Freddy Hamilton, a middle-aged bachelor whose undogmatic gentleness and tolerance, while a suitable antidote to the violent passions of Arab and Jew, nonetheless provoke the committed pilgrim Barbara into attacking him for being 'lukewarm . . . neither cold nor hot'; and the emancipated young Arab girl Suzi Ramdez who finds a fullness of life precisely in escaping from the stifling hot and cold of religion and politics. For Barbara the pilgrimage into Jordan, where her Jewish blood endangers her, is as important for the affirmation of her own individual identity as the disinterested, personally motivated assistance given by Suzi is for the latter; but for Freddy the violence done to his personality by his own bid for identity through a liberating commitment—organising Barbara into carrying out her journey clothed as an Arab servant-woman, playing truant from his work in order to help her, and eventually sleeping with Suzi in the course of a night spent in spontaneous counter-espionage—is too great, and he suffers a lapse of memory.

Other titles include *Girls of Slender Means* (1963), a lightweight novel; *Doctors of Philosophy* (1963), a play; *Collected Poems* (1967); *Collected Stories* (1967); and a further novel, *The Public Image* (1968). K. R. R.

Spencer, Bernard (1909–), English poet. Spencer uses the clarity of his perception and firmness of intellect to compose verse that records the immediate and the sensuous in individual human lives. His first volume *Aegean Islands* (1946) is not concerned with classical Greece nor with the richness of history but simply records the sea and the sky, the warmth of the earth and the heat of the sun. He is involved with a hedonist enjoyment of food and wine and with a liking both for the pattern of peasant life and for the elegance of sophisticated women. He enjoys those aspects of life which please the mind and those which please the flesh. *The Twist in the Plotting* (1960) is less immediate and more melancholy in tone but records still a delight in the grace of human movement and the pleasures of the human environment. Spencer's poetry is both elegant and refreshing in its lightness of touch. D. L. P.

Spender, Stephen (1909–), English poet. Spender was educated at University College, Oxford, and in the 1930s became a member of the Marxist group surrounding Auden and Isherwood. His autobiography *World within World* (1951) carries portraits of Auden, Isherwood, Day-Lewis and MacNeice. With Isherwood he travelled widely in pre-war

Germany and other parts of Europe. Since the war he has been Professor of Poetry at the universities of Cincinnati (1953) and California (1959). Spender was co-editor of the Anglo-American magazine *Encounter* from 1953 until 1967 when he resigned following the discovery that, without his knowledge, the magazine had been backed financially by the American C.I.A.

Spender's early poetry is concerned like that of other members of his Marxist group with the social and economic consequences of the depression. The images in his poetry are the mechanical functions of industry, and his ideals the reforming ideals of socialism. A great deal of this verse of the thirties was contributed to the magazines *New Verse* and *New Writing*. Where Spender differs from Auden and (say) Wyndham Lewis is with the reflection in his work of personal involvement. Instead of interest in ideas for their own sake, and abstract reforming zeal, his work expresses compassion for particular people. Also his eventual swing away from Marxism was not in the grand manner of Auden (to Christianity) or of Isherwood (to mysticism); it was, rather, to a personal involvement in an art that touches upon the lives of individuals, in a way that politics, dealing as it does with the abstract and with the impersonal manipulation of masses, cannot. The experience of Spender's poetry is a process of self-revelation in which the reader joins in the discovery of universal truths in personal depth, rather than the totalities and generalisations of Wyndham Lewis and Auden.

The following lines are from 'Elegy for Margaret', in *Poems of Dedication* (1947):

> I look into your sunk eyes,
> Shafts of wells to both our hearts
>
> It can only prove
> That extremes of love
> Stretch beyond the hideous flesh to hideous bone
> Howling in hyena dark alone.
>
> Oh, but my grief is thought, a dream.
>
> Poverty-stricken hopeless ugliness
> Of the fact that you will soon be dead.

Spender's *Collected Poems 1928–1953* was published in 1954. D. L. P.

Spengler, Oswald (1880–1936), German cultural philospher, was originally a mathematician. His ideas became part of the European heritage with the famous study *Der Untergang des Abendlandes* [*The Decline of the West*] in 1918. Spengler argued that the development of the city as the standard social organism meant the ultimate extinction of civilisation, a theme he was to elaborate in *Der Mensch und die Technik* [*Man and Technics*] (1931), in which man is described not only as suffering from urbanisation, but ultimately the victim of the machine age. Spengler's pursuit of the morphology of culture led him to deny the dependence of one culture upon another; Roman culture was not based on the Greek, but was an independent organism which grew, flowered, withered away and died. This, according to Spengler, was true of modern Western culture. An early work *Preussentum und Sozialismus* ['Prussianism and socialism'] (1920) with its demands for a fusion of nationalism and socialism led to the saying that Spengler 'held Hitler over the baptismal font', but in the aptly named *Jahre der Entscheidung* [*Years of Decision*], published in the year when Hitler came to power (1933), he rejected the ideas of racial purity which were central to national socialism and argued instead that the Jews should be absorbed into the German '*Volk*' because of their intellectual vitality; further, he pleaded for the development of 'heroic pessimism' and urged that the urban proletariat be deprived of any real power in the state. G. W.

Spillane, Micky (Frank Morrison Spillane; 1918–), American writer of detective novels. Spillane's books combine a forceful narrative line with crude sex and blatant sadism. The stories centre on a private investigator, usually Mike Hammer, whose attitudes do not differ materially from those of the criminals he pursues. The difference is created by a conventional line drawn quite arbitrarily between morality and immorality. Blondes are undressed and characters cut in half by machine-guns on both sides of the line with equal regularity. The books are immensely popular. The best known is *I, The Jury* (1947). D. L. P.

Spring, Howard (1889–1965), English novelist. Born in Cardiff, and brought up in poverty, he was forced to leave school at eleven years old because of the death of his father. His first published work was a children's book *Darkie & Co* (1932), which he wrote to amuse his own children, but his first novel *Shabby Tiger* appeared in 1934 and was followed by a sequel *Rachel Rosing* (1935). Then in 1938 he won fame with a world best-seller *O Absalom*, later called *My Son, My Son*, and he was able to retire to Cornwall. Many of his later novels were set in Cornwall and most of them, like *Fame is the Spur*, portray the struggles of a central character from poverty to fame. There is a Dickensian quality about his novels which are thickly and richly peopled and full of melodrama.

He has also written three autobiographical works describing his own fight against adversity: *Heaven Lies About Us* (1939), *In the Meantime* (1942), and *And Another Thing* (1946). K. M. H.

Squire, Sir John Collings (1884–1958), English poet. Squire wrote in the Georgian school of pastoral poetry but introduced parody into his work. As an editor of anthologies he was responsible for *The Comic Muse* (1925) and *The Cambridge Book of Lesser Poets* (1927). His own verse includes *Poems and Baudelaire Flowers* (1909) and *Collected Parodies* (1921). An autobiography *The Honeysuckle and the Bee* was published in 1937.

D. L. P.

Stacpoole, Henry de Vere (1863–1951), Irish-born novelist. His romantic novel *The Blue Lagoon* (1909), set in the south seas, became a best-seller and was followed by a large number of other works in this genre—*The Ship of Coral* (1911), *The Pearl Fishers* (1915), *The Gates of Morning* (1925), *Green Coral* (1935) and many others. R. A. K.

Stapledon, William Olaf (1886–1950), English novelist who was an early exponent of science fiction in the sense of predicting and analysing future human development. This he did to great effect in *Last and First Men* (1931), a provocative first work which was followed by several others in the same vein including *Last Men in London* (1932), *Waking World* (1934) and *Worlds of Wonder* (1949). R. A. K.

Stark, Freya (1893–), English travel-writer born in Paris. An experienced traveller and explorer in little-known parts of Arabia and the eastern Mediterranean, she has been honoured by geographical societies, and worked on government service during 1939–45 helping to enlist Arab support for the Allied cause. She describes her journeys with humour and sensitivity. Her titles include *Baghdad Sketches* (1933), *The Valleys of the Assassins* (1934), *The Southern Gates of Arabia* (1936), *Letters from Syria* (1942) and *East is West* (1945). Autobiographical volumes include *Traveller's Prelude* (1950), *Beyond Euphrates, 1928–33* (1951) and *The Coast of Incense, 1933–39* (1953). G. S.

Stead, Christina (1902–), Australian-born novelist who left the country in 1928 and has since spent periods of her life in America, Paris and London. A novelist of remarkable intelligence, sophistication and style, her first published work was *The Salzburg Tales* (1934). This was followed by *Seven Poor Men of Sydney* (written earlier but published in 1934) concerning young revolutionaries of the 1920s, and interesting for its portrayal of the seedy Sydney waterfront, revealing its international rather than provincial character. The book which most displays her unusual talents is probably *The Man who Loved Children* (1940; reissued to critical acclaim in 1966). It describes unbelievably savage warfare between a husband and wife. Sam Pollitt is an egomaniac, moraliser and collector of facts, whose mind is a vast compendium of natural lore and liberal and philanthropic philosophies—so ill-digested and contradictory that in his elaborations upon them he reveals the primitive and even fascist subconscious desires that lurk beneath. His lack of culture and of true understanding make him an arid travesty of civilised man, the ironic title commenting on his unfitness to be father to his tribe of seven children, the rôle which above all he cherishes. His wife Henny is his opposite, a wild dark furious termagant, dragged down from her rich society background by endless childbearing and her own financial incompetence to a harsh and increasing poverty. The children—in particular Louisa the eldest, an ugly duckling saved by luminous intelligence—devise all manner of self-protective mechanisms to survive the bitter struggles. The book is above all about the microcosm of the family, its private languages and rituals, and its complex relationships; it is utterly unsentimental but deeply moving in its glimpses of lulls in the marital storm, of Sam's occasional true generosity of spirit and of Henny's surprisingly deep love for the children thrust upon her. Despite unmanageably rich and varied material, the structure of the book is firmly controlled: the first half expansive, turbulent and comic, the second retrenched, bitter and tragic.

Her other books include *The Beauties and the Furies* (1936); a work dealing with the rise of international banking, *The House of All Nations* (1938); *For Love Alone* (1944); *A Little Tea, A Little Chat* (1949); *The People with the Dogs* (1951); and *Cotters' England* (1967), which creates a gallery of characters locked in conflict and irresistible bonds of affection, and is on the same scale as *The Man Who Loved Children.* S. R.

Stein, Gertrude (1874–1946), American writer, remembered as a shrewd and encouraging patron of the *avant-garde* both in painting and writing, and as an author whose style reached the ultimate in abstraction. In *Three Lives* (1908) she wrote intelligibly and with sympathetic humour, and where the style of the intractable *Tender Buttons* (1915) was modified from the extreme of intellectual obscurity, as in *The Autobiography of Alice B. Toklas* (1933), she could state her highly self-opinionated views on people and ideas coherently and with a pungency unalloyed with either morality or tact. The value of those views is debatable. Her object was intellectual exactitude and the avoidance of associational emotion in writing, and her real value to posterity is as a provoker of thought and as a scourge of the woolly-minded. H. C.

Steinbeck, John (1902–1968), American novelist, has spent much of his life in and around his birthplace, the beautiful Salinas valley in California. In his first novel, the historical romance *Cup of Gold* (1929), he tried, like the book's hero, the buccaneer Henry Morgan, to transcend the limitations of the small world that he knew intimately; but for most of the succeeding quarter-century his writing was dominated by his experience of his native region—the land with its beauty and fertility (whence the recurring Eden image), its human inhabitants whom he had come to know intimately by working with them in every conceivable capacity from agricultural chemist to labourer in a road gang, and its animal life. His representation of the life of 'the long valley' is at once religious and scientific, with archetypal scriptural images embedded in an awareness of its biological patterns and relationships.

In 1930, after a decade of varied living—for the first five years he had studied intermittently at Stanford University, before trying his hand as a reporter in New York—he married and settled down near Monterey, at the mouth of Salinas river. His next novel in order of writing, *To a God Unknown* (1933), was a nature myth. Although set in California, its characters are no more real than those in *Cup of Gold.* But with *Pastures of Heaven* (1932)—one of the many variations on the Eden theme—he struck a literary form and style which was to produce several of his most famous works: the series of loosely connected stories about various members of a community, strung together so as to create a theme or pattern, written in a manner at once realistic, sentimental and humorous. The first of these was the immensely popular *Tortilla Flat* (1935).

In Monterey, Steinbeck had met the marine biologist Edward Ricketts, and had come to share his interest in the animal life around the coast—in particular in the phenomenon of a group of tiny creatures functioning as one organism. His interest in the animal life of the valley had already led him to see that much of human behaviour could be understood by thinking in terms of animal behaviour (and especially of such principles as the survival of the fittest and the continuity of life); now he saw that the phenomenon of group, family or community behaviour—to be explored in so many of his novels—could be greatly illuminated by a biological approach. In addition, he was influenced by Ricketts's own biological philosophy—which might be summed up by saying that he refused to allow his observations to be coloured by any theory as to nature's purpose. In Steinbeck, this had produced an all-embracing love of every variety of life undistorted by any ideas of what should or should not be: a love which could look with equanimity at human freaks and social outcasts. Such are the community of idle *paisanos* (peasants of mixed blood) who inhabit Tortilla Flat on the outskirts of Monterey. In the America of the 1930s they have lacked as individuals the ruthless self-interest necessary for economic and social survival; but as a group—and even at a more basic level as individuals—they have what Steinbeck was later to call a 'strong survival quotient'. True they cheerfully steal their food from a restaurant, and to obtain a gallon of wine they will resort to all manner of amiable trickery; while Danny, their leader, has nothing more serious to engage in than amatory exploits. But they can also be generous to each other and to anybody in need, and are truly anxious for nothing—least of all for property of any kind. Their adventures are described in mock-Arthurian style, suggesting an almost legendary quality for their sanity and happiness.

However, there is slightly more to it. Set against the social miseries of the great depression, *Tortilla Flat* could not fail—however objective and biological its author was trying to be—to be a comment on American society. In fact, Steinbeck goes so far as to say of Danny and his friends that they are 'clean of commercialism, free of the complicated systems of American business and, having nothing that can be stolen, exploited or mortgaged, that system has not attacked them very vigorously'. And when Danny inherits a pair of houses from his grandfather, his friends feel it necessary to commiserate with him for having become a man of property. 'Let money come and charity flies away,' one of them adds. Any reader detecting a religious overtone in this passage will not be surprised to find that Danny and his friends are privileged to witness a miracle in the course of their adventures. This semi-political, semi-religious aspect of *Tortilla Flat* was to reappear very strongly in Steinbeck's writings during the years that followed.

His next novel, *In Dubious Battle* (1936), was a grim story of strikes and strike-breaking. Although in all sincerity Steinbeck claimed that he was being completely objective, it is difficult not to feel the author's sympathies to be with the strikers. However, it is worth saying that he had been interested in the phenomenon of a strike as another example of group behaviour amongst human beings—and in particular in the ability of the individual to submerge his own separate existence. Then came *Of Mice and Men* (1937), subsequently adapted as a highly successful stage play. Here the group consists of only two people: Lennie, a physical giant with the mind of a child, and George his protector, shrewd and practical. In a world consisting almost entirely of single men—the ranching country of the west, with its system of casual labour—they cut an odd figure. Without the responsibility of caring for Lennie, who does not know his own strength and is always getting into trouble, George would be free to enjoy himself on his month's earnings like the others. But the truth is that he derives as much security and stability from the relationship as does Lennie; and in their plans to set up house together and lead a settled existence, they have a contentment and sense of purpose that is denied to the others. However, 'the best laid plans of mice and men gang aft agley':

and Lennie, himself something of a mouse, is destined to wreck everything by his fondness for playing with soft things. At the beginning of the story we see him pathetically holding a mouse that he has crushed to death; at the end, when he has choked to death a girl who has lured him into fondling her, it is himself who must be killed to save him from being lynched.

Apart from a general consciousness of the unsettled economic and social background, there are no obvious political or religious overtones to the story of George and Lennie. However, this was to be followed by what is certainly Steinbeck's most celebrated work, the massive epic *The Grapes of Wrath* (1939)—the first version of which was scrapped because it was too much a piece of political propaganda. The story of the Joads, a dispossessed farming family from the Oklahoma dustbowl, making their prodigious trek to the promised land of California, only to find themselves ruthlessly exploited and reduced to near-starvation, is rooted in history: and the alternate chapters of the book set their story in perspective by tracing the experiences of the migrant community as a whole. Steinbeck's approach to the story is at once biological and political. Starting with an account of the unbalanced relationship between man and nature that has produced the dustbowl, he proceeds to describe how the unfortunate share-cropping Okies fall victims to the profits system: the evictions cannot be blamed on individual human beings, say the emissaries of the banks that own the land, it's just that banks have to have profits. A bank, it is suggested, has its own collective existence: it is another group organism. However, for all its quasi-biological objectivity, this in itself constitutes a criticism of the American way of life—as did the happiness of the propertyless *paisanos* of Tortilla Flat. And although the collective resilience and durability of the Joads and the strikes which occur at the end of the book can be fairly thought of as objectively studied group behaviour, the passages dealing with the machinations of the Californian employers, to attract by deliberate publicity a pool of reserve labour and then cut wages ruthlessly to near the bread-line—and the even more horrifying accounts of fruit being coated with tar and thrown into the sea in order to maintain a scarcity and keep the prices up—these can only be analysed in political terms. This is not to say that the book reads like a tract: Steinbeck had already rejected one version for that reason. It is to say that it is a work of art with strong political implications.

No fewer than six of Steinbeck's novels have titles with a religious flavour, and the phrase 'the grapes of wrath' comes from Julia Ward Howe's religio-political 'Battle Hymn of the Republic' ('Mine eyes have seen the glory of the coming of the Lord'). Both the story of the trek and the style in which it is told have the strong Old Testament flavour that is to be found so often in Steinbeck's writing, with California in prospect taking on the attributes of 'the land flowing with milk and honey'. But in this novel the religious element is more profound, centring in the rôle of the ex-preacher Jim Casey (his initials are clearly intended to be significant) who travels with the Joads. Having found orthodox Christianity unsatisfactory, he is gradually evolving a new kind of religion, with a flavour of Edward Ricketts reflected in such utterances as 'There ain't no sin and there ain't no virtue. There's just stuff people do' and 'Maybe all men got one big soul ever'body's a part of'. More important is the practical expression given to this last statement: his emergence as leader of the strike movement, and its first martyr.

When the book ends, Tom Joad has set out to follow in Casey's footsteps. But the last action lies with his sister Rose of Sharon, whose child has been born dead as a result of malnutrition: offering her milk to a man who has become demented with starvation through trying to keep his son alive, she asserts in dramatic form the survival of the migrant community through solidarity and interdependence—and, at the most basic level, the continuation of life through every kind of vicissitude, which has been prefigured by the famous early chapter about the progress of a turtle.

During the war years, Steinbeck worked as a journalist. Both the books he published during this period—*Bombs Away* (1942) and *The Moon is Down* (1942)—were conceived as part of the war effort. He returned to one of his own characteristic brands of fiction with *Cannery Row* (1945), another set of stories about a group of social outcasts in Monterey. Since the writing of his pre-war books, he had been on an expedition (in 1940) with Edward Ricketts to study the marine life of the gulf of California; and his biological approach to the new set of characters is more explicit than before, as for instance when he talks of opening the pages and letting them 'crawl out'. Furthermore, the central character, Doc, is himself a marine biologist and one of several portrayals of Ricketts.

The religio-political element is also more marked than in *Tortilla Flat*: at the outset Steinbeck states that from one viewpoint the inhabitants of Cannery Row are 'whores, pimps, gamblers and sons of bitches' but from another they are 'saints and angels and martyrs and holy men'. It may be difficult to think of Mack and the boys either as pimps and gamblers or simply as martyrs and holy men: but to respectable society these amiable creatures are certainly 'no-goods, come-to-bad-ends, blots-on-the-town, thieves, rascals, bums'. To which Steinbeck, looking up at the 'hurried mangled craziness' of Monterey and thinking of 'the cosmic Monterey where men in fear and hunger destroy their stomachs in the fight to secure certain food', replies: 'what can it profit a man to gain the whole world and to come to his property with a gastric ulcer, a blown prostate and bifocals?' Mack and the boys—who 'dine delicately with tigers, fondle the frantic heifers' (more scriptural images)—'avoid the trap and walk round the poison'. Their adventures, mainly centring on their attempts to show their appreciation of Doc, are as comic as those of Danny and his friends; but the combination of New Testament imagery with pungent social criticism makes for much greater weight.

In the two decades that followed *Cannery Row* Steinbeck was constantly experimenting with new material and new techniques. But his prolific writings during this period, though always readable and at times extremely powerful, do not contain anything that is generally accepted as a masterpiece. There is an intensification of the religious element, evident in the anti-capitalist fable *The Pearl* (1947), the morality *The Wayward Bus* (1947) and the epic *East of Eden* (1952). This last work returns to the Eden theme and goes on to explore the problem of evil as embodied in the Cain and Abel myth. However, like *The Grapes of Wrath* it is also semi-documentary—in this case dealing with the author's own antecedents; but the various elements in the book, including a streak of melodrama, are imperfectly fused. Contemporary with these was the dramatic novelette *Burning Bright* (1950), one of Steinbeck's least successful products.

In a more light-hearted vein are the fairly popular *Sweet Thursday* (1954), a nostalgic sequel to *Cannery Row* with Mack and the boys grown self-conscious and near-respectable; and the total contrast of the French political fantasy *The Short Reign of Pippin IV* (1957). In the former, Steinbeck was returning to a well-tried formula after several attempts to break new ground; while the latter represented his most complete break with his native west as a source of inspiration. When he returned again to the American scene, with *The Winter of our Discontent* (1961), it was to a New England setting, and a further attempt to interpret the fall of man with the new material available. In 1962 Steinbeck was awarded the Nobel Prize for Literature. K. R. R.

Stephens, James (1882–1950), Irish poet and novelist. Stephens wrote both prose and poetry of a whimsical and fantastic nature. The content is based on Irish legend, and to an extent both style and content are derived from his Irish contemporary Æ. However, *The Crock of Gold* (1912) is a humorous novel of legend and fantasy that exceeds even the latter's imaginative capacities. *Collected Poems* was published in 1926. D. L. P.

Stern, Gladys B. (1890–), English novelist. Her first novel, *Pantomime*, appeared in 1914, followed in 1917 by *Grand Chain*. Her most significant work consists of the 'Matriarch' novels whose central character is based on the strong personality of her great-aunt. The series opens with *Tents of Israel* (1924) and continues through four further novels, concluding with *The Young Matriarch* (1942). R. A. K.

Stevens, Wallace (1879–1955), American poet. Stevens is one of the most impressive twentieth-century American poets and his work reflects most of the major intellectual and aesthetic problems of literature in his time. He was born in Reading, Pennsylvania, into a family of Dutch origins. He was educated at Harvard and later at the New York Law School, being admitted to the bar in 1904. He later became associated with the Hartford (Connecticut) Accident and Indemnity Company with whom he worked for a lifetime, becoming vice-president in 1934. There appear to have been few tensions between his career in assurance and his work as a poet; Stevens was equally at home in the world of big business as in, say, the atmosphere of Greenwich Village. His published work includes: *Harmonium* (1923), revised in 1931; *Ideas of Order* (1936); *The Man with the Blue Guitar* (1937); *Parts of a World* (1942); *Notes toward a Supreme Fiction* (1942); *Esthétique du Mal* (1945); *Transport to Summer* (1947); *The Auroras of Autumn* (1950); *The Necessary Angel* (essays, 1951); *Collected Poems* (1954); and *Opus Posthumous* (essays and poetry, 1957).

The early Stevens of *Harmonium* is a Romantic owing a great deal to the ideas of Thoreau and Emerson, exhibiting as in the following lines an enjoyment of nature and immersion in the profusion and confusion of images of different quality that strike the eye:

> A red bird flies across the golden floor
> It is a red bird that seeks out his choir
> Among the choirs of wind and wet and wing.

The purpose of the Romantic is essentially to discover meaning from the richness of experience. In the poem 'Sunday Morning' Stevens tries to do just this: to evoke a feeling of satisfaction and fulfilment from the world of visual, tactile and auditory sensation. The heroine of the poem is to feel replete with such satisfactions:

> Like her remembrance of awakened birds
> Or her desire for June and evening tipped
> By the consummation of the swallows' wings.

Unfortunately this is not enough. Stevens requires intellectual and emotional security of a greater order:

> But when the birds are gone, and their warm fields
> Return no more, where then, is Paradise?

The poet becomes concerned to involve himself in a relationship that essentially is transcendental and complete. Though he rejects religion, God and immortality, the context of his whole emotional and intellectual life, expressed in poetry, is the search for meaning. He realises, as in the quotation above, that the heightening of individual emotional experiences is not enough: though each new experience in each new poem is a new contact with reality, there seems no possibility of the general affirmation of experience—as there would be in the continued emotional state of faith.

Aware of his Romantic predicament, Stevens sometimes attempts to sidestep it by making the problems of poetry themselves the subject of poetry. To this extent he is a philosopher. He aims to present intellectual problems in an emotional or aesthetic context, to construct, perhaps, an aesthetic reality. As with Yeats's poetry, this must involve the construction of an artifact over and beyond the flux of life but representing a quality of perfection that is part of it. Such an aesthetic reality tends to become something more significant than life itself because it has greater purity. Contingent with this problem is Stevens's involvement with symbolism especially that represented by the French symbolists such as Baudelaire and Valéry. The object of the symbolists was to use words to evoke an intuitive understanding of the moral and aesthetic world outside the intellectual grasp of men. Since the intellect performs a simplifying process, this other method of using words is necessary to enable one to grasp at the whole of reality instead of small pieces of it. What Stevens sets out to do, then, is to create through symbolism an intellectual and a feeling environment of which the individual is a meaningful part. That is, he wishes to create in a poem a situation where an individual can really feel part of a meaningful environment in a sense of total surrender of his isolation. This problem of man's isolated identity comes up in 'Memoirs of a Magnifico':

> Twenty men crossing a bridge
> Into a village
> Are twenty men crossing twenty bridges
> Into twenty villages
> Or one man crossing one bridge
> Into one village.

(Stevens is concerned, too, with philosophic problems of perception; what can we know and how do we know what we see is real? He remarks: '. . . poetry is to a large extent an act of perception and . . . the problems of perception, as they are developed in philosophy, resemble similar problems in poetry'.)

The poet is thus torn between the imagist idea of observing and describing in detail what is before his eyes, the symbolist doctrine of evoking a higher and non-intellectual reality, and the desire to order and create an aesthetic reality of his own. In the final analysis he finds meaning in the creative act itself.

In an age of belief Stevens's attitudes would be translated into mysticism. But he denies himself anything beyond the lyric contemplation of religious ceremony, as in 'Sunday Morning':

> Supple and turbulent, a ring of men
> Shall chant in orgy on a summer morn
> Their boisterous devotion to the sun,
> Not as a god, but as a god might be
> Naked among them, like a savage source.

Consequently he falls back to the imagination as a creative power next to that of faith. The experience of the poet becomes an act of construction which has its own internal reality. The poet as the constructor becomes his own god. In expressing this, Stevens does not succeed in reuniting emotion with intellect into the single faculty of sensitivity which the seventeenth-century poet Donne achieves:

> Her pure and eloquent blood
> Spoke in her cheeks, and so distinctly wrought
> That one might almost say her body thought.

Instead he places intellectual dilemmas of knowledge and meaningfulness into an aesthetic context and proclaims an individual act of creativity:

> She was the single artificer of the world
> In which she sang. And when she sang, the sea,
> Whatever self it had, became the self
> That was her song, for she was the maker. Then we
> As we beheld her striding here along,
> Knew that there never was a world for her
> Except the one she sang and singing made.
> (from 'Ideas of Order at Key West')

D. L. P.

Stewart, Douglas (1913–), Australian literary figure active in many fields: as editor of the 'Red Page' of the *Bulletin* (since 1941); as a poet (*Green Lions*, 1936; *The Dossier in Springtime*, 1941; *The Birdsville Track*, 1955); and as the author of verse plays suitable for broadcast on the radio, the most famous of which is *Fire on the Snow* (1944). In this, with slow, unforced and very moving poetry, the voices of the five men of Scott's polar expedition enact the events of that heroic and tragic journey. Using the same form, he has also written *The Golden Lover* (1944), *Ned Kelly* (1943) and *Shipwreck* (1947), the last two planned as stage productions but still perhaps better suited to radio. His later publications include the amusing short work *Fisher's Ghost* (1960). S. R.

Stewart, Harold (1916–), Australian poet in whom the unusual combination of influences of oriental culture and western psychology have blended to give poetry of striking originality. He also delights in experimenting with a great number of verse forms, and has a nimbleness and precision with words that gives a crystalline clarity to his generally lyrical tone. He has published *Phoenix Wings* (1948), and the long poem *Orpheus* which was awarded first prize in the *Sydney Morning Herald* competition of 1949, a modern allegory seen in psychological terms. A poem often chosen for inclusion in anthologies is 'A Flight of Wild Geese'. S. R.

Stewart, J. I. M. See **Innes,** Michael.

Stewart, Mary (1916–), English novelist, a lecturer in English at Durham University until her marriage in 1945, scored an immediate success with her first novel *Madame Will You Talk* (1954), and since then has become a well-established writer. Her novels which are a blend of mystery and romance are usually concerned with charming young people involved in adventures in colourful holiday settings. Amongst her most popular novels are *This Rough Magic* (1964) set in Corfu, *My Brother Michael* (1959) also with a Greek setting, and *Airs Above the Ground* (1965), an original story woven around the Lipizzano horses of the Spanish Riding School in Vienna. K. M. H.

Stivens, Dal[las] (1911–), Australian writer whose publications *The Tramp* (1936) and *The Courtship of Uncle Henry* (1946) consist of very short stories, experimental in that they deal with a wide range of subject matter in forms that are varied to suit the topic. A theme common to many of them is man seen at a moment of frustration. Stivens's later collections include *The Gambling Ghost* (1953), *Ironbark Bill* (1953) and *The Scholarly Mouse* (1957). He has also written the novels *Jimmy Brockett* (1951) and *The Wide Arch* (1958). S. R.

Stone, Irving (1903–), American writer of romanticised fictional biography, is best known for *Lust for Life* (1934; based on Van Gogh) and *The Agony and the Ecstasy* (1961; on Michelangelo). K. R. R.

Stone, Louis (1871–1935), Australian novelist, was born in England but came to Australia when he was fourteen. He published two novels, neither of which sold well at first, but which have since come to be regarded as classics of their kind. *Jonah* (1911) was the first novel to take seriously the slum larrikin—the wild boy who flourished in gangs, forerunner of the Chicago hooligan, the English teddy-boy, the Australian bodgie. Though its plot is not very credible, it is fascinating for its description of the larrikins' behaviour and for capturing their vivid and picturesque slang. The second book *Betty Wayside* (1925) is in similar vein. S. R.

Storey, David (1933–), English novelist who made his name with the publication of *This Sporting Life* (1960), the story of a professional rugby-league footballer and his relationship with his withdrawn widowed landlady. The novel derived much of its force from its revelation of the real pain of inarticulacy that lay behind the successful and powerful façade of a football hero. Storey's next novel *Flight into Camden* (1960) also deals with the problems of communication, this time between educated children and working-class parents. *Radcliffe* (1964), an overwhelmingly powerful book, explores, in a quite unprecedented manner, and with a poetry and explicitness reminiscent of D. H. Lawrence, the aggression, violence and struggle for power in a homosexual relationship. Storey has also written the play *The Restoration of Arnold Middleton* (1967). S. R.

Stout, Rex (1886–), American detective novelist, whose most memorable books feature the *bon viveur* armchair sleuth Nero Wolfe and his mobile assistant Archie Goodwin. These include *Fer-de-Lance* (1934), *Three Doors to Death* (1950), *Before Midnight* (1955), and *The Doorbell Rang* (1966) in which Wolfe tangles with the F.B.I. K. R. R.

Stow, Randolph (1935–), Australian novelist and poet. His first volume of verse *Act One* (1957) established him as a lyrical poet of the Australian landscape. In *Outrider* (1962), a collection of poems with illustrations by Sidney Nolan, Stow turns in addition to history, to the explorer and pioneer, and to the outback in order to discover the kernel of human feeling and endeavour that lies behind legend and myth. His first two novels *A Haunted Land* (1956) and *The Bystander* (1957) displayed considerable, perhaps even morbid, psychological insight. He is best known however for the award-winning *To the Islands* (1958) recording on an actual and a symbolic level the journeyings of the chief of an outback mission for the natives and his companion an old aborigine. Similarly constructed on two levels of meaning is *Tourmaline* (1963) which tells of the advent of a mysterious water-diviner on the parched and dying town. Particularly impressive is *The Merry-go-Round in the Sea* (1965), set in Western Australia where Stow's family have been pastoralists for several generations, and thus rich in autobiographical material. It is a tender recreation of childhood and early adolescence: and in a boy's idolisation of his elder cousin, and his dismay at the cousin's disintegration following his experiences as a Japanese prisoner-of-war, is posed the conflict of two ways of life, that of safe, narrow provincial and predictable Australia, and that of unsettling, unknown and unimaginable 'abroad'. S. R.

Strachey [Giles] Lytton (1880–1932), English historian and biographer. Strachey was a member of the Bloomsbury group of intellectuals. In the preface to *Eminent Victorians* (1918) he announces the intention to depart from the conventional form of factual biography and to employ a style of personal attitude and selected insights. The accounts that follow of Cardinal Manning, Florence Nightingale, Dr Arnold and General Gordon are ironic, witty, perceptive, malicious and brilliant. At the time of publication they were shocking. Strachey's best-known biography is of *Queen Victoria* (1921), written with the same criteria as *Eminent Victorians.* The style is so deft and the content so lively that Victoria herself seems to become endowed with Strachey's own qualities. He commented subsequently that he set out to attack but concluded by reluctantly admiring the subject of his book. D. L. P.

Street, Arthur George (1899–1966), English novelist and journalist. Primarily a farmer, he began writing as a hobby in 1931. He also lectured on agriculture and was a frequent broadcaster. His books, whether novels or essays, are mostly quiet sketches set in the English countryside. His titles include *Farmer's Glory* (1932), *Hedge Trimmings* (1933), *Country Calendar* (1935), *Hitler's Whistle* (1943), *Ditchampton Farm* (1946), *Cooper's Crossing* (1962) and *Fish and Chips* (1964). G. S.

Strong, L. A. G. (Leonard Alfred George Strong; 1896–1958), English novelist, poet and critic. A teacher, he gave up his profession on the success of *Dewar Rides* (1929), a rather macabre, brutal novel about a Dartmoor farmer. Cruelty is also portrayed in *The Brothers* (1932). Some of his best short stories are set on the fishing coasts of Ireland. His publications also include the novels *The Garden* (1931), *Sea Wall* (1933) and *Corporal Tune* (1934); a collection of poems *The Body's Imperfections* (1957); and the autobiography *Green Memory* (1960). G. S.

Stuart, Jesse (1907–), American writer about the people of the mountain region of Kentucky, as in the verses of *Man with a Bull-Tongue Plow* (1934), the short stories of *Men of the Mountain* (1941), and the novel *Trees of Heaven* (1940). His later books include *The Good Spirit of Laurel Ridge* (1953). K. R. R.

Stýblová, Valja (1922–), Czech novelist. A neurologist by profession, she deals in her novels with contemporary social problems in Czechoslovakia. Her novel *Mne soudila noc* [*The Abortionists*] (1957), the confession of a medical student, gives a picture of youth demoralised by the Nazi occupation. K. B.

Styron, William (1925–   ), American novelist, whose titles include *Lie Down in Darkness* (1951) and *Set This House on Fire* (1960). The former recounts, against the background of the progress of a funeral, a southern family tragedy in which a chain reaction of unsatisfactory relationships has had its climax in a young girl's suicide, following the destruction of her marriage through her incestuous feelings for her father. Later titles include his Pulitzer prizewinning novel *The Confessions of Nat Turner* (1968). K. R. R.

Supervielle, Jules (1884–1960), French poet and novelist. Born in Montevideo, Uruguay, he spent his early childhood there and divided his life between South America and Paris. Orphaned at an early age, he published about ten collections of verse between 1919 and his death. The most important of these are probably *Gravitations* ['Gravitations'] (1925), *Le Forçat innocent* ['The innocent prisoner'] (1930) and *La Fable du monde* ['Fable of the world'] (1938). His poetry is generally unrhymed but otherwise close to regular verse; his syntax is clear, but he avoids being prosaic by a freshness of vision and originality of feeling.

His novels include *L'Homme de la pampa* ['The man of the pampa'] (1923), *Le Voleur d'enfants* [*The Colonel's Children*] (1926) and *Le Survivant* [*The Survivor*] (1928); the last two forming a unity, in the story of Colonel Bigua of Montevideo who is forced to leave Uruguay and spend some time in Paris. His sterility affects him greatly, and he adopts children who return with him to South America. After an unsuccessful attempt at suicide he flees from his wife and mother, to find his feet eventually on a small estate. This work is symbolic and poetic in atmosphere. Supervielle also published, by contrast, some very light and humorous short stories—*L'Arche de Noé* ['Noah's ark'] (1938), *Orphée* ['Orpheus'] (1948)—and plays including *La Belle au bois* ['Sleeping beauty'] (1932) and *Bolivar* (1936). D. E. A.

Svevo, Italo (1861–1928), Italian novelist. 'Italo Svevo' was the pseudonym of Ettore Schmitz, a prosperous businessman born in Trieste of German-Jewish stock. He died in a motoring accident after a brief fame consequent on the discovery of *La coscienza di Zeno* [*The Confessions of Zeno*] (1924) by James Joyce and Valéry Larbaud. The early novels, *Una vita* [*A Life*] (1893) and *Senilità* [*As a Man Grows Older*] (1898), attracted minimal attention in the flamboyant years of D'Annunzio, although they anticipate *Zeno* much as Proust's *Jean Santeuil* prefigures *Remembrance of Things Past*. Svevo's distinctive, unfurbished language, his preoccupation with the leisure hours of Italians active in the commercial life of an Austro-Hungarian city, his precocious bourgeois interest in Freudian mythology, encouraged by the proximity of Vienna, accidents of birth, geography and temperament, all alienate him from the mainstream of national life and literature. He remains curiously middle-European, his Trieste an Italianate Lübeck, and, as Saba remarked, he might easily have written in German. His examination of the individual consciousness, the neuroses, mistresses, literary and social aspirations of his protagonists, his disenchantment by the formless, purposeless, provincial world, can suggest the influence of Maupassant, Flaubert, psychoanalytical theory and Schopenhauer, invite comparison with Pirandello and still contrive an indubitable originality. *Senilità* and *Una vita* chronicle banal love affairs, Zeno's confessions are prompted by an attempt to stop smoking, but plot is relatively unimportant here and Svevo's diffident appraisal, always ironical, pessimistic, ambivalent, achieves comic grandeur with Zeno: 'Unlike other illnesses life is always mortal. It admits of no cure.' M. D. E.

Swinnerton, Frank (1884–), English novelist and critic. His novels deal mainly with the same strata of society as are portrayed by Wells and Bennett but with a greater awareness of the cheerfulness behind the difficulties of lower-middle-class life. Of his novels, *Nocturne* (1917), *Shops and Houses* (1918), *September* (1919), *Young Felix* (1923) and *Harvest Comedy* (1937) are typical of this style and approach. But he is probably best known for his lively commentaries upon his contemporaries in *The Georgian Literary Scene* (1934), one of the most revealing surveys of writing and writers of his day. Later novels include *Death of a Highbrow* (1961). R. A. K.

Symons, Arthur (1865–1945), English poet and critic. Symons's main contribution to the developments of English literature is the volume *The Symbolist Movement in Literature* (1899) which introduced the French symbolist poets to an Anglo-Saxon audience, deeply affecting the poetic form of writers and the attitudes of readers of English verse. The French symbolists such as Baudelaire and Verlaine and their philosophic spokesman Bergson believed that intellect was a perverting force; they wished the reader to experience meaning through the symbolic effects of images, words and sounds that would give an overall feeling of what the poet meant, rather than be offered the emptiness of a simplified, categorising type of rational conclusion. Of the English-speaking poets, Yeats was particularly influenced by Symons's book.

Symons's own poetry combines this concept of aesthetics with a very real personal nervous disorder which disjoints his work and of which he writes in *Confessions: A Study in Pathology* (1930). D. L. P.

Synge, John Millington (1871–1909), outstanding tragedian of the Irish theatre, who went to the peasant people of the Aran islands in Galway bay for his inspiration and found there 'a popular imagination that is fiery, magnificent and tender'.

He was born in Dublin of an Anglo-Irish landowning family and went to Trinity College, Dublin. He spent many years wandering through France, Germany and Italy, but returned to Ireland at the suggestion of W. B. Yeats, who met him in Paris in 1899. He wrote for the Abbey Theatre, Dublin, and it was without doubt Synge's plays that did the most to establish the popularity of the new Irish drama. From the Aran islanders he assimilated a whole living peasant tradition, complete with its own legends, customs and language, which he reduced to a most precise and concentrated dramatic form.

The core of his plays is man's conflict with his environment, which involves a constant evocation of the ephemeral nature of beauty and the near approach of death. In a grim comedy *The Shadow on the Glen* (1903) natural beauty and the ugliness of old age are directly weighed against each other. The story is of the old cuckold who by feigning death outwits his wife, who is eventually driven out to walk the roads with a passing tramp. The tramp however holds out the prospect of a far fuller life: '. . . you'll be hearing the herons crying out over the black lakes, and you'll be hearing the owls and the grouse with them, and the larks and the big thrushes when the days are warm'. *Riders to the Sea* (1904) is a profound and passionate symbolic one-act tragedy, whose theme is the struggle of the Aran islanders against the sea, which is in this case the personification of the fatality of life. The old woman Maurya has lost all her sons but one, Bartley, to the sea. Bartley is going to sail with the horses to sell them in Connemara and she fears for him and cannot bless him, seeing him haunted by his brother Michael, whom she sees riding behind Bartley on the grey pony 'with fine clothes on him, and new shoes on his feet'. *Deirdre of the Sorrows* (1910) was Synge's attempt to use a more formal, remote legend and it suffers from a corresponding lack of immediacy. The characteristic Irish speech previously so well manipulated becomes a little clumsy when transferred to a traditionally heroic action.

The Playboy of the Western World (1907) combines in the most typical manner possible the tragic theme (a son Christy claims that he has killed his tyrant father, thereby achieving heroic status) with the comic (the supposed-dead father is resurrected and comes to prick the bubble of his son's glory). The mock-epic nature of the play is enhanced by Christy's prowess in the village games (recalling Homer's funeral games), which raises his stature to a high local pitch just at the time when his father appears. The tragic element returns at the end, however, for the hero vanishes and the reconciliation of father and son leaves the innkeeper's daughter Pegeen desolate: 'O my grief, I've lost him surely. I've lost the only playboy of the western world'. The play has a richness which *Riders to the Sea* does not, for the latter being entirely tragic simply transmits a sense of fatality in life, though raised in spite of its down-to-earth speech and reality of setting to the level of poetic image. *The Playboy* on the other hand leaves the audience in an unresolved state of mind and emotion, still only too aware of the richness of life on both levels, tragic and comic.

Synge also wrote some poems, and a most interesting account of his life in the west of Ireland (*The Aran Islands*, 1907). Other plays are *The Well of the Saints* (1905) and *The Tinker's Wedding* (1908). G. C.

T

Taffrail (Captain Henry Taprell Dorling, R.N.; 1883–1968), English novelist and naval historian. A writer of lively sea stories, he also produced readable histories of the war at sea, particularly during the second world war. Titles include *Pirates* (1929), *The Shetland Plan* (1939) and *Arctic Convoy* (1956). R. A. K.

Tagore, Rabindranath (Ravindranath Thakura; 1861–1941), Indian poet, novelist, short-story writer and essayist. Tagore was born in Calcutta and came to England to study in 1878. His native language was Bengali; the first translation into English was of *Gitanjali* [*Song Offering*] which was published with an introduction by Yeats in 1912. It is composed of lyrics and songs on nature, love and childhood. Tagore was awarded the Nobel Prize for Literature, mainly for this work, in 1913. The poet's reputation in his own country is still massive, mainly for the *Ravindrasandeit* which are poems set to music. His early reputation in England was based on a view of his work as mystical and religious, although the centre of Tagore's creativity is in the lyrical mode.

Other English translations include *One Hundred Poems of Kabir* (1914); *Broken Ties and Other Stories* (1925); *Collected Poems and Plays* (1936); and the autobiographical *My Reminiscences* (1917). Tagore's poem 'Lord of the Heart of the People' is now the Indian national anthem. D. L. P.

Tarasov-Rodionov, Alexandr (?–1937?), Soviet writer whose book *Shokolad* [*Chocolate*] (1922) created a spate of controversy when it was published since it explained at some length how the secret police kept the communists in power, and laid bare the truth of 'revolutionary Soviet justice'. Thus he implicitly raised the question of communist morality. The novel anticipated the system used in the purges of the thirties when many old Bolsheviks 'confessed' to fabricated crimes, and the author himself eventually disappeared from the literary scene, branded on account of his novel as an enemy of the people. B. W.

Tarkington, Booth (1869–1946), American novelist, was essentially a scion of the genteel tradition of American fiction who tried in his novels to come to terms with 'progress' and social change. In *The Magnificent Ambersons* (1918; Pulitzer prize) we meet an Indiana family whose failure so to come to terms is a cause of its downfall. However, there is no doubting their magnificence; and there is no question of the essential barbarism of the 'business heroes' of such later novels as *The Plutocrat* (1927), and *The Midlander* (1923)—which, together with *The Turmoil* (1915) and *The Magnificent Ambersons*, completed a trilogy entitled *Growth*. K. R. R.

Tarsis, Valeriy (1906–), Soviet writer who became so critical of the Soviet system that in 1966 he left Russia for the west. He was born in Kiev, and after university he did some writing and translating for a publishing house. During the war he was badly wounded at Stalingrad. The seeds of disillusionment were sown early, for both his father and his father-in-law were obliterated during Stalin's rule. His highly critical writings were not published, and so he sent his stories out of the country. For his own safety *Sinyaya mukha* [*Bluebottle*] (1962) and *Krasnoye i chornoye* [*Red and Black*] (1962) were published in England under the pseudonym Ivan Valeriy, but Tarsis always admitted his authorship. He was eventually incarcerated in a mental hospital, but as a result of protests from the west he was released and his experiences appeared in the autobiographical *Palata No. 7* [*Ward 7*] (1965). It derives its title from Chekhov's *Ward 6* and tells how a writer who has sent critical books abroad to be published finds himself in a psychiatric ward. Nearly all the other inmates are there because they too are so mad that they cannot appreciate the wonders of communism. The writer is eventually released through the help of a sympathetic doctor. Tarsis' novel *Kombinat naslazhdyeniy* [*The Pleasure Factory*]—a study of a proletarian Nice on the Black Sea—appeared in English in 1967. B. W.

Tate, Allen (1899–), American poet and critic, has been concerned to examine the fundamental structure of his society in an era of changing values and beliefs. This examination is carried out against the background of his involvement with the Southern states.

Tate, born in Kentucky, was educated at Vanderbilt University. From the age of twenty-five he has been a freelance writer and teacher. Besides producing poetry and criticism he is a novelist, an editor and a short-story writer. Like Robert Penn Warren he was a member of the 'Fugitive Group' whose subject matter was the countryside and society of the South.

Allen Tate's poetry has the intellectual discipline of Eliot, the turn of conceit of the metaphysicals and the macabre imagery of Poe. This would seem a *pot-pourri* but in fact works well. The poet's involvement with the decline of the South is tied in to his view of a Western world in which tradition and faith have vanished to a point where men are unable to make meaningful distinctions between good and evil. Rather more significantly than Donne, in the late sixteenth century, he is preoccupied with living in a scientific age where man is forced to turn in to himself for values which do not appear to be universal. This is conveyed in the poem contained in most anthologies, 'Ode to the Confederate Dead' (*Poems 1922–1947*).

Both for an understanding of the moral problems of the age and for an understanding of twentieth-century literature in America, Allen Tate is well worth reading, both as a poet and as a critic. Collections of his verse include *Selected Poems* (1937), *Poems 1922–1947* (1948) and *Poems 1920–1945* (published in England, 1947); volumes of criticism include *On the Limits of Poetry, Selected Essays 1928–1948* (1948), *Reason in Madness* (1941), *The Forlorn Demon* (1953) and *Language of Poetry* (1960). Also of interest is his novel *The Fathers* (1938). D. L. P.

Taylor, Elizabeth (1912–), English novelist with an ability to portray with unusual accuracy the behaviour and attitudes of women in contemporary life, as for example in *A Wreath of Roses* (1950) and *In a Summer Season* (1961). In *The Soul of Kindness* (1964) she tells the story of a girl who is wholly self-centred but convinced that she is 'kind', and of the unhappiness she brings to others. *A Dedicated Man* (1965) is a volume of short stories. P. E.

Teasdale, Sara (1884–1933), American poet. Sara Teasdale is a minor poet who published a number of volumes of lyrical verse, possessing delicacy and craftmanship, in the period before and after the first world war.

Born in St Louis, Missouri, her overprotected childhood resulted in a dual attitude to life, of passion and neurotic recoil, which reflects in her poetry. Her first major volume, *Helen of Troy and Other Poems* (1911), was favourably received by Louis Untermeyer and she became a member of the literary group surrounding Harriet Monroe and the publication of *Poetry*. Vachel Lindsay courted her but she married (and later divorced) an elderly businessman. Sara Teasdale died in 1933 from an overdose of drugs, two years after the suicide of Lindsay.

Love Song (1917) ran into a number of editions and won a Pulitzer prize in 1918. The poetry is workmanlike enough to appear artless and the lyrics are simple and attractive. She owes little to the strict imagist theories by which many of her contemporaries were possessed and her work is pleasant but slight. Among collections of her poems are *Selected Poems* (1930), including 'Stars Tonight'; and *Collected Poems* (1937). D. L. P.

Tendryakov, Vladimir Fyodorovich (1923–), Soviet writer. Although a member of the Communist Party he tries in his works to avoid political clichés and tends therefore to restrict his subject matter to simple people and the countryside; these he describes clearly and without moralising.

He tells a good story and makes his characters come alive. His best-known short novels are *Ukhaby* [*Road Holes*] (1957), a daring attack on inhuman bureaucracy; *Troika, semyorka, tuz* [*Three, Seven and Ace*] (1960), a rather sad tale of faint-hearted hero-worship; and *Sud* [*The Trial*] (1961) which shows how justice can be distorted on account of fear. B. W.

Tennant, Kylie (1912–), Australian novelist who attempts to render whole sections of Australian society, sometimes scathingly and sometimes simply with humour. She is skilled in capturing the cadences of dialogue, and in exactly catching distinctive Australian characteristics. *Tiburan* (1938) is set in New South Wales during the depression; *Foveaux* (1939) deals with suburban life. *The Battlers* (1941), written with great exuberance, is somewhat different in that it takes a person rather than an area as its subject; and this trend is continued in *Ride On Stranger* (1943) which tells of the impact of a girl, Shannon Hicks, on the city of Sydney. *Lost Haven* (1946) gives a depressing account of the worst in the national character as it explores the lives of the inhabitants of a dreary coastal town. In 1952, she submitted the prize-winning play, *Tether a Dragon*; and later won an award for her novel *All the Proud Tribesmen* (1960).

S. R.

Tertz, Abram. See **Sinyavsky,** Andrei D.

Tey, Josephine (Elizabeth Mackintosh; 1897–1952), English novelist who also wrote plays under the name of Gordon Daviot. Her first novel *The Man in the Queue* (1929) introduced Inspector Grant, later to become very familiar to her readers. Her mystery stories include *Miss Pym Disposes* (1947) and *The Franchise Affair* (1949), the latter featuring a young girl who claims to have been abducted and imprisoned by an eccentric woman and her daughter. The historical *Daughter of Time* (1951) is an attempt to vindicate the ill-famed King Richard III. The plays written under the name of Gordon Daviot were extremely successful, and her *Richard of Bordeaux* (1933), a drama about Richard II, is especially memorable.

P. E.

Thirkell, Angela (1890–1961), English novelist, the great-niece of the pre-Raphaelite painter Sir Edward Burne-Jones, and mother of the novelist Colin McInnes, settled in Melbourne following her second marriage. Her first book *Three Houses*, the memoirs of her childhood, did not appear until 1936, but she won her great popularity during the war years with her novels of the British upper-middle classes, all of which were pervaded with an air of snobbish gentility. Faced with the hardships and vicissitudes of war, the reading public looked back with nostalgia to the picture she painted of an England gone for ever. Her material was often thin and her treatment of it was sometimes superficial, but her novels remained best-sellers for some years. Her titles include *Pomfret Towers* (1938), *Marling Hall* (1942) and *Happy Returns* (1952). K. M. H.

Thomas, Dylan (1914–1953), Welsh poet, strongly influenced by his native environment but writing within the mainstream of English poetry. He derived much of his inspiration from his native Swansea and later from the little Welsh town of Laugharne. The bulk of his poetry was composed during his 'Swansea period', 1930–34, and during those four years he wrote over 250 poems as well as the short stories collected in the unpublished *The Burning Baby* (1938) and later in *The Man of Love* (1939) and *A Prospect of the Sea* (1955).

In his early poetry and prose he played with themes of a macabre nature. Like Rimbaud he was preoccupied with death, and as a youth often said he would never reach forty. He also experimented with surrealistic and other techniques. In his poems sense was a poor second to word-painting, and, in the fiery mood of Rimbaud, he experimented with sound and colour, and with daring images; in consequence the work is complex and often obscure. The following passage is typical:

> Before the fall from love the flying heartbone,
> Winged like a sabbath ass this children's piece
> Uncredited blows Jericho on Eden.

During the Swansea period he composed most of the works contained in his first volume, *Eighteen Poems* (1934), and most of those included in his second, *Twenty-five Poems* (1935). The individual poems are mostly short, skilfully constructed though with a certain sameness of rhythm, and with a density that accrues from his word-preoccupation. The punning and word-play is as remarkable as that of James Joyce, a bubbling well of physical images that all but overwhelms the reader. The height of this early style is reached in the sonnet sequence 'Altarwise by Owl Light', which has some extreme examples of his involved technique:

> Then, penny-eyed, that gentleman of wounds,
> Old cock from nowheres and the heaven's egg,
> With bones unbuttoned to the half-way winds.

However, it also shows a sign of development towards the longer poems of his later period.

It was *Deaths and Entrances* (1946) that established his reputation as a poet; a critic remarked that Dylan Thomas could do magnificent things with words, 'now he can do magnificent things with poems'. *Collected Poems* (1952) set the seal on his achievement, only a year before his death in America. In what he terms his 'craft or sullen art', Dylan Thomas explores in these mature works wide-ranging aspects of the human situation, albeit often expressed in the mould of his own Welsh youth. Through them runs the firm thread of the life-death synthesis, a reflection of the conflict that seemed to dominate his own personality and eventually to consume him. This expression reaches its peak in the poem that begins

> The force that through the green fuse drives the flower
> Drives my green age: that blasts the roots of trees
> Is my destroyer.

These later poems are also less obscure. 'Poem on His Birthday' still reveals the joy in word-play, but the words now clothe the thought; and in 'Do not go gentle into that good night' the simplicity and pathos strongly contrast with the colourful obscurity of his early work:

> Do not go gentle into that good night,
> Old age should burn and rave at close of day;
> Rage, rage against the dying of the light.
>
> Though wise men at their end know dark is right,
> Because their words had forked no lightning they
> Do not go gentle into that good night.

Thomas's prose works, ebullient and evocative, range over his early childhood and his youthful experiences. Early macabre and surrealist stories gave way to witty commentaries, exemplified in his unfinished novel *Adventures in the Skin Trade* (1955) and in the stories contained in *Portrait of the Artist as a Young Dog* (1940)—a work showing transition between the styles, and the happiest of his prose works. Radio helped to popularise such humorous, noun-and-adjective-laden prose pieces as 'A Child's Christmas in Wales' where he walks with great skill the tightrope between flippancy and true human comedy; and it is for a radio play, a 'play for voices'—produced in the period after the second world war when he was engaged in writing film scripts in addition to B.B.C. broadcasts—that he is best known. As early as 1939, he was at work on *Under Milk Wood*, a poetic evocation of the little town of Laugharne where he had found peace and inspiration. Progress on the work had been very slow and it was not until 1953 that a near-finished version was given its première in America. The play, held together by the dominant figure of the narrator, deals with a day in the life of a small Welsh town, Llareggub, and its seeming collective insanity. The inhabitants enact their little dramas and expose their pettiness and futility, seemingly trapped within the limits of their little society—Lord Cutglass waiting for death; No-good

Boyo forever fishing in the harbour; Polly Garter consistently a 'bad lot' and likely to 'go to 'ell'—until, as night falls on the town, its sanity becomes revealed. This poetic fantasy is a complex container of Dylan Thomas's chief characteristics as a poet—his word-play, verging on buffoonery, and the poetic sympathy that the human situation invariably arouses in his work.

In these later years the shy and insecure poet escaped from his own inner conflict in accepting the image of the bohemian writer. The untidiness of his life—he had no real home of his own until 1949, and was constantly harried by debt—was conducive to this ultimately self-destructive rôle; while his very facility of expression ate into his life as the demands of radio and cinema, and his own financial needs, turned him from those periods of concentration and revision needed for his real work. He died in New York at the age of thirty-nine. He had lived two years longer than Rimbaud. R. A. K.

Thomas, [Philip] Edward (1878–1917), English poet and critic. Thomas is usually categorised as a Georgian pastoral poet with a fairly conventional stylistic form. His work does contain however an understanding of human motivation that is not dissimilar to that of his friend and colleague Robert Frost. The early poetry was published under the name of Edward Eastaway. *Collected Poems* was issued in 1920. Thomas also published, among others, studies of Pater (1913) and Keats (1916).

D. L. P.

Thomas, Gwyn (1913–), Welsh novelist and short-story writer, and a schoolmaster by profession. He published a volume of short stories *Where Did I Put My Pity* in 1946, and in the same year his first novel *Dark Philosophers,* woven around the conversations of four unemployed Welsh miners, was well received by the critics. There is a Rabelaisian quality about his writing, and he has often also been compared with Chaucer or Runyon, although much of his humour is in a minor key.

In *All Things Betray Thee* (1949) Thomas describes an ironworks in industrial Wales in 1855; and his story, written with grim ironic humour, is full of the singing cadences so beloved of the Welsh writer. In a prose miscellany *The Welsh Eye* (1964) he uses his gifts to portray his country and countrymen with gentle mocking humour and insight. His other works include the novels *A Frost on my Frolic* (1953) and *Point of Order* (1956), and a play *The Keep* (1962). K. M. H.

Thomas, R. S. (Ronald Stuart Thomas; 1913–), Welsh poet, and parson in a country parish in Wales. His poetry and his profession are both the expression of his affinitive understanding of ordinary unnoticed people and his sad, possessive love for the Welsh nation now rapidly receding before English encroachment. Born in Cardiff, Thomas learnt to speak Welsh when adult; this helped him to enter into a positive relationship with his reticent hill parishioners and their puritanical nonconformist neighbours. He reveals the harshness of their lives without pity or criticism but always with sympathy. In his style he is clear, terse yet rhythmic, unsententious though sure of his own judgment. His main publications are *Song at the Year's Turning* (1956) which won the Heinemann Award for Literature, *Poetry for Supper* (1958), *Tares* (1961), *The Bread of Truth* (1963) and *Pietà* (1966); *The Minister*, a verse play included in the first volume, was written for broadcasting and published separately in 1953. Thomas also edited the *Penguin Book of Religious Verse* (1963). G. C.

Thurber, James Grover (1894–1961), American humorist. Thurber was born at Columbus, Ohio, partially blinded as a child and educated at Ohio University. He worked as a journalist in France and America before in 1927 becoming one of the tone-setting contributors to the newly founded magazine the *New Yorker*. Thurber's cartoons and writing are a combination of keen humour, fantasy and melancholy. His view of humour is similar to Wordsworth's view of poetry, but whereas the poet recollects emotion in tranquillity, Thurber recollects emotional chaos. Thurber's style is curiously grotesque not in the sense of vulgar exaggeration but in his concentration on the graphically misshapen and the emotionally castrated. His success is due to catching universal human traits enlarged under pressure from irresistible outside forces. His published work includes *Is Sex Necessary* (1929); *The Seal in the Bedroom and Other Predicaments* (1932); *Fables for Our Times* (1940); *The Thurber Carnival* (1945); *The Thurber Country* (1953); and *Credos and Curios* (1962). D. L. P.

Thurston, E[rnest] Temple (1879–1933), English novelist (*The City of Beautiful Nonsense*, 1909) and playwright (*The Wandering Jew*, 1920). His one-time wife Katherine Cecil Thurston wrote the best-selling novel *John Chilcote, M.P.* (1904). K. R. R.

Tiller, Terence (1916–), English poet. Tiller's poetry is complex, academic and heavily symbolic. It derives inspiration from a feeling for European culture but in sensibility and emotional content is essentially English. The form and subject of the verse lean heavily on scholarship. 'Three Case Histories', for example, in *Reading a Medal* (1957) have their source in the seventeenth-century metaphysicals, in the Arcadian poets and in Shakespeare. This scholarship combined with subtlety of expression and oblique intellectual reference makes the poems difficult to penetrate in terms of meaning, a difficulty not made easier by an often esoteric symbolism. However, given that the poems need to be forced, by the reader, to release their content, the rich texture is profound and rewarding. Other volumes include *The Inward Animal* (1943) and *Unknown, Eros* (1957).

D. L. P.

Timmermans, Felix (1886–1947), Flemish author and painter. An autodidact, he produced a prolific stream of novels, short stories, plays and verse and established himself as the doyen of twentieth-century writers in Flemish. His best-known work is *Pallieter* [*Pallieter*] (1916), a sequence of natural settings in praise of all life, in which the central character glories in his surroundings, seeing the natural world as a mirror of its Creator. In similar vein is his *Boerenpsalm* ['The Psalm of the countryman'] (1935), a glorification of man in the person of the peasant Wortel, in the vicissitudes of his life and in his deep religious life. R. C. W.

Tobino, Mario (1910–), Italian poet and novelist. A psychiatrist in charge of a mental hospital in Tuscany, Tobino has published several volumes of verse, fiction and travel books, but his most outstanding work is *Le libere donne di Magliano* [*The Mad Women of Magliano: An Imaginary Journal*] (1953), a compelling account of various types of illnesses as observed in the female wards of an asylum. Tobino's production often betrays a preoccupation with erotic motifs and the problems of mental and physical suffering: his stark realism is however occasionally blended with idyllic tones and is suffused with sympathy and humanity. Also successful was *Il clandestino* [*The Underground*], a novel which won the 1962 Strega prize.

D. B.

Tolkien, J. R. R. (John Ronald Renel Tolkien; 1892–), English novelist and scholar. Tolkien was a professor of English literature and a philologist. But his chief work is the trilogy *The Lord of the Rings* published between 1954 and 1956. The book developed from a small children's volume *The Hobbit* which created a mythical race of gnome-like men in a land inhabited by magicians and monsters and permeated by magical and mysterious forces. In the main work, from the small beginnings of village life with the Hobbits, a dramatic series of events is set into motion which climaxes in a gigantic battle between the forces of good and the forces of evil. Before this climax the little Hobbits have journeyed through shattering experiences accompanied by their chief ally, Gandalf the Grey, a magician of princely proportions who pits himself against the Dark Lord of Mordor and his evil consorts. It is quite impossible adequately to describe the scope of the trilogy, which constructs a self-consistent world

of its own. The force, power and fascination of the work have to be experienced before they can be understood. The completely adult structure of *The Lord of the Rings* has been compared with Spenser's *Fairie Queen.* The individual titles are *The Fellowship of the Ring*, *The Two Towers* and *The Return of the King*.
D. L. P.

Tolstoy, Alexei Nikolayevich (1883–1945), Soviet writer, distantly related to both Leo Tolstoy and Ivan Turgenev. He joined the Social Democratic (Marxist) Party but by the time of the revolution he had become strongly anti-Bolshevik. He was a correspondent during World War I and emigrated in 1919.

His literary career had begun before the war, but it was abroad that he began to write his best work. *Dyetstvo Nikity* [*Nikita's Childhood*] (1921) is based on his own childhood experiences and is full of pleasant memories and the charm of bygone days. Tolstoy also began to write the first and best part of his trilogy *Khozhdeniye po mukam* [*Road to Calvary*] (1921–41), which deals with the difficulties encountered by a group of intellectuals in accepting the Soviet system. The first part had to be altered after Tolstoy's return to the Soviet Union in 1923 because the emphasis was thought wrong. Many are the reasons given for Tolstoy returning home, but basically one must put his nostalgic longing to be in Russia, albeit Soviet Russia, as his prime motive. He completely accepted the new régime, and in the second and third part of *Road to Calvary* the intellectuals he describes also come to accept the Soviet system.

Soon after his return, in an attempt to fit into the new genre, Tolstoy wrote some interesting and sensational science-fiction. *Aelita* [*Aelita*] (1924) tells of a Soviet expedition to Mars to begin a revolution there, and *Giperboloid inzhenyera Garina* [*The Garin Death Ray*] (1925) is a somewhat more serious account of how the inventor of a death ray tries to impose his brand of totalitarianism on society.

However, it is perhaps Tolstoy's other, unfinished, trilogy *Piotr Pervyi* [*Peter I*] (1929–45) for which he will be best remembered. Basing it upon a wealth of detail, Tolstoy lucidly describes the enforced europeanisation of Russia under Peter the Great, whom he tends to idealise—and in so doing to justify implicitly the part played by Stalin in the sovietisation of Russia after the revolution. The novel is a masterpiece of historical research and it does illustrate Tolstoy's real and deep feeling for his country.

Tolstoy died at the height of his powers. During the persecutions of the middle thirties, for peace and quiet, he had distorted history to flatter Stalin by portraying him as the hero of Tsaritsyn (Stalingrad/Volgograd) and denigrating Trotsky; and in the de-Stalinisation period his reputation suffered a setback. However, the beautifully clear narrative style of this talented writer, who also produced several plays, is well preserved in his two trilogies. B. W.

Toman, Josef (1899–), Czech novelist, poet and dramatist. The characters of his novels, such as *Don Juan* [*Don Juan*] (1944), personify moral principles. K. B.

Tomlinson, Charles (1927–), English poet. Tomlinson is an aesthetic poet in the sense that he constructs works of art which reflect the seen world but are separate from it, in the same way that a painter constructs a picture. He has been accused of not being concerned with people and it is true that he looks beyond immediate personal emotions to discover transcendental values in the mysterious world outside. In this he is influenced by the work of Wallace Stevens who seeks to crystallise intellectual ideas in aesthetic constructions and by Marianne Moore whose concern is to evaluate the real world from the perspective of values built into the aesthetic wholes of her own poems.

Charles Tomlinson is in the tradition of Pound and Eliot in the use of indirect reference and quotation, and in using symbolism which makes the meaning of his poetry difficult to penetrate without knowledge of his field of reference. He is an academic and intellectual poet in the application of an intelligence and sensibility that, for all their subtlety, are best described as hard. He is in strong reaction against the provincialism of Larkin. His reply to the accusation that he is not concerned with people or emotions has been that as a human being he is concerned to evaluate the world of his own perception, whether sensory or intellectual, and to do this with integrity is to be an artist.

In *Versions of Feodor Tyutchev* (1960), based on the translations by Henry Gifford, Tomlinson both introduces the reader to an important aspect of the European tradition of literature and creates distinct works of art of his own—which again is what any artist must do with the material under his hand. Charles Tomlinson's published poetry also includes *Relations and Contraries* (1951), *The Necklace* (1955), *Seeing is Believing* (1960) and *American Scenes* (1966). D. L. P.

Tomlinson, H. M. (Henry Major Tomlinson; 1873–1958), English novelist, whose works stem mainly from his travelling and from his interest in the sea. An expedition up the Amazon inspired his first book *The Sea and the Jungle* (1912) which, in spite of its relative lack of popularity at the time, is still his most representative work. A natural style reminiscent of Thoreau and Emerson pervades most of his work—in novels such as *Gallion's*

Reach (1927), *All our Yesterdays* (1930), *All Hands* (1937) and *Morning Light* (1946), as well as in his often better-known travel books which include *London River* (1921), *Turn of the Tide* (1945) and *Malay Waters* (1950).

R. A. K.

Torga, Miguel (1907–), literary pseudonym of Alfredo Rocha, Portuguese poet, dramatist, novelist and diarist and a medical practitioner in Coimbra. In his early years he associated with many young modernist intellectuals, flitting from group to group and from one hopeful but short-lived literary periodical to the next; but by 1940 he emerged as an independent figure, a 'rebel Orpheus'. Since 1928 he has maintained a consistent and prolific literary output and his works run to some forty volumes. Despite the strong and often narrow Iberian spirit of his work, it has the paradoxical quality of universal appeal which has led to its frequent evaluation with regard to the Nobel Prize. Among his more representative verse collections are *O Outro Livro de Job* ['The Other Book of Job'] (1936), *Lamentação* [*Lamentation*] (1943), *Odes* ['Odes'] (1946) and *Orfeu Rebelde* ['Rebel Orpheus'] (1958). Essentially his poetry is a poetry of protest against all existence, its brevity and futility; though he uses transcendental imagery, God he rejects as an irrelevance. His major prose works are *Bichos* [*Farrusco the Blackbird*] (1940), *Vindima* ['Grape-harvest'] (1945) and *Portugal* ['Portugal'] (1950). His most popular work, the first of these is a collection of short stories chiefly about animals to which are attributed quasi-human feelings, and stresses life's eternal cycle, in which death is always stoically accepted. The novel *Vindima* relates a catastrophic grape-harvest on a Douro estate in which a series of harrowing disasters amply illustrates that pessimistic fatalism which also characterises Torga's *Portugal*, a collection of impressionistic regional essays.

R. C. W.

Torrence, Frederick Ridgely (1875–1950), American poet and playwright. Torrence's verse develops from early sentiment to intense mysticism. The latter and more interesting stage is represented by *Hesperides* (1925). Torrence's verse plays include *El Dorado* (1903) and *Abelard and Heloise* (1907). Three plays for the Negro theatre were produced in 1917: *Granny Maumee*, *The Rider of Dreams* and *Simon the Cyrenian*. *Poems* was published in 1941 and *Last Poems* in 1944. D. L. P.

Toynbee, Arnold (1889–), English historian, wrote the monumental *A Study of History* (1934–61) comparing twenty different civilisations and tracing in them the pattern of a life-cycle. For all its gigantic erudition, the work has been criticised as being mythopoeic rather than straightforwardly historical. K. R. R.

Toynbee, [Theodore] Philip (1916–), English novelist and critic. His works include *The Savage Days* (1937), *The Barricades* (1943), *Tea with Mrs Goodman* (1947)—an experiment not only in stream-of-consciousness method but with time and symbolism—and *The Fearful Choice* (1958). Subsequently Toynbee experimented with the idea of a verse-novel, his first two works in this genre being *Pantaloon, or the Valediction* (1961) and its sequel *Two Brothers* (1964). R. A. K.

Treece, Henry (1912–66), English poet and novelist. As a poet he was a leader of the self-christened 'Apocalyptic' movement which reacted against the politically flavoured and realist poetry of the thirties. Amongst his volumes of verse are *The Black Seasons* (1945) and *The Exiles* (1952). Turning then to fiction, and employing his ability to write about the ancient world with the clarity of an eye-witness, he set himself the task of reconstructing the history of Celtic Britain from the Bronze Age to the decline of the Cymry under Arthur. Three novels in this vein are *The Eagles Have Flown* (1954), in which Arthur appears as a leader in an England threatened by savage invaders after the departure of the last Roman legions; *Red Queen, White Queen* (1958) which deals with the insurrection of Boadicea in A.D. 61; and his last novel *The Green Man* (1966). His Greek trilogy *Jason* (1961), *Electra* (1963) and *Oedipus* (1964) has enjoyed great popularity. P. E.

Trevelyan, Robert Calverly (1872–1951), English poet and playwright. The brother of the historian G. M. Trevelyan, he writes verse heavily influenced by his own translations from the classics. Volumes include *Polyphemus* (1901) and *Poems and Fables* (1925). D. L. P.

Trevor, William (1928–), Irish-born novelist, author of *The Old Boys* (1964). This is a funny and macabre story of the machinations of an old-boy committee, each aging member being driven relentlessly by memories of insults, triumphs and rivalries of his public-school years which the interval of adult life has done nothing to soften. Other titles include *The Boarding House* (1965), *The Love Department* (1966) and a volume of short stories entitled *The Day We Got Drunk on Cake* (1967). S. R.

Trilling, Lionel (1905–), American critic. Trilling's criticism is remarkable for its sense of historical perspective and a social and political involvement that is moral in its intensity. To his study of *Matthew Arnold* (1939) Trilling brought psychological and sociological interests that had been made evident in *Freud and the Crisis of Our Culture* (1933). *E. M. Forster* (1943) is treated by a similar method. Trilling's major critical essays *The*

Liberal Imagination (1950) and *The Opposing Self* (1955) continue to use these approaches with considerable success in the field of literary criticism. *Beyond Culture* (1966) deals with the problems of teaching modern literature. D. L. P.

Troyat, Henri (1911–), French biographer, travel-writer, playwright and novelist. Born in Russia but living in Paris since 1920, Henri Troyat has written biographies of Dostoyevsky, Pushkin, Lermontov and Tolstoy, as well as a book of Russian memoirs. His first novel *Faux Jour* [*False Dawn*] (1935) was soon followed by others, and he gained the Prix Goncourt in 1938 for *L'Araigne* [*The Spider's Web*]. But he is best known as the author of novels recalling his Russian background—*Tant que la Terre durera* [*As Long as Earth Lasts*] (3 vols, 1945) and *La Lumière des justes* [*The Light of the Just*] (3 vols, 1962). The intervening *Les Semailles et les moissons* [*The Seed and the Fruit*] (5 vols, 1953–58) has a French setting and relates the story of a family from 1914 to 1945. In 1959 Troyat became a member of the French Academy. D. E. A.

Tuohy, Frank (1925–), English novelist and short-story writer. His volume of stories *The Admiral and the Nuns* (1962), with such diverse settings as England, South America and eastern Europe, illustrates his virtuosity. His early novels *The Animal Game* (1957) and *The Warm Nights of January* (1959) were highly praised; but his most successful work to date was *The Ice Saints* (1964), a story of contemporary Poland and of the effect of an English girl's visit on a cross-section of the society of a People's Democracy. P. E.

Turner, Walter James Redfern (1889–1946), Australian-born English poet and novelist. Turner's exotic verse, heavy with images and rich with metaphor, is seen at its best in *New Poems* (1928), *Songs and Incantations* (1936) and *Fables, Parables and Plots* (1943). His novels include *The Man Who Ate the Popomack* (1922) and *The Aesthetes* (1927). D. L. P.

Tutuola, Amos (1920–), Nigerian writer who achieved international fame with the publication of *The Palm-Wine Drinkard* (1952), a fanciful and magical tale peopled with giants and monsters, which critics felt survived comparison with allegories such as those of Bunyan and Dante. It has been suggested that for European readers the particular charm of this book lies in the excitement of finding that these strange creations correspond with their own myths; as well as in the enjoyment of what seem to be audacious anachronisms—such as cigarettes, and the mention of a telephone. In the same child-like prose style, Amos Tutuola subsequently produced *My Life in the Bush of Ghosts* (1954), *Simbi and the Satyr of the Dark Jungle* (1955), *The Brave African Huntress* (1954) and *Feather Woman of the Jungle* (1961). These have not been greeted with equal enthusiasm, though they are not detectably inferior. This perhaps reveals more about the over-enthusiastic reaction of the public to anything novel, rather than a waning of Tutuola's powers. Later titles include *Ajaiyi and his Inherited Property* (1968). S. R.

Tvardovsky, Alexandr Trifonovich (1910–), Russian peasant poet born in Zagorye in the Smolensk region. His father was a hard-working small-farmer with a considerable interest in literature. Thus the young Tvardovsky received a solid grounding in the historical traditions of his nation's literature. All his life Tvardovsky has retained his love of the countryside and his independence of mind and action. This is evident from his works. He began writing at an early age but his first work did not appear until 1934–36. This was the long poem *Strana Muraviya* ['The land of Muravia'], about a mythical land where people are free of the collective system of farming. During and after World War II Tvardovsky worked on a humorous narrative poem *Vasily Tyorkin* [extract trans. as *Death of a Hero*] (1941–45) about an ordinary happy-go-lucky soldier. The hero is a likeable character and Tvardovsky's reputation was greatly enhanced. In 1960 he completed a long poem *Dal' za dalyu* ['Space beyond Space'; extracts trans. as *Siberia* and *The Two Smithies*] about his childhood. It also contains some remarks about a writer's duty to society and the way that duty had been abnegated through fear under Stalin's rule. It is a most important poem for it shows how the writer has been aware that he was not being true to himself or his readers in writing to order. His poetry available in English also includes 'To my Critics', 'Pioneers' and 'No, Life has not Denied me my Share'. A story worth reading is 'The Stovemakers'. B. W.

Tynan, Katherine (1861–1931), Irish poet, novelist and autobiographer. Tynan like her friend Dora Sigerson was dominated by the joint influences of Catholicism and Irish patriotism. Like Æ and Yeats her involvement in the Irish renaissance also included a fascination with Celtic mythology. *Collected Poems* was published in 1930. Five autobiographical volumes were published: *Twenty-Five Years* (1933), *The Middle Years* (1917), *The Years of the Shadow* (1919), *The Wandering Years* (1922) and *Memories* (1924). Among her hundred or so romantic novels is *The House in the Forest* (1928). D. L. P.

Tzara, Tristan (1896–1964), French poet. Born of a Rumanian Jewish family, reputedly the ringmaster of the Dada movement's 391 presidents, his death passed virtually unnoticed in Britain and America and not one of his numerous works, spanning almost fifty years, was currently available in English, outside of anthologies and ephemera. In the late 1960s the best collection of Dada material in translation was Robert Motherwell's *The Dada Painters and Poets* (1951), containing Tzara's famous *Sept manifestes Dada, 1916–20* [*Seven Dada Manifestoes*] (1924) but none of his poetry; the most intelligent critical account of Dada was Michel Sanouillet's *Dada à Paris* ['Dada in Paris'] (1965). However, with Breton's death exciting academic necrophilia, Duchamp a ready-made cult figure, Ernst honoured by the Venice Biennale and Pierre Albert-Birot newly discovered, it seemed possible that recognition of Tzara's beneficent influence on contemporary European culture would not be much longer delayed.

What Tzara, Huelsenbeck, Ball, Arp, Janco and their co-religionists demanded in 1916 was the ending of that 'shamefaced sex of comfortable compromise and good manners' which had led Europe into one world war and was to plunge it into another. They wanted to administer an enema to a constipated tradition; they wanted to extirpate society not to explain it; they wanted to joke seriously and if that offended people then well and good since art was for living not for hanging on walls. They wanted a return to the unconscious, the dream, the spontaneous, to primeval chaos, *tabula rasa*; they wanted to clear the table but only in order to prepare a feast of the imagination—for if Dada was nihilistic it was a fructifying not a sterilizing nihilism. They wanted to demolish the treadmill so that others might construct 'the fecund wheel of a universal circus'.

M. D. E.

U

Unamuno, Miguel de (1864–1936), Spanish writer and thinker. Unamuno is the leading figure of the 1898 generation which, faced by Spain's final collapse as a world power, attempted to understand the tragedy of Spain in particular and man in general. He probed this national and personal tragedy not only in the essays which form the basis for his international reputation, but also in highly distinctive novels, poetry and plays.

A native of Bilbao, Unamuno was constantly stirred by memories of his youth: by love for his strongly Catholic mother and hatred for his brother, and by the events of the Carlist war when the city was bombarded. After receiving his doctorate from Madrid University (1883), Unamuno wrote and taught for the remainder of his life. Appointed Professor of Greek at Salamanca in 1891, he was already engaged on his first novel *Paz en la guerra* ['Peace in war'] (1897), a partly autobiographical account of the Carlist siege of Bilbao. In the essay *En torno al casticismo* ['About Spanishness'] (1895) he tries to relate Spain's traditions to general European progress. Up to this point Unamuno had approached writing and thought in a rational, deterministic manner.

In 1897, however, he suffered a personal and religious crisis. He emerged with the help of his wife whom he came increasingly to see as a mother-figure, and in all his subsequent work we find a deep suspicion of reason as a criterion, and an anguished view of man and his hope for immortality. Unamuno's pre-existentialist vision is discernible in a number of essays. *Vida de Don Quijote y Sancho* [*Life of Don Quixote and Sancho*] (1905) depicts Don Quixote as the archetypal man fashioning immortality for himself by his own actions and faith, and in *Del sentimiento trágico de la vida* [*The Tragic Sense of Life*] (1913) he again examines man's desire for immortality. Reason can neither bring us to God nor keep us from Him. Man's only solution is to live in such a way that death is an injustice. A fresh statement of Unamuno's religious views is found in *La agonía del cristianismo* [*The Agony of Christianity*] (1925). True Christianity is seen as a religion of agony and struggle. From the essays there emerges a philosophical attitude which one critic has called 'creative doubt'. Unamuno is searching intuitively for his God, for the answer to the problem of man's personality, for a possible victory over death.

But this search is most effectively conveyed in the novels, poetry and drama. As a creative artist Unamuno seeks not elegance but a complete communication of his anguish. His poetry is particularly virile and unyielding: he was out of sympathy both with Darío's modernism, and, later, with the new poetry of the 1920s. But in *Poesía* ['Poetry'] (1907), *Rosario de sonetos líricos* ['Rosary of lyrical sonnets'] (1911) and *El Cristo de Velázquez* [*The Christ of Velázquez*] (1920) his religious doubts are evoked with sententious precision. His novels are equally rich in content, if diffuse in form. Indeed *Amor y pedagogía* ['Love and pedagogy'] (1902) and *Cómo se hace una novela* ['How a novel is made'] (1927) are really essays. *Niebla* [*Mist*] (1914) deals with the problem of personality and the autonomous character in a way reminiscent of Pirandello. Augusto Pérez, the central character who takes on a life of his own, is a disturbing reminder of the dislocation in the spirit of modern man. *Abel Sánchez* ['Abel Sánchez'] (1917) is the most effective treatment of the Cain-Abel theme which preoccupied Unamuno.

The tragic dichotomy seen in Abel Sánchez and Joaquín Monegro reappears in the play *El otro* [*The Other One*] (1932), written in 1926 when Unamuno was experiencing a fresh crisis. Involved in politics by his opposition to Primo de Rivera and his subsequent exile, Unamuno was again perplexed by his own personality: who was he? writer or politician? The Unamuno the world knew, or the Unamuno he wished to be? In *El otro* one of two twins kills the other and the play is an allegory of the disruption in the writer's personality. In another play *El hermano Juan* ['Brother Juan'] (1934) the Don Juan legend is used to suggest once more that man must engage in shaping his own personality, his reputation being a form of immortality. Thus Unamuno's writings are cyclical in character. He consistently reverts to the same themes—doubt and religious faith, the survival after death of man's personality. These preoccupations and his anguished sense of man's tragedy place Unamuno in the forefront of European pre-existentialist thought. D. H. G.

Underhill, Evelyn (1875–1941), English mystic, poet and novelist. Her works include *Mysticism* (1911), *Practical Mysticism* (1914) and *Man and the Supernatural* (1927). Volumes of poetry include *Immanence* (1912), and among her novels are *The Column of Dust* (1909). Her *Collected Papers* were published in 1946. D. L. P.

Undset, Sigrid (1882–1949), Norwegian novelist and winner of the 1928 Nobel Prize for Literature. She was born in Kalundborg, Denmark, the daughter of a prominent archaeologist whose death in 1893 led to a fall in the family fortunes and to the curtailment of young Sigrid's education. Work as a clerk in an Oslo office was an important seminal factor in the production of her first novel *Jenny* [*Jenny*] (1911) which analysed the problems of the young middle-class woman. Fortified by its success she was encouraged to devote herself more fully to literature, concentrating particularly on the historical novel. Writing in a conventional yet monumental style and with an impressive knowledge of the Norwegian Middle Ages, which lent dignity to her work, she evolved her masterpiece, the fourteenth-century trilogy *Kristin Lavransdatter* [*Kristin Lavransdatter*] (1920–22). Only relatively less successful were the four volumes of her *Olav Audunssøn* [*The Master of Hestviken*] (1925–27). Subsequently Sigrid Undset turned to writing novels of contemporary Norwegian life, of which more than a dozen were published. Particularly noteworthy in their composition was the strong influence of her conversion to Catholicism in 1924. Many of them have been translated into English by A. G. Chater, the eminent translator of the Scandinavian literatures, but none recaptured the majestic impact of *Kristin Lavransdatter*. R. C. W.

Ungaretti, Giuseppe (1888–), Italian poet born in Alexandria of Italian parents. He studied in Egypt then at the Sorbonne and Collège de France where he befriended Apollinaire and other *avant-garde* figures, and actively participated in the literary and artistic circles of Paris. During the first world war he fought in the army and saw action at Carso and Champagne. In 1919 he married Jeanne Dupoix and settled in Italy in 1920. From 1936 until 1943 Ungaretti taught Italian literature at the University of São Paulo (Brazil) and, after his return to Italy, at the University of Rome.

His early poems coincide with a period of experimentation in Italian letters. *Il porto sepolto* ['The buried port'] (1916) and *Allegria di naufragi* ['Happiness of shipwrecks'] (1919) reveal the characteristics of his particular kind of impressionism. Influenced by Mallarmé, Valéry and their French contemporaries, Ungaretti too is intent upon capturing in his poetry the secret rapport between his inner self and the wonders of the outside world. *L'Allegria* ['Happiness'] (1932) and *Sentimenti del tempo* ['Sentiments of time'] (1936) established his significance as the supreme exponent of the so-called *poesia pura*—tense, pulsating and hermetic poems which give the impression of transcending common experience; a poetry of subtle insights enhanced by immediacy of expression. In time his impressionism orders its sensations and his poetry achieves balance between instinct and reason.

The poems of *Il dolore* ['Sorrow'] (1947) and *Un grido e paesaggi* ['A cry and landscapes'] (1952) are more complex and intense. In lyrics of great purity, Ungaretti expresses the solitude of modern man, and his vision of human suffering is at once eloquent and profound. In 1957 his complete works were published and entitled *Vita d'un uomo* [*Life of a Man*]. His remarkable translations of other poets include Shakespeare's sonnets, poems by Blake, Mallarmé and Góngora, and Racine's *Phèdre*. In 1961 he was awarded the important Premio Penna d'oro for his contribution to modern Italian poetry. G. P.

Untermeyer, Louis (1885–), American man of letters, divides his own work into four sections: poetry, parodies, translations and critical collections. He is probably best known for the latter, having produced a long series of opinion-moulding anthologies. The most outstanding of these come under the title *Modern American Poetry,* a recent revised edition of which was issued in 1962.

Untermeyer, born in New York, entered his father's business in 1900 and continued in it until he retired as vice-president in 1923. He then spent two years studying abroad before returning to New York to devote himself to literature. He has been married four times.

Apart from the often brilliant parodies, his verse is lyrical, vigorous and technically outstanding. It is certainly not great poetry but refreshingly exuberant and often capable of high seriousness in the expression of contemporary social problems. Published titles include *Collected Parodies* (1926); *Challenge* (1914); *Burning Bush* (1928); and *Food and Drink* (1932). His critical collections and anthologies also include *Modern American and British Poetry* (with Karl Shapiro and Richard Wilbur, 1955); and *For You with Love* (1961). *From Another World* (1939) is an autobiography.

D. L. P.

Updike, John (1932–), American novelist and poet, sprang to renown with his novel *The Poorhouse Fair* (1959), set in a poor-law institution. This was followed by *Rabbit Run* (1960), a book aflame with tenderness for the youthful spirit prematurely stifled in arid suburban domesticity.

What the fundamentally good but irresponsible 'Rabbit' Angstrom—once the deft speedster of the high-school sportsfield—runs from is a joyless world (a dreary job; the girl he once made pregnant now become a graceless housewife; and a mesh of unsought personal and social responsibilities), a world which appears to offer no scope for him to flower and be fruitful as a human being. Just what his creative potentialities are is amply confirmed when he revives the well-springs of emotion and of full female sexuality in the hardened, apathetic prostitute Ruth whom he meets in a café. However, the pattern is to repeat itself: if he knows how to make love to Ruth in a way that gives both of them the intensest satisfaction, he has also ignored the likely consequences; and for all his capacity to create a warm human relationship, he has reckoned without the now duplicated set of responsibilities. Never having begun to 'grow up', he can only resort to headlong flight.

There is a complementary pattern in *The Centaur* (1963), where the hero, the schoolmaster Caldwell, represents the opposite extreme of total responsibility. The attempt to give the story a mythological dimension, by making it simultaneously the story of the gentle, learned and wounded centaur Chiron, is of dubious value. Caldwell is in one sense too good for this world; in another it can be said that his goodness—like that of Rabbit Angstrom—is a social liability. His self-deprecation, for instance, can be acutely embarrassing to his son; and his total lack of care for his own well-being puts a burden on those who love him. Most important of all, were he just George Caldwell and not also Chiron the centaur, his sacrificial death would certainly be ambivalent. This moving account of the heroically misguided life and death of a sensitive, tormented, endlessly burden-shouldering teacher in the bleak world of rural Pennsylvania is as powerful as its predecessor.

Updike's other publications include *Of the Farm* (1966) and *The Music School* (1967); *Pigeon Feathers* (1962), a collection of short stories; and several volumes of verse including *Hoping for a Hoopoe* (1954), in which the poem 'Ex-Basketball Player' clearly prefigures the creation of the hero of *Rabbit Run*. K. R. R.

Uris, Leon (1924–), American novelist. Uris joined the United States Marines when he was seventeen. His first novel *Battle Cry* (1953) is a lengthy narrative of the part played in the second world war by a fictional group of marines. *The Angry Hill* (1955) is concerned with the Palestine Brigade in Greece. *Exodus* (1958) is a best-selling account of the creation of the state of Israel after the war. *Mila 18* (1961) tells the story of the Jewish uprising in the Warsaw ghetto created by the Nazis. D. L. P.

Ustinov, Peter (1921–), English actor, producer, dramatist, novelist, short-story writer and *raconteur*. Ustinov, well known for his impromptu television conversations, and joint director of the Nottingham Playhouse, has written popular and sometimes experimental plays including *House of Regrets* (1940), *The Tragedy of Good Intentions* (1944), *The Love of Four Colonels* (1951) and *Romanoff and Juliet* (1956). *Add a Dash of Pity* (1959) and *The Frontiers of the Sea* (1966) are volumes of short stories; *The Loser* (1961) is a novel. He has also acted in, scripted and directed a variety of films. D. L. P.

V

Vachell, Horace Annesley (1861–1955), prolific English writer best known for *The Hill* (1905) which is an idealised account of school life at Harrow, and *Quinneys* (1914), the gently humorous story of an antique dealer and his family. P. E.

Vailland, Roger (1907–1967), French novelist and dramatist, whose career presents a sentimental paradigm to the francophile foreigner. Born in 1907, he studied philosophy, flirted with the surrealist movement, worked as a journalist for several years, fought courageously in the resistance—the period of his first, excellent novel, the 1945 winner of the journalists' Prix Interallié, *Drôle de jeu* [*Playing with Fire*] (1945)—and joined the Communist Party. Now, enthusiasm, conversion and recantation behind him, replete with paradox and satanic charm, the Vailland hero lives in the remote countryside, bored even with sex which is at best no more than a stylish manoeuvre, an intellectual gavotte danced by a blasé seducer and a tempting nymph, as in *Les Mauvais Coups* [*Turn of the Wheel*] (1948) and *La Fête* [*The Sovereigns*] (1960). Occasionally, the elegantly sadistic ploy is reversed and the delectable provincial adroitly infibulates her pursuer, as in *La Truite* [*The Young Trout*] (1964), an amusing tilt at expense-account sophistication. *La Loi* [*The Law*] (1957), a lucid study of the inexorable game of insult and humiliation played in southern Italian villages, is probably Vailland's most successful novel. A compelling, imaginative venture into the social and psychological ramifications of a vicious ritual which is also a philosophy, it won the Prix Goncourt.

M. D. E.

Valéry, Paul (1871–1945), French poet. Valéry was born in Sète of a Corsican father and Italian mother. He went to high school in Montpellier from 1884 to 1888, and took up literature and especially poetry (Hugo, Gautier, Baudelaire). By the time he entered the law faculty at the University of Montpellier he was already writing poetry. He also made contact with the writers Pierre Louys, Mallarmé, Hérédia, Gide and later the composer Debussy. Valéry's literary vocation seemed clear, but in 1892 he went through a profound crisis which caused him to decide to give up literature entirely in favour of pure thought. So he settled in Paris in 1894, worked in the war ministry for several years, after which he became the private secretary of Edouard Lebey, one of the directors of the Havas Agency. He remained in this post for twenty-two years. It left him plenty of leisure for his personal research into the nature of intellect. He was 'silent' for twenty years, he lived in 'the cloister of the intellect', as Berne-Joffroy said. He got rid of most of his books and lived in an austere room in Paris equipped with a blackboard which he covered with mathematical calculations. Every morning for several hours from dawn onwards he noted down his reflections on mental phenomena, on attention, the ego, dreams, time, language. He did this every day till the end of his life, filling 257 *cahiers* (notebooks). The results of this rigorous mental discipline can be seen in the works which Valéry did publish during his first two years in Paris: *Introduction à la méthode de Léonard de Vinci* [*Introduction to the Method of Leonardo da Vinci*] (1895) and *La Soirée avec M. Teste* [*An Evening with Mr Teste*] (1896). Monsieur Teste is a 'sort of intellectual animal', he is 'intelligence carried to its furthest limit', he has become 'master of his memory and all the operations of his mind'. He observes the world and other people with implacable lucidity. His language is one of rigorous precision. He never says anything vague. He is an unknown genius because a true genius would never waste his time on the public relations necessary to get known.

Finally at the instigation of Gide and Gaston Gallimard, Valéry published *La Jeune Parque* [*The Youngest of the Fates*] (1917), and became a famous lyrical poet almost overnight. For a number of years (1918–22) he composed poems freely, including the famous *Le Cimetière marin* [*The Graveyard by the Sea*] (1920). *Album de vers anciens* [*Album of Old Verses*], Valéry's juvenilia, was published in 1920, and was followed in 1922 by his last volume of poems, *Charmes* [*Incantations*]. The *Album* contains such poems as *La Fileuse* ['Woman spinning'], about a young woman spinning and falling asleep in the dusk by the window. An impression of sweetness and evanescent grace is communicated through the use of *terza rima* and of generally very skilful versification: purely feminine rhymes, adroit use of enjambment and caesura, and expressive alliteration. The influence of Mallarmé is clear. Other poems in the *Album* show symbolist influence: such as *Naissance de Vénus* ['Birth of Venus'] and *Le Bois amical* ['The friendly wood']. *La Jeune Parque* is perhaps Valéry's most typical poem, together with *Le Cimetière marin*. The former took four years to write (1913–17) and consists of 512 lines. There were a hundred drafts of it which, if printed, would run to 600 pages. Its subject is 'the changing of a conscience during one night', and it is obscure and difficult. The poem is a monologue of the youngest of the three Fates, uttered when she wakes during the night. It represents the crisis of adolescence: the awakening of the mind, in love with the absolute, and its struggle against the instinctive appeal of the senses. It is philosophical poetry couched in pure, beautiful and classical French, as is also *Le Cimetière marin* which is a meditation on life and death, summed up in the epigraph from Pindar: 'O my soul, do not aspire to immortal life, but exhaust the field of the possible'. In this poem, as he says, Valéry brings together 'the simplest and most constant themes of (his) emotional and intellectual life, as they had imposed themselves on (his) adolescence in association with the sea and the light of a certain spot on the shores of the Mediterranean'. With the publication of this poem, Valéry became a great national figure, member of the French Academy, President of the Pen Club etc., and was given a national funeral when he died. A. L. W.

Valle-Inclán, Ramón María del (Ramón del Valle y Peña; 1866–1936), Spanish novelist and playwright. An exotic figure who affected a distinctive style both in his own life and in his writings, Valle-Inclán was a member of the Galician squirearchy. His mordant tongue, proud bearing and unique appearance—with flowing beard and one arm amputated—contrasted vividly with the rigours of his day-to-day existence, whose real merit lay in the steadfast search for stylistic perfection in his writing. His output is difficult to classify since there is a marked cross-fertilisation of genres. Thus the published texts of plays such as the trilogy *Comedias bárbaras* ['Barbarous comedies'] (1907–22) or his dramatic masterpiece *Divinas palabras* ['Divine words'] (1920) have the appearance of dialogued novels. However, the major lines of his development are plainly discernible. As a young man in Galicia, Valle-Inclán became deeply imbued with the French literary fashions of the 1880s—the sniggering perversities of decadent symbolism, the terrorific admixture of horror and farce of *grand guignol*. These form a constant undercurrent in his work; they are never gratuitous elements, however, but a coherent part of his disabused view of the world. The early novels are modernist in tone: *Flor de santidad* ['Flower of sanctity'] (1904) is a tale of witchcraft and superstition in Galicia while the four *Sonatas* [*Four Sonatas*] (1902–05) are the 'pleasant memoirs' of the Marqués de Bradomín, a Galician Casanova, 'ugly, Catholic and sentimental'. The characteristic vision of sinning humanity is most tellingly displayed, however, in the trilogy *La guerra carlista* ['The Carlist war'] (1908–22) and *Tirano Banderas* [*Tyrant*], the vivid portrait of a South American dictator. The same embittered mood runs through *Divinas palabras,* a parable of the universality of sin, set in a Galician village. Both as novelist and playwright Valle-Inclán created a new language and a new technique. He is one of the great seminal influences on contemporary Spanish literature. D. H. G.

Vallejo, César (1892–1938), Peruvian poet, a *mestizo* whose work represents a personal, anguished rebellion against the established order: aesthetic, metaphysical, and social. His first poems, *Heraldos negros*

['Black heralds'] (1918), were already, most of them, a step away from 'modernism'. After being unjustly imprisoned he voiced his bitterness and revolt in *Trilce* ['Trilce'] (1922). The capricious liberty of syntax and spelling, and the frank illogical imagery, are vehicles for the expression of a chaotic state of mind faced with the absurdity of a chaotic world.

From 1923 until his death he lived in poverty in Paris. Neglecting poetry, he produced prose works stimulated by a dedication to the communist cause. But the Spanish civil war stirred him to return to his true vocation, precipitating the poetry of *Poemas humanos* ['Human poems'] (1939), with its themes of death, anguish, love, human solidarity. More orderly than *Trilce*, it is perhaps his most passionate and moving work.

In English there exist the translations of John Knoepfle, James Wright and Robert Bly in *Twenty Poems of César Vallejo* (1963); he is also represented in Dudley Fitts's *Anthology of Contemporary Latin American Poetry* (1947) and in H. R. Hays's *Twelve Spanish American Poets* (1943).

P. R. B.

Vančura, Vladislav (1891–1942), Czech novelist. A doctor of medicine he devoted himself wholly to literature; he was executed by the Germans during the occupation of Czechoslovakia. A writer of firm communist beliefs, Vančura was a great master and innovator in style. *Konec starych Časů* [*The End of the Old Times*] (1934) depicts with irony the experiences of a Russian aristocratic emigré among Czechoslovak landowners. K. B.

Van der Post, Laurens (1906–), South African writer of novels and travel-journals. An unresolved split between the imaginative, mystical visionary and the responsive observer makes Van der Post equally observing—or frustrating—in both genres. He is, for Africa, a seer of the Lawrence of Arabia type, in whom Africa and Europe, artist and scientist, philosopher and poet, explorer and political thinker seem so constantly at war that the result appears as schizoid art: hieratic, heroic or inflated, disproportionate. This, despite the magnificence of the writing, mars *Venture to the Interior* (1952) as well as the novel *Flamingo Feather* (1955). The earlier novels *In a Province* (1934) and *The Face beside the Fire* (1953) and a third travel account *The Lost World of the Kalahari* (1958) show less strain. Subsequent writings include the novel *The Heart of the Hunter* (1961). C. P.

Van Dine, S. S. (Willard H. Wright; 1888–1939), American writer of intellectual detective stories featuring the sophisticated Philo Vance. Titles include *The Benson Murder Case* (1926) and *The 'Canary' Murder Case* (1926). K. R. R.

Van Doren, Carl (1885–1950), American man of letters, born in Hope, Illinois, was a biographer, critic, scholar and teacher. The elder brother of the poet Mark Van Doren, his careful scholarship and concern with American culture helped to establish American literature and history as serious subjects in the universities. His literary journalism helped to bridge the gap between scholarship and the public at large.

Carl Van Doren produced critical work on the American novel as well as a history of American and English literature. He wrote a book of short stories *Other Provinces* (1925) and a novel *The Ninth Wave* (1926). His many biographies include the classic *Benjamin Franklin* (1938) which won a Pulitzer prize. D. L. P.

Van Doren, Mark (1894–   ), American poet. Mark Van Doren is an academic attempting to follow the poetic tradition of Robert Frost. The younger brother of Carl Van Doren, he was born in Hope, Illinois, took his degree at Illinois University and subsequently, with a break for war service, finished his postgraduate education at Columbia where he went on to teach. His writing includes novels, short stories and a play; and he is a Shakespearian scholar and an anthologist as well as the author of critical investigations of contemporary figures such as Edward Arlington Robinson. As a teacher he is a liberal educationalist somewhat in reaction to the pragmatism of Dewey.

Van Doren's poetry, like that of Wordsworth, is concerned with the universal truths to be garnered from everyday life. His feeling for the countryside has a quality similar to that of Frost and he is capable of penetrating to the identity between man and soil. 'Foreclosure' in *Collected Poems* (1939) is an example of this deeply felt sympathy, in this case with a farmer forced to leave the substance of his life behind him and clinging to memories:

> So his lost land went with him, pulling
> Its tatters close around.

Van Doren has been accused of lacking emotional depth, but his emotion, again like that of Robert Frost, is not so much lacking as restrained and matches the unobtrusive quality of his imagination. He is not a major poet nor an original one but his verse has sufficient depth and significance to endure. His published volumes of verse include *Collected Poems* (1939); Pulitzer prize, 1940; *Spring Birth* (1953); and *Morning Worship and Other Poems* (1960). Amongst his prose works are the novels *The Transients* (1935) and *Tilda* (1943); the volumes of short stories *Nobody Say a Word and Other Stories* (1953); the biographies *Thoreau* (1916) and *Shakespeare* (1939); the dramatic work *Last Days of Lincoln* (1959); and his *Autobiography* (1958). D. L. P.

Van Druten, John (1901–57), Anglo-American playwright whose early works included the popular *Young Woodley* (1928) but who became best known to a later generation for his witchcraft-comedy *Bell, Book and Candle* (1950). His later successes were in some cases adaptations, *I am a Camera* (1952) being based on the Berlin stories of Christopher Isherwood (q.v.). K. R. R.

Vane, Sutton (1888–1963), English playwright who is remembered for his most unusual and very successful play *Outward Bound* (1923) in which a group of passengers who find themselves on a ship which is otherwise deserted realise that they are in fact dead, and bound for the other world which is both heaven and hell. P. E.

Vargas Llosa, Mario (1936–), Peruvian novelist who lives and works in Paris. In 1958 he received the Spanish Premio Leopoldo Alas for his collection of short stories *Los jefes* ['The men in charge']; later his first novel *La ciudad y los perros* [*The Time of the Hero*] (1963) narrowly failed to win the 1963 Formentor Prize, receiving three votes out of seven. The manuscript had already carried off the Spanish Premio Biblioteca Breve in 1962. The setting of this socially mordant novel is the Leoncio Prado military academy in Lima with its brutal, savage and sensual traditions. The theme centres on the hushing-up of the murder of a timid, sensitive cadet by its treatment as an accident on an exercise. Vargas Llosa uses this as a springboard for a penetrating examination of the confused moral codes of cadets and officers alike and for successively peeling off the various social layers from which the cadets came. *La casa verde* ['The green house'] (1966) was a brave attempt at an epic novel, embracing the social climates of the 'three Perus'—the jungle, the *sierra*, the urbanised coast; the characterisation here was less successful. Much more convincing in this regard was his third novel *Los cachorros* ['The pups'] (1967), a sensitive study of the problem of sexual impotence in a young man. R. C. W.

Veblen, Thorstein (1857–1929), American historian and social scientist whose writings have had a profound influence on American literature. His criticisms of society—its institutions and types of individuals—are contained in ten books, of which his first *The Theory of the Leisure Class* (1899) is still the most read. Both Veblen's scepticism and his prose style have been influential. Other titles include *The Theory of Business Enterprise* (1904). R. A. K.

Vercors (Jean Bruller; 1902–), French writer, was known only to a small circle of friends and acquaintances until the clandestine publication of *Le Silence de la mer* [*The Silence of the Sea*] (1942), a short story which exactly fitted the mood of defeated France under the occupation. The pseudonym 'Vercors' was kept by the author for his subsequent works—*La Marche à l'étoile* ['March to the star'] (1943) which established him as one of the major writers of the resistance, and the more ambitious novels *Les Armes de la nuit* ('Weapons of the night'] (1946), *La Puissance du jour* ['Power of the day'] (1951), *Les Animaux dénaturés* [*Borderline*] (1952) and *Sylva* (1961). He has also written a play, *Zoo* (1964), and essays —*Le Sable du temps* ['The sands of time'] (1945), *Les Pas dans le sable* ['Footsteps in the sand'] (1954) and *P.P.C.* (1957). D. E. A.

Veresayev, V. V. (Vikenti Vikentievich Smidovich; 1867–1945), Russian writer, was a radical, a Menshevik and a doctor, and belonged to no particular literary group. His horror at the atrocities committed during the civil war is conveyed in his novel *V tupikye* [*Deadlock*] (1923), which features an idealistic girl who will have no truck with either the Reds or the Whites. B. W.

Veríssimo, Erico (1905–), Brazilian novelist and critic born in Alta Cruz (Rio Grande do Sul). Veríssimo is a prolific writer who has been widely translated. A controversial figure, he sees himself as a simple '*contador de histórias*' and follows no specific literary or philosophical current. Considering himself an artisan rather than artist, more magician than logician, he is in fact a frustrated painter who paints with words and is particularly enthusiastic about poetry and music. Socially committed in most of his writing, he explains the realism of his novels by invoking a writer's duty to be sincere. His penetrating eye is constantly focused upon a world of violence, injustice and absurdity. Significant works include *Caminhos Cruzados* [*Crossroads and Destinies*] (1935], *Música ao Longe* ['Music in the distance'] (1935), *Olhai os Lírios do Campo* ['Behold the lilies of the field'] (1938) and *O Resto é Silêncio* [*The Rest is Silence*] (1943), which draw psychological and social tensions together. This drama of the individual and society reappears with new vigour in his later and most extensive work *O Tempo e o Vento* ['Time and the wind'] which comprises three separate volumes: *O Continente* (1948–49), *O Retrato* (1951) and *Arquipélago* (1961–62) in which he traces the historical formation of his native Rio Grande do Sul. Veríssimo is also interesting as the Brazilian writer who has most clearly assimilated the techniques of modern English and American novelists—the naturalism of Faulkner, Caldwell and Huxley which reveals '*o homem total*'. In addition to his novels, Veríssimo has written short stories, a biography of Joan of Arc, travelogues (notably a study on Mexico) and numerous works of fiction for children. Other works by Veríssimo translated into English include his brief outline of *Brazilian Literature* (1945) and *Noite* [*Night*] (1954) which provides an interesting example of his originality and experiments with prose technique. G. P.

Vidal, Gore (1925–), American novelist and playwright with a penchant for social and political themes. His long-running play *The Best Man* (1960) featured the national convention of a political party assembled to nominate its candidate for the presidency. His fiction includes the much-praised war novel *Williwaw* (1946); *The City and the Pillar* (1949), a once-controversial portrait of a male homosexual; the Byzantine historical novel *Julian* (1964); and *Washington, D.C.* (1967), in which he portrays both the public and private sides of American political life. He has also written short stories notable for their craftsmanship, and detective fiction under the name of Edgar Box. K. R. R.

Viereck, Peter (1916–), American poet. Viereck is an academic in reaction against what he regards as the obscurity of twentieth-century verse. He was born in New York, and educated at Harvard and Oxford; he served in the second world war in Italy and Africa and returned to take up a teaching career. He is a poet of wit and intelligence writing mainly within a traditional structure for a middle-class audience of non-specialists. The verse can be amusing, analytic and occasionally lyrically beautiful. He deliberately retains conservative form in his writing and rejects the lines mapped out by Eliot and Pound, and his poetry retains clarity at the expense of real depth and originality. His published work includes *Terror and Decorum* (1948), *Strike Through the Mask* (1950), *The First Morning* (1952) and *The Persimmon Tree* (1957). The first-named volume won a Pulitzer prize. D. L. P.

Vilakazi, Benedict Wallet (1906–47), South African poet, some of whose Zulu poems have been published, in English renderings by D. McK. Malcolm and F. L. Friedman, as *Zulu Horizons* (1962). A powerful poet, whose work has also been translated for anthologies and magazines, Vilakazi wields a muscular, orotund style that is supple and flexible enough to accommodate social and personal themes with equal dignity and beauty. His idiomatic, proverbial and historical allusiveness is direct, calm, open, in contrast with the complex, involuted, explosive style of the younger, also anthologised, Raymond Mazisi Kunene. C. P.

Villiers, Alan John (1903–   ), Australian author of books about the sea and the sailing ships which have been his life since the age of fifteen. His works include *The Cruise of the 'Conrad'* (1937), the story of a 60,000-mile journey in a full-rigged ship crewed by cadets; the prize-winning *The Quest of the Schooner 'Argus'* (1952); *The Way of a Ship* (1953); and his autobiography, *The Set of the Sails* (1949). S. R.

Vittorini, Elio (1908–66), Italian writer. Born in Sicily and self-taught, he held a variety of jobs ranging from bridge-building to journalism, and was editor of various periodicals and collections of literary works. His early production, which includes *Il garofano rosso* [*The Red Carnation*] (1935), an account of the experiences of a group of young people at the time of the march on Rome, and the short novel *Erica e i suoi fratelli* [*Erica*] (written in 1936 but withheld until 1954), represents an attempt at fusing purely literary motifs with tough objectiveness. But not until *Conversazione in Sicilia* [*Conversation in Sicily*] (1941) did Vittorini receive the accolade of critics and readers alike. This work, in which Vittorini relates a Sicilian's return to his native island and visit to his mother, evokes from the childhood memories of a close family life the images of a captivatingly unadulterated world in a harmonious combination of realism and symbolism, humour and tragedy. These themes also appear in other works such as *Il Sempione strizza l'occhio al Fréjus* [*Tune For an Elephant*] (1947) and *La Garibaldina* [*La Garibaldina*] (1950) which however lack the impassioned gusto of *Conversazione in Sicilia.* D. B.

Vladimov, Georgiy (1931–   ), Soviet writer, began his career in literary criticism after completing his law studies in Leningrad. He is concerned that literature should be about the individuality of people rather than either a condemnation of the Soviet system or a propaganda leaflet. His short novel *Ruda* [*The Ore*] (1955) portrays an independent Russian worker whose pride in doing a job well lays him open to ostracism from the members of his *kollectiv* for not fitting in with the rest of the community. B. W.

Voinovich, Vladimir (1926–   ), Soviet writer whose sincerity and transparent desire to be a realist has led to violent official criticism. His first novel *This is Where we Live* (1961) was blamed for presenting a false portrait of Soviet life. His second, *I'd be Honest if they'd Let me* (1962), also occasioned severe censure. This story too gives a provocative picture of the boredom of Soviet life—the petty individuals among the petty masses. Its exaggeration of the truth is probably a compensating reaction to demands that reality be distorted to satisfy a credo. B. W.

Voznesensky, Andrei (1933–), Soviet poet who had originally intended upon a career in architecture. He began publishing his work in 1958. Perhaps he symbolises better than Yevtushenko the growing demand for intellectual and creative freedom. His work is more unorthodox than the latter's and technically better constructed. Voznesensky enjoys listening to the sound of words and often includes unusual vocabulary in his poems simply for their phonic value or because of their similarity with more common words. This experimentalism together with unusual subject matter has led to his being criticised mainly because they produce elusive images. Voznesensky produced a sort of poetic manifesto with his poem *Parabolicheskaya ballada* [*Parabolic Ballad*] (1961). Other translated works include his account of the fate of his architectural career in *Pozhar v Arkhitekturnom institutye* [*Fire in the Architectural Institute*] (1958), and such stimulating poems as *Poyut negry* [*We are Negroes*] (1961), *Lobnaya ballada* [*The Skull Ballad*] (1962) and *Antimiry* [*Antiworlds*] (1961). Two English anthologies, *Selected Poems* (trans. Herbert Marshall) and *Poems 1950–1965* (trans. Robert Creeley), appeared in 1966. B. W.

Waddell, Helen (1889–1965), English mediaeval scholar and author of the novel *Peter Abelard* (1933), which portrays the small society of the twelfth-century Paris schools, successfully using characteristic dialogue and contemporary situations, rather than descriptive passages. The sudden intense love between the chaste ascetic Abelard, aged thirty-seven, and Heloise, seventeen-year-old niece of the gullible old canon Fulbert, triumphantly changes the whole outlook for both. A son is born and they are secretly married in an attempt to appease Fulbert, who becomes insane, forces Heloise into a convent and organises the castration of Abelard. He becomes a monk, continues to teach and is condemned for heresy. Finally as a hermit he finds spiritual comfort in his new apprehension of the Atonement.

The Wandering Scholars (1927) and *Mediaeval Latin Lyrics* (1929) are both concerned with the unbroken Latin cultural tradition. G. C.

Wain, John (1925–), English novelist and poet, best known for his first, comic novel *Hurry on Down* (1953) which belongs with Amis's *Lucky Jim*, published the following year, in giving a comic expression to some of the preoccupations of the 'angry young men' of the time. Its principal target is the English class system, and its hero (or anti-hero) Charles Lumley, concerned to emancipate himself from the trappings of his upper-middle-class background in order to establish his own individuality, embarks on a course of social down-climbing. This proves both hilariously difficult and also ineffectual, each rung of the ladder fixing him in a different economic class with its corresponding social ramifications as firmly as did his initial position near the top. The book ends with Lumley having come to terms with the need for socio-economic involvement, his individuality no longer menaced.

Wain's subsequent novels tend to be thematically repetitive, with the provinces-versus-metropolis issue appearing from time to time as in Amis. Titles include *Living in the Present* (1955), *The Contenders* (1958) and *The Young Visitors* (1965). He has also expressed his preoccupations in short stories—of which *Nuncle and Other Stories* (1960) and *Death of the Hind Legs* (1966) are collections—and in verse. Some of his poems were included in Robert Conquest's anthology *New Lines* (1956). As with Donald Davie's poetry, the eighteenth century has had an effect on his verse in that form and reason are dominant in his rejection of the extremes of romanticism; like Amis's, it has some elements of the ordinary man coming to terms with the real world in a common-sense manner. Volumes of verse include *Mixed Feelings* (1951), *A Word Carved on a Sill* (1956) and *Weep Before God* (1961). K. R. R.; D. L. P.

Wakeman, Frederic (1909–), American novelist, wrote *The Hucksters* (1946) satirising the advertising business. Other titles include *De Luxe Tour* (1956). K. R. R.

Waley, Arthur (1889–1966), English translator and poet. Waley was for some time Assistant Keeper of the Department of Prints and Drawings at the British Museum. He is principally known for his translations of Chinese and Japanese poetry, as in *170 Chinese Poems* (1917) and *Japanese Poems* (1919). Waley himself describes these translations as literal but in fact considerable poetic skill is required to convey the effects of simplicity and rhythmic movement contained in the originals. His prose translations include *The Nō Plays of Japan* (1921), and the novel by Baroness Murasaki, *The Tale of Genji* (1925–32). A selection of his work was published in *Chinese Poems* (1946); and his book *The Opium War through Chinese Eyes* came out in 1958.

Waley must be accounted an important figure in twentieth-century literature, and be credited, as substantially as Ezra Pound, with bringing the influence of oriental literature to bear on English and American poetry during the period after the first world war. D. L. P.

Wallace, Edgar (1875–1932), English novelist. Born in London the illegitimate son of an actress, and adopted by a Billingsgate porter, he lived in poverty doing menial jobs until at eighteen he enlisted and went to South Africa. He began writing articles and became a Reuter correspondent in the Boer War. His first novel *The Four Just Men* (1905) was a murder mystery. It was followed by *Sanders of the River* (1911), a series of west African stories. In the next twenty-seven years he wrote more than one hundred and fifty best-selling thrillers and plays, of little literary value but immensely popular, including *Bones* (1915), *The Green Archer* (1923), *The Crimson Circle* (1922) and *The Ringer* (1929). G. S.

Wallace, Irving (1916–), American novelist, best known for his very long novel *The Prize* (1963) which brings together the various Nobel prizewinners for a particular year—these including a married couple who at a time when their marriage is at breaking-point have won the prize for medicine with their research into the vitrification of spermatozoa. The book contains much accurate detail about the machinations of Nobel prizewinner selection. His other novels include *The Chapman Report*

(1962), which exposes the pseudo-sociological methods of a research team investigating the sex lives of American women, by probing the actual love-life of four supposedly typical individuals; and *The Three Sirens* (1964), an account of a group of anthropologists who study an isolated race of happy primitives on a Polynesian island and begin to doubt their own (particularly sexual) values. Later titles include *The Plot* (1967). P. E.

Walmsley, Leo (1892–1966), English novelist. Most of his stories are set against a background of fishing ports and his favourite countryside of Cornwall. His works include *Phantom Lobster* (1933), *Love in the Sun* (1939), *Master Mariner* (1948) and *So Many Loves* (1954). R. A. K.

Walpole, Hugh (1884–1941), English novelist, born in New Zealand. He began his working life as a schoolmaster and published his first novel *The Wooden Horse* in 1909. Then came *Mr Perrin & Mr Traill* (1911), a sensitive study of two schoolmasters. He served in the first world war with the Red Cross in Russia, and later wrote several novels with Russia as a background, notably *Dark Forest* (1916) and *Secret City* (1919). These were followed by his stories of boyhood which were in part autobiographical, including *Jeremy* (1919), *Jeremy and Hamlet* (1923) and *Jeremy at Crale* (1927). *The Cathedral* (1922) dealing with the Cornish town of Polchester was probably inspired by his own ecclesiastical background and his admiration for Trollope. In the early thirties came the four volumes of the Herries saga, regarded by many as his best work: *Rogue Herries* (1930), *Judith Paris* (1931), *The Fortress* (1932) and *Vanessa* (1933).

Walpole's literary output was extensive: he wrote and eventually had published over forty novels besides many volumes of short stories, studies on Conrad and Trollope and three volumes of literary confession—*The Crystal Box* (1924), *The Apple Trees* (1932) and *Roman Fountain* (1940). A somewhat spiteful portrait of this admittedly middle-brow writer is to be found in the character of Alroy Kear in Somerset Maugham's *Cakes and Ale*. K. M. H.

Walser, Martin (1928–), German author. His first literary success was his sociologically trenchant novel *Ehen in Philippsburg* ['Marriage in Philippsburg'] which won the 1957 Hermann Hesse Prize. His work includes short stories and plays, most notably the play *Eiche und Angora* [*The Rabbit Race*] (1962), the first part of a trilogy attempting to portray village life in south Germany after the end of the second world war. Sociological vision and penetrative analysis of character are Walser's strongpoints. R. C. W.

Warner, Rex (1905–), English novelist and Greek-scholar. Though one of a number of writers whose works may be characterised by their reaction to war and chaos, he has shown a distinct originality of temperament as well as the disciplinary influence of his classical scholarship. He experimented, in such novels as *The Professor* (1938) and *The Aerodrome* (1941), in allegorical forms and in a purposeful symbolism. His translations from the Greek are numerous and he has produced a significant set of essays entitled *The Cult of Power* (1946). Later novels centre on figures from ancient history, including *The Young Caesar* (1958), *Pericles the Athenian* (1963) and, in *The Converts* (1967), St Augustine.

R. A. K.

Warner, Sylvia Townsend (1893–), English novelist and short-story writer many of whose books have fantastic themes and are peopled by various strange creatures, such as benevolent witches. Typical is *The Cat's Cradle Book* (1960), a collection of stories embodying feline ethics as told by mother cats to their kittens for generations; others include *Lolly Willowes* (1926) and *The Corner that Held them* (1948), the latter a witty amusing novel of mediaeval convent life. Her manner of treating the fantastic as normal is perhaps best seen in her mature volume of stories *A Stranger with a Bag* (1966). P. E.

Waterhouse, Keith (1929–), English writer, left school at fifteen, working at various jobs before becoming a journalist in Yorkshire; when twenty-two he moved to Fleet Street and travelled widely as a feature writer. His first novel *There is a Happy Land* (1957), a pathetic, perceptive story of childhood and child murder told by a small boy, was enthusiastically reviewed. *Billy Liar* (1959), the study of a lad who compensates for his tawdry life by fantastic daydreams, was dramatised by Waterhouse and his friend Willis Hall and was highly successful as a play and a film. They have since collaborated on several plays and film scripts and written together for radio and television. Waterhouse's subsequent publications include his third novel *Jubb* (1963). G. S.

Watkins, Vernon (1906–), Welsh poet. Watkins is a poet preoccupied with the symbolic, the universal, the mystical, the visionary; he ignores the immediate changing world of people to concentrate on the unchanging pattern of reality. Watkins is a heavily symbolic romantic, without the wit and humour and human interest of Dylan Thomas, concentrating on mysticism centred in life, birth, death, light, dark, the moving force and pattern behind the order of the cosmos. The Welsh land and seascapes are caught up in a symbolic representation of nature; birth is not an agonising, natural or sweated labour but an indication of the sacredness of the womb. Watkins's poetry is not personal or immediate but ethereal in the grand style. Published work includes *Ballad of the Mari Lwyd* (1941); *The Lamp and the Veil* (1945); *The Lady with the Unicorn* (1948); *The Death Bell* (1954); *Cypress and Acacia* (1959); and *Affinities* (1962). *Letters to Vernon Watkins by Dylan Thomas* was published in 1957. D. L. P.

Waugh, Alec (1898–), English novelist, brother of Evelyn Waugh. His name was removed from his school roll when his first novel *The Loom of Youth* (1917), an exposé of public school life, was published. The best-known of his novels is probably *Island in the Sun* (1956) on the subject of the emotional and political problems which arise between black and white in a West Indian island. Also notable is *The Rule of the Minaret* (1965), a story of British counter-intelligence in the middle east. *My Brother Evelyn and Other Portraits* was published in 1967. P. E.

Waugh, Evelyn (1903–66), English novelist, is best known for his very popular satirical novels of the 1930s—to be precise, from *Decline and Fall* (1928) to *Put Out More Flags* (1942). In his post-World War II novels, with the exception of *The Loved One* (1948), there is not the same gusto: pungent social criticism having given way to a mixture of nostalgia and distaste, with a stiffening of personal distress and religious undertones. What remains is his undiminished capacity for creating truly memorable characters.

Evelyn Waugh was educated at Lancing, an Anglican public school, and Oxford. From his novels, and especially from his self-portrait in *The Ordeal of Gilbert Pinfold* (as well as from his autobiography), we get a clear picture of his feelings about the world he grew up in—essentially a blend of ridicule and disgust. Like Graham Greene, he was converted to Catholicism in 1930, his first marriage having been dissolved a few months previously. Ridicule and farce are the chief characteristics of his pre-war novels, the first of which, the immensely popular *Decline and Fall*, may be taken as typical. Innocence, in the form of the earnest and guileless Paul Pennyfeather, falls an easy prey to a world full of fools and knaves. The opening is characteristic: attacked and stripped by a gang of drunken aristocrats in his college quadrangle he is promptly sent down for indecent exposure. Subsequently, while teaching at Llanabba Castle, a private school staffed largely by people who have had their studies similarly terminated, he is beguiled into a liaison (initially, and on paper, an ill-defined business relationship) with Margot Beste-Chetwynde, the mother of one of his pupils: with the result that he finds himself arrested and jailed for being involved in the white slave traffic (Margot, of course, escaping). The story at times borders on the preposterous: but both the farcical and preposterous issue logically enough from the satirical characterisation of all the people that Paul encounters—from the depraved aristocrats and the dubious schoolmasters who tutor their less intelligent offspring, to the 'progressive' prison governor whose policies precipitate a murder. And through it all there runs the theme of universal folly and knavery, and of the injustices perpetrated on the innocent—extending to such random disasters as little Lord Tangent's death from a poisoned foot, the legacy of a mis-shooting by the master in charge of the starting-pistol at the Llanabba sports.

The treatment of little Lord Tangent might suggest that Evelyn Waugh's concern is much wider than merely to castigate human behaviour; and that it is not just a question of the 'decline and fall' of another great civilisation. There is something here of the gratuitously evil, as with the elephant's killing of the child in *A Handful of Dust* (1934). Certainly in his African novels—to which he turned after the London society satire of his second novel *Vile Bodies* (1930)—we find a strong sense of evil: *Black Mischief* (1932) and *Scoop* (1938) opposing to the corruption and decadence of the sophisticated European metropolis not the simple purity of a world of 'noble savages' but the viciousness of a society become depraved without even ceasing to be barbarous. The inhabitants of Ishmaelia, a country governed entirely by one ruling family, the Jacksons, whose members occupy every post in the administration, and at present embroiled in a confused civil turmoil on which the English press magnate Lord Copper wishes to get a 'scoop', have nothing to learn from the Beste-Chetwyndes—though 'the better sort of Ishmaelites have been Christian for some time and will not publicly eat human flesh uncooked in Lent without special and costly dispensation from their bishop'.

The series that had begun with *Decline and Fall* ended with *Put Out More Flags*—which was also the first of a group of books set in the period of the second world war. Here the brilliant, near-farcical satirising of mankind's folly and knavery in times of peace has given way to something approaching the sick humour of more recent times; and it is easy to react with near-loathing to the chicanery of Basil Seal and Ambrose Silk when set against the background of the war against Hitler. The picture of the world and its inhabitants given in these six novels is one that is almost entirely lacking in positive values, and may be compared to that painted by Graham Greene in the same period.

Like Greene, Waugh was to find an escape from this nihilism as a result of his conversion to Roman catholicism. *Brideshead Revisited* (1945), in many ways the mid-point of his career (and to many readers the point where he begins to lose his characteristic literary talent), is the first book to have a specifically religious theme. The Oxford of these 'sacred and profane memories' of the non-Catholic Capt. Charles Ryder is still recognisable as the Oxford of Paul Pennyfeather, though there is more emphasis on frivolity and degeneracy—notably in the portrayal of the teddy-bear cult—than on boorish irresponsibility and social injustice. What is new is a softer, more sympathetic attitude, culminating in the suggestion that the totally depraved Sebastian, precisely in the climax of his self-abandonment, is not far from that sanctity which, consciously or unconsciously, Ryder is seeking.

There followed the war trilogy, *Men at Arms* (1952), *Officers and Gentlemen* (1954) and *Unconditional Surrender* (1961): and here the central figure is a Catholic, Guy Crouchback. The trilogy was described in *The Times* as 'the most important piece of fiction to emerge from the second world war'. And yet to many readers it is a depressing work. The exuberant, savage ridicule of the earlier books has given way to a lofty distaste for the modern world *in toto*; and the new positive values have dwindled to those of an aristocratic English Catholicism seeking solace in a disdainful, nostalgic withdrawal from it. Crouchback, undistinguished member of an old but now insignificant Catholic family, is as ill-at-ease with his protestant fellow-officers in a smart regiment as he is with the plebeian Irish parish priest. In *Men at Arms* we see him enlisting in the army because, having identified Hitler and Stalin as the twin pillars of 'the modern world', he is thus able to discover some sense of purpose in his life. Disillusion is inevitable, and as the tone of the trilogy becomes increasingly one of snobbishness and pessimism, the humour becomes ever more thin. At the end of the road there can only lie 'unconditional surrender'.

Evelyn Waugh's other post-war novels include *The Loved One* (1948), a brilliant satire in the pre-war style on what has been called the 'American way of death', and *The Ordeal of Gilbert Pinfold* (1957), a poignant, largely autobiographical account of a mental illness. Shortly before his death the trilogy was reissued under the title *Sword of Honour* (1965). K. R. R.

Webb, Alice F. (1876–), New Zealand short-story writer, both in the delicacy of her style and in her experiments with technique (particularly the monologue) may be compared with Katherine Mansfield. However, she never developed to a similar extent, perhaps because she remained confined to one locality. Her work is collected in *Miss Peter's Special* (1926). S. R.

Webb, Mary (1881–1927), English novelist, had written stories and poems ever since she was a child, and her first novel *Golden Arrow* appeared in

1916 followed by *Gone to Earth* in 1917. Her early novels aroused little general interest, although a few discerning critics praised her writing, but she won the Femina Vie Heureuse Prize in 1924 with *Precious Bane*. Stanley Baldwin, then prime minister, read and admired this book and it was his eulogy after her death that finally brought her fame.

Mary Webb had a passionate love of nature, and this coupled with the sense of overhanging doom which is present in most of her writing invites comparison with Thomas Hardy. Her style, so full of cadences and poetic imagery, has a lyrical quality which probably owes much to her Celtic ancestry, but at times her work is marred by overintensity and a tendency towards stylistic floridness.

Her other works include *Spring of Joy*, a collection of essays (1917); *House in Dormer Forest* (1920); and *Seven for a Secret* (1922). K. M. H.

Webster, Jean (1876–1916), American novelist best known for *Daddy-Long-Legs* (1912), the story of an orphan's romance told in a series of letters. Its sequel *Dear Enemy* (1915) did not achieve the same popularity. P. E.

Webster, Mary Morison (–), Scottish-born poet, sister of the novelist Elizabeth Jean Webster (*The Expiring Frog*, 1946), domiciled in South Africa since 1920. A fine poetess, whose work has the beauty and passion of an Emily Dickinson or a Christina Rossetti, she is also an original critic. C. P.

Wedekind, Frank (1864–1918), German playwright, born in Hanover, the son of a doctor. Educated in Switzerland he was a freelance journalist for some time before entering an advertising agency in Munich. At the age of thirty-three he became an actor, formed his own company and toured Germany. His first important play *Frühlings Erwachen* [*Spring Awakening*] (1891) is a tragedy of puberty; he broke many of the accepted social conventions of the time by the frank treatment of sex on the stage, and was prevented by censorship from staging it until 1906. *Der Erdgeist* [*The Earth Spirit*] (1895) and *Die Büchse der Pandora* [*Pandora's Box*] (1904) were originally written as one play. The latter was not performed until after his death; its central character is a woman driven by sex, bringing disaster on her men until she herself is killed by Jack the Ripper. The theme of the conflict between youth and old age, central to the expressionist theatre, was also dwelt upon by Wedekind; but it was not until the censorship disappeared with the defeat of imperial Germany in 1918 that his ideas could be really examined. G. W.

Weil, Simone (1909–43), French writer. Born in Paris, she specialised early in philosophy. A fervent Christian, she attempted to find the answer to problems of the day, that of the working class, of the Spanish civil war, of the second world war. The intensity of experience into which her religious beliefs led her, and the matching intensity of her literary activity, brought on her early death. During her life she published articles and reviews which have been collected and published posthumously. Titles include *La Pesanteur et la grâce* [*Gravity and Grace*] (1947), *L'Enracinement* [*The Need for Roots*] (1949), *L'Attente de Dieu* [*Waiting on God*] (1950), *Cahiers* ['Notebooks'] (1951, 1953 and 1956) and *Oppression et liberté* [*Oppression and Liberty*] (1955). A. L. W.

Weiss, Peter Ulrich (1916–), German-Swedish writer. Born in Prussia of Jewish parents, he moved to England with his family for two years before studying at the Art Academy in Prague. After the Czechoslovak crisis of 1938 he moved to Switzerland, but finally settled in Sweden; he has lived there since 1939 and is now naturalised. He first of all was a painter and a film producer; but since 1960 he has devoted himself to literature and drama. His prose work *Der Schatten des Körpers des Kutschers* ['The shadow of the body of the coachman'] (1960) was regarded as stylistically extremely promising; *Abschied von den Eltern* (1961) and *Fluchtpunkt* (1962) [jointly trans. as *Leavetaking and Vanishing Point*], which were based on his own early experiences, were also praised. *Das Gespräch der drei Gehenden* ['The conversation of the three walkers'] (1963) is an experimental prose work; three men meet on a bridge, and despite their talking fail to communicate.

But Weiss is known in England much more as a dramatist. *Die Verfolgung und Ermordung Jean Paul Marat* [*The Marat-Sade*] appeared in 1964 and was promptly produced in London the following year. Its full title in English—*The Persecution and Assassination of Marat as performed by the inmates of the Asylum of Charenton under the direction of the Marquis de Sade*—makes it easy to appreciate the stir it caused. In 1965 *Die Ermittlung* [*The Investigation*] promptly passed into the English repertoire. An inquiry into the extermination of the Jews, it brings out the complicity and guilt of Europe by having the judges and the accused changing places. G. W.

Welch, Denton (1915–48), English novelist of unusual promise and originality who died at thirty-three after many years of illness following a road accident. He is chiefly remembered for his novels of adolescence

Maiden Voyage (1943) and *In Youth is Pleasure* (1944) which are distinguished by their spontaneity, perception and imagination. His posthumous *Journals* contain accounts of the wide travels he undertook in spite of ill-health. The volume *Denton Welch: Selections from his Published Works* was published in 1963 with a notable introduction by Jocelyn Brooke.

P. E.

Wells, Carolyn (1869–1942), American anthologist of humorous verse (*A Nonsense Anthology*, 1902) and writer of detective stories featuring the sleuth Fleming Stone (*The Fleming Stone Omnibus*, 1933). K. R. R.

Wells, H. G. (Herbert George Wells; 1866–1946), English novelist, the son of a small shopkeeper who went bankrupt. His childhood was spent in a dim poverty which stimulated, rather than suppressed, his expansive vision and imagination, and left him with a sense of ambitious purpose. At the age of sixteen he gave up his apprenticeship in the drapery trade and became a teacher; he took a degree in zoology and joined the Fabian Society. In 1893 he abandoned teaching to become a full-time writer.

His first fiction, including the long short-story *The Time Machine* (1895), may be described as fantastic, in that he chose great distances of time and space as his medium. Wells used this method not for the inherent adventure but as a means to objectivity; from a distance he could portray a coherent, massive picture of the society he sought to reform. *Tono-Bungay* (1909), a humorous character novel rather than a romance, and the work that combines his qualities to the best advantage, provides a portrait of his early years: the mother of his hero, George Ponderevo, has been 'in service' so long that her idea of life is confined to 'knowing one's place'; the general deprivation of the ghastly Frapp family makes of an oppressive religion their only liberty; and Aunt Susan is one of the most endearing and bravest people in fiction, whose mockery conceals not only her terror of obliteration but her own serenity while she is whirled from penury to prosperity on a wave of spurious patent medicine. As a social document the book regrets the passing of tradition and privilege, not for themselves but for the lack of anything better than charlatanism to take their place.

Love and Mr Lewisham (1900), *Kipps* (1905) and *Ann Veronica* (1909) do much the same. In *The History of Mr Polly* (1910) Wells introduced his best-loved hero—the 'little man' with the soul of greatness, whose pitifully small but hard-won achievement is to live his own happy, useful life. These books exemplify Wells's essay 'The Contemporary Novel' (1911), in which he demanded a form adaptable enough to indicate the whole of life. The novel, he asserted, must be 'the initiator of knowledge, the seed of fruitful self-questioning', and amongst the discursiveness necessary for the one there must be a clear elucidation of the direction to be taken by the other. His best work however, which fulfils these demands, precedes this essay. Wells's later work, which includes *The Outline of History* (1920) and *The Shape of Things to Come* (1933), was dominated by the idea of the one-world state and more often took the form of an expanded tract than a novel. It suffers from prolixity (his earlier work, though indeed discursive, was still economical), and from being beyond the comprehension of the general reader both in subject and language. It was also out of tune with the politics and strident nationalism of the twenties and thirties. Another defect, from *Joan and Peter* (1918) onwards, is his peevishness and even hopelessness (as in *The Fate of Homo Sapiens*, 1939; and in *Mind at the End of its Tether*, 1945).

His indefatigable energy resulted in a great number of books on a wide range of subjects, often of ephemeral interest; his best work, though of its time, still contains food for thought as well as delight in its humour and diversity. H. C.

Wentworth, Patricia (born Dora Amy Elles; –1961), English novelist. Her first novel was a romance of the French revolution and then came the first of her romantic thrillers *The Astonishing Adventure of Jane Smith* (1923). She continued to write in this vein with the accent on romance until the advent of Miss Silver in the 1940s. This mild-mannered old lady, cast in the same mould as Agatha Christie's Miss Marple, has appeared in most of Miss Wentworth's later thrillers, unravelling mysteries and unmasking murderers to the accompaniment of clicking knitting needles. Among her many works are *Miss Silver Intervenes* (1943), *Miss Silver Comes to Stay* (1949) and *The Watersplash* (1953). K. M. H.

Werfel, Franz (1890–1945), Austrian writer. Born in Prague, the son of a wealthy Jewish manufacturer, his poems, plays and novels are a constant advocacy of a millennial universal brotherhood. *Poems*, some fifty English translations made from the collected *Gedichte aus dreissig Jahren* (1939), gives an indication of his distinguished, lyrical contribution to the religious, ecstatic, 'communistic' aspect of expressionism, especially if considered in relation to his principal plays *Spiegelmensch* [*Mirror Man*] (1920), *Bocksgegang* [*Goat Song*] (1921) and *Juarez und Maximilian* [*Juarez and Maximilian*] (1924); but it was as a novelist that Werfel found his greatest audience. Three novelettes, *Nicht der Mörder* [*Not the Murderer*] (1920), *Der Tod des Kleinbürgers* [*The Man Who Conquered Death*] (1927) and *Der Abituriententag* [*The Class Reunion*] (1928), all in the English collection *Twilight of the World*, merit attention, artistically, as do *Verdi* [*Verdi*]

(1924), an acute, musically intelligent, fictional comparison of Verdi with Wagner; the engrossing moral and psychological drama involving an army officer in charge of a firing squad, *Barbara, oder die Frömmigkeit* [*The Pure in Heart*] (1929), an excellent portrait of pre-war Austrian society; and *Die Geschwister von Neapel* [*The Pascarella Family*] (1931), a study of a domineering father which explores further the typically expressionist conflict of father and son previously attempted in *Not the Murderer*. Popular acclaim, however, has been reserved, largely, for *Die vierzig Tage des Musa Dagh* [*The Forty Days*] (1933), an account of Armenian heroism and Turkish brutality in World War I, and *Das Lied von Bernadette* [*The Song of Bernadette*] (1941). M. D. E.

Wescott, Glenway (1901–   ), American novelist, achieved some reputation in the twenties with his novels and stories inspired by his native Wisconsin. The grimness of its puritanism and the pioneering of the frontier days are evoked in *The Apple of the Eye* (1924); the latter again in *The Grandmothers, A Family Portrait* (1927). With the volume of stories *Goodbye, Wisconsin* (1928) Wescott reached a high-water mark, withdrawing to Europe in the hope of freeing himself from its influence. His subsequent writings failed to make a comparable impact, although one or two later works—*The Pilgrim Hawk* (1940), *Apartment in Athens* (1944)—have enjoyed a limited popularity. K. R. R.

Wesker, Arnold (1932–   ), English playwright, first attracted attention with a production of *Roots* (1959), the middle part of a trilogy about a Jewish family from the East End of London. The subsequent performances of the whole trilogy and of his earlier play *The Kitchen* (1959), later filmed, confirmed his reputation, which was further enlarged with the long West End run of *Chips with Everything* (1962). In the years that followed he applied his energies to the development of 'Centre 42', an organisation with trade-union backing for bringing the arts into the life of the industrial worker; and his play *Their Very Own and Golden City* (1966) has a trade-union setting.

The Kitchen portrays the life behind and below a smart restaurant—a life which Wesker had himself experienced. Of widely varied and sometimes mutually hostile national backgrounds, the restaurant's workers are united in their wearisome drudgery for an essentially uncomprehending boss: they have jobs and food, 'what is there more?' he asks. Whatever 'more' there might be, it has been enough to produce one exceptionally violent personal outburst; the mounting communal frustration that precedes it being conveyed in a ritualistic, near-musical build-up of the tempo and sound-volume of their work, and giving it something of a sacrificial quality.

The trilogy takes up this question of the 'more'. In *Chicken Soup with Barley* (1960) we meet the members of the hard-pressed Kahn family, notably the key figure of the self-educated Ronny, and his indomitable mother. The socialist implications of *The Kitchen* are presented here in more explicit form, but it becomes clear that the full answer to the Kahns' needs will never come simply through politics. It is in *Roots*, in which he never actually appears, that we learn more of Ronny's distinctive ideas about what more is needed for a full and satisfying life—through the dramatic development in the personality of Beatie Bryant, the East Anglian girl who has come under his influence while in London. In *I'm Talking about Jerusalem* (1960) we meet Ronny's sister Ada and her husband who have moved out into the country to escape the spiritual corruption endemic to city life, but are in turn disillusioned by the intellectual and emotional constriction of rural society—a constriction from which Beatie had been liberated by Ronny.

If the trilogy's time sequence is too strongly emphasised, its ending must seem an anti-climax: if, on the other hand, the thematic interrelationships of the three plays are adequately experienced, the disillusionment of the two outer parts will be seen to be balanced by the positive qualities of *Roots*. However, the pessimism of *Chips With Everything* is unmistakable. The important thing about Beatie was that she emerged as an authentic individual: in the latter play, written for a society already meek and indiscriminating that is epitomised in its acceptance of the uniform, ubiquitous fried potatoes, we witness (in an R.A.F. setting) the ruthless extinction of individuality by those who cannot tolerate it.

K. R. R.

West, Morris (1916–), Australian novelist. His first book *Gallows on the Sand* was published in 1955 but it was in 1957 that one of his most notable books, the non-fiction *Children of the Sun*, appeared. This passionate protest against the conditions of poverty in the Naples slums was also an appeal for help for the priest Borelli who worked alone for so long to bring hope to the slum dwellers. Since then Morris West has become established as a powerful Catholic writer and in *The Devil's Advocate* (1959) and *The Shoes of the Fisherman* (1963) he writes with great authority and insight about the politics of the Roman Catholic Church. In the former a dying English priest is sent to a southern Italian village to investigate, and discredit, claims for the canonisation of a mysterious inhabitant now dead; while the latter is the story of the choosing of a Ukrainian cardinal as pope and the far-reaching effects of this choice. These were followed by *The Ambassador* (1965), a novel of the war in South Vietnam. K. M. H.; P. E.

West, Nathanael (Nathan Weinstein; 1904–40), American novelist. West's satire of the American way of life, contained in four novels published in the 1930s, is sociologically severe, savage and scatological. His style and attitudes remind one irresistibly of Voltaire. The first, *The Dream Life of Balso Snell* (1931), strikes out grotesquely at the values both of art and of society. In *Miss Lonelyhearts* (1933), the best known of the novels, a reporter takes over the 'sob' column of his newspaper and is drawn into the barrenness and individual loneliness to be found in twentieth-century America. The novel progresses against a background of self-pity and ineffectual sex until finally 'Miss Lonelyhearts' is accidentally killed by the crippled husband of one of his correspondents, a nymphomaniac wife who has seduced the increasingly inadequate newspaperman.

A Cool Million (1934) is very much in the genre of Voltaire's *Candide*. Lemuel Pitkin, a young American pursuing the goal of wordly success through free enterprise, is taken up by Shagpole Whipple, an ex-president of the United States and a believer in opportunist politics. Pitkin moves in and out of intrigues and brothels, retains some innocence but loses in rapid succession his teeth, an eye, his scalp, a leg and finally his life. He is a witness to rapes, riots and the inhumanity of man to man.

The Day of the Locust (1939) is set in the Hollywood of the 'extra' and the 'hanger on'. It is a novel of middle-aged boredom, of lust and loitering, and of the frustration of meaningless minds and mis-used bodies. The running down of American society as represented in California explodes in blood and riot.

West's novels juxtapose coolness and passion in a grotesque exposure of the political, economic and social bankruptcy of his society. D. L. P.

West, Rebecca (Cicily Isabel Fairfield; 1892–), English journalist, novelist and critic. She began her career in the theatre (acting the part in Ibsen's *Rosmersholm* that was to become her literary pseudonym), but turned to journalism, and in 1916 wrote her first book, a study of Henry James. Her novels include *The Judge* (1922), an interesting example of the influence of Freudian psychology on novelists of the period; *The Thinking Reed* (1936), which conveys memorably, through the experiences of a girl married to a wealthy industrialist, the moral dangers involved in being very rich; *The Fountain Overflows* (1957), in which real (i.e. non-worldly) values are represented in a family's single-minded devotion to the world of music; and *The Birds Fall Down* (1966). She is probably more widely known for two books she wrote about the Nuremberg trials, *The Meaning* *of Treason* (1947), which deals with William Joyce and John Amery, and *A Train of Powder* (1955). Other titles include *D. H. Lawrence, an Elegy* (1930); and *Black Lamb and Grey Falcon* (1941), an account of a pre-war Yugoslavian journey. R. A. K.

Wharton, Edith (1862–1937), American novelist, whose material, style and tone suggest affinities with Henry James. However, her satirical attacks on the almost tribal conventions of the late nineteenth-century fashionable New York society in which she grew up, and her exploration of the potentialities for personal tragedy inherent in too rigid an adherence to them, mark her out as a writer of originality and distinction. For instance, the orphaned and impoverished Lily Bart in *The House of Mirth* (1905) will not marry the man she loves because he cannot redeem her material fortunes, and this refusal dooms her to a disastrous descent into abysmal penury and premature death. *Ethan Frome* (1911), the book by which she is now most remembered—and which was published after she had moved to France following the termination of her own unhappy marriage with the death of her husband—is in various ways less typical: here it is the marriage bond that stands between two lovers and the fulfilment of their love.

While in France Edith Wharton tried to break away from the social background which she had exploited in her early novels, but was unable to do so convincingly; and it is once more to her New York childhood that she returns in *Age of Innocence* (1920)—another story of love frustrated by convention. What distinguishes her most clearly from James in her portrayal of this society is a greater willingness to see through to its economic foundations, coupled with an awareness of the moral contradictions implicit in the lives of even its most exemplary members. This is perhaps most evident in *The Custom of the Country* (1913). Her misfortune was that her moral strictures were not radical enough for the readers of the mainstream of post-Jamesian social fiction. K. R. R.

Wheatley, Dennis (1897–), English novelist who has produced thrillers with a wide range of background, historical and geographical. Crooks, spies and gallants move through his pages, with recurring characters such as Gregory Sallust and Roger Brook. His attention to background and detail is striking in such novels as *The Devil Rides Out* (1935), with a theme of black magic, and *They Found Atlantis* (1936). R. A. K.

White, E. B. (Elwyn Brooks White; 1899–), American journalist (*New Yorker*, *Harper's*), essayist and humorist, collaborated with Thurber in *Is Sex Necessary?* (1929) and has published volumes of verse including *The Fox of Peapack and Other Poems* (1933). K. R. R.

White, Patrick (1915–), Australian novelist. He grew up in New South Wales in a third-generation family of pastoralists, was educated in England, fought in the second world war, and eventually returned to Australia to live on a small property outside Sydney. His early books, *The Living and the Dead* (1941) and the ironically entitled *Happy Valley* (1938), are to a certain extent psychological novels in that he uses the stream-of-consciousness technique to record the interior monologues of his characters, both children and adults. This attempt to capture a personal view of reality and set it against the external world is developed more subtly in what he feels to be his most completely realised novel, *The Aunt's Story* (1948), in which we are drawn in to share the fantasy world created by a mad woman. *The Tree of Man* (1956), which made him known outside Australia, is the lengthy saga of the pioneering Stan and Amy Parker and the book recreates with tremendous richness and actuality the living presence of the Australian bush. It is important in reading White's novels to appreciate how completely he has absorbed both the physical environment and the mental traits of the people of Australia, and when this background appears in his writing it has a precise symbolism—it is a world in which nature has a long, rich, profound and only dimly understood heritage and civilisation is raw, crude and purblind, its recent graft an angry scar.

White's next novel *Voss* (1957) can be seen on two levels—firstly, the record of the German explorer Voss's tragic expedition into the desert interior; secondly and symbolically, a soul's pilgrimage and penetration into an uncharted region of experience. Each man on the expedition has a private reason for going and Voss's is the strongest of all—he is testing himself. Throughout the novel runs the counterpoint of Laura, the girl who though she does not accompany him nevertheless shares his experiences—in dream and reverie as well as through letter-writing. At times Voss takes on the attributes of Christ or even God himself; at others, he seems to become the Devil.

Despite the priase they received, these books were to many people unreadable because of their impenetrable prose, and it was not until the triumphant and absorbing *Riders in the Chariot* (1961) that White acquitted himself of this charge. The scope of this novel is vast; it weaves together four bulky, complex and disparate strands, each sufficient for a separate novel, yet without straining credulity. It concerns four 'outcasts', each with a personal visionary philosophy-religion, that nourishes, sustains and illumines lives that the world despises. There is the mad woman Mary Hare, living in a crumbling ruined Xanadu, an architectural fantasy built by her semi-aristocratic father, guided in her relationships with people by the pantheism that she derives from her love for plants and animals; the intellectual Jew Himmelfarb, who has survived by a series of miraculous events the German persecution, purges and concentration camps of World War II, and leads a devout and ascetic life of poverty and humility; the laundress Mrs Goldbold, with her drunken husband Tom and their numerous daughters, who has evolved her simple beliefs from her early experiences of non-conformity in England; and finally the aborigine Alf Dubbo whose fascination for paint has led him in his search for subjects to an apocalyptic intensity of vision. These four people, who between them represent the varied ingredients of the Australian population, come across each other in White's Sydney suburb of Sarsaparilla and clash with its inhabitants, who are themselves prejudiced, frightened, and frightening, parodies of the main characters. The resolution is a crucifixion, and in this repetition of an event 2,000 years old White provides an indictment of civilisation and its lack of true spiritual progress.

He has since published *Four Plays* (1965), including the interesting work *The Ham Funeral*, a mixture of farce and tragedy, with dialogue somewhat like that of Harold Pinter; and a novel, again set in Sarsaparilla, *The Solid Mandala* (1966). In this he explores the lives of the middle-aged twins Waldo and Arthur Brown, personifying in their separate but parallel existences two facets—the interior and exterior manifestations—of a single personality. Though often bitterly received, especially by Australian critics, White's work is now recognised as of world stature, and each of the novels reveals a further ambitious extension in scope and style. S. R.

White, T. H. (Terence Hanbury White; 1906–), English novelist, transformed Malory's *Morte d'Arthur* into a series of novels whose light and sometimes very funny style does not conceal his observation of the modern human condition and, in particular, his melancholy comment on man's solitude within society. *The Sword in the Stone* (1938), *The Ill-made Knight* (1941) and others were edited by White and republished in one volume *The Once and Future King* (1958). He also wrote an account of his own practice in falconry, *The Goshawk* (1951). H. C.

Whiting, John (1917–63), English playwright. His earlier plays *A Penny for a Song* (1951), *Saint's Day* (1951) and *Marching Song* (1954) were written during a period in which the greatest influences in the English theatre were still T. S. Eliot and Christopher Fry. Therefore these plays are more literary and coldly intellectual than others by modern dramatists, and Whiting himself has condemned 'theatrical journalism' and spoken of the need in theatre for a sense of literature.

In these three plays, as in *The Devils* (1961), the author is concerned with moral problems: responsibility for violence and suffering viewed in the hallucinatory world of the old poet Paul Southman in *Saint's Day*, the absurdity of war in the sometimes biting Dorset Napoleonic comedy *Penny for a Song*. But in Whiting the most absorbing theme is that of self-destruction: when and how does a man destroy himself? This is most closely analysed in the life of the ex-General Forster in *Marching Song*, and more especially in the priest Grandier and his relationship with the devil-ridden nuns in *The Devils*. The promise of these plays is such that it was a tragic loss for British theatre when John Whiting died of cancer at the age of forty-five. J. B. M.

Wickham, Anna (1884–), English poet of Australian parentage and education. Her poetry includes *The Man with a Hammer* (1916) and *The Little Old House* (1921). D. L. P.

Widdemer, Margaret (1890–), American poet and novelist. Widdemer first attracted attention with a poem 'Factories' later published in 1915 in the volume *Factories and Other Poems*. The poem denounces child labour and the volume as a whole shows a humanitarian regard for maltreated workers. The later verse contained in *Collected Poems* (1928 and 1957) is less hard and more sentimental. Among the author's romantic novels is the best-seller *The Rose Garden Husband* (1915). D. L. P.

Wiechert, Ernst (1887–1950), East Prussian writer and outspoken critic of the Nazis. His works include symbolic plays, conventional lyric verse and stories of which the most successful include *Die Magd des Jürgen Doscocil* [*The Girl and the Ferryman*] (1932) and *Die Majorin* [*The Baroness*] (1934). R. C. W.

Wilbur, Richard (1921–), American poet. Richard Wilbur's poetry belongs with the best of the period following the second world war. It is not consumed with passion nor deeply involved with social issues; it is formal and academic. In depth, it might be described as aesthetic in the sense that Wallace Stevens and Marianne Moore are concerned with aesthetics.

Wilburn was born in New York, brought up in New Jersey and graduated in 1942 from Amhurst College, Massachusetts. He spent two years abroad in the army and then returned to postgraduate studies at Harvard and subsequently a career lecturing in English literature. His published volumes of verse include *Things of This World* for which he won a Pulitzer prize in 1957.

The wit and grace of his poetry have led to comparison with the metaphysicals; he is certainly a master of the conceit and like the work of the latter his poetry is precise and technically brilliant. Wilbur, like Marianne Moore, is capable of assembling into an aesthetic whole a jumble of apparently disparate particles. His writing, like that of Wallace Stevens, can also be obliquely philosophical.

The elegance of the poetry is not of the cold variety. In a sense Wilbur has, more successfully than Moore, turned ethics into aesthetics and his value judgments are no less meaningful for that. A short piece from *Ceremony and Other Poems* (1948), while not his most outstanding work, well represents the brilliance of the poet's style:

'A Simile for Her Smile'

Your smiling, or the hope, the thought of it,
Makes in my mind such pause and abrupt ease
As when the highway bridge gates fall,
Balking the hasty traffic, which must sit
On each side massed and staring while
Deliberately the drawbridge starts to rise;

Then horns are hushed, the oil smoke rarifies
Above the idling motors one can tell
The packet's smooth approach, the slip,
Slip of the silken river past the sides,
The ringing of clear bells, the dip
And slow cascading of the paddle wheel.

Published volumes of his verse include *The Beautiful Changes* (1947), *Ceremony and Other Poems* (1950), *Things of This World* (1956), *Poems 1943–1956* (published in England, 1957) and *Advice to a Prophet and Other Poems* (1961). Also of interest is his translation of Molière's *The Misanthrope* (1953). D. L. P.

Wilder, Thornton (1897–), American novelist and playwright, one of the most distinguished and individual minor writers of his time, has won three Pulitzer prizes: for his novel *The Bridge of San Luis Rey* (1927) and his plays *Our Town* (1938) and *The Skin of our Teeth* (1943). Through these three works, and much of Wilder's other writing, runs a preoccupation with the goal or purpose of human life. *The Bridge of San Luis Rey* is based on the collapse of a bridge in Peru in 1704, plunging five people to their death, and poses the question 'was it an accident?'. The novel examines the lives of five characters suggested to Wilder by the victims, indicating a possible significance in certain events preceding and following the disaster: had each of the five perhaps just passed through some critical experience? and was the disaster perhaps necessary for the spiritual progress of others who knew them?

Our Town, which created a sensation by dispensing almost entirely with scenery and by opening with the curtain up, looks for significance not so much in the events surrounding death (though there is a death in it) as in the fabric of everyday life, finding it with the aid of a partial elimination of the particularities of place and time. Similar techniques are used in the more elaborate *The Skin of our Teeth,* a play which carries much more precise meanings on a number of distinct levels. Mr Antrobus, for instance, may be seen simultaneously as *Homo sapiens,* as a composite universal patriarch-pioneer figure, and as a modern Everyman. The adventures of his family—which in addition to wife and daughter includes a son Henry, alias Cain, and their maid Sabina, a Lilith-figure (but also described as 'the voice of the people in their confusion and their need')—are at the same time the history of the human race: commencing with the struggle for physical survival in the ice age, going through a phase when man has become lord of nature and his very prosperity and ease lead him to the brink of moral destruction, and finally showing him emerging by the skin of his teeth from the apotheosis of his innate wickedness, a modern war.

Wilder's other works include the novels *The Cabala* (1920), *The Woman of Andros* (1930) and *Heaven is my Destination* (1935), the last two with a strong Christian element; the farce *The Merchant of Yonkers* (1939) subsequently renamed as *The Matchmaker* (1955); a group of playlets, intended as part of two cycles to be entitled *The Seven Deadly Sins* and *The Seven Ages of Man*; and a further novel, *The Eighth Day* (1967).

K. R. R.

Williams, Charles (1886–1945), English novelist, poet, dramatist and writer of several theological works. The theme of his seven strangely fascinating novels is the struggle between good and evil, and supernatural experiences and spiritual torments are vividly described. The titles include *Many Dimensions* (1931); *Shadows of Ecstasy* (1931), the story of a mass African uprising and invasion of Europe inspired by a white man who claims to have triumphed over death; and *The Greater Trumps* (1932), a weird story of the mystic symbolism and influence of the Tarot cards. P. E.

Williams, Emlyn (1905–), Welsh actor and playwright. His dramatic works include several effective macabre plays of the pattern of his first success *A Murder Has Been Arranged* (1930). Particularly popular were *Night Must Fall* (1935), *The Corn is Green* (1938) and *Druid's Rest* (1944). He has also received public acclaim for his readings of Dickens and Dylan Thomas.

R. A. K.

Williams, Raymond (1921–), English writer on sociological topics and author of the widely read *Culture and Society* (1958), entered the realms of fiction with the solid but subtle *Border Country* (1960). The central character of this novel is a London lecturer of Welsh working-class background, whose father's imminent death brings him back to the culture of his origin and gives him the opportunity to come to terms with and take possession of his heritage. This was followed by *Second Generation* (1964).

K. R. R.

Williams, Tennessee (Thomas Lanier Williams; 1914–), American playwright of the post-World War II period, generally considered second in importance only to Arthur Miller. More prolific than Miller, he is also more erratic, and his treatment of the explosive forces of sexuality, chiefly in his native South (from one of whose states he took his adopted name), can sometimes overbalance into crude and sensational melodrama. However, at his best he is a master of the total theatrical experience.

His first success came with *The Glass Menagerie* (1945). In this, his gentlest play, he presents the theme that was to occupy him for two decades; that of reality versus illusion or fantasy. Mrs Wingfield and her daughter Laura both live in a fantasy world: the former in an imaginary past of Southern social grandeur populated by endless admirers which insulates her from her present impoverished loneliness; the latter in a brittle artificial world she has created for herself with her menagerie of glass animals as an escape from a world that her crippled leg and plain features inhibit her from entering. On the daughter is placed the burden of enacting the mother's fantasies: and the centrepiece of the play is the visit of a 'gentleman caller' (in fact a friend of her brother Tom) who, out of a genuine if mild compassion and the lack of anything better to do, pays court to Laura. He makes her dance and gives her confidence: symbolically they bump against the table with the animals and break the horn off the unicorn, with whose freakishness she has identified herself. But with his interest waning (he is in fact already committed elsewhere) he cannot follow up his rescue act; and the play ends with Laura's further retreat into fantasy, which is set against her brother's success in making his own dream—of running away to sea—come true.

With *Streetcar Named Desire* (1947)—the title referring to a New Orleans tramcar whose destination is the street actually named Desire—the fantasies and delusions of Williams's characters become specifically related to the highways of sexual desire. There is also here the intense, extreme element so characteristic of Southern writing, in the neurotic nymphomania of the 'genteel' belle Blanche who arrives on the streetcar to visit her married sister, together with something of the violence with which Southern repressions are apt to erupt, in her provoking her brother-in-law Stanley to rape her. With her final removal to a mental institution the play has taken on a similar, only more emphatic, pattern to its predecessor.

This was followed by *Summer and Smoke* (1948) and *The Rose Tattoo* (1951), where the chief characters' fantasies take the form not so much of a denial of desire as of an obsession with purity. In the former this leads to the heroine rejecting the man she loves and becoming a lonely spinster; in the latter the widow Serafima is a prisoner of an idealisation of her marriage which she will not allow to be tarnished by truth. Like Mrs Wingfield, she tries to force her teenage daughter to enact her own fantasy, in this case by applying her own standards of imaginary perfection to the girl's boy-friends. She is rescued from her own frustrations, and from the danger of ruining her daughter's life, by a man who, while himself adopting the same rose tattoo that her late husband carried (which has become a symbol of their 'ideal' marriage), is also possessed of information concerning the latter's infidelities—with which he is finally able to liberate Serafima and restore her to a living reality. The title of the expressionist *Camino Real* (1953) puns on the English and Spanish words real and *real* ('royal'): and the play focuses on the point at which for its varied group of characters the *camino real* ('royal highway', i.e. of dreams) becomes the *camino* real, the path of truth. The group includes such historical personages as Lord Byron, Casanova, Don Quixote and Sancho Panza, together with the ubiquitous modern American everyman Kilroy, a boxer with a faulty heart. Their arid death-ridden town at the meeting of the roads, a town peopled also with perverts, prostitutes and the riff-raff of society, is beyond time and space (it is significantly over the border): for each of them it is situated at the critical stage of their lives, *nel mezzo del cammin di nostra vita.* For most, the way out is too frightening, threatening to lead only to disgust: Byron alone at least having the courage of his romanticism and being still prepared to 'make voyages, attempt them'. It is left to Kilroy to acquire Christ-like dimensions and to provide miraculously—simply through his unquenched faith in the potential goodness of man—a redemption that obviates the road that leads only to disgust. The fountains flow again in the piazza, and saving love returns to the *camino.*

After the richness and variety of *Camino Real*, there is a return to a simpler, starker version of the illusion-reality theme in *Cat on a Hot Tin Roof* (1955), with sexuality again a central issue together with the problem of death. Big Daddy is dying of cancer; everyone conspires to deny it. Brick, his younger son, is homosexual and alcoholic; everyone tries to ignore this too, including his frustrated wife Maggie (the 'cat') who even goes so far as to feign a pregnancy. The gigantic shouting matches between father and son, in which the truth is ruthlessly bared, solve nothing; only Maggie—like Tom Wingfield—eventually succeeds in translating her dream into reality. There is no hint here, as there has been in the previous play, that there could be any solution of the illusion-reality problems in situations where reality equals disgust or even death.

What continues from this play into the weird and horrific events of *Suddenly Last Summer* (1958) is an increasing preoccupation with the byways of sex together with an inquiry into the nature of the sexuality; and there is now also a mounting pitch of violence. Here we encounter every conceivable expression of the sexual instinct together with a peculiarly revolting piece of cannibalism on the part of a group of hungry boys and a deliberate mutilation of the girl Catherine's brain at her mother's behest in order to demolish her belief in the events that have occurred. Sebastian, the rich young American victim of the cannibals, has been engaged in a search for reality, for God, for a way of living; and while much of the material of this play suggests that its author's increasingly tormented preoccupations have now become obsessional, this quest of Sebastian's—at least partly answered in the image of the land-marooned turtle as a creature out of its element and a prey to God—does at least point a way forward.

The corner was seemingly turned with the aptly named *Period of Adjustment* (1960); and with *Night of the Iguana* (1961) Williams produced what to many people was one of his best plays to date. It is set, like *Camino Real*, over the border—this time more explicitly in Mexico, whose tropical jungle provides him with an image for the real nature of human instinct. This time the true reality is juxtaposed with the unreal 'reality' accepted by a busload of religious American women tourists, who are led by the self-deceiving lesbian Miss Fellows and driven by the unfrocked clergyman Shannon. The tour comes to a standstill when Shannon makes an unscheduled visit to the hostelry run by his recently widowed friend Mrs Falk: he has reached the end of his tether in his struggle with the two realities and will not budge forward or backward. There now arrive on the scene two people apparently possessed of the secret of happiness: the New England spinster Hannah Jelks and her grandfather Nono, 'the oldest living poet'. The former is remarkable both for her own self-fulfilment in such a bizarre relationship, and for her acceptance in others of every conceivable form of relationship: 'nothing disgusts me', she is to declare, 'except unkindness and violence'. When Shannon, desperately trying to adjust to the so-called 'realities' of everyday life—the need to control desire, to keep a job—eventually despairs and embarks on the 'long swim' of oblivion by jumping into the sea, he is brought back and trussed up like the hostelry's pet iguanas, and for the whole night Miss Jelks battles for his sanity. She is eventually able to set him, 'one of God's creatures', free; and she also provides him with a pattern for living in a world in which, in the words of the poem Nono is composing, 'creatures of a golden kind' must endure in an alien element of universal decay and mortality: a pattern of relationship (however bizarre) and services which he is quick to imitate in his charity to Miss Fellows and in his relationship with the widow Falk, and which appears to provide him with all he really needs. Nono's completed poem, which allows the old man to die contented, states with great beauty the need to endure this being out of one's element with patience and courage.

Williams's other titles include *The Milk Train Doesn't Stop Here Any More* (1963), the novel *The Roman Spring of Mrs Stone* (1950) and the short-story volume *The Knightly Quest* (1968). K. R. R.

Williams, William Carlos (1883–1963), American poet and novelist, can be described as an imagist and objectivist, but in the context of the American scene he is a poet trying to create a native mode of expression removed from what he feels to be the academic form of a verse like Eliot's *The Waste Land.* His later poetry is informed by the necessity to construct, from the American language, elemental values removed both from the European tradition and the scrap-book methods of his contemporaries.

Apart from qualifying in New York to practise medicine and a brief trip to Europe, Williams has spent the rest of his life in his home town, Rutherford, New Jersey, working as a doctor and writing. He issued a volume of fairly ordinary verse in 1909 and then came under the influence of the imagists, producing several volumes in that tradition until the publication of *Spring and All* in 1923. This establishes his conscious attempt at a definitive American technique. Although vastly different in style from Marianne Moore, Williams has, like her, the distinction of forging a singular and not easily described verse form—which works. His style narrows but shapes that form.

Williams is a novelist and an essayist as well as a poet. *In the American Grain* (1925) is a volume of essays arraigning the cheapness of much of American experience. Like Thoreau, he is concerned that the American land is to be profoundly experienced and enjoyed, and not merely exploited by commercial and industrial interests. This attitude in prose is consistent with the quality of his shorter poems. 'By the road to the contagious hospital', in *Spring and All,* is concerned with the objective definition of how things look. The style is precise:

One by one objects are defined . . .
It quickens: clarity, outline of leaf . . .

The poet himself has described his poetry as composing words 'into an intense expression of his perceptions and ardors'. Randall Jarrell in the introduction to *Selected Poems* (1949) talks of the true delight of how things look, the empathy and emotional identification with the subject. In the longer poems such as the epic *Paterson* published in four sections between 1946 and 1951 the poet's concern extends from definition to communication. Inevitably he becomes less involved with the need for visual objectivity than with the universal need for a man to establish a meaningful relationship with his self-constructed world.

Collections of Williams's poetry are *The Collected Earlier Poems of William Carlos Williams* (1951), *The Collected Later Poems of William Carlos Williams* (1950) and *The Lost Poems of William Carlos Williams or The Past Recaptured* (1957). His novels include *A Voyage to Pagany* (1928), *White Mule* (1937), *In the Money—White Mule, Part Two* (1940), and *The Build Up* (1952). Also of interest is a volume of short stories *The Knife of the Times and Other Stories* (1932). D. L. P.

Williams-Ellis, Amabel (1894–), English novelist (*Volcano*, 1931; *Learn to Love First*, 1939), has also written critical works (*Exquisite Tragedy*, a life of Ruskin; 1928), sociological studies (*Art of Being a Woman*; 1951) and children's books (*Princesses and Trous*; 1950). P. E.

Williamson, Henry (1897–), English novelist. Although he first came to notice with a series of novels under the general title of *The Flax of Dreams*, written between 1921 and 1928, he is best known for his nature writings, particularly two books with non-human heroes that invoke human sympathies: *Tarka the Otter* (1927) and *Salar the Salmon* (1935). These novels show great sensitivity and a sympathy with natural surroundings similar to that found in the work of Richard Jefferies. A further, more extended series of novels, spanning several decades of contemporary English life, has the general title *A Chronicle of Ancient Sunlight*, individual volumes including *The Dark Lantern* (1951), *Love and the Loveless* (1958) and *A Solitary War* (1966). R. A. K.

Willingham, Calder (1922–), American novelist. A Southern writer, his books include *End as a Man* (1947), *Geraldine Bradshaw* (1950), *The Gates of Hell* (1951), *Reach to the Stars* (1952), *Natural Child* (1952) and *To Eat a Peach* (1955). D. L. P.

Willis, Ted (Lord Willis; 1914–), English playwright. Probably best known for his work as script writer of the *Dixon of Dock Green* television series which began in 1953, he is a prolific writer for television and was a founder member of the TV and Screenwriters Guild. His play *Woman in a Dressing Gown* was filmed in 1958 and received the Berlin Award. His other plays include *Hot Summer Night* (1957), filmed as *Flame in the Streets* (1961); *No Trees in the Street* (1955; filmed 1959); and *God Bless the Guv'nor* (1959). He was created a life peer in 1963. G. S.

Wilson, Angus (1913–), English novelist, became a writer through developing short-story writing as a weekend distraction from his career as a public servant. When his first collection of stories, *The Wrong Set* (1949), was published, he was still working at the British Museum, where —apart from a war-time spell at the foreign office—he had been since 1936. In this volume, and its successor *Such Darling Dodos* (1958), the strongest element is the characteristic social satire whose occasional virulence caused Wilson to be grouped by some critics with the 'angry young men' of the 1950s. But there is also evidence of the agnostic humanism that was to become the chief preoccupation of his novels.

The first of these was *Hemlock and After* (1952). In the writer Bernard Sands we meet a typical Wilson character—a theoretical humanist who founders on the rocks of the harsh realities of human nature. In particular his own progress to Socratic self-knowledge is tantamount, ironically, to drinking hemlock. Bernard genuinely tries to help people—one of his schemes is to assist young writers—but he has become increasingly crippled and ineffectual through his knowledge that in his various relationships, particularly those with young men, the good he does is counterbalanced by a trail of damage. Here we meet another characteristic Wilson theme: responsibility for the consequences of one's behaviour. However, his collapse is not the end of the matter: for his death is preceded by the recovery of his neuroris-stricken wife, Ella, whose illness has been the symptom of the complete breakdown of a relationship. Where Bernard cannot survive knowledge of the evil in human nature, and of the pain that must be inflicted in any true relationship, Ella is able to make a fresh start. She brings Bernard's work for the young writers to some measure of fruition, and is also able to help people where he has failed through qualms about his own motives.

Bernard Sands is made impotent through knowledge of the responsibility for causing pain that must inevitably be borne by any active man; Gerald Middleton in *Anglo-Saxon Attitudes* (1956) is crippled by knowledge of a particularly painful responsibility that he has failed to discharge. As a scholar his most solemn obligation is to the truth; but for years he has brushed off the nagging thought that there may have been an unintentional fraud in the sensational discovery by his late friend Lionel Stokesay of pagan idols in an Anglo-Saxon bishop's tomb. It is not just the likelihood of becoming a laughing stock in view of the flimsiness of the evidence (simply a claim made while drunk and subsequently retracted by Stokesay's son Gilbert—later killed in the war—that he himself had inserted the idols as a practical joke); there are other people who stand to be hurt—such as Stokesay's widow Dollie, who has been his mistress, and a mentally unbalanced fellow-scholar Rose Lorimer who has become personally involved in the theory that the English bishops embraced the pagan idol-worship, and who makes a return to sanity and active scholarship when the theory receives apparent support from a German find in Heligoland.

Like that of Bernard Sands, Gerald Middleton's failure to come to terms with truth is reflected in the state of his marriage, where a conspiracy of self-deception over an injury caused by his neurotic wife to their daughter in childhood has had a similar paralysing effect. The falseness and compromise typified by the family Christmas reunion has also ruined his relationship with Dollie. Part of his return to purposeful, constructive living, which begins when he takes the decision to follow up his suspicion about the idols, is a realisation that he must be prepared to go forward alone.

Although Gerald's recovery is the central theme of the book, it is set off by several more or less related sub-plots involving a truly Dickensian wealth of minor characters exhibiting a wide variety of 'Anglo-Saxon attitudes' to the problems of living. Gerald's squeamishness, for instance, finds its opposite in the unctuous crusading zeal of his son John, a Labour M.P. who parades his self-righteousness in the popular press; and with the coffee-bar world of John's secretary Elvira we enter yet another social stratum. Many of the minor characters provide opportunities for Wilson's satirical genius; but there is also the more sombre story of Rose Lorimer, who finally collapses into certifiable insanity when Gerald demolishes the basis of her early recovery.

The apparent impossibility of developing a personal relationship without becoming responsible for hurting the other person has been a cause of Bernard Sands's downfall; and the acceptance of loneliness has been an essential part of Gerald Middleton's recovery. Both of these ideas find further expression in *The Middle Age of Mrs Eliot* (1958). Meg Eliot's brother David has withdrawn as completely as is practicable from human relationships, and leads a semi-monastic (though productive) life as a nursery gardener; but for Meg herself, whose life as the wife of a successful businessman has consisted of a mesh of personal relationships with her marriage at the centre, the emptiness that is left by her husband's sudden death is terrifying. Her first attempts to fill the void involve a translation of what have hitherto been her hobbies and 'good works' into possible full-time occupations; but lack of professional knowledge, and the impossibility of entering into relationships with strangers without the patronising demeanour of the society hostess, make her unsuitable to do either. After various vicissitudes, she finds a new rôle for herself in an employee-employer relationship as 'an employed person in a largely employed world', and trains to become a private secretary.

Meg's brother David finds solace in tending plants; Simon Carter in *The Old Men at the Zoo* (1961) finds it in tending animals. His direct contact and sympathy with a realm of instinctive behaviour, free of human squeamishness and dishonesty, is mirrored in the healthy and 'natural' relationship that he enjoys with his American wife Martha. As in *Anglo-Saxon Attitudes*, here is a direct relationship between the state of his personal relationships and the way he discharges his public responsibilities; and the book is largely concerned with the dilemmas that the latter place him in. When an inexperienced young keeper is killed by a sick giraffe, his first reaction is to seek the culprit; but while he rejects the idea that it is in the zoo's interests to hush up the affair, he later capitulates in order to spare the feelings of the boy's mother. This is the beginning of his deterioration.

The next critical event is the removal of large numbers of animals to an open zoo in Wales. He has always supported the director, Edwin Leacock, in his aspirations to create a second Whipsnade; and when the opportunity is offered by the Zoological Society's president, the politician-cum-newspaperman Lord Godmanchester, he allows himself to be persuaded that it is in the zoo's interests to turn a blind eye to the possibility that Godmanchester has engineered the evacuation largely to create a war scare and procure his own return to office. In Wales too we see the first manifestation of Simon's failure at a personal level, when he mishandles the opportunity of saving the sanity of Leacock's near-nymphomaniac daughter Harriet, as a result of his chief's request that he should not interfere. Shortly afterwards Harriet is killed by her Alsatian dog in the act of intercourse, and the climax of the whole episode is Carter's connivance, to spare Mrs Leacock's feelings, in the story that she has been killed by an escaped animal. This gives Godmanchester, now back in power, an excuse for terminating the experiment in 'limited liberty' and returning the zoo to London—a disaster too great for Leacock to bear, and which results in his resignation.

With the zoo back in London, Simon finds himself working to realise the policy of the new director, Sir Robert Falcon, a man obsessed with restoring the style and pageantry of the Victorian zoo. Although there are now signs of unease in Martha, she accepts that it is after all his job to follow the director's policy. But when Falcon is succeeded by men with much less innocuous *idées fixes*, Simon's 'Vicar of Bray' act is seen as the natural development of the erosion that his values have undergone. The climax comes when we see him working for a man who is himself compromising with the barbarous schemes of a fascist-type government; and he is brought to his senses by the desertion of the horrified Martha. When the book ends it is an open question whether he will be able to make a fresh start and save his marriage: whether, in the last phrase of the book, he has himself been 'killed by a giraffe'.

In *Late Call* (1964) Wilson returns to another study of a woman faced with the challenge of a new life—posed in this case by her retirement from the seaside town where she has for many years managed a boarding-house, to the new town where her son Harold is headmaster of a secondary-modern school. The characterisation—of the pompous, earnest, self-important, would-be 'with-it' Harold Calvert, of his three mixed-up children, and of his rootless, superficially civilised neighbours—is as sure (and lethal) as ever; as also is his evocation of locales (supermarkets and ten-pin bowling alleys) not previously encountered in his fiction. But the 'late call' of Harold's mother Sylvia—to bring to her son's world a breath of the earthy commonsense and honesty that are seemingly represented both by her own rural childhood and by the new-world attitudes of a Canadian farming family by whom she is befriended—is only tenuously communicated.

Angus Wilson has also published a third set of stories *A Bit off the Map* (1957); a play, *The Mulberry Bush* (1955); and a further novel, *No Laughing Matter* (1967). K. R. R.

Wilson, Colin (1931–), English writer. Wilson achieved wide critical and public acclamation in 1956 with the publication of *The Outsider* which deals with the concept of the social misfit as a potential individual hero, rejected by the community and seeking a meaningful rôle in a transcendent creativity. Wilson places Lawrence of Arabia, Nijinsky and Van Gogh in this category. The book is impressive rather than profound; it makes sound intellectual points and literary generalisations, rather than revealing universal truth. *Religion and the Rebel* followed in 1957, receiving unduly harsh treatment from critics who had allowed themselves to be carried away with excessive enthusiasm for its predecessor.

Other work includes a novel *Adrift in Soho* (1961); part-authorship of an *Encyclopaedia of Murder* (1961), which records the case histories of many famous murderers and illustrates Wilson's preoccupation with the psychology of violence; and a book of literary essays *The Strength to Dream* (1962). Wilson subsequently directed his attention to a spy novel, to which genre he hoped to give intellectual respectability. D. L. P.

Wilson, Edmund (1895–   ), American critic and novelist, formerly married to Mary McCarthy. One of the major literary critics of this century, his lively and trenchant comments have appeared in *Vanity Fair*, *New Republic* and the *New Yorker*, for which he was book critic from 1944 to 1948. His first major work was *Axel's Castle* (1931), a study of the symbolist movement. In *The Triple Thinkers* (1938) there appear stimulating and important essays on Flaubert and Henry James; and Wilson makes a penetrating study of artistic creativity in *The Wound and the Bow* (1941) which contains studies of Dickens, Kipling and Hemingway. *To the Finland Station* (1940) is a study of Marxism and the development of the Russian revolution portrayed through short biographies of the leading figures.

Two memorable novels, *I Thought of Daisy* (1929)—a tale of life in Greenwich Village in the twenties—and the best-selling *Memoirs of Hecate County* (1946), reveal his own originality in fiction. The memoirs are really six stories of the intellectual and emotional life of characters in the New York suburbs—witty, wealthy and with their own particular problems. Two literary chronicles shed a stimulating and provocative light on three important decades: *Classics and Commercials* (1950) is a collection of essays and reviews dealing with those literary figures who came to the author's attention during the 1940s; while *The Shores of Light* (1952) is a collection of his written work from the twenties and thirties, interspersed with letters, dialogues and short sketches, which combine to give a panorama of the cultural activities of those decades, ranging from Ring Lardner to Bakunin. *The Bit Between My Teeth* (1966) is a sequel to these volumes. R. A. K.

Wilson, Ethel (1890–   ), Canadian novelist, has a highly personal and idiosyncratic style in that her books are not so concerned with plot as with a poetic reaction to, and exploration of, a theme. In her first novel, *Hetty Dorval* (1947), she explores the contradiction of a girl who gives herself so freely that she is unable to enter into a real relationship. This was followed by *The Innocent Traveller* (1949) and *Equation of Love* (1952). The latter, an experimental work, attempts to give an extra dimension by first describing the nature of love as it appears to a dozen characters, and then tracing its forms in the life of one person. Another of her major works is *Swamp Angel* (1954), notable for two magnificent literary creations—Mrs Severance and Maggie Lloyd. S. R.

Wilson, Guthrie (1914–   ), popular New Zealand novelist, best known for his war novel *Brave Company* (1951) which portrays with great honesty and power the private's view of war. S. R.

Winsor, Kathleen (1919–   ), American author of the long and unflaggingly erotic Restoration novel *Forever Amber* (1944). Her later titles include *Wanderers Eastward, Wanderers West* (1965). K. R. R.

Winters, Yvor (1900–   ), American poet and critic. Winters believes strongly that reason must be a positive factor not only in the progressive materialism of twentieth-century society but in literature and poetry. He reacts strongly against the negative approach of Frost to the values of the technological revolution as well as to the views of critics like Henry Adams who insist that art must be chaotic to express the chaos of life. *In Defense of Reason* (1947) is a combination of Winters's first three critical works and is perhaps one of the most important critical books to be published since 1945; it is certainly one of the most influential. The critic's concern for rationality is echoed in the form of his own poetry. *Collected Poems* was published in 1952. D. L. P.

Wodehouse, P. G. (Pelham Grenville Wodehouse; 1881–   ), English humorous novelist, whose creation of Jeeves, the perfect manservant, has made him as deathless as his own host of characters. Jeeves and his master Bertie Wooster first appeared about 1911, and in 1965 their adventures were successfully televised. They are in company with Psmith, who elevates the stock school-story to Etonian status, and Mulliner with his reminiscences of his remarkable relatives, as well as many others. War, moral problems, social change and even the necessity to earn a living do not exist in any of the innumerable stories. All the young men have private incomes, and expectations from even richer, older relatives. They are 'mentally insignificant' but entirely good-natured, and their accidents of fortune entailed by the former quality, together with their fantastic efforts to extricate themselves by way of the other, are told with verve: the action never sagging because nobody ever thinks—except Jeeves. What was originally the subject matter for a parody has long been an anachronism, but the author has transformed it into a dream-life where the amiable and honourable prosper while pomposity and tyranny are deflated. Every scene is presented with a fine and farcical sense of theatre, a felicity of phrase and professional skill. In the context of his life's work, his broadcasts from Germany, expressing the German view, at the start of World War II must be accounted little more than an indiscretion.

Titles include *Leave it to Psmith* (1923), *The Inimitable Jeeves* (1924), *The Code of the Woosters* (1938), *Galahad at Blandings* (1965) and *Plum Pie* (1966). H. C.

Wolfe, Humbert (1885–1940), English poet. Wolfe's professional career was in the civil service, to which he was appointed in 1908, becoming deputy secretary to the Ministry of Labour in the period before the second world war. He was a writer of light satirical verse. His work includes *Lampoons* (1925); *Requiem* (1927); and *Kensington Gardens in War Time* (1940). D. L. P.

Wolfe, Thomas (1900–38), American novelist. Wolfe's novels represent the climax of romantic self-expression in the pursuit of meaning within the context of American experience. They are a vast autobiographical outpouring.

Wolfe was born in Asheville, North Carolina, in 1900. He attended the state university between 1916 and 1920, took his master's degree at Harvard in 1922 and became an instructor in English at New York University; his novels are placed either in the setting of his Carolina birthplace or in New York. The best-known, *Look Homeward Angel* (1929), is a sprawling account of the childhood of Eugene Gant, although the latter is less the hero of the novel than the narrator of his family's history. The central characters are his parents Oliver and Eliza Gant, who are caught in endless conflict between the submergence in experience of the former and the security in property of the latter. The reality of the characters is Dickensian. The virtue of the novel lies in its force, its vigour, its excitement, its lyricism and its exaggeration. The excesses of Wolfe's tide of prose, as with all his books, were cut and ordered by his editors. What remains is not perfect but striking. *Of Time and the River* (1935) takes Eugene Gant to New York, to the city of wealth and culture, to reach out for the American literary dream which finds meaning away from rude experience in urbane and urban order. The later novels change the name of the hero from Gant to Webber and attempt to rework the same ground with greater objectivity and clarity of outline; but they depend, in fact, on the same autobiographical force.

Wolfe is well represented by Henry Adams's dictum that art must be chaotic to express the chaos of life. His characters, as he himself, are trying to force their way through the confusion of life's experience into some central core of meaning. What emerges from the novels is the impact of the struggle which is the force of life itself. Other novels than those mentioned are *The Web and the Rock* (1939) and *You Can't go Home Again* (1940). D. L. P.

Woolf, Leonard (1880–   ), English writer and publisher, husband of the novelist Virginia Woolf. He wrote on a wide range of topics for the *International Review*, the *Political Quarterly*, the *Nation*, and was for a time editor of those journals. He has been active in the genres of the novel

(*The Village in the Jungle*, 1913), and the theatre (*The Hotel*, 1939), in addition to economic and political commentary (*Principia Politica*, 1953); but it is for his editing of his wife's writings and for his memorable volumes of autobiography (notably *Beginning Again*, 1965; *Downhill all the Way*, 1967) that he is best known. R. A. K.

Woolf, Virginia (née Stevens; 1882–1941), English novelist, occupies a secure and central position in the history of the English novel: from which it would no more be possible to omit mention of her own actual achievements in the art (principally *Mrs Dalloway* and *To the Lighthouse*), than it would be to exclude an account of the revolution she pioneered in fictional technique.

Virginia Stevens was a member of a distinguished literary family, and there is a strong traditional element in her writing. When she published her early works (*The Voyage Out*, 1915; *Night and Day*, 1919; *Jacob's Room*, 1922), E. M. Forster—a fringe member of the Bloomsbury intellectual group of which she was the central figure—had already written four out of his five great humanist novels with their characteristic opposition of the inner life and 'the outer world of telephones and anger'; while two out of the three great experimental works of the exiled Irishman James Joyce were completed well before she had herself performed anything of importance. Nonetheless, she it was who proclaimed in England in 1919 that the life of the mind—the inner life so valued by Forster, so thoroughly explored by the psychologists, and already so distinctively represented in the early fiction of Dorothy Richardson (of which the term 'stream of consciousness' was first used)—required to be treated in a form of novel totally different from the social fiction of the leading Edwardians. Her own works were to dwarf Dorothy Richardson's *Pilgrimage*, and at the same time to remain much less far-ranging in their technical experimentation than Joyce's *Ulysses* and *Finnegan's Wake*: and it is she who has thus come to be identified with the straightforward stream-of-consciousness method (which, however, she used in a highly specialised way) and with the kind of novel in which the events of the outer world take second place to the inner 'epiphanies' of the human psyche.

There is not much evidence of radical change in method in the three early novels already mentioned. What does transpire is their author's intense feeling that the fabric of the upper-middle-class society into which she herself was born denied to those individuals who composed it the kind of self-fulfilment at the deepest level of the personality that she and her Bloomsbury friends looked for. In the first two books, the intelligent sensitive heroines remain largely in a state of idealistic disengagement; in the third, the hero Jacob Flanders is fully involved and is consequently destroyed. In the biblical associations of the latter's name and in the various allusions in the novel to the Jacob-Esau story, one may sense an affirmation that the civilisation now seen to be so life-destroying has derived from a culture that was once spiritually fruitful: a culture which the Jacobs of this world could revivify if only they were given the inheritance. This essentially traditionalist framework of Virginia Woolf's cultural radicalism is something that requires to be emphasised.

Septimus Warren-Smith in *Mrs Dalloway* (1925), the first of the group of novels on which Virginia Woolf's literary reputation rests, has it in him to be another Jacob. Broken by his experience of the first world war (which had killed off Jacob Flanders) he has returned alive to the world from which he had come, there to represent in his suffering the demand for a new spirit of personal honesty and responsiveness, of peace-making love and understanding. But if he and his like are the potential inheritors and redeemers of their civilisation, they also constitute a threat to its existing patriarchs: to men like the eminent Harley Street psychiatrist Sir William Bradshaw, who must deal with Septimus's illness and see to it that society does not suffer from his 'unsocial impulses'. Unable to regain 'a sense of proportion', Bradshaw's troublesome victim takes his own life.

The Bradshaw-Septimus story mirrors and externalises the drama within the psyche of the society-hostess Clarissa Dalloway, the central figure of the book. The life of her mind—the ceaseless stream of impressions, associations and conscious thought-processes that compose its activity—is conveyed in a way that makes it impossible to level at this book the charges made with regard to its predecessors: namely that having preached technical innovation, Mrs Woolf wrote her novels in a thoroughly conventional manner. Previously, too, the mental processes of the disengaged hero or heroine have been set alongside the external events in the lives of the other characters; whereas here, such external events as occur (and there are few of them) appear almost entirely as they impinge on Clarissa's mind, which is distinguished from those of the characters of other stream-of-consciousness writers by its high degree of self-consciousness. In terms of events, the climax of the book is the appearance of the prime minister at her party, in full view of the people she most wants to be impressed; the true climax, however, is her realisation of the essential hollowness of her triumph. Also, we immediately see her give vent to a burst of irrational hatred—as if to express the violence done to her psyche in the contortions that have produced this hollowness. She is both Bradshaw and Septimus; in her are the potentialities for both death and life, for destruction and re-creation.

In Virginia Woolf's next two novels, it is not the behaviour-patterns of the upper-middle-class England that are opposed to the spiritual fulfilment of the individual: rather it is external reality itself which threatens the latter—and threatens it not so much with psychological frustrations and misdirections, as with the questioning of its significance. The inner joys of Mrs Ramsay in *To the Lighthouse* (1927) are not in danger from the pattern of her own life, nor from that of her husband, children, and friends; but the validity of her faith in the reality and importance of these experiences is apparently denied both by the fact-ridden rationalism of Mr Ramsay and by the constant flux of the physical world. Here, as in *The Waves* (1931), Virginia Woolf takes the sea as a matrix for a group of interrelated physical symbols with which to make a poetic statement both of the challenge posed by nature and ultimately of the resolution that the novel proclaims.

The lighthouse itself, which to Mrs Ramsay is a symbol of an illumination that transcends the meaningless chaos of life, but to her husband is merely a building on a rock, is the most important of these symbols. In the first part of the book, in which Mrs Ramsay's almost mystical apprehensions receive their most positive statement, a projected excursion is frustrated by the weather; in the third and last part it is eventually reached, ten years later, and becomes a focus for the reconciliation of husband and wife. In the short middle section, where the subject matter is not the material of the human mind but of external reality, and where the forces of nature have made their counter-statement to the previous spiritual affirmations of Mrs Ramsay, we have been made to feel the universality of time and mortality: three deaths occur, including that of Mrs Ramsay herself, who is to survive into the third part, and the reaching of the lighthouse, only inasmuch as she lives on in the minds of others.

If it is in the minds of others that Mrs Ramsay lives on to have her inner world reconciled with her husband's world of facts, it is also in the mind of another—the artist Lily Briscoe—that the reconciliation itself takes place; and it is she who, at the end of the book, is left to give it expression in a painting of husband and wife as she remembers them. It is arguable that this reconciliation is only made possible through the medium of art: that, in fact, the novel's conclusion is that only art can give permanence to those significant moments of which Mrs Ramsay's inner life is composed. In *The Waves*, however, the character who is best endowed with the capacity to create a meaningful pattern—the inveterate phrase-maker Bernard—is made to be fully aware of the relative nature of any pattern he perceives; and it is on the symbolic ambivalences of the physical world —the cycle of day and the night, the seasons, and principally the flux of the sea—that Virginia Woolf falls back in her attempt to find a true reconciliation of the meaningful and the meaningless. Whether her imposition of this triple symbolism on the sensory, emotional, imaginative and intellectual lives of her six characters—the suggestion, in particular, that the significant moment of human experience stands in the same relation to the meaningless infinities of time as the waves do to the sea—does achieve this is a matter of disagreement, and for many readers the book has proved a heartrending poem of futility.

Whatever one's views about *The Waves*, there is little dispute that *The Years* (1937) marks a very clear decline in Virginia Woolf's creative talents. Here, as in her last unfinished novel *Between the Acts* (1941), she appears to have turned her back on the quest for the reconciliation of inner sense and outer nonsense, concentrating rather—in a way that sometimes recalls the early novels—on the obstacles presented by contemporary society to the development of that inner life of whose value she, at least, had no doubt. The difference is that here she seeks a historical perspective for the situation of the present: in the former novel, by writing a piece of social history that, for all its lack of inspiration, gave the book a certain popularity; in the latter, by writing the story round a historical pageant. There was nothing in these last books to suggest that the motivation of her suicide in 1941—subsequently explained in the memoirs of her husband Leonard Woolf in terms of recurring illness—included any loss of faith in the values she had expressed consistently over a quarter-century.

Apart from her novels, her output had included a 'biography' of the spirit of England, entitled *Orlando* (1928), and one of Elizabeth Barrett Browning's dog *Flush* (1933); as well as a wide range of essays, and diaries.
K. R. R.

Wouk, Herman (1915–   ), American novelist, best known for *The Caine Mutiny* (1951), a long novel set on a dilapidated minesweeper in World War II. The novel is interesting not for the mutiny itself which is effected quite calmly by one man at the height of a typhoon, but for the detailed and psychological analysis of the characters of the group of officers responsible for such an event taking place. The story is told as it is seen, and only dimly understood, by Willie Keith, and covers the period of his development from brash midshipman to mature captain. The novel examines the hierarchical and authoritarian structure of the Navy, the effect such power has on the men who wield it and on those who are subject to it. But it is in its conclusion that the book deals most readers a slap in the face. For almost all its length, the novel has seemed to support the indignation aroused in the intellectual Keefer by the obsessions, injustices and inertia of the new captain Queeg. It is Keefer's steady cataloguing of these abnormalities that lead the other officers to mutiny. But after the court-martial proceedings, the brilliant young Jewish lawyer who has successfully defended the mutineers gives vent to a passionate and furious attack on these men who have in this way undermined an institution (the Navy and its chain of command, its tradition of unquestioning obedience) which whatever its flaws is dedicated to the greater good of stamping out German and Japanese fascism. In short, Wouk's moral would seem to be that the end justifies the means. The real imbalance in the novel consists in its suggesting so very convincingly quite the opposite—that Queeg's insane despotism is enough to lose America the moral right to win the war. In this, as in his later works, it should be noted that one of Wouk's concerns is to present a specifically Jewish viewpoint, which he does with considerable success.

In each of his other novels, he has again chosen to portray an area of life that has a popular mystique, which he invites his readers to enter vicariously through his main characters. Thus *Aurora Dawn* (1947) deals with business life; *The City Boy* (1948) with a summer holiday camp; *Marjorie Morningstar* (1955) with show business; and *Youngblood Hawke* (1962) with the world of the writer. S. R.

Wren, P. C. (Percival Christopher Wren; 1885–1941), English novelist, whose military experience, particularly in the French Foreign Legion, gave rise to a number of romantic novels in the heroic style. Of these the most popular were the Geste series—*Beau Geste* (1924), *Beau Sabreur* (1926), *Beau Ideal* (1928) and *The Good Gestes* (1929). These created a romantic image of the Legion which pervaded much similar popular literature. R. A. K.

Wright, Judith Arundell (Mrs J. P. McKinney; 1915–), Australian poet of international stature who established her reputation with the four volumes *The Moving Image* (1946), *Woman to Man* (1949), *The Gateway* (1953) and *The Two Fires* (1955). Her poetry, always simple, condensed, has moved outward in content from themes intrinsic to woman—love for a man, the bearing of children,

> The eyeless labourer in the night,
> the selfless, shapeless seed I hold—

to the more general philosophical questions of being:

> The dried body of winter is hard to kill.
> Frost crumbles the dead bracken, greys the old grass, . . .
>
> For it is anguish to be reborn and reborn:
> at every return of the overmastering season
> to shed our lives in pain, to waken into the cold, . . .
>
> Easier, far easier, to stand with downturned eyes
> and hands hanging, to let age and mourning cover us
> with their dark rest . . .

Throughout her work her greatest strength has been a really fresh and intuitive insight into the Australian landscape, its history and myth, and its characters; and she is able to introduce the occasional aboriginal term or swagman's phrase without archness. However, her exquisitely controlled language is richly allusive, and she extends her theme of man in nature from its Australian setting to a universal application.

She has also edited *Australian Poetry* (1948) and *The Oxford Book of Australian Verse* (1956). S. R.

Wright, Richard (1908–60), American novelist and short-story writer who was one of the greatest spokesmen for his fellow Negroes. His works include *Uncle Tom's Children* (1938), a collection of four shorter pieces; *Black Boy* (1945), an autobiography of his boyhood; and *Listen!* (1957), an important novel of racial intolerance and injustice. P. E.

Wylie, Elinor (1885–1928), American poet. Elinor Wylie is a poet of elegance and intellect whose developing maturity was cut short by early death. She was born in New Jersey but came of an old Pennsylvania family; her grandfather was Governor of that state. Despite her severe family background she left her first husband to live unmarried in London with her lover Horace Wylie; their union was eventually legalised. She was married again in 1923, to William Rose Benèt.

Wylie's first volume *Nets to Catch the Wind* (1921) showed an individual sharpness and elegance of technique which has brilliance despite its lack of emotional depth. *Black Armour* (1923) developed the depth and *Trivial Breath* (1928) demonstrated a transition from the exquisite craftsman to a poet involved, with passion and intensity, in metaphysical issues. Her last work *Angels and Earthly Creatures*, published posthumously in 1929, matures these trends in a sequence of sonnets which while they show an acquaintance with Donne, the seventeenth-century metaphysicals and the dramatist Webster, are not derivatively dependent upon them. Wylie develops a maturer poetic style than the residual romanticism contained in the work of her colleague Edna St Vincent Millay. She goes her own way. The *Collected Poems* were published in 1932; the *Collected Prose* in 1933. D. L. P.

Wylie, Philip (1902–), American writer, best known for his novel *Generation of Vipers* (1942) which vigorously attacked 'momism', the sentimental cult of the American mother. Other novels include *Opus 21* (1949), a diagnosis of American sexual malaise; and he also wrote books attacking organised Christianity and foretelling the horrors of atomic war. K. R. R.

Wyndham, John (John Beynon Harris; 1903–   ), English author of science-fiction novels, who concerns himself with human behaviour and therefore with moral and ethical codes, postulating their modification in totally new and unforeseen circumstances. For example, *The Day of the Triffids* (1951) describes the chaos which results when all but a few hundred of the earth's entire population are blinded simultaneously, in order to deal with the behaviour of and problems faced by these survivors in this hypothetical setting—particularly in relation to, first, responsibility for the short-term alleviation of the hopeless suffering of the blind masses; and subsequently to the predatory attacks of the 'triffids', curious biological hybrids created to yield oil, which since the catastrophe have pulled up their roots and taken on an independent existence and in face of whose formidable powers they must construct a new civilisation. In general Wyndham's work is strong in invention and philosophical implications, weak in characterisation. Other titles include *The Kraken Wakes* (1953), *The Chrysalids* (1953), *The Midwych Cuckoos* (1957; filmed as *The Village of the Damned*) and a collection of short stories *The Seeds of Time* (1956).

S. R.

Wynter, Sylvia Rufinia (c.1927–   ), Caribbean novelist and writer of plays for television and radio. Married to the author Jan Carew (b. 1922), with whom she has collaborated, she is best known for her novel *The Hills of Hebron* (1962), describing the intrigues, personality clashes and conflicts of outlook and temperament that attend the activities of Moses, a messianic prophet in the hills of Jamaica. A powerful work, it has a richly varied prose and universally valid overtones. C. P.

Y

Yates, Dornford (Cecil William Mercer; 1885–1960), English novelist whose work became immensely popular, particularly during the twenties and thirties. His stories are mainly light adventures, often farcical, and mainly featuring the slightly improbable character Berry, who appeared first in *Berry and Co.* (1921) and subsequently in a number of books stretching into the early fifties. R. A. K.

Yeats, William Butler (1865–1939), Irish poet and dramatist. Yeats was born near Dublin, the son of an artist. He was educated at Godolphin School, Hammersmith, and later at Erasmus School, Dublin. He studied art for a number of years before going to London in 1887. There he wrote for the *Yellow Book* and helped found the Rhymer's Club. He published during the 1890s a number of narrative poems and verse plays which were focused on the mythology of Ireland and involved in the magical and mysterious. These included *The Wanderings of Oisin and Other Poems* (1899), *The Countess Kathleen* (1892) and *The Land of Heart's Desire* (1894). *The Celtic Twilight* (1893) is a volume of essays. His edition of the *Works of William Blake* appeared in 1893.

Yeats published a volume of his *Collected Poems* in 1895. The poetry here demonstrates his main literary and philosophic involvements. He employs the soft images and dreams of the Celtic background, deriving symbols from history and art. Besides expression of intense personal feeling he manifests the desire to create some kind of enduring object of aesthetic value, a hard beauty logically separate from self. The following year Yeats returned to Ireland and became the leader of the Irish renaissance in literature and drama. With Lady Gregory, Synge, Æ, George Moore and others he helped to found the Irish Literary Theatre which became the Abbey Theatre. Plays he himself wrote for it included *Kathleen ni Hoolihan* (1902) and *The King's Threshold* (1904).

Yeats's mature poetic development derives also from a number of other influences. In 1887 he had become involved with theosophy through a Madame Blavatsky. Theosophy in the seventeenth century was a semi-religious movement pursuing, in depth, knowledge of nature by means of mysticism. The nineteenth-century movement in which Yeats became immersed was concerned to develop man's latent spiritual depth by studying eastern religions and literature as well as the mystical laws of nature. *Among the Reeds* (1899) shows the influence both of this school of theosophy and of contemporary literary movements such as French symbolism. Another, later influence of a different sort was Ezra Pound who revised a whole collection of Yeats's poems, at one time even acting as his secretary; and who created a tendency in Yeats towards ritualistic drama, to be evidenced in his translations of two dramas from Sophocles in 1928, *King Oedipus* and *Oedipus at Colonus.*

A reading of the poetry that Yeats was now writing shows him clearly as an anti-materialist. The subject matter of his personal philosophy is a complex mysticism difficult to break down into simple intellectual terms. It is a compound of theosophy, Irish mythology, oriental spiritualism, *Yellow Book* aestheticism and primitive sensuality, a compound which almost miraculously produces a richness of symbolism, density of imagery and clarity of intellect that are quite breathtaking. And there is at times a sense of the ambivalences, the contradictions and the paradoxes of human life, as for example in the mystery of the opposed sweetness and ugliness of sex. In 'Crazy Jane Talks with the Bishop' he observes:

But Love has pitched his mansion in
The place of excrement;
For nothing can be sole or whole
That has not been rent.

The solid foundations of Yeats's attitudes in his later poetry can be found in *A Vision*, the first version of which was published in 1925. In 1917 he had married George Hyde Lees, a spiritualist and medium, who, he claimed, was the vehicle through which spirits enunciated the substance of *A Vision* when she was in trance states. In the book is expressed a view of the cyclical character of the lives of both individual men and whole civilisations. Yeats is also concerned with a theory of opposites. As with 'love' and 'excrement', 'whole' and 'rent', in the quotation above, the poet contrasts time and timelessness, spirit and substance. These two ideas find expression in some key concepts: the most important being those of 'gyres' and 'vortices'. A gyre is a spiral, a circular movement upwards which represents the development of a man or of a civilisation. The vortex is the contrasting decline and fall. All men and all civilisations alternate between gyre and vortex. Together with this goes the idea that human individuals have opposites or 'masks'. A complete man assimilates the characteristics of himself and of his opposing mask; the complete soul at death transmigrates into another form and continues with a pattern of existence. Yeats believed, too, that the relations between science and religion could be manipulated by art. These views anchor his symbolism in this and all the subsequent volumes of poetry.

Yeats's poems embrace a diversity of moods and subjects—love, politics and philosophic speculation. His verse is a combined expression of complexity and simplicity. His later writing is at its best where all the complex threads come together. The most anthologised poems are 'Byzantium' and 'Sailing to Byzantium'. In the latter Yeats transfers the image of an old man into the possibility of a new pattern of existence, not in life but in the universal artifice of art:

> . . . and gather me
> Into the artifice of eternity.
>
> One out of nature I shall never take
> My bodily form from any natural thing
> But such a form as Grecian goldsmiths make
> Of hammered gold and gold enamelling . . .

'Byzantium' reworks this theme, setting the context of the poem richly and sensuously:

> Night resonance recedes, night walker's song
> After great cathedral gong;

The poem invokes a golden image in which art captures life and symbolises a more effective eternity than life itself has to offer. The spirit world breaks the complexity and fury of the life-force, leaving a more tranquil albeit ritualistic representation:

> And all complexities of fury leave
> Dying into a dance,
> An agony of trance,
> An agony of flame that cannot singe a sleeve.

His volumes of mature writing include *The Green Helmet* (1910); *Responsibilities* (1914); *The Wild Swans at Coole* (1917); *Michael Robartes and the Dancer* (1920); *The Tower* (1928); *The Winding Stair* (1929); and *Last Poems* (1939). Yeats was also involved in revising his poetry in the light of subsequent guiding attitudes: he did this with the *Collected Poems* editions of 1908 and 1933. During these years many honours came to him including membership of the Irish Senate, of which he became an active member, and the Nobel Prize for Literature in 1923. D. L. P.

Yeats-Brown, Francis (1886–1944), English novelist, wrote the famous *Lives of a Bengal Lancer* (1930). He was highly adventurous and fascinated by eastern thought and religions and his book, parts of which are taken from his own Indian army experiences, was inspired by this great interest.

P. E.

Yesenin, Sergei Alexandrovich (1895–1925), Russian poet, was born into a peasant family in Ryazan. When he was only nine he began to write poems and eventually at eighteen he went to study in Moscow. He joined a peasant literary circle and in 1915 managed to get a collection of his poems published. Because of his upbringing and temperament many of his early works were influenced by popular folk-verse and religious allusions, but in welcoming the revolution he turned to anti-religious themes. This change made Yesenin's poetry well known, though his best work is not in the pretentious verse with which he greeted the revolution but rather in the nostalgic poems recalling, in simple melodious verse, the countryside he had known as a youth.

For a while Yesenin belonged to the imagist circle, but he later discarded literary associations. In seven years he had married three times, but he could not find the security he longed for in a changing world. He became dissatisfied with the rowdy company in the bars. This and a growing disillusionment with post-revolutionary attitudes led to a mental breakdown and his committing suicide. He had a desire to be a new Pushkin, expressed in *Pushkinu* ['To Pushkin'] (1924), and if appreciative readership be the criterion he certainly came very close. The lost, disillusioned, yet remarkably honest later poetry about his tavern life contains some of his best mature and reflective work, notably *Ispovyed' khuligana* ['Confession of a hooligan'] (1924) and *Chorniy chelovyek* ['Black man'] (1925). B. W.

Yevtushenko, Yevgeny Alexandrovich (1933–), Soviet poet. His 'Let us be most outspoken, and tell truth about ourselves' may be used as the motto of the new generation of Soviet writers, epitomised in many ways by Yevtushenko himself. He was born in the remote town of Zima on the Trans-Siberian Railway and brought up in a firmly established Soviet Russia. Nevertheless he early acquired a militant questing outlook and his refusal to accept long-established principles in his poetry made him a celebrated figure; although with some aspects of his work he seems to have reached a working compromise with officialdom. He is a great favourite with the younger generation who enjoy listening to him reciting his poems. Yevtushenko owes much to Mayakovsky's declamatory style, though his work lacks the older poet's fire and imagery, and in his softer lyrics moves closer to Yesenin. Despite the inflation of his reputation, Yevtushenko's work is of a high standard, especially when he is reminiscing about his home, as in *Stantsiya Zima* [*Zima Station*] (1956), or striking a blow at prejudice and injustice, as in *Baby Yar* [*Baby Yar*] (1961). Most significantly, it does show a resurgence of the kind of writing which attaches importance to personal emotion. There exist several anthologies in English translation of his *Poems*. B. W.

Young, Andrew John (1883–   ), English clergyman and poet. Young was made a canon of Chichester cathedral in 1948. His poetry, mainly concerned with descriptions of the natural scene, includes *Songs of Night* (1910); *The Bird Cage* (1926); *Winter Harvest* (1933); and *Into Hades* (1952). He was awarded the Queen's Medal for Poetry in 1952.

D. L. P.

Young, Francis Brett. See **Brett Young,** Francis.

Z

Zamyatin, Yevgeni Ivanovich (1884–1937), Russian novelist, was a remarkably analytical satirist, whose early life had been spent in Lebedyan in the Tambov province. The works of Dostoyevsky and Turgenev produced a strong impression on him but he nevertheless began his working life as a naval engineer. His literary career began in 1911 while in exile with *Uyezdnoye* [*Tales of a District*], a short novel. By 1913 his merciless powers of analysis had become so manifest that the publication of *Na kulichkakh* [*At the World's End*] (1913) brought about his detention by the tsarist authorities. Zamyatin wrote many such satirical works, but perhaps he is best known in the west for his brilliant post-revolutionary attack on totalitarianism in a negative utopia, in the novel *My* [*We*] (1924); he was generally opposed to the Soviet régime's regimentation of life, and mounting friction between himself and the state after the publication abroad of this work led to Zamyatin's eventual exile to France. The novel describes the totalitarian state of the 2600s and shows how much the state has control over its inhabitants and how two 'lover-criminals' are punished. The state rids its people of unhappiness by finally removing their imagination. In many respects this novel anticipated Orwell's *1984* and loudly expressed Zamyatin's plea for freedom of expression.

While in exile he began writing the novel *Bich Bozhiy* [*Scourge of God*] based on his play *Attila* [*Attila*] (1926) which was a direct allusion to the Soviet Union. His other play, *Blokha* [*The Flea*] (1923), had been an enormous success. B. W.

Zangwill, Israel (1864–1926), Jewish novelist and playwright born in England of Russian parentage, wrote some moving studies of Jewish life and history including *The Children of the Ghetto* (1892–93) and *Dreamers of the Ghetto* (1898), the latter a collection of essays about famous Jews of history. A popular, less weighty work was his *Merely Mary Ann* (1893), the story of a servant-girl who becomes rich through inheritance. Later titles include the novels *The Grey Wig* (1903) and *Jinny the Carrier* (1919), and plays such as *Too Much Money* (1918) and *The Cockpit* (1922). P. E.

Zoshchenko, Mikhail Mikhailovich (1895–1958), Soviet writer, was, after Chekhov, the best-liked humorous writer in Russia. He was born in the Ukraine, of noble parentage, but soon moved to St Petersburg. After the civil war he began writing his mordant satirical sketches, exploding pomposity and hypocrisy wherever he saw it. In them Zoshchenko takes the part of the all-knowing narrator who colourfully describes ridiculous and trivial events. His language is very ornamental and exaggerated, although he claimed that he wrote in the simple language of the lower classes.

Zoshchenko was subject to fits of melancholy and hypochondria. In *Pered voskhodom solntsa* [*Before Sunrise*] (1943) he attempts to trace the reasons for this melancholy with humorous excerpts from his own life. His hypochondria is reflected in *Vozvrashchonnaya molodost'* [*Restored Youth*] (1933) where he describes how an aged professor refinds his youth, marries a young girl, but is shocked into paralysis when she deserts him. After World War II Zoshchenko was removed from the Writers' Union ostensibly for a satirical attack on the Soviet Union with his children's story *Priklyucheniya obezyany* [*Adventures of a Monkey*] (1946), which was interpreted as meaning that there was more liberty in the zoo than outside. He was restored to favour shortly before his death, though then a shadow of his former self. B. W.

Zuckmayer, Carl (1896–), prolific German playwright, born in Nackenheim, went straight to the western front on leaving school, publishing his first verse in 1917. After the war he studied science at Frankfurt and Heidelberg. His first play *Kreuzweg* ['Cross-way'] (1902) failed, and his later attempts to earn a living as a play producer were also unsuccessful. However, *Der fröhliche Weinberg* ['The merry vineyard'] (1925) won him acclaim for its delightful peasant comedy. *Der Hauptmann von Köpenick* [*The Captain from Köpenick*] (1931) fixed his reputation firmly in popular esteem. A witty and satirical play, it describes how an ex-jailbird in despair of not being able to find a job dresses as an officer and finds that everyone sits up and takes notice of him. Filmed twice, it seemed to be his best work, until *Des Teufels General* [*The Devil's General*] appeared in 1946. Written in America where he had emigrated in 1939, this deals with the growth of the resistance movement to Hitler. General Harras, convinced he has been serving the devil, takes to the air in a plane which has been sabotaged. He is killed, and given a state funeral. It is a grimmer play than his normal productions; where *The Captain* satirised the Kaiser's *Reich, The General* satirised Hitler's. Many of his earlier plays have been dismissed as being too facile; but the serious theme of *Der Gesang im Feurofen* ['The song in the flames'] (1950) has caused him to be revalued. His prose works also showed power: *Herr über Leben und Tod* ['Master of life and death'] (1938) faced the agonising question as to whether defective babies should be allowed to live. His success has been considerable because of his wit and his undoubted versatility. G. W.

Zweig, Arnold (1887–1968), German novelist, born at Kattowitz of a German-Jewish family, studied philosophy and literature before joining the army in 1915. He fought before Verdun and his army experiences were to be a constant source of material. In politics he was a socialist and this together with his Jewish blood caused him to seek final refuge in Palestine after being exiled by the Nazis in 1934. He returned to East Germany in 1948 and became a member of the People's Chamber.

His first publication *Novellen um Claudia* [*Claudia*] (1912) was an interesting compilation of short stories which together made a novel about two young intellectual lovers. The novel *Der Streit um den Sergeanten Grischa* [*The Case of Sergeant Grischa*] (1926) was based on an earlier play; it formed part of a series designed to epitomise the war and post-war years, the chronological start being *Junge Frau von 1914* [*Young Women of 1914*] (1931), a love story about a Berlin banker's daughter and a young penniless author conscripted for the war. The series moved on with *Erziehung vor Verdun* [*Education before Verdun*] (1935) and *Einsetzung eines Königs* [*The Crowning of a King*], the latter concerning the candidature of the duke of Teck for the throne of Lithuania. The whole series is a masterly panorama of the Kaiser's Germany. After the second war, Zweig attacked the corruption of Nazi Germany in *Das Beil von Wandsbeck* [*The Axe of Wandsbeck*] (1947). Here a master butcher, highly respected, becomes in secret the executioner to the Nazis, in order to restore his business fortunes; for this purpose he uses an axe which is a family heirloom. G. W.

Zweig, Stefan (1881–1942), Austrian writer, was born in Vienna of Jewish parents. No relative of Arnold Zweig, he first became known as much for his translations of Baudelaire, Verlaine and Ben Jonson as for his own lyrics collected in *Die gesammelten Gedichte* ['Collected poems'] (1924). Very much influenced by the psycho-analysis then currently in vogue in Vienna, his studies of great authors, such as those on Balzac, Dickens and Dostoyevsky in *Drei Meister* ['Three masters'] (1919), showed deep psychological insight. His short stories showed mastery of form and an acute interest in the problems of sexuality: *Erstes Erlebnis* ['First experience'] (1911) dealt with awakening sexual knowledge in young boys and girls; *Amok* ['Amok'] (1923) was more sordid and adult; *Verwirrung der Gefühle* ['Confusion of feelings'] (1926) was concerned with the mental rather than the physical aspects of passion. It was, however, in the genre of the historical novel that Zweig founded his world reputation. *Marie Antoinette* (1932) was successfully filmed; but *Maria Stuart* [*Mary Stuart*] (1935), which contrasted the passionate Queen of Scots with the erotically malformed Elizabeth of England, is probably his most widely known work.

In 1935 Zweig emigrated to England and became a British subject. He committed suicide together with his second wife in Brazil in 1942. His memoirs *Die Welt von Gestern* [*The World of Yesterday*] were published posthumously in 1944, but it was his first wife Frederike Zweig who revealed the secrets of his private life in *Stefan Zweig wie ich ihn erlebte* ['Stefan Zweig as I knew him'] (1947). G. W.

Index of English Titles

List of Principal Entries by Countries

Since the articles in this guide are arranged alphabetically, there is no index of authors. However, the following lists of the principal entries for each country are provided as guidance for readers who wish to study the literature of a particular country, region or language.

ENGLISH-LANGUAGE AUTHORS

BRITISH ISLES

England

Aldington, Richard
Amis, Kingsley
Arden, John
Auden, W. H.
Beerbohm, Max
Belloc, Hilaire
Bennett, Arnold
Betjeman, John
Binyon, Laurence
Blunden, Edmund
Bowen, Elizabeth
Bradbury, Malcolm
Braine, John
Bridges, Robert
Brooke, Rupert
Cary, Joyce
Chesterton, G. K.
Compton-Burnett, Ivy
Connolly, Cyril
Conquest, Robert
Conrad, Joseph
Cooper, William
Davie, Donald
Davies, W. H.
Day-Lewis, Cecil
De la Mare, Walter
Dennis, Nigel
Douglas, Norman
Durrell, Lawrence
Eliot, T. S.
Empson, William
Enright, D. J.
Firbank, Ronald
Flecker, James Elroy
Ford, Ford Madox
Forster, E. M.
Fry, Christopher
Fuller, Roy
Galsworthy, John
Golding, William
Graves, Robert
Green, Henry
Greene, Graham
Gunn, Thom
Hardy, Thomas
Hartley, L. P.
Housman, A. E.
Hughes, Richard
Hughes, Ted
Huxley, Aldous
Isherwood, Christopher
Jellicoe, Ann
Jennings, Elizabeth
Kipling, Rudyard
Koestler, Arthur (Hungarian born)
Larkin, Philip
Lawrence, D. H.
Leavis, F. R.
Lee, Laurie
Lewis, Wyndham
Livings, Henry
Lowry, Malcolm
Macauley, Rose
MacNeice, Louis
Masefield, John
Maugham, William Somerset
Morgan, Charles
Murdoch, Iris
Orwell, George
Osborne, John
Owen, Wilfrid

Pinter, Harold
Powell, Anthony
Powys, John Cowper
Powys, T. F.
Priestley, J. B.
Rosenberg, Isaac
Russell, Bertrand
Sansom, William
Sassoon, Siegfried
Shaffer, Peter
Sillitoe, Alan
Simpson, N. F.
Sitwell, Edith
Sitwell, Osbert
Snow, C. P.
Spender, Stephen
Storey, David
Strachey, Lytton
Tiller, Terence
Tomlinson, Charles
Wain, John
Waugh, Evelyn
Wells, H. G.
Wesker, Arnold
Wilson, Angus
Woolf, Virginia
Wyndham, John

Scotland

Barrie, J. M.
McDiarmid, Hugh
Muir, Edwin
Spark, Muriel

Wales

Jones, David
Thomas, Dylan
Thomas, R. S.
Watkins, Vernon

Ireland

Beckett, Samuel
Behan, Brendan
Childers, Erskine (Anglo-Irish)
Joyce, James
Moore, George
O'Brien, Flann
O'Casey, Sean
Shaw, George Bernard
Synge, John Millington
Trevor, William
Yeats, William Butler

U. S. A.

Adams, Henry Brooks
Adams, Léonie
Aiken, Conrad
Albee, Edward
Algren, Nelson
Anderson, Sherwood
Auchincloss, Louis
Baldwin, James
Barnes, Djuna
Barth, John
Bellow, Saul
Benét, Stephen Vincent
Bowles, Paul
Bradbury, Ray
Buck, Pearl
Burroughs, William
Cabell, James Branch
Caldwell, Erskine
Capote, Truman
Cather, Willa
Corso, Gregory
Cozzens, James Gould
Crane, Hart
Cummings, E. E.
Dahlberg, Edward
Donleavy, James Patrick
Dos Passos, John
Dreiser, Theodore
Farrell, James T.
Faulkner, William
Ferlinghetti, Lawrence
Fitzgerald, Francis Scott
Frost, Robert
Ginsberg, Allen
H. D.
Heller, Joseph
Hemingway, Ernest
James, Henry
Jarrell, Randall
Jeffers, Robinson
Jones, James

Kerouac, Jack
Keyes, Frances Parkinson
Lardner, Ring
Lewis, Sinclair
Lindsay, Vachell
Lowell, Amy
Lowell, Robert
McCarthy, Mary
McCullers, Carson
Mailer, Norman
Malamud, Bernard
Marquand, John Phillips
Millay, Edna St Vincent
Miller, Arthur
Miller, Henry
Moore, Marianne
Nash, Ogden
Norris, Frank
O'Connor, Flannery
Odets, Clifford
O'Hara, John
O'Neill, Eugene
Penn Warren, Robert
Perelman, S. J.
Plath, Sylvia
Porter, Katherine Anne
Pound, Ezra
Purdy, James
Ransom, John Crowe
Robinson, Edward Arlington
Roethke, Theodore
Rukeyser, Muriel
Runyon, Damon
Salinger, J. D.
Sandburg, Carl
Santayana, George
Saroyan, William
Shapiro, Karl
Sinclair, Upton
Singer, Isaac Bashevis
Stein, Gertrude
Steinbeck, John
Stevens, Wallace
Styron, William
Tarkington, Booth
Tate, Allen
Thurber, James
Trilling, Lionel
Updike, John
Van Doren, Carl
Van Doren, Mark
Veblen, Thorstein
Vidal, Gore
West, Nathanael
Wharton, Edith
Wilbur, Richard
Wilder, Thornton
Williams, Tennessee
Williams, William Carlos
Wilson, Edmund
Winters, Yvor
Wolfe, Thomas
Wouk, Herman

AUSTRALIA

Adams, Arthur H.
Boyd, Martin
Brennan, Christopher J.
Brent of Bin Bin
Brickhill, Paul
Casey, Gavin S.
Cato, Nancy
Cusack, Dymphna
Dark, Eleanor
Davison, Frank Dalby
Dennis, C. J.
Dyson, Edward
Eldershaw, Barnard M.
Fitzgerald, Robert David
Franklin, Miles
Furphy, Joseph
Gaskin, Catherine
Gilmore, Mary
Gunn, Mrs Aneas
Hardy, Frank
Harris, Max
Herbert, Xavier
Hope, A. D.
Idriess, Ion
Ingamells, Rex
Keesing, Nancy
Lawler, Ray
Lawson, Henry
Lindsay, Norman
Lindsay, Jack
Macartney, Frederick T.
McAuley, James
McInnes, Colin
Mackenzie, Kenneth

CANADA

NEW ZEALAND

SOUTH AFRICA

Krige, Uys
La Guma, Alex
Langley, Noel
Lytton, David
Mackenzie, Kenneth
Millin, Sarah Gertrude
Modisane, Bloke
Mofolo, Thomas
Mphahlele, Ezekial
Nkosi, Lewis
Packer, Joy
Paton, Alan
Plaatje, Sol T.
Plomer, William
Prince, Frank Templeton
Rive, Richard
Rooke, Daphne
Schreiner, Olive
Segal, Ronald
Slater, Francis Carey
Smith, Pauline
Van der Post, Laurens
Vilakazi, Benedict Wallet

WEST, CENTRAL AND EAST AFRICA

Gambia

Peters, Lenrie

Ghana

Aidoo, Christina Ama Ata
Awoonor-Williams, George

Kenya

Ngugi, James T.

Nigeria

Achebe, Chinua
Aluko, Timothy Mofolorunsho
Clark, John Pepper
Egbuna, Obi B.
Ekwensi, Cyprian
Fagunwa, Daniel Olorunsemi
Henshaw, James Ene
Ladipo, Duro
Nzekwu, Onuora
Okara, Gabriel
Okigbo, Christopher
Soyinka, Wole
Tutuola, Amos

Rhodesia

Lessing, Doris

Sierra Leone

Nicol, Abioseh D.

WEST INDIES

Braithwaite, E. R.
Lamming, George
Mittelholzer, Edgar
Naipaul, Vidiadhar Surajpsasad
Wynter, Sylvia Rufinia

FOREIGN-LANGUAGE AUTHORS

AUSTRIA

Bachmann, Ingeborg
Baum, Vicki
Broch, Herman
Celan, Paul
Doderer, Heimito von
Freud, Sigmund
Hochwälder, Fritz
Hofmannsthal, Hugo von
Musil, Robert
Werfel, Franz
Zweig, Stefan

BELGIUM

Flemish

Timmermans, Felix

French

Ghelderode, Michel de
Maeterlinck, Maurice
Mallet, Françoise
Michaux, Henri
Simenon, Georges

BRAZIL

Amado, Jorge
Bandeira, Manuel
Drummond de Andrade, Carlos
Freyre, Gilberto
Ivo, Lêdo
Jesus, Carolina Maria de
Lima, Jorge de
Lins do Rêgo, José
Meireles, Cecilia
Queiroz, Rachel de
Ramos, Graciliano
Veríssimo, Erico
For other Latin American countries see SPANISH AMERICA

CZECHOSLOVAKIA

Bass, Eduard
Čapek, Karel
Durych, Jaroslav
Glazarová, Jarmila
Hašek, Jaroslav
Hostovský, Egon
Jesenský, Janko
Kožik, František
Lustig, Arnošt
Majerová, Marie
Mnacko, Ladislav
Mucha, Jiri
Olbracht, Ivan
Otcenásek, Jan
Řezáč, Václav
Styblová, Valja
Toman, Josef
Vančura, Vladislav

DENMARK

Brandes, Georg
Branner, Hans Christian
Dinesen, Isak
Gjellerup, Karl
Jensen, Johannes Vilhelm
Michaëlis, Karin
Munk, Kaj
Nexø, Martin Andersen
Petersen, Nis
Soya, Carl Erik Martin

FINLAND

Sillanpää, Frans Femil

FRANCE

Alain-Fournier
Anouilh, Jean
Apollinaire, Guillaume
Aragon, Louis
Artaud, Antonin
Aymé, Marcel
Barbusse, Henri
Bazin, Hervé
Beauvoir, Simone de
Berger, Yves
Bergson, Henri
Bernanos, Georges
Boulle, Pierre
Breton, André
Butor, Michel
Camus, Albert
Castillo, Michel del
Cau, Jean
Céline, Louis Ferdinand
Cendrars, Blaise
Char, René
Chevallier, Gabriel
Claudel, Paul
Clostermann, Pierre
Cocteau, Jean
Colette, Sidonie-Gabrielle
Daninos, Pierre
Duhamel, Georges
Duras, Marguerite
Eluard, Paul
Feydeau, Georges
France, Anatole
Gary, Romain
Genet, Jean
Gide, André
Giono, Jean
Giraudoux, Jean
Golon, Sergeanne
Langfus, Anna (Franco-Polish)
Larbaud, Valéry
Lartéguy, Jean
Le Clézio, Jean-Marie Gustave (Anglo-French)

Malraux, André
Marcel, Gabriel
Martin du Gard, Roger
Mauriac, Claude
Mauriac, François
Maurois, André
Mistral, Frédéric
Montherlant, Henry de
Oldenbourg, Zoë
Pagnol, Marcel
Palle, Albert
Perse, Saint-John
Peyrefitte, Roger
Pieyre de Mandiargues, André
Prévert, Jacques
Proust, Marcel
Queneau, Raymond
Robbe-Grillet, Alain
Rochefort, Christiane
Rolland, Romain
Romains, Jules
Sagan, Françoise
Saint-Excupéry, Antoine de
Sarraute, Nathalie
Sartre, Jean-Paul
Schwarz-Bart, André
Simon, Claude
Supervielle, Jules
Troyat, Henri
Vailland, Roger
Valéry, Paul
Vercors, Jean Bruller
Weil, Simone
See also under BELGIUM *and* SWITZERLAND

FRENCH-SPEAKING NORTH AFRICA

Tunisia

Memmi, Albert

FRENCH-SPEAKING WEST AFRICA

Cameroons

Beti, Mongo
Laye, Camara
Rabearivelo, Jean

Senegal

Senghor, Léopold Sédar

FRENCH WEST INDIES

Césaire, Aimé

GREECE

Cavafy, Constantine
Kazantzakis, Nikos
Seferis, Giorgos

GERMANY

Andres, Stefan
Beier, Ulli
Bergengruen, Werner
Böll, Heinrich
Brecht, Bertolt
Canetti, Elias
Carossa, Hans
Eich, Günter
Elsner, Gisela
Enzensberger, Hans Magnus
Gaiser, Gerd
George Stefan
Grass, Günter
Hauptmann, Gerhart
Heidegger, Martin
Hesse, Hermann
Hochhuth, Rolf
Holthusen, Hans Egon
Jaspers, Karl
Johnson, Uwe
Jünger, Ernst
Kafka, Franz
Kessel, Martin
Kirst, Hans Hellmut
Mann, Heinrich
Mann, Thomas
Nossack, Hans Erich
Piontek, Heinz
Remarque, Erich Maria
Rilke, Rainer Maria
Rinser, Luise

Sachs, Nelly
Schröder, Rudolf Alexander
Schweitzer, Albert
Spengler, Oswald
Walser, Martin
Wedekind, Frank
Wiechert, Ernst
Zuckmayer, Carl
Zweig, Arnold
See also under AUSTRIA *and* SWITZERLAND

HUNGARY

Ady, Endre
Déry, Tibor
Illyés, Gyulu
József, Attila
Németh, László

ICELAND

Gunnarsson, Gunnar
Laxness, Halldór Killjan

ISRAEL

Agnon, Samuel Joseph

ITALY

Bacchelli, Riccardo
Bassani, Giorgio
Betti, Ugo
Buzzati, Dino
Calvino, Italo
Cassola, Carlo
Cialente, Fausta
Coccioli, Carlo
Croce, Benedetto
D'Annunzio, Gabriele
Deledda, Grazia
Dolci, Danilo
Gadda, Carlo Emilio
Guareschi, Giovanni
La Capria, Raffaele
Lampedusa, Prince Giuseppe Tomasi di
Levi, Carlo
Malaparte, Curzio
Maraini, Dacia
Montale, Eugenio
Morante, Elsa
Moravia, Alberto
Papini, Giovanni
Pascoli, Giovanni
Pasinetti, Pier-Maria
Pasolini, Pier Paolo
Pavese, Cesare
Pirandello, Luigi
Pirro, Ugo
Pratolini, Vasco
Quasimodo, Salvatore
Silone, Ignazio
Soldati, Mario
Svevo, Italo
Tobino, Mario
Ungaretti, Giuseppe
Vittorini, Elio

NETHERLANDS

Couperus, Louis
Frank, Anne

NORWAY

Grieg, Nordahl
Hamsun, Knut
Heyerdahl, Thor
Krog, Helge
Mykle, Agnar
Rolvaag, Ole
Undset, Sigrid

POLAND

Andrzejewski, Jerzy
Choromański, Michel
Goetel, Ferdynand
Gombrowicz, Witold
Hlasko, Marek
Kasprowicz, Jan
Peterkiewicz, Jerzy
Reymont, Wladyslaw Stanislaw

PORTUGAL

Ferreira de Castro, José Maria
Galvão, Henrique

Lacerdo, Alberto de
Paco D'Arcos, Joaquim
Pessoa, Fernando Nogueira
Ribeiro, Aquilino
Torga, Miguel
See also under BRAZIL

RUMANIA

Dumitriu, Petru
Gheorghiu, C. Virgil
Horia, Vintila
Istrati, Panait
Rebreanu, Liviu
Sadoveanu, Mihail

SPAIN

Alberti, Rafael
Aleixandre, Vicente
Alvarez Quintero, Serafín and Joaquín
Arrabel
Aub, Max
Ayala, Francisco
Azorín
Barea, Arturo
Baroja, Pio
Benavente, Jacinto
Blasco, Ibáñez
Buero Vallejo, Antonio
Casona, Alejandro
Cela, Camilo José
Cernuda, Luis
Delibes, Miguel
Echegaray, José
Garcia Hortelano, Juan
Garcia Lorca, Federico
Gironella, José María
Goytisolo, Juan
Guillén, Jorge
Hernández, Miguel
Jiménez, Juan Ramón
Lera, Angel Maria de
Machado, Antonio
Madariaga, Salvador de
Martín Descalzo, Ignacio
Martínez Sierra, Gregorio
Matute, Ana María
Mihura, Miguel
Miró Ferrer, Gabriel
Ortega y Gasset, José
Otero, Blas de
Pérez de Ayala, Ramón
Salinas, Pedro
Sánchez Ferlosio, Rafael
Semprún, Jorge
Sander, Ramón
Unamuno, Miguel de
Valle-Inclán, Ramón Maria del

SPANISH AMERICA

Argentina

Borges, Jorge Luis
Cortázar, Julio
Gálvez, Manuel
Güiraldes, Ricardo
Mallea, Eduardo

Chile

Barrios, Eduardo
Huidobro, Vicente
Mistral, Gabriela
Neruda, Pablo

Cuba

Carpentier, Alejo

Guatemala

Asturias, Miguel Angel

Mexico

Azuela, Mariano
Fuentes, Carlos
Paz, Octavio
Reyes, Alfonso
Rulfo, Juan

Nicaragua

Darío, Rubén

Paraguay

Bastos, Augusto Roa

Peru

Alegría, Ciro
Vallejo, César
Vargas Llosa, Mario

Tarasov-Rodionov, Alexandr
Tarsis, Valeriy
Tendryakov, Vladimir
Tolstoy, Alexei
Tvardpvsly, Alexandr
Veresayev, V. V.
Vladimov, Georgiy
Voinovich, Vladimir
Voznesensky, Andrei
Zamyatin, Yevgeni
Zoshchenko, Mikhail

YUGOSLAVIA

Andríc, Ivo
Bulatović, Miodrag
Krleža, Miroslav
Popa, Vasko

The Editors

GENERAL EDITOR: Kenneth Ridley Richardson, M.A. (Cantab.). Formerly on the editorial staff of *Chambers's Encyclopaedia*, and subsequently freelance editor and writer; now Senior Lecturer in Liberal Studies, Kingston Polytechnic, teaching contemporary American and English literature.
Special editorial responsibility: Britain and the United States (novelists and dramatists).

ASSOCIATE EDITOR: R. Clive Willis, M.A. (Cantab.), Ph.D. (Manchester). Lecturer in Portuguese, University of Manchester. Publications include *Langenscheidt-Methuen Universal Dictionary, Portuguese-English, English-Portuguese* (1960) and *An Essential Course in Modern Portuguese* (1965).
Special editorial responsibility: Europe excluding Slavonic & Hungarian languages, and Latin America.

ASSISTANT EDITORS: David L. Parkes, B.A. (Bristol). Formerly Lee Conway Postgraduate Scholar in American Studies at the University of Bristol and subsequently on the teaching staff of Tulane University (New Orleans) and Kingston Polytechnic; now Staff Tutor at the Further Education Staff College, Blagdon.
Editorial responsibility: Britain and the United States (poets).

Sallyann Richardson, B.A. (Melbourne). Has taught in schools and colleges in Australia and England, and broadcast for the BBC; now freelance lecturer and writer.
Editorial responsibility: the Commonwealth.

Bryan Woodriff, B.A. (Sheffield). Formerly a grammar-school teacher; now Senior Lecturer in Liberal Studies, Kingston Polytechnic, teaching Russian Language and Literature.
Editorial responsibility: Slavonic and Hungarian languages.

The Contributors

D. E. A. D. E. Ager, B.A. Formerly a schoolmaster; now Lecturer in French, University of Salford.

C. B. Charles Barr, B.A. Teacher (formerly at Eton College), freelance lecturer and writer. Publications include *Laurel and Hardy* (1968).

P. R. B. Peter R. Beardsell, B.A. Assistant Lecturer in Spanish, University of Sheffield.

D. B. Dino Bressan, L. in Lett. (Pisa). Has taught in the universities of Aberdeen and Birmingham and is now Lecturer in Italian, University of Salford.

K. B. Karel Brušák, M.A. Visiting lecturer in Czech, University of Cambridge.

G. C. Gay Crace, B.A. Formerly on the editorial staff of *Chambers's Encyclopaedia*, now a freelance editor.

H. C. Hugh Crace. Has worked in a public library, for several publishing houses, and now manages a London bookshop.

G. F. C. G. F. Cushing, M.A., Ph.D. Reader in Hungarian Language and Literature, University of London School of Slavonic and East European Studies. Publications include *Hungarian Prose and Verse* (1956), and 'Hungary' in *Contrasts in Emerging Societies* (1965).

M. D. E. Malcolm D. Evans, B.A. Lecturer in Liberal Studies, Oldham College of Further Education.

P. E. Pamela Evans. Lecturer in Liberal Studies, Southgate Technical College.

D. H. G. Derek H. Gagen, B.A. Lecturer in Spanish, University of Manchester.

M. G. Meir Gertner, M.A., Ph.D. Reader in Modern Hebrew, University of London School of Oriental and African Studies. Publications include '*S. J. Anons episches Werk*' in *Almanach i für Literatur u. Theologie* (Wuppertal-Barmen, 1967).

K. G-Y. Kevin Gough-Yates, B.A. Has taught in various London colleges and is now freelance lecturer and writer.

G. D. G. David Gow, B. Mus. Composer and lecturer. Has taught for the extra-mural departments of Oxford and London universities, and in various London colleges.

K. M. H. Kathleen M. Hancock, A.L.A. Formerly on the staff of Middlesex County Libraries and the National Central Library; now Librarian, Willesden College of Technology.

R. A. K. Robin A. Kelly, B.A. Educationalist and writer. Formerly Principal Lecturer in Liberal Studies, Kingston Polytechnic. Author of *The Sky was their Roof* (1953), *The Big Fifties* (1957) and *Inshore Heroes* (with W. Granville; 1961).

J. L. James Leahy, B.A. Freelance lecturer and writer, now in Chicago. Author of *The Cinema of Joseph Losey* (1968).

S. M. Sheila Marsland, B.A. (Soc.). Lecturer in Liberal Studies, Kingston Polytechnic, teaching sociology.

J. B. M. Brian Matthews, M.A. Senior Lecturer in French, Kingston Polytechnic.

B. M. B. Mazur, B.A. Assistant Lecturer in Polish Language and Literature, University of London School of Slavonic and East European Studies.

J. T. M. John T. Mead, B.A. Has worked for the National Coal Board and the National Association for Mental Health, and is now Lecturer in Social Psychology, Borough Polytechnic.

D. L. P. David L. Parkes, B.A. Formerly Lee Conway Postgraduate Scholar in American Studies at the University of Bristol and subsequently on the teaching staff of Tulane University (New Orleans) and Kingston Polytechnic; now Staff Tutor at the Further Education Staff College, Blagdon.

C. P. Cosmo Pieterse, M.A. (Capetown). Freelance writer, broadcaster and actor. Has edited *Ten One-Act Plays from Africa* (1968) and *Eight South African Poets* (1968).

G. P. Giovanni Pontiero, M.A., Ph.D. Lecturer in Latin American Studies, University of Liverpool.

K. R. R. Kenneth Ridley Richardson, M.A. Formerly on the editorial staff of *Chambers's Encyclopaedia*, and subsequently freelance editor and writer; now Senior Lecturer in Liberal Studies, Kingston Polytechnic, teaching contemporary American and English literature.

S. R. Sallyann Richardson, B.A. (Melbourne). Has taught in schools and colleges in Australia and England, and broadcast for the BBC; now freelance lecturer and writer.

G. S. Gwynneth Stern, B.A. Bibliographical Assistant, BBC Reference Library.

M. T. Margaret Tarratt, B.A., B.Litt. Teaches English literature at the University of Reading.

A. L. W. Alan L. Walker, B.A. Lecturer in French, University of Salford.

G. W. G. Weischedel, Dipl. Dolm. (Mainz). Formerly an interpreter; now Lecturer in German, University of Salford.